# CLYMER®

# *HONDA*

## *CRF250R, CRF250X, CRF450R & CRF450X •*
## *2002-2005*

## CLYMER®

P.O. Box 12901, Overland Park, Kansas 66282-2901

Copyright ©2005 Penton Media, Inc.

FIRST EDITION
First Printing October, 2005
Second Printing May, 2007

Printed in U.S.A.

CLYMER and colophon are registered trademarks of Penton Media, Inc.

ISBN-10: 0-89287-928-9

ISBN-13: 978-0-89287-928-1

Library of Congress: 2005925023

MEMBER

*AUTHOR: Ron Wright.*

*TECHNICAL PHOTOGRAPHY: Ron Wright.*

*TECHNICAL ILLUSTRATIONS: Steve Amos.*

*WIRING DIAGRAMS: Bob Meyer and Lee Buell.*

*EDITOR: Lee Buell.*

*PRODUCTION: Susan Hartington.*

*TOOLS AND EQUIPMENT: K & L Supply Co. at www.klsupply.com.*

*COVER: 2005 CRF250X by Mark Clifford Photography at www.markclifford.com.*

# CLYMER®

**Publisher** Shawn Etheridge

## EDITORIAL

*Managing Editor*
James Grooms

*Associate Editors*
Rick Arens
Steven Thomas

*Authors*
Jay Bogart
Michael Morlan
George Parise
Mark Rolling
Ed Scott
Ron Wright

*Technical Illustrators*
Steve Amos
Errol McCarthy
Mitzi McCarthy
Bob Meyer

*Group Production Manager*
Dylan Goodwin

*Production Manager*
Greg Araujo

*Senior Production Editor*
Darin Watson

*Production Editors*
Justin Marciniak
Holly McComas
Adraine Roberts

*Production Designer*
Jason Hale

## MARKETING/SALES AND ADMINISTRATION

*Marketing and Sales Representative*
Erin Gribbin

*Sales Managers*
Justin Henton
Matt Tusken

*Director, Operations–Books*
Ron Rogers

*Customer Service Manager*
Terri Cannon

*Customer Service Account Specialist*
Courtney Hollars

*Customer Service Representatives*
Dinah Bunnell
April LeBlond

*Warehouse & Inventory Manager*
Leah Hicks

# CLYMER®

P.O. Box 12901, Overland Park, KS 66282-2901 • 800-262-1954 • 913-967-1719

**More information available at *clymer.com***

# CONTENTS

# QUICK REFERENCE DATA

## MOTORCYCLE INFORMATION

MODEL:_____YEAR:_____

VIN NUMBER:_____

ENGINE SERIAL NUMBER:_____

CARBURETOR SERIAL NUMBER OR I.D. MARK:_____

## TIRE INFLATION PRESSURE

| | Front and rear |
|---|---|
| Tire pressure | |
| CRF250R | 98 kPa (14.2 psi) |
| CRF250X | 100 kPa (14.5 psi) |
| CRF450R | |
| 2002-2004 | 100 kPa (14.5 psi) |
| 2005 | 98 kPa (14.2 psi) |
| CRF450X | 100 kPa (14.5 psi) |

## RECOMMENDED LUBRICANTS AND FUEL

| | |
|---|---|
| Air filter | Foam air filter oil |
| Brake fluid | DOT 4 |
| Control cables[1] | Cable lube |
| Coolant[2] | Pro Honda HP Coolant or equivalent |
| Engine oil | |
| Type | Pro Honda GN4 and HP4 (without molybdenum disulfide additives) or equivalent 4-stroke engine oil |
| API service classification[3] | SG or higher |
| JASO T903 standards | MA or MB |
| Viscosity | SAE 10W-40 |
| Transmission oil | |
| Type | Pro Honda HP Transmission oil, Pro Honda GN4 or PH4 (without molybdenum additives) or equivalent 4-stroke engine oil |
| API service classification | SG or higher |
| JASO T903 standards | MA |
| Viscosity | SAE 10W-40 |

(continued)

## RECOMMENDED LUBRICANTS AND FUEL (continued)

| | |
|---|---|
| Fork oil | |
|   Type | Pro-Honda HP fork oil or equivalent |
|   Viscosity | 5W |
| Fuel | Unleaded fuel with octane number of 91 or higher |
| Steering and suspension lubricant | Multipurpose waterproof grease |

1. Do not use drive chain lubricant on control cables. Do not lubricate original equipment throttle cables. Refer to text for further information.
2. Coolant must not contain silicate inhibitors as they can cause premature wear to the water pump seals. Refer to text for further information.
3. API SG or higher classified oils not specified as ENERGY CONSERVING can be used. Refer to text for additional information.

### Table 6 ENGINE OIL CAPACITY

| | ml | U.S. oz. |
|---|---|---|
| Engine oil change only | | |
|   CRF450X | 670 | 22.7 |
|   All other models | 660 | 22.3 |
| Engine oil and filter change | | |
|   CRF450X | 700 | 23.7 |
|   All other models | 690 | 23.3 |
| Engine disassembly | | |
|   CRF450X | 870 | 29.4 |
|   All other models | 850 | 28.8 |

### Table 7 TRANSMISSION OIL CAPACITY

| | ml | U.S. oz. |
|---|---|---|
| CRF250R | | |
|   Transmission oil change | | |
|     2004 | 720 | 24.3 |
|     2005 | 600 | 20.3 |
|   After engine disassembly | | |
|     2004 | 770 | 26.0 |
|     2005 | 700 | 23.7 |
| CRF250X | | |
|   Transmission oil change | 670 | 22.7 |
|   After engine disassembly | 750 | 25.4 |
| CRF450R | | |
|   Transmission oil change | 590 | 20.0 |
|   After engine disassembly | 670 | 22.7 |
| CRF450X | | |
|   Transmission oil change | 650 | 22.0 |
|   After engine disassembly | 750 | 25.4 |

## ENGINE COMPRESSION, DECOMPRESSOR AND VALVE CLEARANCE

| | |
|---|---|
| Decompressor clearance | |
|   CRF450R | 0.35 mm (0.014 in.) |

(continued)

## ENGINE COMPRESSION, DECOMPRESSOR AND VALVE CLEARANCE (continued)

| | |
|---|---|
| Engine compression | |
| CRF250R and CRF250X | 392 kPa (57 psi) at 800 rpm |
| CRF450R | |
| 2002-2003 | 441 kPa (64 psi) at 600 rpm |
| 2004-on | 539 kPa (78 psi) at 600 rpm |
| CRF450X | 402 kPa (58 psi) at 360 rpm |
| Valve clearance | |
| Intake | |
| CRF250R and CRF250X | 0.09-0.15 mm (0.004-0.006 in.) |
| CRF450R and CRF450X | 0.13-0.19 mm (0.005-0.007 in.) |
| Exhaust | 0.25-0.31 mm (0.010-0.012 in.) |

## SPARK PLUG TYPE AND GAP

| | |
|---|---|
| Spark plug gap | |
| Operating gap | |
| CRF250R | |
| 2004 | 0.8-0.9 mm (0.032-0.035 in.) |
| 2005 | 0.6-0.7 mm (0.024-0.028 in.) |
| CRF250X | 0.8-0.9 mm (0.032-0.035 in.) |
| CRF450R and CRF450X | 1.0-1.1 mm (0.039-0.043 in.) |
| Service limit | |
| 2004 CRF250R and all CRF250X | 1.0 mm (0.039 in.) |
| 2005 CRF250R | 0.8 mm (0.032 in.) |
| CRF450R and CRF450X | 1.2 mm (0.047 in.) |
| Spark plug type | |
| CRF250R | |
| Standard | |
| 2004 | DENSO VUH24D |
| | NGK IMR8C9H |
| 2005 | NGK R0409 B8 |
| Optional (colder) | |
| 2004 | DENSO VUH27D |
| | NGK IMR9C9H |
| 2005 | NGK R0409 B9 |
| CRF250X | |
| Standard | DENSO VUH24D |
| | NGK IMR8C9H |
| Optional (colder) | DENSO VUH27D |
| | NGK IMR9C9H |
| CRF450R and CRF450X | |
| Standard | DENSO VK24PRZ11 |
| | NGK IFR8H11 |
| Optional (colder) | DENSO VK27PRZ11 |
| | NGK IFR9H11 |

## IDLE SPEED ADJUSTMENT

| | |
|---|---|
| All models | 1600-1800 RPM |

## COOLANT CAPACITY

|  | Liters | U.S. qt. |
|---|---|---|
| Coolant change | | |
| CRF250R | 0.93 | 0.98 |
| CRF250X | 1.13 | 1.19 |
| CRF450R | | |
| 2002-2004 | 1.03 | 1.09 |
| 2005 | 1.11 | 1.17 |
| CRF450X | 1.11 | 1.17 |
| Engine disassembly | | |
| CRF250R | 1.00 | 1.06 |
| CRF250X | 1.20 | 1.27 |
| CRF450R | | |
| 2002-2004 | 1.12 | 1.18 |
| 2005 | 1.20 | 1.27 |
| CRF450X | 1.20 | 1.27 |

## DRIVE CHAIN AND ROLLER SPECIFICATIONS

| | |
|---|---|
| Drive chain free play | 25-35 mm (1.0-1.4 in.) |
| Drive chain inner plate width service limit | |
| CRF250X and CRF450X | 13.4 mm (0.53 in.) |
| Drive chain 17-pin length service limit | |
| CRF250R and CRF450R | 259 mm (10.2 in.) |
| Drive chain slider thickness | 5.0 mm (0.2 in.) |
| Drive chain roller outside diameter | |
| service limit | |
| CRF250R | |
| 2004 | 39 mm (1.54 in.) |
| 2005 | |
| Upper | 38 mm (1.5 in.) |
| Lower | 31 mm (1.2 in.) |
| CRF250X | |
| Upper | 25 mm (1.0 in.) |
| Lower | 39 mm (1.54 in.) |
| CRF450R | |
| 2002-2004 | 39 mm (1.54 in.) |
| 2005 | |
| Upper | 39 mm (1.54 in.) |
| Lower | 35 mm (1.4 in.) |
| CRF450X | |
| Upper | 39 mm (1.54 in.) |
| Lower | 35 mm (1.4 in.) |

## MAINTENANCE TORQUE SPECIFICATIONS

|  | N•m | in.-lb. | ft.-lb. |
|---|---|---|---|
| Coolant drain bolt | | | |
| CRF250R, 2005 CRF450R and | | | |
| CRF450X | – | – | – |
| All other models | 9.8 | 87 | – |
| Crankshaft hole cap* | 15 | 133 | – |
| Decompressor adjuster locknut | | | |
| CRF450R and CRF450X | 10 | 88 | – |
| Drive chain roller nut and bolt | 12 | 106 | – |

(continued)

## MAINTENANCE TORQUE SPECIFICATIONS

| | N•m | in.-lb. | ft.-lb. |
|---|---|---|---|
| **Engine oil drain bolt** | | | |
| CRF250R and CRF250X | 22 | – | 16 |
| CRF450R | | | |
| 2002-2003 | 22 | – | 16 |
| 2004-on | 16 | 142 | – |
| CRF450X | 16 | 142 | – |
| **Oil filter cover bolt** | | | |
| CRF250R | – | – | – |
| CRF250X | 12 | 106 | – |
| CRF450R | | | |
| 2002-2004 | 9.8 | 87 | – |
| 2005 | 12 | 106 | – |
| CRF450X | – | – | – |
| **Rear axle locknut** | 127 | – | 94 |
| **Rim lock nuts** | 12 | 106 | – |
| **Spark plug** | See text | | |
| **Spokes** | 3.7 | 32.7 | |
| **Ignition timing hole cap*** | | | |
| CRF250R and CRF250X | 5.9 | 52 | – |
| CRF450R | | | |
| 2002-2003 | 9.9 | 87 | – |
| 2004 | 5.9 | 52 | – |
| 2005 | 6.0 | 53 | |
| CRF450X | 10 | 88 | – |
| **Transmission oil check bolt** | | | |
| CRF250R | – | – | – |
| CRF250X | 9.8 | 87 | – |
| CRF450R | | | |
| 2002-2004 | 9.8 | 87 | – |
| 2005 | – | – | – |
| CRF450X | – | – | – |
| **Transmission oil drain bolt** | 22 | – | 16 |

***Lubricate threads with grease.**

# CHAPTER ONE

# GENERAL INFORMATION

This detailed comprehensive manual covers the Honda CRF250R (2004-2005), CRF250X (2004-2005), CRF450R (2002-2005) and the CRF450X (2005).

The text provides complete information on maintenance, tune-up, repair and overhaul. Hundreds of photographs and illustrations created during the complete disassembly of the motorcycle guide the reader through every job. All procedures are in step-by-step format and designed for the reader who may be working on the motorcycle for the first time.

## MANUAL ORGANIZATION

A shop manual is a tool and, as in all Clymer manuals, the chapters are thumb tabbed for easy reference. Main headings are listed in the table of contents and the index. Frequently used specifications and capacities from the tables at the end of each individual chapter are listed in the *Quick Reference Data* section at the front of the manual. Specifications and capacities are provided in U.S. standard and metric units of measure.

During some of the procedures, there will be references to headings in other chapters or sections of the manual. When a specific heading is called out in

a step it will be *italicized* as it appears in the manual. If a sub-heading is indicated as being "in this section" it is located within the same main heading. For example, the sub-heading *Handling Gasoline Safely* is located within the main heading *SAFETY*.

This chapter provides general information on shop safety, tools and their usage, service fundamentals and shop supplies. **Tables 1-8**, at the end of the chapter, list the following:

**Table 1** lists engine and frame serial numbers.

**Table 2** lists motorcycle dimensions.

**Table 3** lists motorcycle weight.

**Table 4** lists metric, inch and fractional equivalents.

**Table 5** lists conversion formulas.

**Table 6** lists general torque specifications.

**Table 7** lists technical abbreviations.

**Table 8** lists metric tap and drill sizes.

## WARNINGS, CAUTIONS AND NOTES

The terms WARNING, CAUTION and NOTE have specific meanings in this manual.

A WARNING emphasizes areas where injury or even death could result from negligence. Mechanical damage may also occur. WARNINGS *are to be taken seriously*.

A CAUTION emphasizes areas where equipment damage could result. Disregarding a CAUTION could cause permanent mechanical damage, though injury is unlikely.

A NOTE provides additional information to make a step or procedure easier or clearer. Disregarding a NOTE could cause inconvenience, but would not cause equipment damage or injury.

## SAFETY

Professional mechanics can work for years and never sustain a serious injury or mishap. Follow these guidelines and practice common sense to safely service the motorcycle.

1. Do not operate the motorcycle in an enclosed area. The exhaust gasses contain carbon monoxide, an odorless, colorless and tasteless poisonous gas. Carbon monoxide levels build quickly in small enclosed areas and can cause unconsciousness and death in a short time. Make sure to properly ventilate the work area or operate the motorcycle outside.

2. Never use gasoline or any extremely flammable liquid to clean parts. Refer to *Cleaning Parts and Handling Gasoline Safely* in this section.

3. Never smoke or use a torch in the vicinity of flammable liquids, such as gasoline or cleaning solvent.

4. If welding or brazing on the motorcycle, remove the fuel tank to a safe distance at least 50 ft. (15 m) away.

5. Use the correct type and size of tools to avoid damaging fasteners.

6. Keep tools clean and in good condition. Replace or repair worn or damaged equipment.

7. When loosening a tight fastener, be guided by what would happen if the tool slips.

8. When replacing fasteners, make sure the new fasteners are the same size and strength as the original ones.

9. Keep the work area clean and organized.

10. Wear eye protection *anytime* the safety of the eyes is in question. This includes procedures that involve drilling, grinding, hammering, compressed air and chemicals.

11. Wear the correct clothing for the job. Tie up or cover long hair so it does not get caught in moving equipment.

12. Do not carry sharp tools in clothing pockets.

13. Always have an approved fire extinguisher available. Make sure it is rated for gasoline (Class B) and electrical (Class C) fires.

14. Do not use compressed air to clean clothes, the motorcycle or the work area. Debris may be blown into the eyes or skin. *Never* direct compressed air at anyone. Do not allow children to use or play with any compressed air equipment.

15. When using compressed air to dry rotating parts, hold the part so it does not rotate. Do not allow the force of the air to spin the part. The air jet is capable of rotating parts at extreme speed. The part may disintegrate or become damaged, causing serious injury.

16. Do not inhale the dust created by brake pad and clutch wear. These particles may contain asbestos. In addition, some types of insulating materials and gaskets may contain asbestos. Inhaling asbestos particles is hazardous to one's health.

17. Never work on the motorcycle while someone is working under it.

18. When placing the motorcycle on a stand, make sure it is secure before walking away.

### Handling Gasoline Safely

Gasoline is a volatile flammable liquid and is one of the most dangerous items in the shop. Because gasoline is used so often, many people forget it is hazardous. Only use gasoline as fuel for gasoline internal combustion engines. Keep in mind when working on the machine, gasoline is always present in the fuel tank, fuel line and carburetor. To avoid a disastrous accident when working around the fuel system, carefully observe the following precautions:

1. *Never* use gasoline to clean parts. Refer to *Cleaning Parts* in this section.

2. When working on the fuel system, work outside or in a well-ventilated area.

3. Do not add fuel to the fuel tank or service the fuel system while the motorcycle is near open flames, sparks or where someone is smoking. Gasoline vapor is heavier than air; it collects in low areas and is more easily ignited than liquid gasoline.

4. Allow the engine to cool completely before working on any fuel system component.

5. Do not store gasoline in glass containers. If the glass breaks, a serious explosion or fire may occur.

6. Immediately wipe up spilled gasoline with rags. Store the rags in a metal container with a lid until they can be properly disposed of, or place them outside in a safe place for the fuel to evaporate.

7. Do not pour water onto a gasoline fire. Water spreads the fire and makes it more difficult to put out. Use a class B, BC or ABC fire extinguisher to extinguish the fire.

8. Always turn off the engine before refueling. Do not spill fuel onto the engine or exhaust system. Do not overfill the fuel tank. Leave an air space at the top of the tank to allow room for the fuel to expand due to temperature fluctuations.

## Cleaning Parts

Cleaning parts is one of the more tedious and difficult service jobs performed in the home garage. Many types of chemical cleaners and solvents are available for shop use. Most are poisonous and extremely flammable. To prevent chemical exposure, vapor buildup, fire and serious injury, observe each product warning label and note the following:

1. Read and observe the entire product label before using any chemical. Always know what type of chemical is being used and whether it is poisonous and/or flammable.

2. Do not use more than one type of cleaning solvent at a time. If mixing chemicals is required, measure the proper amounts according to the manufacturer.

3. Work in a well-ventilated area.

4. Wear chemical-resistant gloves.

5. Wear safety glasses.

6. Wear a vapor respirator if the instructions call for it.

7. Wash hands and arms thoroughly after cleaning parts.

8. Keep chemical products away from children and pets.

9. Thoroughly clean all oil, grease and cleaner residue from any part that must be heated.

10. Use a nylon brush when cleaning parts. Metal brushes may cause a spark.

11. When using a parts washer, only use the solvent recommended by the manufacturer. Make sure the parts washer is equipped with a metal lid that will lower in case of fire.

## Warning Labels

Most manufacturers attach information and warning labels to the motorcycle. These labels contain instructions that are important to personal safety when operating, servicing, transporting and storing the motorcycle. Refer to the owner's manual for the description and location of labels. Order replacement labels from the manufacturer if they are missing or damaged.

## SERIAL NUMBERS

Serial and identification numbers are stamped on various locations on the frame, engine and carburetor body. Record these numbers in the *Quick Reference Data* section in the front of the manual. Have these numbers available when ordering parts.

The frame serial number (**Figure 1**) is stamped on the right side of the steering head.

The engine serial number (**Figure 2**) is stamped on a raised pad on the left crankcase.

The carburetor identification number (**Figure 3**) is stamped on the left side of the carburetor body.

## FASTENERS

Proper fastener selection and installation is important to ensure the motorcycle operates as designed and can be serviced efficiently. The choice of original equipment fasteners is not arrived at by chance. Make sure replacement fasteners meet all the same requirements as the originals.

### Threaded Fasteners

Threaded fasteners secure most of the components on the motorcycle. Most are tightened by turning them clockwise (right-hand threads). If the normal rotation of the component being tightened would loosen the fastener, it may have left-hand threads. If a left-hand threaded fastener is used, it is noted in the text.

Two dimensions are required to match the thread size of the fastener: the number of threads in a given distance and the outside diameter of the threads.

The two systems currently used to specify threaded fastener dimensions are the U.S. standard system and the metric system (**Figure 4**). Pay particular attention when working with unidentified fasteners; mismatching thread types can damage threads.

> *NOTE*
> *To ensure that the fastener threads are not mismatched or cross-threaded, start all fasteners by hand. If a fastener is hard to start or turn, determine the cause before tightening with a wrench.*

The length (L, **Figure 5**), diameter (D) and distance between thread crests (pitch) (T) classify metric screws and bolts. A typical bolt may be identified by the numbers, 8—1.25 × 130. These numbers indicate the bolt has a diameter of 8 mm, the distance between thread crests is 1.25 mm and the length is 130 mm. Always measure bolt length as shown in L, **Figure 5** to avoid purchasing replacements of the wrong length.

The numbers on the top of the fastener (**Figure 5**) indicate the strength of metric screws and bolts. The higher the number, the stronger the fastener is. Typically, unnumbered fasteners are the weakest.

Many screws, bolts and studs are combined with nuts to secure particular components. To indicate

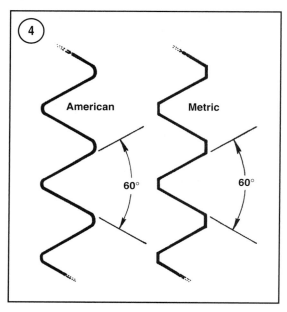

the size of a nut, manufacturers specify the internal diameter and the thread pitch.

The measurement across two flats on a nut or bolt indicates the wrench size.

> *WARNING*
> *Do not install fasteners with a strength classification lower than what was originally installed by the manufacturer. Doing so may cause equipment failure and/or damage.*

### Torque Specifications

The materials used in the manufacturing of the motorcycle may be subjected to uneven stresses if the fasteners of the various subassemblies are not

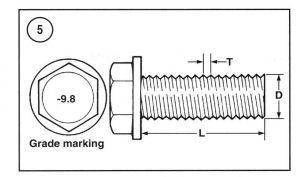

Grade marking

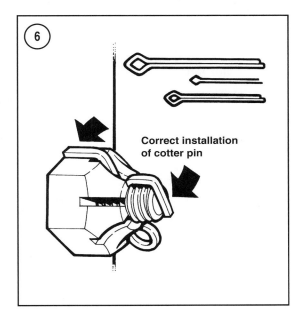

Correct installation
of cotter pin

installed and tightened correctly. Fasteners that are improperly installed or work loose can cause extensive damage. It is essential to use an accurate torque wrench as described in this chapter.

Specifications for torque are provided in Newton-meters (N•m), foot-pounds (ft.-lb.) and inch-pounds (in.-lb.). Refer to **Table 6** for general torque specifications. To determine the torque requirement, first determine the size of the fastener as described in *Threaded Fasteners* in this section. Torque specifications for specific components are at the end of the appropriate chapters. Torque wrenches are covered in *Basic Tools* in this chapter.

## Self-Locking Fasteners

Several types of bolts, screws and nuts incorporate a system that creates interference between the two fasteners. Interference is achieved in various ways. The most common types are the nylon insert nut and a dry adhesive coating on the threads of a bolt.

Self-locking fasteners offer greater holding strength than standard fasteners, which improves their resistance to vibration. All self-locking fasteners cannot be reused. The materials used to form the lock become distorted after the initial installation and removal. Discard and replace self-locking fasteners after removing them. Do not replace self-locking fasteners with standard fasteners.

## Washers

The two basic types of washers are flat washers and lockwashers. Flat washers are simple discs with a hole to fit a screw or bolt. Lockwashers are used to prevent a fastener from working loose. Washers can be used as spacers and seals, or can help distribute fastener load and prevent the fastener from damaging the component.

As with fasteners, when replacing washers make sure the replacement washers are of the same design and quality.

## Cotter Pins

A cotter pin is a split metal pin inserted into a hole or slot to prevent a fastener from loosening. In certain applications, such as the rear axle on an ATV or motorcycle, the fastener must be secured in this way. For these applications, a cotter pin and castellated (slotted) nut is used.

To use a cotter pin, first make sure the diameter is correct for the hole in the fastener. After correctly tightening the fastener and aligning the holes, insert the cotter pin through the hole and bend the ends over the fastener (**Figure 6**). Unless instructed to do so, never loosen a tightened fastener to align the holes. If the holes do not align, tighten the fastener enough to achieve alignment.

Cotter pins are available in various diameters and lengths. Measure the length from the bottom of the head to the tip of the shortest pin.

## Snap Rings and E-clips

Snap rings (**Figure 7**) are circular-shaped metal retaining clips. They secure parts and gears in place on parts such as shafts, pins or rods. External type snap rings are used to retain items on shafts. Internal type snap rings secure parts within housing bores. In some applications, in addition to securing the component(s), snap rings of varying thicknesses also determine endplay. These are usually called selective snap rings.

The two basic types of snap rings are machined and stamped snap rings. Machined snap rings (**Figure 8**) can be installed in either direction, because both faces have sharp edges. Stamped snap rings (**Figure 9**) are manufactured with a sharp and a round edge. When installing a stamped snap ring in a thrust application, install the sharp edge facing away from the part producing the thrust.

E-clips are used when it is not practical to use a snap ring. Remove E-clips with a flat blade screwdriver by prying between the shaft and E-clip. To install an E-clip, center it over the shaft groove and push or tap it into place.

Observe the following when installing snap rings:

1. Remove and install snap rings with snap ring pliers. Refer to *Basic Tools* in this chapter.

2. In some applications, it may be necessary to replace snap rings after removing them.

3. Compress or expand snap rings only enough to install them. If overly expanded, they lose their retaining ability.

4. After installing a snap ring, make sure it seats completely.

5. Wear eye protection when removing and installing snap rings.

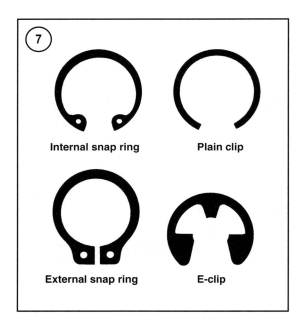

Internal snap ring          Plain clip

External snap ring          E-clip

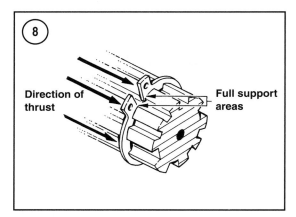

Direction of thrust          Full support areas

### SHOP SUPPLIES

**Lubricants and Fluids**

Periodic lubrication helps ensure a long service life for any type of equipment. Using the correct type of lubricant is as important as performing the lubrication service, although in an emergency the wrong type is better than not using one. The following section describes the types of lubricants most often required. Make sure to follow the manufacturer's recommendations for lubricant types.

*Engine oils*

Engine oil for four-stroke motorcycle engine use is classified by three standards: the American Petroleum Institute (API) service classification, the Society of Automotive Engineers (SAE) viscosity rating and the Japanese Automobile Standards Organization (JASO) T 903 Standard classification.

The API and SAE information is on all oil container labels. The JASO information is found on oil containers sold by the oil manufacturer specifically for motorcycle use. Two letters indicate the API service classification. The number or sequence of numbers and letter (10W-40 for example) is the oil's viscosity rating. The API service classification

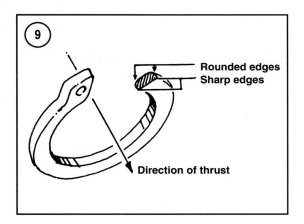

Rounded edges
Sharp edges
Direction of thrust

and the SAE viscosity index are not indications of oil quality.

The API service classification indicates that the oil meets specific lubrication standards. The first letter in the classification S indicates that the oil is for gasoline engines. The second letter indicates the standard the oil satisfies.

The JASO certification label identifies two separate oil classifications and a registration number to ensure the oil has passed all JASO certification standards for use in four-stroke motorcycle engines. The classifications are: MA (high friction applications) and MB (low friction applications). Only oil that has passed JASO standards can carry the JASO certification label.

*NOTE*
*Refer to Engine Oil and Filter in Chapter Three for further information on API, SAE and JASO classifications.*

Always use an oil with a classification recommended by the manufacturer. Using an oil with a different classification can cause engine damage.

Viscosity is an indication of the oil's thickness. Thin oils have a lower number while thick oils have a higher number. Engine oils fall into the 5- to 50-weight range for single-grade oils.

Most manufacturers recommend multi-grade oil. These oils perform efficiently across a wide range of operating conditions. Multi-grade oils are identified by a W after the first number, which indicates the low-temperature viscosity.

Engine oils are most commonly mineral (petroleum) based, but synthetic and semi-synthetic types are used more frequently. When selecting engine oil, follow the manufacturer's recommendation for type, classification and viscosity.

### Greases

Grease is lubricating oil with thickening agents added to it. The National Lubricating Grease Institute (NLGI) grades grease. Grades range from No. 000 to No. 6, with No. 6 being the thickest. Typical multipurpose grease is NLGI No. 2. For specific applications, manufacturers may recommend water-resistant type grease or one with an additive such as molybdenum disulfide ($MoS_2$).

### Brake fluid

Brake fluid is the hydraulic fluid used to transmit hydraulic pressure (force) to the wheel brakes. Brake fluid is classified by the Department of Transportation (DOT). Current designations for brake fluid are DOT 3, DOT 4 and DOT 5. This classification appears on the fluid container.

Each type of brake fluid has its own definite characteristics. Do not intermix different types of brake fluid as this may cause brake system failure. DOT 5 brake fluid is silicone based. DOT 5 is not compatible with other brake fluids or in systems for which it was not designed. Mixing DOT 5 fluid with other fluids may cause brake system failure. When adding brake fluid, *only* use the fluid recommended by the manufacturer.

Brake fluid will damage any plastic, painted or plated surface it contacts. Use extreme care when working with brake fluid and remove any spills immediately with soap and water.

Hydraulic brake systems require clean and moisture free brake fluid. Never reuse brake fluid. Keep containers and reservoirs properly sealed.

*WARNING*
*Never put a mineral-based (petroleum) oil into the brake system. Mineral oil causes rubber parts in the system to swell and break apart, causing complete brake failure.*

### Coolant

Coolant is a mixture of water and antifreeze used to dissipate engine heat. Ethylene glycol is the most common form of antifreeze. Check the motorcycle manufacturer's recommendations when selecting antifreeze. Most require one specifically designed for aluminum engines. These types of antifreeze have additives that inhibit corrosion.

Only mix antifreeze with distilled water. Impurities in tap water may damage internal cooling system passages.

## Cleaners, Degreasers and Solvents

Many chemicals are available to remove oil, grease and other residue from the motorcycle. Before using cleaning solvents, consider how they will be used and disposed of, particularly if they are not water-soluble. Local ordinances may require special procedures for the disposal of many types of cleaning chemicals. Refer to *Safety* in this chapter.

Use brake parts cleaner to clean brake system components. Brake parts cleaner leaves no residue. Use electrical contact cleaner to clean electrical connections and components without leaving any residue. Carburetor cleaner is a powerful solvent used to remove fuel deposits and varnish from fuel system components. Use this cleaner carefully, as it may damage finishes.

Generally, degreasers are strong cleaners used to remove heavy accumulations of grease from engine and frame components.

Most solvents are designed to be used with a parts washing cabinet for individual component cleaning. For safety, use only nonflammable or high flash point solvents.

## Gasket Sealant

Sealant is used in combination with a gasket or seal. In other applications, such as between crankcase halves, only a sealant is used. Follow the manufacturer's recommendation when using a sealant. Use extreme care when choosing a sealant different from the type originally recommended. Choose sealant based on its resistance to heat, various fluids and its sealing capabilities.

A common sealant is room temperature vulcanization sealant, or RTV. This sealant cures at room temperature over a specific time period. This allows the repositioning of components without damaging gaskets.

Moisture in the air causes the RTV sealant to cure. Always install the tube cap as soon as possible after applying RTV sealant. RTV sealant has a limited shelf life and will not cure properly if the shelf life has expired. Keep partial tubes sealed and discard them if they have surpassed the expiration date.

### *Applying RTV sealant*

Clean all old gasket residue from the mating surfaces. Remove all gasket material from blind threaded holes to avoid inaccurate bolt torque. Spray the mating surfaces with aerosol parts cleaner and then wipe with a lint-free cloth. The area must be clean for the sealant to adhere.

Apply RTV sealant in a continuous bead 2-3 mm (0.08-0.12 in.) thick. Circle all the fastener holes unless otherwise specified. Do not allow any sealant to enter these holes. Assemble and tighten the fasteners to the specified torque within the time frame recommended by the sealant manufacturer.

## Gasket Remover

Aerosol gasket remover can help remove stubborn gaskets. This product can speed up the removal process and prevent damage to the mating surface that may be caused by using a scraping tool. Most of these types of products are very caustic. Follow the gasket remover manufacturer's instructions for use.

## Threadlocking Compound

A threadlocking compound is a fluid applied to the threads of fasteners. After tightening the fastener, the fluid dries and becomes a solid filler between the threads. This makes it difficult for the fastener to work loose from vibration or heat expansion and contraction. Some threadlocking compounds also provide a seal against fluid leaks.

Before applying a threadlocking compound, remove any old compound from both thread areas and clean them with aerosol parts cleaner. Use the compound sparingly. Excess fluid can run into adjoining parts.

*CAUTION*
*Threadlocking compounds are anaerobic and will stress, crack and attack most plastics. Use caution when using*

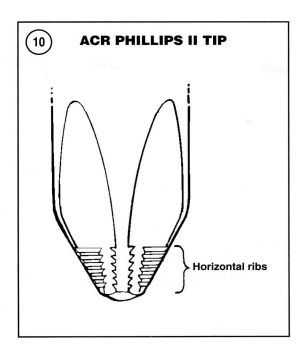

(10) **ACR PHILLIPS II TIP**

Horizontal ribs

*these products in areas where there are plastic components.*

Threadlocking compounds are available in a wide range of compounds for various strength, temperature and repair applications. Follow the manufacturer's recommendations regarding compound selection.

## BASIC TOOLS

Most of the procedures in this manual can be carried out with basic hand tools and test equipment familiar to the home mechanic. Always use the correct tools for the job. Keep tools organized and clean. Store them in a tool chest with related tools organized together.

Quality tools are essential. The best are constructed of high-strength alloy steel. These tools are light, easy to use and resistant to wear. Their working surface is devoid of sharp edges and carefully polished. They have an easy-to-clean finish and are comfortable to use. Quality tools are a good investment.

Some of the procedures in this manual specify special tools. In many cases the tool is illustrated in use. Those with a large tool kit may be able to use a suitable substitute or fabricate a suitable replacement. However, in some cases, the specialized

equipment or expertise may make it impractical for the home mechanic to attempt the procedure. When necessary, such operations are recommended to have a dealership or specialist perform the task. It may be less expensive to have a professional perform these jobs, especially when considering the cost of equipment.

When purchasing tools to perform the procedures covered in this manual, consider the tool's potential frequency of use. If a tool kit is just now being started, consider purchasing a basic tool set from a quality tool supplier. These sets are available in many tool combinations and offer substantial savings when compared to individually purchased tools. As work experience grows and tasks become more complicated, specialized tools can be added.

### Screwdrivers

Screwdrivers of various lengths and types are mandatory for the simplest tool kit. The two basic types are the slotted tip (flat blade) and the Phillips tip. These are available in sets that often include an assortment of tip sizes and shaft lengths.

As with all tools, use a screwdriver designed for the job. Make sure the size of the tip conforms to the size and shape of the fastener. Use them only for driving screws. Never use a screwdriver for prying or chiseling metal. Repair or replace worn or damaged screwdrivers. A worn tip may damage the fastener, making it difficult to remove.

Phillips-head screws are often damaged by incorrectly fitting screwdrivers. Quality Phillips screwdrivers are manufactured with their crosshead tip machined to Phillips Screw Company specifications. Poor quality or damaged Phillips screwdrivers can back out (camout) and round over the screw head. In addition, weak or soft screw materials can make removal difficult.

The best type of screwdriver to use on Phillips screws is the ACR Phillips II screwdriver, patented by the Phillips Screw Company. ACR stands for the horizontal anti-camout ribs found on the driving faces or flutes of the screwdriver's tip (**Figure 10**). ACR Phillips II screwdrivers were designed as part of a manufacturing drive system to be used with ACR Phillips II screws, but they work well on all common Phillips screws. A number of tool companies offer ACR Phillips II screwdrivers in different tip sizes and interchangeable bits to fit screwdriver bit holders.

*NOTE*
*Another way to prevent camout and to increase the grip of a Phillips screw-driver is to apply valve grinding com-pound or Permatex Screw & Socket Gripper onto the screwdriver tip. Af-ter loosening/tightening the screw, clean the screw recess to prevent en-gine oil contamination.*

**Wrenches**

Open-end, box-end and combination wrenches (**Figure 11**) are available in a variety of types and sizes.

The number stamped on the wrench refers to the distance between the work areas. This size must match the size of the fastener head.

The box-end wrench is an excellent tool because it grips the fastener on all sides. This reduces the chance of the tool slipping. The box-end wrench is designed with either a 6 or 12-point opening. For stubborn or damaged fasteners, the 6-point provides superior holding because it contacts the fastener across a wider area at all six edges. For general use, the 12-point works well. It allows the wrench to be removed and reinstalled without moving the handle over such a wide arc.

An open-end wrench is fast and works best in ar-eas with limited overhead access. It contacts the fas-tener at only two points and is subject to slipping if under heavy force, or if the tool or fastener is worn. A box-end wrench is preferred in most instances, especially when breaking loose and applying the fi-nal tightness to a fastener.

The combination wrench has a box-end on one end and an open-end on the other. This combination makes it a convenient tool.

**Adjustable Wrenches**

An adjustable wrench or Crescent wrench (**Fig-ure 12**) can fit nearly any nut or bolt head that has clear access around its entire perimeter. An adjust-able wrench is best used as a backup wrench to keep a large nut or bolt from turning while the other end is being loosened or tightened with a box-end or socket wrench.

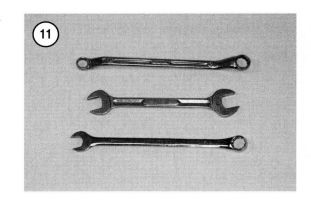

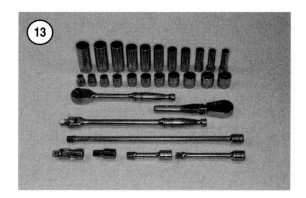

Adjustable wrenches contact the fastener at only two points, which makes them more subject to slip-ping off the fastener. Because one jaw is adjustable and may become loose, this shortcoming is aggra-vated. Make certain the solid jaw is the one trans-mitting the force.

**Socket Wrenches, Ratchets and Handles**

Sockets that attach to a ratchet handle (**Figure 13**) are available with 6-point or 12-point openings

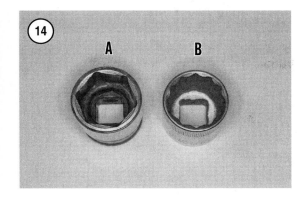

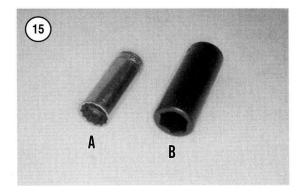

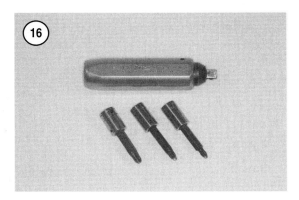

more durability. Compare the size and wall thickness of a 19-mm hand socket (A, **Figure 15**) and the 19-mm impact socket (B). Use impact sockets when using an impact driver or air tools. Use hand sockets with hand-driven attachments.

> *WARNING*
> *Do not use hand sockets with air or impact tools because they may shatter and cause injury. Always wear eye protection when using impact or air tools.*

Various handles are available for sockets. Use the speed handle for fast operation. Flexible ratchet heads in varying lengths allow the socket to be turned with varying force and at odd angles. Extension bars allow the socket setup to reach difficult areas. The ratchet is the most versatile. It allows the user to install or remove the nut without removing the socket.

Sockets combined with any number of drivers make them undoubtedly the fastest, safest and most convenient tool for fastener removal and installation.

### Impact Drivers

An impact driver provides extra force for removing fasteners by converting the impact of a hammer into a turning motion. This makes it possible to remove stubborn fasteners without damaging them. Impact drivers and interchangeable bits (**Figure 16**) are available from most tool suppliers. When using a socket with an impact driver, make sure the socket is designed for impact use. Refer to *Socket Wrenches, Ratchets and Handles* in this section.

> *WARNING*
> *Do not use hand sockets with air or impact tools because they may shatter and cause injury. Always wear eye protection when using impact or air tools.*

### Allen Wrenches

Use Allen or setscrew wrenches (**Figure 17**) on fasteners with hexagonal recesses in the fastener head. These wrenches are available in L-shaped bar, socket and T-handle types. A metric set is required

(**Figure 14**) and different drive sizes. The drive size indicates the size of the square hole that accepts the ratchet handle. The number stamped on the socket is the size of the work area and must match the fastener head.

As with wrenches, a 6-point socket provides superior-holding ability, while a 12-point socket needs to be moved only half as far to reposition it on the fastener.

Sockets are designated for either hand or impact use. Impact sockets are made of thicker material for

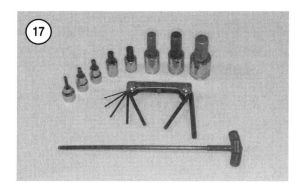

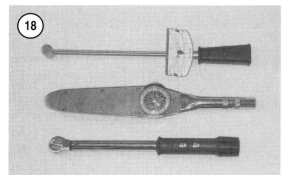

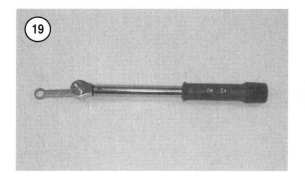

when working on most motorcycles. Allen bolts are sometimes called socket bolts.

**Torque Wrenches**

Use a torque wrench with a socket, torque adapter or similar extension to tighten a fastener to a measured torque. Torque wrenches come in several drive sizes (1/4, 3/8, 1/2 and 3/4) and have various methods of reading the torque value. The drive size indicates the size of the square drive that accepts the socket, adapter or extension. Common methods of reading the torque value are the deflecting beam, the dial indicator and the audible click (**Figure 18**).

When choosing a torque wrench, consider the torque range, drive size and accuracy. The torque specifications in this manual provide an indication of the range required.

A torque wrench is a precision tool that must be properly cared for to remain accurate. Store torque wrenches in cases or separate padded drawers within a toolbox. Follow the manufacturer's instructions for their care and calibration.

**Torque Adapters**

Torque adapters or extensions extend or reduce the reach of a torque wrench. The torque adapter shown in **Figure 19** is used to tighten a fastener that cannot be reached because of the size of the torque wrench head, drive, and socket. If a torque adapter changes the effective lever length (**Figure 20**), the torque reading on the wrench will not equal the actual torque applied to the fastener. It is necessary to recalibrate the torque setting on the wrench to compensate for the change of lever length. When using a torque adapter at a right angle to the drive head,

calibration is not required, because the effective length has not changed.

To recalculate a torque reading when using a torque adapter, use the following formula and refer to **Figure 20**:

$$TW = \frac{TA \times L}{L + A}$$

*TW* is the torque setting or dial reading on the wrench.

*TA* is the torque specification and the actual amount of torque that is applied to the fastener.

*A* is the amount that the adapter increases (or in some cases reduces) the effective lever length as measured along the centerline of the torque wrench.

*L* is the lever length of the wrench as measured from the center of the drive to the center of the grip.

The effective length is the sum of *L* and *A*.

Example:

TA = 20 ft.-lb.
A = 3 in.
L = 14 in.
$$TW = \frac{20 \times 14}{14 + 3} = \frac{280}{17} = 16.5 \text{ ft.-lb.}$$

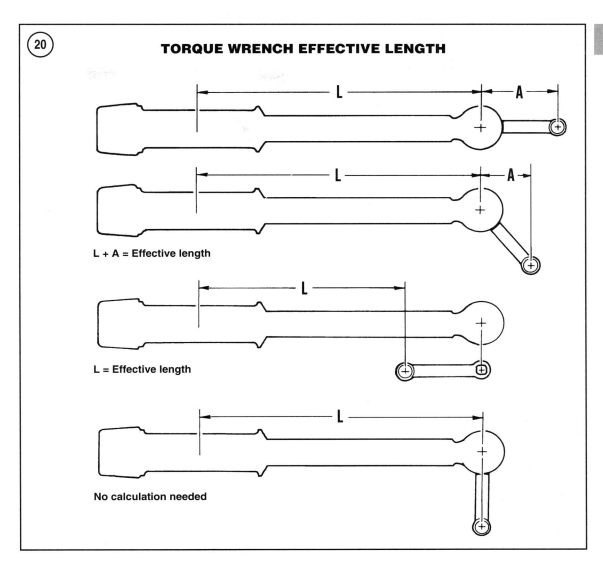

**(20)**

## TORQUE WRENCH EFFECTIVE LENGTH

L + A = Effective length

L = Effective length

No calculation needed

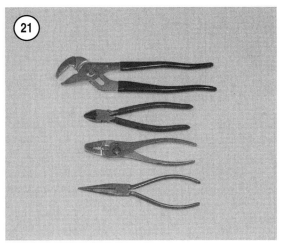

**(21)**

In this example, the torque wrench would be set to the recalculated torque value (TW = 16.5 ft.-lb.). When using a beam-type wrench, tighten the fastener until the pointer aligns with 16.5 ft.-lb. In this example, although the torque wrench is pre set to 16.5 ft.-lb., the actual torque is 20 ft.-lb.

### Pliers

Pliers come in a wide range of types and sizes. Pliers are useful for holding, cutting, bending, and crimping. Do not use them to turn fasteners. **Figure 21** and **Figure 22** show several types of useful pliers. Each design has a specialized function. Slip-joint pliers are general-purpose pliers used for gripping and bending. Diagonal cutting pliers are needed to cut wire and can be used to remove cotter pins. Use needlenose pliers to hold or bend small objects. Locking pliers (**Figure 22**), sometimes called Vise-Grips, are used to hold objects very tightly. They have many uses ranging from holding two parts together, to gripping the end of a broken stud. Use caution when using locking pliers, as the sharp jaws will damage the objects they hold.

### Snap Ring Pliers

Snap ring pliers are specialized pliers with tips that fit into the ends of snap rings to remove and install them.

Snap ring pliers (**Figure 23**) are available with a fixed action (either internal or external) or convertible (one tool works on both internal and external snap rings). They may have fixed tips or interchangeable ones of various sizes and angles. For general use, select a convertible type pliers with interchangeable tips (**Figure 23**).

> *WARNING*
> *Snap rings can slip and fly off when removing and installing them. Also, the snap ring pliers' tips may break. Always wear eye protection when using snap ring pliers.*

### Hammers

Various types of hammers are available to fit a number of applications. Use a ball-peen hammer to strike another tool, such as a punch or chisel. Use soft-faced hammers when a metal object must be struck without damaging it. *Never* use a metal-faced hammer on engine and suspension components because damage occurs in most cases.

Always wear eye protection when using hammers. Make sure the hammer face is in good condition and the handle is not cracked. Select the correct hammer for the job and make sure to strike the object squarely. Do not use the handle or the side of the hammer to strike an object.

### Ignition Grounding Tool

Some test procedures require turning the engine over without starting it. To prevent damage to the

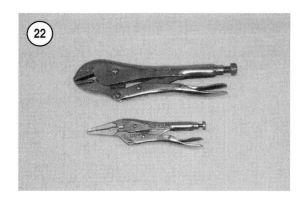

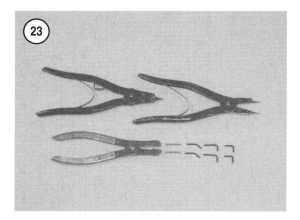

ignition system from excessive resistance or the possibility of fuel vapor being ignited by an open spark, remove the spark plug cap and ground it directly to a good engine ground with the tool shown in **Figure 24**.

Make the tool shown from a No. 6 screw and nut, two washers, length of tubing, alligator clip, electrical eyelet and a length of wire.

## PRECISION MEASURING TOOLS

The ability to accurately measure components is essential to perform many of the procedures described in this manual. Equipment is manufactured to close tolerances, and obtaining consistently accurate measurements is essential to determine which components require replacement or further service.

Each type of measuring instrument is designed to measure a dimension with a certain degree of accuracy and within a certain range. When selecting the measuring tool, make sure it is applicable to the task.

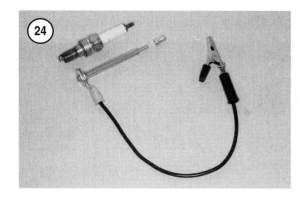

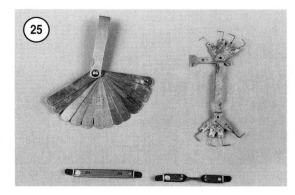

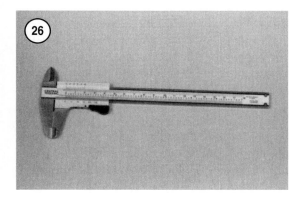

Heavy-handed use of measuring tools produces less accurate results. Hold the tool gently by the finger-tips to easily feel the point at which the tool contacts the object. This feel for the equipment produces more accurate measurements and reduces the risk of damaging the tool or component. Refer to the following sections for specific measuring tools.

### Feeler Gauge

Use feeler or thickness gauges (**Figure 25**) for measuring the distance between two surfaces.

A feeler gauge set consists of an assortment of steel strips of graduated thickness. Each blade is marked with its thickness. Blades can be of various lengths and angles for different procedures.

A common use for a feeler gauge is to measure valve clearance. Use wire (round) type gauges to measure spark plug gap.

### Calipers

Calipers (**Figure 26**) are excellent tools for obtaining inside, outside and depth measurements. Although not as precise as a micrometer, they allow reasonable precision, typically to within 0.05 mm (0.001 in.). Most calipers have a range up to 150 mm (6 in.).

Calipers are available in dial, vernier or digital versions. Dial calipers have a dial readout that provides convenient reading. Vernier calipers have marked scales that must be compared to determine the measurement. The digital caliper uses a liquid-crystal display (LCD) to show the measurement.

Properly maintain the measuring surfaces of the caliper. There must not be any dirt or burrs between the tool and the object being measured. Never force the caliper to close around an object. Close the caliper around the highest point so it can be removed with a slight drag. Some calipers require calibration. Always refer to the manufacturer's instructions when using a new or unfamiliar caliper.

To read a vernier caliper refer to **Figure 27**. The fixed scale is marked in 1-mm increments. Ten individual lines on the fixed scale equal 1 cm. The movable scale is marked in 0.05 mm (hundredth) increments. To obtain a reading, establish the first number by the location of the 0 line on the movable scale in relation to the first line to the left on the

As with all tools, measuring tools provide the best results if cared for properly. Improper use can damage the tool and cause inaccurate results. If any measurement is questionable, verify the measurement using another tool. A standard gauge is usually provided with micrometers to check accuracy and calibrate the tool if necessary.

Precision measurements can vary according to the experience of the person performing the procedure. Accurate results are only possible if the mechanic possesses a feel for using the tool.

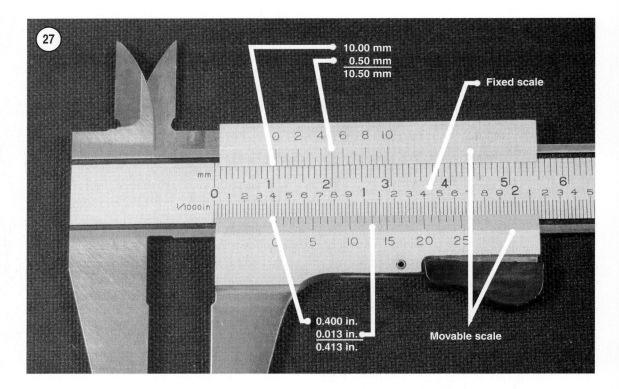

fixed scale. In this example, the number is 10 mm. To determine the next number, note which of the lines on the movable scale align with a mark on the fixed scale. A number of lines will seem close, but only one will align exactly. In this case, 0.50 mm is the reading to add to the first number. Adding 10 mm and 0.50 mm equals a measurement of 10.50 mm.

## Micrometers

A micrometer is an instrument designed for linear measurement using the decimal divisions of the inch or meter (**Figure 28**). While there are many types and styles of micrometers, most of the procedures in this manual call for an outside micrometer. Use the outside micrometer to measure the outside diameter of cylindrical forms and the thickness of materials.

A micrometer's size indicates the minimum and maximum size of a part that it can measure. The usual sizes (**Figure 29**) are 0-25 mm (0-1 in.), 25-50 mm (1-2 in.), 50-75 mm (2-3 in.) and 75-100 mm (3-4 in.).

Micrometers that cover a wider range of measurements are available. These use a large frame with interchangeable anvils of various lengths. This type of micrometer offers a cost savings, but its overall size may make it less convenient.

When reading a micrometer, numbers are taken from different scales and added together. The following sections describe how to adjust, care for and read the measurements of various types of outside micrometers.

For accurate results, properly maintain the measuring surfaces of the micrometer. There cannot be any dirt or burrs between the tool and the measured object. Never force the micrometer to close around an object. Close the micrometer around the highest point so it can be removed with a slight drag.

### *Adjustment*

Before using a micrometer, check its adjustment as follows:

1. Clean the anvil and spindle faces.

2A. To check a 0-1 in. or 0-25 mm micrometer:

   a. Turn the thimble until the spindle contacts the anvil. If the micrometer has a ratchet stop, use it to ensure that the proper amount of pressure is applied.

**28**

| DECIMAL PLACE VALUES* | |
|---|---|
| 0.1 | Indicates 1/10 (one tenth of an inch or millimeter) |
| 0.01 | Indicates 1/100 (one one-hundreth of an inch or millimeter) |
| 0.001 | Indicates 1/1000 (one one-thousandth of an inch or millimeter) |

*This chart represents the values of figures placed to the right of the decimal point. Use it when reading decimals from one-tenth to one one-thousandth of an inch or millimeter. It is not a conversion chart (for example: 0.001 in. is not equal to 0.001 mm).

**29**

b. If the adjustment is correct, the 0 mark on the thimble will align exactly with the 0 mark on the sleeve line. If the marks do not align, the micrometer is out of adjustment.

c. Follow the manufacturer's instructions to adjust the micrometer.

2B. To check a micrometer larger than 1 in. or 25 mm use the standard gauge supplied by the manufacturer. A standard gauge is a steel block, disc or rod that is machined to an exact size.

a. Place the standard gauge between the spindle and anvil, and measure its outside diameter or length. If the micrometer has a ratchet stop, use it to ensure that the proper amount of pressure is applied.

b. If the adjustment is correct, the 0 mark on the thimble will align exactly with the 0 mark on the sleeve line. If the marks do not align, the micrometer is out of adjustment.

c. Follow the manufacturer's instructions to adjust the micrometer.

*Care*

Micrometers are precision instruments. They must be used and maintained with great care. Note the following:

1. Store micrometers in protective cases or separate padded drawers in a toolbox.

2. When in storage, make sure the spindle and anvil faces do not contact each other or another object. If they do, temperature changes and corrosion may damage the contact faces.

3. Do not clean a micrometer with compressed air. Dirt forced into the tool will cause wear.

4. Lubricate micrometers with WD-40 to prevent corrosion.

*Metric micrometer*

The standard metric micrometer (**Figure 30**) is accurate to one one-hundredth of a millimeter (0.01 mm). The sleeve line is graduated in millimeter and half millimeter increments. The marks on the upper half of the sleeve line equal 1.00 mm. Each fifth mark above the sleeve line is identified with a number. The number sequence depends on the size of the micrometer. A 0-25 mm micrometer, for example, will have sleeve marks numbered 0 through 25 in 5 mm increments. This numbering sequence continues with larger micrometers. On all metric micrometers, each mark on the lower half of the sleeve equals 0.50 mm.

The tapered end of the thimble has 50 lines marked around it. Each mark equals 0.01 mm. One complete turn of the thimble aligns its 0 mark with

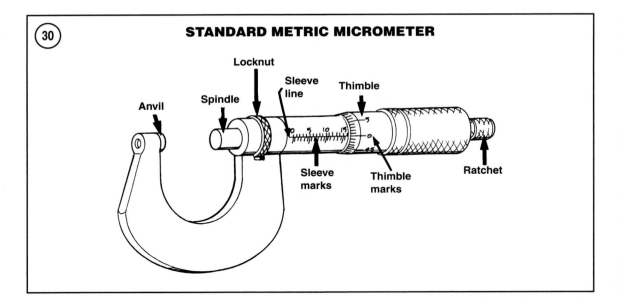

**STANDARD METRIC MICROMETER**

the first line on the lower half of the sleeve line or 0.50 mm.

When reading a metric micrometer, add the number of millimeters and half-millimeters on the sleeve line to the number of one one-hundredth millimeters on the thimble. Perform the following steps while referring to **Figure 31**.

1. Read the upper half of the sleeve line and count the number of lines visible. Each upper line equals 1 mm.

2. See if the half-millimeter line is visible on the lower sleeve line. If so, add 0.50 mm to the reading in Step 1.

3. Read the thimble mark that aligns with the sleeve line. Each thimble mark equals 0.01 mm.

> *NOTE*
> *If a thimble mark does not align exactly with the sleeve line, estimate the amount between the lines. For accurate readings in two-thousandths of a millimeter (0.002 mm), use a metric vernier micrometer.*

4. Add the readings from Steps 1-3.

### Standard inch micrometer

The standard inch micrometer (**Figure 32**) is accurate to one-thousandth of an inch or 0.001. The sleeve is marked in 0.025 in. increments. Every fourth sleeve mark is numbered 1, 2, 3, 4, 5, 6, 7, 8,

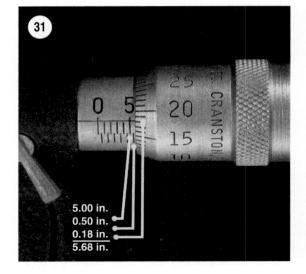

9. These numbers indicate 0.100, 0.200, 0.300, and so on.

The tapered end of the thimble has 25 lines marked around it. Each mark equals 0.001 in. One complete turn of the thimble will align its zero mark with the first mark on the sleeve or 0.025 in.

To read a standard inch micrometer, perform the following steps and refer to **Figure 33**.

1. Read the sleeve and find the largest number visible. Each sleeve number equals 0.100 in.

2. Count the number of lines between the numbered sleeve mark and the edge of the thimble. Each sleeve mark equals 0.025 in.

**STANDARD INCH MICROMETER**

3. Read the thimble mark that aligns with the sleeve line. Each thimble mark equals 0.001 in.

*NOTE*
*If a thimble mark does not align exactly with the sleeve line, estimate the amount between the lines. For accurate readings in ten-thousandths of an inch (0.0001 in.), use a vernier inch micrometer.*

4. Add the readings from Steps 1-3.

**Telescoping and Small Bore Gauges**

Use telescoping gauges (**Figure 34**) and small bore gauges (**Figure 35**) to measure bores. Neither gauge has a scale for direct readings. Use an outside micrometer to determine the reading.

To use a telescoping gauge, select the correct size gauge for the bore. Compress the movable post and

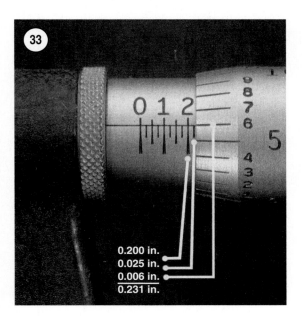

0.200 in.
0.025 in.
0.006 in.
0.231 in.

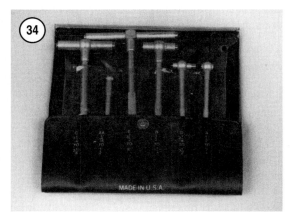

MADE IN U.S.A.

carefully insert the gauge into the bore. Carefully move the gauge in the bore to make sure it is centered. Tighten the knurled end of the gauge to hold the movable post in position. Remove the gauge and measure the length of the posts. Telescoping gauges are typically used to measure cylinder bores.

To use a small bore gauge, select the correct size gauge for the bore. Carefully insert the gauge into the bore. Tighten the knurled end of the gauge to carefully expand the gauge fingers to the limit within the bore. Do not overtighten the gauge because there is no built-in release. Excessive tightening can damage the bore surface and damage the tool. Remove the gauge and measure the outside dimension (**Figure 36**). Small bore gauges are typically used to measure valve guides.

### Dial Indicator

A dial indicator (**Figure 37**) is a gauge with a dial face and needle used to measure variations in dimensions and movements. Measuring brake rotor runout is a typical use for a dial indicator.

Dial indicators are available in various ranges and graduations and with three basic types of mounting bases: magnetic (B, **Figure 37**), clamp, or screw-in stud. When purchasing a dial indicator, select one with a continuous dial (A, **Figure 37**).

### Cylinder Bore Gauge

A cylinder bore gauge is similar to a dial indicator. The gauge set shown in **Figure 38** consists of a dial indicator, handle, and different length adapters (anvils) to fit the gauge to various bore sizes. The bore gauge is used to measure bore size, taper and out-of-round. When using a bore gauge, follow the manufacturer's instructions.

### Compression Gauge

A compression gauge (**Figure 39**) measures combustion chamber (cylinder) pressure, usually in psi or $kg/cm^2$. The gauge adapter is either inserted or screwed into the spark plug hole to obtain the reading. Disable the engine so it does not start and hold the throttle in the wide-open position when performing a compression test. An engine that does not have adequate compression cannot be properly tuned. Refer to Chapter Three.

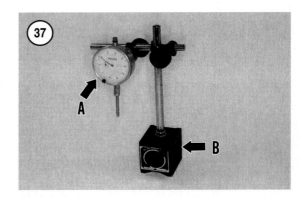

### Multimeter

A multimeter (**Figure 40**) is an essential tool for electrical system diagnosis. The voltage function indicates the voltage applied or available to various electrical components. The ohmmeter function tests circuits for continuity, or lack of continuity, and measures the resistance of a circuit.

Some manufacturers' specifications for electrical components are based on results using a specific test meter. Results may vary if using a meter not recommended by the manufacturer. Such requirements are noted when applicable.

### *Ohmmeter (analog) calibration*

Each time an analog ohmmeter is used or if the scale is changed, the ohmmeter must be calibrated.

Digital ohmmeters do not require calibration.

1. Make sure the meter battery is in good condition.
2. Make sure the meter probes are in good condition.
3. Touch the two probes together and observe the needle location on the ohms scale. The needle must

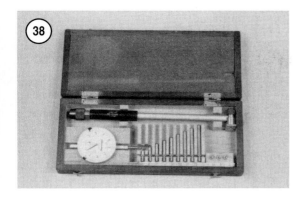

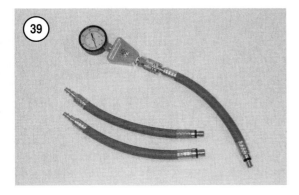

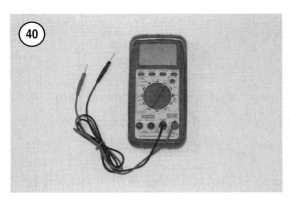

align with the 0 mark to obtain accurate measurements.

4. If necessary, rotate the meter ohms adjust knob until the needle and 0 mark align.

## ELECTRICAL SYSTEM FUNDAMENTALS

A thorough study of the many types of electrical systems used in today's motorcycles is beyond the scope of this manual. However, a basic understanding of electrical basics is necessary to perform simple diagnostic tests.

Refer to *Electrical Testing* in Chapter Two for typical test procedures and equipment. Refer to Chapter Ten for specific system test procedures.

### Voltage

Voltage is the electrical potential or pressure in an electrical circuit and is expressed in volts. The more pressure (voltage) in a circuit, the more work can be performed.

Direct current (DC) voltage means the electricity flows in one direction. All circuits powered by a battery are DC circuits.

Alternating current (AC) means the electricity flows in one direction momentarily and then switches to the opposite direction. Alternator output is an example of AC voltage. This voltage must be changed or rectified to direct current to operate in a battery powered system.

### Resistance

Resistance is the opposition to the flow of electricity within a circuit or component and is measured in ohms. Resistance causes a reduction in available current and voltage.

Resistance is measured in an inactive circuit with an ohmmeter. The ohmmeter sends a small amount of current into the circuit and measures how difficult it is to push the current through the circuit.

An ohmmeter, although useful, is not always a good indicator of a circuit's actual ability under operating conditions. This is because of the low voltage (6-9 volts) the meter uses to test the circuit. The voltage in an ignition coil secondary winding can be several thousand volts. Such high voltage can cause the coil to malfunction, even though it tests acceptable during a resistance test.

Resistance generally increases with temperature. Perform all testing with the component or circuit at room temperature. Resistance tests performed at high temperatures may indicate high resistance readings and cause unnecessary replacement of a component.

### Amperage

Amperage is the unit of measurement for the amount of current within a circuit. Current is the actual flow of electricity. The higher the current, the more work can be performed up to a given point. If the current flow exceeds the circuit or component capacity, it will damage the system.

### BASIC SERVICE METHODS

Most of the procedures in this manual are straightforward and can be performed by anyone reasonably competent with tools. However, consider personal capabilities carefully before attempting any operation involving major disassembly.

1. *Front*, in this manual, refers to the front of the motorcycle. The front of any component is the end closest to the front of the motorcycle. The left and right sides refer to the position of the parts as viewed by the rider sitting on the seat facing forward.

2. Whenever servicing an engine or suspension component, secure the motorcycle in a safe manner.

3. Tag all similar parts for location and mark all mating parts for position. Record the number and thickness of any shims when removing them. Identify parts by placing them in sealed and labeled plastic sandwich bags.

4. Tag disconnected wires and connectors with masking tape and a marking pen. Do not rely on memory alone.

5. Protect finished surfaces from physical damage or corrosion. Keep gasoline and other chemicals off painted surfaces.

6. Use penetrating oil on frozen or tight bolts. Avoid using heat where possible. Heat can warp, melt or affect the temper of parts. Heat also damages the finish of paint and plastics.

7. When a part is a press fit or requires a special tool to remove, the information or type of tool is identified in the text. Otherwise, if a part is difficult to remove or install, determine the cause before proceeding.

8. To prevent objects or debris from falling into the engine, cover all openings.

9. Read each procedure thoroughly and compare the illustrations to the actual components before starting the procedure. Perform the procedure in sequence.

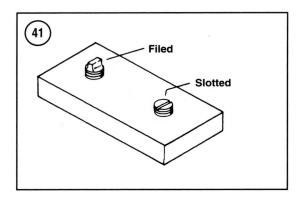

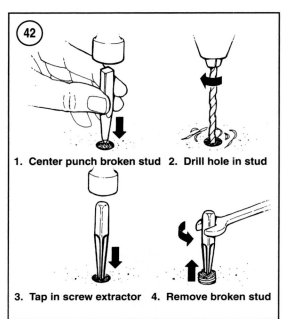

1. Center punch broken stud   2. Drill hole in stud

3. Tap in screw extractor   4. Remove broken stud

10. Recommendations are occasionally made to refer service to a dealership or specialist. In these cases, the work can be performed more economically by the specialist than by the home mechanic.

11. The term *replace* means to discard a defective part and replace it with a new part. *Overhaul* means to remove, disassemble, inspect, measure, repair and/or replace parts as required to recondition an assembly.

12. Some operations require using a hydraulic press. If a press is not available, have these operations performed by a shop equipped with the necessary equipment. Do not use makeshift equipment that may damage the motorcycle.

13. Repairs are much faster and easier if the motorcycle is clean before starting work. Degrease the

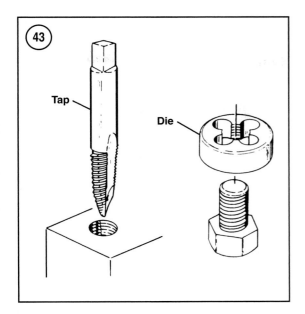

motorcycle with a commercial degreaser; follow the directions on the container for the best results. Clean all parts with cleaning solvent when removing them.

*CAUTION*
*Do not direct high-pressure water at steering bearings, fuel hoses, wheel bearings, suspension and electrical components. Water may force grease out of the bearings and possibly damage the seals.*

14. If special tools are required, have them available before starting the procedure. When special tools are required, they are described at the beginning of the procedure.

15. Make diagrams of similar-appearing parts. For instance, crankcase bolts are often not the same lengths. Do not rely on memory alone. Carefully laid out parts can become disturbed, making it difficult to reassemble the components correctly.

16. Make sure all shims and washers are reinstalled in the same location and position.

17. Whenever rotating parts contact a stationary part, look for a shim or washer.

18. Use new gaskets if there is any doubt about the condition of old ones.

19. If using self-locking fasteners, replace them with new ones. Do not install standard fasteners in place of self-locking ones.

20. Use grease to hold small parts in place if they tend to fall out during assembly. Do not apply grease to electrical or brake components.

**Removing Frozen Fasteners**

If a fastener cannot be removed, several methods may be used to loosen it. First, apply a penetrating fluid. Apply it liberally and let it penetrate for 10-15 minutes. Rap the fastener several times with a small hammer. Do not hit it hard enough to cause damage. Reapply the penetrating fluid if necessary.

For frozen screws, apply penetrating fluid as described, then insert a screwdriver in the slot and rap the top of the screwdriver with a hammer. This loosens the rust so the screw can be removed in the normal way. If the screw head is too damaged to use this method, grip the head with locking pliers and twist the screw out.

Avoid applying heat unless specifically instructed. Heat may melt, warp or remove the temper from parts.

**Removing Broken Fasteners**

If the head breaks off a screw or bolt, several methods are available for removing the remaining portion. If a large portion of the remainder projects out, try gripping it with locking pliers. If the projecting portion is too small, file it to fit a wrench or cut a slot in it to fit a screwdriver (**Figure 41**).

If the head breaks off flush, use a screw extractor. To do this, centerpunch the exact center of the remaining portion of the screw or bolt. Drill a small hole in the screw and tap the extractor into the hole. Back the screw out with a wrench on the extractor (**Figure 42**).

**Repairing Damaged Threads**

Occasionally, threads are stripped through carelessness or impact damage. Often the threads can be repaired by running a tap (for internal threads on nuts) or die (for external threads on bolts) through the threads (**Figure 43**). To clean or repair spark plug threads, use a spark plug tap.

If an internal thread is damaged, it may be necessary to install a Helicoil or some other type of thread insert. Follow the manufacturer's instructions when installing their insert.

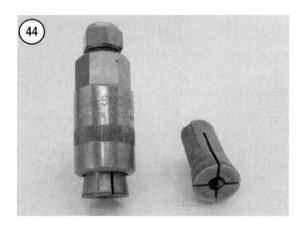

If it is necessary to drill and tap a hole, refer to **Table 8** for metric tap and drill sizes.

### Stud Removal/Installation

A stud removal tool (**Figure 44**) is available from most tool suppliers. This tool makes the removal and installation of studs easier. If one is not available, thread two nuts onto the stud and tighten them against each other. Remove the stud by turning the lower nut (**Figure 45**).

1. Measure the height of the stud above the surface.
2. Thread the stud removal tool onto the stud and tighten it, or thread two nuts onto the stud.
3. Remove the stud by turning the stud remover or the lower nut.
4. Remove any threadlocking compound from the threaded hole. Clean the threads with an aerosol parts cleaner.
5. Install the stud removal tool onto the new stud or thread two nuts onto the stud.
6. Apply threadlocking compound to the threads of the stud.
7. Install the stud and tighten with the stud removal tool or the top nut.
8. Install the stud to the height noted in Step 1 or its torque specification.
9. Remove the stud removal tool or the two nuts.

### Removing Hoses

When removing stubborn hoses, do not exert excessive force on the hose or fitting. Remove the hose clamp and carefully insert a small screwdriver or pick tool between the fitting and hose. Apply a

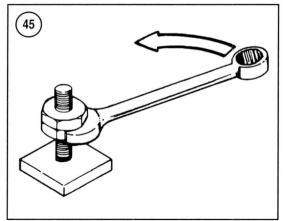

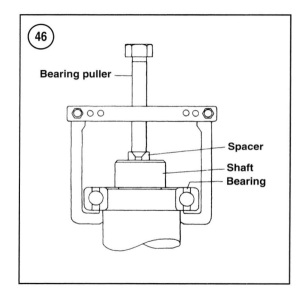

spray lubricant under the hose and carefully twist the hose off the fitting. Clean the fitting of any corrosion or rubber hose material with a wire brush. Clean the inside of the hose thoroughly. Do not use any lubricant when installing the hose (new or old). The lubricant may allow the hose to come off the fitting, even with the clamp secure.

### Bearings

Bearings are used in the engine and transmission assembly to reduce power loss, heat and noise resulting from friction. Because bearings are precision parts, they must be maintained with proper lubrication and maintenance. If a bearing is damaged, replace it immediately. When installing a new

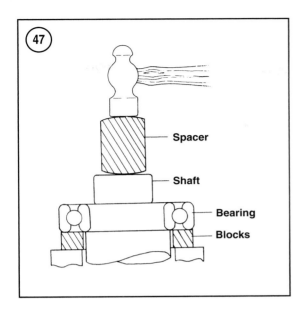

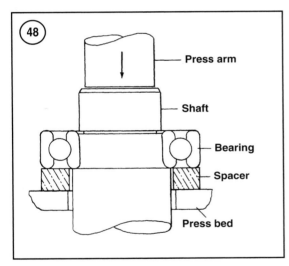

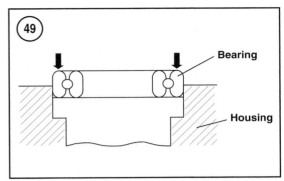

remove a bearing that is in good condition. However, improper bearing removal will damage the bearing and possibly the shaft or case. Note the following when removing bearings:

1. When using a puller to remove a bearing from a shaft, take care that the shaft is not damaged. Always place a piece of metal between the end of the shaft and the puller screw. In addition, place the puller arms next to the inner bearing race. See **Figure 46**.

2. When using a hammer to remove a bearing from a shaft, do not strike the hammer directly against the shaft. Instead, use a brass or aluminum rod between the hammer and shaft (**Figure 47**) and make sure to support both bearing races with wooden blocks as shown.

3. The ideal method of bearing removal is with a hydraulic press. Note the following when using a press:

   a. Always support the inner and outer bearing races with a suitable size wooden or aluminum spacer (**Figure 48**). If only the outer race is supported, pressure applied against the balls and/or the inner race will damage them.

   b. Always make sure the press arm (**Figure 48**) aligns with the center of the shaft. If the arm is not centered, it may damage the bearing and/or shaft.

   c. The moment the shaft is free of the bearing, it drops to the floor. Secure or hold the shaft to prevent it from falling.

bearing, take care to prevent damaging it. Bearing replacement procedures are included in the individual chapters where applicable; however, use the following sections as a guideline.

> *NOTE*
> *Unless otherwise specified, install bearings with the manufacturer's mark or number facing outward.*

### Removal

While bearings are normally removed only when damaged, there may be times when it is necessary to

### Installation

1. When installing a bearing in a housing, apply pressure to the *outer* bearing race (**Figure 49**). When installing a bearing on a shaft, apply pressure to the *inner* bearing race (**Figure 50**).

2. When installing a bearing as described in Step 1, some type of driver is required. Never strike the bearing directly with a hammer or it will damage the bearing. When installing a bearing, use a piece of pipe or a driver with a diameter that matches the bearing inner race. **Figure 51** shows the correct way to use a driver and hammer to install a bearing.

3. Step 1 describes how to install a bearing in a case half or over a shaft. However, when installing a bearing over a shaft and into the housing at the same time, a tight fit is required for both outer and inner bearing races. In this situation, install a spacer underneath the driver tool so that pressure is applied evenly across both races. See **Figure 52**. If the outer race is not supported as shown, the balls will push against the outer bearing race and damage it.

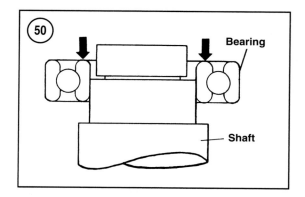

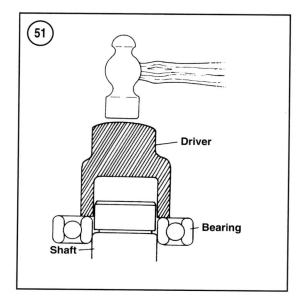

### Interference fit

1. Follow this procedure when installing a bearing over a shaft. When a tight fit is required, the bearing inside diameter is smaller than the shaft. In this case, driving the bearing on the shaft using normal methods may cause bearing damage. Instead, heat the bearing before installation. Note the following:

   a. Secure the shaft so it is ready for bearing installation.

   b. Clean all residues from the bearing surface of the shaft. Remove burrs with a file or sandpaper.

   c. Fill a suitable pot or beaker with clean mineral oil. Place a thermometer rated above 120° C (248° F) in the oil. Support the thermometer so it does not rest on the bottom or side of the pot.

   d. Remove the bearing from its wrapper and secure it with a piece of heavy wire bent to hold it in the pot. Hang the bearing in the pot so it does not touch the bottom or sides of the pot.

   e. Turn the heat on and monitor the thermometer. When the oil temperature rises to approximately 120° C (248° F), remove the bearing from the pot and quickly install it. If necessary, place a socket on the inner bearing race and tap the bearing into place. As the bearing chills, it will tighten on the shaft, so install it quickly. Make sure the bearing is installed completely.

2. Follow this step when installing a bearing in a housing. Bearings are generally installed in a housing with a slight interference fit. Driving the bearing

into the housing using normal methods may damage the housing or cause bearing damage. Instead, heat the housing before the bearing is installed. Note the following:

> *CAUTION*
> *Before heating the housing in this procedure, wash the housing thoroughly with detergent and water. Rinse and rewash the cases as required to remove all traces of oil and other chemical deposits.*

   a. Heat the housing to approximately 100° C (212° F) in an oven or on a hot plate. An easy way to check that it is the proper temperature is to place tiny drops of water on the housing; if they sizzle and evaporate immediately, the

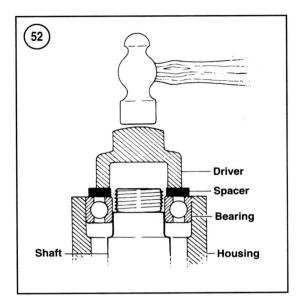

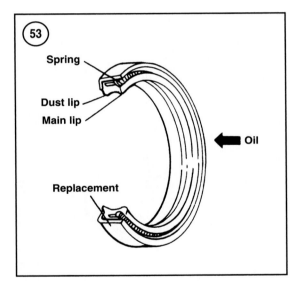

*NOTE*
*Remove and install the bearings with a suitable size socket and extension.*

c. Hold the housing with the bearing side down and tap the bearing out. Repeat for all bearings in the housing.

d. Before heating the bearing housing, place the new bearing in a freezer if possible. Chilling a bearing slightly reduces its outside diameter while the heated bearing housing assembly is slightly larger due to heat expansion. This makes bearing installation easier.

*NOTE*
*Always install bearings with the manufacturer's mark or number facing outward.*

e. While the housing is still hot, install the new bearing(s) into the housing. Install the bearings by hand, if possible. If necessary, lightly tap the bearing(s) into the housing with a driver placed on the outer bearing race (**Figure 49**). Do not install new bearings by driving on the inner-bearing race. Install the bearing(s) until it seats completely.

**Seal Replacement**

Seals (**Figure 53**) contain oil, water, grease or combustion gasses in a housing or shaft. Improperly removing a seal can damage the housing or shaft. Improperly installing the seal can damage the seal. Note the following:

1. Prying is generally the easiest and most effective method of removing a seal from the housing. However, always place a rag underneath the pry tool (**Figure 54**) to prevent damage to the housing. Note the seal's installed depth or if it is installed flush.

2. Pack waterproof grease in the seal lips before the seal is installed.

3. In most cases, install seals with the manufacturer's numbers or marks facing out.

4. Install seals with a socket or driver placed on the outside of the seal as shown in **Figure 55**. Drive the seal squarely into the housing until it is to the correct depth or flush (**Figure 56**) as noted during removal. Never install a seal by hitting against the top of it with a hammer.

temperature is correct. Heat only one housing at a time.

*CAUTION*
*Do not heat the housing with a propane or acetylene torch. Never bring a flame into contact with the bearing or housing. The direct heat will destroy the case hardening of the bearing and will likely warp the housing.*

b. Remove the housing from the oven or hot plate, and hold onto the housing with welding gloves. It is hot!

## STORAGE

Several months of non-use can cause a general deterioration of the motorcycle. This is especially true in areas of extreme temperature variations. This deterioration can be minimized with careful preparation for storage. A properly stored motorcycle is much easier to return to service.

### Storage Area Selection

When selecting a storage area, consider the following:

1. The storage area must be dry. A heated area is best, but not necessary. It should be insulated to minimize extreme temperature variations.
2. If the building has large window areas, mask them to keep sunlight off the motorcycle.
3. Avoid buildings in industrial areas where corrosive emissions may be present. Avoid areas close to saltwater.
4. Consider the area's risk of fire, theft or vandalism. Check with an insurer regarding motorcycle coverage while in storage.

### Preparing the Motorcycle for Storage

The amount of preparation a motorcycle should undergo before storage depends on the expected length of non-use, storage area conditions and personal preference. Consider the following list the minimum requirement:

1. Wash the motorcycle thoroughly. Make sure all dirt, mud and other debris are removed.
2. Lubricate the drive chain.
3. Start the engine and allow it to reach operating temperature. Drain the engine oil regardless of the riding time since the last service. Fill the engine with the recommended type of oil.
4. Drain the fuel tank, fuel lines and carburetor.
5. Remove the spark plug and ground the ignition system with a grounding tool as described in this chapter. Then pour a teaspoon (15-20 ml) of engine oil into the cylinder. Place a rag over the opening and kick the engine over to distribute the oil. Remove the grounding tool and reinstall the spark plug.
6. On CRF250X and CRF450X models, remove and service the battery as described under *Battery Storage* in Chapter Ten.

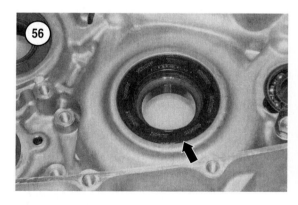

7. When the engine has cooled to room temperature, drain the cooling system as described in Chapter Three. On CRF250X and CRF450X models, drain the coolant in the coolant reserve tank and all tank lines.

8. Cover the exhaust and intake openings.

9. Apply a protective substance to the plastic and rubber components. Make sure to follow the manufacturer's instructions for each type of product being used.

10. Place the motorcycle on a workstand with both wheels off the ground.

11. Cover the motorcycle with old bed sheets or something similar. Do not cover it with any plastic material that will trap moisture.

**Returning the Motorcycle to Service**

The amount of service required when returning a motorcycle to service after storage depends on the length of non-use and storage conditions. In addition to performing the reverse of the above procedure, note the following:

1. Remove the covers from the intake and exhaust openings.

2. On CRF250X and CRF450X models, service and install the battery as described in Chapter Ten.

3. Service the air filter as described in Chapter Three.

4. Inspect the cooling system as described in Chapter Three. Check the coolant drain plug and all hose connections for leaks.

5. Refill the fuel tank. Turn the fuel shutoff valve on and check for fuel leaks.

6. Make sure the brakes, clutch, throttle and engine stop switch work properly before operating the motorcycle. Refer to Chapter Three and evaluate the service intervals to determine which areas require service.

7. If the motorcycle has been in storage for longer than four months, change the engine oil and filter, and the transmission oil as described in Chapter Three.

### Table 1 ENGINE AND FRAME IDENTIFICATION NUMBERS

| Model/year | Engine | Frame |
|---|---|---|
| **CRF250R** | | |
| 2004 | ME10E-2000001-2049999 | JH2ME103*4M000001-4M049999 |
| 2005 | ME10E-2100001-on | JH2ME103*5M100001-on |
| **CRF250X** | | |
| 2004 | | |
| 49-state | ME11E-5000001-on | JH2ME110*4K000001-on |
| California | ME11E-5000001-on | JH2ME111*4K000001-on |
| 2005 | NA | NA |
| 49-state | ME11E-5100001-on | JH2ME110*5M100001-on |
| California | ME11E-5100001-on | JH2ME111*5M100001-on |
| **CRF450R** | | |
| 2002 | PE05E-2000001-2099999 | JH2PE053*2M000001-2M099999 |
| 2003 | PE05E-2100001-2199999 | JH2PE053*3M100001-3M199999 |
| 2004 | | |
| First production run | PE05E-2200001-2249999 | JH2PE053*4M200001-4M249999 |
| Second production run | PE05E-2250001-2299999 | JH2PE053*4K250001-4K299999 |
| 2005 | PE05E-2300001-on | JH2PE053*5M300001-on |
| **CRF450X** | | |
| 2005 | | |
| 49-state | PE06E-5000001-on | JE2PE060*5K000001-on |
| California | PE06E-5000001-on | JH2PE061*5K000001-on |

### Table 2 GENERAL MOTORCYCLE DIMENSIONS

| | mm | in. |
|---|---|---|
| **Footpeg height** | | |
| **CRF250R** | | |
| 2004 | 434 | 17.1 |
| 2005 | 446 | 17.6 |
| **CRF250X** | 483 | 19.0 |
| **(continued)** | | |

**Table 2 GENERAL MOTORCYCLE DIMENSIONS (continued)**

| | mm | in. |
|---|---|---|
| **Footpeg height (continued)** | | |
| **CRF450R** | | |
| 2002 | 420 | 16.5 |
| 2003 | 429 | 16.9 |
| 2004 | 430 | 16.9 |
| 2005 | 431 | 17.0 |
| **CRF450X** | 431 | 17.0 |
| **Ground clearance** | | |
| **CRF250R** | | |
| 2004 | 349 | 13.7 |
| 2005 | 361 | 14.2 |
| **CRF250X** | 346 | 13.6 |
| **CRF450R** | | |
| 2002 | 331 | 13.0 |
| 2003 | 337 | 13.3 |
| 2004 | 338 | 13.3 |
| 2005 | 339 | 13.3 |
| **CRF450X** | 345 | 13.6 |
| **Overall height** | | |
| **CRF250R** | | |
| 2004 | 1263 | 49.7 |
| 2005 | 1277 | 50.3 |
| **CRF250X** | 1261 | 49.6 |
| **CRF450R** | | |
| 2002 | 1254 | 49.4 |
| 2003 | 1257 | 49.5 |
| 2004-on | 1262 | 49.7 |
| **CRF450X** | 1273 | 50.1 |
| **Overall length** | | |
| **CRF250R** | 2172 | 85.5 |
| **CRF250X** | 2174 | 85.6 |
| **CRF450R** | | |
| 2002 | 2187 | 86.1 |
| 2003 | 2186 | 86.1 |
| 2004 | 2194 | 86.4 |
| 2005 | 2191 | 86.3 |
| **CRF450X** | 2180 | 85.8 |
| **Overall width** | | |
| **CRF250R and CR250X** | 827 | 32.6 |
| **CRF450R** | | |
| 2002-2003 | 825 | 32.5 |
| 2004 | 827 | 32.6 |
| 2005 | 825 | 32.5 |
| **CRF450X** | 821 | 32.3 |
| **Seat height** | | |
| **CRF250R** | | |
| 2004 | 957 | 37.7 |
| 2005 | 965 | 38.0 |
| **CRF250X** | 958 | 37.7 |
| **CRF450R** | | |
| 2002 | 945 | 37.2 |
| 2003 | 953 | 37.5 |
| 2004 | 954 | 37.6 |
| 2005 | 955 | 37.6 |
| **CRF450X** | 963 | 37.9 |
| **Wheelbase** | | |
| **CRF250R** | 1479 | 58.2 |

(continued)

**Table 2 GENERAL MOTORCYCLE DIMENSIONS (continued)**

|  | mm | in. |
|---|---|---|
| Wheelbase (continued) | | |
| CRF250X | 1483 | 58.4 |
| CRF450R | | |
| 2002 | 1488 | 58.6 |
| 2003 | 1486 | 58.5 |
| 2004 | 1495 | 58.9 |
| 2005 | 1492 | 58.7 |
| CRF450X | 1483 | 58.4 |

**Table 3 WEIGHT SPECIFICATIONS**

|  | kg | lb. |
|---|---|---|
| Dry weight | | |
| CRF250R | | |
| 2004 | 93.5 | 206.1 |
| 2005 | 92.7 | 204.4 |
| CRF250X | 107.0 | 235.9 |
| CRF450R | | |
| 2002 and 2004 | 102.0 | 224.9 |
| 2003 | 103.1 | 227.3 |
| 2005 | 101.9 | 224.7 |
| CRF450X | 116.0 | 255.7 |

**Table 4 METRIC, INCH AND FRACTIONAL EQUIVALENTS**

| mm | in. | Nearest fraction | mm | in. | Nearest fraction |
|---|---|---|---|---|---|
| 1 | 0.0394 | 1/32 | 26 | 1.0236 | 1 1/32 |
| 2 | 0.0787 | 3/32 | 27 | 1.0630 | 1 1/16 |
| 3 | 0.1181 | 1/8 | 28 | 1.1024 | 1 3/32 |
| 4 | 0.1575 | 5/32 | 29 | 1.1417 | 1 5/32 |
| 5 | 0.1969 | 3/16 | 30 | 1.1811 | 1 3/16 |
| 6 | 0.2362 | 1/4 | 31 | 1.2205 | 1 7/32 |
| 7 | 0.2756 | 9/32 | 32 | 1.2598 | 1 1/4 |
| 8 | 0.3150 | 5/16 | 33 | 1.2992 | 1 5/16 |
| 9 | 0.3543 | 11/32 | 34 | 1.3386 | 1 11/32 |
| 10 | 0.3937 | 13/32 | 35 | 1.3780 | 1 3/8 |
| 11 | 0.4331 | 7/16 | 36 | 1.4173 | 1 13/32 |
| 12 | 0.4724 | 15/32 | 37 | 1.4567 | 1 15/32 |
| 13 | 0.5118 | 1/2 | 38 | 1.4961 | 1 1/2 |
| 14 | 0.5512 | 9/16 | 39 | 1.5354 | 1 17/32 |
| 15 | 0.5906 | 19/32 | 40 | 1.5748 | 1 9/16 |
| 16 | 0.6299 | 5/8 | 41 | 1.6142 | 1 5/8 |
| 17 | 0.6693 | 21/32 | 42 | 1.6535 | 1 21/32 |
| 18 | 0.7087 | 23/32 | 43 | 1.6929 | 1 11/16 |
| 19 | 0.7480 | 3/4 | 44 | 1.7323 | 1 23/32 |
| 20 | 0.7874 | 25/32 | 45 | 1.7717 | 1 25/32 |
| 21 | 0.8268 | 13/16 | 46 | 1.8110 | 1 13/16 |
| 22 | 0.8661 | 7/8 | 47 | 1.8504 | 1 27/32 |
| 23 | 0.9055 | 29/32 | 48 | 1.8898 | 1 7/8 |
| 24 | 0.9449 | 15/16 | 49 | 1.9291 | 1 15/16 |
| 25 | 0.9843 | 31/32 | 50 | 1.9685 | 1 31/32 |

**Table 5 CONVERSION TABLES**

| Multiply: | By: | To get the equivalent of: |
|---|---|---|
| Length | | |
| Inches | 25.4 | Millimeter |
| Inches | 2.54 | Centimeter |
| Miles | 1.609 | Kilometer |
| Feet | 0.3048 | Meter |
| Millimeter | 0.03937 | Inches |
| Centimeter | 0.3937 | Inches |
| Kilometer | 0.6214 | Mile |
| Meter | 3.281 | Feet |
| Fluid volume | | |
| U.S. quarts | 0.9463 | Liters |
| U.S. gallons | 3.785 | Liters |
| U.S. ounces | 29.573529 | Milliliters |
| Imperial gallons | 4.54609 | Liters |
| Imperial quarts | 1.1365 | Liters |
| Liters | 0.2641721 | U.S. gallons |
| Liters | 1.0566882 | U.S. quarts |
| Liters | 33.814023 | U.S. ounces |
| Liters | 0.22 | Imperial gallons |
| Liters | 0.8799 | Imperial quarts |
| Milliliters | 0.033814 | U.S. ounces |
| Milliliters | 1.0 | Cubic centimeters |
| Milliliters | 0.001 | Liters |
| Torque | | |
| Foot-pounds | 1.3558 | Newton-meters |
| Foot-pounds | 0.138255 | Meters-kilograms |
| Inch-pounds | 0.11299 | Newton-meters |
| Newton-meters | 0.7375622 | Foot-pounds |
| Newton-meters | 8.8507 | Inch-pounds |
| Meters-kilograms | 7.2330139 | Foot-pounds |
| Volume | | |
| Cubic inches | 16.387064 | Cubic centimeters |
| Cubic centimeters | 0.0610237 | Cubic inches |
| Temperature | | |
| Fahrenheit | $(°F - 32) \times 0.556$ | Centigrade |
| Centigrade | $(°C \times 1.8) + 32$ | Fahrenheit |
| Weight | | |
| Ounces | 28.3495 | Grams |
| Pounds | 0.4535924 | Kilograms |
| Grams | 0.035274 | Ounces |
| Kilograms | 2.2046224 | Pounds |
| Pressure | | |
| Pounds per square inch | 0.070307 | Kilograms per square centimeter |
| Kilograms per square centimeter | 14.223343 | Pounds per square inch |
| Kilopascals | 0.1450 | Pounds per square inch |
| Pounds per square inch | 6.895 | Kilopascals |
| Speed | | |
| Miles per hour | 1.609344 | Kilometers per hour |
| Kilometers per hour | 0.6213712 | Miles per hour |

**Table 6 GENERAL TORQUE SPECIFICATIONS**

| Fastener size or type | N•m | in.-lb. | ft.-lb. |
|---|---|---|---|
| 5 mm screw | 4 | 35 | — |
| 5 mm bolt and nut | 5 | 44 | — |
| 6 mm screw | 9 | 80 | — |

(continued)

### Table 6 GENERAL TORQUE SPECIFICATIONS (continued)

| Fastener size or type | N•m | in.-lb. | ft.-lb. |
|---|---|---|---|
| 6 mm bolt and nut | 10 | 88 | – |
| 6 mm flange bolt (8 mm head, small flange) | 9 | 80 | – |
| 6 mm flange bolt (10 mm head) and nut | 12 | 106 | – |
| 8 mm bolt and nut | 22 | – | 16 |
| 8 mm flange bolt and nut | 27 | – | 20 |
| 10 mm bolt and nut | 35 | – | 26 |
| 10 mm flange bolt and nut | 40 | – | 30 |
| 12 mm bolt and nut | 55 | – | 41 |

### Table 7 TECHNICAL ABBREVIATIONS

| | |
|---|---|
| ABDC | After bottom dead center |
| ATDC | After top dead center |
| BBDC | Before bottom dead center |
| BDC | Bottom dead center |
| BTDC | Before top dead center |
| C | Celsius (centigrade) |
| cc | Cubic centimeters |
| cid | Cubic inch displacement |
| CDI | Capacitor discharge ignition |
| cu. in. | Cubic inches |
| F | Fahrenheit |
| ft. | Feet |
| ft.-lb. | Foot-pounds |
| gal. | Gallons |
| hp | Horsepower |
| ICM | Ignition control module |
| in. | Inches |
| in.-lb. | Inch-pounds |
| I.D. | Inside diameter |
| Kg | Kilograms |
| Kgm | Kilogram meters |
| Km | Kilometer |
| KPa | Kilopascals |
| L | Liter |
| LED | Light-emitting diode |
| m | Meter |
| mA | Milliampere |
| ml | Milliliter |
| mm | Millimeter |
| N•m | Newton-meters |
| O.D. | Outside diameter |
| OHC | Overhead cam |
| oz. | Ounces |
| PAIR | Pulse secondary air injection system |
| psi. | Pounds per square inch |
| pt. | Pint |
| qt. | Quart |
| rpm | Revolutions per minute |
| RTV | Room temperature vulcanizing |
| TPS | Throttle position sensor |

## Table 8 METRIC TAP AND DRILL SIZES

| Metric size | Drill equivalent | Decimal fraction | Nearest fraction |
|---|---|---|---|
| 3 × 0.50 | No. 39 | 0.0995 | 3/32 |
| 3 × 0.60 | 3/32 | 0.0937 | 3/32 |
| 4 × 0.70 | No. 30 | 0.1285 | 1/8 |
| 4 × 0.75 | 1/8 | 0.125 | 1/8 |
| 5 × 0.80 | No. 19 | 0.166 | 11/64 |
| 5 × 0.90 | No. 20 | 0.161 | 5/32 |
| 6 × 1.00 | No. 9 | 0.196 | 13/64 |
| 7 × 1.00 | 16/64 | 0.234 | 15/64 |
| 8 × 1.00 | J | 0.277 | 9/32 |
| 8 × 1.25 | 17/64 | 0.265 | 17/64 |
| 9 × 1.00 | 5/16 | 0.3125 | 5/16 |
| 9 × 1.25 | 5/16 | 0.3125 | 5/16 |
| 10 × 1.25 | 11/32 | 0.3437 | 11/32 |
| 10 × 1.50 | R | 0.339 | 11/32 |
| 11 × 1.50 | 3/8 | 0.375 | 3/8 |
| 12 × 1.50 | 13/32 | 0.406 | 13/32 |
| 12 × 1.75 | 13/32 | 0.406 | 13/32 |

# CHAPTER TWO

# TROUBLESHOOTING

Diagnose electrical and mechanical problems by following an orderly procedure and remembering the basic operating requirements.

1. Define symptoms.

2. Determine which areas could exhibit those symptoms.

3. Test and analyze the suspect areas.

4. Isolate the problem.

By following a systematic approach, the possibility of unnecessary parts replacement can be avoided. Always start with the simple and most obvious checks when troubleshooting. This would include the engine stop switch, fuel quantity and condition, fuel valve position, and spark plug cap tightness.

Proper maintenance as described in Chapter Three reduces the necessity for troubleshooting. Even with the best of care, however, the motorcycle may develop problems that require troubleshooting.

If the problem cannot be solved, stop and evaluate all conditions prior to the problem. If the motor-cycle must be taken to a repair facility, the mechanic will want to know as many details as possible.

For removal, installation and test procedures for some components, refer to the specific chapter. When applicable, tables at the end of each chapter also provide specifications and service limits.

## ENGINE PRINCIPLES AND OPERATING REQUIREMENTS

An engine needs three basics to run properly: correct air/fuel mixture, compression and a spark at the right time (**Figure 1**). If one basic requirement is missing, the engine will not run.

## STARTING THE ENGINE

When experiencing engine-starting troubles, it is easy to work out of sequence and forget basic starting procedures. The following sections describe the recommended starting procedures.

Before starting the engine, perform the pre-ride inspection as described in Chapter Three.

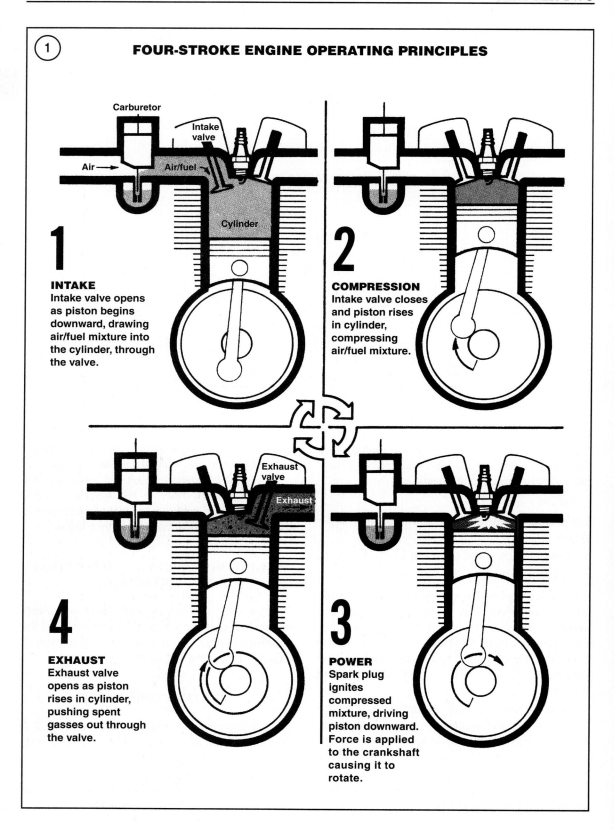

2

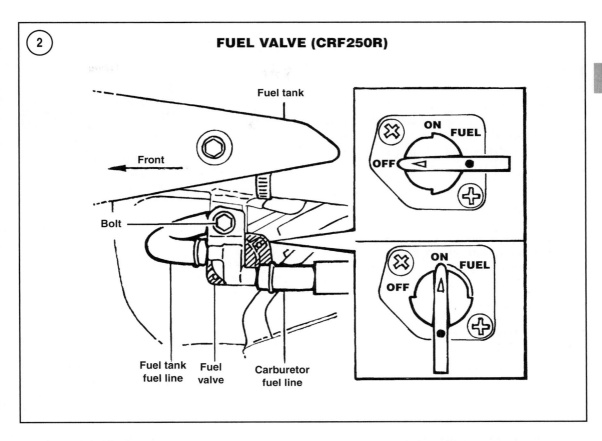

**FUEL VALVE (CRF250R)**

Fuel tank

Front

Bolt

Fuel tank fuel line   Fuel valve   Carburetor fuel line

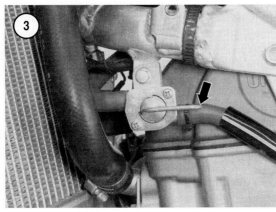

**Starting Procedure
(CRF250R and CRF450R)**

*Engine is cold*

1. Shift the transmission into neutral.

2. Turn the fuel valve on. See **Figure 2** (CRF250R) or **Figure 3** (CRF450R).

3A. If the air temperature is below 0° C (32° F), open the throttle two or three times to allow the accelerator pump to feed additional fuel to the engine.
3B. If the air temperature is below 35° C (95° F), pull the choke knob (**Figure 4**) all the way out to richen the air/fuel mixture.

*NOTE*
*Do not open the throttle when kicking
the engine over in Step 4. This allow the accelerator pump to feed*

*more fuel to the engine, possibly foul-*
*ing the spark plug.*

4. While keeping the throttle *closed*, firmly kick the kickstarter through its entire stroke.

5. When the engine starts, allow it to idle for approximately one minute, then push the choke all the way in (**Figure 4**). If the idle is not smooth, use the throttle to keep the engine running until it warms up.

> *NOTE*
> *Do not race the engine during the warm-up period. The carburetor accelerator pump can overly richen the air/fuel mixture, which would cause the engine to stall.*

**Engine is warm**

1. Shift the transmission into neutral.
2. Turn the fuel valve on. See **Figure 2** (CRF250R) or **Figure 3** (CRF450R).

> *NOTE*
> *Do not open the throttle when kicking the engine over in Step 3. This will allow the accelerator pump to feed more fuel to the engine, possibly fouling the spark plug.*

3. Pull the hot start lever (**Figure 5**) and while keeping the throttle *closed*, firmly kick the kickstarter through its entire stroke.
4. Release the hot start lever as soon as the engine starts.

**Starting the engine after a fall or after the engine stalls**

1. Shift the transmission into neutral.

> *NOTE*
> *Do not open the throttle when kicking the engine over in Step 2. This will allow the accelerator pump to feed more fuel to the engine, possibly fouling the spark plug.*

2. Pull the hot start lever (**Figure 5**) and while keeping the throttle *closed*, firmly kick the kickstarter through its entire stroke.

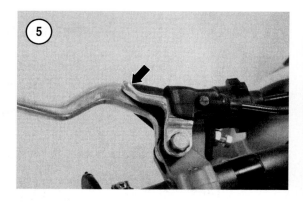

3. Release the hot start lever as soon as the engine starts.
4. If the engine fails to start, refer to *Flooded Engine* in this section.

**Flooded engine**

If the engine fails to start after several attempts, it is probably flooded. This occurs when too much fuel is drawn into the engine and the spark plug fails to ignite it. The smell of gasoline is often evident when the engine is flooded. Troubleshoot a flooded engine as follows:

1. Look for gasoline overflowing from the carburetor or overflow hose. If gasoline is evident, the engine is flooded and/or the float in the carburetor bowl is stuck. If the carburetor float is stuck, remove and repair the float assembly as described in Chapter Nine.
2. Shift the transmission into neutral.
3. Check that the choke knob (**Figure 4**) is fully closed (pushed in).
4. Open the throttle fully and hold in this position. Then kick the kickstarter firmly through its entire stroke ten times to clear the engine. Close the throttle.

> *NOTE*
> *Do not open the throttle when kicking the engine over in Step 5. This will allow the accelerator pump to feed more fuel to the engine, possibly fouling the spark plug.*

5. Pull the hot start lever (**Figure 5**) and while keeping the throttle *closed*, firmly kick the kickstarter through its entire stroke.

6. Release the hot start lever as soon as the engine starts.

7. If the engine still does not start, refer to *Engine Will Not Start* in this chapter.

**Starting Procedure
(CRF250X and CRF450X)**

> *CAUTION*
> *On CRF250X models, do not kick-start the engine without the battery connected in the circuit. Doing so can damage the lighting system. If it is necessary to start the engine without the battery, first remove the main relay from the wiring harness (Chapter Ten).*

> *NOTE*
> *Do not operate the starter for more than 5 seconds at a time. Wait approximately 10 seconds between starting attempts to prevent overheating and damaging the starter.*

*Engine cold with air temperature
between 10-35° C (50-95° F)*

1. Shift the transmission into neutral.
2. Turn the fuel valve on (**Figure 6**).
3. Pull the choke knob (**Figure 4**) all the way out to richen the air/fuel mixture.

> *NOTE*
> *Do not open the throttle when starting the engine in Step 4. This will allow the accelerator pump to feed more fuel to the engine, possibly fouling the spark plug.*

4. While keeping the throttle *closed*, pull the clutch lever fully in and press the starter button (**Figure 7**), or firmly kick the kickstarter through its entire stroke.

5. When the engine starts, allow it to idle for approximately 15 seconds, then push the choke all the way in (**Figure 4**). If the idle is not smooth, use the throttle to keep the engine running until it warms up.

> *NOTE*
> *Do not race the engine during the warm-up period. The carburetor accelerator pump can overly richen the air/fuel mixture, which may cause the engine to stall.*

*Engine cold with air temperature
above 35° C (95° F)*

1. Shift the transmission into neutral.
2. Turn the fuel valve on (**Figure 6**).

> *NOTE*
> *Do not open the throttle when starting the engine in Step 3. This will allow the accelerator pump to feed more fuel to the engine, possibly fouling the spark plug.*

3. While keeping the throttle *closed*, pull the clutch lever fully in and press the starter button (**Figure 7**), or firmly kick the kickstarter through its entire stroke.

4. When the engine starts, allow it to idle until it warms up.

### Cold engine with air temperature below 10° C (50° F)

1. Shift the transmission into neutral.
2. Turn the fuel valve on (**Figure 6**).
3. On CRF450X models, if the temperature is below 32° F (0° C), open the throttle two or three times to allow the accelerator pump to feed additional fuel to the engine.
4. Pull the choke knob (**Figure 4**) all the way out to richen the air/fuel mixture.

*NOTE*
*Do not open the throttle when starting the engine in Step 4. This will allow the accelerator pump to feed more fuel to the engine, possibly causing the spark plug to foul.*

5. While keeping the throttle *closed*, pull the clutch lever fully in and press the starter button (**Figure 7**), or firmly kick the kickstarter through its entire stroke.
6. When the engine starts, use the throttle to keep the engine running until the engine warms up and the choke (**Figure 4**) can be fully closed.

*NOTE*
*Do not race the engine during the warm-up period. The carburetor accelerator pump can overly richen the air/fuel mixture and cause the engine to stall.*

### Engine is hot

1. Shift the transmission into neutral.
2. Turn the fuel valve on (**Figure 6**).

*NOTE*
*Do not open the throttle when starting the engine in Step 3. This will allow the accelerator pump to feed more fuel to the engine, possibly fouling the spark plug.*

3. Pull the hot start lever (**Figure 5**). Then while keeping the throttle *closed*, pull the clutch lever fully in and press the starter button (**Figure 7**), or firmly kick the kickstarter through its entire stroke.
4. Release the hot start lever as soon as the engine starts.

### Starting the engine after a fall or after the engine stalls

1. Shift the transmission into neutral.

*NOTE*
*Do not open the throttle when kicking the engine over in Step 2. This will allow the accelerator pump to feed more fuel to the engine, possibly fouling the spark plug.*

2. Pull the hot start lever (**Figure 5**). Then while keeping the throttle *closed*, pull the clutch lever fully in and press the starter button (**Figure 7**), or firmly kick the kickstarter through its entire stroke.
3. Release the hot start lever as soon as the engine starts.
4. If the engine fails to start, refer to *Flooded Engine* in this section.

### Flooded engine

If the engine fails to start after several attempts, it is probably flooded. This situation occurs when too much fuel is drawn into the engine and the spark plug fails to ignite it. The smell of gasoline is often evident when the engine is flooded. Troubleshoot a flooded engine as follows:

1. Look for gasoline overflowing from the carburetor or overflow hose. If gasoline is evident, the engine is flooded and/or the float in the carburetor bowl is stuck. If the carburetor float is stuck, remove and repair the float assembly as described in Chapter Nine.
2. Shift the transmission into neutral.
3. Check that the choke knob (**Figure 4**) is fully closed (pushed in).

*NOTE*
*Do not open the throttle when kicking the engine over in Step 4. This will allow the accelerator pump to feed more fuel to the engine, possibly fouling the spark plug.*

4A. Kickstarter—Perform the following:
  a. Open the throttle fully and hold in this position. Then kick the kickstarter firmly through its entire stroke ten times to clear the engine. Close the throttle.

b. Pull the hot start lever (**Figure 5**) and while keeping the throttle *closed*, firmly kick the kickstarter through its entire stroke.

c. Release the hot start lever as soon as the engine starts.

4B. Starter—Perform the following:

a. Pull the hot start lever (**Figure 5**). Then pull the clutch lever fully in, open the throttle fully and press the starter button (**Figure 7**) for 5 seconds.

b. If the engine starts, close the throttle and release the hot start lever. If the engine starts but idles roughly, vary the throttle position slightly until the engine idles and responds smoothly.

c. If the engine did not start, wait 10 seconds and repeat the starting procedure.

5. If the engine still does not start, refer to *Engine Will Not Start* in this chapter.

## ENGINE WILL NOT START

### Identifying the Problem

If the engine does not start, perform the following steps in order while remembering the *Engine Principals and Operating Requirements* described in this chapter. If the engine fails to start after performing these checks, refer to the troubleshooting procedures indicated in the steps. If the engine starts, but idles or runs roughly, refer to *Poor Engine Performance* in this chapter.

1. Refer to *Starting the Engine* in this chapter to make sure all starting procedures are correct.

2. On CRF250X and CRF450X models, if the starter does not turn over, refer to *Starting System Testing in Chapter Ten*.

3. If the engine seems flooded, refer to *Starting The Engine* in this chapter. If the engine is not flooded, continue with Step 4.

4. Remove the cap from the fuel tank and make sure the fuel tank has a sufficient amount of fuel to start the engine.

5. If there is sufficient fuel in the fuel tank, remove the spark plug immediately after attempting to start the engine. The plug's insulator should be wet, indicating that fuel is reaching the engine. If the plug tip is dry, fuel is not reaching the engine. Refer to *Fuel System* in this chapter. If there is fuel on the spark plug and the engine will not start, the engine may not have adequate spark. Continue with Step 6.

*NOTE*
*When examining the direct ignition coil or spark plug cap in the following steps, check for the presence of water.*

6. Make sure the direct ignition coil or spark plug wire is secure. Push the direct ignition coil or spark plug cap and slightly rotate it to clean the electrical connection between the plug and the connector. If the engine does not start, continue with Step 7.

*NOTE*
*A cracked or damaged direct ignition coil or spark plug cap and cable can cause intermittent problems that are difficult to diagnose. If the engine occasionally misfires or cuts out, use a spray bottle to wet the direct ignition coil or plug cap and plug cable while the engine is running. Water that enters one of these areas causes an arc through the insulating material, causing an engine misfire.*

*NOTE*
*Engine misfire can also be caused by water that enters through connectors. Check the connectors for loose wire ends. On waterproof connectors, check for damage where the wires enter the connector.*

7. Perform the *Spark Test* in this section. If there is a strong spark, perform Step 8. If there is no spark or if the spark is very weak, refer to *Ignition System Testing* in Chapter Ten.

8. If the fuel and ignition systems are working correctly, perform a leakdown test (this chapter) and cylinder compression test (Chapter Three). If the leakdown test indicates a problem, or the compression is low, refer to *Low Engine Compression* under *Engine* in this chapter.

### Spark Test

Perform a spark test to determine if the ignition system is producing adequate spark. This test should be performed with a spark tester. A spark tester looks like a spark plug with an adjustable gap between the center electrode and grounded base.

Because the voltage required to jump the spark tester gap is sufficiently larger than that of a normally gapped spark plug, the test results are more accurate than with a spark plug. Do not assume that because a spark jumped across a spark plug gap, the ignition system is working correctly.

Perform this test on the engine when it is both cold and hot, if possible. If the test results are positive for each test, the ignition system is working correctly.

*CAUTION*
*After removing the direct ignition coil or spark plug cap and before removing the spark plug in Step 1, clean the area around the spark plug with compressed air. Dirt that falls into the cylinder causes rapid engine wear.*

*NOTE*
*The spark tester used in this procedure is available from Motion Pro (part No. 08-0122) and can be purchased through motorcycle dealerships.*

1. Remove the fuel tank (Chapter Nine).
2. Disconnect the direct ignition coil or spark plug cap. Check for the presence of water.
3. Visually inspect the spark plug for damage.
4. Connect a spark tester to the direct ignition coil or spark plug cap. Ground the spark tester base (or spark plug) to a good ground (**Figure 8**). Position the spark tester or spark plug firing tip away from the open spark plug hole. Position the spark tester so the electrodes are visible.

*WARNING*
*Mount the spark tester or spark plug away from the spark plug hole in the cylinder head so the spark plug or tester cannot ignite gasoline vapors in the cylinder. If the engine is flooded, do not perform this test. The spark generated by the spark plug or spark tester can ignite fuel ejected through the spark plug hole.*

5. Shift the transmission into neutral.

*WARNING*
*Do not hold the spark tester, spark plug or connector or a serious electrical shock may result.*

6. Turn the engine over with the kickstarter. If using the starter on CRF250X and CRF450X models, pull the clutch lever in and push the starter button. A fat blue spark must be evident between the spark tester or spark plug terminals.
7. If there is a strong, blue spark, the ignition system is functioning properly. Check for one or more of the following possible malfunctions:
   a. Faulty fuel system component.
   b. Flooded engine.
   c. Engine damage (low compression).
8. If the spark was weak (white or yellow) or if there was no spark, perform the peak voltage checks described under *Ignition System Testing* in Chapter Ten.
9. Reinstall the fuel tank.

**Starter Does Not Turn Over or Turns Over Slowly (CRF250X and CRF450X)**

Refer to *Starting System Testing* in Chapter Ten.

**POOR ENGINE PERFORMANCE**

If the engine runs, but performance is unsatisfactory, refer to the following section that best describes the symptoms.

**Engine Starts But Stalls and is Hard to Restart**

Check for the following:
1. Incorrect choke operation. This can be due to improper use or a stuck choke valve in the carburetor.
2. Incorrect hot start valve operation. This situation can be due to improper use or incorrect hot start valve adjustment.

3. Plugged fuel tank vent hose (**Figure 9**).
4. Plugged fuel hose, fuel shutoff valve or fuel filter.
5. Incorrect carburetor adjustment.
6. Incorrect float level adjustment.
7. Plugged carburetor jets.

*NOTE*
*If a warm or hot engine will start with the choke on, or if a cold engine starts and runs until the choke is turned off, the pilot jet is probably plugged.*

8. Contaminated or stale fuel.
9. Clogged air filter.
10. Intake pipe air leak.
11. Plugged exhaust system. Check the silencer or muffler, especially if the motorcycle was just returned from storage.
12. Faulty ignition system component.

### Engine Backfires, Cuts Out or Misfires During Acceleration

A backfire occurs when fuel is burned or ignited in the exhaust system.
1. A lean air/fuel mixture can cause these engine performance problems. Check for the following conditions:
  a. Incorrect float level adjustment.
  b. Plugged pilot jet or pilot system.
2. Faulty accelerator pump.
3. Loose exhaust pipe-to-cylinder head connection.
4. Intake air leak.
5. Incorrect ignition timing or a damaged ignition system can cause these conditions. Perform the *Peak Voltage Tests* in Chapter Ten to isolate the

damaged ignition system component. Check the ignition timing as described in Chapter Ten.

*NOTE*
*The ignition timing is controlled by the ICM and cannot be adjusted. However, checking the ignition timing can be used to diagnose problems.*

6. Check the following engine components:
  a. Broken valve springs.
  b. Stuck or leaking valves.
  c. Worn or damaged camshaft lobes.
  d. Incorrect valve timing due to incorrect camshaft installation or a mechanical failure.

### Engine Backfires on Deceleration

If the engine backfires when the throttle is released, check the following:
1. Lean carburetor pilot system.
2. Loose exhaust pipe-to-cylinder head connection.
3. On CRF250X and CRF450X California models: Faulty secondary air supply system.
4. Faulty ignition system component.
5. Check the following engine components:
  a. Broken valve springs.
  b. Stuck or leaking valves.
  c. Worn or damaged camshaft lobes.
  d. Incorrect valve timing due to incorrect camshaft installation or a mechanical failure.

### Poor Fuel Mileage

1. Clogged fuel system.
2. Dirty or clogged air filter.
3. Incorrect ignition timing (defective ICM or ignition pulse generator).

### Engine Will Not Idle or Idles Roughly

1. Clogged air filter element.
2. Poor fuel flow resulting from a partially clogged fuel valve, fuel filter or fuel hose.
3. Faulty accelerator pump assembly.
4. Contaminated or stale fuel.
5. Incorrect carburetor adjustment.
6. Leaking head gasket.
7. Intake air leak.

8. Incorrect ignition timing (defective ICM or ignition pulse generator).
9. Low engine compression.

## Low Engine Power

1. Support the motorcycle on a stand with the rear wheel off the ground, then spin the rear wheel by hand. If the wheel spins freely, perform Step 2. If the wheel does not spin freely, check for the following conditions:
   a. Dragging brakes. Check for this condition immediately after riding the motorcycle.

*NOTE*
*After riding the motorcycle, come to a stop on a level surface. Turn the engine off and shift the transmission into neutral. Walk or push the motorcycle forward. If the motorcycle is harder to push than normal, check for dragging brakes.*

   b. Damaged or binding drive chain.
   c. Damaged wheel bearings.
2. Test ride the motorcycle and accelerate quickly from first to second gear. If the engine speed increased according to throttle position, perform Step 3. If the engine speed did not increase, check for one or more of the following problems:
   a. Slipping clutch.
   b. Warped clutch plates/discs.
   c. Worn clutch plates/discs.
   d. Weak or damaged clutch springs.
3. Test ride the motorcycle and accelerate lightly. If the engine speed increased according to throttle position, perform Step 4. If the engine speed did not increase, check for one or more of the following problems:
   a. Clogged air filter.
   b. Restricted fuel flow.
   c. Pinched fuel tank breather hose (**Figure 9**).
   d. Clogged or damaged silencer or muffler.

*NOTE*
*A clogged exhaust system will prevent some of the burned exhaust gasses from exiting the exhaust port at the end of the exhaust stroke. This condition effects the incoming air/fuel mixture on the intake stroke and reduces engine power.*

4. Check for retarded ignition timing as described in Chapter Ten. A decrease in power results when the plugs fire later than normal.
5. Check for one or more of the following problems:
   a. Low engine compression.
   b. Worn spark plug.
   c. Fouled spark plug.
   d. Incorrect spark plug heat range.
   e. Weak ignition coil.
   f. Incorrect ignition timing (defective ICM or ignition pulse generator).
   g. Plugged carburetor passages.
   h. Incorrect oil level (too high or too low).
   i. Contaminated oil.
   j. Worn or damaged valve train assembly.
   k. Engine overheating.
6. If the engine knocks when it is accelerated or when running at high speed, check for one or more of the following possible malfunctions:
   a. Incorrect type of fuel.
   b. Lean fuel mixture.
   c. Advanced ignition timing (defective ICM).

*NOTE*
*Other signs of advanced ignition timing are engine overheating and hard or uneven engine starting.*

   d. Excessive carbon buildup in combustion chamber.
   e. Worn piston and/or cylinder bore.

## Poor Idle or Low Speed Performance

1. Check for an incorrect pilot screw adjustment.
2. Check for damaged or loose intake pipe and air filter housing hose clamps. These conditions will cause an air leak.
3. Perform the spark test in this chapter. Note the following:
   a. If the spark is good, go to Step 4.
   b. If the spark is weak, perform the *Peak Voltage Testing* described in Chapter Ten.
4. Check the ignition timing as described in Chapter Ten. If ignition timing is correct, perform Step 5. If the timing is incorrect, perform the *Peak Voltage Testing* in Chapter Ten.
5. Check the fuel system as described in this chapter.

## Poor High Speed Performance

1. Check ignition timing as described in Chapter Three. If the ignition timing is correct, perform Step 2. If the timing is incorrect, perform the *Peak Voltage Tests* in Chapter Ten.
2. Check the fuel system as described in this chapter.
3. Check the valve clearance as described in Chapter Three. Note the following:
   a. If the valve clearance is correct, perform Step 4.
   b. If the clearance is incorrect, adjust the valves as described in Chapter Three.
4. Incorrect valve timing and worn or damaged valve springs can cause poor high-speed performance. If the camshaft was timed just before the motorcycle experiencing this type of problem, the cam timing may be incorrect. If the cam timing was not set or changed, and all the other inspection procedures in this section failed to locate the problem, inspect the camshaft and valve assembly.

### FUEL SYSTEM

The following section isolates common fuel system problems under specific complaints. If there is a good spark, poor fuel flow may be preventing the correct amount of fuel from being supplied to the spark plug. Troubleshoot the fuel system as follows:

1. Clogged fuel tank breather hose (**Figure 9**).
2. Check that there is a sufficient amount of fuel in the tank.
3. After attempting to start the engine, remove the spark plug (Chapter Three) and check for fuel on the plug tip. Note the following:
   a. If there is no fuel visible on the plug, check for a clogged fuel shutoff valve, fuel filter or fuel line.
   b. If there is fuel present on the plug tip, and the engine has spark, check for an excessive intake air leak or the possibility of contaminated or stale fuel.

> *NOTE*
> *If the motorcycle was not used for some time, and was not properly stored, the fuel may have gone stale, where lighter parts of the fuel have evaporated. Depending on the condition of the fuel, a no-start condition can result.*

   c. If there is an excessive amount of fuel on the plug, check for a clogged air filter or flooded carburetor.

### Rich Mixture

The following conditions can cause a rich air/fuel mixture:
1. Clogged air filter.
2. Choke valve stuck open.
3. Float level too high.
4. Contaminated float valve seat.
5. Worn or damaged float valve and seat.
6. Leaking or damaged float.
7. Clogged carburetor jets.
8. Incorrect carburetor jetting.

### Lean Mixture

The following conditions can cause a lean air/fuel mixture:
1. Intake air leak.
2. Float level too low.
3. Clogged fuel line, fuel filter or fuel shutoff valve.
4. Partially restricted fuel tank breather hose.
5. Plugged carburetor air vent hose.
6. Damaged float.
7. Damaged float valve.
8. Incorrect carburetor jetting.

### ENGINE

## Engine Smoke

The color of engine smoke can help diagnose engine problems or operating conditions.

### *Black smoke*

Black smoke is an indication of a rich air/fuel mixture.

### *Blue smoke*

Blue smoke indicates that the engine is burning oil in the combustion chamber as it leaks past worn valve stem seals and piston rings. Excessive oil consumption is another indicator of an engine that is burning oil. Perform a compression test (Chapter Three) to isolate the problem.

### White smoke or steam

It is normal to see white smoke or steam from the exhaust after first starting the engine in cold weather. This is actually condensed steam formed by the engine during combustion. If the motorcycle is ridden far enough, the water cannot collect in the crankcase and should not become a problem. Once the engine heats up to normal operating temperature, the water evaporates and exits the engine through the crankcase vent system. However, if the motorcycle is ridden for short trips or repeatedly started and stopped and allowed to cool off without the engine getting warm enough, water will start to collect in the crankcase. With each short run of the engine, more water collects. As this water mixes with the oil in the crankcase, sludge is produced. Sludge can eventually cause engine damage as it circulates through the lubrication system and blocks off oil passages.

Large amounts of steam can also be caused by a cracked cylinder head or cylinder block surface that allows coolant to leak into the combustion chamber. Perform a *Coolant System Pressure Test* as described in Chapter Eleven.

## Low Engine Compression

Problems with the engine top end will affect engine performance. When the engine is suspect, perform the leakdown procedure in this chapter and make a compression test as described in Chapter Three. Interpret the results as described in each procedure to troubleshoot the suspect area. An engine can lose compression through the following areas:
1. Valves:
    a. Incorrect valve adjustment.
    b. Incorrect valve timing.
    c. Worn or damaged valve seat surfaces.
    d. Bent valves.
    e. Weak or broken valve springs.
2. Cylinder head:
    a. Loose spark plug or damaged spark plug hole.
    b. Damaged cylinder head gasket.

    c. Warped or cracked cylinder head.
3. Damaged decompressor assembly.

## High Engine Compression

1. Faulty decompressor assembly.
2. Excessive carbon buildup in the combustion chamber.

## Engine Overheating (Cooling System)

*WARNING*
*Do not remove the radiator cap, coolant drain plug or disconnect any coolant hose immediately after or during engine operation. Scalding fluid and steam may be blown out under pressure and cause serious injury. When the engine has been operated, the coolant is very hot and under pressure. Attempting to remove the items when the engine is hot can cause the coolant to spray violently from the radiator, water pump or hose, causing severe burns and injury.*

1. Low coolant level.
2. Air in cooling system.
3. Clogged radiator, hose or engine coolant passages.
4. Worn or damaged radiator cap.
5. Damaged water pump.

## Engine Overheating (Engine)

1. Improper spark plug heat range.
2. Low oil level.
3. Oil not circulating properly.
4. Valves leaking.
5. Heavy carbon deposits in the combustion chamber.
6. Dragging brake(s).
7. Slipping clutch.

## Preignition

Preignition is the premature burning of fuel and is caused by hot spots in the combustion chamber. Glowing deposits in the combustion chamber, inadequate cooling or an overheated spark plug can all cause preignition. This is first noticed as a power loss but eventually causes damage to the internal parts of the engine because of the high combustion chamber temperature.

## Detonation

Detonation is the violent explosion of fuel in the combustion chamber before the proper time of ignition. Using low octane gasoline is a common cause of detonation.

Even when using a high octane gasoline, detonation can still occur. Other causes are over-advanced ignition timing, lean air/fuel mixture at or near full throttle, inadequate engine cooling, or the excessive accumulation of carbon deposits in the combustion chamber.

Continued detonation can result in engine damage.

## Power Loss

Refer to *Poor Engine Performance* in this chapter.

## Engine Noises

Unusual noises are often the first indication of a developing problem. Investigate any new noises as soon as possible. Something that may be a minor problem, if corrected, could prevent the possibility of more extensive damage.

Use a mechanic's stethoscope or a small section of hose held near your ear (not directly on your ear) with the other end close to the source of the noise to isolate the location. Determining the exact cause of a noise can be difficult. If this is the case, consult with a professional mechanic to determine the cause. Do not disassemble major components until all other possibilities have been eliminated.

Consider the following when troubleshooting engine noises:

1. Knocking or pinging during acceleration can be caused by using a lower octane fuel than recommended. May also be caused by poor fuel. Pinging can also be caused by an incorrect spark plug heat range or carbon buildup in the combustion chamber.

2. Slapping or rattling noises at low speed or during acceleration—May be caused by excessive piston-to-cylinder wall clearance (piston slap).

*NOTE*
*Piston slap is easier to detect when the engine is cold and before the piston has expanded. Once the engine has warmed up, piston expansion reduces piston-to-cylinder clearance.*

3. Knocking or rapping while decelerating—Usually caused by excessive rod bearing clearance.
4. Persistent knocking and vibration occurring every crankshaft rotation—Usually caused by worn rod or main bearing(s). Can also be caused by broken piston rings or a damaged piston pin.
5. Rapid on-off squeal—Compression leak around cylinder head gasket or spark plug(s).
6. Valve train noise—Check for the following:
   a. Excessive valve clearance.
   b. Worn or damaged camshaft.
   c. Damaged camshaft.
   d. Worn or damaged valve train components.
   e. Damaged valve lifter bore(s).
   f. Valve sticking in guide.
   g. Broken valve spring.
   h. Low oil pressure.
   i. Clogged cylinder oil hole or oil passage.

### ENGINE LUBRICATION

An improperly operating engine lubrication system quickly leads to engine seizure. Check the engine oil level and oil pressure as described in Chapter Three. Oil pump service is described in Chapter Four and Chapter Five.

## High Oil Consumption or Excessive Exhaust Smoke

1. Worn valve guides.
2. Worn valve guide seals.
3. Worn or damaged piston rings.
4. Incorrect piston ring installation.

## Low Oil Pressure

1. Low oil level.
2. Worn or damaged oil pump.
3. Clogged oil strainer screen.

4. Clogged oil filter.
5. Internal oil leakage.
6. Oil relief valve stuck open.
7. Incorrect type of engine oil.

**High Oil Pressure**

1. Oil relief valve stuck closed.
2. Clogged oil filter.
3. Clogged oil gallery or metering orifices.

**No Oil Pressure**

1. Low oil level.
2. Oil relief valve stuck closed.
3. Damaged oil pump.
4. Incorrect oil pump installation.
5. Internal oil leak.

**Oil Level Too Low**

1. Oil level not maintained at correct level.
2. Worn piston rings.
3. Worn cylinder.
4. Worn valve guides.
5. Worn valve guide seals.
6. Piston rings incorrectly installed during engine overhaul.
7. External oil leakage.
8. Oil leaking into the cooling system.

**Oil Contamination**

1. Blown head gasket allowing coolant to leak into the engine.
2. Coolant leak.
3. Oil and filter not changed at specified intervals or when operating conditions demand more frequent changes.

### CYLINDER LEAKDOWN TEST

A cylinder leakdown test can accurately pinpoint engine leakage problems from the head gasket, water jackets in the cylinder head and cylinder, valves and valve seats, and piston rings. This test is performed by applying compressed air to the cylinder through a special tester and then measuring the percent of leakage. A cylinder leakdown tester and an

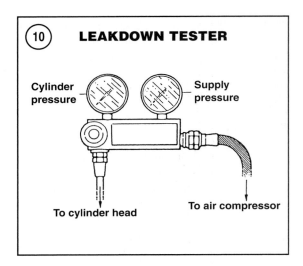

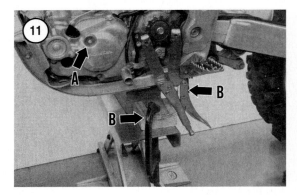

air compressor are needed to perform this test (**Figure 10**).

When performing a leakdown test, the engine is first set at TDC on its compression stroke so that all the valves are closed. When the combustion chamber is pressurized, very little air should escape. However, the difficulty in performing a leakdown test on a single cylinder engine (especially on the engines described in this manual with low static engine compression) is in preventing the piston from moving as the combustion chamber starts to pressurize. Any piston movement will force the crankshaft to turn away from TDC and allow air to escape past an open valve seat.

In this procedure it will be necessary to lock the engine at TDC on its compression stroke and then perform the leakdown test. Follow the manufacturer's directions along with the following information when performing a cylinder leakdown test.

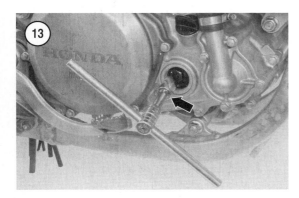

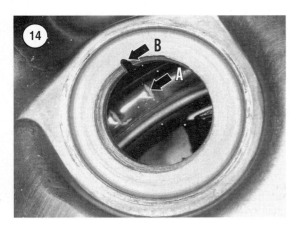

1. Support the motorcycle on a work stand with the rear wheel off the ground.

2. Remove the air filter assembly (Chapter Three). Open and secure the throttle so it is at its wide-open position.

3A. On CRF250R and CRF450R models, remove the master link and slide the drive chain off the drive sprocket.

3B. CRF250X and CRF450X models are equipped with an endless drive chain, loosen the rear axle nut

and move the rear wheel forward to obtain as much chain slack as possible. Then remove the drive sprocket cover and the drive sprocket as described in Chapter Twelve. Reinstall the drive sprocket without the drive chain.

4. Remove the fuel tank (Chapter Nine).

5. Remove the spark plug (Chapter Three).

6. Install the threaded hose adapter from the leakdown kit. Then install the leakdown gauge onto the hose.

7. Remove the ignition timing hole cap (A, **Figure 11**) from the left crankcase cover.

8. Remove the crankshaft hole cap (**Figure 12**) from the right crankcase cover.

> *NOTE*
> *Because the following test is performed with the cylinder head cover installed on the engine, the camshaft lobes cannot be viewed to ensure that the engine is positioned at TDC on its compression stroke. To determine when the engine is approaching TDC on its compression stroke, or whether it is 360° off, observe the following two indicators to predict engine position. First, when aligning the index marks in Step 9, listen for pressure building inside the combustion chamber, indicating that the piston is moving to TDC on its compression stroke. Second, view the gauge on the leakdown tester when turning the engine. As the piston moves toward TDC on its compression stroke, compression building inside the combustion chamber may cause the gauge needle to move slightly. If the crankshaft is 360° off, these indicators will not be present.*

> *NOTE*
> *The decompressor mechanism will click loudly once during each crankshaft revolution. This is normal.*

9. Use an 8 mm hex socket on the primary drive gear mounting bolt (**Figure 13**) and turn the crankshaft *clockwise* and align the TDC mark on the flywheel (A, **Figure 14**) with the index mark on the left crankcase cover (B). Remove the hex socket from the primary drive gear.

10. Perform the following to lock the transmission so the engine remains at TDC on its compression stroke when performing the leakdown test:

> *WARNING*
> *Do not attempt to lock the engine by trying to use a tool to hold the Allen bolt on the end of the crankshaft. Once the combustion chamber becomes pressurized, any crankshaft movement can throw the tool away from the engine under considerable force. Attempting to hold the tool can cause serious injury. Engine damage may also occur to the crankshaft or right crankcase cover. Lock the engine as described in this procedure.*

  a. Turn the drive sprocket by hand and shift the transmission into top gear with the shift pedal.

  b. Mount a holding tool (Motion Pro Clutch Holding Tool [part No. 08-0008]) or equivalent onto the drive sprocket. Use a wooden block and clamp to hold the holding tool so it cannot move when the combustion chamber becomes pressurized. See the tool setup in B, **Figure 11**.

  c. Check that the TDC marks are still aligned as described in Step 9. If not, turn the crankshaft as required, then relock the holding tool in position.

11. Remove the radiator cap and the oil filler cap.

12. Perform a cylinder leakdown test by applying air pressure to the combustion chamber. Follow the manufacturer's instructions while reading the percent of leakage on the gauge (**Figure 15**). Listen for air leaking while noting the following:

> *NOTE*
> *Because of play in the transmission gears, it is unlikely the engine will stay at TDC on the first try. If the crankshaft turns, reposition the countershaft slightly and then relock it in position with the holding tool. After several attempts, you will get a feel of the transmission play and know what direction the countershaft should be turned and locked.*

> *NOTE*
> *If a large amount of air escapes from the exhaust pipe or through the carburetor, the air is leaking through an open valve. Check the index mark (**Figure 14**) to make sure the engine is at TDC on the compression stroke. If the engine is remaining at TDC but there is still a large amount of air escaping from the engine, the crankshaft is off one revolution. Turn the engine 360° and realign the TDC mark as described in Step 9, then relock it as described in Step 10.*

  a. Air leaking through the exhaust pipe indicates a leaking exhaust valve.

  b. Air leaking through the carburetor indicates a leaking intake valve.

  c. Air leaking through both the intake and exhaust valves indicates the engine is not set at TDC on its compression stroke.

  d. Air leaking through the coolant filler neck indicates a leaking cylinder head gasket or a cracked cylinder head or cylinder liner.

  e. Air leaking through the oil filler hole indicates the rings are not sealing properly in the bore.

13. If the cylinder leakdown is 10 percent or higher, further service is required.

14. Disconnect the test equipment and install all the parts previously removed. On CRF250X and CRF450X models, readjust the drive chain (Chapter Three).

## CLUTCH

Basic clutch troubleshooting is listed in this section. Clutch service is covered in Chapter Six and Chapter Seven.

**No Pressure at Clutch Lever**

1. Incorrect clutch adjustment.
2. Broken clutch cable.
3. Damaged clutch lifter mechanism.

**Clutch Lever Hard to Pull In**

1. Dry or damaged clutch cable.
2. Kinked or stuck clutch cable.

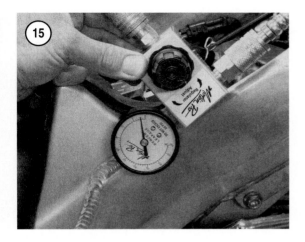

3. Incorrect clutch cable routing.
4. Damaged clutch lifter mechanism.
5. Damaged clutch lifter thrust washer and needle bearing.

**Rough Clutch Operation**

Worn, grooved or damaged clutch hub and clutch housing slots.

**Clutch Slip**

If the engine speed increases without an increase in motorcycle speed, the clutch is probably slipping. The main causes of clutch slippage are:
1. No clutch lever free play.
2. Worn clutch plates.
3. Weak clutch springs.
4. Sticking or damaged clutch lifter.
5. Clutch plates contaminated by engine oil additive.

**Clutch Drag**

If the clutch does not disengage or if the motorcycle creeps with the transmission in gear and the clutch disengaged, the clutch is dragging. Some main causes of clutch drag are:
1. Excessive clutch lever free play.
2. Warped clutch plates.
3. Damaged clutch lifter assembly.
4. Loose clutch housing locknut.
5. High oil level.
6. Incorrect oil viscosity.

7. Engine oil additive being used.
8. Damaged clutch hub and clutch housing splines.

## GEARSHIFT LINKAGE

The gearshift linkage assembly connects the shift pedal (external shift mechanism) to the shift drum (internal shift mechanism). See Chapter Six and Chapter Seven to identify the components called out in this section.

**Transmission Jumps Out of Gear**

1. Damaged stopper arm.
2. Damaged stopper arm spring.
3. Loose stopper arm mounting bolt.
4. Loose guide plate mounting bolts.
5. Damaged shifter collar.
6. Worn or damaged shift drum cam.
7. Damaged shift shaft spring.

**Difficult Shifting**

1. Incorrect clutch operation.
2. Incorrect oil viscosity.
3. Loose or damaged stopper arm assembly.
4. Bent shift fork shaft(s).
5. Bent or damaged shift fork(s).
6. Worn gear dogs or slots.
7. Damaged shift drum grooves.
8. Damaged shift shaft spindle.
9. Incorrect gearshift linkage installation.
10. Damaged shift lever assembly.

**Shift Pedal Does Not Return**

1. Bent shift shaft spindle.
2. Bent shift shaft engagement arm.
3. Damaged shift lever assembly.
4. Weak or damaged shift shaft arm return spring.
5. Shift shaft incorrectly installed (return spring not indexed around pin).

**Excessive Engine/Transmission Noise**

1. Damaged primary drive and driven gears or bearing.
2. Incorrect balancer shaft installation.

3. Incorrect primary drive and drive gear installation.

4. Damaged transmission or balancer shaft bearings or gears.

## TRANSMISSION

Transmission symptoms are sometimes hard to distinguish from clutch symptoms. Basic transmission troubleshooting is listed below. Refer to Chapter Eight for transmission service procedures. Before working on the transmission, make sure the clutch and gearshift linkage assembly are not causing the problem.

### Difficult Shifting

1. Incorrect clutch operation.
2. Bent shift fork(s).
3. Damaged shift fork guide pin(s).
4. Bent shift fork shaft(s).
5. Damaged shift drum grooves.
6. Damaged gears.

### Jumps Out of Gear

1. Loose or damaged shift drum cam mounting bolt.
2. Bent or damaged shift fork(s).
3. Bent shift fork shaft(s).
4. Damaged shift drum grooves.
5. Worn gear dogs or slots.

### Incorrect Shift Lever Operation

1. Bent shift pedal or linkage.
2. Stripped shift pedal splines.
3. Damaged shift linkage.
4. Damaged shift shaft spindle.

### Excessive Gear Noise

1. Worn or damaged transmission bearings.
2. Worn or damaged gears.
3. Excessive gear backlash.

### Engine Vibration

1. Incorrect balancer shaft timing.

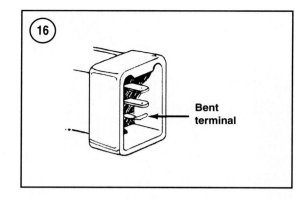

2. Excessive crankshaft runout.

3. Damaged crankshaft and balancer shaft bearings.

## ELECTRICAL TESTING

This section describes basic electrical testing and test equipment use.

### Preliminary Checks and Precautions

Refer to the color wiring diagrams at the end of the manual for component and connector identification. Use the wiring diagrams to determine how the circuit should work by tracing the current paths from the power source through the circuit components to ground. Also, check any circuits that share the same fuse (if used), ground or switch. If the other circuits work properly and the shared wiring is good, the cause must be in the wiring used only by the suspect circuit. If all related circuits are faulty at the same time, the probable cause is a poor ground connection or a blown fuse (if used).

As with all troubleshooting procedures, analyze typical symptoms in a systematic manner. Never assume anything and do not overlook the obvious like a blown fuse or an electrical connector that has separated. Test the simplest and most obvious items first and try to make tests at easily accessible points on the motorcycle.

Before starting any electrical troubleshooting, perform the following:

1. On CRF250X and CRF450X models, check the fuse (Chapter Ten). If the fuse is blown, replace it.

2. On CRF250X and CRF450X models, inspect the battery. Make sure it is fully charged, and the

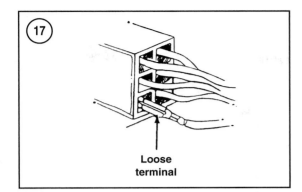

Loose
terminal

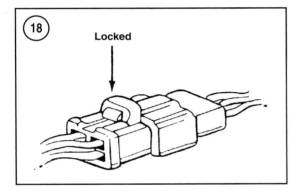

Locked

battery leads are clean and securely attached to the battery terminals. Refer to *Battery* in Chapter Ten.

3. Disconnect each electrical connector in the suspect circuit and make sure there are no bent terminals in the electrical connector (**Figure 16**).

4. Make sure the terminals on the end of each wire are pushed all the way into the connector (**Figure 17**). If not, carefully push them in with a narrow blade screwdriver.

5. Check the wires where they connect to the terminals for damage.

6. Make sure all terminals within the connector are clean and free of corrosion. Clean them, if necessary, and pack the connectors with dielectric grease.

7. Push the connector halves together. Make sure the connectors are fully engaged and locked together (**Figure 18**).

8. Never pull the electrical wires when disconnecting an electrical connector—pull only on the connector.

*NOTE*
*Always consider electrical connectors the weak link in the electrical system. Dirty, loose fitting and corroded*

connectors cause numerous electrical related problems, especially on off-road motorcycles. When troubleshooting an electrical problem, carefully inspect the connectors and wiring harness.

**Intermittent Problems**

Intermittent problems are problems that do not occur all the time and can be difficult to locate. For example, when a problem only occurs when the motorcycle is ridden over rough roads (vibration) or in wet conditions (water penetration), it is intermittent. To locate and repair intermittent problems, simulate the condition when testing the components. Note the following:

1. Vibration—This is a common problem with loose or damaged electrical connectors.
   a. Perform a continuity test as described in the appropriate service procedure, or under *Continuity Test* in this section.
   b. Lightly pull or wiggle the connectors while repeating the test. Do the same when checking the wiring harness and individual components, especially where the wires enter a housing or connector.
   c. A change in meter readings indicates a poor connection. Find and repair the problem or replace the part. Check for wires with cracked or broken insulation.

*NOTE*
*An analog ohmmeter is useful when making this type of test. Slight needle movements are apparent when indicating a loose connection.*

2. Heat—This is another common problem with connectors or plugs that have loose or poor connections. As these connections heat up, the connection or joint expands and separates, causing an open circuit. Other heat related problems occur when a component creates its own heat as it starts to fail or go bad.
   a. Troubleshoot the problem to help isolate the problem or area.
   b. To check a connector, perform a continuity test as described in the appropriate service procedure, or under *Continuity Test* in this chapter. Then repeat the test while heating the

connector with a heat gun or hair dryer. If the meter reading was normal (continuity) when the connector was cold, then fluctuated or read infinity when heat was applied, the connection is bad.

c. To check a component, wait until the engine is cold, then start and run the engine. Note operational differences when the engine is cold and hot.

d. If the engine does not start, isolate and remove the component. First test it at room temperature, and then after heating it with a hair dryer. A change in meter readings indicates a temperature problem.

*CAUTION*
*A heat gun or hair dryer will quickly raise the heat of the component being tested. Do not apply heat directly to the ICM or use heat in excess of 60° C (140° F) on any electrical component. If available, monitor heat with an infrared thermometer.*

3. Water—When this problem occurs in wet conditions, or in areas with high humidity, start and run the engine in a dry area. Then, with the engine running, spray water onto the suspected component. Often times, water related problems repair themselves after the component becomes hot enough to dry itself.

### Electrical Component Replacement

Most motorcycle dealerships and parts suppliers will not accept the return of any electrical part. If you cannot determine the *exact* cause of any electrical system malfunction, have a Honda dealership retest that specific system to verify your test results. If you purchase a new electrical component(s), install it, and then find that the system still does not work properly, you will probably be unable to return the unit for a refund.

Consider any test results carefully before replacing a component that tests only *slightly* out of specification, especially resistance. A number of variables can affect test results dramatically. These include: the testing meter's internal circuitry, ambient temperature and conditions under which the machine has been operated. All instructions and specifications have been checked for accuracy;

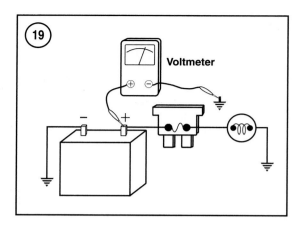

however, successful test results depend to a great degree upon individual accuracy.

### Test Equipment

#### *Test light or voltmeter (CRF250X and CRF450X)*

A test light can be constructed from a 12-volt light bulb with a pair of test leads carefully soldered to the bulb. To check for battery voltage in a circuit, attach one lead to ground and the other lead to various points along the circuit. The bulb lights when battery voltage is present.

A voltmeter is used in the same manner as the test light to find out if battery voltage is present in any given circuit. The voltmeter, unlike the test light, also indicates how much voltage is present at each test point. When using a voltmeter, attach the positive lead to the component or wire to be checked and the negative lead to a good ground (**Figure 19**).

#### *Ammeter (CRF250X and CRF450X)*

An ammeter measures the flow of current (amps) in a circuit (**Figure 20**). When connected in series in a circuit, the ammeter determines if current is flowing through the circuit and if that current flow is excessive because of a short in the circuit. Current flow is often referred to as current draw. Comparing actual current draw in the circuit or component to the manufacturer's specified current draw provides useful diagnostic information.

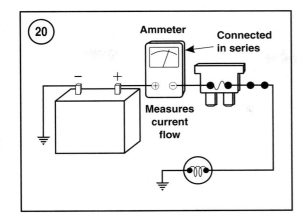

### Self-powered test light (continuity tester)

A self-powered test light can be constructed from a 12-volt light bulb, a pair of test leads and a 12-volt battery. When the test leads are touched together, the light bulb should go on.

Use a self-powered test light as follows:

1. Touch the test leads together to make sure the light bulb goes on. If not, correct the problem before using it in a test procedure.

2. On CRF250X and CRF450X models, disconnect the battery or remove the fuse.

3. Select two points within the circuit where there should be continuity.

4. Attach one lead of the self-powered test light to each point.

5. If there is continuity, the self-powered test light bulb will come on.

6. If there is no continuity, the self-powered test light bulb will not come on, indicating an open circuit.

### Ohmmeter

An ohmmeter measures the resistance (in ohms) to current flow in a circuit or component. Like the self-powered test light, an ohmmeter contains its own power source and should not be connected to a live circuit.

Ohmmeters may be analog type (needle scale) or digital type (LCD or LED readout). Both types of ohmmeters have a switch that allows the user to select different ranges of resistance for accurate readings. The analog ohmmeter also has a set-adjust control which is used to zero or calibrate the meter (digital ohmmeters do not require calibration).

An ohmmeter is used by connecting its test leads to the terminals or leads of the circuit or component to be tested (**Figure 21**). If an analog meter is used, it must be calibrated by touching the test leads together and turning the set-adjust knob until the meter needle reads zero. When the leads are uncrossed, the needle should move to the other end of the scale indicating infinite resistance.

During a continuity test, a reading of infinity indicates that there is an open in the circuit or component. A reading of zero indicates continuity, that is, there is no measurable resistance in the circuit or component being tested. If the meter needle falls between these two ends of the scale, this indicates the actual resistance to current flow that is present. To determine the resistance, multiply the meter reading by the ohmmeter scale. For example, a meter reading of 5 multiplied by the R × 1000 scale is 5000 ohms of resistance.

> *CAUTION*
> *Never connect an ohmmeter to a circuit which has power applied to it. Always disconnect the battery negative lead before using an ohmmeter.*

### Jumper wire (CRF250X and CRF450X)

A jumper wire is a simple way to bypass a potential problem and isolate it to a particular point in a circuit. If a faulty circuit works properly with a jumper wire installed, an open exists between the two jumper points in the circuit.

To troubleshoot with a jumper wire, first use the wire to determine if the problem is on the ground side or the load side of a device. Test the ground by connecting a jumper between the lamp and a good ground. If the lamp comes on, the problem is the connection between the lamp and ground. If the lamp does not come on with the jumper installed, the lamp's connection to ground is good so the problem is between the lamp and the power source.

To isolate the problem, connect the jumper between the battery and the lamp. If it comes on, the problem is between these two points. Next, connect the jumper between the battery and the fuse side of the switch. If the lamp comes on, the switch is good. By successively moving the jumper from one point to another, the problem can be isolated to a particular place in the circuit.

Pay attention to the following when using a jumper wire:

1. Make sure the jumper wire gauge (thickness) is the same as that used in the circuit being tested. Smaller gauge wire will rapidly overheat and could melt.

2. Install insulated boots over alligator clips. This prevents accidental grounding, sparks or possible shock when working in cramped quarters.

3. Jumper wires are temporary test measures only. Do not leave a jumper wire installed as a permanent solution. This creates a severe fire hazard that could easily lead to complete loss of the motorcycle.

4. When using a jumper wire always install an inline fuse/fuse holder (available at most auto supply stores or electronic supply stores) to the jumper wire. Never use a jumper wire across any load (a component that is connected and turned on). This would result in a direct short and will blow the fuse(s).

**Test Procedures**

*Voltage test (CRF250X and CRF450X)*

Unless otherwise specified, make all voltage tests with the electrical connectors still connected. Insert the test leads into the backside of the connector and make sure the test lead touches the electrical wire or metal terminal within the connector housing. If the test lead only touches the wire insulation, there will be a false reading.

Always check both sides of the connector as one side may be loose or corroded, thus preventing electrical flow through the connector. This type of test can be performed with a test light or a voltmeter. A voltmeter gives the best results.

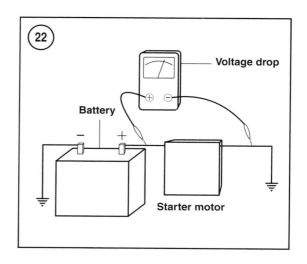

*NOTE*
*If using a test light, it does not make any difference which test lead is attached to ground.*

1. Attach the voltmeter negative test lead to a good ground (bare metal). Make sure the part used for ground is not insulated with a rubber gasket or rubber grommet.

2. Attach the voltmeter positive test lead to the point to be tested (**Figure 19**).

3. Turn the ignition switch on. If using a test light, the test light will come on if voltage is present. If using a voltmeter, note the voltage reading. The reading should be within 1 volt of battery voltage. If the voltage is less, there is a problem in the circuit.

*Voltage drop test (CRF250X and CRF450X)*

The wires, cables, connectors and switches in an electrical circuit are designed to carry current with low resistance. This ensures that current can flow through the circuit with a minimum loss of voltage. Voltage drop indicates where there is resistance in a circuit. A higher than normal amount of resistance in a circuit decreases the flow of current and causes the voltage to drop between the source and destination in the circuit.

Because resistance causes voltage to drop, a voltmeter is used to measure voltage drop when current is running through the circuit. If the circuit has no resistance, there is no voltage drop so the voltmeter indicates 0 volts. The greater the resistance in a circuit, the greater the voltage drop reading.

To perform a voltage drop:

1. Connect the positive meter test lead to the electrical source (where electricity is coming from).

2. Connect the voltmeter negative test lead to the electrical load (where the electricity is going). See **Figure 22**.

3. If necessary, activate the component(s) in the circuit. For example, if checking the voltage in the starter circuit, it would be necessary to push the starter button.

4. Read the voltage drop (difference in voltage between the source and destination) on the voltmeter. Note the following:

    a. The voltmeter should indicate 0 volts. If there is a drop of 0.5 volts or more, there is a problem within the circuit. A voltage drop reading of 12 volts indicates an open in the circuit.

    b. A voltage drop of 1 or more volts indicates that a circuit has excessive resistance.

    c. For example, consider a starting problem where the battery is fully charged but the starter motor turns over slowly. Voltage drop would be the difference in the voltage at the battery (source) and the voltage at the starter (destination) as the engine is being started (current is flowing through the battery cables). A corroded battery cable would cause a high voltage drop (high resistance) and slow engine cranking.

    d. Common sources of voltage drop are loose or contaminated connectors and poor ground connections.

### Peak voltage test

Peak voltage tests check the voltage output of the ignition coil and ignition pulse generator at normal cranking speed. These tests make it possible to identify ignition system problems quickly and accurately.

Peak voltage tests require a peak voltage adapter or tester. See Chapter Ten, *Ignition System Testing*.

### Continuity test

A continuity test is used to determine the integrity of a circuit, wire or component. A circuit has continuity if it forms a complete circuit, that is, if there are no opens in either the electrical wires or components within the circuit. A circuit with an open, on the other hand, has no continuity.

This type of test can be performed with a self-powered test light or an ohmmeter. An ohmmeter gives the best results. If using an analog ohmmeter, calibrate the meter by touching the leads together and turning the calibration knob until the meter reads zero.

1. Disconnect the negative battery cable.
2. Attach one test lead (test light or ohmmeter) to one end of the part of the circuit to be tested.
3. Attach the other test lead to the other end of the part or the circuit to be tested.
4. The self-powered test light comes on if there is continuity. An ohmmeter reads 0 or very low resistance if there is continuity. A reading of infinite resistance indicates no continuity; the circuit is open.

### Testing for a short with a self-powered test light or ohmmeter (CRF250X and CRF450X)

1. Disconnect the negative battery cable.
2. Remove the blown fuse (**Figure 23**).
3. Connect one test lead of the test light or ohmmeter to the load side (battery side) of the fuse terminal in the starter relay.
4. Connect the other test lead to a good ground (bare metal). Make sure the part used for a ground is not insulated with a rubber gasket or rubber grommet.
5. With the self-powered test light or ohmmeter attached to the fuse terminal and ground, wiggle the wiring harness relating to the suspect circuit at various intervals. Start next to the fuse terminals and work away from the fuse terminal. Watch the

self-powered test light or ohmmeter while progressing along the harness.

6. If the test light blinks or the needle on the ohmmeter moves, there is a short-to-ground at that point in the harness.

### *Testing for a short with a test light or voltmeter (CRF250X and CRF450X)*

1. Remove the blown fuse (**Figure 23**).
2. Connect the test light or voltmeter across the fuse terminals in the starter relay. Turn the ignition switch ON and check for battery voltage.
3. With the test light or voltmeter attached to the fuse terminals, wiggle the wiring harness relating to the suspect circuit at various intervals. Start next to the fuse terminal and work systematically away from the fuse terminal. Watch the test light or voltmeter while progressing along the harness.
4. If the test light blinks or if the needle on the voltmeter moves, there is a short-to-ground at that point in the harness.

### FRONT SUSPENSION AND STEERING

#### Steering is Sluggish

1. Tight steering adjustment.
2. Damaged steering head bearings.
3. Low tire pressure.
4. Damaged tire.

#### Motorcycle Steers to One Side

1. Bent axle.
2. Bent frame.
3. Worn or damaged wheel bearings.
4. Worn or damaged swing arm pivot bearings.
5. Damaged steering head bearings.
6. Bent swing arm.
7. Incorrectly installed wheels.
8. Front and rear wheels are not aligned.
9. Front fork legs positioned unevenly in steering stem.
10. Damaged tire.

#### Front Suspension Noise

1. Loose mounting fasteners.
2. Damaged fork.

3. Low fork oil capacity.

#### Front Wheel Wobble/Vibration

1. Loose front wheel axle.
2. Loose or damaged wheel bearing(s).
3. Damaged wheel rim(s).
4. Damaged tire(s).
5. Loose or damaged spokes.

#### Front End Too Stiff

1. Decrease the fork compression damping.
2. Decrease the fork oil capacity.
3. Change to a lighter weight fork oil.
4. Install softer fork springs.

#### Front End Oversteers

1. Install stiffer fork springs.
2. Increase fork oil capacity.

#### Front End Washes Out or Understeers

1. Decrease fork oil capacity.
2. Install softer fork springs.

#### Front End Shakes or Jumps Under Heavy Braking

1. Increase fork oil capacity.
2. Increase shock rebound damping.
3. Reduce the shock spring preload.

#### Front End is Unstable at High Speed

1. Increase fork oil capacity.
2. Increase rear shock spring preload.

### REAR SUSPENSION

#### Poor Traction During Acceleration

1. Decrease shock compression damping adjustment.
2. Decrease shock spring preload.

**Rear End Hops During Acceleration**

1. Decrease shock compression damping adjustment.
2. Decrease shock spring preload.

## BRAKE SYSTEM

The front and rear brake units are critical to riding performance and safety. Inspect the front and rear brakes frequently and repair any problem immediately. When replacing or refilling the brake fluid, use only DOT 4 brake fluid from a closed container. See Chapter Three for additional information on brake fluid selection and routine brake inspection and service.

Always check the brake operation before riding the motorcycle.

**Soft or Spongy Brake Lever or Pedal**

Operate the front brake lever or rear brake pedal and check to see if the lever travel distance increases. If the lever travel does increase while being operated, or feels soft or spongy, there may be air in the brake line. In this condition, the brake system is not capable of producing sufficient brake force. When there is an increase in lever or pedal travel or when the brake feels soft or spongy, check the following possible causes:

1. Air in system.

*WARNING*
*If the fluid level drops too low, air can enter the hydraulic system through the master cylinder. Air can also enter the system from loose or damaged hose fittings. Air in the hydraulic system causes a soft or spongy brake lever action. This condition is noticeable and reduces brake performance. When it is suspected that air has entered the hydraulic system, flush the brake system and bleed the brakes as described in Chapter Fifteen.*

2. Low brake fluid level.

*WARNING*
*As the brake pads wear, the brake fluid level in the master cylinder res-*

*ervoir drops. Whenever adding brake fluid to the reservoir, visually check the brake pads for wear. If it does not appear that there is an increase in pad wear, check the brake hoses, lines and banjo bolts for leaks.*

3. Leak in the brake system.
4. Contaminated brake fluid.
5. Plugged brake fluid passages.
6. Damaged brake lever or pedal assembly.
7. Worn or damaged brake pads.
8. Worn or damaged brake disc.
9. Warped brake disc.
10. Contaminated brake pads and disc.

*WARNING*
*A leaking fork seal can allow oil to contaminate the brake pads and disc.*

11. Worn or damaged master cylinder cups and/or cylinder bore.
12. Worn or damaged brake caliper piston seals.
13. Contaminated master cylinder assembly.
14. Contaminated brake caliper assembly.
15. Brake caliper not sliding correctly on slide pins.
16. Sticking master cylinder piston assembly.
17. Sticking brake caliper pistons.

**Brake Drag**

When the brakes drag, the brake pads are not capable of moving away from the brake disc when the brake lever or pedal is released. Any of the following causes, if they occur, would prevent correct brake pad movement and cause brake drag.

1. Warped or damaged brake disc.
2. Brake caliper not sliding correctly on slide pins.
3. Sticking or damaged brake caliper pistons.
4. Contaminated brake pads and disc.
5. Plugged master cylinder port.
6. Contaminated brake fluid and hydraulic passages.
7. Restricted brake hose joint.
8. Loose brake disc mounting bolts.
9. Damaged or misaligned wheel.
10. Incorrect wheel alignment.
11. Incorrectly installed brake caliper.
12. Damaged front or rear wheel.

## Hard Brake Lever or Pedal Operation

When applying the brakes and there is sufficient brake performance but the operation of brake lever feels excessively hard, check for the following possible causes:

1. Clogged brake hydraulic system.
2. Sticking caliper piston.
3. Sticking master cylinder piston.
4. Glazed or worn brake pads.
5. Mismatched brake pads.
6. Damaged front brake lever.
7. Damaged rear brake pedal.
8. Brake caliper not sliding correctly on slide pins.
9. Worn or damaged brake caliper seals.

## Brake Grabs

1. Damaged brake pad pin bolt. Look for steps or cracks along the pad pin bolt surface.
2. Contaminated brake pads and disc.
3. Incorrect wheel alignment.
4. Warped brake disc.
5. Loose brake disc mounting bolts.
6. Brake caliper not sliding correctly on slide pins.
7. Mismatched brake pads.
8. Damaged wheel bearings.

## Brake Squeal or Chatter

1. Contaminated brake pads and disc.
2. Incorrectly installed brake caliper.
3. Warped brake disc.
4. Incorrect wheel alignment.
5. Mismatched brake pads.
6. Incorrectly installed brake pads.

7. Damaged or missing brake pad spring or pad retainer.

## Leaking Brake Caliper

1. Damaged dust and piston seals.
2. Damaged cylinder bore.
3. Loose caliper body bolts.
4. Loose banjo bolt.
5. Damaged banjo bolt washers.
6. Damaged banjo bolt threads in caliper body.

## Leaking Master Cylinder

1. Damaged piston secondary seal (**Figure 24**).
2. Damaged piston snap ring/snap ring groove.
3. Worn or damaged master cylinder bore.
4. Loose banjo bolt.
5. Damaged banjo bolt washers.
6. Damaged banjo bolt threads in master cylinder body.
7. Loose or damaged reservoir cap.

# CHAPTER THREE

# LUBRICATION, MAINTENANCE AND TUNE-UP

This chapter covers periodic service procedures that do not require major disassembly. Regular, careful maintenance is the best guarantee for a trouble-free, long-lasting motorcycle. All motorcycles, especially those designed for competition and off-road use, require proper lubrication, maintenance and tune-up to maintain a high level of performance and to extend engine, suspension and chassis life.

Perform lubrication, maintenance and tune-ups following the correct procedures and exercising common sense. Always remember that damage can result from improper tuning and adjustment. In addition, if special tools or testers are required to perform a particular maintenance or adjustment procedure, use the correct tool or refer service to a qualified Honda dealership or repair shop.

Perform procedures in a logical order. For example, some procedures must be done with the engine cold and others with the engine at operating temperature. Check the valve adjustment when the engine is cold; adjust the carburetor and drain the engine oil and transmission oil when the engine is hot. Also, because the engine needs to run as well as

possible when adjusting the carburetor, service the air filter and spark plug first. If the carburetor is adjusted and then the air filter is found to need service, the carburetor will require readjustment.

**Tables 1-13** are at the end of this chapter.

## MAINTENANCE INTERVALS

*WARNING*
*When performing any service work to the engine or cooling system, never remove the radiator cap, coolant drain bolt or disconnect any hose while the engine and radiator are hot. Scalding fluid and steam may be blown out under pressure and cause serious injury.*

Follow the maintenance in **Tables 1-3** to help maintain motorcycle performance and ensure reliability. The following explains the function of each table.

1. Check the *Pre-ride Inspection* items in **Table 1** before the first ride of the day. If the motorcycle was

cleaned and serviced after its last ride, some of these steps will have been performed at that time.

2. The competition schedule in **Table 2** provides a guide for maintaining the motorcycle under racing conditions. The intervals are based on the number of races completed as well as the number of hours of operation. Follow these intervals to maintain engine and suspension performance and overall reliability under severe operating conditions.

3. The maintenance schedule listed in **Table 3** is a guide for CRF250X and CRF450X models when used for typical off-road and trail riding. However, follow the service intervals in **Table 2** when operating the motorcycle in competition or under other severe conditions.

### Recording Maintenance and Engine Operating Times

Perform all competition and non-competition maintenance services at the intervals outlined in this chapter. Because frequent and extensive maintenance is required to keep the motorcycle fit, it is important to keep records on engine operating time, number of races completed and when and what services are performed.

The CRF250X and CRF450X models are equipped with a tripmeter, which can be used to keep track of mileage. However, for the CRF250R and CRF450R models and the CRF250X and CRF450X models when used in competition, it is necessary to keep track of engine operating time (**Table 2**). An easy way to do this is to divide the amount of time that the engine is operating into hours and tenths of an hour, where each five minutes represents 1/10 of an hour. For example, if the engine is run for approximately 45 minutes, 0.8 tenths would be recorded in a logbook. When the engine is run for approximately one hour and 25 minutes, 1.4 hours would be recorded. **Figure 1** shows how to divide one hour into tenths of an hour.

Record the date, the motorcycle operating time interval or number of races completed, and the type of service performed in a logbook or in the maintenance log at the back of this manual. This record can also be used to schedule future service procedures at the correct time.

| ENGINE OPERATING TIME IN MINUTES | TIME RECORDED IN TENTHS OF AN HOUR |
|---|---|
| 5 | 0.1 |
| 10 | 0.2 |
| 15 | 0.3 |
| 20 | 0.3 |
| 25 | 0.4 |
| 30 | 0.5 |
| 35 | 0.6 |
| 40 | 0.7 |
| 45 | 0.8 |
| 50 | 0.8 |
| 55 | 0.9 |
| 60 | 1.0 |

Example: If engine is run for approximately 1 hour and 45 minutes, the time recorded in a logbook would be 1.8.

### Emission Labels

On CRF250X and CRF450X models sold in California, emission control labels are attached to the rear fender. The vehicle emission control information label (A, **Figure 2**) lists tune-up information. The vacuum hose routing diagram label (B, **Figure 2**) shows a schematic of the emission control system. This information is useful when identifying hoses used in the emission control system.

### Test Ride

The test ride is an important part of the maintenance procedure because it is during this step that it is determined whether the motorcycle is

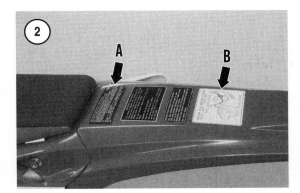

3

ready to ride or if it needs additional work. When test riding a motorcycle, always start slowly and ride it in a safe place away from other vehicles and people. Concentrate on the areas that were adjusted and notice how these components affect other systems. If the brakes were serviced, check their operation at slower speeds and with moderate pressure before testing at higher speeds. Do not continue to ride the motorcycle if the engine, brakes or any suspension or steering component is not working correctly.

## AIR FILTER

Never run the engine without a properly oiled and installed air filter element. Likewise, running the engine with a dry or damaged air filter element allows unfiltered air to enter the engine. A well-oiled but dirty or clogged air filter reduces the amount of air that enters the engine and causes a rich air/fuel mixture, causing poor engine starting, spark plug fouling and reduced engine performance. Frequent air filter inspection and cleaning is a critical part of minimizing engine wear and maintaining engine

performance. **Figure 3** shows how dirt can pass through an improperly serviced or damaged air filter.

**Table 2** and **Table 3** lists intervals for cleaning the air filter. Clean the air filter more often when riding in sand or dusty conditions.

*NOTE*
*For competition riding, it is a good idea to have one or more pre-oiled air filters stored in plastic bags that can be installed between motos when racing in severe dust or sand conditions. Do not attempt to clean an air filter and reuse it between motos because there may not be enough time to properly dry the filter. A filter that was damp when oiled will not trap fine dust. Make sure the filter element is dry before oiling it.*

### Removal/Installation

#### CRF250X and CRF450X

The air filter is installed behind the left side cover.

1. Lift the ring (A, **Figure 4**) and turn it counterclockwise to unlock the air box cover (B).

2. Remove the air filter mounting bolt (**Figure 5**).

3. Pull the air filter off the air box flange, then turn it clockwise until the bottom part of the air filter (**Figure 6**) is pointing toward the 8 o'clock or 9 o'clock position. Remove the air filter, noting that the alignment tab (**Figure 7**) on the filter should be pointing up.

4. Check inside the air box for debris that may have passed through or around the air filter.

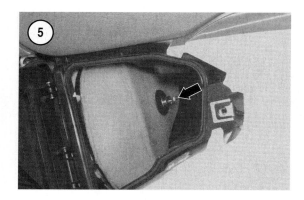

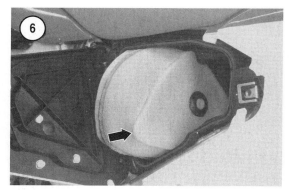

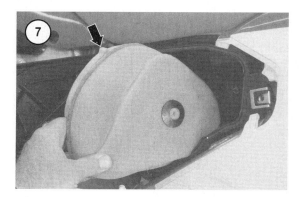

5. Wipe the inside of the air box with a clean rag. If the air box cannot be cleaned while it is installed on the motorcycle, remove and then clean it.

6. Clean and reoil the air filter as described in this section.

7. Apply a thin coat of white lithium grease onto the filter sealing surface (**Figure 8**).

8. Align the air filter with the air box opening so the alignment tab is pointing up (**Figure 7**) and install it into the airbox. Without seating the filter (**Figure 7**), turn it the air filter counterclockwise until its alignment tab aligns with the alignment mark on the air box, then seat the filter. **Figure 9** shows the air filter tab and air box alignment mark properly aligned.

9. Install the air filter mounting bolt (**Figure 5**). Check that the air filter element seats evenly against the sealing surface of the air box and tighten the bolt securely.

10. Close the air box cover (B, **Figure 4**) and turn the key (A) to lock the cover.

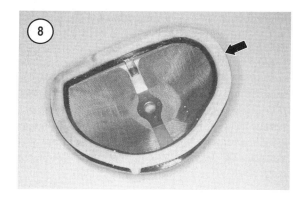

## *2002 CRF450R*

1. Remove the seat (Chapter Sixteen).

2. Remove the air filter mounting bolt (**Figure 10**).

3. Pull the air filter off the air box flange and remove it through the top of the air box.

4. Check inside the air box for dirt and other debris that may have passed through or around the air filter.

5. Wipe the inside of the air box with a clean rag. If the air box cannot be cleaned while it is installed on the motorcycle, remove and then clean it.

6. Clean and reoil the air filter as described in this section.

7. Apply a thin coat of white lithium grease onto the filter sealing surface (**Figure 8**, typical).

8. Install the air filter by positioning the tab on the air filter against the alignment tab on the air box as shown in **Figure 10**.

9. Install the air filter mounting bolt (**Figure 10**). Check that the air filter element seats evenly against the sealing surface of the air box and tighten the bolt securely.

10. Install the seat (Chapter Sixteen).

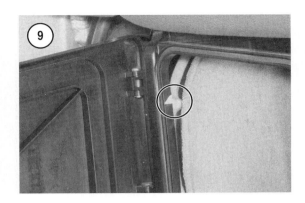

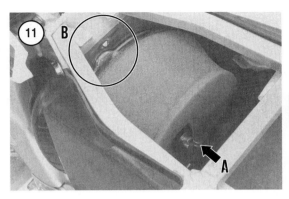

3

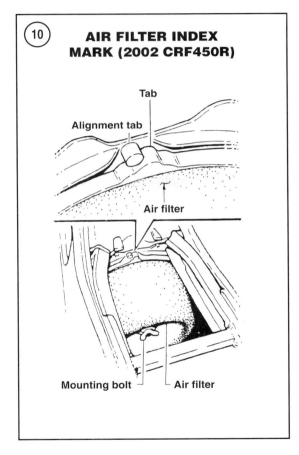

AIR FILTER INDEX
MARK (2002 CRF450R)

Tab

Alignment tab

Air filter

Mounting bolt — — Air filter

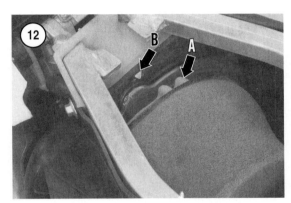

*CRF250R and 2003-on CRF450R*

The air filter is equipped with two sets of raised alignment tabs: a single tab and two tabs positioned side-by-side. The single tab aligns the air filter with the air box. When this tab is properly aligned, the air filter is positioned in its normal operating position. The two side-by-side tabs are used to align the air filter when removing and installing it.

1. Remove the seat (Chapter Sixteen).
2. Remove the air filter mounting bolt (A, **Figure 11**).

*CAUTION*
*Removing the air filter without aligning the two filter tabs as described in Step 3 could cause air filter damage.*

3. Pull the air filter off the air box and turn it counterclockwise until the two filter tabs (side-by-side [A, **Figure 12**]) align with the alignment mark on the air box (B, **Figure 12**). Remove the air filter.
4. Check inside the air box for debris that may have passed through or around the air filter.
5. Wipe the inside of the air box with a clean rag. If the air box cannot be cleaned while it is installed on the motorcycle, remove and then clean it.
6. Clean and reoil the air filter as described in this section.
7. Apply a thin coat of white lithium grease onto the filter sealing surface (**Figure 8**, typical).
8. Install the air filter into the air box by aligning the two tabs on the filter (A, **Figure 12**) with the air box alignment mark (B). Then turn the air filter

clockwise and align the single tab with the air box alignment mark (B, **Figure 11**) and position the air filter onto the air box flange.

9. Install the air filter mounting bolt (A, **Figure 11**). Check that the air filter element seats evenly against the sealing surface of the air box and tighten the bolt securely.

10. Install the seat (Chapter Sixteen).

### Cleaning

1. Remove the air filter as described in this section.

2A. On 2002 CRF450R models, remove the air filter from the holder (**Figure 13**).

2B. On all other models, lift the tab on the filter off the tab on the holder (**Figure 14**), then remove the filter from the holder. See **Figure 15**.

3. Before cleaning the air filter element, check it for brittleness, separation or other damage. Replace the element if it is excessively worn or damaged. If there is no visible damage, clean the air filter element as follows.

*WARNING*
*Do not clean the air filter element or holder with gasoline.*

4. Soak the air filter element in a container filled with a high flash point solvent, kerosene or an air filter cleaning solution. Gently squeeze the filter to dislodge and remove the oil and dirt from the filter pores. Swish the filter around in the cleaner while repeating this step a few times, then remove the air filter and set it aside to dry.

5. Fill a clean pan with warm soapy water.

6. Submerge the filter element into the cleaning solution and gently work the soap solution into the filter pores. Soak and squeeze the filter element *gently* to clean it.

*CAUTION*
*Do not wring or twist the filter element when cleaning it. This could damage a filter pore or tear the filter element loose at a seam and allow unfiltered air to enter the engine.*

7. Rinse the filter element under clear water while gently squeezing it.

8. Repeat these steps until there are no signs of dirt being rinsed from the filter element.

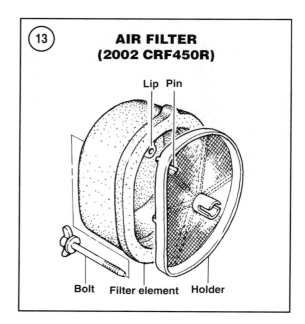

**AIR FILTER (2002 CRF450R)**

Lip  Pin

Bolt    Filter element    Holder

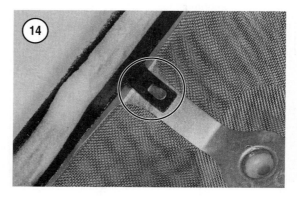

9. After cleaning the filter element, inspect it carefully and replace it if it is torn or damaged. Do not run the engine with a damaged air filter element, as it allows dirt to enter the engine.

10. Set the air filter element aside and allow it to dry thoroughly.

*CAUTION*
*A filter that was damp when oiled will not trap fine dust. Make sure the filter element is dry before oiling it.*

11. Properly oiling an air filter element is a messy job. Wear a pair of disposable rubber gloves when performing this procedure. Oil the filter element as follows:

   a. Place the air filter element into a one gallon-sized storage bag.

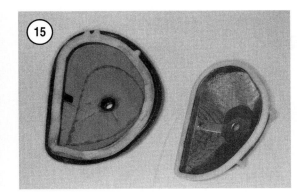

3

12A. On 2002 CRF450R models, install the air filter element over the holder. Fit the pin on the outer edge of the holder into the lip sewn into the filter element (**Figure 13**).

12B. On all other models, align and install the air filter over the holder. Hook the tab on the filter over the tab on the holder (**Figure 14**).

*CAUTION*
*If the air filter element lip is not properly installed over the holder, the element will not properly seal against the air box. This will allow dirt to enter the engine.*

13. Apply a coat of white lithium grease onto the filter element sealing surface (**Figure 8**).
14. Install the air filter as described in this section.
15. Pour the leftover filter element oil from the bag back into the bottle for future use.

### CRANKCASE BREATHER INSPECTION

Periodically or after riding in wet conditions, remove the plug from the crankcase breather hose (**Figure 16**) to drain the hose of water and other contaminants. Reinstall the plug.

### ENGINE OIL AND FILTER

**Engine Oil Selection**

Regular oil and filter changes contribute more to engine longevity than any other maintenance. **Table 2** and **Table 3** list the recommended oil and filter change intervals. The time interval is more important than the mileage interval because combustion acids, formed by gasoline and water vapor, contaminates the oil even if the motorcycle is not run for several months. If a motorcycle is operated under dusty conditions, the oil gets dirty quicker and should be changed more frequently than recommended.

Oil requirements for motorcycle engines are more demanding than for automobile engines. Oils specifically designed for motorcycles contain special additives to prevent premature viscosity breakdown, protect the engine from oil oxidation resulting from higher engine operating temperatures and provide lubrication qualities designed for engines operating at higher rpm. Consider the following when selecting engine oil:

*CAUTION*
*Do not use motor oils to lubricate foam air filters. Foam air filter oil is specifically formulated for easy and thorough application into the filter pores and provides a tacky viscous medium to filter air borne contaminants. Motor oils are too thin to remain suspended in the filter; the oil will be drawn into the engine and allow dirt to pass through the filter.*

   b. Pour foam air filter oil into the bag and onto the filter element to soak it.
   c. Gently squeeze and release the filter element, from the outside of the bag, to soak the filter oil into the filter element pores. Repeat until all of the pores are saturated.
   d. Remove the filter element from the bag and check the pores for uneven oiling. Light or dark areas on the filter indicate this condition. If necessary, work more oil into the filter and repeat substep c.
   e. When the filter is oiled evenly, squeeze the filter a final time to remove excess oil.
   f. Remove the air filter element from the bag.

1. Do not use oil with oil additives or oil with graphite or molybdenum additives. These may adversely affect clutch operation.

2. Do not use vegetable, non-detergent or castor based racing oils.

3. The Japanese Automobile Standards Organization (JASO) has established an oil classification for motorcycle engines. JASO motorcycle specific oils are identified by the JASO T 903 Standard. The JASO label (**Figure 17**) appears on the oil container and identifies the two separate motorcycle oil classifications—MA and MB. Honda recommends both the MA and MB classification for the CRF250 and CRF450 engines. JASO classified oil also uses the Society of Automotive Engineers (SAE) viscosity ratings.

4. When selecting an American Petroleum Institute (API) classified oil, use only a high-quality motorcycle oil with an SG or higher classification that does not display the term *Energy Conserving* on the oil container circular API service label (**Figure 18**).

5. **Figure 19** indicates when different viscosity oils can be used, depending on the ambient temperature.

*NOTE*
*There are a number of ways to discard used oil safely. The easiest way is to pour it from the drain pan into a gallon plastic bleach, juice or milk container for disposal. Some service stations and oil retailers will accept used oil for recycling. Do not discard oil in household trash or pour it onto the ground. Never add brake fluid, fork oil or any other type of petroleum-based fluid to any engine oil to be recycled. To locate a recycler, contact the American Petroleum Institute (API) at **www.recycleoil.org**.*

**Engine Oil Level Check**

*WARNING*
*Because the engine must be warmed up before checking the oil level, do not start and run the engine in a closed area. The exhaust gasses contain carbon monoxide, a colorless, ordorless, poisonous gas. Carbon monoxide levels build quickly in a closed area and can cause unconsciousness and death in a short time. When running the engine in the fol-*

**JASO CERTIFICATION LABEL**

Sales company oil code number

M001XXXXX

**MA**

**OIL CLASSIFICATION**
**MA: Designed for high-friction applications**
**MB: Designed for low-friction applications**

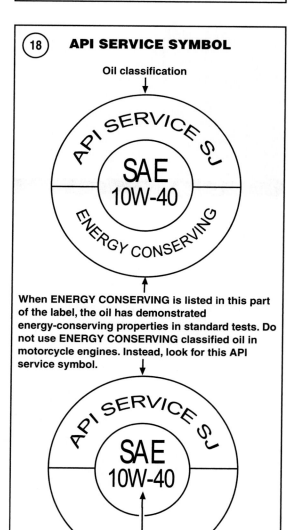

**API SERVICE SYMBOL**

Oil classification

API SERVICE SJ
**SAE 10W-40**
ENERGY CONSERVING

When **ENERGY CONSERVING** is listed in this part of the label, the oil has demonstrated energy-conserving properties in standard tests. Do not use **ENERGY CONSERVING** classified oil in motorcycle engines. Instead, look for this API service symbol.

API SERVICE SJ
**SAE 10W-40**

Oil viscosity

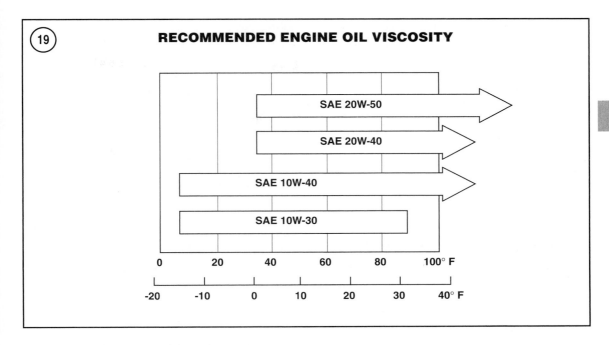

**RECOMMENDED ENGINE OIL VISCOSITY**

SAE 20W-50

SAE 20W-40

SAE 10W-40

SAE 10W-30

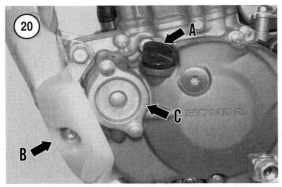

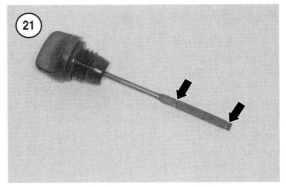

*lowing sections, always do so in an area with adequate ventilation.*

1. Start the engine and allow it to warm up for 3 to 5 minutes. In colder weather, allow the engine to idle for at least 5 minutes.

2. Support the motorcycle so it is vertical and level. Allow the engine to rest in this position for 2 to 3 minutes before checking the oil level.

*NOTE*
*On CRF250X and CRF450X models, do not check the oil level when the motorcycle is supported on its side stand.*

3A. On CRF250R, CRF250X and CRF450X models, check the oil level as follows:

a. Unscrew the dipstick (A, **Figure 20**) and wipe it clean.

b. Reinsert and seat the dipstick against the hole opening, but do not screw it into the cover (A, **Figure 20**).

c. Remove the dipstick and check the oil level. The oil level should be between the lower and upper marks on the dipstick (**Figure 21**). The oil level should not exceed the upper mark.

d. If the oil level is correct, insert and tighten the dipstick.

e. If the oil level is too low, add the appropriate amount of oil to bring the level to within the upper mark on the dipstick. Add oil in small quantities and check the level often. After reaching the proper level, reinstall the dipstick and start the engine. Recheck the oil level after the engine has run for a few minutes. Do not overfill.

3B. On CRF450R models, check the oil level as follows:

a. The oil level should be between the lower and upper marks on the crankcase cover (**Figure 22**). The oil level should not exceed the upper mark.

b. If the oil level is too low, remove the oil fill cap (A, **Figure 23**) and add the appropriate weight oil to bring the level to within the upper mark on the cover. Add oil in small quantities and check the level often. When the oil level is correct, reinstall the oil fill cap and start the engine. Recheck the oil level after the engine has run for a few minutes. Do not overfill.

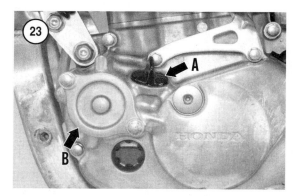

**Engine Oil and Filter Change**

Change the engine oil and filter at the intervals recommended in **Table 2** or **Table 3**. Use the appropriate grade of oil as recommended in this section.

Always change the oil when the engine is warm. Contaminants will remain suspended in the oil and it will drain more completely and quicker. The following procedure includes oil filter replacement. If the oil filter does not require replacement or removal, skip those steps.

1. Remove the engine guard (B, **Figure 20**, typical).

2. Start the engine and allow it to warm up for several minutes. Shut off the engine.

3A. On CRF250R and CRF250X models, drain the engine oil as follows:

a. Remove the dipstick (A, **Figure 20**).

b. Place a drain pan below the oil drain bolt (**Figure 24**). Remove the drain bolt and washer and allow the oil to drain.

3B. On CRF450R and CRF450X models, drain the engine oil as follows:

a. Remove the oil fill cap (A, **Figure 23**) or dipstick (A, **Figure 20**).

b. Place a drain pan below the oil drain bolt (**Figure 25**) on the left side of the crankcase. Remove the oil drain bolt and washer and allow the oil to drain.

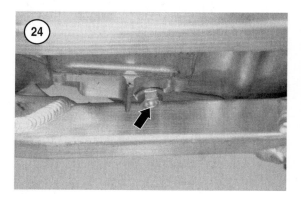

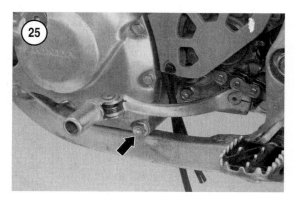

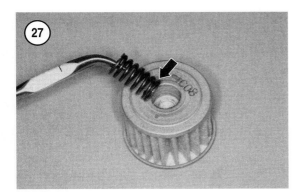

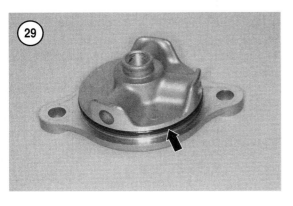

4. After the oil has stopped draining from the oil drain bolt hole, press the engine stop switch and turn the engine over several times with the kickstarter to remove as much oil as possible.

5. Remove the oil filter as follows:

  a. Remove the bolts, oil filter cover and its O-ring. See C, **Figure 20** (CRF250R and CRF250X) or B, **Figure 23** (CRF450R and CRF450X).

  b. Remove the oil filter and spring (**Figure 26**). Discard the oil filter.

6. Reinstall the oil drain bolt and a new washer (**Figure 24** or **Figure 25**) and tighten to the torque specification in **Table 13**.

7. Apply grease onto one side of the spring and insert this side into the filter (**Figure 27**).

8. Install the oil filter into the cover with its OUT SIDE mark facing out (**Figure 28**).

*CAUTION*
*Installing the oil filter backward will*
*cause engine damage.*

9. Replace the oil filter cover O-ring (**Figure 29**) if damaged. Lubricate the O-ring with engine oil and install in the cover groove.

10. Install the oil filter cover. On CRF250R and CRF450X models, tighten the bolts securely. On CRF250X and CRF450R models, tighten the bolts as specified in **Table 13**.

11. Fill the engine with the correct weight (**Table 5**) and quantity (**Table 6**) oil.

12. On CRF450R models, install and tighten the oil fill cap (A, **Figure 23**). On all other models, install and tighten the dipstick (A, **Figure 20**).

13. Start the engine and allow it to idle. Check for any leaks.

14. Recheck the oil level as described in this section.

15. Install the engine guard and tighten the bolt securely.

## ENGINE OIL STRAINER

All engines are equipped with an engine oil strainer mounted behind the left side cover. Periodic cleaning of the strainer is not part of normal maintenance. However, remove and clean the strainer whenever the left crankcase cover is removed from the engine, or whenever the engine has experienced a lubricating or overheating problem. Refer to Chapter Four or Chapter Five.

## TRANSMISSION OIL

Service the transmission oil at the intervals specified in **Table 2** or **Table 3**. Refer to **Table 5** for the recommended type and viscosity transmission oil and **Table 7** for transmission oil capacity.

### Transmission Oil Level Inspection

*WARNING*
*Because the engine must be warmed up before checking the oil level, do not start and run the engine in a closed area. The exhaust gasses contain carbon monoxide, a colorless, ordorless, poisonous gas. Carbon monoxide levels build quickly in a closed area and can cause unconsciousness and death in a short time. When running the engine in the following sections, always do so in an area with adequate ventilation.*

1. Start the engine and allow it to warm up for 3 minutes. In cold weather, allow the engine to idle for at least 5 minutes.
2. Support the motorcycle so it is vertical and level. Allow the engine to rest in this position for 2 minutes before checking the oil level.

*NOTE*
*On CRF250X and CRF450X models, do not check the oil level with the motorcycle supported on its sidestand.*

3. Remove the oil fill cap and the transmission oil check bolt from the right crankcase cover. See **Figure 30** (CRF250R and CRF250X), **Figure 31** (CRF450R) or **Figure 32** (CRF450X). A small amount of oil should flow out the check hole. If oil flows out of the hole, reinstall the check bolt and washer and tighten to the specification in **Table 13**. On models without a manufacturer's specification, tighten the bolt securely. Then install and tighten the oil fill cap. If oil does not flow out of the check hole, continue with Step 4.
4. If no oil flowed from the check hole, slowly add the appropriate weight of oil (**Table 5**) until oil starts to flow through the check hole. Reinstall the

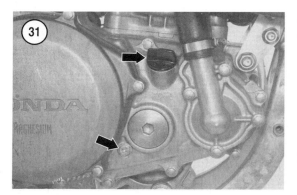

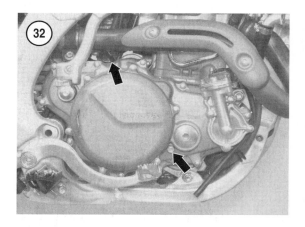

check bolt and washer and tighten to the specification in **Table 13**. Then install and tighten the oil fill cap.
5. Clean the cover of all drained oil. Then check the bolt for leaks.

### Transmission Oil Change

1. Start the engine and allow it to warm up for several minutes. Shut off the engine.

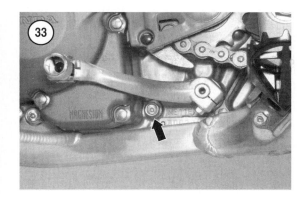

5. Fill the transmission with the correct weight (**Table 5**) and quantity (**Table 7**) oil. Install and tighten the oil fill cap.

6. Start the engine and allow it to idle. Check for any leaks.

7. Recheck the oil level as described in this section.

### ENGINE COMPRESSION CHECK

A cranking compression test is one of the quickest ways to check the internal condition of the engine (piston rings, piston, head gasket, valves and cylinder). It is a good idea to check compression at each tune-up, record it and compare it with the reading obtained at the next tune-up.

Use a screw-in type compression gauge with a flexible adapter. Before using the gauge, check that the rubber gasket on the end of the adapter is not cracked or damaged; this gasket seals the cylinder to ensure accurate compression readings.

1. On CRF250X and CRF450X models, make sure the battery is fully charged to ensure proper engine cranking speed.

2. Run the engine until it reaches normal operating temperature, then turn it off.

3. Remove the spark plug as described in this chapter.

4. Lubricate the threads of the compression gauge adapter with a *small* amount of antiseize compound and carefully thread the gauge (**Figure 35**) into the spark plug hole. Tighten the hose by hand to form a good seal.

*CAUTION*
*When the spark plug lead is disconnected, the electronic ignition will produce the highest voltage possible. This can damage the ICM or other ignition component. To protect the ignition system, install a grounding tool in the spark plug cap. Refer to* **Ignition Grounding Tool** *in Chapter One. Do not crank the engine more than necessary.*

5A. Kickstart—Open the throttle completely, press the engine stop switch and kick the engine over while reading the compression gauge until there is no further rise in pressure. The compression reading should increase on each stroke. Record the reading.

2. Remove the oil fill cap (**Figures 30-32**).

3. Place a drain pan below the oil drain bolt on the left side of the crankcase. Remove the drain bolt and washer and allow the oil to drain. See **Figure 33** (CRF250R or CRF250X) or **Figure 34** (CRF450R and CRF450X).

4. Reinstall the oil drain bolt and a new washer (**Figure 33** or **Figure 34**) and tighten to 22 N•m (16 ft.-lb.).

5B. Electric start—Open the throttle completely and operate the starter to turn the engine over while reading the compression gauge until there is no further rise in pressure. The compression reading should increase on each stroke. Record the reading. If the starter does not turn the engine over fast enough, press the engine stop switch and use the kickstarter.

6. Refer to **Table 8** for the compression specification. If the compression reading is low, go to Step 8. If the compression reading is high, go to Step 9.

7. A low compression reading can be caused by the following:

    a. Incorrect valve adjustment.

    b. Worn piston rings, piston or cylinder bore.

    c. Leaking valve seat.

    d. Damaged cylinder head gasket.

*NOTE*
*An engine with low compression cannot*
*be tuned to maximum performance.*

8. A high compression reading can be caused by the following:

    a. Damaged decompressor assembly.

    b. Excessive carbon deposits on the piston crown or combustion chamber.

9. To isolate the problem to a valve or ring problem, perform a wet compression test. Pour about a teaspoon of engine oil into the spark plug hole. Repeat the compression test and record the reading. If the compression increases significantly, the valves are good but the rings are defective. If compression does not increase, the valves require servicing.

10. Reverse the steps to complete installation. Reinstall the spark plug as described under *Spark Plug* in this chapter.

## PISTON AND PISTON RING REPLACEMENT

Replace the piston and piston rings at the intervals specified in **Table 2**. Refer to Chapter Four or Chapter Five for service procedures.

## PISTON PIN REPLACEMENT

Replace the piston pin at the intervals specified in **Table 2**. Refer to Chapter Four or Chapter Five for service procedures.

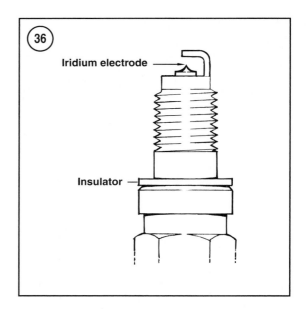

Iridium electrode

Insulator

## IGNITION TIMING

Refer to Chapter Ten.

## SPARK PLUG

### Service Notes

The spark plugs have an iridium center electrode and a platinum tip in the side electrode (**Figure 36**). These spark plugs must be serviced differently than conventional type spark plugs. Note the following:

1. Use only a wire type feeler gauge to measure the spark plug gap. Never use a blade or leaf type feeler gauge as it may damage the electrode's iridium tip or the side electrode's platinum tip.

2. The spark plug gap *cannot* be adjusted. If the gap is out of specification, replace the spark plug.

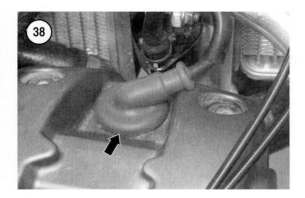

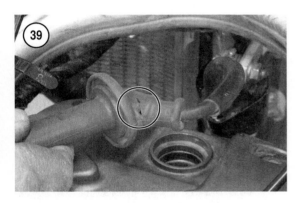

3A. On CRF250R and CRF250X models, grasp the ignition coil (**Figure 37**) and twist it slightly to break it loose, then pull it from the spark plug.

3B. On CRF450R and CRF450X models, grasp the plug cap (**Figure 38**) and twist it slightly to break it loose, then pull it from the spark plug.

*CAUTION*
*On CRF450R and CRF450X models, do not remove the plug cap by pulling on the secondary wire. This will weaken the plug cap and cause it to crack (**Figure 39**). Water can then enter the cap and cause a misfire when it contacts the terminal.*

4. Fit a spark plug wrench onto the spark plug, then remove it by turning the wrench counterclockwise. If the plug is seized or difficult to remove, stop and perform the following:

 a. Apply penetrating lubricant and allow it to stand for about 15 minutes.

 b. If the plug is completely seized, apply moderate pressure in both directions with the wrench. Only attempt to break the seal so lubricant can penetrate the spark plug threads. If this does not work, and the engine can still be started, install the ignition coil or spark plug cap and start the engine. Allow it to completely warm up. The heat of the engine may be enough to expand the parts and allow the plug to be removed.

 c. If the spark plug is loose, but is difficult to remove, apply penetrating lubricant around the spark plug threads. Slowly work the plug in and out of the cylinder head while continuing to add lubricant.

 d. Inspect the threads in the cylinder head for damage. Clean and true the threads with a spark plug thread-chaser. Apply a thick grease onto the thread-chaser threads before using it. The grease will help trap some of the debris cut from the threads to prevent it from falling into the engine.

*NOTE*
*Damaged spark plug threads will require removal of the cylinder head (Chapter Four or Chapter Five) and repair.*

3. The spark plug firing tip *cannot* be cleaned. If the plug tip is contaminated or partially fouled, replace the spark plug.

4. Use only the spark plugs specified in **Table 9**. Using a non-resistor type spark plug can cause ignition problems.

5. Tighten new and used spark plugs carefully as described in this section.

**Removal**

Careful removal of the spark plug is important in preventing dirt from entering the combustion chamber. It is also important to know how to remove a plug that is seized, or is resistant to removal. Forcing a seized plug can damage the threads in the cylinder head.

1. Remove the fuel tank (Chapter Nine).

2. Blow away any dirt that has accumulated around the spark plug.

*CAUTION*
*Dirt that falls through the spark plug hole causes engine wear and damage.*

5. Inspect the plug carefully as described in this section.

> *CAUTION*
> *The porcelain cover, found on the top of the spark plug, actually extends into the plug to prevent the spark from grounding through the plug metal body and threads. The porcelain cover can be easily damaged from mishandling. Make sure the spark plug socket fits the plug fully before turning the plug.*

**Gap Measurement**

The spark plug gap cannot be adjusted. Refer to *Service Notes* in this section.

1. If installing a new spark plug, make sure the terminal nut is installed on the end of the plug.

2. Refer to the spark plug gap in **Table 9**. Select the correct size wire feeler gauge and try to slide it past the gap between both electrodes (**Figure 40**). If there is a slight drag as the wire gauge passes through the gap, the setting is correct. If the gap is too large, note the following:

    a. 2004 CRF250R and all CRF250X: If a 1.00 mm (0.039 in.) wire feeler gauge can slide past the gap, replace the spark plug.

    b. 2005 CRF250R: If a 0.8 mm (0.032 in.) wire feeler gauge can slide past the gap, replace the spark plug.

    c. CRF450R and CRF450X: If a 1.2 mm (0.047 in.) wire feeler gauge can slide past the gap, replace the spark plug.

> *CAUTION*
> *If the gap is not within the clearance range listed in **Table 9**, replace the spark plug. Do not attempt to adjust it.*

**Installation**

1. Wipe a *small* amount of antiseize compound to the plug threads before installing the spark plug. Do not allow the compound to get on the electrodes.

2. Screw the spark plug in by hand until it seats. Very little effort should be required; if force is necessary, the plug may be cross-threaded. Unscrew it and try again.

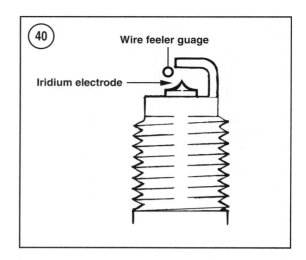

**Wire feeler guage**

**Iridium electrode**

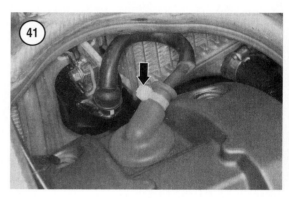

3A. Installing a used spark plug without a torque wrench—Tighten the spark plug an additional 1/8 turn after it seats.

3B. Installing a used spark plug with a torque wrench—After seating the spark plug, tighten it to 16 N•m (12 ft.-lb.).

4. New spark plug—Tighten the spark plug twice to prevent it from loosening:

    a. Denso spark plug: Tighten the spark plug 1/2 turn after it seats.

    b. NGK spark plug: Tighten the spark plug 3/4 turns after it seats.

    c. Loosen the spark plug.

    d. Tighten the spark plug until it seats, then tighten an additional 1/8 turn.

> *CAUTION*
> *Do not overtighten the spark plug. This may crush the gasket and cause a compression leak or damage the cylinder head threads.*

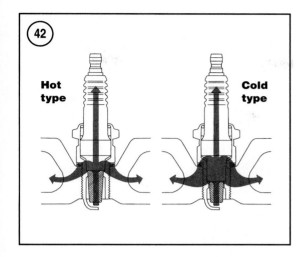

Hot type

Cold type

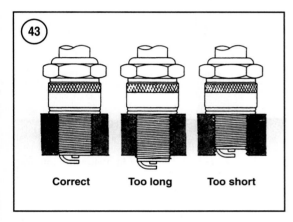

Correct    Too long    Too short

5. Align and press the ignition coil (**Figure 37**) or plug cap (**Figure 38**) onto the spark plug.

*NOTE*
*On CRF450R and CRF450X models, secure the spark plug cap with a plastic tie as shown in **Figure 41**. This will help prevent water from seeping past the cap and onto the terminals where it can cause a misfire.*

6. Install the fuel tank (Chapter Nine).

**Selection**

The proper spark plug is very important in obtaining maximum performance and reliability. The condition of a used spark plug can reveal a lot about engine condition and carburetion.

The spark plugs used on these models use an iridium center electrode and a platinum tip in the side electrode (**Figure 36**). The spark plugs in **Table 9** are the only spark plugs that should be used in the CRF models covered in this manual.

If the engine is run in hot climates, at high speed or under heavy loads for prolonged periods, a spark plug with a colder heat range may be required. A colder plug quickly transfers heat away from its firing tip and to the cylinder head. This is accomplished by a short path up the ceramic insulator and into the body of the spark plug (**Figure 42**). By transferring heat quickly, the plug remains cool enough to avoid overheating and preignition problems. If the engine is run slowly for prolonged periods, this type of plug will foul and cause poor performance. A colder plug does not cool down a hot engine.

If the engine is run in cold climates or at a slow speed for prolonged periods, a spark plug with a hotter heat range may be required. A hotter plug slowly transfers heat away from its firing tip and to the cylinder head. This is accomplished by a long path up the ceramic insulator and into the body of the plug (**Figure 42**). By transferring heat slowly, the plug remains hot enough to avoid fouling and buildup. If the engine is run in hot climates for fast or prolonged periods, this type of plug will overheat, cause preignition problems and possibly melt the electrode. Damage to the piston and cylinder assembly is possible.

Changing to a different heat range plug is normally not required. Changing to a different heat range plug may be necessary when operating a motorcycle with a modified engine. This type of change is usually based on a recommendation made by the engine builder. Experience in reading spark plugs is also required when trying to determine if a different heat range plug is required. When installing a different heat range plug, go one step hotter or colder from the *recommended* plug. Do not try to correct poor carburetor or ignition problems by using different spark plugs. This only compounds the existing problem(s) and possibly leads to engine damage.

The reach (length) of a plug is also important (**Figure 43**). A shorter than normal plug causes hard starting and reduces engine performance and can result in carbon buildup on the exposed cylinder head threads. These same conditions can occur if the correct length plug is used without a gasket. Trying to thread a spark plug into threads with carbon buildup may damage the threads in the cylinder head.

### Reading/Inspection

The spark plug is an excellent indicator of how the engine is operating. By correctly evaluating the condition of the plug, engine problems can be diagnosed. To correctly read a spark plug, perform the following:

1. If using a new spark plug, remove it from the box and inspect it. Measure the gap as described in this section. If the gap is too large, return the spark plug as the gap on these spark plugs cannot be adjusted. Refer to *Service Notes* in this section for further information.

2. Refer to *Installation* in this section when removing and installing the spark plug during this procedure.

3. If a new plug was installed, ride the motorcycle for approximately 15 to 20 minutes so it will begin to color. Then continue with Step 4.

4. Accelerate on a straight road at full throttle. Then push the engine stop button, pull the clutch lever in and coast to a stop. Do not stop by downshifting the transmission.

5. Remove the spark plug and examine its firing tip while noting the following:

   a. Inspect the spark plug with a magnifying glass or spark plug reader.

   b. Because the spark plug used in these models uses an iridium center electrode, replace the spark plug if the electrode is worn or contaminated. Do not clean or regap the spark plug.

   c. **Figure 44** and **Figure 45** and the following sections provide a description, as well as common causes for each of the conditions.

> *CAUTION*
> *In all cases, when a spark plug is abnormal, find the cause of the problem before continuing engine operation. Engine damage is possible when abnormal plug readings are ignored.*

### Normal condition

The porcelain insulator around the center electrode is clean and colorless. There should be a gray

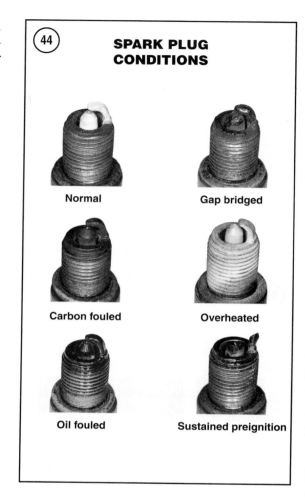

**44**

### SPARK PLUG CONDITIONS

Normal

Gap bridged

Carbon fouled

Overheated

Oil fouled

Sustained preignition

ring around the center electrode where it separates from the porcelain. No erosion or rounding of the electrodes or abnormal gap is evident. This indicates an engine that has properly adjusted ignition timing and fuel mixture. This heat range of the plug is appropriate for the conditions in which the engine has been operated. The plug can be reused.

### Oil fouled

The plug is wet with black, oily deposits on the electrodes and insulator. The electrodes do not show wear. Replace the spark plug.

1. Incorrect carburetor jetting.
2. High float level.
3. Clogged air filter.
4. Faulty ignition component.
5. Spark plug heat range too cold.
6. Low engine compression.

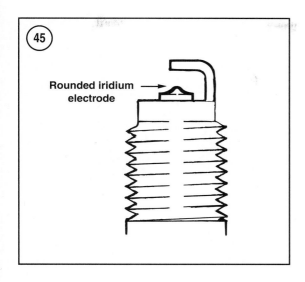

7. Engine not properly broken in.

### Carbon fouled

The plug is black with a dry, sooty deposit on the entire plug surface. This dry, sooty deposit is conductive and can create electrical paths that bypass the electrode gap. This often causes misfiring of the plug. Replace the spark plug.
1. Rich fuel mixture.
2. Spark plug heat range too cold.
3. Clogged air filter.
4. Too much oil applied to air filter during service.
5. Faulty ignition component.
6. Low engine compression.
7. Prolonged idling.

### Overheating

The plug is dry and the insulator has a white or light gray cast. The insulator may also appear blistered. The electrodes may have a burnt appearance and there may be metallic specks on the center electrode and porcelain. This material is being removed from the piston crown. Replace the spark plug.
1. Lean fuel mixture.
2. Spark plug heat range too hot.
3. Faulty ignition component.
4. Air leak at the exhaust port or in the intake boot.
5. Overtightened spark plug.
6. No crush washer on spark plug.
7. Spark plug heat range too hot.

8. Modified air box (holes drilled in sides of air box).
9. Less-restrictive exhaust system.

### Gap bridging

The plug is clogged with deposits between the electrodes. The engine may run with a bridged spark plug, but it will misfire. Replace the spark plug.
1. Incorrect oil type.
2. Incorrect fuel or fuel contamination.
3. Excessive carbon deposits in combustion chamber.

### Preignition

The plug electrodes are severely eroded or melted. This condition can lead to engine damage. Replace the spark plug.
1. Faulty ignition system component.
2. Spark plug heat range too hot.
3. Air leak.
4. Excessive carbon deposits in combustion chamber.

### Worn out

The center electrode is rounded from normal combustion. There is no indication of abnormal combustion or engine conditions. If the center electrode is rounded like that shown in **Figure 45**, replace the spark plug.

## VALVE CLEARANCE AND DECOMPRESSOR SYSTEM INSPECTION

### Valve Clearance Measurement

Valve clearance is adjusted by changing the thickness of the shims, which are located under the rocker arm and valve lifters.

### CRF250R and CRF250X

Check valve clearance when the engine temperature is below 35° C (95° F).
1. Support the motorcycle so it is stable and secure.

2. Remove the cylinder head cover as described in Chapter Four.

> *NOTE*
> *To eliminate any error when setting the crankshaft at TDC, use the ignition timing marks on the flywheel instead of the timing marks on the crankshaft. Refer to **Crankshaft Timing Marks** in Chapter Four or Chapter Five.*

3. Remove the crankshaft hole cap (**Figure 46**) from the right crankcase cover.

4. Remove the ignition timing hole cap (**Figure 47**) from the left crankcase cover.

5. Remove the spark plug to make turning the crankshaft easier.

> *NOTE*
> *Use an 8 mm hex socket on the primary drive gear mounting bolt to turn the crankshaft (**Figure 48**).*

6. Set the engine at TDC on its compression stroke as follows:

> *NOTE*
> *The decompressor mechanism will click loudly once during each crankshaft revolution. This is normal.*

  a. Turn the crankshaft *clockwise* and align the TDC mark on the flywheel (A, **Figure 49**) with the index mark on the left crankcase cover (B). Then check that both index lines on the cam sprocket align with the cylinder head surface (**Figure 50**).

  b. The engine is now at TDC on either its compression stroke or exhaust stroke. The engine

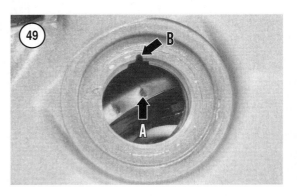

is on its compression stroke if the rocker arm (**Figure 51**) can be moved slightly by hand, indicating that exhaust and intake valves are closed. If the rocker arm is tight, the engine is on its exhaust stroke and the exhaust valves are open. If the rocker arm is tight, turn the crankshaft clockwise one full turn and realign the TDC marks described in substep a. The rocker arm should now be loose.

> *CAUTION*
> *If the cam sprocket timing marks do not align as described in Step 6 the*

b. Select and insert a flat feeler gauge between the rocker arm and shim (exhaust side [**Figure 52**]) or between the cam lobe and valve lifter (intake side [**Figure 53**]). Clearance is correct when a slight resistance is felt as the gauge is inserted and withdrawn. If clearance is incorrect, use a feeler gauge to determine the actual clearance. Record the measurement for that valve. The recorded clearance measurements will be used if valve adjustment is necessary.

8. If any of the valve clearance dimensions are incorrect, it is necessary to replace the shim with a shim of a different thickness. The shims are available from Honda in 0.025 increments that range from 1.20 to 2.90 mm in thickness. To adjust the valve clearance, refer to *Valve Clearance Adjustment* in this section.

9. If all the valve clearances are correct, continue with Step 10.

10. Check the decompressor system as described in this section.

11. Reinstall the spark plug as described in this chapter.

12. Lubricate the crankshaft hole cap (**Figure 46**) threads and O-ring with grease and tighten to 15 N•m (133 in.-lb.).

13. Lubricate the ignition timing hole cap (**Figure 47**) threads and O-ring with grease and tighten to 5.9 N•m (52 in.-lb.).

### *CRF450R and CRF450X*

Check valve clearance when the engine temperature is below 35° C (95° F).

1. Support the motorcycle so it is stable and secure.

*cam timing is incorrect. A damaged or incorrectly adjusted cam chain tensioner or excessively stretched cam chain can cause the camshaft to jump time. This condition can cause bent valves and loss of compression.*

7. With the engine positioned at TDC on its compression stroke, check and record the valve clearances for each valve as follows:

a. Refer to **Table 8** for the correct valve clearance.

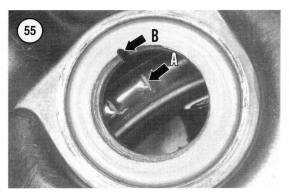

2. Remove the cylinder head cover as described in Chapter Five.

> *NOTE*
> *To eliminate any error when setting the crankshaft at TDC, use the ignition timing marks on the flywheel instead of the timing marks on the crankshaft. Refer to **Crankshaft Timing Marks** in Chapter Four or Chapter Five.*

3. Remove the crankshaft hole cap (**Figure 46**, typical) from the right crankcase cover.
4. Remove the ignition timing hole cap (**Figure 47**, typical) from the left crankcase cover.
5. Remove the spark plug to make turning the crankshaft easier.

> *NOTE*
> *Use an 8 mm hex socket on the primary drive gear mounting bolt to turn the crankshaft (**Figure 54**).*

6. Set the engine at TDC on its compression stroke as follows:

> *NOTE*
> *The decompressor mechanism will click loudly once during each crankshaft revolution. This is normal.*

  a. Turn the crankshaft *clockwise* and align the TDC mark on the flywheel (A, **Figure 55**) with the index mark on the left crankcase cover (B). Then check that the index line on the cam sprocket (A, **Figure 56**) aligns with the triangle mark on the cam holder (B).

  b. The engine is now at TDC on either its compression stroke or exhaust stroke. The engine

is on its compression stroke if the rocker arm (C, **Figure 56**) can be moved slightly by hand, indicating that exhaust and intake valves are closed. If the rocker arm is tight, the engine is on its exhaust stroke and the exhaust valves are open. If the rocker arm is tight, turn the crankshaft clockwise one full turn and realign the TDC marks described in substep a. The rocker arm should now be loose.

> *CAUTION*
> *If the cam sprocket timing marks do not align as described in Step 6, the cam timing is incorrect. A damaged or incorrectly adjusted cam chain tensioner or excessively stretched cam chain can cause the camshaft to jump time. This condition can cause bent valves and loss of compression.*

7. With the engine positioned at TDC on its compression stroke, check and record the valve clearances for each valve as follows:

  a. Refer to **Table 8** for the correct valve clearance.

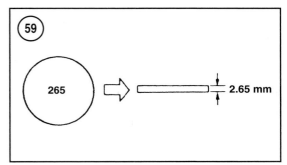

b. Select and insert a flat feeler gauge between the rocker arm and shim (exhaust side [**Figure 57**]) or between the cam lobe and valve lifter (intake side [**Figure 58**]). Clearance is correct when a slight resistance is felt as the gauge is inserted and withdrawn. If clearance is incorrect, use a feeler gauge to determine the actual clearance. Record the measurement for that valve. The recorded clearance measurements will be used if valve adjustment is necessary.

*NOTE*
*The right exhaust valve clearance measurement is required when determining the decompressor clearance as described under **Decompressor Clearance Adjustment and System Inspection (CRF450R and CRF450X)** in this section. Record this clearance on a piece of paper.*

8. If any of the valve clearance dimensions are incorrect, it is necessary to replace the shim with a shim of a different thickness. The shims are available from Honda in 0.025 increments that range from 1.20 to 3.00 mm in thickness. To adjust the valve clearance, refer to *Valve Clearance Adjustment* in this section.

9. If all the valve clearances are correct, continue with Step 10.

10. Check and adjust the decompressor clearance and inspect the system as described in this section.

11. Reinstall the spark plug as described in this chapter.

12. Lubricate the crankshaft hole cap (**Figure 46**, typical) threads and O-ring with grease and tighten to 15 N•m (133 in.-lb.).

13. Lubricate the ignition timing hole cap threads (**Figure 47**) and O-ring with grease and tighten to the torque specification in **Table 13**. If no torque specification is listed, tighten the hole cap securely.

**Valve Clearance Adjustment**
**(All Models)**

1. Remove the camshaft as described in Chapter Four or Chapter Five.

2. Reinstall the spark plug (to prevent a shim from falling through the spark plug hole).

3. Before removing the valve lifters and shims, note the following:

a. Identify and store the valve lifters and shims in a manner that allows them to be identified and installed in their original locations. This step is critical to ensure correct valve clearance adjustment and reassembly.

b. The number on the shim surface (**Figure 59**) is the thickness of the shim. For example, a 265 designation indicates the shim is 2.65 mm thick.

c. Always measure the thickness of the old shim with a micrometer to make sure of the exact thickness of the shim. On some shims, the numbers may be indecipherable. Shims worn to less than their indicated thickness (**Figure 59**) will effect calculations for a new shim. Measure the new shim to make sure it is marked correctly and not worn.

   d. The intake shims are mounted underneath the valve lifters. Because the shims may stick to the lifters when removing the lifters, remove the lifters carefully to prevent the shims from falling into the engine.

   e. Use a magnet to remove the lifters and shims.

   f. Clean the shims and valve lifters with solvent or contact cleaner and dry with compressed air.

4. Cover the chain tunnel with a rag (to prevent a shim from falling into the crankcase).

5A. On CRF250R and CRF250X models, note the following when removing the valve lifters and shims for each valve to be adjusted:

   a. The exhaust shims can be removed without having to remove the rocker arm (**Figure 60**).

   b. Remove the intake valve lifters (A, **Figure 61**) and shims (B).

5B. On CRF450R and CRF450X models, note the following when removing the valve lifters and shims for each valve to be adjusted:

   a. The intake valve lifters will probably come out with the camshaft holder. The intake valve shims will either stay inside the valve lifters or remain in the spring seats at the end of the valves.

   b. Remove the intake (A, **Figure 62**) and exhaust (B, **Figure 62**) shims as required.

6. Measure the thickness of the old shim with a micrometer.

7. Using the recorded valve clearance, the specified valve clearance (**Table 8**) and the old shim thickness, determine the new shim thickness with the following equation: $a = (b - c) + d$.

   a. $a$ is the new shim thickness.

   b. b is the measured valve clearance.

   c. c is the specified valve clearance.

   d. d is the old shim thickness.

*NOTE*
*The following numbers are used for example only. Use the actual clearance, correct clearance specification and existing shim thickness for the engine.*

8. Refer to the following as an *example*:

   a. If the measured exhaust valve clearance is 0.33 mm, the old shim thickness is 2.450 mm

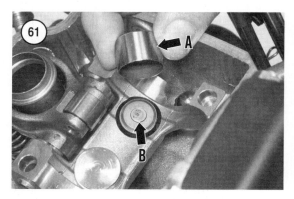

and the specified valve clearance is 0.28 mm (midpoint of specification).

   b. Then: $(0.33 - 0.28) + 2.45 = 2.500$ (new shim thickness).

*NOTE*
*If the required shim thickness exceeds 2.800 mm (CRF250F and CRF250X) or 3.000 mm (CRF450R and CRF450X), the valve seat is heavily carboned and must be cleaned or refaced.*

*NOTE*
*Some dealership service departments will allow customers to trade shims when they do their own valve adjustments. When obtaining shims in this manner, many of which will be used, measure their thickness with a micrometer before installing them in the engine. Shim kits are also available from K&L Supply and can be ordered through most motorcycle dealerships.*

9. Apply clean engine oil to both sides of the new shim.

2. Check the decompressor system (**Figure 63**) mounted on the camshaft for any visible damage.

3. Move and release the weight arm (A, **Figure 63**) on the end of the decompressor cam. It should move and return under spring pressure. When moving the weight arm, inspect the cam area (B, **Figure 63**) on the end of the decompressor cam for any visible wear or damage. Check the raised part of the cam for any flat spots, cracks or other damage.

4. Check the roller (C, **Figure 63**) on the rocker arm for any cracks, flat spots or other damage.

5. Turn the crankshaft clockwise as described under *Valve Clearance Measurement* in this section. The decompressor cam should click loudly once during each complete revolution of the camshaft. If not, remove and inspect the decompressor cam assembly as described in Chapter Four.

6. Install the cylinder head cover (Chapter Four).

**Decompressor Clearance Adjustment and System Inspection (CRF450R and CRF450X)**

Check and adjust the decompressor clearance after adjusting the right exhaust valve clearance. This section describes how to check and adjust the decompressor clearance using two separate feeler gauges.

1. Check and adjust both exhaust valve clearances as described under *Valve Clearance Measurement* in this section.

2. If the engine was turned over after adjusting the exhaust valve clearances, reset the engine at TDC on its compression stroke as described under *Valve Clearance Measurement* in this section.

3. Insert the feeler gauge used to set the right exhaust valve clearance between the right exhaust valve shim and rocker arm as shown in **Figure 64**.

> *CAUTION*
> *When checking and adjusting the decompressor clearance in Step 4, the feeler gauge used to set the right exhaust valve clearance **must** remain in place (**Figure 64**). If the decompressor clearance is set without the feeler gauge in place, the resulting decompressor clearance will be too small. This will cause hard starting, abnormal decompressor arm and exhaust rocker arm noise, and valve damage.*

10. Install the new shim with its marked side facing down. Make sure the shim seats flush in the upper spring seat bore. See **Figure 62**, typical.

11. Install the intake valve lifters and camshaft as described in Chapter Four or Chapter Five.

12. Rotate the camshaft several times, then recheck the valve clearances as described in this section. Repeat this procedure until the valve clearances are correct.

13A. On CRF250R and CRF250X models, inspect the decompressor assembly as described in this section.

13B. On CRF450R and CRF450X models, check and adjust the decompressor clearance and inspect the system as described in this section.

14. Reinstall the spark plug as described in this chapter.

15. Install the cylinder head cover as described in Chapter Four or Chapter Five.

**Decompressor Inspection (CRF250R and CRF250X)**

1. Remove the cylinder head cover (Chapter Four).

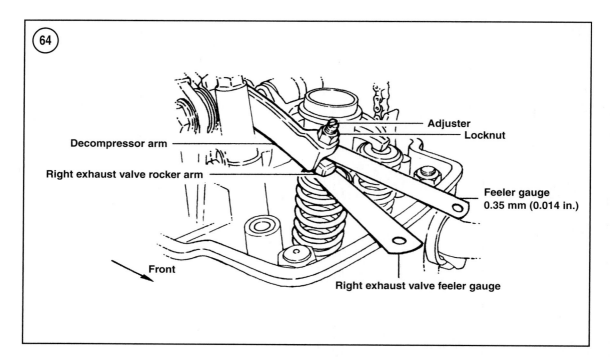

4. Insert a 0.35 mm (0.014 in.) feeler gauge between the decompressor adjusting screw and the right side rocker arm (**Figure 64**). Clearance is correct when a slight resistance is felt as the gauge is inserted and withdrawn. If clearance is incorrect, loosen the locknut and turn the adjusting screw as required until there is a slight resistance on the feeler gauge. Lubricate the adjusting screw threads with oil. Then hold the adjusting screw and tighten the locknut to 10 N•m (88 in.-lb.).

5. Recheck the decompressor clearance.

6. When the decompressor clearance is correct, remove both feeler gauges (**Figure 64**).

7. Check the decompressor system (A, **Figure 65**) mounted on the camshaft for any visible damage.

8. Move and release the weight arm (B, **Figure 65**) on the end of the decompressor cam. It should move and return under spring pressure.

9. Check the roller on the rocker arm for any cracks, flat spots or other damage.

10. Turn the crankshaft clockwise as described under *Valve Clearance Measurement* in this section. The decompressor cam should click loudly once during each complete revolution of the camshaft. If not, remove and inspect the decompressor cam assembly as described in Chapter Five.

11. Install the cylinder head cover (Chapter Five).

## CARBURETOR

This section describes service to the fuel hose, shutoff valve, intake tube, starting circuits and carburetor.

### Fuel Hose and Shutoff Valve Inspection

Inspect the fuel hose (A, **Figure 66**, typical) for cracks, leaks, soft spots and deterioration. Make sure each end of the hose is installed to the proper depth on the fuel tank and carburetor fittings. Secure each end of the hose with a clamp. Replace the fuel hose and hose clamps if damaged.

Inspect the fuel shutoff valve (B, **Figure 66**, typical) for any leaks or damage. O-rings in the valve can deteriorate and cause the valve to leak fuel. If there is insufficient fuel flow, the fuel filter mounted on the fuel valve may be partially clogged. To service the fuel shutoff valve, refer to Chapter Nine.

> *WARNING*
> *A leaking fuel hose may cause a fire; do not start the engine with a leaking or damaged fuel hose or fuel shutoff valve.*

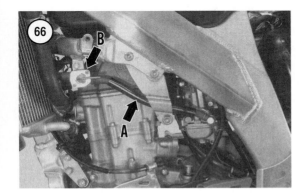

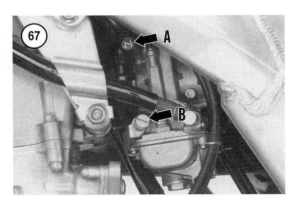

## Fuel Filter
## (CRF250X and CRF450X)

At the intervals specified in **Table 3**, remove and clean the fuel filter screen. Refer to Chapter Nine for service procedures.

## Carburetor Cleaning

Periodically disassemble, clean and reassemble the carburetor as described in Chapter Nine.

### Choke Valve Inspection

Inspect the choke valve (A, **Figure 67**) for proper operation. When operated, the knob must fully seat when it is pushed in. If the knob does not fully seat, the valve is open and will cause a rich air/fuel mixture. If the choke valve knob cannot be fully seated (pushed in), replace the valve.

> *NOTE*
> *Opening the choke valve richens the air/fuel mixture for starting a cold engine. If the valve is stuck in either of its closed or open position, the engine will be difficult to start and will not run after it warms up.*

### Hot Start Valve (Air Valve) Inspection

Refer to *Hot Start Cable Adjustment* in this chapter.

### Engine Idle Speed Adjustment

1. Check the air filter for cleanliness. Clean if necessary as described in this chapter.
2. Connect a tachometer to the engine following the manufacturer's instructions.
3. Make sure the throttle cable free play is correct. Check and adjust as described in this chapter.
4. Start and allow the engine to reach operating temperature.
5. Adjust the idle speed with the throttle stop screw (B, **Figure 67**) to the specification in **Table 10**. Open and close the throttle a few times to make sure the idle speed returns to the rpm set in Step 5.
6. Turn off the engine and disconnect the tachometer.
7. Test ride the motorcycle. If throttle response is poor from an idle, check the pilot screw adjustment. Refer to Chapter Nine.

### SECONDARY AIR SUPPLY SYSTEM
### (CRF250X AND CRF450X CALIFORNIA
### MODELS)

At the intervals specified in **Table 3**, check the secondary air supply system as follows:
1. Check the following hoses for deterioration, damage or loose connections:

a. Air supply hose. See A, **Figure 68** (CRF250X) or A, **Figure 69** (CRF450X).
b. Air suction hose. See B, **Figure 68** (CRF250X) or B, **Figure 69** (CRF450X).
c. Vacuum hose. See C, **Figure 68** (CRF250X) or C, **Figure 69** (CRF450X). Make sure this hose is not kinked or pinched.

2. Refer to Chapter Nine for further information and testing procedures.

### EXHAUST SYSTEM

Refer to Chapter Four or Chapter Five for service and repair procedures.

### Inspection

1. Inspect the exhaust pipe for cracks or dents that could alter performance. Refer all repairs to a qualified dealership or welding shop.
2. Check all the exhaust pipe fasteners and mounting points for loose or damaged parts.

### Spark Arrestor Cleaning
### (CRF250X and CRF450X)

Remove and clean the spark arrestor at the intervals specified in **Table 3**. Refer to Chapter Four or Chapter Five for service procedures.

### Muffler Repacking
### (CRF250R and CRF450R)

Replace the glass wool in the muffler periodically. Refer to Chapter Four or Chapter Five for service procedures.

### COOLING SYSTEM

At the intervals specified in **Table 2** and **Table 3**; inspect and service the cooling system as described in this section.

> *WARNING*
> *Never remove the radiator cap, the coolant drain plug or disconnect any coolant hose while the engine and radiator are hot. Scalding fluid and steam may blow out under pressure and cause serious injury.*

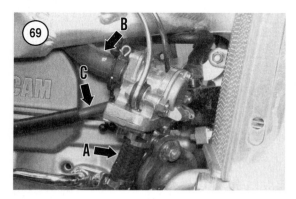

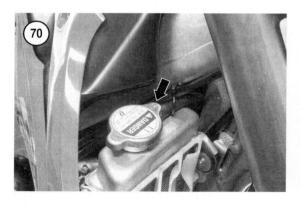

### Cooling System Inspection

1. With the engine cold, remove the radiator cap (**Figure 70**).

2. Check the rubber washers on the radiator cap (**Figure 71**). Replace the cap if the washers show signs of deterioration, cracking or other damage. If the radiator cap is good, perform Step 3.

3. To test the cooling system for leaks or to test the radiator cap, perform the *Pressure Test* in Chapter Eleven.

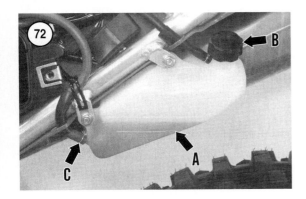

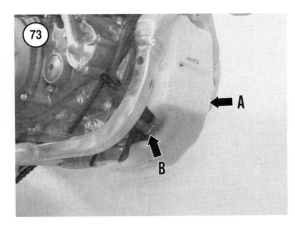

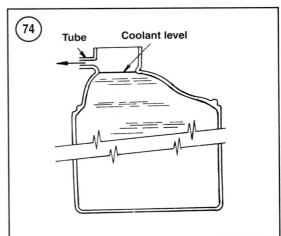

serve tank (A, **Figure 73**) and connecting hoses for leaks and damage.

6. Carefully clean the radiator core. Use a whisk broom, compressed air, or low pressure water. Straighten bent radiator fins with a screwdriver.

7. Check for signs of coolant or coolant stains from the inspection hole in the bottom of the right crankcase cover as described in Chapter Eleven. If there is leakage, the mechanical seal is damaged. Rebuild the water pump as described in Chapter Eleven.

**Coolant Check**

*CRF250R and CRF450R*

When the engine is cold, check the coolant level in the radiator. Remove the radiator cap (**Figure 70**). The coolant level must be at the bottom of the radiator filler neck (**Figure 74**). If the level is low, add a sufficient amount of antifreeze and distilled water (in a 50:50 ratio) as described under *Coolant*. Reinstall the radiator cap.

*CRF250X and CRF450X*

1. Start the engine and warm up to normal operating temperature.

2. With the engine running at idle speed, support the machine in an upright position. Do not support it on its sidestand. The coolant level must be between the maximum and minimum level marks on the coolant reserve tank. See **Figure 75** (CRF250X) or **Figure 76** (CRF450X).

4. Check all cooling system hoses for damage or deterioration. Replace any questionable hose. Make sure all hose clamps are tight.

5A. On CRF250X models, remove the left side cover (Chapter Sixteen). Check the coolant reserve tank (A, **Figure 72**) and connecting hoses for leaks and damage.

5B. On CRF450X models, remove the center engine guard (Chapter Sixteen). Check the coolant re-

3. Turn the engine off. If the level is low, add coolant to the coolant reserve tank.

4. On CRF250X models, remove the left side cover as described in Chapter Sixteen.

5. Remove the cap (B, **Figure 72** [CRF250X] or **Figure 77** [CRF450X]) and add a sufficient amount of antifreeze and distilled water (in a 50:50 ratio) as described under *Coolant*. Reinstall the cap.

6. On CRF250X models, reinstall the left side cover (Chapter Sixteen).

## Coolant Type

Use only a high quality ethylene glycol-based antifreeze designed for aluminum engines. Mix the antifreeze with water, making sure to use only distilled (or purified) water. Never use tap or salt water as this damages engine parts. Distilled water is available at supermarkets or drug stores.

## Coolant Change

Completely drain and refill the cooling system at the interval in **Table 2** or **Table 3**.

> *WARNING*
> *Waste antifreeze is toxic and must never be discharged into storm sewers, septic systems, waterways, or onto the ground. Place used antifreeze in the original container and dispose of it according to local regulations. Do not store coolant where it is accessible to children or pets.*

> *CAUTION*
> *Be careful not to spill antifreeze on painted surfaces as it damages the surface. Wash immediately with soapy water and rinse thoroughly with clean water.*

1. Remove the radiator cap (**Figure 70**).

2. On CRF250X and CRF450X models, perform the following:

   a. Remove the left side cover (CRF250X) or center engine guard (CRF450X) as described in Chapter Sixteen.

   b. Disconnect the siphon hose at the tank and drain the coolant into a drain pan. See C, **Figure 72** (CRF250X) or B, **Figure 73** (CRF450X).

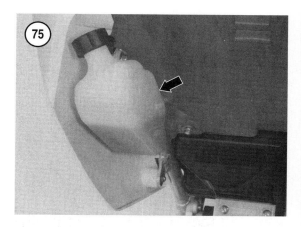

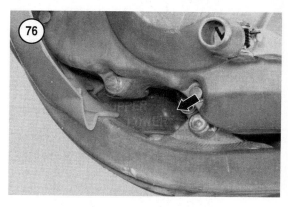

   c. Flush the coolant reserve tank with clean water.

   d. Reconnect the siphon hose and secure it with its clamp.

3. Place a drain pan underneath the right side of the engine.

4. Remove the coolant drain bolt and sealing washer from the water pump cover and drain the coolant. Discard the sealing washer if leaking or damaged. See **Figure 78** (CRF250R and CRF250X) or **Figure 79** (CRF450R and CRF450X).

5. Flush the cooling system with water directed through the radiator filler neck until the water exiting the drain bolt is clear and free from contaminants. Allow this water to drain completely.

6A. On CRF250R, 2005 CRF450R and CRF450X models, install the coolant drain bolt and washer and tighten securely.

6B. On all other models, install the coolant drain bolt and washer and tighten to 9.8 N•m (87 in.-lb.).

7. Refill the radiator by adding a 50:50 mixture of antifreeze and distilled water through the radiator

10. On CRF250X and CRF450X models, fill the coolant reserve tank to the minimum mark on the tank. See **Figure 72** (CRF250X) or **Figure 76** (CRF450X). Do not install the cap at this time.

11A. On CRF250R and CRF450R models, start the engine and allow it to idle for a few minutes, then shut it off. After the engine cools down, remove the radiator cap and check the coolant level in the radiator (**Figure 74**). Add coolant up to the filler neck, if necessary. Reinstall the radiator cap (**Figure 70**).

11B. On CRF250X and CRF450X models, bleed air from the system as follows:

  a. Start the engine and allow it to idle for 2-3 minutes.

  b. Snap the throttle three to four times to bleed air from the cooling system.

  c. With the motorcycle sitting level and engine running at idle speed, check the coolant level in the coolant reserve tank (**Figure 72** or **Figure 76**). Turn the engine off. Add coolant to bring the level between the maximum and minimum marks on the tank. Reinstall the cap and tighten securely. Reinstall the left side cover or center engine guard (Chapter Sixteen).

12. Check the coolant drain bolt and hoses for leaks.

## CONTROL CABLE INSPECTION AND LUBRICATION

This section describes lubrication procedures for the control cables. Clean and lubricate the throttle, clutch and hot start cables whenever the cable operation becomes sluggish or stiffens. At the same time, check the cables for wear and damage or fraying that could cause the cables to bind or break. The most positive method of cable lubrication involves using a cable lubricator like the one shown in **Figure 80** and a can of cable lubricant.

*CAUTION*
*Do not use chain lubricant to flush and lubricate the control cables.*

1. Disconnect both clutch cable ends as described under *Clutch Cable Replacement* in Chapter Six or Chapter Seven.

2. Disconnect both throttle cable ends as described under *Throttle Cable Replacement* in Chapter Nine.

filler neck. See **Table 11** for coolant capacity. Do not install the radiator cap at this time.

8. Lean the motorcycle from side to side (approximately 20°) to remove air trapped in the cooling system. When the motorcycle is level, observe the coolant level in the radiator (**Figure 74**). Repeat this step until the coolant level stops dropping in the radiator.

9. Install the radiator cap (**Figure 70**).

3. Disconnect both hot start cable ends as described under *Hot Start Cable Replacement* in Chapter Nine.

> *WARNING*
> *Do not lubricate the throttle cables or hot start cable with their lower cable ends mounted at the carburetor. Debris that flushes out of the end of the cable will contaminate the area behind the cable cover or the hot start valve.*

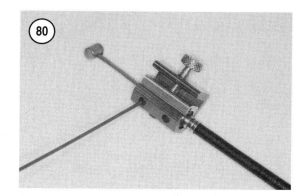

4. Attach a cable lubricator to one end of the cable, following the manufacturer's instructions (**Figure 80**).

5. Tie a plastic bag around the opposite cable end to catch the lubricant.

6. Fit the nozzle of the cable lubricant into the hole in the lubricator.

7. Hold a rag over the lubricator, then press and hold the button on the lubricant can. Continue until lubricant drips from the opposite end.

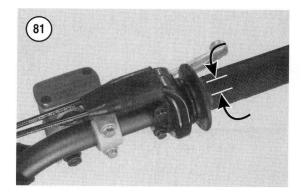

8. Disconnect the cable lubricator, then pull the inner cable back and forth to help distribute the lubricant.

9. Allow time for excess lubricant to drain from the cable before reconnecting it.

10. Apply a light coat of grease to the upper throttle cable balls before reconnecting them.

11. Lubricate the clutch and hot start cable pivot bolts with grease.

12. Reverse Steps 1-3 to reconnect the cables.

13. Adjust the cables as described in this chapter.

## THROTTLE CABLE ADJUSTMENT

Cable wear and stretch affect the operation of the carburetor. Normal amounts of cable wear and stretch can be controlled by the free play adjustments described in this section. If the cables cannot be adjusted within their limits, the cables are excessively worn or damaged and require replacement.

Free play is the distance the throttle grip can be rotated, measured at the throttle grip flange, until resistance from the throttle shaft can be felt.

### Throttle Cable Adjustment and Operation

Throttle cable free play is necessary to prevent variation in the idle speed when turning the handle-

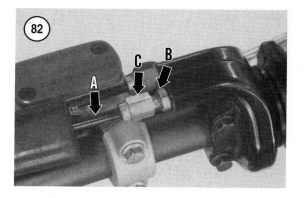

bars. In time, the throttle cable free play increases as the cable stretches. This delays throttle response and affects low speed operation. On the other hand, if there is no throttle cable free play, an excessively high idle speed can result.

1. Rotate the throttle grip (**Figure 81**) from low idle position as if accelerating, with the handlebar pointed in different steering positions. In each position, the throttle must open and close smoothly and completely. If the throttle cables bind or move roughly, inspect the cables for kinks, bends or other

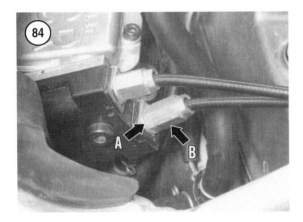

82). *Make minor adjustments at the upper end of the pull cable. Make major adjustments at the lower end of the pull cable.*

3. Slide the rubber cover (**Figure 81**) away from the throttle housing.

4. Loosen the pull cable locknut (B, **Figure 82**) and turn the cable adjuster (C) in or out to achieve the correct free play. Tighten the locknut.

5. Recheck the free play and note the following:

 a. If the free play is correct, reposition the rubber cover (**Figure 81**) over the throttle housing.

 b. If further adjustment is required, continue with Step 6.

6. Remove the fuel tank (Chapter Nine).

7. See **Figure 83** (CRF250R or CRF250X) or **Figure 84** (CRF450R and CRF450X). Loosen the pull cable locknut (A) and turn the adjuster (B) in or out to achieve the correct free play. Tighten the locknut.

8. If the correct free play cannot be achieved, the throttle cables have stretched to the point where they need to be replaced. Replace both throttle cables as described in Chapter Nine.

9. Reinstall the fuel tank (Chapter Nine).

10. Recheck the throttle cable free play.

11. Slide the rubber cover (**Figure 81**) over the throttle housing.

12. Make sure the throttle grip rotates freely from a fully closed to fully open position.

13. Start the engine and allow it to idle in neutral. Turn the handlebar from side to side. If the idle increases, the throttle cable is routed incorrectly or there is not enough throttle cable free play. Repair this condition before riding the motorcycle.

## HOT START CABLE ADJUSTMENT

1. Operate the hot start lever (**Figure 85**) several times. If there is any roughness or binding, lubricate the hot start cable as described in this chapter. At the same time, inspect the hot start valve and spring (**Figure 86**) installed on the end of the cable and replace if damaged. Reinstall the hot start cable, valve and spring if removed.

2. Pull the hot start lever to determine the lever's free play as shown in **Figure 85**. If the free play is more or less than 2-3 mm (1/16-1/8 in.), continue with Step 3 to adjust the cable.

damage. Replace damaged cables. If the cables move smoothly and are not damaged, continue with Step 2.

2. Determine the throttle grip free play as shown in **Figure 81**. If the free play is more or less than 3-5 mm (1/8-3/16 in.), adjust the cables as described in the following steps.

*NOTE*
*Throttle cable adjustment is made at either end of the pull cable (A, **Figure***

3. Loosen the cable adjuster locknut (A, **Figure 87**) and turn the adjuster (B) either in or out as required, to achieve the specified amount of free play. Tighten the locknut and recheck the free play adjustment. If the proper amount of free play cannot be obtained, the hot start cable has stretched to the point where it needs to be replaced. Replace the hot start cable. See Chapter Nine.

## CLUTCH LEVER ADJUSTMENT

The clutch lever free play is continually changing due to the clutch cable wearing and stretching over time, as well as clutch plate wear. Maintain the clutch lever free play within the specification listed in this procedure. Insufficient free play causes clutch slippage and premature clutch plate wear. Excessive free play causes clutch drag and rough shift pedal operation.

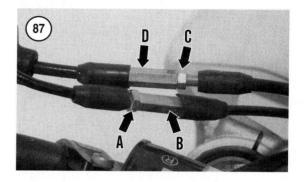

### CRF250X, 2002-2003 CRF450R and CRF450X

1. Determine the clutch lever free play at the end of the clutch lever as shown in **Figure 88**. If the free play is more or less than 10-20 mm (3/8-3/4 in.), adjust the cable as described in the following steps.

2A. On CRF250X and CRF450X models, turn the cable end adjuster (A, **Figure 89**) toward the front of the motorcycle to decrease free play or toward the rear of the motorcycle to increase free play within the specifications in Step 1.

2B. On 2002-2003 CRF450R models, slide the cover (A, **Figure 90**) away from the adjuster. Loosen the locknut (B, **Figure 90**) and turn the cable end adjuster (C) either in or out as required to achieve the specified amount of free play. Tighten the locknut.

3. If the proper amount of free play cannot be achieved by adjusting the cable end adjuster, the cable midline adjuster must be changed. Perform the following:

  a. Turn the cable end adjuster (A, **Figure 89** or C, **Figure 90**) in all the way and then back out one turn.

  b. Loosen the clutch cable midline adjuster locknut (B, **Figure 89**) and turn the adjuster (C) as required to obtain the free play specified in Step 1. Tighten the locknut (B, **Figure**

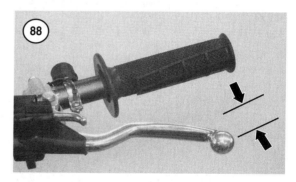

89). If necessary, fine-tune the adjustment at the cable end adjuster.

4. If the correct free play cannot be achieved, either the cable has stretched to the point that it needs to be replaced or the clutch discs are worn. Refer to Chapter Six or Chapter Seven for clutch cable and clutch service.

5. Make sure the locknut(s) are tight.

6. Reposition the adjuster cover(s).

### CRF250R and 2004-on CRF450R

Two different clutch adjustments are provided on these models: 1) clutch lever position and clutch lever free play, and 2) clutch lever free play.

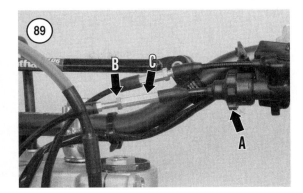

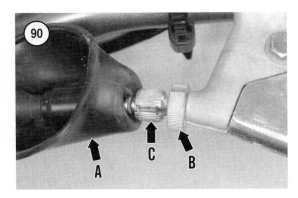

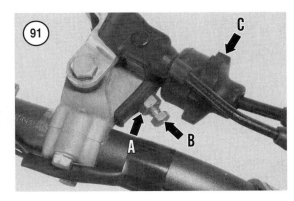

*Clutch lever position and*
*clutch lever free play*

This procedure describes how to reposition the clutch lever (toward or away from the handlebar) and then adjust the clutch lever free play. If it is only necessary to adjust the clutch lever free play, perform the *Clutch Lever Free Play* procedure in this section.

1. Loosen the locknut (A, **Figure 91**) and turn the adjuster (B) clockwise (moves lever closer to han-

dlebar) or counterclockwise (moves lever farther away from handlebar). Tighten the locknut.

2. Turn the clutch cable end adjuster (C, **Figure 91**) counterclockwise until it lightly seats, then turn it clockwise five turns.

3. Loosen the clutch cable midline adjuster locknut (C, **Figure 87**) and turn the adjuster (D, **Figure 87**) as required to obtain 10-20 mm (3/8-3/4 in.) free play at the tip of the clutch lever as shown in **Figure 88**. Tighten the locknut.

### Clutch lever free play

This procedure describes how to adjust the clutch lever free play. If the clutch lever position must also be changed, perform the prior adjustment procedure.

1. Determine the clutch lever free play at the end of the clutch lever as shown in **Figure 88**. If the free play is more or less than 10-20 mm (3/8-3/4 in.), adjust the cable as described in the following steps.

2. Turn the cable end adjuster (C, **Figure 91**) toward the front of the motorcycle to decrease free play or toward the rear of the motorcycle to increase free play to achieve the free play specified in Step 1.

3. If the proper amount of free play cannot be achieved at the cable end adjuster, the cable midline adjuster must be changed. Perform the following:

    a. Turn the cable end adjuster (C, **Figure 91**) in all the way and then back out one turn.

    b. Loosen the clutch cable midline adjuster locknut (C, **Figure 87**) and turn the adjuster (D) as required to obtain the free play specified in Step 1. Tighten the locknut (C, **Figure 87**). If necessary, fine-tune the adjustment at the cable end adjuster.

4. If the correct free play cannot be achieved, either the cable has stretched to the point that it needs to be replaced or the clutch discs are worn. Refer to Chapter Six or Chapter Seven for clutch cable and clutch service.

5. Make sure the locknut is tight.

### BRAKES

This section describes routine service procedures for the front and rear disc brakes. Refer to **Table 2** and **Table 3** for service intervals.

## Disc Brake Pad Wear

Inspect the brake pads for wear, scoring, grease or fork oil contamination or other damage. Refer to **Figure 92** for the front pads and **Figure 93** for the rear pads. Inspect the thickness of the friction material on each pad. If any one pad on the front or rear is worn to its wear limit grooves, or measures 1.0 mm (0.04 in.) or less, replace both pads. Refer to Chapter Fifteen for brake pad service.

## Front Brake Lever Adjustment

Brake pad wear in the front brake caliper is automatically compensated as the pistons move outward in the caliper. However, the brake lever's position in relation to the handlebar can be adjusted.

1. Remove the dust cover from the adjuster.
2. To move the brake lever closer to or farther away from the handlebar, loosen the locknut (A, **Figure 94**) and turn the adjuster (B) in or out. Tighten the locknut.
3. Check the front brake lever free play as shown in **Figure 95**. The free play should be less than 20 mm. If the brake lever free play (**Figure 95**) exceeds 20 mm (0.80 in.), there is probably air in the brake system and it must be bled. Refer to Chapter Fifteen.
4. Support the motorcycle with the front wheel off the ground. Rotate the front wheel and check for brake drag. Operate the front brake lever several times to make sure it returns to the at-rest position after releasing it.
5. Tighten the locknut, making sure the adjuster does not move, and recheck the free play.
6. Move the brake lever away from the handlebar and lubricate the end of the adjuster and piston contact surfaces with silicone brake grease.
7. Install the dust cover.

## Rear Brake Pedal Height Adjustment

1. Apply the rear brake a few times and allow the pedal to come to rest. Make sure the return spring is installed and in good condition.
2. Measure the pushrod height dimension as shown in **Figure 96**. The correct height dimension is 79.6 mm (3.13 in.).
3. If necessary, loosen the locknut (**Figure 96**) and turn the pushrod to adjust its height position.

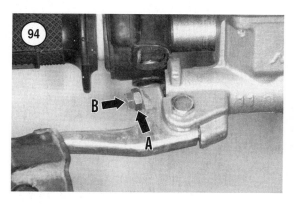

Tighten the locknut securely and recheck the height dimension.

## Brake Fluid Level Inspection

The brake fluid level in the front and rear master cylinder reservoirs must be kept above the minimum level line. If the fluid level is low in either reservoir, check for loose or damaged hoses or loose banjo bolts. If there are no visible fluid leaks, check the brake pads for excessive wear. As the brake

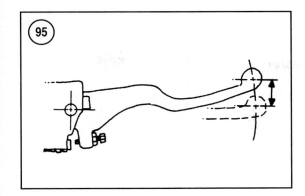

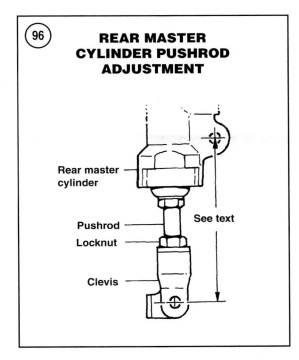

**REAR MASTER CYLINDER PUSHROD ADJUSTMENT**

Rear master cylinder

Pushrod

Locknut

Clevis

See text

pads wear, the caliper piston(s) moves farther out of the bore(s), thus causing the brake fluid level to drop in the reservoir. Also, check the master cylinder bore and the brake caliper piston areas for signs of leaking brake fluid. If there is a noticeable fluid leak, that component requires overhaul to replace the damaged part. Check the brake pads for wear as described in this section. Refer to Chapter Fifteen for brake service.

*WARNING*
*If any reservoir is empty, or if the brake fluid level is so low that air is entering the brake system, bleed the brake system as described in Chapter*

*Fifteen. Simply adding brake fluid to the reservoir does not restore the brake system to its full effectiveness.*

1. Park the motorcycle on level ground.
2. Clean the master cylinder area before removing the cover to avoid contaminating the reservoir.

3

*WARNING*
*Use brake fluid clearly marked DOT 4 and specified for disc brakes. Others may vaporize and cause brake failure. Do not intermix different brands or types of brake fluid, as they may not be compatible. Do not intermix a silicone-based (DOT 5) brake fluid, as it can cause brake component damage leading to brake system failure.*

*CAUTION*
*Be careful when handling brake fluid. Do not spill it on painted or plastic surfaces, as it will damage them. Wash the area immediately with soap and water and rinse thoroughly.*

*CAUTION*
*Do not remove the cap on either the front or rear brake reservoirs unless the reservoirs are level.*

*CAUTION*
*When adding brake fluid to the reservoirs, inspect the master cylinder reservoir diaphragm for tearing, cracks or other damage. A damaged diaphragm will allow moisture to enter the reservoir and contaminate the brake fluid.*

3A. Front—Perform the following:
   a. Turn the handlebar so the master cylinder reservoir is level.
   b. Observe the brake fluid level through the inspection window (A, **Figure 97**) on the master cylinder reservoir.
   c. The brake fluid level must be above the lower level line.
   d. Remove the two screws and remove the cover (B, **Figure 97**) and diaphragm.
   e. Add DOT 4 brake fluid up to the upper level mark inside the reservoir (**Figure 98**).
   f. Replace the cover and diaphragm if damaged.

g. Install the diaphragm and cover and tighten the screws securely.

3B. Rear—Perform the following:

a. Check that the brake fluid level is above the lower level mark on the reservoir (A, **Figure 99**). To add brake fluid, continue with the following steps.

b. Remove the two screws, cover (B, **Figure 99**), plate (**Figure 100**) and diaphragm.

c. Add DOT 4 brake fluid up to the upper level mark inside the reservoir (**Figure 101**).

d. Replace the cover and diaphragm if damaged.

e. Install the diaphragm, plate and cover and tighten the screws securely.

## Disc Brake Hose Replacement

Replace the brake hoses when they become swollen or damaged. Refer to Chapter Fifteen for service procedures.

## Brake Fluid Change

Every time a fluid reservoir cap is removed, a small amount of dirt and moisture enters the brake system. The same thing happens if a leak occurs or any part of the hydraulic system is loosened or disconnected. Dirt can clog the system and cause unnecessary wear. Water in the brake fluid can vaporize at high brake system temperatures, impairing the hydraulic action and reducing stopping ability.

To maintain peak performance, change the brake fluid every year and when rebuilding a caliper or master cylinder. To change brake fluid, follow the brake bleeding procedure in Chapter Fifteen.

> *WARNING*
> *Use brake fluid clearly marked DOT 4 only. Others may vaporize and cause brake failure. Dispose of any unused fluid according to local regulations. never reuse brake fluid. Contaminated brake fluid can cause brake failure.*

## DRIVE CHAIN AND SPROCKETS

CRF250R and CRF450R models were originally equipped with standard or non-O-ring drive chains.

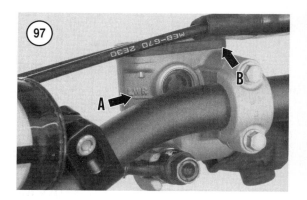

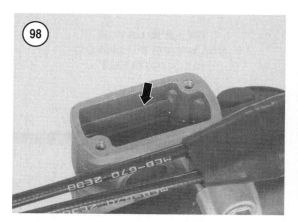

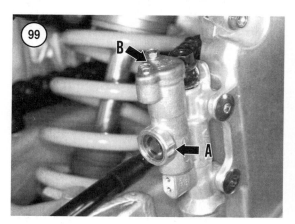

CRF250X and CRF450X models were equipped with an O-ring drive chain. O-ring drive chains are internally lubricated and sealed by O-rings (**Figure 102**).

Refer to **Table 2** or **Table 3** for drive chain and sprocket service intervals. Perform the maintenance procedures more often when riding in mud and sand.

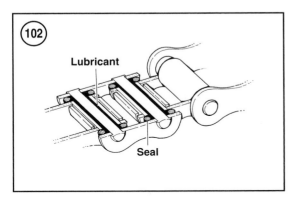

Lubricant

Seal

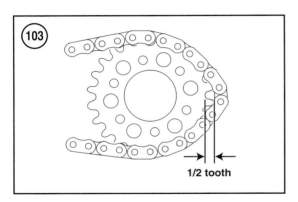

1/2 tooth

**Drive Chain Cleaning**

1. Remove the drive chain (Chapter Twelve).
2A. O-ring chain—Clean the drive chain in a plastic pan partially filled with kerosene. Work the links to loosen and dissolve dirt. Lightly scrub the chain with a soft-bristle brush.

> *CAUTION*
> *Brushes with coarse or wire bristles will damage the O-rings.*

> *CAUTION*
> *Do not clean an O-ring drive chain with anything but kerosene. Most solvents and gasoline will cause the O-rings to swell and deteriorate, permanently damaging the chain.*

2B. Non-O-ring chain—Immerse the chain in a plastic pan containing kerosene and flex the links to loosen the dirt. Allow the chain to soak for approximately one half-hour. If necessary, remove dirt from the outside of the chain with a stiff brush.
3. Rinse the chain with clean kerosene. Hang the chain up to allow the cleaning solution to drain. Place a drain pan under the chain.
4. Lay the chain on a workbench and check for binding or kinked links and damaged pins.
5. Before installing the drive chain, clean the driven sprocket of all dirt and residue.
6. Install the drive chain (Chapter Twelve).

**Drive Chain and Sprocket Wear Inspection**

A worn drive chain and sprockets are both unreliable and potentially dangerous. Inspect the chain and both sprockets for wear and replace if necessary. If there is wear, replace both sprockets and the chain. Mixing old and new parts will prematurely wear the new parts.

1. Perform a quick inspection of the chain by pulling one link away from the rear sprocket. If more than half the height of the tooth is visible (**Figure 103**), the chain is probably worn out. Confirm by measuring the chain as described in Step 2.

> *NOTE*
> *Clean the chain before measuring chain wear in the following steps.*

2A. On CRF250X and CRF450X models, measure the drive chain inner plate width with a caliper

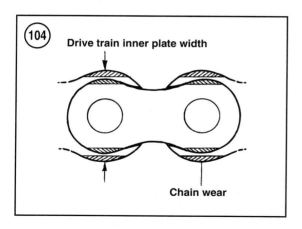

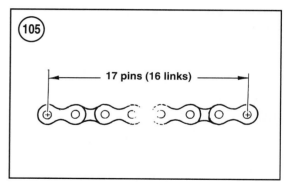

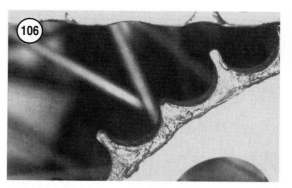

(**Figure 104**). Measure at several different places along the chain. Replace the drive chain if any width measurement is less than 13.4 mm (0.53 in.).

2B. On CRF250R and CRF450R models, measure the drive chain wear as follows:

    a. Loosen the axle nut and turn the chain adjusters until the chain is tight.

    b. Measure the length of any 17-pin (16 links) span along the top chain run (**Figure 105**).

    c. Turn the rear wheel and repeat the measurement at different points around the chain.

    d. If any measured distance exceeds the service limit (**Table 12**), replace the chain and both sprockets.

3. If the chain is not worn, inspect the inside surfaces on both sides of the chain. The plates should be shiny at both ends of the chain roller. If one side of the chain is worn, the chain has been running out of alignment. This also causes premature wear of the rollers and pins. Replace the chain and both sprockets if there is uneven wear. Also check for a damaged chain guide and worn bushings and bearings in the swing arm and drive system.

4. Inspect the teeth on each sprocket. The teeth should be symmetrical and uniform. Look for hooked and broken teeth (**Figure 106**). Check the rear sprocket for cracks and damaged Allen bolt recesses.

*NOTE*

*If both sprockets and chain were replaced as a set, and the driven sprocket wore out quickly, inspect the condition of the sprocket teeth. If the worn area is halfway up on the sprocket teeth, the chain was adjusted too tightly. Sprocket wear contained*

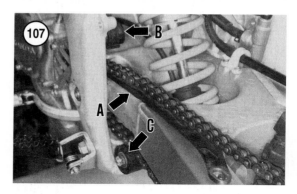

*to one side of the sprocket is normally caused by incorrect chain alignment. A bent or damaged chain guide will also cause the sprocket to wear on one side. Also, consider the condition of the swing arm bearings. Worn or damaged bearings will affect swing arm and chain alignment, even when the chain adjuster marks are correctly aligned.*

5. CRF250R and CRF450R models, adjust the drive chain and tighten the rear axle nut as described in this section.

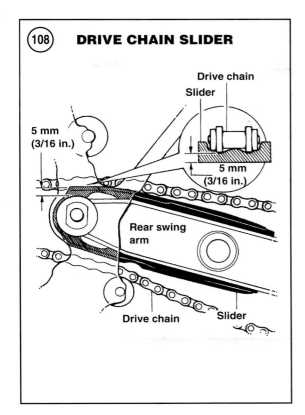

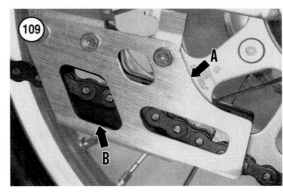

3

## Drive Chain Slider Inspection

The slider (or rub plate) protects the swing arm from chain damage.

1. Remove the drive sprocket cover.
2. Inspect the chain slider (A, **Figure 107**) for excessive wear or damage.
3. Measure the chain slider wear grooves as shown in **Figure 108**. Replace the chain slider if the measurement is 5 mm (3/16 in.) or less from the upper surface. If there is extensive damage or wear, inspect the swing arm. To replace the slider and inspect the swing arm, remove the swing arm as described in Chapter Fourteen.
4. Install the drive sprocket cover.

## Chain Guide Slider Inspection

1. Inspect the chain guide (A, **Figure 109**) for loose mounting bolts or damage.
2. Inspect the chain guide slider for wear and damage. Replace the chain guide slider when the chain has worn the slider to its wear limit groove (B, **Figure 109**).

## Drive Chain Roller Inspection

1. Inspect the drive chain rollers (B and C, **Figure 107**) for excessive wear or damage, a loose pivot bolt or excessively worn or damaged bushing. Replace as follows:
2. Measure each roller outside diameter. Replace the rollers when their outside diameter is less than the service limit in **Table 12**.
3A. On CRF250R models, identify and replace the rollers as follows:
   a. The upper roller is green. The lower roller is black.
   b. Install all 2004 rollers and the 2005 upper roller with their arrow mark facing out (**Figure 110**).
   c. Install the 2005 lower roller with its recessed side facing out.
3B. On CRF250X models, identify and install the rollers as follows:
   a. The upper roller is green. The lower roller is black.
   b. Install the rollers with their arrow mark facing out (**Figure 110**).

3C. On CRF450R and CRF450X models, identify and install the rollers as follows:

    a. On 2002-2003 models, the upper roller uses an orange bearing seal. The lower bearing seal is black.

    b. On 2004-on models, the upper roller is green. The lower roller is black.

    c. Install the rollers with their arrow mark facing out (**Figure 110**).

4. Tighten the roller mounting bolts and nut to 12 N•m (106 in.-lb.).

**Drive Chain Lubrication**

Lubricate the drive chain throughout the day as required. A properly maintained chain provides maximum service life and reliability.

1. Ride the motorcycle approximately 5 minutes to heat the chain.

2. Support the motorcycle on a work stand with the rear wheel off the ground.

3. Shift the transmission into neutral.

4A. Non-O-ring chain:

    a. Turn the rear wheel and lubricate the chain with an SAE 80 or 90-weight gear oil or a chain spray lubricant. Do not over-lubricate, as this causes dirt to collect on the chain and sprockets.

    b. Wipe off all excess oil from the rear hub, wheel and tire.

4B. O-ring chain:

> *CAUTION*
> *An O-ring chain is pre-lubricated during manufacturing. External oiling is only required to prevent chain rust and to keep the O-rings pliable. Do not use a tacky chain lubricant on O-ring chains. Dirt and other abrasive material that sticks to the lubricant also sticks against the O-rings and damages them. Clean the chain as described in this chapter.*

    a. Lubricate the chain with a lubricant specified by the chain manufacturer. If unavailable, lubricate the chain with an SAE 80 or 90-weight gear oil or a chain lubricant (non-tacky) specifically formulated for O-ring chains.

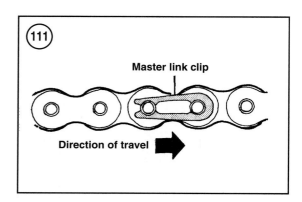

Master link clip

Direction of travel

    b. Wipe off all excess oil from the rear hub, wheel and tire.

    c. After lubricating the chain with gear oil, support the motorcycle with the rear wheel off the ground. Then hold a cloth against the chain and rear sprocket and slowly turn the wheel to remove excess oil.

5. Check that the master link is properly installed and secured (**Figure 111**).

**Drive Chain Adjustment**

The drive chain must have adequate free play to accommodate swing arm movement. A tight chain causes unnecessary wear to the drive line components, while a loose chain may jump off the sprockets, possibly causing damage and injury.

Consider weather and track conditions when checking and adjusting chain free play. Mud and sand will build up on a chain, reducing free play. Check and loosen the chain if necessary.

Check chain free play before riding the motorcycle and after each race. **Table 12** lists drive chain specifications.

1. Support the motorcycle with the rear wheel off the ground.

2. Slowly turn the rear wheel and check the chain for binding and tight spots by moving the links up and down by hand. If a link or group of links does not move freely, remove and clean the chain. On CRF250X and CRF450X models, check for swollen or damaged O-rings.

3. Check the amount of free play by measuring midway between the two sprockets at the upper chain run (**Figure 112**). Since chains do not wear evenly, check several sections of the chain to find the tightest length (least amount of play) and mea-

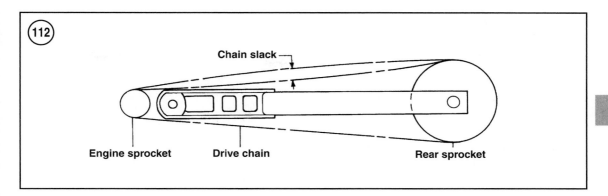

Chain slack

Engine sprocket    Drive chain    Rear sprocket

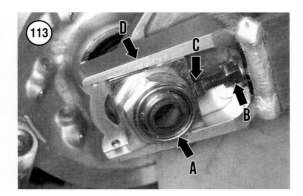

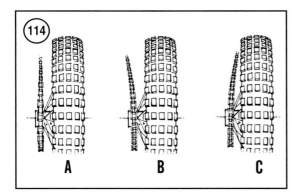

A    B    C

sure free play at this point. The correct amount of free play is 25-35 mm (0.98-1.38 in.). If the free play is out of specification, continue with Step 4.

*CAUTION*
*Excessive free play (50 mm/2.0 in. or more) may damage the frame.*

4. Mark the chain's tight spot with chalk. After adjusting and spinning the chain, recheck free play at the same spot. Because drive chains do not wear

evenly, always measure and adjust the chain at its tightest spot.

*CAUTION*
*When adjusting the drive chain, maintain rear wheel alignment. A misaligned rear wheel can cause poor handling and pulling to one side or the other, as well as increased chain and sprocket wear. All models have wheel alignment marks on the swing arm and chain adjuster plates.*

5. Loosen the rear axle nut (A, **Figure 113**).
6. Loosen the chain adjuster locknut (B, **Figure 113**) on each side of the swing arm and turn the adjuster bolts (C) to adjust the chain. Turn the adjuster bolts equally so the chain adjuster plate index marks (D, **Figure 113**) align with the same index marks on each side of the swing arm. Remeasure chain free play at the original spot (chalk mark).
7. When the chain slack is correct, verify proper wheel alignment by sighting along the chain from the rear sprocket. The chain must leave the sprocket in a straight line (A, **Figure 114**). If it is turned to one side or the other (B and C, **Figure 114**), perform the following:
   a. Adjust wheel alignment by turning one adjuster or the other. Recheck chain free play.
   b. Confirm swing arm index mark accuracy, if necessary, by measuring from the center of the swing arm pivot shaft to the center of the rear axle.
8. Tighten the rear axle locknut (A, **Figure 113**) to 127 N•m (94 ft.-lb.).
9. Snug the adjuster bolts (C, **Figure 113**) against the adjuster plates. Then hold the adjuster bolts and tighten the locknuts (B, **Figure 113**) securely.

10. Spin the wheel several times and note the following:

    a. Recheck the free play at its tightest point. Make sure the free play is within specification.

    b. Check the chain alignment as it runs through the chain guide.

    c. Check rear brake operation.

    d. Check that the drive sprocket cover and case saver are installed and tightened securely.

## TIRES AND WHEELS

### Tire Pressure

Check and set the tire pressure to maintain good traction and handling and to prevent rim damage. Keep an accurate tire gauge in the toolbox. **Table 4** lists the standard tire pressure for the front and rear wheels. Check the tire pressure when the tires are cold.

### Tire Inspection

The tires take a lot of punishment due to the variety of terrain and racing conditions. Inspect them weekly for damage. To check for internal sidewall damage, remove the tire from the rim as described in Chapter Twelve. Inspect the inner tire casing for tears or sharp objects embedded in the tire.

Check the valve stem. If a valve stem is turned sideways (**Figure 115**), the tire and tube have slipped on the rim. The valve will eventually pull out of the tube, causing a flat. Straighten the tube as described under *Tube Alignment* in this section.

### Tube Alignment

Check the valve stem alignment. **Figure 115** shows a valve stem that has slipped with the tire. If the tube is not repositioned, the valve stem will eventually pull away from the tube, causing a flat. To realign the tube and tire:

1. Wash the tire and rim.

2. Remove the valve stem core to deflate the tire.

3. Loosen the rim lock nuts.

4. With an assistant steadying the motorcycle, break the tire-to-rim seal all the way around the wheel on both sides.

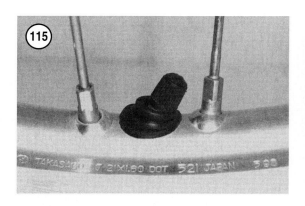

5. Put the motorcycle on a stand with the wheel off the ground.

6. Spray soapy water along both tire beads.

7. Have an assistant apply the brake.

8. Grab the tire at two opposite places and turn it and the tube to straighten the valve stem.

9. Install the valve stem core and inflate the tire. If necessary, reapply the soap and water to help the tire seat on the rim. Check the tire to make sure it seats evenly around the rim.

> *WARNING*
> *Do not over-inflate the tire and tube. If the tire does not seat properly, remove the valve stem core and re-lubricate the tire with soap and water again.*

10. Tighten the rim lock nut(s) to 12 N•m (106 in.-lb.).

11. Adjust the tire pressure (**Table 4**) and install the valve stem nut and cap.

### Wheel Spoke Tension and Wheel Inspection

Inspect wheel runout and check spoke tension as follows:

> *NOTE*
> *During break-in for a new or a re-spoked wheel, check the spoke tension at the end of each 15-minute interval for the first hour of riding. Most spoke seating takes place during initial use.*

1. Inspect the rims for cracks, warp or dents. Replace damaged rims.

2. Support the motorcycle with the wheel off the ground, then spin it while watching the rim. If there is appreciable rim wobble or runout, note the following:

    a. Refer to *Wheel Bearings* in this chapter to check the bearings.

    b. If the wheel bearings are good, check the wheel runout and true the wheel as described in Chapter Twelve.

3. Tap each spoke in the same spot with a spoke wrench. Tight spokes will ring and loose spokes will make a dull, flat sound.

4. If only a few spokes are loose, tighten them with a spoke wrench. If a group of spokes are loose, tighten them while truing the wheel as described in Chapter Twelve.

5. When using a spoke torque wrench, tighten the spokes to 3.7 N•m (32.7 in.-lb.).

> *NOTE*
> *Most spokes loosen as a group rather than individually. Tighten loose spokes carefully. Over-tightened spokes put excessive pressure across the wheel. Never tighten spokes so tight that the spoke wrench rounds off the spoke nipples. If the spokes are stuck, apply penetrating oil into the top of each nipple and allow time for it to soak in and dissolve rust and corrosion on the mating threads.*

### WHEEL BEARING INSPECTION

At the intervals listed in **Table 2** or **Table 3**, check the condition of the seals and bearings. If the seals are reusable, wipe off their outer surface, then pack the lip of each seal with grease. To replace the seals and wheel bearings, refer to the service procedures in Chapter Twelve.

Check the front and rear wheel bearings as follows:

1. Support the motorcycle with the wheel off the ground.

2. Push the caliper in to push the piston(s) into its bore. This will move the pads away from the disc.

3. Spin the wheel while checking for excessive wheel bearing noise or other damage. Stop the wheel.

4. Grab the wheel at two points and rock it. There should be no perceptible play at the wheel bearings.

If any movement can be seen or felt, check the wheel bearings for excessive wear or damage (Chapter Twelve).

5. Spin the wheel while applying the brake several times to reposition the pads against the disc.

> *WARNING*
> *Do not ride the motorcycle until the front and rear brakes work correctly.*

### STEERING

**Steering Head Bearing Inspection**

Inspect the steering head bearings at the intervals specified in **Table 2** or **Table 3**. Lubricate the bearings when necessary. Remove the steering stem to clean and lubricate the bearings. Refer to Chapter Thirteen for complete service procedures.

**Steering Head Adjustment**

The steering head assembly consists of upper and lower tapered roller bearings, the steering stem and the steering head. Because the motorcycle is subjected to rough terrain and conditions, check the bearing play at the specified intervals (**Table 2** or **Table 3**) or whenever it feels loose. A loose bearing adjustment hampers steering and causes premature bearing and race wear. In extreme conditions, a loose bearing adjustment can cause loss of control. Refer to *Steering Play Check and Adjustment* in Chapter Thirteen.

To check steering play:

1. Apply the front brake while compressing the fork. If the steering head pulls away from the frame, or looseness is felt, the steering is too loose.

2. Support the motorcycle with the front wheel off the ground. Turn the handlebar from side to side. Roughness or binding indicates a too tight steering adjustment or damaged bearings.

**Front Suspension Inspection**

1. With the front wheel touching the ground, apply the front brake and pump the fork up and down vigorously. Check fork movement, paying attention to any abnormal noises or oil leaks.

2. Check that the upper and lower fork tube pinch bolts are secure (Chapter Thirteen).

3. Check that the handlebar holder bolts are secure (Chapter Thirteen).
4. Check that the front axle nut is secure (Chapter Twelve).

**FRONT FORK**

**Pressure Adjustment**

Fork pressure should be released before riding the motorcycle.
1. Place the motorcycle on a work stand with the front wheel off the ground.
2. Loosen the pressure release screws (**Figure 116**) to release air pressure from each fork tube.
3. Periodically check that the O-ring on each pressure release screw is in good condition.
4. Reinstall the pressure release screws and tighten securely.

**Front Fork Oil Change
(Except Fork Damper)**

Change the fork oil at the intervals specified in **Table 2** as described in Chapter Thirteen.

**Fork Damper Oil Change**

Change the fork oil in the fork damper at the intervals specified in **Table 2** as described in Chapter Thirteen.

**REAR SHOCK ABSORBER
INSPECTION**

1. Remove or raise and lock the subframe as described in Chapter Sixteen.
2. Check that the damper rod is not bent and that there is no oil leaking from the damper rod seal.
3. Check the shock mounting nuts and bolts for tightness (Chapter Fourteen).

**REAR SWING ARM AND LINKAGE**

**Rear Suspension Inspection**

1. Support the motorcycle on a stand with the rear wheel off the ground.
2. Check swing arm bearing play as described in Chapter Fourteen.

3. Check the tightness of all rear suspension mounting bolts (Chapter Fourteen).
4. Check that the rear axle nut is tight (Chapter Fourteen).

**Swing Arm and Shock Linkage
Bearing Lubrication**

Service and lubricate the swing arm and shock linkage bearings and pivot bolts at the intervals specified in **Table 2**. Do not remove the needle bearing cages to lubricate them. Refer to Chapter Fourteen for complete service procedures.

**HEADLIGHT ADJUSTMENT
(CRF250X AND CRF450X)**

When necessary, adjust the headlight's vertical adjustment by turning the adjusting screw (**Figure 117**) on the front visor.

**SIDESTAND INSPECTION
(CRF250X AND CRF450X)**

Inspect the sidestand and its return spring for loose or missing parts. Service the sidestand as described in Chapter Sixteen.

**FASTENERS INSPECTION**

Constant vibration can loosen many of the fasteners on the motorcycle. Check the tightness of all fasteners, especially those on:
1. Engine mounting hardware.
2. Cylinder head hanger bolts.
3. Engine crankcase covers.

4. Handlebar and front fork.
5. Shift pedal.
6. Kick pedal.
7. Brake pedal and lever.
8. Exhaust system.
9. Fuel tank.
10. Seat and side covers.
11. Lights (CRF250X and CRF450X).
12. Check all hose and cable guides and clamps.

## ENGINE BREAK-IN

If the engine bearings, crankshaft, piston, piston rings or cylinder have been serviced, perform the following break-in procedure.

1. Observe the following conditions when breaking in the engine:
   a. Operate the motorcycle on flat ground. Do not run in sand, mud or up hills. This will overload and possibly overheat the engine.
   b. Vary the throttle position. Do not keep the throttle in the same position for more than a few seconds.
   c. Check the spark plug frequently. Refer to the *Spark plug* in this chapter to identify spark plug condition.
2. Perform the *Pre-Ride Inspection* in this chapter.
3. Service the air filter as described in this chapter.
4. Check the engine and transmission oil levels.
5. Make sure the cooling system is full.
6. Start the engine and allow it to warm up. During this time, check for proper idle speed and leaks.
7. Break-in time consists of the motorcycle's first 15 miles (24 km).

**Table 1 PRE-RIDE INSPECTION***

| |
|---|
| Check spark plug condition. Check secondary wire and plug cap or ignition coil for tightness. |
| Check air filter and clean if necessary. |
| Check engine oil level. |
| Check transmission oil level. |
| CRF250R and CRF450R: Check coolant level in radiator. |
| CRF250X and CRF450X: Check coolant level in reserve tank. |
| Check cooling system for loose or damaged hoses. Check hose clamp tightness. |
| Check breather hose for contamination. Remove plug and drain contaminants if necessary. |
| Check clutch cable free play and operation. |
| Check hot start cable free play and operation. |
| Check throttle cable free play and operation. Throttle must return when released. |
| Check for loose or damaged spokes. |
| Check rim lock tightness. |
| Check tire inflation pressure. Check for tire damage. |
| Check front and rear brake operation and brake fluid level. |
| Check front and rear suspension operation. |
| Check drive chain guide sliders and rollers for missing or damaged parts. |
| Check drive chain adjustment. |
| Check drive chain lubrication. |
| Check all exposed and accessible fasteners for loose or missing parts. |
| Start engine and allow to idle. Check that engine idles correctly. |
| *Perform the pre-ride inspection before the first ride of the day. |

**Table 2 COMPETITION SCHEDULE (ALL MODELS)**

Each race or approximately 2.5 hours of engine operation
  Clean air filter[1]
  Inspect the spark plug
  Check the coolant level
  Inspect the cooling system
  Check the engine idle speed[2]
  Inspect the drive chain slider and rollers
  Inspect the drive and driven sprocket
  Inspect and lubricate the drive chain
  Inspect the brake system
  Check brake fluid level
  Check brake pad wear
  Inspect control cables
  Lubricate clutch and hot start cable
  Check clutch cable adjustment
  Check throttle operation and adjustment
  Check hot start operation and adjustment
  Inspect the exhaust system
  Inspect the wheels and tires
  Check all exposed fasteners
Every three races or approximately 7.5 hours of engine operation
  Replace drive chain
  Lubricate swing arm and shock linkage
  Replace fork oil (not the damper oil)[3]
Every six races or approximately 15 hours of engine operation
  Change the engine oil and replace the oil filter[3]
  Change the transmission oil[4]
  Replace the piston and rings
  Replace the piston pin (CRF250R and CRF250X)
  Check the valve clearance and decompressor system[2]
Every nine races or approximately 22.5 hours of engine operation
  Replace the oil in the fork damper
  Check the steering bearing adjustment
Every twelve races or approximately 30 hours of engine operation
  Replace the piston pin (CRF450R and CRF450X)
Every two years
  Change engine coolant
  Change brake fluid

1. Install a clean air filter after every moto when racing in dusty conditions.
2. Check after initial break-in ride or after rebuilding engine.
3. Change after initial break-in ride.
4. Change transmission oil after replacing clutch discs and plate.

**Table 3 GENERAL MAINTENANCE SCHEDULE (CRF250X AND CRF450X)**

Every 300 miles (500 km) or three months
  Inspect the drive chain slider and rollers*
  Lubricate the drive chain*
  Check drive chain adjustment
Initial maintenance after 100 miles (150 km)
  Check valve clearance and decompressor system
  Change the engine oil and replace the oil filter
  Change the transmission oil
  Check engine idle speed
  Inspect the cooling system
  Check all exposed fasteners
  Inspect the wheels and tires
  Check the steering bearing adjustment

(continued)

**Table 3 GENERAL MAINTENANCE SCHEDULE (CRF250X AND CRF450X) (continued)**

Every 600 miles (1000 km) or every six months
  Clean the air filter*
  Inspect the crankcase breather
  Inspect the spark plug
  Check valve clearance and decompressor system
  Change the engine oil and replace the oil filter
  Change the transmission oil
  Check engine idle speed
  Inspect the cooling system
  Check brake fluid level
  Check brake pad wear
  Inspect brake system
  Check clutch cable adjustment
  Inspect the wheels and tires
Every 1000 miles (1600 km) or 100 hours of engine operation
  Remove and clean the spark arrestor
Every 1200 miles (2000 km) or twelve months
  Inspect the fuel line
  Clean the fuel filter
  Check throttle operation and adjustment
  Check the coolant
  Check the headlight adjustment
  Check the front and rear suspension operation
  Check all exposed fasteners
  Check the steering bearing adjustment
  Check the sidestand
Every 2400 miles (4000 km) or twenty-four months
  Inspect the secondary air supply system (California CRF250X and CRF450X models)
Every two years
  Change engine coolant
  Change brake fluid

*Check more often when riding in dusty or set conditions.

**Table 4 TIRE INFLATION PRESSURE**

| | Front and rear |
| --- | --- |
| Tire pressure | |
|   CRF250R | 98 kPa (14.2 psi) |
|   CRF250X | 100 kPa (14.5 psi) |
|   CRF450R | |
|     2002-2004 | 100 kPa (14.5 psi) |
|     2005 | 98 kPa (14.2 psi) |
|   CRF450X | 100 kPa (14.5 psi) |

**Table 5 RECOMMENDED LUBRICANTS AND FUEL**

| | |
| --- | --- |
| Air filter | Foam air filter oil |
| Brake fluid | DOT 4 |
| Control cables[1] | Cable lube |

(continued)

## Table 5 RECOMMENDED LUBRICANTS AND FUEL (continued)

| | |
|---|---|
| Coolant[2] | Pro Honda HP Coolant or equivalent mixed with distilled water at a 50:50 ratio |
| Engine oil | |
|   Type | Pro Honda GN4 and HP4 (without molybdenum disulfide additives) or equivalent 4-stroke engine oil |
|   API service classification[3] | SG or higher |
|   JASO T903 standards | MA or MB |
|   Viscosity | SAE 10W-40 |
| Transmission oil | |
|   Type | Pro Honda HP Transmission oil, Pro Honda GN4 or PH4 (without molybdenum additives) or equivalent 4-stroke engine oil |
|   API service classification | SG or higher |
|   JASO T903 standards | MA |
|   Viscosity | SAE 10W-40 |
| Fork oil | |
|   Type | Pro-Honda HP fork oil or equivalent |
|   Viscosity | 5W |
| Fuel | Unleaded fuel with octane number of 91 or higher |
| Steering and suspension lubricant | Multipurpose waterproof grease |

1. Do not use drive chain lubricant on control cables. Do not lubricate original equipment throttle cables. Refer to text for further information.
2. Coolant must not contain silicate inhibitors as they can cause premature wear to the water pump seals. Refer to text for further information.
3. API SG or higher classified oils not specified as ENERGY CONSERVING can be used. Refer to text for additional information.

## Table 6 ENGINE OIL CAPACITY

| | ml | U.S. oz. |
|---|---|---|
| Engine oil change only | | |
|   CRF450X | 670 | 22.7 |
|   All other models | 660 | 22.3 |
| Engine oil and filter change | | |
|   CRF450X | 700 | 23.7 |
|   All other models | 690 | 23.3 |
| Engine disassembly | | |
|   CRF450X | 870 | 29.4 |
|   All other models | 850 | 28.8 |

## Table 7 TRANSMISSION OIL CAPACITY

| | ml | U.S. oz. |
|---|---|---|
| CRF250R | | |
|   Transmission oil change | | |
|     2004 | 720 | 24.3 |
|     2005 | 800 | 20.3 |
|   After engine disassembly | | |
|     2004 | 770 | 26.0 |
|     2005 | 700 | 23.7 |
| (continued) | | |

**Table 7 TRANSMISSION OIL CAPACITY (continued)**

|  | ml | U.S. oz. |
|---|---|---|
| CRF250X |  |  |
| Transmission oil change | 670 | 22.7 |
| After engine disassembly | 750 | 25.4 |
| CRF450R |  |  |
| Transmission oil change | 590 | 20.0 |
| After engine disassembly | 670 | 22.7 |
| CRF450X |  |  |
| Transmission oil change | 650 | 22.0 |
| After engine disassembly | 750 | 25.4 |

**Table 8 ENGINE COMPRESSION, DECOMPRESSOR AND VALVE CLEARANCE**

| | |
|---|---|
| Decompressor clearance | |
| CRF450R | 0.35 mm (0.014 in.) |
| Engine compression | |
| CRF250R and CRF250X | 392 kPa (57 psi) at 800 rpm |
| CRF450R | |
| 2002-2003 | 441 kPa (64 psi) at 600 rpm |
| 2004-on | 539 kPa (78 psi) at 600 rpm |
| CRF450X | 402 kPa (58 psi) at 360 rpm |
| Valve clearance | |
| Intake | |
| CRF250R and CRF250X | 0.09-0.15 mm (0.004-0.006 in.) |
| CRF450R and CRF450X | 0.13-0.19 mm (0.005-0.007 in.) |
| Exhaust | 0.25-0.31 mm (0.010-0.012 in.) |

**Table 9 SPARK PLUG TYPE AND GAP**

| | |
|---|---|
| Spark plug gap | |
| Operating gap | |
| CRF250R | |
| 2004 | 0.8-0.9 mm (0.032-0.035 in.) |
| 2005 | 0.6-0.7 mm (0.024-0.028 in.) |
| CRF250X | 0.8-0.9 mm (0.032-0.035 in.) |
| CRF450R and CRF450X | 1.0-1.1 mm (0.039-0.043 in.) |
| Service limit | |
| 2004 CRF250R and all CRF250X | 1.0 mm (0.039 in.) |
| 2005 CRF250R | 0.8 mm (0.032 in.) |
| CRF450R and CRF450X | 1.2 mm (0.047 in.) |
| Spark plug type | |
| CRF250R | |
| Standard | |
| 2004 | DENSO VUH24D |
| | NGK IMR8C9H |
| 2005 | NGK R0409 B8 |
| Optional (colder) | |
| 2004 | DENSO VUH27D |
| | NGK IMR9C9H |
| 2005 | NGK R0409 B9 |
| CRF250X | |
| Standard | DENSO VUH24D |
| | NGK IMR8C9H |
| Optional (colder) | DENSO VUH27D |
| | NGK IMR9C9H |

(continued)

**Table 9 SPARK PLUG TYPE AND GAP (continued)**

| | |
|---|---|
| Spark plug type (continued) | |
| CRF450R and CRF450X | |
| Standard | DENSO VK24PRZ11 |
| | NGK IFR8H11 |
| Optional (colder) | DENSO VK27PRZ11 |
| | NGK IFR9H11 |

**Table 10 IDLE SPEED ADJUSTMENT**

| | |
|---|---|
| All models | 1600-1800 RPM |

**Table 11 COOLANT CAPACITY**

| | Liters | U.S. qt. |
|---|---|---|
| Coolant change | | |
| CRF250R | 0.93 | 0.98 |
| CRF250X | 1.13 | 1.19 |
| CRF450R | | |
| 2002-2004 | 1.03 | 1.09 |
| 2005 | 1.11 | 1.17 |
| CRF450X | 1.11 | 1.17 |
| Engine disassembly | | |
| CRF250R | 1.00 | 1.06 |
| CRF250X | 1.20 | 1.27 |
| CRF450R | | |
| 2002-2004 | 1.12 | 1.18 |
| 2005 | 1.20 | 1.27 |
| CRF450X | 1.20 | 1.27 |

**Table 12 DRIVE CHAIN AND ROLLER SPECIFICATIONS**

| | |
|---|---|
| Drive chain free play | 25-35 mm (0.98-1.38 in.) |
| Drive chain inner plate width service limit | |
| CRF250X and CRF450X | 13.4 mm (0.53 in.) |
| Drive chain 17-pin length service limit | |
| CRF250R and CRF450R | 259 mm (10.2 in.) |
| Drive chain slider thickness | 5.0 mm (0.20 in.) |
| Drive chain tensioner roller outside diameter | |
| service limit | |
| CRF250R | |
| 2004 | 39 mm (1.53 in.) |
| 2005 | |
| Upper | 38 mm (1.50 in.) |
| Lower | 31 mm (1.22 in.) |
| CRF250X | |
| Upper | 25 mm (0.98 in.) |
| Lower | 39 mm (1.53 in.) |
| CRF450R | |
| 2002-2004 | 39 mm (1.53 in.) |
| 2005 | |
| Upper | 39 mm (1.53 in.) |
| Lower | 35 mm (1.38 in.) |
| CRF450X | |
| Upper | 39 mm (1.53 in.) |
| Lower | 35 mm (1.38 in.) |

Table 13 **MAINTENANCE TORQUE SPECIFICATIONS**

|  | N•m | in.-lb. | ft.-lb. |
|---|---|---|---|
| Coolant drain bolt | | | |
|   CRF250R, 2005 CRF450R and | | | |
|     CRF450X | – | – | – |
|   All other models | 9.8 | 87 | – |
| Crankshaft hole cap* | 15 | 133 | – |
| Decompressor adjuster locknut | | | |
|   CRF450R and CRF450X | 10 | 88 | – |
| Drive chain roller nut and bolt | 12 | 106 | – |
| Engine oil drain bolt | | | |
|   CRF250R and CRF250X | 22 | – | 16 |
|   CRF450R | | | |
|     2002-2003 | 22 | – | 16 |
|     2004-on | 16 | 142 | – |
|   CRF450X | 16 | 142 | – |
| Oil filter cover bolt | | | |
|   CRF250R | – | – | – |
|   CRF250X | 12 | 106 | – |
|   CRF450R | | | |
|     2002-2004 | 9.8 | 87 | – |
|     2005 | 12 | 106 | – |
|   CRF450X | – | – | – |
| Rear axle locknut | 127 | – | 94 |
| Rim lock nuts | 12 | 106 | – |
| Spark plug | See text | | |
| Spokes | 3.7 | 32.7 | – |
| Ignition timing hole cap* | | | |
|   CRF250R and CRF250X | 5.9 | 52 | – |
|   CRF450R | | | |
|     2002-2003 | 9.9 | 87 | – |
|     2004 | 5.9 | 52 | – |
|     2005 | 6.0 | 53 | – |
|   CRF450X | 10 | 88 | – |
| Transmission oil check bolt | | | |
|   CRF250R | – | – | – |
|   CRF250X | 9.8 | 87 | – |
|   CRF450R | | | |
|     2002-2004 | 9.8 | 87 | – |
|     2005 | – | – | – |
|   CRF450X | – | – | – |
| Transmission oil drain bolt | 22 | – | 16 |

*Lubricate threads with grease.

3

# CHAPTER FOUR

# ENGINE (CRF250R AND CRF250X)

This chapter provides engine service information for CRF250R and CRF250X models. Read the appropriate section before attempting any repair. Become familiar with the procedures to understand the skill and equipment required. Refer to Chapter One for tool usage and techniques. When special tools are required or recommended, the Honda part number is provided.

Always clean the engine before starting repairs. If the engine remains in the frame, clean the surrounding framework and under the fuel tank. Do not allow dirt to enter the engine.

Keep the work environment as clean as possible. Store parts and assemblies in well-marked plastic bags and containers. Keep new parts wrapped until installation.

Refer to Chapter Three for break-in procedures.

**Tables 1-7** are at the end of this chapter.

## SERVICING ENGINE IN FRAME

The following components can be serviced with the engine installed in the frame:
1. Cylinder head cover, camshaft and cylinder head.
2. Cylinder and piston.

3. Alternator (Chapter Ten).
4. Clutch, external shift linkage and kickstarter (Chapter Six).
5. Water pump (Chapter Eleven).
6. Starter clutch (CRF250X [Chapter Six]).
7. Starter (CRF250X [Chapter Ten]).
8. Emission control system (CRF250X [Chapter Nine]).

## ENGINE

### Removal

This procedure describes the steps to remove the complete engine assembly. If desired, remove the sub-assemblies attached to the crankcase while the engine is still in the frame.
1. Support the motorcycle securely.
2. If possible, perform a compression test (Chapter Three) and leakdown test (Chapter Two) before dismantling the engine.
3. Remove the skid plate, engine guards, side covers and seat (Chapter Sixteen).
4. On CRF250X models, disconnect the negative battery cable at the battery (**Figure 1**).
5. Drain the engine oil (Chapter Three).

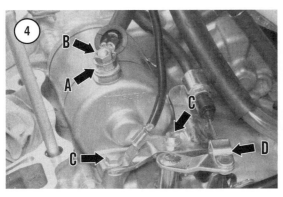

6. Drain the transmission oil (Chapter Three).

7. Drain the coolant (Chapter Three).

8. Remove the seat (Chapter Sixteen).

9. Remove the fuel tank (Chapter Nine).

10. Remove the exhaust system (this chapter).

11. Remove the carburetor (Chapter Nine).

12. Remove the shift pedal (**Figure 2**).

13A. On CRF250R models, disconnect the drive chain. If necessary, remove the drive sprocket (Chapter Twelve).

13B. On CRF250X models, an endless drive chain is used. Remove the drive sprocket (Chapter Twelve) to disconnect the drive chain from the engine.

14. Remove the brake pedal (Chapter Fifteen).

15. Disconnect the direct ignition coil (A, **Figure 3**) from the spark plug.

16. Disconnect the crankcase breather hose (B, **Figure 3**) at the cylinder head cover.

17A. On 2004 CRF250R models, remove the bolts and the clutch cable stay from the left crankcase cover. On all models, disconnect the clutch cable from the clutch release lever.

17B. On CRF250X models:

   a. California models—Remove the PAIR control valve (Chapter Nine).

   b. Hold the lower nut (A, **Figure 4**) at the starter terminal, then remove the upper nut (B) and disconnect the starter cable.

*NOTE*
*Holding the lower nut prevents the positive terminal from turning and damaging its wire connector inside the starter. Refer to **Starter** in Chapter Ten.*

   c. Remove the bolt (C, **Figure 4**) and the ground cable.

   d. Remove the clutch cable nut and remove the clutch cable from the starter stay (D, **Figure 4**).

18A. On CRF250R models, disconnect the ignition pulse generator and stator connectors (**Figure 5**).

18B. On CRF250X models, disconnect the regulator/rectifier and ignition pulse generator connectors (**Figure 6**).

19. Remove the engine hanger plate nuts, bolts, plates and washer (**Figure 7**). Note the hose routing through the plates before removing them.

4

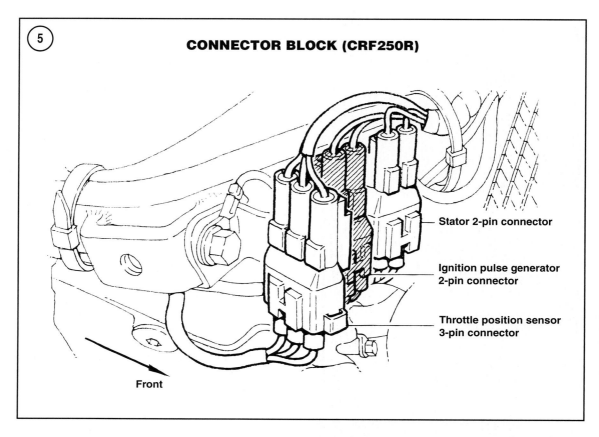

⑤

**CONNECTOR BLOCK (CRF250R)**

Stator 2-pin connector

Ignition pulse generator
2-pin connector

Throttle position sensor
3-pin connector

Front

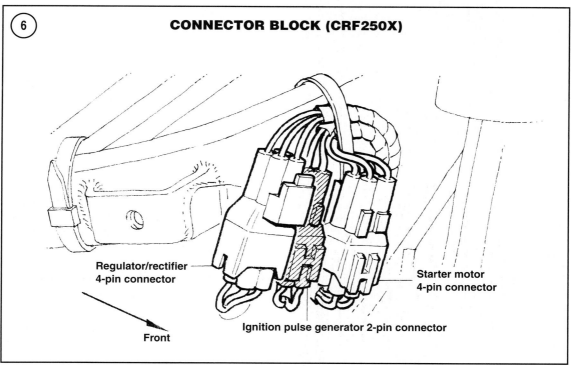

⑥

**CONNECTOR BLOCK (CRF250X)**

Regulator/rectifier
4-pin connector

Starter motor
4-pin connector

Ignition pulse generator 2-pin connector

Front

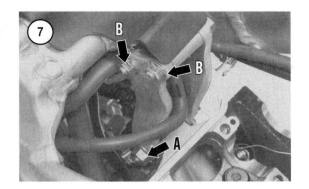

20B. If the engine is to be removed as an assembly, perform the following:

    a. Disconnect the upper radiator hose at the cylinder head.

    b. Disconnect the lower radiator hose at the water pump.

    c. Remove the kick pedal.

21. Remove the pivot shaft nut and washer (**Figure 8**).

22. Remove the front engine mount nut, washer and bolt (A, **Figure 9**).

23. Remove the lower engine mounting nut, washer and bolt (B, **Figure 9**).

*NOTE*
*When the pivot shaft is removed, the swing arm will come loose. Pull the shaft out only far enough to free the engine. After the engine is removed, push the shaft back through the frame and swing arm.*

24. Remove the pivot shaft (C, **Figure 9**) until it is free of the engine but still installed in the right side of the swing arm.

*WARNING*
*If necessary, have an assistant help remove the engine.*

25. Remove the engine from the right side.

26. Push the pivot shaft back through the frame.

27. Clean and inspect the frame and all exposed hardware, hoses and wiring. Check for cracks and damage, particularly at welded joints.

28. Refer to the procedures in this chapter for servicing the crankcase assembly.

20A. If the engine is to be disassembled, remove the following components while the engine is mounted in the frame:

    a. Cylinder head, cylinder and piston (this chapter).

    b. Starter (CRF250X [Chapter Ten]).

    c. Clutch (Chapter Six).

    d. Starter clutch (CRF250X [Chapter Six]).

    e. Kickstarter and idle gear (Chapter Six).

    f. External shift mechanism (Chapter Six).

    g. Flywheel (Chapter Ten).

    h. Balancer shaft (Chapter Six).

    i. Primary drive gear (Chapter Six).

**Installation**

1. Check all coolant hoses and hose connections for looseness or damage. Make sure the hose clamps are tight. Check for deterioration on the inside of the hoses.

2. Make sure the wiring harness, vent hoses and rear brake hose are routed and secured properly.

3. Replace damaged engine mounting fasteners.

4. Lubricate the pivot shaft with grease and insert it partway through the right side of the frame and swing arm (A, **Figure 10**). Do not grease the threads on the end of the pivot bolt.

4

5. Make sure the bushings (B, **Figure 10**) are installed inside the swing arm.

6. Install the engine into the frame from the right side, then push the pivot shaft through the frame and engine from the right side. Make sure the flat on the head of the pivot shaft seats into the frame recess (C, **Figure 9**).

> *CAUTION*
> *The threads on all engine mounting fasteners and the swing arm pivot shaft must be dry when tightened.*

> *CAUTION*
> *Tighten the engine mount fasteners finger-tight in the following steps. Do not tighten the bolts until all of the bolts and hanger plates have been installed.*

7. Install the pivot shaft washer and nut (**Figure 8**).

8. Install the lower engine mounting bolt, washer and nut (B, **Figure 9**). Install the bolt from the left side.

9. Install the front engine mounting bolt, washer and nut (A, **Figure 9**). Install the bolt from the left side.

10. If the engine was disassembled, reverse Step 20A under *Removal* to install the parts.

11. Identify the engine hanger plates by their L (left side) or R (right side) marks (**Figure 11**). Install the hanger plates (**Figure 7**) with these marks facing to the outside. Install the bolts from the left side.

12. Tighten the swing arm pivot shaft nut (**Figure 8**) to 88 N•m (65 ft.-lb.).

13. Tighten the engine hanger plate engine side nut (A, **Figure 7**) to 54 N•m (40 ft.-lb.).

14. Tighten the engine hanger plate frame side nuts (B, **Figure 7**) to the torque specification in **Table 7**.

15. Tighten the front engine mounting nut (A, **Figure 9**) to 54 N•m (40 ft.-lb.).

16. Tighten the lower engine mounting nut (B, **Figure 9**) to 64 N•m (47 ft.-lb.).

17. Reverse Steps 1-18 under *Removal* to complete engine installation. Note the following.

18. Tighten the kickstarter pedal mounting bolt to 37 N•m (27 ft.-lb.).

19. Fill the engine with new oil (Chapter Three).

20. Fill the transmission with new oil (Chapter Three).

21. Fill the cooling system with coolant (Chapter Three).

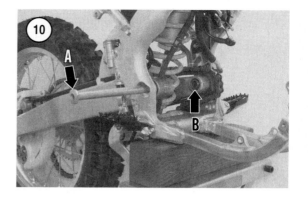

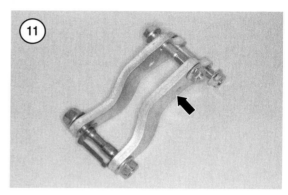

22. Start the engine and check for leaks.

23. Check throttle operation.

24. Check the shift pedal mounting position, clutch adjustment and gear engagement.

25. If the engine top end was rebuilt, perform a compression check. Record the results for future reference.

26. Review the *Engine Break-In* procedure in Chapter Three.

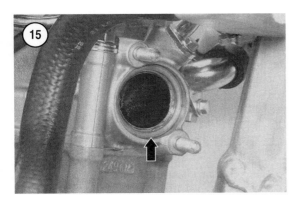

## EXHAUST SYSTEM

### Removal and Installation

1. Support the motorcycle on a workstand.
2. Remove the right side cover (Chapter Sixteen).
3. Remove the muffler as follows:
   a. Loosen the muffler joint band bolt (**Figure 12**).
   b. Remove the bolts securing the muffler pipe to the subframe and remove the muffler (**Figure 13**).

4. Remove the exhaust pipe as follows:
   a. Remove the exhaust pipe joint nuts (**Figure 14**) and exhaust pipe.
   b. Remove and discard the gasket from the exhaust port.
5. Reverse these steps to install the exhaust system, plus the following steps.
6. Install a new exhaust pipe gasket (**Figure 15**). If necessary, apply a small amount of grease to the gasket to hold it in place. The grease will burn off once the engine is started.
7. Replace the exhaust pipe-to-muffler gasket if leaking or damaged.
8. Install the exhaust pipe while leaving the joint nuts finger-tight.
9. Install the muffler while leaving the mounting bolts loose.
10. Tighten the exhaust pipe joint nuts (**Figure 14**) in a crossing pattern and in several steps to 21 N•m (15 ft.-lb.).
11. Tighten the muffler mounting bolts (**Figure 13**) to 26 N•m (19 ft.-lb.).
12. Tighten the muffler joint clamp bolt (**Figure 12**) to 21 N•m (15 ft.-lb.).
13. Start the engine and check for exhaust leaks.

### Muffler Repacking (CRF250R)

The glass wool in the muffler can be replaced (**Figure 16**).
1. Remove the muffler as described in this section.

*CAUTION*
*When removing rivets, drill through the rivet head and not into the muffler housing. Remove the loose rivet ends when cleaning out the muffler.*

2. Remove the rivets by drilling off the rivet heads. Then remove the end cap, end cover, housing and front band.
3. Pull the glass wool off the inner pipe and discard it. Remove any residue remaining inside the muffler housing and on the inner pipe.
4. Clean the inner pipe and muffler housing with a wire brush to remove all rust and exhaust residue. Make sure all the inner pipe core holes are clear.
5. Remove the new glass wool packing from its container and compare it with the inner pipe and the

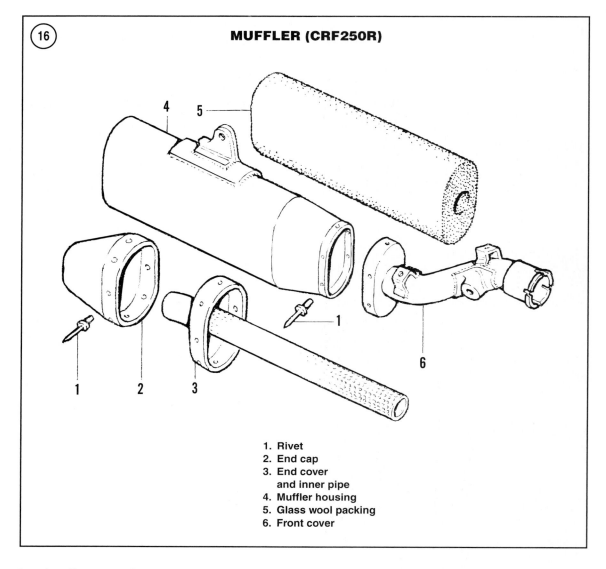

**MUFFLER (CRF250R)**

1. Rivet
2. End cap
3. End cover
   and inner pipe
4. Muffler housing
5. Glass wool packing
6. Front cover

housing diameters. If necessary, cut the wool glass to fit the housing.

6. Wrap the new wool glass packing around the inner pipe core. Pack as much material around the inner pipe as possible without making it too tight. When correctly packed around the inner pipe, the glass wool should be slightly larger than the muffler housing.

7. Slide the muffler housing carefully over the wool glass and into position. Make sure the housing does not push the wool glass forward and leave a gap at the end of the muffler.

8. Rivet the front band, end cover and end cap to the muffler housing.

**Spark Arrestor Cleaning (CRF250X)**

1. Support the motorcycle on its sidestand.

2. Remove the bolts (**Figure 17**), spark arrestor (**Figure 18**) and gasket. Replace the gasket if leaking.

3. Clean the spark arrestor with a wire brush and replace if the screen is damaged.

4. Installation is the reverse of removal. Tighten the spark arrestor mounting bolts securely. Start the engine and check for leaks.

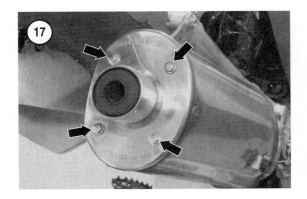

## CYLINDER HEAD COVER

### Removal

1. Support the motorcycle on a workstand.

2. Remove the fuel tank (Chapter Nine).

3. Disconnect the direct ignition coil (A, **Figure 19**) and the breather hose (B). Slide the clamp down the hose so it cannot fall into the engine.

*NOTE*
*Before removing the cylinder head cover bolts, check for oil leaks around the cover and bolt gaskets.*

4. Remove the bolts, gaskets and cylinder head cover (C, **Figure 19**).

5. Remove the plug hole seal (**Figure 20**) if it did not come off with the cylinder head cover.

### Installation

1. Remove any sealer residue remaining along the cylinder head cutout (**Figure 21**). Remove the material carefully so it does not fall into the engine.

2. After removing the gasket residue from the cylinder head cutout, clean the entire cylinder head gasket surface with contact cleaner.

3. Replace the bolt gaskets if leaking or damaged. Reuse the gaskets if in good condition.

4. Replace the cylinder head cover gasket (A, **Figure 22**) if leaking or damaged. Reuse the gasket if in good condition.

5. Perform the following to reuse the original cylinder head cover gasket or to install a new gasket:

   a. Carefully pull the gasket (A, **Figure 22**) from the cover. Discard the gasket if damaged.

b. Remove all sealer residue from the groove in the cylinder head cover. Clean the cover in solvent and dry thoroughly.

c. If reusing the original gasket, pull hardened strips of the old sealer from the top of the gasket and along the half-moon extension (B, **Figure 22**).

d. Apply Gasgacinch to the cover groove (A, **Figure 23**) and to the side of the gasket (B) that will seat against the cover when installed. Do not apply sealer to the side of the gasket that will seat against the cylinder head. Follow the manufacturer's instructions for drying time before installing the gasket into the cover groove.

e. Install the gasket by inserting its raised surface into the cover groove. Check that the gasket seats in the groove completely.

6. Install the plug hole seal (**Figure 20**) onto the spark plug tunnel. Do not apply sealer to the seal.

7. Apply an RTV sealer to the cylinder head corner surfaces identified in **Figure 21**. Do not apply an excessive amount of sealer. Allow the sealer to set for 10-15 minutes (or follow manufacturer's directions) before installing the cylinder head cover and gasket.

8. Install the cylinder head cover onto the cylinder head. Make sure the lip around the half-moon gasket extension fits squarely in the cylinder head groove.

9. Install the gaskets onto the bolts with their UP mark facing up (**Figure 24**). Do not apply sealer to the gaskets.

10. Install the cylinder head cover bolts and gaskets and tighten to 9.8 N•m (87 in.-lb.).

11. Reconnect the direct ignition coil (A, **Figure 19**) onto the spark plug.

12. Reconnect the breather hose onto the cylinder head cover and secure the hose with the clamp.

13. Install the fuel tank (Chapter Nine).

14. Follow the sealer manufacturer's recommendations for drying time before starting the engine.

### CAMSHAFT AND ROCKER ARM

The camshaft and rocker arm assembly can be removed with the engine mounted in the frame.

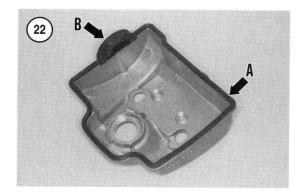

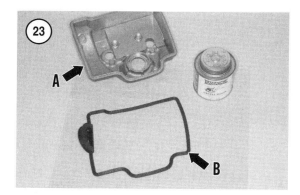

### Crankshaft Timing Marks

A chain and two sprockets drive the camshaft. One sprocket is mounted on the camshaft and the other sprocket is permanently fixed to the crankshaft. To ensure proper valve timing in relation to piston travel, the camshaft must be timed to the crankshaft. This is done by positioning the crankshaft with the piston at TDC and then aligning the camshaft TDC timing marks before installing the chain onto the camshaft.

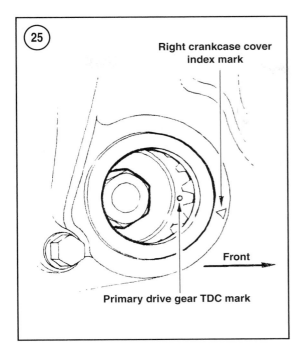

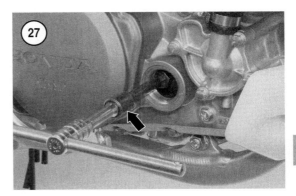

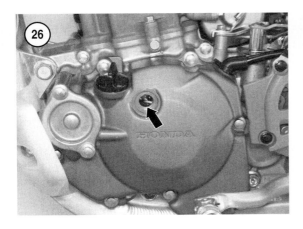

Index marks on the primary drive gear and right crankcase cover are used to position the crankshaft at TDC (**Figure 25**). However, because these index marks are located to one side of each other (cannot be viewed straight on), the precise viewing of both marks may be difficult and cause a viewing error (or parallax). In this case the error can be significant and cause it to appear that the index marks are incorrectly aligned when they are correct or vice versa.

To eliminate any error when setting the crankshaft at TDC, view the ignition timing marks on the flywheel (**Figure 26**) through the left crankcase cover timing hole.

## Camshaft/Rocker Arm Removal

1. Remove the cylinder head cover as described in this chapter.

2. Remove the crankshaft hole cap from the right crankcase cover.

3. Remove the ignition timing hole cap from the left crankcase cover.

4. Remove the spark plug to make turning the crankshaft easier.

*NOTE*
*Use an 8 mm hex socket on the primary drive gear mounting bolt to turn the crankshaft (**Figure 27**).*

5. If it is necessary to service the decompressor assembly, hold the crankshaft with the hex socket (**Figure 27**) and loosen, but do not remove, the decompressor cam stopper plate bolt (**Figure 28**). If the bolt is very tight, wait and remove the camshaft first. Then loosen the bolt as described under

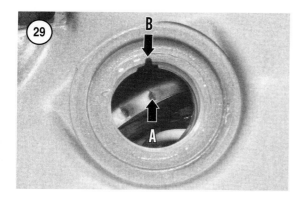

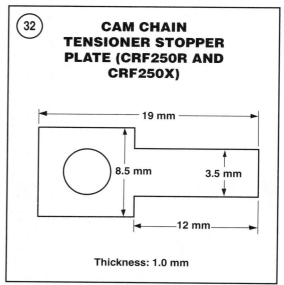

## CAM CHAIN TENSIONER STOPPER PLATE (CRF250R AND CRF250X)

19 mm

8.5 mm

3.5 mm

12 mm

**Thickness: 1.0 mm**

*Decompressor Inspection/Removal/Installation* in this section.

6. Set the engine at TDC on its compression stroke as follows:

> *NOTE*
> *The decompressor mechanism will click loudly once during each crankshaft revolution. This is normal.*

a. Turn the crankshaft *clockwise* and align the TDC mark on the flywheel (A, **Figure 29**) with the index mark on the left crankcase cover (B). Then check that both index lines on the cam sprocket align with the cylinder head surface (**Figure 30**).

> *NOTE*
> *If using the primary drive gear and right crankcase cover timing marks, align the TDC mark on the primary drive gear with the index mark on the right crankcase cover (**Figure 25**).*

b. The engine is now at TDC on either the compression stroke or exhaust stroke. The engine is on the compression stroke if the rocker arm (**Figure 31**) can be moved slightly by hand,

indicating that exhaust and intake valves are closed. If the rocker arm is tight, the engine is on the exhaust stroke and the exhaust valves are open. If the rocker arm is tight, turn the crankshaft clockwise one full turn and realign the TDC marks described in substep a. The rocker arm should now be loose.

> *NOTE*
> *Before removing the camshaft, turn the engine over several times while checking the camshaft and flywheel timing marks. Confirm that the timing marks and camshaft positions are correct and note how the camshaft lobes are positioned when the engine is at TDC on its compression stroke.*

> *CAUTION*
> *If the cam sprocket timing marks do not align as described, the cam timing*

4

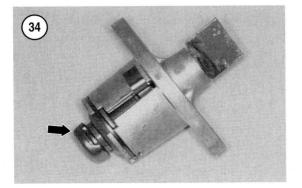

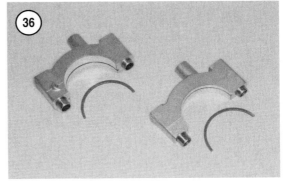

*is incorrect. A damaged or incorrectly adjusted cam chain tensioner or excessively stretched cam chain can cause the camshaft to jump time. This condition can cause bent valves and loss of compression. Before removing the tensioner, lift the chain to check its tension—it should be tight.*

7. With the engine positioned at TDC on its compression stroke, check and record the valve clearances as described in Chapter Three. If one or more clearances are incorrect, it will be necessary to install the appropriate size shims during reassembly.

8. Loosen the cam chain tension as follows:

*NOTE*
*A stopper plate is required to turn and lock the cam chain tensioner in its retracted position. Fabricate the stopper plate to the dimensions shown in* **Figure 32**.

a. Remove the bolt and sealing washer from the center of the tensioner housing.

b. Insert the small end of the stopper plate (**Figure 33**) into the tensioner and turn the pushrod clockwise until it stops. Then insert the stopper plate into one set of notches machined in the tensioner housing to lock the tensioner.

*NOTE*
**Figure 34** *shows the tensioner assembly removed with the pushrod locked in its retracted position. Spring pressure should be felt when turning the stopper plate in substep c. If the tensioner turns easily, it is most likely damaged.*

c. Check that the cam chain is loose.

9. Tie a piece of wire to the cam chain.

10. Loosen the camshaft bolts (**Figure 35**) in a crossing pattern and in two or three steps.

*CAUTION*
*Each camshaft holder is equipped with a set ring and two dowel pins* (**Figure 36**). *Remove the camshaft*

*holders carefully so these parts do not
fall into the engine.*

11. Remove the camshaft holder bolts, holders,
dowel pins (**Figure 35**) and set rings.

12. Slide the left cam bearing off its journal in the
cylinder so the camshaft drops slightly in the cylinder head. Then disconnect the cam chain from the
cam sprocket and remove the camshaft (**Figure 37**).

13. Before removing the valve lifters and shims,
note the following:

    a. Use a divided container to store the intake
    valve lifters and the four intake and exhaust
    valve shims in their original mounting posi-
    tion.

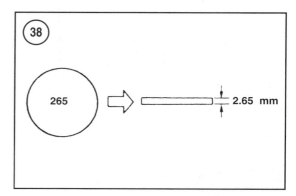

    b. The intake valve shims will either stay inside
    the valve lifters or remain in the spring seats
    at the end of the valves. Remove the valve
    lifters carefully so the shims do not dislodge
    and fall into the engine.

    c. The exhaust valve shims can be removed
    without having to remove the rocker arm.

    d. Each shim was originally marked with a num-
    ber indicating its thickness (**Figure 38**). If a
    shim number is indecipherable, measure the
    shim's thickness with a micrometer and re-
    cord it to identify the shim with its original
    mounting position.

14. Remove the intake valve lifters (A, **Figure 39**)
and shims (if they are stuck inside the valve lifters).
Store them in a divided container.

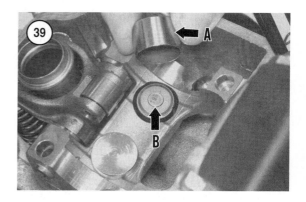

15. Remove the intake (B, **Figure 39**) and exhaust
valve shims (**Figure 40**) and install them in a divided container.

16. Remove the rocker arm as follows:

    a. Remove the rocker arm shaft cap and O-ring
    (**Figure 41**) from the cylinder head.

    b. Thread one of the camshaft holder bolts (7
    mm thread) into the rocker arm shaft and re-
    move the shaft (**Figure 42**).

    c. Remove the rocker arm (**Figure 42**).

17. Clean and inspect the camshaft, camshaft
holder, decompressor assembly and rocker arm as
described in this section.

**Camshaft/Rocker Arm Installation**

1. If the decompressor cam stopper plate bolt is loose, tighten it as described under *Decompressor Inspection/Removal/Installation* in this section.

   a. Lubricate the rocker arm shaft and rocker arm bore with engine oil.

   b. Install the rocker arm and rocker arm shaft. Align the holes in the rocker arm and shaft with the cam holder threads in the cylinder head.

   c. Remove the bolt (**Figure 42**) from the end of the rocker arm shaft.

   d. Lubricate the rocker arm shaft cap O-ring with oil.

   e. Lubricate the rocker arm shaft cap (**Figure 41**) threads with grease and tighten to 5.9 N•m (52 in.-lb.).

3. Review *Crankshaft Timing Marks* in this section. Then set the engine at TDC by turning the crankshaft *clockwise* and aligning the TDC mark on the flywheel (A, **Figure 29**) with the index mark on the left crankcase cover (B). The engine must be held in this position when installing and timing the camshaft sprocket.

*NOTE*
*If using the timing marks on the primary drive gear and right crankcase cover, align the TDC mark on the primary drive gear with the index mark on the right crankcase cover (**Figure 25**).*

4. If removed, lubricate the valve shims with engine oil and install them into the spring seats. See B, **Figure 39** and **Figure 40**. Install the shims in their original position. If one or more of the original shims are to be replaced for valve adjustment, install the new shims in their correct position in the spring seats.

5. Apply molybdenum disulfide oil solution to the outer surface of each intake valve lifter and install the valve lifters in their original mounting position (A, **Figure 39**) in the cylinder head. Make sure each lifter (A, **Figure 43**) seats flush against its intake valve shim.

6. Make sure the rocker arm (B, **Figure 43**) is seating flush against the exhaust valve shims.

7. Lubricate the cam lobes and cam journals with molybdenum oil solution.

*CAUTION*
*Do not lubricate the camshaft holder mating surface, camshaft holder mounting bolt threads or cylinder head-to-cam holder threads with molybdenum oil solution as it will affect the camshaft holder torque reading.*

8. Before installing the camshaft, note the following:

   a. Make sure the cam chain tensioner pushrod is held in its retracted position with the stopper plate. See Step 8 under *Camshaft/Rocker Arm Removal* in this section.

b. Keep the front of the cam chain taut so there is no play in the chain when the chain is installed over the sprocket. Maintain all the chain slack at the back of the chain.

c. Do not install the left camshaft bearing into its journal until after installing the cam chain over the cam sprocket. Otherwise, the camshaft will sit too high, reducing the amount of chain slack available for installation. See **Figure 44**.

9. Install the camshaft and time the cam sprocket as follows:

> *CAUTION*
> *When installing the camshaft, check the position of the flywheel timing marks (**Figure 29**). The engine must be set at TDC on its compression stroke when the camshaft is timed in this step.*

a. Slide the left bearing so it rests against the cam sprocket on the camshaft and is not installed on its journal.

b. Install the camshaft through the cam chain and turn it so that the intake cam lobes face up and rearward (A, **Figure 45**), then align the timing marks on the sprocket with the cylinder head gasket surface (**Figure 46**). Install the chain onto the sprocket.

c. Position the camshaft into the cylinder head.

d. Recheck the timing marks. The index marks on the cam sprocket must align with the cylinder head surface (**Figure 46**) when the flywheel TDC index marks align with the left crankcase index mark (**Figure 29**). If not, reposition the camshaft until the marks align.

e. When both sets of marks align, lift the camshaft and slide the left bearing onto its cylinder head journal (**Figure 47**).

f. Recheck the timing marks.

> *CAUTION*
> *If the timing marks are not in these exact locations with the engine at TDC, cam timing will be incorrect. Engine damage could occur if the camshaft is not properly installed.*

10. Install the camshaft holders (**Figure 36**) as follows:

> *CAUTION*
> *Make sure the oil passage running through the left camshaft holder is clear.*

a. Apply grease to the set rings and install a set ring in each camshaft holder groove (A, **Figure 48**).

b. Make sure the dowel pins are installed in the camshaft holders (B, **Figure 48**).

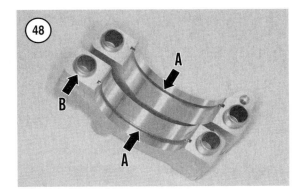

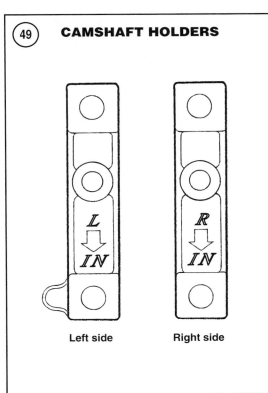

**CAMSHAFT HOLDERS**

Left side        Right side

c. Identify the camshaft holders by their L (left side) and R (right side) identification marks (**Figure 49**).

d. Install the camshaft holders by positioning the set rings into the bearing grooves. The IN mark and arrow on each camshaft holder must face toward the intake side of the engine (**Figure 49**). Make sure each camshaft holder seats flush against its bearing and cylinder head surface.

e. Lubricate the camshaft holder bolt threads and flange seating surfaces with engine oil and install them. The front bolts are longer than the rear bolts (**Figure 35**). Tighten the camshaft holder mounting bolts in a crossing pattern and in two steps to 16 N•m (142 in.-lb.).

11. Listen for an audible *snap* while watching the rear chain run at the cam sprocket, then remove the stopper plate (**Figure 33**) from the tensioner. The chain should tighten while the noise indicates that the tensioner pushrod has extended. If this noise did not occur, remove and inspect the tensioner.

12. Turn the crankshaft *clockwise* several times, then place it at TDC on its compression stroke. Make sure the timing marks on the cam sprocket align with the cylinder head gasket surface (**Figure 46**). If not, the camshaft timing is incorrect.

13. Install a new sealing washer and tighten the cam chain tensioner bolt securely.

14. Check the valve clearance (Chapter Three).

15. Install and tighten the spark plug.

16. Apply grease to the crankshaft hole cap threads and tighten to 15 N•m (133 in.-lb.).

17. Apply grease to the ignition timing hole cap threads and tighten to 5.9 N•m (52 in.-lb.).

18. Install the cylinder head cover as described in this chapter.

**Camshaft Inspection**

Replace parts that show obvious damage, or meet or exceed the service limits in **Table 2**.

1. Clean and dry the camshaft and decompressor assembly.

2. Check that the camshaft bearings turn freely and do not exhibit any noticeable noise or roughness. The right bearing (A, **Figure 50**) can be replaced after removing the decompressor assembly. If the left

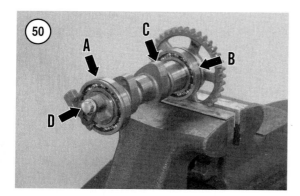

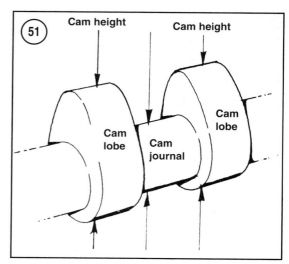

bearing (B, **Figure 50**) is damaged, replace the camshaft assembly.

3. Inspect the cam sprocket for cracks and damaged teeth.

4. Inspect the machined surfaces on the camshaft for cracks or roughness.

5. Inspect the cam lobes (C, **Figure 50**) for pitting, scoring or damage.

6. Measure each cam lobe height (**Figure 51**) with a micrometer. Refer to **Table 2** for specifications.

## Decompressor
## Inspection/Removal/Installation

1. Operate the decompressor weight (A, **Figure 52**), making sure it moves and returns freely. Check the return spring (**Figure 53**). If necessary, remove and service the decompressor assembly.

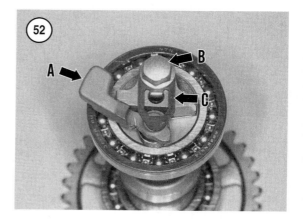

> *CAUTION*
> *The decompressor cam stopper plate bolt (B, **Figure 52**) is secured with a threadlock and is tightened securely to the camshaft. Heating the camshaft helps prevent the bolt threads from stripping and possibly damaging the camshaft.*

2. Loosen the decompressor cam stopper plate bolt and remove the decompressor assembly as follows:

   a. Support the cam sprocket in a vise with soft jaws (**Figure 50**) and heat the area around the decompressor mounting bolt with a heat gun.

   b. After a sufficient amount of time, loosen and remove the decompressor cam stopper plate bolt, stopper plate, decompressor weight and spring, and right bearing (**Figure 54**). Discard the mounting bolt.

   c. Allow the parts to cool before handling them.

3. Inspect the decompressor weight shaft (A, **Figure 55**) for bending and other damage.

4. Inspect the cam area (B, **Figure 55**) for pitting, wear and other damage.

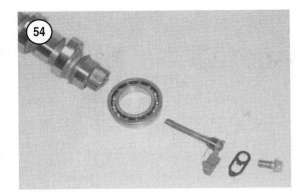

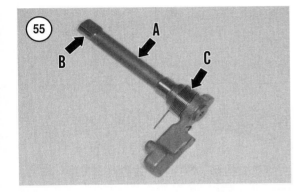

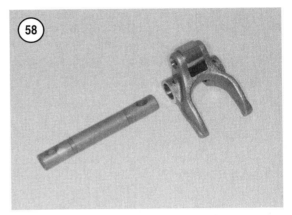

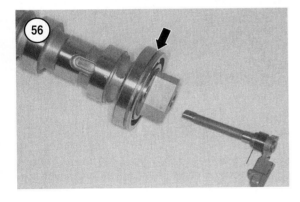

b. Install the spring (C, **Figure 55**) onto the decompressor weight shaft.

c. Install the decompressor weight shaft into the camshaft and set the spring arm against the camshaft as shown in **Figure 57**.

d. Install the stopper plate (C, **Figure 52**) by inserting its tab into the hole in the camshaft.

e. Apply a medium strength threadlock onto the bolt threads and install the bolt (B, **Figure 52**).

f. Support the cam sprocket in a vise with soft jaws (**Figure 50**) and tighten the decompressor cam stopper plate bolt (D, **Figure 50**) to 9.8 N•m (87 in.-lb.).

5. Replace the decompressor spring (C, **Figure 55**) if damaged.

6. If wear was previously detected with the right bearing, replace it.

7. Inspect the bearing operating area on the camshaft for pitting and other damage.

8. Install the decompressor assembly and tighten the decompressor cam stopper plate bolt as follows:

a. Install the right side bearing with its groove side (**Figure 56**) facing out.

## Rocker Arm and Shaft Inspection

Replace parts that show obvious damage, or meet or exceed the service limit in **Table 2**.

1. Clean and dry the rocker arm and shaft (**Figure 58**). Make sure the rocker arm oil holes are clear.

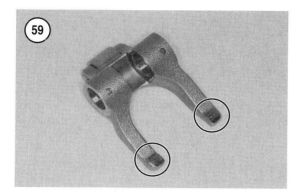

2. Inspect the rocker arm contact surfaces (**Figure 59**) for wear and damage. If the camshaft contact surfaces on the rocker arm are damaged, inspect the adjustment shims and camshaft lobes for damage.

3. Measure the rocker arm inside diameter.

4. Inspect the rocker arm shaft for scoring and other damage. The shaft must be smooth.

5. Measure the rocker arm shaft outside diameter.

6. Subtract the rocker arm shaft outside diameter measurement (Step 5) from the rocker arm inside diameter (Step 3) to determine the rocker arm-to-shaft clearance. Replace the rocker arm and shaft if the clearance is too large.

### Valve Lifter Inspection

Replace the valve lifters if they are obviously damaged, or not within specification.

1. Inspect the valve lifters for scoring or other damage. If there is damage or uneven wear, remove the exhaust valves from the cylinder head and inspect the mating bores for damage.

2. Measure each valve lifter outside diameter (**Table 2**).

### CAM CHAIN TENSIONER, GUIDES AND CAM CHAIN

The engine is equipped with a cam chain tensioner mounted on the cylinder block, a front and rear chain guide and cam chain. The cam chain tensioner, cam chain and both guides can be replaced with the engine mounted in the frame.

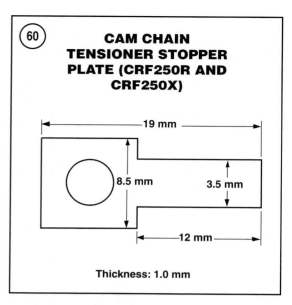

### Cam Chain Tensioner Removal/Inspection/Installation

The cam chain tensioner controls cam chain tension with an adjustable spring-loaded pushrod. As the cam chain wears and stretches, the tensioner's pushrod automatically adjusts to maintain the proper amount of cam chain slack. When the cam chain tensioner no longer provides the correct amount of tension against the chain, the chain slack can increase and allow the chain to jump one or more teeth on the camshaft sprocket. This will change the cam timing and possibly cause loss of engine compression and severe engine damage.

1. Position the engine at TDC on its compression stroke as described under *Valve Adjustment* in Chapter Three. This step removes tension from the

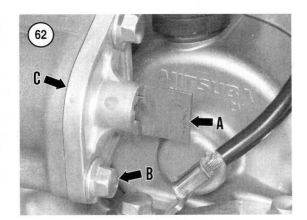

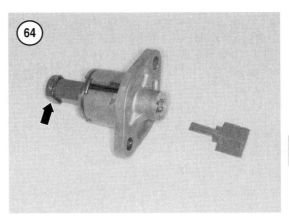

4

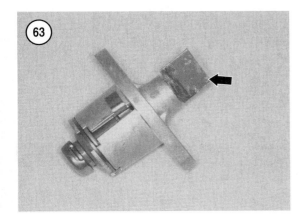

valve springs to help prevent camshaft movement and the cam chain jumping time.

2. Clean the area around the cam chain tensioner.

3. Retract the cam chain tensioner pushrod tension against the cam chain as follows:

> *NOTE*
> *A stopper plate is used to turn and lock the tensioner pushrod in its retracted position. Fabricate the stopper plate to the dimensions shown in **Figure 60**.*

  a. Remove the bolt (**Figure 61**) and sealing washer from the tensioner housing.

  b. Insert the small end of the stopper plate (A, **Figure 62**) into the tensioner and turn the pushrod clockwise until it stops. Then insert the outer portion of the stopper plate into one set of notches machined in the tensioner housing to lock the tensioner.

4. Remove the mounting bolts (B, **Figure 62**) and the tensioner housing (C). Remove and discard the gasket.

> *CAUTION*
> *Do not turn the engine over once the cam chain tensioner has been removed.*

5. Remove the stopper plate (**Figure 63**). The pushrod should click and extend (**Figure 64**).

6. Inspect the cam chain tensioner as follows:

  a. Inspect the pushrod and tensioner housing for damage.

  b. With the pushrod extended (**Figure 64**), try to push the pushrod by hand. It should not move.

  c. Use the stopper plate to turn the tensioner and retract the pushrod. It should move evenly under spring pressure. If the pushrod moves, but does not feel like it is under spring tension, the tensioner is most likely damaged.

  d. The cam chain tensioner is available only as a unit assembly. Do not attempt to disassemble it. Replace the tensioner assembly if necessary.

7. Remove all gasket residue from the cam chain tensioner and cylinder block gasket surfaces.

> *CAUTION*
> *The cam chain tensioner must be installed with the pushrod locked in its retracted position.*

8. Turn and lock the pushrod in its retracted position as described in Step 3 (**Figure 63**).

9. Install a new gasket onto the tensioner.

10. Install the tensioner (C, **Figure 62**) and tighten its mounting bolts (B) to 12 N•m (106 in.-lb.).

11. Remove the stopper plate (A, **Figure 62**) to allow the pushrod to extend.

*NOTE*
*The tensioner should click after removing the stopper plate, which indicates the pushrod has extended. If not, remove the tensioner and check the pushrod operation.*

12. Install a new sealing washer and tighten the bolt (**Figure 61**).

**Cam Chain Guides and Cam Chain Removal/Installation**

1. Remove the cylinder head as described in this chapter.

2. Remove the front chain guide (**Figure 65**).

3. To remove the rear chain guide and cam chain (**Figure 66**) perform the following:

    a. Remove the flywheel (Chapter Ten).

    b. Remove the bolt (A, **Figure 66**), washer, collar and rear chain guide (B).

    c. Remove the bolt (C, **Figure 66**), stopper plate (D) and cam chain (E).

4. Inspect the chain guides, cam chain (**Figure 67**) and sprockets as follows:

    a. Check the chain fit on the cam and crankshaft sprockets. The chain should completely seat between the sprocket teeth and not have a tendency to slide up the teeth.

    b. Inspect the crankshaft sprocket for wear or damage. The profile of each tooth should be symmetrical.

    c. Check the chain for excessive play between the links, indicating worn rollers and pins.

    d. Visually inspect the chain guides for excessive wear (grooves), cuts or other damage.

*NOTE*
*If there is damage with any of these parts, check the cam chain tensioner as described in this section.*

5. Install the cam chain (E, **Figure 66**) around the crankshaft sprocket.

6. Install the stopper plate (D, **Figure 66**) and tighten the mounting bolt (C) securely.

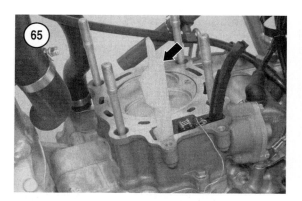

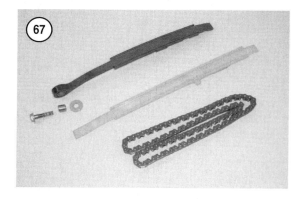

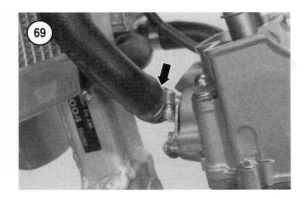

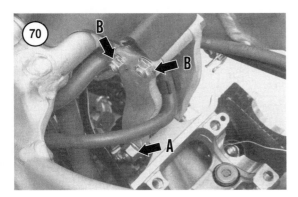

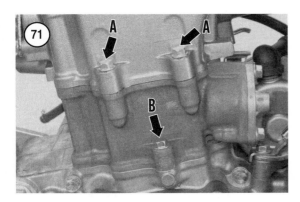

7. Apply a medium strength threadlock onto the rear chain guide mounting bolt threads. Install the rear chain guide (B, **Figure 66**), collar, washer and tighten the bolt (A) to 12 N•m (106 in.-lb.).

8. Install the front cam chain guide (**Figure 65**). Seat the upper part of the guide into the cylinder notch and its lower end into the guide channel (**Figure 68**).

9. Install the flywheel (Chapter Ten).

10. Install the cylinder head as described in this chapter.

## CYLINDER HEAD

This section describes removal, inspection and installation of the cylinder head. After the cylinder head is removed, refer to the appropriate sections in this chapter for further disassembly, inspection and assembly procedures. The cylinder head can be removed with the engine mounted in the frame.

### Removal

1. Drain the coolant (Chapter Three).

2. Remove the exhaust pipe as described in this chapter.

3. On CRF250X models, remove the PAIR control valve and air supply pipe (Chapter Nine).

4. Remove the carburetor (Chapter Nine).

5. Remove the cylinder head cover as described in this chapter.

6. Remove the camshaft and rocker arm as described in this chapter. Make sure to remove the valve adjustment shims after removing the camshaft.

7. Disconnect the coolant hose (**Figure 69**) at the cylinder head.

8. Remove the engine hanger plate nuts, bolts, plates and washer (**Figure 70**). Note the hose routing through the plates before removing them.

9. Remove the two cylinder head 6 mm mounting bolts (A, **Figure 71**).

10. Loosen the cylinder 6 mm mounting bolt (B, **Figure 71**).

11. Loosen the four cylinder head mounting nuts (**Figure 72**) in several stages and in a crossing pattern. Remove the nuts and washers.

12. Loosen the cylinder head by lightly tapping around its base with a soft mallet. Lift the head from

the engine and remove it sideways through the top of the frame (**Figure 73**).

13. Remove the head gasket (A, **Figure 74**) and the two dowel pins (B) from the cylinder.

14. Secure the cam chain with a piece of wire.

15. Cover the engine openings with clean shop rags to prevent debris from entering.

16. Inspect the cylinder head assembly as described in this section.

**Installation**

1. Clean the gasket surfaces of all gasket residue. All cylinder head and cylinder block surfaces must be clean and dry.

2. Check both cylinder head ports for loose parts. Plug the intake port with a rubber stopper.

3. Make sure the front chain guide is installed in the cylinder block (**Figure 65**).

4. Insert the two dowel pins (B, **Figure 74**) and a new cylinder head gasket (A) onto the cylinder.

5. Turn and lower the cylinder head onto the engine, routing the cam chain through the head.

6. Lubricate the cylinder head washers, nuts and stud threads with engine oil.

7. Install the washers and nuts and tighten finger-tight.

8. Tighten the nuts (**Figure 72**) in two or three steps and in a crossing pattern to 39 N•m (29 ft.-lb.).

9. Tighten the cylinder 6 mm mounting bolt (B, **Figure 71**) to 9.8 N•m (87 in.-lb.).

10. Install and tighten the cylinder head 6 mm mounting bolts (A, **Figure 71**) to 9.8 N•m (87 in.-lb.).

11. Install and tighten the engine hanger plates as follows:

   a. Identify the engine hanger plates by their L (left side) or R (right side) mark. Install the hanger plates with these marks facing to the outside. Install the bolts from the left side.

   b. Tighten the engine hanger plate engine side nut (A, **Figure 70**) to 54 N•m (40 ft.-lb.).

   c. Tighten the engine hanger plate frame side nuts (B, **Figure 70**) to the torque specification in **Table 7**.

12. Reconnect the coolant hose (**Figure 69**) onto the cylinder head water pipe. Tighten the clamp securely.

13. Reverse Steps 1-6 under *Removal* to complete installation, while noting the following:

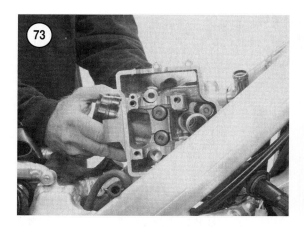

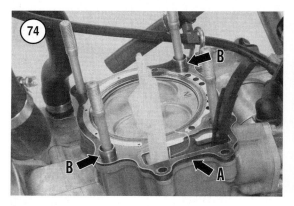

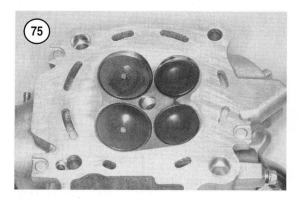

   a. Check the valve clearance (Chapter Three).

   b. Refill and bleed the cooling system (Chapter Three).

**Inspection**

1. Test the valves for leakage by performing a solvent test as described under *Valves* in this chapter.

2. Remove all gasket residue from the cylinder

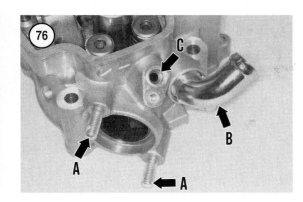

head mating surfaces. Do not scratch or gouge the surfaces.

*CAUTION*
*If the valves are removed from the head, the valve seats are exposed and can be damaged from careless cleaning. A damaged valve seat will not seal properly.*

3. Remove all carbon deposits from the combustion chamber and valve ports (**Figure 75**). Use solvent and a fine wire brush or hardwood scraper. Do not use sharp-edged tools such as screwdrivers or putty knives.

4. Inspect the spark plug hole threads and note the following:

   a. If the threads are dirty or mildly damaged, use a spark plug thread tap to clean and straighten the threads. Use kerosene or aluminum tap-cutting fluid to lubricate the threads.

   b. If the threads are galled, stripped or cross-threaded, repair with a steel thread insert (Heli-Coil).

*CAUTION*
*Prevent thread damage by applying antiseize compound to the spark plug threads before installation. Do not overtighten the spark plug.*

5. Inspect the exhaust pipe studs (A, **Figure 76**) for thread damage. Replace damaged studs as described in Chapter One.

6. Clean the entire cylinder head assembly in fresh solvent.

*CAUTION*
*If the head was bead-blasted, wash the entire assembly in hot soapy water to remove all blasting grit that is lodged in crevices and threads. Clean and chase all threads to ensure no grit remains. Grit that remains in the head will contaminate the engine oil and damage other parts of the engine.*

7. Inspect the cylinder head for cracks in the combustion chamber, water jackets and exhaust port (**Figure 76**). If cracks are found, have a dealership or machine shop determine if the cylinder head can be repaired. If not, replace the head.

8. Inspect the cylinder head for warp as follows:

   a. Place a straightedge across the cylinder head as shown in **Figure 77**.

   b. Attempt to insert a flat feeler gauge between the straightedge and the machined surface of the head. If clearance exists, record the measurement.

   c. Repeat substeps a and b several times, laying the straightedge both across and diagonally on the head.

9. Compare the measurements in Step 8 to the warp service limit in **Table 2**. If the clearance is not within the service limit, have a dealership or machine shop inspect and possibly resurface the cylinder head. If the head warpage is minor, true the head as follows:

   a. Tape a sheet of 400-600 grit emery paper to a thick sheet of glass or surface plate.

   b. Place the head on the emery paper and move the head in a figure-eight pattern.

   c. Rotate the head at regular intervals so material is removed evenly.

   d. Check the progress often, measuring the clearance with the straightedge and feeler gauge. If clearance is excessive, or increases, stop the procedure and have a dealership or machine shop determine if the cylinder head can be repaired.

e. Reclean the cylinder head.

10. Clean and inspect the cylinder head nuts and washers:

a. Check the stud threads for damage.

b. Check the washers for cracks and warpage. The washers must be flat.

11. Check the intake tube (A, **Figure 78**) for damage. If there is any dirt on the inside of the tube, check the carburetor and air box. Install the intake tube by aligning its notch with the tab on the side of the cylinder head (B, **Figure 78**). Tighten the hose clamp securely.

12. On CRF250X California models, clean the secondary air intake port (C, **Figure 76**) of all carbon deposits.

## VALVES

*CAUTION*
*The intake valves are titanium and protected with a thin oxide coating. Handle these valves carefully during all cleaning and inspection procedures.*

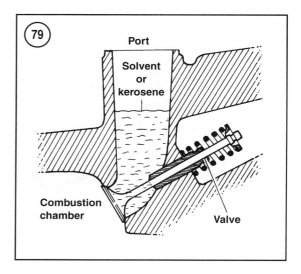

### Solvent Test

Perform a solvent test with the valves installed in the cylinder head. The test can reveal if valves are fully seating, as well as expose undetected cracks in the cylinder head.

1. Remove the cylinder head as described in this chapter.

2. Make sure the combustion chamber is dry and the valves are seated.

3. Pour solvent or kerosene into the intake or exhaust port as shown in **Figure 79**.

4. Inspect the combustion chamber for leakage around the valve.

5. Clean and dry the combustion chamber and repeat for the other valves.

6. If there is leakage, inspect for:

a. A worn or damaged valve face.

b. A worn or damaged valve seat.

c. A bent valve stem.

d. A crack in the combustion chamber.

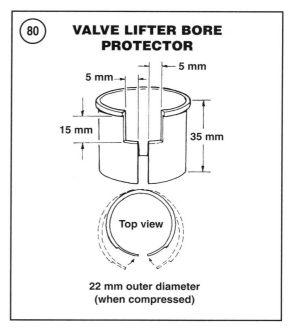

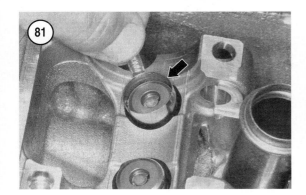

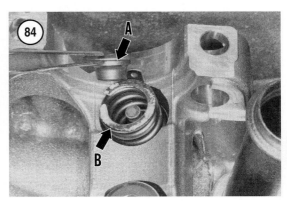

**Valve Service Tools**

The following tools are required to remove and install the valves in this section:

1. Valve spring compressor. The Motion Pro Valve Spring Compressor (part No. 08-0247) is shown in the following section.

2. Valve lifter bore protector. This tool is used to protect the valve lifter bore when removing and installing the intake valves. This tool can be made

from a 35 mm film container cut to the dimensions shown in **Figure 80**.

**Valve Removal**

1. Remove the cylinder head as described in this chapter.

2. Perform a solvent test on the intake and exhaust valves as described in this section.

3. When removing the intake valves, install the valve lifter bore protector into the bore (**Figure 81**).

4. Install a valve spring compressor over the valve assembly. Place one end of the tool squarely over the valve head. Place the other end of the tool squarely on the spring seat (**Figure 82**).

> *CAUTION*
> *Do not overtighten the valve spring. This can cause loss of valve spring tension.*

5. Tighten the compressor until the spring seat no longer holds the valve keepers in position. Remove the keepers (**Figure 83**) from the valve stem.

6. Slowly relieve the pressure on the valve spring and remove the valve compressor from the head.

7. Remove the upper spring seat (A, **Figure 84**) and spring (B).

8. Inspect the valve stem for sharp and flared metal around the groove (**Figure 85**). Deburr the valve stem before removing the valve from the head.

> *CAUTION*
> *Burrs on the valve stem can damage the valve guide.*

9. Remove the valve from the cylinder head.

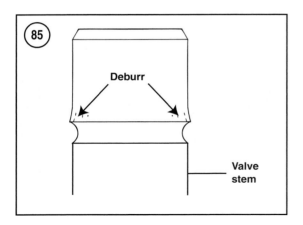

10. Remove and discard the valve stem seal (**Figure 86**).

> *CAUTION*
> *Do not damage the lifter bore when removing the intake valve stem seals.*

11. Remove the lower spring seat (**Figure 87**).

12. Store the valve parts (**Figure 88**, typical) in a divided container so they can be reinstalled in their original position.

> *CAUTION*
> *Do not intermix the valve components or poor valve seating may result.*

13. Repeat to remove the remaining valves.

14. Inspect the valve components and cylinder head valve seats as described in this section.

## Valve Installation

Perform the following procedure for each set of valve components.

1. Refer to your disassembly notes to identify the valve assemblies and install them in their original mounting position.

2. Clean the cylinder head in solvent and dry with compressed air.

3. Install the lower spring seat (**Figure 87**).

4. Coat the inside of a new valve stem seal with engine oil and push it squarely over the end of the valve guide until it snaps into the groove on the outside of the guide (**Figure 89**).

5. Coat the valve stem shaft with molybdenum oil solution.

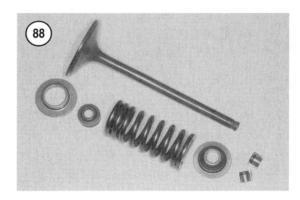

6. Insert the appropriate valve into the cylinder head. Hold the top of the valve stem seal, then rotate the valve to pass it through the seal. Check that the seal remains seated in the valve guide groove.

7. Install the valve spring with the closely spaced coil pitch end (**Figure 90**) facing down (toward cylinder head). See B, **Figure 84**.

8. Install the upper spring seat (A, **Figure 84**).

9. Before compressing the intake valve springs, install the valve lifter bore protector into the bore (**Figure 81**).

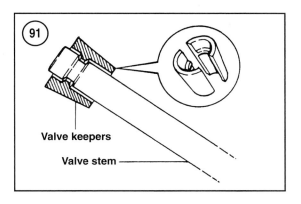

Valve keepers

Valve stem

10. Install a valve spring compressor over the valve assembly. Place the tool squarely over the valve head and spring seat (**Figure 82**).

11. Tighten the compressor enough to install the valve keepers.

*CAUTION*
*Do not overtighten and compress the valve spring. This can cause a loss of valve spring tension.*

12. Insert the keepers around the groove in the valve stem (**Figure 91**), then slowly relieve the

pressure on the valve spring and remove the compressor from the head.

13. Tap the end of the valve stem with a soft mallet to ensure that the keepers are locked in the valve stem groove. See **Figure 92** (intake) and **Figure 93** (exhaust).

14. After installing all the valves, perform a solvent test as described in this chapter.

15. Install the cylinder head as described in this chapter.

**Valve Inspection**

Refer to the troubleshooting chart in **Figure 94** when performing valve inspection procedures in this section. When measuring the valves and valve components, compare the actual measurements to the specifications in **Table 2**. Replace parts that are damaged or out of specification as described in this section. Maintain the alignment of the valve components as they must be reinstalled in their original position.

1. Soak the valves in solvent to soften the carbon deposits. Then clean and dry carefully. Do not damage the valve seating surface.

2. Inspect the valve face (**Figure 95**) for burning, pitting or other signs of wear. Unevenness of the valve

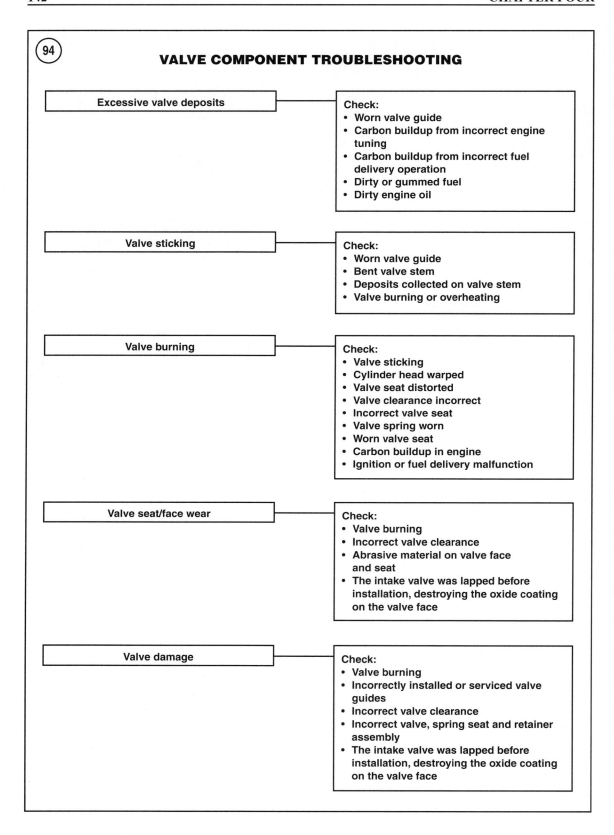

94

# VALVE COMPONENT TROUBLESHOOTING

**Excessive valve deposits**

Check:
- Worn valve guide
- Carbon buildup from incorrect engine tuning
- Carbon buildup from incorrect fuel delivery operation
- Dirty or gummed fuel
- Dirty engine oil

**Valve sticking**

Check:
- Worn valve guide
- Bent valve stem
- Deposits collected on valve stem
- Valve burning or overheating

**Valve burning**

Check:
- Valve sticking
- Cylinder head warped
- Valve seat distorted
- Valve clearance incorrect
- Incorrect valve seat
- Valve spring worn
- Worn valve seat
- Carbon buildup in engine
- Ignition or fuel delivery malfunction

**Valve seat/face wear**

Check:
- Valve burning
- Incorrect valve clearance
- Abrasive material on valve face and seat
- The intake valve was lapped before installation, destroying the oxide coating on the valve face

**Valve damage**

Check:
- Valve burning
- Incorrectly installed or serviced valve guides
- Incorrect valve clearance
- Incorrect valve, spring seat and retainer assembly
- The intake valve was lapped before installation, destroying the oxide coating on the valve face

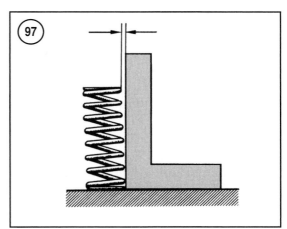

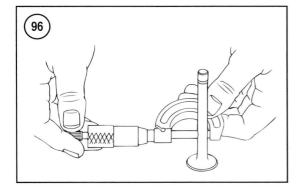

*all particles and dry with compressed air.*

5. Insert each valve into its respective valve guide and move it up and down by hand. The valve should move smoothly.

6. Measure each valve guide inside diameter with a small hole gauge and record the measurements. Note the following:

*NOTE*
*Because valve guides wear unevenly (oval shape), measure each guide at different positions. Use the largest diameter measurement when determining its size.*

    a. If a valve guide is out of specification, replace it as described in this section.

    b. If a valve guide is within specification, record the measurement so it can be used to determine the valve stem-to-guide clearance in Step 7.

7. Subtract the measurement made in Step 4 from the measurement made in Step 6 to determine the valve stem-to-guide clearance. Note the following:

    a. If the clearance is out of specification, determine if a new guide would bring the clearance within specification.

    b. If the clearance would be out of specification with a new guide, replace the valve and guide as a set.

8. Inspect the valve springs as follows:

    a. Inspect each spring for any cracks or other visual damage.

    b. Use a square and check the spring for distortion or tilt (**Figure 97**).

face is an indication that the valve is not serviceable. If the wear on an exhaust valve is too extensive to be corrected by hand-lapping the valve into its seat, replace the valve. The titanium intake valves cannot be lapped. Replace these valves if defective.

3. Inspect the valve stems for wear and roughness. Check the valve keeper grooves for damage.

4. Measure each valve stem outside diameter with a micrometer (**Figure 96**). Note the following:

    a. If a valve stem is out of specification, discard the valve.

    b. If a valve stem is within specification, record the measurement so it can be used to determine the valve stem-to-guide clearance in Step 7.

*NOTE*
*Honda recommends reaming the valve guides to remove any carbon buildup before checking and measuring the guides. For the home mechanic it is more practical to remove carbon and varnish from the valve guides with a stiff spiral wire brush. Then clean the valve guides with solvent to wash out*

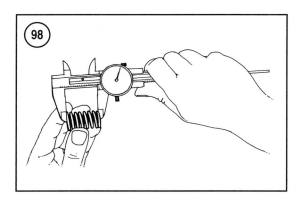

c. Measure the free length of each valve spring with a vernier caliper (**Figure 98**).

d. Replace defective springs.

9. Check the valve keepers. If they are in good condition, they may be reused; replace in pairs as necessary.

10. Inspect the spring seats for damage.

11. Inspect the valve seats as described under *Valve Seat Inspection* in this section.

12. Inspect the intake valve lifter bores (**Figure 99**) for scoring and other damage. Then measure the valve lifter bore inside diameter and compare to the service limit in **Table 2**. If the bore is damaged or if its diameter is too large, replace the cylinder head.

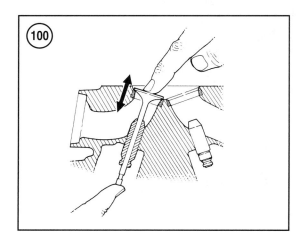

### Valve Seat Inspection

The most accurate method for checking the valve seal is to use a marking compound (machinist's dye), available from auto parts and tool stores. Marking compound is used to locate high or irregular spots when checking or making close fits. Follow the manufacturer's directions.

> *NOTE*
> *Because of the close operating tolerances within the valve assembly, the valve stem-to-guide clearance guide must be within specification; otherwise, the inspection results will be inaccurate.*

1. Remove, clean and inspect the valves as described in this chapter. The valve face must be in good condition for the inspection results to be accurate.

2. Clean the valve seat in the cylinder head and valve mating areas with contact cleaner.

3. Thoroughly clean all carbon deposits from the valve face with solvent and dry thoroughly.

4. Spread a thin layer of marking compound evenly on the valve face.

5. Slowly insert the valve into its guide and tap the valve against its seat several times (**Figure 100**) without spinning it.

6. Remove the valve and examine the impression left by the marking compound. If the impression (on the valve or in the cylinder head) is not even and continuous, and the valve seat width (**Figure 101**) is not within the specified tolerance listed in **Table 2**, the valve seat in the cylinder head must be reconditioned.

7. Closely examine the valve seat in the cylinder head (**Figure 102**). It should be smooth and even with a polished seating surface.

8. If the valve seat is not in good condition, recondition the valve seat as described in this section.

9. Repeat for the other valves.

### Valve Guide Replacement

Replace worn or damaged valve guides. Special tools and considerable experience are required to

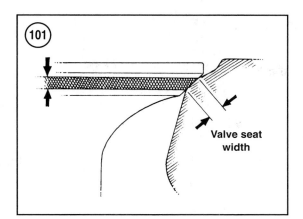

head. Chilling them slightly reduces the outside diameter, while the cylinder head is slightly larger due to heat expansion. This makes valve guide installation much easier. Remove the guides, one at a time, as needed.

*NOTE*
*Flangeless valve guides are used. Step 3 confirms that the original guides were installed to the correct valve guide projection height specified in **Table 2**. If the projection height measurement is incorrect, the valve guide bore(s) in the cylinder head may have widened, allowing the guide to move.*

properly replace the valve guides in the cylinder head. If these tools are unavailable, have a Honda dealership perform this procedure. Removing the cylinder head, then taking it to a dealership to have the valve guides replaced, can save a considerable amount of money. When replacing a valve guide, also replace the valve.

Read the entire procedure before attempting valve guide replacement. When using heat in the following steps, it will be necessary to work quickly and have the correct tools on hand.

3. Measure the valve guide projection height above the cylinder head surface with a vernier caliper (**Figure 103**) and record for each valve guide. Compare to the valve guide projection height specification in **Table 2**. If a valve guide is positioned incorrectly, check its bore for damage.

4. Place the cylinder head on a hot plate and heat to a temperature of 130-140° C (266-284° F). Do not exceed 150° C (300° F). Monitor the temperature with heat sticks, available at welding supply stores, or use an infrared thermometer.

*Tools*

See a Honda dealership for the correct valve guide and valve guide reamer.

*WARNING*
*Wear welding gloves or similar insulated gloves when handling the cylinder head. It will be very hot.*

*Procedure*

1. Remove all the valves and valve guide seals from the cylinder head.
2. Place the new valve guides in the freezer for approximately one hour before heating the cylinder

*CAUTION*
*Do not heat the cylinder head with a torch; never bring a flame into contact with the cylinder head or valve guide. The direct heat will destroy the*

*case hardening of the valve guide and
may warp the cylinder head.*

5. Remove the cylinder head from the hot plate and
place on wooden blocks with the combustion chamber facing *up*.

6. From the combustion chamber side of the head,
drive out the valve guide with the valve guide remover (**Figure 104**). Quickly repeat this step for
each guide to be replaced. Reheat the head as required. Discard the valve guides after removing
them.

*CAUTION
Because the valve guides are installed
with an interference fit, do not attempt
to remove them if the head is not hot
enough. Doing so may damage
(widen) the valve guide bore in the
cylinder head and require replacement of the head.*

7. Allow the cylinder head to cool.

8. Inspect and clean the valve guide bores. Check
for cracks or any scoring along the bore wall.

9. Reheat the cylinder head as described in Step 4,
then place onto wooden blocks with the valve
spring side facing *up*.

10. Remove one new valve guide, either intake or
exhaust, from the freezer.

11. Align the valve guide in the bore. Using the
valve guide driver tool and a hammer, drive in the
valve guide into the cylinder head until the valve
guide projection height (**Figure 103**) is within the
specification in **Table 2**.

12. Repeat to install the remaining valve guides.

13. Allow the cylinder head to cool to room temperature.

14. Ream each valve guide as follows:

  a. Place the cylinder head on wooden blocks
     with the combustion chamber facing *up*. The
     guides are reamed from this side.

  b. Coat the valve guide and valve guide reamer
     with cutting oil.

*CAUTION
Always rotate the reamer **clockwise**
through the entire length of the guide,
both when reaming the guide and
when removing the reamer. Rotating
the reamer counterclockwise will reverse cut and damage (enlarge) the
valve guide bore.*

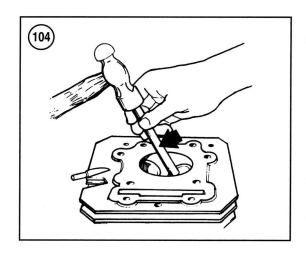

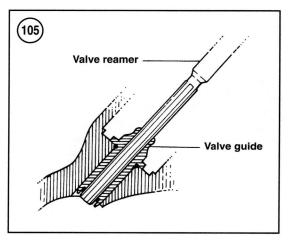

*CAUTION
Do not allow the reamer to tilt. Keep
the tool square to the hole and apply
even pressure and twisting motion
during the entire operation.*

  c. Rotate the reamer clockwise into the valve
     guide (**Figure 105**).

  d. Slowly rotate the reamer through the guide,
     while periodically adding cutting oil.

  e. As the end of the reamer passes through the
     valve guide, maintain the clockwise motion
     and work the reamer back out of the guide
     while continuing to add cutting oil.

  f. Clean the reamer of all chips and relubricate
     with cutting oil before starting on the next
     guide. Repeat for each guide as required.

15. Thoroughly clean the cylinder head and all
valve components in solvent, then with detergent

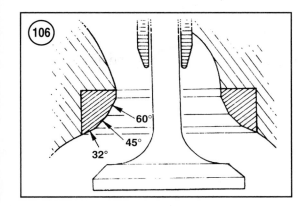

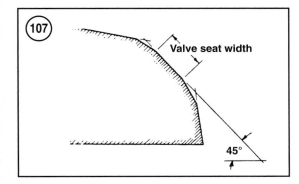

Valve seat width

45°

and hot water to remove all cutting residue. Rinse in cold water and dry with compressed air.
16. Measure the valve guide inside diameter with a small hole gauge. The measurement must be within the specification in **Table 2**.
17. Apply engine oil to the valve guides to prevent rust.
18. Lubricate a valve stem with engine oil and pass it through its valve guide, verifying that it moves without any roughness or binding. Repeat for each valve and guide.
19. After installing a new valve guide, the valve seat must be refaced with a 45° seat cutter as described under *Valve Seat Reconditioning* in this section.

**Valve Seat Reconditioning**

*Tools*

To cut the cylinder head valve seats the following tools are required:
1. Valve seat cutters (**Figure 106**). See a Honda dealership.
2. Vernier caliper.

3. Gear-marking compound.
4. Valve lapping tool.

*Procedure*

Before reconditioning the valve seats, inspect and measure them as described under *Valve Seat Inspection* in this section.
If the intake valve seats must be cut, discard the original intake valves and use new intake valves during this procedure.

> *NOTE*
> *Follow the manufacturer's instructions when using valve facing equipment.*

1. Carefully rotate and insert the solid pilot into the valve guide. Make sure the pilot is correctly seated.
2. Install the 45° cutter and cutter holder onto the solid pilot.

> *CAUTION*
> *Work slowly and make light cuts during reconditioning. Overcutting the valve seats will recede the valves into the cylinder head, reducing the valve adjustment range. If cutting is excessive, the ability to set the valve adjustment may be lost. This condition requires cylinder head replacement.*

3. Using the 45° cutter (**Figure 107**), de-scale and clean the valve seat with one or two turns.
4. If the seat is still pitted or burned, turn the 45° cutter additional turns until the surface is clean. Avoid removing too much material from the cylinder head.
5. Measure the valve seat with a vernier caliper (**Figure 101**). Record the measurement to use as a reference point when performing the following.

> *CAUTION*
> *The 32° cutter removes material quickly. Work carefully and check the progress often.*

6. Install the 32° cutter onto the solid pilot and lightly cut the seat to remove 1/4 of the existing valve seat (**Figure 108**).
7. Install the 60° cutter onto the solid pilot and lightly cut the seat to remove 1/4 of the existing valve seat (**Figure 109**).

8. Measure the valve seat with a vernier caliper (**Figure 101**). Then fit the 45° cutter onto the solid pilot and cut the valve seat to the specified width (**Figure 107**) in **Table 2**.

9. When the valve seat width is correct, check valve seating as follows:

    a. Clean the valve seat with contact cleaner.

    b. Spread a thin layer of marking compound evenly on the valve face.

    c. Slowly insert the valve into its guide.

    d. Support the valve with two fingers (**Figure 100**) and tap the valve up and down in the cylinder head several times. Do not rotate the valve or a false reading will result.

    e. Remove the valve and examine the impression left by the marking compound (**Figure 110**).

    f. Measure the valve seat width as shown in **Figure 101**. Refer to **Table 2** for specified valve seat width.

    g. The valve contact should be approximately in the center of the valve seat area (**Figure 110**).

10. If the contact area is too high on the valve, or if it is too wide, use the 32° cutter and remove a portion of the top area of the valve seat material to lower and narrow the contact area on the valve (**Figure 110**).

11. If the contact area is too low on the valve, or too wide, use the 60° cutter and remove a portion of the lower area of the valve seat material to raise and narrow the contact area on the valve (**Figure 110**).

12. After obtaining the desired valve seat position and width, use the 45° cutter to lightly clean off any burrs that may have been caused by previous cuts.

13A. Exhaust valves—When the contact area is correct, lap the valve as described in this chapter.

13B. Intake valves—The titanium intake valves have a thin oxide coating on their face and must not be lapped. When new intake valve seats are cut in the cylinder head, install new intake valves without lapping them.

14. Repeat Steps 1-13A for all remaining valve seats.

15. Thoroughly clean the cylinder head and all valve components in solvent, then with detergent and hot water. Rinse in cold water and dry with compressed air. Apply a light coat of clean engine oil to all non-aluminum surfaces to prevent rust.

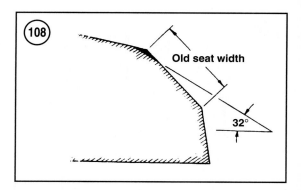

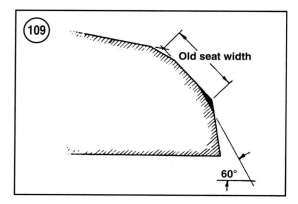

### Valve Lapping

#### *Intake valves*

Do not lap the intake valves. These valves are titanium and have a thin oxide coating (approximately 1.0 micron thick) on their face. Lapping removes the oxide coating and causes the valve face to wear faster. This causes short valve and seat life and a significant power loss. When new intake valve seats are cut in the cylinder head, install new intake valves without lapping them.

#### *Exhaust valves*

Valve lapping can restore the valve seat without machining if the amount of wear or distortion is not too great.

Perform this procedure after determining that the valve seat width and outside diameter are within specifications. A valve lapping tool and compound are required.

1. Smear a light coating of fine grade valve lapping compound on the valve face seating surface.

2. Insert the valve into the head.

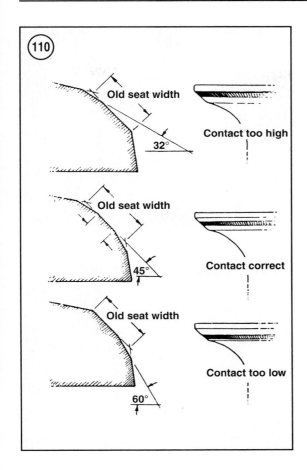

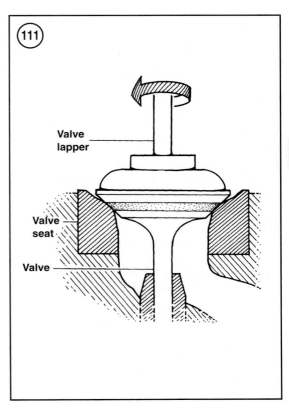

7. Install the valve assemblies as described in this chapter.

3. Wet the suction cup of the lapping stick and stick it onto the head of the valve. Spin the tool in both directions, while pressing it against the valve seat and lap the valve to the seat. Every 5 to 10 seconds, lift and rotate the valve 180° in the valve seat. Continue until the gasket surfaces on the valve and seat are smooth and equal in size. See **Figure 111**.

8. After completing the lapping and reinstalling the valves in the head, perform the *Solvent Test* described under *Valves* in this chapter. There should be no leakage past the seat. If leakage occurs, the combustion chamber will appear wet. If fluid leaks past any of the exhaust valve seats, disassemble that valve assembly and repeat the lapping procedure until there is no leakage. If fluid leaks past an intake valve seat, remove the valve and inspect the valve face and seat.

4. Closely examine the valve seat in the cylinder head (**Figure 101**). It should be smooth and even with a smooth, polished seating ring.

5. Repeat Steps 1-4 for the other exhaust valve.

6. Thoroughly clean the cylinder head and all valve components in solvent, then with detergent and hot water. Rinse in cold water and dry with compressed air. Apply a light coat of clean engine oil to all non-aluminum surfaces to prevent rust.

9. If the cylinder head and valve components are cleaned in detergent and hot water, apply a light coat of engine oil to all bare metal surfaces to prevent rust formation.

> *CAUTION*
> *Any compound left on the valves or in the cylinder head will cause engine wear.*

## CYLINDER

The cylinder and piston can be removed with the engine installed in the frame.

**Removal**

> *CAUTION*
> *Before removing the top end, clean the area above the cylinder so dirt and other abrasive material cannot fall into the engine.*

1. Remove the cylinder head as described in this chapter.
2. Remove the front chain guide (A, **Figure 112**).
3. Remove the bolts, cam chain tensioner housing (B, **Figure 112**) and gasket.
4. Remove the 6 mm cylinder mounting bolt (C, **Figure 112**).
5. Loosen the cylinder by tapping around the base.
6. Remove the cylinder from the crankcase, routing the cam chain through the chain tunnel. Do not dislodge and drop the three dowel pins into the crankcase.
7. Remove the base gasket (A, **Figure 113**).
8. Remove the coolant passage dowel pin (B, **Figure 113**) and the two cylinder dowel pins (C).
9. Slide pieces of cut hose down the cylinder studs to protect the piston rings from damage.
10. Cover the cam chain tunnel and piston to prevent small parts from falling into the engine.
11. Check for damaged or broken piston rings. Check the piston as described under *Piston Inspection* in this chapter.
12. Clean and inspect the cylinder as described in this section.

**Installation**

1. On CRF250X models, if removed, install the starter as described in Chapter Ten. The starter cannot be installed with the cylinder mounted on the engine.
2. Clean the cylinder and crankcase gasket surfaces. Note the following:
    a. If the crankcase halves were reassembled, remove all protruding gasket material from the crankcase joint surfaces.
    b. Do not drop gasket material into the coolant passage (B, **Figure 113**).
    c. Do not drop gasket material into the engine oil passage (A, **Figure 114**). Doing so may plug the crankcase oil jet used on 2004 CRF250R and all CRF250X models (**Figure 115**).

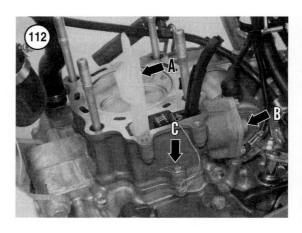

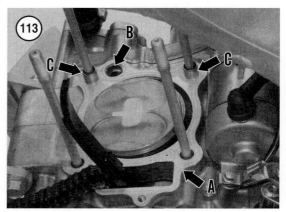

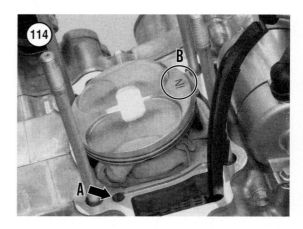

    d. Make sure the cylinder block oil passage is clear. This passage provides oil to the engine top end.
3. If used, remove the hoses from the cylinder studs.
4. Install the coolant passage dowel pin (B, **Figure 113**) and the two cylinder dowel pins (C).

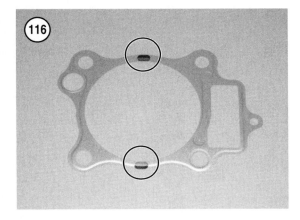

*NOTE*
*The base gasket is equipped with two*
*sealer pads (**Figure 116**) to help seal*
*the crankcase mating areas.*

5. Install a new base gasket (A, **Figure 113**) onto the crankcase. Check that the gasket seats flush around the dowel pins.

6. Lubricate the following components with engine oil.
    a. Piston and rings.
    b. Piston pin and small end of connecting rod.
    c. Cylinder bore.

7. Rest the piston on a wooden holding fixture. On CRF250X models, because of the starter location behind the cylinder, support the piston with separate wooden blocks as shown in A, **Figure 117**.

8. Make sure the piston circlips (B, **Figure 117**) are properly installed.

9. Stagger the piston ring gaps on the piston as shown under *Piston Installation* in this chapter.

10. Lower the cylinder over the piston, routing the cam chain and rear cam chain guide (if installed) through the chain tunnel. Compress each ring so it can enter the cylinder. When the bottom ring is in the cylinder, remove the holding fixture or wooden blocks and lower the cylinder onto the crankcase. Secure the cam chain so it cannot fall into the engine.

11. Install the 6 mm cylinder mounting bolt (C, **Figure 112**) but do not tighten it. This bolt will be tightened during cylinder head installation.

12. Pull up on the cam chain so it cannot bind against the crankshaft sprocket and turn the engine over slowly by operating the kick pedal by hand. If there is any excessive noise or roughness, remove the cylinder and check for a broken piston ring.

13. Install the cam chain tensioner (B, **Figure 112**) and a new gasket. Tighten the mounting bolts to 12 N•m (106 in.-lb.).

14. Install the front chain guide (A, **Figure 112**).

15. Install the cylinder head as described in this chapter.

**Inspection**

1. Remove all gasket residue from the cylinder and crankcase surfaces. Use solvent and a soft scraper to remove residue. Do not use sharp-edge tools that can scratch surfaces. If necessary, soak the surfaces with a solvent-soaked rag to soften deposits.

2. Wash the cylinder in solvent and dry with compressed air. Clean all deposits from the water jacket.

3. Inspect the cylinder bore (**Figure 118**) for obvious scoring or gouges. If damage is evident, replace or resleeve the cylinder.

4. Measure and check the cylinder for wear, taper and out-of-round. Measure the inside diameter of

the cylinder with a bore gauge or inside micrometer (**Figure 119**) as follows:

   a. Measure the cylinder at three points along the bore axis (**Figure 120**). At each point, measure in line (X measurement) with the piston pin, and 90° to the pin (Y measurement). Record and identify the six measurements.

   b. Cylinder wear—Use the largest measurement recorded (X or Y) and compare it to the specifications and service limit in **Table 3**. If the cylinder bore is not within the service limit, replace or resleeve the cylinder.

   c. Cylinder out-of-round—Determine the largest Y measurement made in substep a. Determine the smallest X measurement made in substep a. Determine the difference between the two measurements. Compare the result to the service limit in **Table 3**. If the cylinder bore is not within the service limit, replace or resleeve the cylinder.

> *NOTE*
> *An out-of-round cylinder bore will cause ring scuffing, thus accelerating piston ring and bore wear.*

   d. Cylinder taper—Determine the largest X or Y measurement made at the top of the cylinder. Determine the largest X or Y measurement made at the bottom of the cylinder. Determine the difference between the two measurements. Compare the result to the service limit in **Table 3**. If the cylinder bore is not within the service limit, replace or resleeve the cylinder.

> *NOTE*
> *If the cylinder bore is out of specification, either replace or resleeve the cylinder. When replacing the cylinder, install new piston and rings as a set. If the cylinder is resleeved, the machine shop will fit a new piston to the new cylinder.*

> *NOTE*
> *If the cylinder is within all service limits, and the current piston and rings are reusable, do not deglaze or hone the cylinder bore. This procedure may damage the hardened bore. If the cylinder has been resleeved, the cast iron bore can be deglazed. In all instances,*

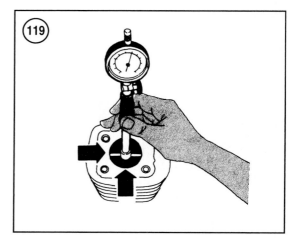

*do not remove the carbon ridge at the top of the cylinder bore. Removal of the buildup will promote oil consumption.*

5. Use a straightedge and feeler gauge set (**Figure 121**) and check the top of the cylinder for warp. Replace the cylinder if the warp exceeds the service limit in **Table 3**.

6. Wash the cylinder in hot soapy water and rinse with clear water. Then check the cleanliness by passing a clean, white cloth over the bore. No residue should be evident. When the cylinder is thoroughly clean and dry, lightly coat the cylinder bore with oil and wrap it in plastic until reassembly.

> *CAUTION*
> *The cylinder must be washed in hot soapy water. Solvents do not remove the fine grit left in the cylinder. This*

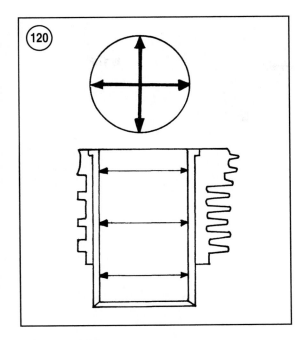

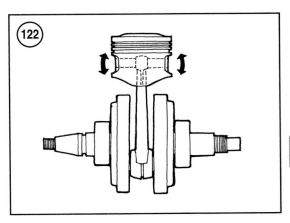

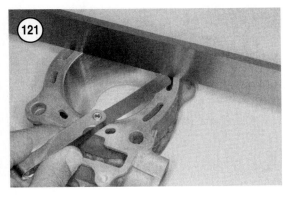

grit will cause premature wear of the rings and cylinder.

## PISTON AND PISTON RINGS

The piston is made of aluminum alloy and fitted with two rings. The piston is attached to the connecting rod with a chrome-plated, steel piston pin. The pin is a precision fit in the piston and rod, and held in place with plain circlips.

As each component of the piston assembly is cleaned and measured, record and identify all measurements. Refer to the measurements and **Table 3** when calculating clearances and checking wear limits.

**Piston Removal**

*CAUTION*
*When it is necessary to rotate the crankshaft, pull up the cam chain so it cannot bind against the crankshaft sprocket. Guide and protect the piston so it does not get damaged when retracted into the crankcase.*

1. Remove the cylinder as described in this chapter.

2. Before removing the piston, hold the rod and try to rock the piston from side to side (**Figure 122**). A rocking (not sliding) motion indicates wear on either the piston pin, pin bore, rod bushing or a combination of all three parts. Careful inspection is required to determine which parts require replacement.

3. Stuff shop rags around the connecting rod and in the cam chain tunnel to prevent debris and small parts from falling into the crankcase.

4. Slide a rubber hose over the front cylinder studs to protect the piston and rings.

5. Find the IN piston identification mark on the piston crown (B, **Figure 114**). If there is no mark, scribe an alignment mark on top of the piston.

6. Remove the circlips from the piston pin bore (**Figure 123**). Discard the circlips.

7. Push the piston pin out of the piston by hand (**Figure 124**). If the pin is tight, use a pin puller (Motion Pro part No. 08-0068) or a homemade removal tool (**Figure 125**).

*CAUTION*
*Do not attempt to drive the pin out with a hammer and drift. The piston*

*and connecting rod assembly may be damaged.*

8. Lift the piston off the connecting rod.

9. Inspect the piston, piston rings and piston pin as described in this section.

### Piston Installation

1. Install the piston rings onto the piston as described in this chapter.

2. Make sure all parts are clean and ready to install. Install new piston circlips (**Figure 126**).

> *CAUTION*
> *Never install used circlips, although they appear reusable, as they fatigue and distort during removal. Severe engine damage will occur if a circlip pops out of its groove during engine operation.*

3. Install a new circlip into one side of the piston. Rotate the circlip in the groove until the end gap is facing down.

4. Lubricate the following components with molybdenum disulfide oil.

    a. Piston pin.
    b. Piston pin bores.
    c. Connecting rod bore.

5. Start the piston pin into the open piston pin bore (**Figure 127**). Place the piston over the connecting rod so the IN mark (B, **Figure 114**) faces the intake side of the engine. If the IN mark is unreadable, use your identification mark made before piston removal.

> *CAUTION*
> *The piston must be installed correctly to accommodate piston pin offset and prevent the valves from striking the piston. Failure to install the piston correctly can lead to severe engine damage.*

6. Align the piston with the rod and slide the pin through the piston and rod (**Figure 124**).

7. Install a wooden holding fixture under the piston to steady the piston when installing the circlip.

8. Install the second circlip into the piston groove (**Figure 123**). Rotate the circlip in the groove until the end gap is facing down.

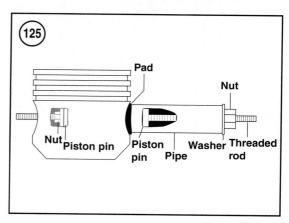

9. Stagger the ring end gaps as shown in **Figure 128**.

10. Install the cylinder as described in this chapter.

### Piston Inspection

The recommended piston replacement interval is every six races or after 15 hours of engine operation.

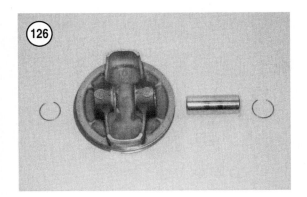

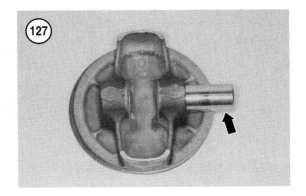

Inspect the used piston at this time interval to detect any possible engine or tuning problems that could damage the new piston.

1. Remove the piston rings as described in this section.

2. Slide a finger along the piston's intake skirt. The surface should feel smooth. If the surface feels coarse or grainy, dirt may be passing through the air filter. Check for a dirty or damaged air filter or leaking air box.

3. Check the piston crown (**Figure 129**) for wear or damage. If the piston crown is pitted, overheating is likely occurring. This can be caused by a lean fuel mixture and/or preignition. If damage is evident, perform the troubleshooting procedures as described in Chapter Two. Recheck the crown after cleaning it.

*CAUTION*
*If the piston crown was damaged by pre-ignition or other causes, inspect the connecting rod for damage. Heat passing through the piston may have weakened the rod. If there is any doubt, replace the crankshaft (this chapter).*

*CAUTION*
*Clean the piston carefully as tools can scratch or chip the valve pockets and damage the piston. This will cause hot spots on the piston when the engine is running.*

4. Soak the piston in solvent to soften the carbon buildup. Then clean the piston crown using a soft scraper. Do not use tools that can damage the surface. Clean the oil holes in the oil ring groove and at

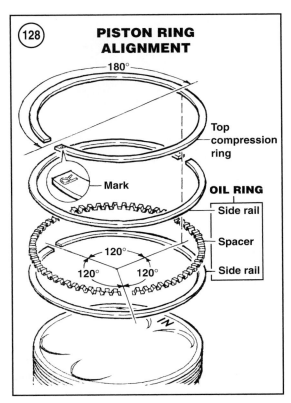

**PISTON RING ALIGNMENT**

180°

Top compression ring

Mark

OIL RING
Side rail
Spacer
Side rail

120°
120° 120°

IN

the top of the piston skirt, directly below the oil ring groove. Do not enlarge the holes.

5. Clean the piston pin bore, ring grooves and piston skirt. Clean the ring grooves with a soft brush, or use a broken piston ring (same shape and thickness as original ring [**Figure 130**]) to remove carbon and oil residue. Polish any mild galling or discoloration off the piston skirt with fine emery cloth and oil.

> *CAUTION*
> *Do not wire brush piston skirts or ring lands. The wire brush removes aluminum and increases piston clearance. It also rounds the corners of the ring lands, which causes decreased support for the piston rings.*

6. Inspect the ring grooves for dents, nicks, cracks or other damage. The grooves should be square and uniform for the circumference of the piston. Particularly inspect the top compression ring groove. It is lubricated the least and is nearest the combustion chamber and has higher operating temperatures. If the oil ring appears worn, or if the oil ring was difficult to remove, the piston has likely overheated and distorted. Replace the piston if any type of damage is detected.

7. Inspect the piston skirt (**Figure 131**). If the skirt shows signs of severe galling or partial seizure (bits of metal embedded in the skirt), replace the piston.

8. Inspect the interior of the piston. Check the crown, skirt, piston pin bores and bosses for cracks or other damage. Check the circlip grooves for cleanliness and damage. Replace the piston if necessary.

9. Measure the piston pin bore diameter (A, **Figure 132**) with a small hole gauge and micrometer. Measure each bore horizontally and vertically. Record the measurements. Compare the largest measurement to the specifications in **Table 3**. Record this measurement to determine the piston pin bore-to-piston pin clearance described in *Piston Pin and Connecting Rod Inspection* in this section.

10. Inspect the piston ring-to-ring groove clearance as described in *Piston Ring Inspection and Removal* in this section. This check helps locate a dented or damaged ring groove.

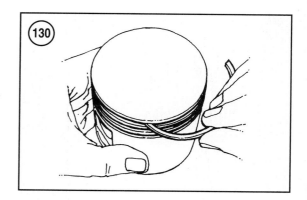

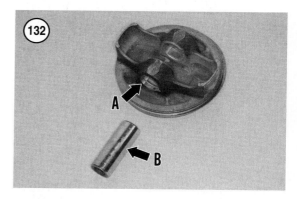

### Piston-to-Cylinder Clearance Check

Calculate the clearance between the piston and cylinder as follows:

1. Clean and dry the piston and cylinder before measuring.

2. Determine the cylinder inside diameter as described under *Cylinder Inspection* in this chapter. If the measurement exceeds the specification in **Table 3**, either install a new cylinder or resleeve the cylinder. If the cylinder bore is within specification, continue with Step 3.

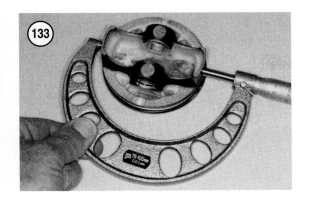

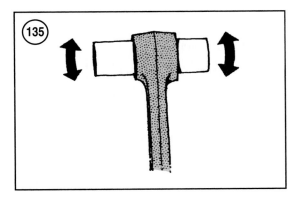

3. Measure the piston skirt outside diameter at a position 90° to the direction of the piston pin (**Figure 133**), while measuring up from the bottom edge of the piston skirt at the dimension specified in **Table 3**. Record the measurement. If the piston diameter is within specification, continue with Step 4. If the piston diameter is too small, install a new piston and ring set and perform Step 4.

4. Determine the clearance by subtracting the piston measurement from the largest cylinder measurement. If the clearance is too large, either replace or

resleeve the cylinder. When replacing the cylinder, install a new piston and ring set. If the cylinder is resleeved, the machine shop will fit a new piston to the new cylinder.

**Piston Pin and Connecting Rod Inspection**

1. Clean and dry the piston pin.
2. Inspect the piston pin (B, **Figure 132**) for chrome flaking, wear or discoloration from overheating.
3. Inspect the piston pin bore in the connecting rod (**Figure 134**). Check for scoring, uneven wear, and discoloration from overheating or excessive wear.
4. Lubricate the piston pin and slide it into the connecting rod. The pin is a slip fit and should slide through the rod with no resistance. Slowly pivot the pin and check for radial play (**Figure 135**). If play is detectable, one or both of the parts are worn. Measure the parts in the following steps to determine their condition and operating clearance.
5. Determine the connecting rod-to-piston pin clearance as follows:
   a. Measure the connecting rod small end inside diameter (**Figure 134**) and compare against the specifications in **Table 3**. If the inside diameter is too large, replace the crankshaft (this chapter).
   b. Measure the piston pin at its middle point (B, **Figure 132**). Replace the piston pin if the measurement exceeds the service limit in **Table 3**.
   c. If both parts are within specification, subtract the piston pin measurement from the connecting rod measurement. If the measurement exceeds the service limit and the connecting rod inside diameter is within specification, replace the piston pin.

*CAUTION*
*If the piston crown was damaged by pre-ignition or other causes, heat passing through the piston may have weakened the rod. If there is any doubt, replace the crankshaft (this chapter).*

6. Determine the piston pin bore-to-piston pin clearance as follows:
   a. Measure the piston pin at both ends (B, **Figure 132**). Record the measurements. Replace

the pin if any measurement exceeds the service limit listed in **Table 3**.

b. Subtract the smallest piston pin measurement from the piston pin bore measurement. This measurement is described under *Piston Inspection* in this section. Replace the piston and pin if they exceed the service limit in **Table 3**.

### Piston Ring Inspection and Removal

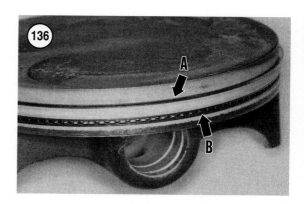

The recommended replacement interval for the piston rings is every six races or after 15 hours of engine operation. During these time intervals, the operational life of the piston rings depends greatly on periodic oil and filter changes and air filter service. Poor service and dirty oil will shorten ring life and reduce engine performance.

The ring assembly consists of a single compression ring (A, **Figure 136**) and an oil control ring assembly (B). The oil ring assembly consists of two side rails and a spacer. See **Figure 128**.

1. Check the piston ring sealing surfaces (**Figure 136**) for abrasive wear and scuffing. Vertical scratches on the rings indicates that dirt is passing through the air filter. Scuffing is usually caused by excessive engine temperatures or an out-of-round cylinder bore.

2. Check the compression piston ring-to-ring groove clearance as follows:

a. Clean the ring and groove (A, **Figure 136**) so accurate measurements can be made with a flat feeler gauge.

b. Press the top ring into the groove, so the ring is nearly flush with the piston.

c. Insert a flat feeler gauge between the ring and groove (**Figure 137**). Record the measurement. Repeat this step at other points around the piston. Replace the ring if any measurement exceeds the service limit in **Table 3**. If excessive clearance remains after installing a new ring, replace the piston.

3. Spread the compression ring by hand (**Figure 138**) and remove it from the piston. Mark the topside of the ring if the original R mark is not visible. If the ring is to be reused, it must be installed facing in its original direction.

*CAUTION*
*Piston ring edges are sharp. Be careful when handling.*

*CAUTION*
*Piston rings are brittle. Do not overspread rings when removing.*

4. Remove the oil ring assembly by first removing the topside rail, followed by the bottom side rail. Remove the spacer last (**Figure 128**). Identify the side rails so they can be installed facing in their original position.

5. Clean and inspect the piston as described in *Piston Inspection* in this section.

6. Measure the piston ring end gap as follows:

*NOTE*
*When measuring the oil control ring, only measure the side rails. Do not measure the spacer.*

a. Inspect the ring ends for any carbon buildup and remove with a fine-cut file. Do not remove metal from the ring ends.

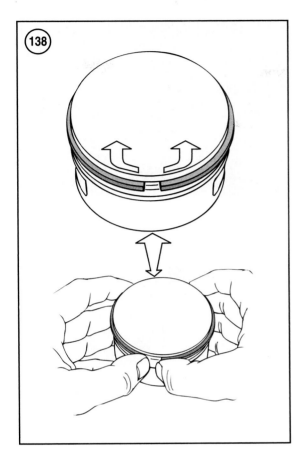

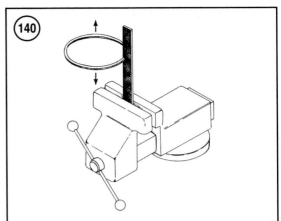

Replace the rings as a set if any gap measurement exceeds the service limit in **Table 3**.

d. If new rings are installed, gap the new rings after the cylinder has been serviced. If the new ring gap is too small, carefully widen the gap using a fine-cut file as shown in **Figure 140**. Work slow and measure often.

7. Roll the compression ring around its piston groove and check for carbon and binding from a damaged ring groove. Remove carbon with a broken piston ring as described under *Piston Inspection* in this section. Repair minor damage with a fine-cut file. If damage is excessive, replace the piston and rings as a set.

**Piston Ring Installation**

1. Check that the piston and rings are clean and dry.

*CAUTION*
*Install the rings by hand (**Figure 138**). Piston rings are brittle. Spread them only enough to clear the piston.*

*NOTE*
*If reusing the piston rings, refer to your identification marks to install them facing in their original direction.*

2. Install the oil control ring assembly (**Figure 128**) as follows:

a. New oil control rings are not marked. The side rails and spacer can be installed with either side facing up.

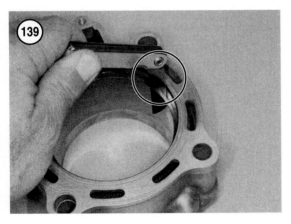

b. Place the ring into the middle of the cylinder and square it with the piston. The accuracy of this measurement depends on how square the ring is in the cylinder.

c. Measure the ring gap with a flat feeler gauge (**Figure 139**). Record the measurement and compare to the specified gap in **Table 3**.

b. Install the oil control ring assembly into the bottom ring groove. Install the spacer first, then the lower and upper side rail. Make sure the ends of the spacer butt together. They must not overlap.

c. Squeeze the ring assembly by hand. Make sure the assembly compresses properly into the ring groove. If not, the spacer ends are overlapping.

3. Install the compression ring into the top ring groove with its manufacturer's R mark facing up.

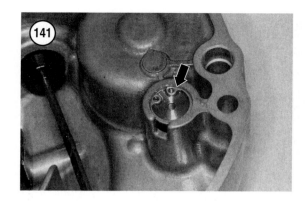

## COUNTERSHAFT SEAL REPLACEMENT

Refer to *Countershaft Seal Replacement* in Chapter Five.

## SHIFT SHAFT SEAL REPLACEMENT

Refer to *Shift Shaft Seal Replacement* in Chapter Five.

## LUBRICATION SYSTEM

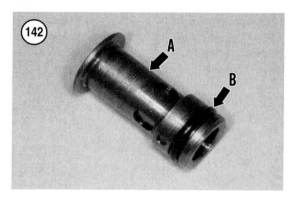

The oil relief valve, oil pump drive gear and oil strainer can be serviced with the engine mounted in the frame. The oil pump and one-way valve are installed inside the engine. Refer to *Crankcase* in this chapter to service these components.

### Oil Relief Valve
### Removal/Inspection/Installation

The oil relief valve is mounted inside the left crankcase cover.

1. Remove the left crankcase cover (Chapter Ten).

2. Remove the snap ring (**Figure 141**) and oil relief valve from the left crankcase cover.

3. Before cleaning the oil relief valve (A, **Figure 142**), check it for clogging and other debris. Make sure the passage holes in the valve are clear.

4. Discard the O-ring (B, **Figure 142**) and clean the valve in solvent. Dry thoroughly.

5. Replace the oil relief valve if damaged. Do not disassemble the valve as replacements parts are not available.

6. Clean the left crankcase cover oil passages as described under *Left Crankcase Cover* in Chapter Ten.

7. Lubricate a new O-ring and install it into the valve groove.

8. Lubricate the valve with engine oil and install it into the left crankcase cover, O-ring end first. Install the snap ring with its flat side facing out.

9. Install the left crankcase cover (Chapter Ten).

10. Install a new oil filter and refill the engine with oil (Chapter Three).

### Oil Strainer
### Removal/Cleaning/Installation

The oil strainer is mounted behind the left crankcase cover.

1. Remove the left crankcase cover (Chapter Ten).

2. Remove the oil strainer (**Figure 143**).

3. Check the strainer for contamination, tearing and damage, then clean in solvent and blow dry. Replace the screen if damaged.

4. Installation is the reverse of these steps.

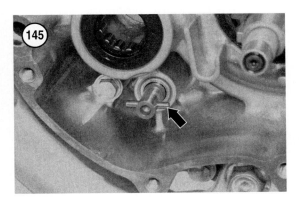

**Oil Pump Drive Gear
Removal/Inspection/Installation**

The oil pump drive gear is mounted behind the left crankcase cover.

1. Remove the flywheel (Chapter Ten).

2. Remove the balancer shaft (Chapter Six).

3. Turn the oil pump drive gear (**Figure 144**) by hand. The shaft should turn freely. If there is any roughness, disassemble the crankcase and inspect the oil pump assembly.

4. Remove the oil pump drive gear (**Figure 144**) and pin (**Figure 145**) from the oil pump shaft.

5. Clean and dry the oil pump drive gear and pin.

6. Replace the gear and pin if damaged. If the pin is damaged, check the mating hole in the oil pump shaft for damage.

7. Install the pin (**Figure 145**) through the hole in the oil pump shaft.

8. Install the oil pump drive gear by aligning the cutout in the backside of the gear with the pin.

9. Turn the gear (**Figure 144**) to make sure the shaft and oil pump rotors turn smoothly.

10. Reverse Step 1 and Step 2 to complete installation.

**CRANKCASE**

The following procedures detail the disassembly and reassembly of the crankcase. When the two halves of the crankcase are disassembled or split, the oil pump, one-way valve, crankshaft and transmission assemblies can be removed.

The crankcase halves are made of cast aluminum alloy. Do not hammer or excessively pry on the crankcase. The halves will fracture or break. The halves are aligned and sealed at the joint by dowels and a gasket.

The crankshaft consists of two full-circle flywheels pressed onto the crankpin. The assembly is supported at each end by a ball bearing. Crankshaft overhaul requires the use of a hydraulic press and a number of special measuring tools.

The oil pump and one-way valve are mounted in the left crankcase.

**Special Tools**

No special tools are required to disassemble and reassemble the crankcase halves, or to remove and install the crankshaft. However, bearing removal and installation tools are required to replace the crankcase bearings.

**Disassembly**

This procedure describes disassembly of the crankcase halves and removal of the crankshaft, internal shift mechanism, transmission, oil pump and one-way valve.

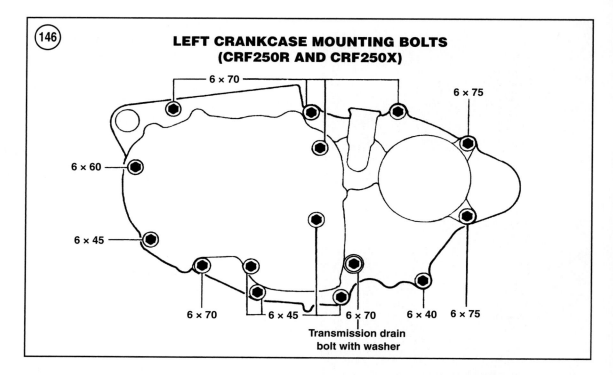

(146)
**LEFT CRANKCASE MOUNTING BOLTS
(CRF250R AND CRF250X)**

6 × 70

6 × 75

6 × 60

6 × 45

6 × 70　　　6 × 45　　　6 × 70　　6 × 40　　6 × 75

**Transmission drain
bolt with washer**

Identify parts or make written notes as required to help with reassembly. Note any damaged or worn parts.

*NOTE*
*References to the **right** and **left** side of the engine refer to the engine as it sits in the frame, not as it sits on the workbench.*

1. Remove all exterior engine assemblies as follows:
   a. Cylinder head, cam chain and guides, cylinder, and piston (this chapter).
   b. Starter (CRF250X [Chapter Ten]).
   c. Flywheel (Chapter Ten).
   d. Oil pump drive gear and oil strainer (this chapter).
   e. Drive sprocket (Chapter Twelve).
   f. Clutch, kickstarter, external shift linkage (Chapter Six).
   g. Starter clutch (CRF250X [Chapter Six]).
   h. Primary drive gear and balancer assembly (Chapter Six).
2. Place the engine on wooden blocks with the left side facing up.

*NOTE*
*To ensure that the crankcase bolts are correctly located during assembly, make an outline of the left crankcase on a piece of cardboard. Punch holes in the cardboard at the same locations as the bolts. After removing each bolt from the crankcase, place the bolt in its respective hole in the template (**Figure 146**).*

3. Remove the transmission drain bolt and washer (**Figure 146**).

4. Loosen each crankcase 6 mm bolt (**Figure 146**) 1/4 turn, working in a crossing pattern. Loosen the bolts in two or thee steps until they can be removed by hand.

5. Grasp both crankcase halves (so they cannot separate) and turn the engine over so the right side faces up.

6. Lightly tap the right crankcase half and remove it. All the internal crankcase components will remain in the left case half. If necessary, alternately tap on the ends of the transmission shafts to prevent them from binding the right crankcase half. See **Figure 147**.

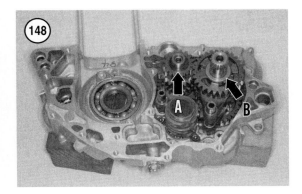

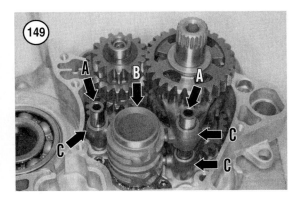

*CAUTION*
*Do not hammer or pry on areas of the crankcase that are not reinforced. Do not pry on gasket surfaces.*

7. Immediately check for the outer washer installed on the countershaft (A, **Figure 147**). If the washer is not on the countershaft, remove it from the right case half and reinstall it.

8. Remove the crankshaft (B, **Figure 147**).

9. Remove the one-way valve (C, **Figure 147**) and the oil pump rotors and shaft (D).

10. Reinstall the right crankcase half on the left case half. Then grasp both crankcase halves (so they cannot separate) and turn the engine over so the left side faces up. Remove the left case half.

11. Immediately check for the outer mainshaft (A, **Figure 148**) and countershaft (B) washers. If not installed on their respective shafts, remove them from the left case half and reinstall them.

12. Remove the two dowel pins and crankcase gasket.

13. Remove the transmission assembly (**Figure 149**) from the right case half as follows:

*NOTE*
*If the engine was experiencing shifting problems, examine the transmission assembly before removing it. Look for wear or damaged parts. Spin the countershaft and turn the shift drum by hand to shift the transmission. Check the movement and operation of each shift fork and sliding gear. Look for hard shifting and incomplete gear dog engagement. Check also for seized gears and bushings.*

a. Remove the two shift fork shafts (A, **Figure 149**). Note any binding or roughness when removing the shafts.

b. Move the shift forks away from the shift drum, then remove the shift drum (B, **Figure 149**).

c. Remove the shift forks (C, **Figure 149**).

*NOTE*
*The transmission shafts (**Figure 150**) are removed at the same time.*

d. Position the right crankcase so that the transmission shafts are parallel with the workbench. Then tap the shafts and remove them (**Figure 151**).

e. Inspect and service the transmission assembly as described in Chapter Eight.

14. Inspect the crankshaft assembly as described in this chapter.

15. Inspect the oil pump as described in this chapter.

16. Clean and inspect the cases and bearings as described in this chapter.

**Assembly**

1. Before assembly:

a. Make sure a new center case gasket is on hand. Do not reuse the original gasket.

b. Lubricate the seal lips with grease.

c. Confirm that the transmission shafts are properly assembled (Chapter Eight). Then apply grease to the outer washers on each transmission shaft to help hold them in place.

d. Lubricate the crankshaft, bearings and transmission sliding surfaces with engine oil.

2. Support the right crankcase assembly on wooden blocks (**Figure 152**).

3. Install the transmission and internal shift mechanism as follows:

a. Mesh the transmission shafts (**Figure 151**) and install them into the right crankcase at the same time. See **Figure 150**.

b. Identify the shift forks by the letter cast on each fork. The L (left) and R (right) shift forks engage with the countershaft, while the C (center) shift fork engages with the mainshaft. See **Figure 153** (CRF250R) or **Figure 154** (CRF250X).

c. Install the R shift fork into the countershaft fifth gear groove (R, **Figure 155**). On CRF250R, the R mark should face up. On CRF250X, the R mark should face down.

d. Install the L shift fork into the countershaft fourth gear groove (L, **Figure 155**). On CRF250R, the L mark should face up. On CRF250 X, the L mark should face down.

e. Install the C shift fork into the mainshaft third gear groove (C, **Figure 155**). The C mark should face down on all models.

f. Install the shift drum (A, **Figure 156**) into the right case bearing.

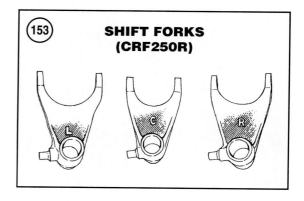

**SHIFT FORKS (CRF250R)**

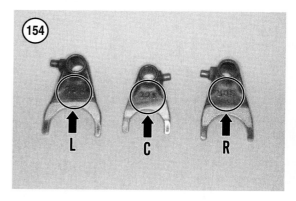

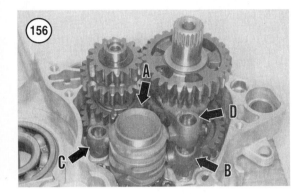

4

g. Install the R shift fork pin into the lower shift drum groove (B, **Figure 156**).

h. Install the C shift fork pin into the center shift drum groove (C, **Figure 156**).

i. Install the L shift fork pin into the upper shift drum groove (D, **Figure 156**).

j. Lubricate the shift fork shafts with engine oil. Install the long shift fork shaft (A, **Figure 157**) through the L and R shift forks. Install the other shaft (B, **Figure 157**) through the C shift fork. Make sure both shafts bottom out in the right case half.

k. Spin the transmission shafts and turn the shift drum by hand to check transmission operation. Check that each shift fork travels through its operating groove in the shift drum and bottoms against both ends of the groove (**Figure 158**).

*NOTE*
*It is difficult to identify the different gear positions when turning the shift drum without the stopper lever installed on the engine. Substep k only determines if the shift forks can move through their complete operational range.*

4. Temporarily install the left case half and seat it against the right case half (**Figure 147**).

5. Grasp both case halves so they cannot separate and turn the engine over so the right case half faces up. Then carefully remove the right case half. Immediately locate the outer countershaft washer (B, **Figure 148**) and reinstall it, if necessary.

6. Install the crankshaft so the spline end faces out (A, **Figure 159**).

7. Lubricate the oil pump rotors and shaft and install them into the left crankcase bore (B, **Figure 159**). Make sure the rotors seat flush with the left crankcase.

8. Clean both case surfaces so they are clean and dry.

9. Install the dowel pins (A, **Figure 160**) and a new gasket (B).

10. Center the one-way valve in the gasket cutout as shown in C, **Figure 160** and **Figure 161**.

*NOTE*
*Figure 161 shows how the center case gasket is used to align the one-way valve in the left case half. However, when the engine is assembled, the one-way valve actually mounts into a cutout in the right case half. The one-way valve is installed on the left case half first because it may fall out of the right case half when the engine cases are assembled. In Step 11, install the right case carefully so that the one-way valve enters the cutout correctly.*

11. Make sure the right crankcase gasket surface is clean and dry. Then install the right case half onto the left case half. Tap the right case to seat it flush against the gasket. Excessive force should not be necessary as there are no press-fits between the crankshaft and its main bearings.

12. Grasp both case halves so they cannot separate and turn the engine over so the left case half faces up.

13. Install and tighten the crankcase mounting bolts as follows:

   a. Clean and dry the crankcase mounting bolts.

   b. Install the crankcase mounting bolts into their original mounting position, using the template made during disassembly and **Figure 162**. Tighten the bolts finger-tight.

*CAUTION*
*The crankcase bolts must be installed correctly. Tightening a too long or short bolt will strip the crankcase threads.*

*CAUTION*
*Throughout the tightening process, occasionally turn the crankshaft and countershaft. If there is any binding,*

*STOP. Take the crankcase apart and find the trouble. Usually it is a gear installed backward or an incorrectly installed dowel pin.*

   c. Turn the engine upright and check that a corner of the one-way valve is visible between the crankshaft halves (**Figure 163**). This indicates the one-way valve was correctly installed. Check the left crankshaft seal to make sure part of its sealing lip did not fold under during crankshaft installation (**Figure 164**).

   d. Tighten all crankcase bolts (**Figure 162**), working in a crossing pattern and in several steps until they are all tight.

   e. Install a new washer on the transmission drain bolt and lubricate the bolt threads with oil. Install and tighten to 22 N•m (16 ft.-lb.).

   f. Turn the crankshaft and both transmission shafts. If there is binding, separate the cases to determine the cause.

   g. Cover the crankcase opening.

14. Carefully trim the center case gasket at the cylinder base surface (**Figure 165**). Do not allow any of the gasket material to fall into the crankcase.

15. Check the transmission for proper shifting as follows:

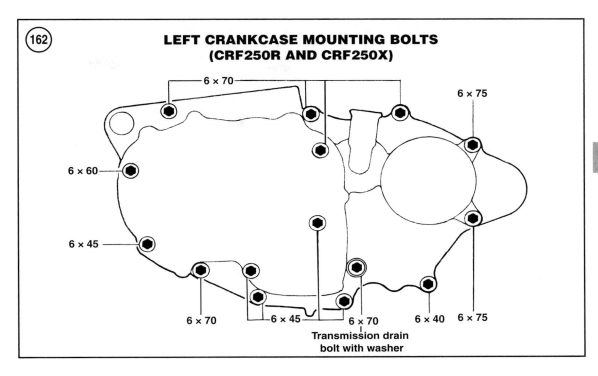

**LEFT CRANKCASE MOUNTING BOLTS
(CRF250R AND CRF250X)**

6 × 70

6 × 75

6 × 60

6 × 45

6 × 70

6 × 45

6 × 70

6 × 40

6 × 75

**Transmission drain
bolt with washer**

4

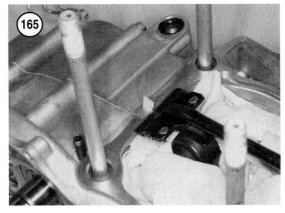

a. Install the shift drum cam, small locating pin and mounting bolt (A, **Figure 166**). Then install the stopper lever (B, **Figure 166**) and its mounting bolt. The spring and washer used with the stopper lever is not required. Use your fingers to engage the stopper lever with the shift drum cam when checking shifting.

*NOTE*
*If necessary, refer to Chapter Six for additional information on installing the shift drum cam and stopper lever assembly.*

b. Turn the mainshaft while turning the shift drum cam and align its raised ramp with the stopper lever (C, **Figure 166**). This is the transmission's *neutral* position. The mainshaft and countershaft should turn independently of one another.

c. Turn the mainshaft while turning the shift drum cam *clockwise*. Stop when the stopper lever can seat between the ramps of the shift drum cam. This is the first gear position. The mainshaft and countershaft should be meshed together.

d. Turn the shift drum cam *counterclockwise*. Turn the shift drum cam past neutral, then place the stopper lever between the ramps to check the remaining gears for proper engagement. The mainshaft and countershaft should mesh whenever the transmission is in gear.

e. Remove the shift drum cam and stopper lever when the check is completed. If the transmission did not engage properly, disassemble the crankcase and inspect the transmission for proper assembly or damaged parts.

16. Reverse Step 1 under *Disassembly*.

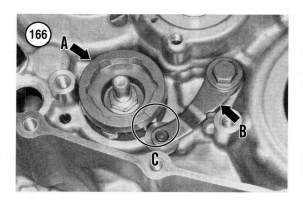

## Inspection

1. Remove the crankcase seals as described in this chapter.

2. Remove all gasket residue from the gasket surfaces.

3. Clean the crankcase halves in solvent.

4. Using clean solvent, flush each bearing. Make sure all gasket residue is removed from the bearings, oil passages and bolt holes.

5A. On 2004 CRF250R and all CRF250X models, check the oil jet (**Figure 167**) installed in the left case half and clean the oil jet and its crankcase passage with compressed air. If the oil jet is removed, reinstall it by applying a medium strength threadlock onto the oil jet threads and tighten to 2.0 N•m (17 in.-lb.).

5B. On 2005 CRF250R models, check the oil jet installed in the left case half. To clean, remove the mounting bolt and the oil jet. Clean the oil jet and its crankcase passage with compressed air. Reinstall the oil jet by applying a medium strength threadlock onto the mounting bolt threads and tighten to 9.8 N•m (87 in.-lb.).

6. Dry the cases with compressed air.

*WARNING*
*When drying a bearing with compressed air, do not allow the inner bearing race to rotate. The air can spin the bearing at excessive speed, possibly causing the bearing to destruct.*

7. Blow through each oil passage with compressed air.

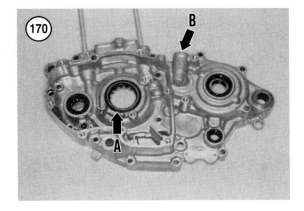

8. Lightly oil the engine bearings before inspecting their condition. A dry bearing exhibits more sound and looseness than a properly lubricated bearing.

9. Inspect the bearings for roughness, pitting, galling and play. Replace any bearing that is not in good condition. Always replace the opposite bearing at the same time. When inspecting the clutch release lever bearing, insert the release lever into the bearing and check for roughness.

10. Inspect the cases for fractures around all mounting and bearing bosses, stiffening ribs and threaded holes. If repair is required, have a dealership or machine shop inspect the cases.

11. Check all threaded holes for damage or buildup. Clean threads with the correct size metric tap. Lubricate the tap with kerosene or aluminum tap fluid.

12. Inspect the oil pump and one-way valve as described under *Oil Pump and One Way Valve* in this chapter.

## CRANKCASE SEAL AND BEARING REPLACEMENT

Refer to *Basic Service Methods* in Chapter One for bearing removal and installation techniques. Also refer to *Interference Fit* if it is necessary to use heat for the removal and installation of the bearings in the housings.

Refer to this section for specific removal and installation techniques for bearings that are unique to this engine.

### Seal Replacement

Replace all the crankcase seals during an engine overhaul.

> *CAUTION*
> *Do not allow the pry tool to contact the seal bore when removing the seal. It may gouge the bore and cause the new seal to leak.*

1. Pry out the old seal with a seal puller or wide-blade screwdriver, as shown in **Figure 168**. Place a folded shop cloth under the tool to prevent damage to the case.

2. If a new bearing is going to be installed, replace the bearing before installing the new seal.

3. Inspect the seal bore. Sand or file any raised grooves in the bore surface, then clean thoroughly.

4. Pack grease into the lip of the new seal.

5. Place the seal in the bore, with the closed side of the seal facing out. The seal must be square to the bore.

6. Install the new seal with a seal driver (**Figure 169**) to the dimensions specified below:

   a. Left crankshaft seal (A, **Figure 170**): 0.5-1.5 mm (0.02-0.06 in.).

   b. All other engine seals: Install the seal so its upper edge is flush with the top of the seal bore.

> *CAUTION*
> *When driving seals, the driver must fit at the perimeter of the seal. If the driver presses toward the center of the seal, the seal can distort and the internal garter spring can become dislodged, causing the seal to leak.*

## Crankcase Bearing Identification

1. When replacing crankcase bearings, note the following:

    a. Phillips, Torx and Allen head screws secure the crankcase bearing retainers. All of these bearing retainer screws are secured with a threadlock and tightened securely. Heat the area around the screws with a heat gun before loosening them. Loosen Phillips screws with a hand-impact driver with the appropriate size Phillips bit (**Figure 171**, typical). The cross-slot part of these screws strip easily, which makes removal difficult. Use the correct size Torx bit when removing Torx screws.

> *NOTE*
> *Refer to **Screwdrivers** in Chapter One for additional information on removing Phillips screws using ACR Phillips II screwdriver bits, and tips on how to increase the grip of a Phillips bit.*

    b. Before installing the bearing retainer screws, clean the screw threads and threaded holes of all threadlock residue. To ensure accurate torque readings, the screw threads must be clean and in good condition. Replace the screw if the driving part of the screw head is damaged.

    c. Install the bearing crankcase bearing retainer screws using threadlocking compound and tighten to 9.8 N•m (87 in.-lb.). Use a high strength threadlocking compound on the right main bearing retainer screws. Use a medium strength threadlocking compound on all other retainer screws.

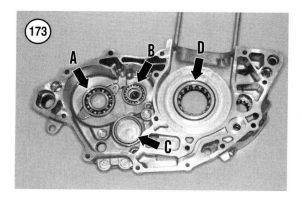

    d. Identify and record the size code of each bearing before removing it from the case. This will eliminate confusion when installing the bearings in their correct bores.

    e. Record the orientation of each bearing in its bore. Note if the size code faces toward the inside or outside of the case. Some bearings are also machined with a shoulder on one side to accept bearing retainer plates. If these bearings are installed backward, the retainer will not seat correctly against the bearing.

    f. Use a hydraulic press or a set of bearing drivers to remove and install bearings. Bearings can also be removed and installed using heat, as described in Chapter One.

    g. Bearings that are only accessible from one side of the case are removed with a blind bearing puller. The puller is fitted through the bearing, then expanded to grip the back side of the bearing (**Figure 172**).

> *NOTE*
> *The tool shown in **Figure 172** is the Motion Pro Blind Bearing and Bushing Remover (part No. 08-0292). Re-*

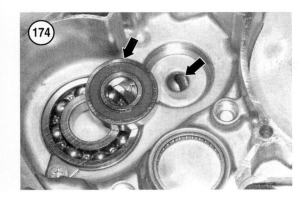

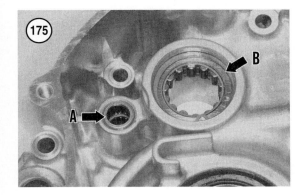

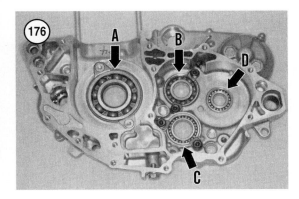

4

*fer to **www.motionpro.com** for a description of this tool.*

2. The following (**Figure 173**) identifies the *left* crankcase bearings:

   a. Countershaft bearing (A, **Figure 173**).

   b. Mainshaft bearing (B, **Figure 173**). The side of the bearing that faces toward the left case half is sealed (**Figure 174**) to protect it from dirt and water that passes through the clutch release lever bore.

   c. Shift drum bearing (C, **Figure 173**).

   d. Crankshaft bearing (D, **Figure 173**).

   e. Clutch release lever bearings (B, **Figure 170**).

   f. Oil pump bearing (A, **Figure 175**).

   g. Balancer shaft bearing (B, **Figure 175**). Remove the snap ring before removing the bearing. During installation, install the snap ring with its flat side facing out.

3. The following list identifies the *right* crankcase bearings:

   a. Crankshaft bearing (A, **Figure 176**).

   b. Mainshaft bearing (B, **Figure 176**).

   c. Shift drum bearing (C, **Figure 176**).

   d. Countershaft bearing (D, **Figure 176**).

   e. Balancer shaft bearing (**Figure 177**).

**Crankcase Bearing Replacement**

All crankcase bearings can be replaced during the following steps.

*NOTE*
*Before removing the bearings, refer to the **Crankcase Bearing Identification** section to determine if there is specific information related to the bearing being replaced.*

1. Place the new bearing(s) in a freezer and chill for at least one hour.

2. Remove the crankcase seal, if applicable.

3. Remove the snap ring from the bearing bore, if applicable. Discard the snap ring if weak, rusted or damaged.

4. Remove the bearing retainers, if applicable.

5. Make note of which side of the bearing is facing out.

6. Heat the crankcase as described in *Interference Fit* in Chapter One. Observe all safety and handling procedures when the case is heated.

> *CAUTION*
> *Do not heat the housing or bearing with a propane or acetylene torch. The direct heat will destroy the case hardening of the bearing and may warp the case.*

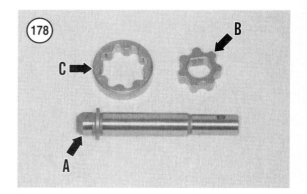

7. Support the heated crankcase on wooden blocks, allowing space for the bearing to fall from the bore.

8. Remove the bearing(s) from the bore, using a press, bearing-driver set or bearing puller. Discard the bearing(s).

9. Allow the case to cool.

10. Clean and inspect the bearing bore. Check that all oil holes (where applicable) are clean.

11. When the bearing(s) have chilled, reheat the crankcase.

12. Support the heated crankcase on wooden blocks, checking that the case is supported directly below the bearing bore.

13. Place the bearing squarely over the bore and check that it is properly oriented as noted before removal and under *Crankcase Bearing Identification*. Center the bearing into the bore. If the bearing drops into the bore, carefully apply pressure to the bearing (Step 14) to make sure it bottoms correctly.

14. Press the bearing into place using a driver that fits on the outer bearing race.

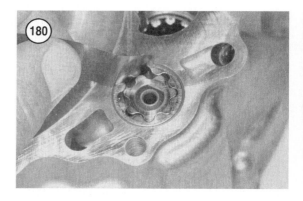

15. Install the seal (if applicable) as described in this chapter.

## OIL PUMP AND ONE-WAY VALVE

The oil pump and one-way valve are removed and installed during crankcase *Disassembly* and *Reassembly*.

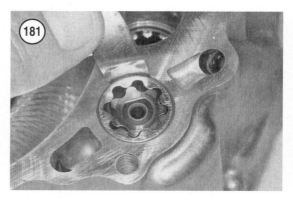

### Inspection

The oil pump operates in a bore in the left crankcase. If the pump is badly worn, it cannot maintain oil pressure. While the oil pump components can be replaced separately, it is best to replace all the parts (**Figure 178**) at the same time if there is any worn or damaged parts, or if the oil pump clearances in **Table 4** are excessive.

1. Clean all parts in fresh solvent. Blow dry with compressed air and place on a clean cloth.

2. Inspect the oil pump drive gear as described under *Lubrication System* in this chapter.

3. Inspect the oil pump shaft (A, **Figure 178**) for:
   a. Worn, scored or damaged surfaces.
   b. Damaged drive pin hole. Check for cracks leading from the hole on both sides of the shaft.
   c. Damaged inner rotor drive shoulder.
   d. Damaged snap ring groove.

4. Inspect the inner (B, **Figure 178**) and outer (C) rotors for:

   a. Scratches, scoring, wear grooves, flaking and other damage.
   b. Wear or damage on the rotor engagement teeth.
   c. Inner rotor shoulder for wear and damage.

5. Inspect the oil pump bore in the left crankcase (**Figure 179**) for scoring, cracks or other damage. If the bore is damaged, replace the left case half.

*NOTE*
*If there is no visible wear on the rotor or bore surfaces, continue with Step 6 to measure the oil pump operating clearances.*

6. Measure and record the oil pump operating clearances as follows. Refer to **Table 4** to determine if the measurements are within specification:
   a. Install the oil pump shaft, inner rotor and outer rotor into the left crankcase oil pump bore.
   b. Measure the tip clearance between the rotors as shown in **Figure 180**. If out of specification, replace both rotors and remeasure.
   c. Measure the side clearance (**Figure 181**). Measure at several places around the housing bore. If the clearance is excessive, repeat the measurement with a new outer rotor. If the clearance is still excessive, replace the left case half.
   d. Install the center case gasket on the left case half. Then place a straightedge across the pump housing and measure the rotor end clearance (**Figure 182**). If the clearance is excessive, replace the rotors and remeasure the clearance.

7. Remove the oil pump assembly from the case bore. Then clean and place in a plastic bag until assembly.

**One-Way Valve Inspection**

1. The one-way valve (**Figure 183**) is not designed to be disassembled. Do not attempt to remove the screw (**Figure 183**) that secures the valve to the holder as the screw head may snap off. This screw is secured with threadlock.

2. Inspect the one way valve plate (**Figure 184**) for bending or other damage. The plate should seat flush against its seat.

3. Replace the one-way valve if there is any detectable wear or damage.

## CRANKSHAFT

### Connecting Rod Big End Bearing Lubrication

Oil forced under pressure through a passageway in the left crankcase cover enters a hole in the left end of the crankshaft (**Figure 185**) and lubricates the connecting rod big end bearing assembly. A seal installed in the left crankcase cover seals the end of the crankshaft and the oil passageway. Refer to *Left Crankcase Cover* in Chapter Ten to service the oil seal and clean the cover oil passageway.

### Inspection

Carefully handle the crankshaft assembly during inspection. Do not place the crankshaft where it could accidentally roll off the workbench. The crankshaft is an assembly-type, with its two halves joined by the crankpin. The crankpin is pressed into the flywheels and aligned, both vertically and horizontally, with calibrated equipment. If the crankshaft assembly shows signs of wear, or is out of alignment, have a dealership inspect the crankshaft. While Honda does not sell OEM parts to rebuild the crankshaft, aftermarket overhaul kits are available.

Inspect the crankshaft assembly as follows:

1. Clean the crankshaft with solvent.

2. Dry the crankshaft with compressed air.

3. Blow through all oil passages with compressed air.

4. Inspect the crankshaft bearing surfaces (**Figure 186**) for scoring, heat discoloration or other damage. Repair minor damage with 320 grit carborundum cloth.

5. Inspect the splines, sprocket and shaft taper for wear or damage.

> *NOTE*
> *If the sprocket is damaged, check the cam chain, upper cam sprocket, chain guides and cam chain tensioner for damage.*

6. Inspect the connecting rod small end (A, **Figure 187**) as described under *Piston Pin and Connecting Rod Inspection* in this chapter.

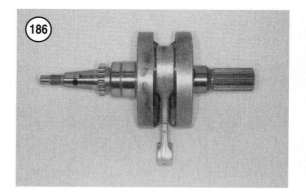

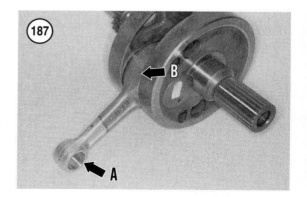

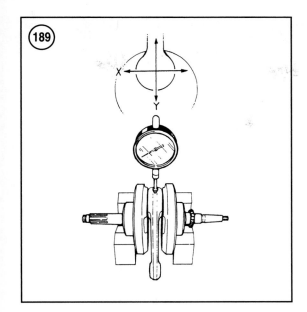

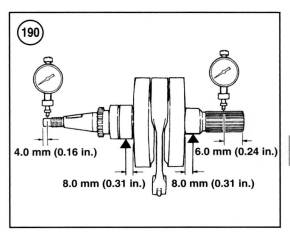

4.0 mm (0.16 in.)  6.0 mm (0.24 in.)

8.0 mm (0.31 in.)  8.0 mm (0.31 in.)

7. Inspect the connecting rod big end bearing (B, **Figure 187**) as follows:

  a. Turn the rod and inspect the bottom bearing and rod for scoring, galling or heat damage. Roughness indicates a damaged bearing and rod.

  b. Slide the connecting rod to one side and measure the connecting rod side clearance with a flat feeler gauge (**Figure 188**). Refer to **Table 5** for service limits.

  c. Support the crankshaft on a set of V-blocks and position the pointer of a dial indicator in the middle of the connecting rod lower end (**Figure 189**). Hold the crankshaft and then move the connecting rod as shown in **Figure 189**. Replace the crankshaft if the clearance exceeds the radial clearance service limit in **Table 5**.

8. Place the crankshaft on a set of V-blocks at the points indicated in **Figure 190**. Rotate the crankshaft two revolutions and measure crankshaft runout with a dial indicator at the two points indicated in **Figure 190**. If the runout exceeds the service limit in **Table 5**, have a dealership evaluate and possibly true the crankshaft.

**Table 1 ENGINE GENERAL SPECIFICATIONS (CRF250R AND CRF250X)**

| | Specification |
|---|---|
| Engine type | 4-stroke, single cylinder, liquid cooled, chain-driven OHC with rocker arm |
| Engine displacement | 249.4 cc (15.21 cu. in.) |
| Bore and stroke | 78.0 × 52.2 mm (3.07 × 2.06 in.) |
| Compression ratio | 12.9:1 |
| Engine dry weight | |
|   CRF250R | 23.9 kg (52.7 lbs.) |
|   CRF250X | 26.6 kg (58.6 lbs.) |
| (continued) | |

**Table 1 ENGINE GENERAL SPECIFICATIONS (CRF250R AND CRF250X) (continued)**

|  | Specification |
|---|---|
| Valve timing* | |
| CRF250R | |
| Intake valve opens | 15° BTDC |
| Intake valve closes | 50° ABDC |
| Exhaust valve opens | 50° BBDC |
| Exhaust valve closes | |
| 2004 | 20° ATDC |
| 2005 | 15° ATDC |
| CRF250X | |
| 49-state and Canada | |
| Intake valve opens | 10° BTDC |
| Intake valve closes | 40° ABDC |
| Exhaust valve opens | 40° BBDC |
| Exhaust valve closes | 10° ATDC |
| California | |
| Intake valve opens | 0° BTDC |
| Intake valve closes | 45° ABDC |
| Exhaust valve opens | 45° BBDC |
| Exhaust valve closes | 0° ATDC |
| *At 1 mm (0.04 in.) lift. | |

**Table 2 CYLINDER HEAD, CAMSHAFT AND VALVE SPECIFICATIONS (CRF250R AND CRF250X)**

|  | New mm (in.) | Service limit mm (in.) |
|---|---|---|
| Cylinder head warp limit | – | 0.05 (0.002) |
| Camshaft | | |
| Lobe height | | |
| CRF250R | | |
| Intake | 36.000-36.240 (1.4173-1.4268) | 35.86 (1.412) |
| Exhaust | | |
| 2004 | 25.667-25.907 (1.0105-1.0120) | 25.56 (1.006) |
| 2005 | 25.501-25.741 (1.0040-1.0134) | 24.40 (0.961) |
| CRF250X | | |
| 49-state and Canada | | |
| Intake | 35.580-35.660 (1.4008-1.4039) | 35.44 (1.395) |
| Exhaust | 25.081-25.161 (0.9874-0.9906) | 24.98 (0.983) |
| California | | |
| Intake | 35.280-35.360 (1.3890-1.3921) | 35.14 (1.383) |
| Exhaust | 24.959-25.038 (0.9826-0.9858) | 24.86 (0.979) |
| Rocker arm | | |
| Inside diameter | 12.016-12.034 (0.4731-0.4738) | 12.07 (0.475) |
| Rocker arm shaft outside diameter | 11.977-11.985 (0.4715-0.4719) | 11.93 (0.470) |
| Rocker arm-to-shaft clearance | 0.031-0.057 (0.0012-0.0022) | 0.11 (0.004) |
| Valves | | |
| Stem outside diameter | | |
| Intake | 4.975-4.990 (0.1959-0.1965) | – |
| Exhaust | 4.960-4.985 (0.1953-0.1963) | 4.955 (0.195) |
| Valve guide inside diameter | | |
| Intake and exhaust | 5.000-5.012 (0.1969-0.1973) | 5.052 (0.199) |
| Valve seat width | | |
| Intake and exhaust | 0.90-1.10 (0.035-0.043) | 1.7 (0.07) |
| (continued) | | |

**Table 2 CYLINDER HEAD, CAMSHAFT AND VALVE SPECIFICATIONS (CRF250R AND CRF250X) (continued)**

| | New mm (in.) | Service limit mm (in.) |
|---|---|---|
| Valves (continued) | | |
| Valve stem-to-guide clearance | | |
| Intake | 0.010-0.037 (0.0004-0.0015) | – |
| Exhaust | 0.015-0.052 (0.0006-0.0020) | – |
| | | |
| Valve guide projection height | | |
| Intake | 14.8-15.0 (0.58-0.59) | – |
| Exhaust | 19.8-20.0 (0.78-0.79) | – |
| Valve spring free length | | |
| Intake | 39.47 (1.554) | 38.5 (1.52) |
| Exhaust | 43.07 (1.696) | 42.1 (1.66) |
| Valve lifter outside diameter | 22.478-22.493 (0.8850-0.8855) | 22.47 (0.885) |
| Valve lifter bore inside diameter | 22.510-22.526 (0.8862-0.8868) | 22.54 (0.887) |

**Table 3 CYLINDER, PISTON AND PISTON RING SERVICE SPECIFICATIONS (CRF250R AND CRF250X)**

| | New mm (in.) | Service limit mm (in.) |
|---|---|---|
| Cylinder | | |
| Bore diameter | 78.000-78.015 (3.0709-3.0715) | 78.04 (3.072) |
| Out-of-round | – | 0.010 (0.004) |
| Taper | – | 0.010 (0.004) |
| Warp | – | 0.05 (0.002) |
| Piston-to-cylinder clearance | 0.020-0.045 (0.0008-0.0018) | 0.18 (0.007) |
| Piston and piston pin | | |
| Piston outside diameter | 77.970-77.980 (3.0697-3.0701) | 77.89 (3.067) |
| Piston pin bore inside diameter | 16.002-16.008 (0.6300-0.6302) | 16.03 (0.631) |
| Piston pin outside diameter | 15.994-16.000 (0.6297-0.6299) | 15.98 (0.629) |
| Piston pin bore-to-piston pin clearance | 0.002-0.014 (0.0001-0.0006) | 0.04 (0.002) |
| Piston measuring point from bottom of piston skirt | 7.0 (0.28) | – |
| Piston rings | | |
| Piston ring-to-ring groove clearance | | |
| Top compression ring | 0.065-0.100 (0.0026-0.0039) | 0.115 (0.0045) |
| Oil ring | – | |
| Ring end gap | | |
| Top compression ring | 0.20-0.30 (0.008-0.012) | 0.44 (0.017) |
| Oil ring side rails | 0.20-0.70 (0.008-0.028) | 0.90 (0.035) |
| Connecting rod | | |
| Small inside diameter | 16.016-16.034 (0.6305-0.6313) | 16.04 (0.6315) |
| Connecting rod-to-piston pin clearance | 0.016-0.040 (0.0006-0.0016) | 0.06 (0.002) |

**Table 4 OIL PUMP SERVICE SPECIFICATIONS (CRF250R AND CRF250X)**

| | New mm (in.) | Service limit mm (in.) |
|---|---|---|
| Body clearance | 0.15-0.20 (0.006-0.008) | – |
| Tip clearance | 0.15 (0.006) | 0.20 (0.008) |
| Side clearance | 0.05-0.12 (0.002-0.005) | – |

**Table 5 CRANKSHAFT SERVICE SPECIFICATIONS (CRF250R AND CRF250X)**

|  | New<br>mm (in.) | Service limit<br>mm (in.) |
| --- | --- | --- |
| Connecting rod side clearance | 0.30-0.75 (0.01-0.03) | 0.8 (0.03) |
| Radial clearance | 0.006-0.018 (0.0002-0.0007) | 0.05 (0.002) |
| Runout |  |  |
|   Left side | – | 0.05 (0.002) |
|   Right side | – | 0.03 (0.001) |

**Table 6 ENGINE TORQUE SPECIFICATIONS (CRF250R AND CRF250X)**

|  | N•m | in.-lb. | ft.-lb. |
| --- | --- | --- | --- |
| Cam chain stopper plate bolt | 12 | 106 | – |
| Cam chain tensioner housing mounting bolt | 12 | 106 | – |
| Camshaft holder mounting bolt[1] | 16 | 142 | – |
| Countershaft bearing set plate screws[2] | 9.8 | 87 | – |
| Crankshaft bearing set plate Torx screw[3] | 12 | 106 | – |
| Crankshaft hole cap[4] | 15 | 133 | – |
| Cylinder head cover bolt | 9.8 | 87 | – |
| Cylinder head 6 mm mounting bolt | 9.8 | 87 | – |
| Cylinder head nut[1] | 39 | – | 29 |
| Cylinder 6 mm mounting bolt | 9.8 | 87 | – |
| Decompressor cam stopper plate bolt[2] | 9.8 | 87 | – |
| Engine oil drain bolt[1] | 22 | – | 16 |
| Exhaust pipe heat shield bolt | 12 | 106 | – |
| Exhaust pipe joint nut | 21 | – | 15 |
| Exhaust pipe protector bolt | 12 | 106 | – |
| Ignition timing hole cap[4] | 5.9 | 52 | – |
| Kick pedal bolt | 37 | – | 27 |
| Mainshaft bearing set plate Allen head screw[2] | 9.8 | 87 | – |
| Muffler joint clamp bolt | 21 | – | 15 |
| Muffler mounting bolts | 26 | – | 19 |
| Oil check bolt | 9.8 | 87 | – |
| Oil jet[2] |  |  |  |
|   CRF250R |  |  |  |
|     2004 | 2.0 | 18 | – |
|     2005 (oil jet mounting bolt) | 9.8 | 87 | – |
|   CRF250X | 2.0 | 18 | – |
| Rear chain guide mounting bolt[2] | 12 | 106 | – |
| Rocker arm shaft cap | 5.9 | 52 | – |
| Shift drum bearing set plate Allen head screw[2] | 9.8 | 87 | – |
| Spark arrestor mounting bolt (CRF250X) | 13 | 115 | – |
| Transmission oil drain bolt[1] | 22 | – | 16 |

1. Lubricate threads and seating surface with engine oil.
2. Apply medium strength threadlock to fastener threads.
3. Apply a high strength threadlock to fastener threads.
4. Lubricate threads with grease.

**Table 7 ENGINE MOUNT TORQUE SPECIFICATIONS (CRF250R AND CRF250X)**

|  | N•m | ft.-lb. |
|---|---|---|
| Engine hanger plate nut | | |
|   Engine side | 54 | 40 |
|   Frame side | | |
|     CRF250R | | |
|       2004 | 26 | 19 |
|       2005 | 34 | 25 |
|     CRF250X | 26 | 19 |
| Engine mounting nut | | |
|   Front | 54 | 40 |
|   Lower | 64 | 47 |
| Swing arm pivot shaft nut | 88 | 65 |

4

# CHAPTER FIVE

# ENGINE (CRF450R AND CRF450X)

This chapter provides engine service information for the CRF450R and CRF450X. Read the appropriate section before attempting any repair. Become familiar with the procedures to understand the skill and equipment required. Refer to Chapter One for tool usage and techniques. When special tools are required or recommended, the Honda part number is provided.

Always clean the engine before starting repairs. If the engine will remain in the frame, clean the surrounding framework and under the fuel tank. Do not allow dirt to enter the engine.

Keep the work environment as clean as possible. Store parts and assemblies in well-marked plastic bags and containers. Keep new parts wrapped until installation.

Refer to Chapter Three for break-in procedures.

**Tables 1-7** are at the end of this chapter.

## SERVICING ENGINE IN FRAME

The following components can be serviced with the engine installed in the frame:
1. Cylinder head cover, camshaft and cylinder head.
2. Cylinder and piston.
3. Alternator (Chapter Ten).

4. Clutch, external shift linkage and kickstarter (Chapter Seven).
5. Water pump (Chapter Eleven).
6. Starter clutch (CRF450X [Chapter Seven]).
7. Starter motor (CRF450X [Chapter Ten]).
8. Emission control system (CRF450X [Chapter Nine]).

The following components are serviced after removing the engine from the frame:
1. Crankcase.
2. Crankshaft.
3. Transmission and internal shift mechanism.
4. Oil pump and one-way valve.

## ENGINE

### Removal

This procedure describes the steps required to remove the complete engine assembly. If desired, remove the sub-assemblies attached to the crankcase while the engine is still in the frame. Refer to **Figure 1** (2002-2004) or **Figure 2** (2005).
1. Support the motorcycle securely.
2. If possible, perform a compression test (Chapter Three) and leakdown test (Chapter Two) before dismantling the engine.

## ① ENGINE MOUNT ASSEMBLY (2002-2004 CRF450R)

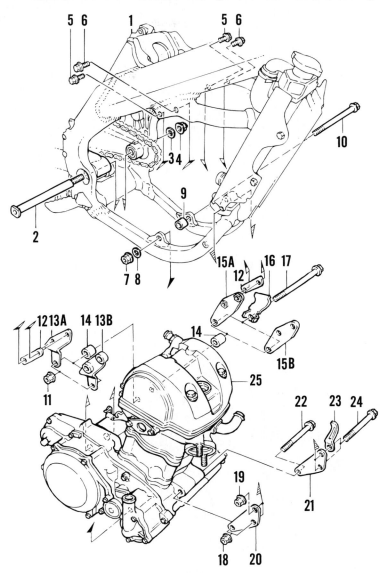

5

1. Frame
2. Swing arm pivot shaft
3. Washer
4. Pivot shaft nut
5. Upper engine hanger plate bolt (frame side rear)
6. Upper engine hanger plate bolt (frame side front)
7. Lower engine mount nut
8. Washer
9. Collar (2002-2003)
10. Lower engine mount bolt
11. Upper engine mount nut
12. Washer (2002)
13A. Right side upper engine hanger plate (2002)
13B. Right side upper engine hanger plate (2003-on)
14. Collar
15A. Left side upper engine hanger plate (2002)
15B. Left side upper engine hanger plate (2003-on)
16. Fuel hose bracket
17. Upper engine mount bolt
18. Front engine hanger plate nut (engine side)
19. Front engine hanger plate nut (frame side)
20. Right front engine hanger plate
21. Left front engine hanger plate
22. Front engine mount bolt
23. Cable guide
24. Front engine mount bolt
25. Engine

② **ENGINE MOUNT ASSEMBLY (2005 CRF450R)**

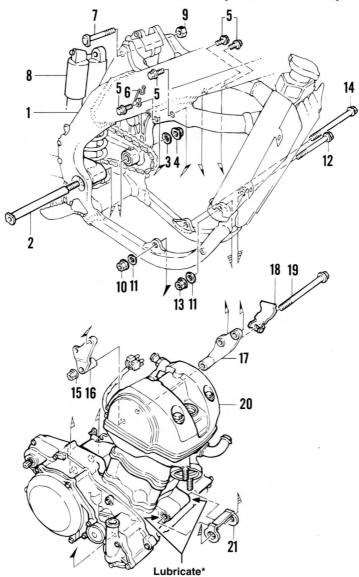

Lubricate*

1. Frame
2. Swing arm pivot shaft
3. Washer
4. Pivot shaft nut
5. Upper engine hanger plate bolt
6. Hose guide (CRF450X)
7. Upper shock absorber mounting bolt
8. Shock absorber
9. Upper shock absorber mounting nut
10. Front engine mount nut
11. Washer
12. Front engine mount bolt
13. Lower engine mount nut
14. Lower engine mount bolt
15. Upper engine hanger plate nut
16. Right front engine hanger plate
17. Left front engine hanger plate
18. Fuel hose bracket
19. Upper engine mount bolt
20. Engine
21. Washer (CRF450R)
*Lubricate front engine mount contact
surfaces with molybdenum disulfide
paste

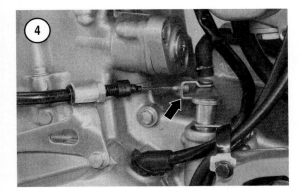

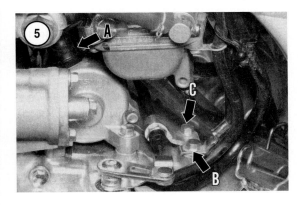

5

3. Remove the skid plate, engine guards, side covers and seat (Chapter Sixteen).

4. On CRF450X models, disconnect the negative battery cable at the battery (**Figure 3**).

5. Drain the engine oil (Chapter Three).

6. Drain the transmission oil (Chapter Three).

7. Drain the coolant (Chapter Three).

8. Remove the fuel tank (Chapter Nine).

9. Remove the exhaust system (this chapter).

10. Remove the carburetor (Chapter Nine).

11. On 2002-2004 models, remove the radiators (Chapter Eleven) if the engine is going to be removed with the top end (cylinder head and cylinder) installed on the engine. Do not remove the radiators if the top end assembly will be removed first.

*NOTE*
*On 2005 models, the assembled engine can be removed with the radiators installed on the frame.*

12. Remove the shift pedal.

13A. On CRF450R models, disconnect the drive chain. If necessary, remove the drive sprocket (Chapter Twelve).

13B. On CRF450X models, an endless drive chain is used. Remove the drive sprocket (Chapter Twelve) to disconnect the drive chain from the engine.

14. Remove the brake pedal (Chapter Fifteen).

15A. On CRF450R models, disconnect the clutch cable from the clutch lifter at the engine (**Figure 4**).

15B. On CRF450X models, perform the following:
   a. Remove the coolant reserve tank (Chapter Eleven).
   b. California models—Remove the PAIR control valve (Chapter Nine).
   c. Hold the lower nut at the starter terminal, then remove the upper nut (A, **Figure 5**) and disconnect the starter cable.

*NOTE*
*Holding the lower nut prevents the positive terminal from turning and damaging its insulator installed inside the starter. Refer to **Starter** in Chapter Ten.*

   d. Remove the bolt (B, **Figure 5**) and the ground cable.
   e. Remove the bolt (C, **Figure 5**) and the clutch cable stay and cable.

16A. On 2002-2004 models, disconnect the alternator connectors (A, **Figure 6**).

16B. On 2005 models, disconnect the ignition pulse generator and exciter coil (CRF450R) or alternator (CRF450X) connectors from the connector block located behind the left radiator (**Figure 7**, typical).

17. On 2005 models, remove the upper shock absorber mounting nut and bolt (**Figure 2**).

18A. If the engine is to be disassembled, remove the following components while the engine is mounted in the frame:

a.  Cylinder head, cylinder and piston (this chapter).

b.  Starter (CRF450X [Chapter Ten]).

c.  Clutch (Chapter Seven).

d.  Starter clutch (CRF450X [Chapter Seven]).

e.  Kickstarter and idle gear (Chapter Seven).

f.  External shift mechanism (Chapter Seven).

g.  Flywheel (Chapter Ten).

h.  Balancer gear and balancer (Chapter Seven).

i.  Primary drive gear (Chapter Seven).

18B.  If the engine is to be removed as an assembly, perform the following:

a.  Disconnect the spark plug wire (B, **Figure 6**).

b.  Disconnect the breather hose (C, **Figure 6**) at the cylinder head cover.

c.  Remove the kick pedal.

d.  Remove the upper engine hanger plate assembly as shown in **Figure 1** or **Figure 2**. On CRF450X models, remove the hose guide (16, **Figure 2**).

19.  Remove the pivot shaft nut and washer (**Figure 1** or **Figure 2**).

20A.  On 2002-2004 models, remove the front engine mount nuts, bolts, brackets and cable guide (A, **Figure 8**).

20B.  On 2005 models, remove the front engine mount nut and bolt (**Figure 2**).

21A.  On 2002-2004 models, remove the lower engine mounting nut, washer, bolt and collar (B, **Figure 8**). The collar is not used on 2004 models.

21B.  On 2005 models, remove the lower engine mounting nut, washer and bolt (**Figure 2**).

*NOTE*
*When the pivot shaft is removed, the swing arm will come loose. Pull the shaft out only far enough to free the engine. After the engine is removed, push the shaft back through the frame and swing arm.*

22.  Partially remove the pivot shaft (C, **Figure 8**).

*WARNING*
*If necessary, have an assistant help remove the engine.*

23.  Remove an assembled engine from the right side. If the engine has been disassembled down to the crankcase, it can be removed from either side.

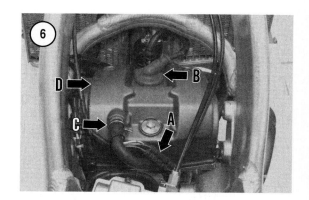

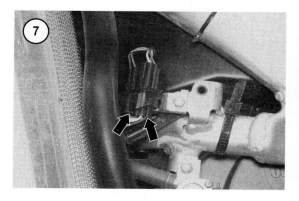

24.  On 2005 CRF450R models, remove the washer (21, **Figure 2**) from the front engine mounting bracket on the engine.

25.  Push the pivot shaft back through the frame (A, **Figure 9**).

26.  Clean and inspect the frame and all exposed hardware, hoses and wiring. Check for cracks and damage, particularly at welded joints.

27.  Refer to the procedures in this chapter for servicing the crankcase assembly.

### Installation

1.  Check all coolant hoses and hose connections for looseness or damage. Make sure the hose clamps are tight. Check for deterioration on the inside of the hoses.

2.  Make sure the wiring harness, vent hoses and rear brake hose are routed and secured properly.

3.  Replace damaged engine mounting fasteners.

4.  Lubricate the pivot shaft with grease and insert it partway through the right side of the frame and swing arm (A, **Figure 9**). Do not grease the threads on the end of the pivot shaft.

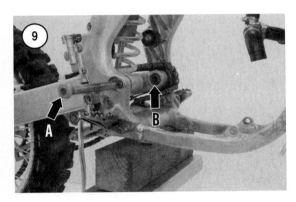

5. Make sure the bushings (B, **Figure 9**) are installed inside the swing arm.

6. On 2005 CRF450R and CRF450X models, lubricate the front engine mounting bracket contact surfaces with molybdenum disulfide paste as indicated in **Figure 2**.

*CAUTION*
*The molybdenum disulfide paste applied in Step 6 prevents the front engine mounting bracket from cracking due to engine movement.*

7. On 2005 CRF450R models, install the washer (21, **Figure 2**) onto the front engine mounting bracket.

8. Install the engine into the frame from the right side, then push the pivot shaft through the frame and engine from the right side. Make sure the flat on the head of the pivot shaft seats into the frame recess (C, **Figure 8**).

*CAUTION*
*The threads on all engine mounting fasteners and the swing arm pivot shaft must be dry when tightened.*

*CAUTION*
*Tighten the engine mount fasteners finger-tight in the following steps. Do not tighten the bolts until all of the bolts and hanger plates have been installed.*

9. Install the pivot shaft washer and nut (**Figure 1** or **Figure 2**).

10A. On 2002-2004 models, install the lower engine mounting bolt, collar, washer and nut (B, **Figure 8**). Install the bolt from the left side. The collar is not used on 2004 models.

10B. On 2005 models, install the lower engine mounting bolt, washer and nut. Install the bolt from the left side (**Figure 2**).

11A. On 2002-2004 models, install the front engine hanger plates, (A, **Figure 8**), bolts and nuts. Install the bolts from the left side. Install the cable guide (**Figure 10**).

11B. On 2005 CRF450R models, install the front engine mounting bolt, washer and nut. Install the bolt from the left side, making sure it passes through the washer installed in Step 7. See 21, **Figure 2**.

12. If the engine was disassembled, reverse Step 18A under *Removal* to install the parts.

13. On 2002 models, apply Honda Moly 60 Paste (or equivalent) to the outside of the left and right side hanger plates as shown in **Figure 11**.

14. Install the upper engine hanger plate assembly as shown in **Figure 1** or **Figure 2**.

15. Tighten the swing arm pivot shaft nut (4, **Figure 1** or 4, **Figure 2**) to 88 N•m (65 ft.-lb.).

16A. On 2002-2004 models, tighten the engine mount bolts as follows:

   a. Front engine hanger plate nut (engine side [18, **Figure 1**]) to 54 N•m (40 ft.-lb.).
   b. Front engine hanger plate nut (frame side [19, **Figure 1**]) to 26 N•m (19 ft.-lb.).

5

c. Lower engine mount nut (7, **Figure 1**) to 54 N•m (40 ft.-lb.).

d. Upper engine hanger plate nut (11, **Figure 1**) to 54 N•m (40 ft.-lb.).

e. On all 2002-2004 models, upper engine hanger plate front frame side bolt (6, **Figure 1**) to 26 N•m (19 ft.-lb.).

f. On 2002 models, upper engine hanger plate rear frame side bolt (5, **Figure 1**) to 29 N•m (21 ft.-lb.).

g. On 2003-2004 models, upper engine hanger plate rear frame side bolt (5, **Figure 1**) to 26 N•m (19 ft.-lb.).

16B. On 2005 models, tighten the engine mount bolts as follows:

a. Front engine mount nut (10, **Figure 2**) to 59 N•m (44 ft.-lb.).

b. Lower engine mount nut (13, **Figure 2**) to 59 N•m (44 ft.-lb.).

c. Upper engine hanger plate nut (15, **Figure 2**) to 59 N•m (44 ft.-lb.).

d. Upper engine hanger plate bolts (5, **Figure 2**) to 26 N•m (19 ft.-lb.).

17. On 2005 models, tighten the upper shock absorber nut (9, **Figure 2**) to 44 N•m (33 ft.-lb.).

18. Reverse Steps 1-16 under *Removal* to complete engine installation.

19. Tighten the kick pedal mounting bolt to the specification in **Table 6**.

20. Fill the engine with new oil (Chapter Three).

21. Fill the transmission with new oil (Chapter Three).

22. Fill the cooling system with coolant (Chapter Three).

23. Start the engine and check for leaks.

24. Check throttle operation.

25. Check the shift pedal mounting position, clutch adjustment and gear engagement.

26. If the engine top-end was rebuilt, perform a compression check. Record the results for future reference.

27. Review the *Engine Break-In* procedure in Chapter Three.

## EXHAUST SYSTEM

### Removal and Installation

1. Support the motorcycle on a workstand.

2. Remove the right side cover (Chapter Sixteen).

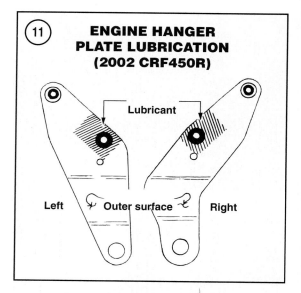

**ENGINE HANGER PLATE LUBRICATION (2002 CRF450R)**

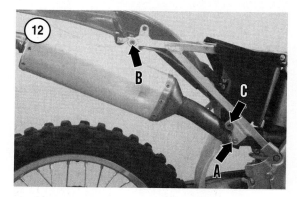

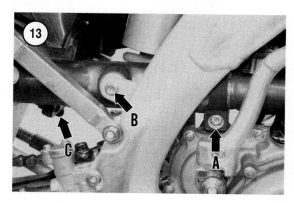

3. Remove the muffler as follows:

a. Loosen the muffler joint band bolt. See A, **Figure 12** (CRF450R) or A, **Figure 13** (CRF450X).

b. Remove the bolts securing the muffler to the subframe and/or frame and remove the muf-

fler. See B and C, **Figure 12** (CRF450R) or B and C, **Figure 13** (CRF450X).

4. Remove the exhaust pipe as follows:

   a. Remove the exhaust pipe joint nuts (**Figure 14**) and exhaust pipe.

   b. Remove and discard the gasket from the exhaust port.

5. Reverse these steps to install the exhaust system, plus the following steps.

6. Install a new exhaust pipe gasket (**Figure 15**). If necessary, apply a small amount of grease to the gasket to hold it in place. The grease will burn off after starting the engine.

7. Replace the exhaust pipe-to-muffler gasket if leaking or damaged.

8. Install the exhaust pipe while leaving the joint nuts finger-tight.

9. Install the muffler while leaving the mounting bolts loose.

10. Tighten the exhaust pipe joint nuts in a crossing pattern and in several steps to 21 N•m (15 ft.-lb.).

11. Tighten the muffler joint band bolt to 21 N•m (15 ft.-lb.).

12A. On CRF450R models, tighten the muffler mounting bolts to 22 N•m (16 ft.-lb.).

12B. On CRF450X models, tighten the muffler mounting bolts to 26 N•m (19 ft.-lb.).

13. Start the engine and check for exhaust leaks.

**Muffler Repacking (CRF450R)**

The glass wool in the muffler can be replaced. See **Figure 16** (2002-2003) or **Figure 17** (2004-on).

1. Remove the muffler as described in this section.

*CAUTION*
*When removing rivets, drill through the rivet head and not into the muffler housing. Remove the loose rivet ends when cleaning out the muffler.*

2. Remove the rivets by drilling off the rivet heads. Then remove the end cap (2004-on), end cover, housing and front band.

3. Pull the glass wool off the inner pipe and discard it. Remove any residue remaining inside the muffler housing and on the inner pipe.

4. Clean the inner pipe and muffler housing with a wire brush to remove all rust and exhaust residue. Make sure all the inner pipe core holes are clear.

5. Remove the new glass wool packing from its container and compare it with the inner pipe and the housing diameters. If necessary, cut the wool glass to fit the housing.

6. Wrap the new wool glass packing around the inner pipe core. Pack as much material around the inner pipe as possible without making it too tight. When correctly packed around the inner pipe, the glass wool should be slightly larger than the muffler housing.

7. Slide the muffler housing carefully over the wool glass and into position. Make sure the housing does not push the wool glass forward and leave a gap at the end of the muffler.

8. Rivet the front band, end cover and end cap (2004-on) to the muffler housing.

**Muffler Service (CRF450X)**

*Diffuser cleaning*

1. Support the motorcycle on its sidestand.

5

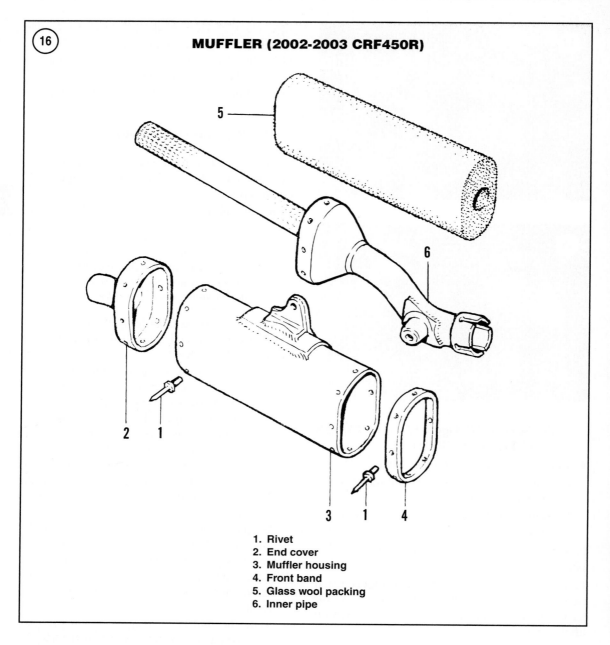

**MUFFLER (2002-2003 CRF450R)**

1. Rivet
2. End cover
3. Muffler housing
4. Front band
5. Glass wool packing
6. Inner pipe

2. Remove the Torx screw and washer securing the diffuser inside the spark arrester (**Figure 18**).

3. Remove the diffuser from the spark arrester.

4. Clean the diffuser of all carbon and sealer residue. Inspect the diffuser for damage and replace if necessary.

5. Apply a muffler sealant to the diffuser sealing surface as shown in **Figure 18**.

6. Installation is the reverse of these steps. Tighten the diffuser Torx screw to 11 N•m (97 in.-lb.). Allow the sealant to set before starting the engine.

*Spark arrester cleaning*

1. Support the motorcycle on its sidestand.
2. Remove the bolts (**Figure 19**), spark arrester (**Figure 20**) and gasket. Replace the gasket if leaking.

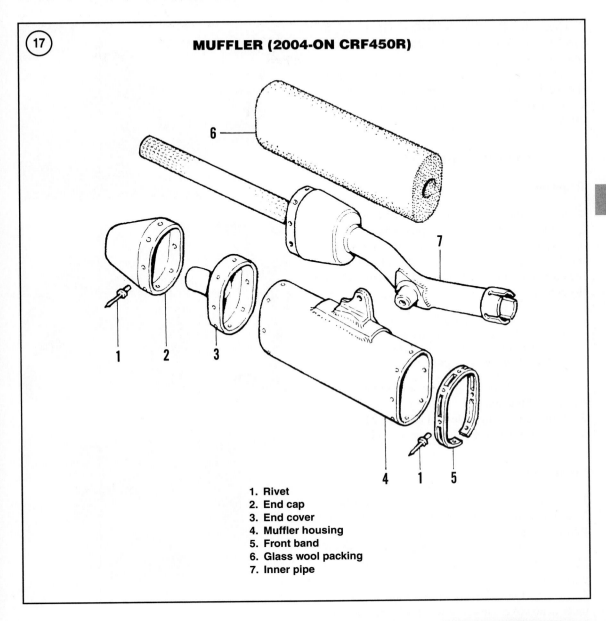

**⑰ MUFFLER (2004-ON CRF450R)**

1. Rivet
2. End cap
3. End cover
4. Muffler housing
5. Front band
6. Glass wool packing
7. Inner pipe

5

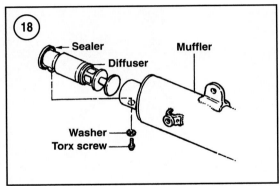

⑱ Sealer  Muffler
Diffuser
Washer
Torx screw

⑲

3. Clean the spark arrester with a wire brush. Replace the spark arrester if the screen is punctured or otherwise damaged.

4. Installation is the reverse of removal. Tighten the spark arrester mounting bolts securely. Start the engine and check for exhaust leaks around the spark arrester.

## CYLINDER HEAD COVER

### Removal

1. Support the motorcycle on a workstand.
2. Remove the fuel tank (Chapter Nine).
3. Disconnect the spark plug cap (B, **Figure 6**) and the breather hose (C). Slide the clamp on the breather hose down the hose so it does not fall into the engine.

> *NOTE*
> *Before removing the cylinder head cover bolts, check for oil leaks around the cover and bolt gaskets.*

4. Remove the bolts, gaskets and cylinder head cover (D, **Figure 6**).
5. Remove the plug hole seal (**Figure 21**) if it did not come off with the cylinder head cover.

### Installation

1. Clean the gasket surfaces on the cylinder head.
2. Replace the bolt gaskets if leaking or damaged. Reuse the gaskets if in good condition.
3. Replace the cylinder head cover gasket (**Figure 22**) if leaking or damaged. Reuse the gasket if in good condition.

4. Perform the following to reuse the original cylinder head cover gasket or to install a new gasket:
   a. Carefully pull the gasket from the cover. Discard the gasket if damaged.
   b. Remove all sealer residue from the groove in the cylinder head cover. Clean the cover in solvent and dry thoroughly.
   c. If reusing the original gasket, pull hardened strips of the old sealer from the gasket.
   d. Apply Gasgacinch to the cover groove (A, **Figure 23**) and to the side of the gasket (B) that will seat against the cover when installed. Do not apply sealer to the side of the gasket that will seat against the cylinder head. Fol-

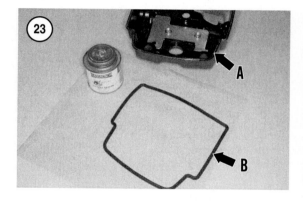

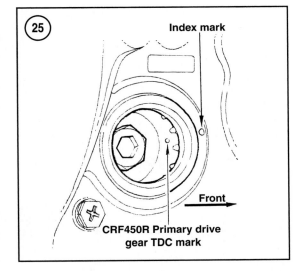

CRF450R Primary drive
gear TDC mark

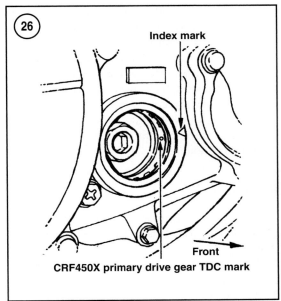

CRF450X primary drive gear TDC mark

## CAMSHAFT HOLDER

This section describes removal and installation of the camshaft holder.

To remove the camshaft from the holder and service the camshaft, camshaft holder and decompressor assembly, refer to *Camshaft Holder Service* in this chapter.

The camshaft and camshaft holder can be removed with the engine mounted in the frame. The camshaft is mounted in the camshaft holder and operates on two ball bearings. The left side bearing is permanently installed on the camshaft. The right side bearing is pressed into the camshaft holder.

### Crankshaft Timing Marks

A chain and two sprockets drive the camshaft. One sprocket is mounted on the camshaft and the other sprocket is permanently fixed to the crankshaft. To ensure proper valve timing in relation to piston travel, the camshaft must be timed to the crankshaft. This is done by positioning the crankshaft with the piston at TDC and then aligning the camshaft TDC timing marks before installing the chain and sprocket onto the camshaft.

Index marks on the primary drive gear and right crankcase cover are used to position the crankshaft at TDC. See **Figure 25** (CRF450R) or **Figure 26** (CRF450X). However, because these index marks

low the manufacturer's instructions for drying time before installing the gasket into the cover groove.

   e. Install the gasket into the cover groove. Check that the gasket seats in the groove completely.

5. Install the plug hole seal (**Figure 21**) onto the spark plug tunnel. Do not apply sealer to the seal.

6. Install the cylinder head cover onto the cylinder head.

7. Install the gaskets onto the bolts with their UP mark facing up (**Figure 24**). Do not apply sealer to the gaskets.

8. Install the cylinder head cover bolts and gaskets and tighten to 9.8 N•m (87 in.-lb.).

9. Reconnect the spark plug cap (B, **Figure 6**) and breather hose (C).

10. Install the fuel tank (Chapter Nine).

are located to one side of each other (cannot be viewed straight on), the precise viewing of both marks may be difficult and result in a viewing error (or parallax). In this case the error can be significant and make it to appear that the index marks are incorrectly aligned when they are correct or vice versa.

To eliminate any error when setting the crankshaft at TDC, view the ignition timing marks on the flywheel (**Figure 27**) through the left crankcase cover timing hole.

## Removal

1. Remove the engine mounting plates at the cylinder head as described under *Engine Removal* in this chapter.
2. Remove the cylinder head cover as described in this chapter.
3. Remove the crankshaft hole cap from the right crankcase cover.
4. Remove the ignition timing hole cap from the left crankcase cover.
5. Remove the spark plug to make turning the crankshaft easier.

> *NOTE*
> *Use an 8 mm hex socket on the primary drive gear mounting bolt to turn the crankshaft (**Figure 28**).*

6. Turn the crankshaft clockwise to expose a cam sprocket bolt (A, **Figure 29**) and loosen it. Turn the crankshaft clockwise again and loosen the other cam sprocket bolt.
7. Set the engine at TDC on its compression stroke as follows:

> *NOTE*
> *The decompressor mechanism will click loudly once during each crankshaft revolution. This is normal.*

a. Turn the crankshaft *clockwise* and align the TDC mark on the flywheel (A, **Figure 30**) with the index mark on the left crankcase cover (B). Then check that the index line on the cam sprocket aligns with the triangle mark on the cam holder (**Figure 31**).

> *NOTE*
> *If you are using the primary drive gear and right crankcase cover tim-*

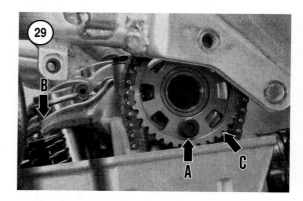

*ing marks, align the TDC mark on the primary drive gear with the index mark on the right crankcase cover (**Figure 25** or **Figure 26**).*

b. The engine is now at TDC on either the compression stroke or exhaust stroke. The engine is on the compression stroke if the rocker arm (B, **Figure 29**) can be moved slightly by hand, indicating that exhaust and intake valves are closed. If the rocker arm is tight, the engine is on its exhaust stroke and the ex-

**CAM CHAIN TENSIONER**
**STOPPER PLATE**
**(CRF450R AND CRF450X)**

**2002-2003**

16.5 mm

8.5 mm      3.5 mm

9.5 mm

Thickness: 1.0 mm

**2004-ON**

19 mm

8.5 mm      3.5 mm

12 mm

Thickness: 1.0 mm

haust valves are open. If the rocker arm is tight, turn the crankshaft clockwise one full turn and realign the TDC marks described in substep a. The rocker arm should now be loose.

*NOTE*
*Before removing the camshaft holder, turn the engine over several times while checking the camshaft and flywheel timing marks. Doing so is important for two reasons. First, it confirms that the timing marks and camshaft positions are correct. This step is helpful when troubleshooting a valve timing problem. Second, checking the timing marks makes you aware of how the camshaft lobes are positioned when the engine is at TDC on its compression stroke.*

*NOTE*
*If the cam sprocket timing marks do not align correctly as described in Step 7 when the engine is at TDC on its compression stroke, the cam timing is incorrect. A damaged or incorrectly adjusted cam chain tensioner or excessively stretched cam chain can cause the camshaft to jump time. This condition can cause bent valves and loss of compression. Before removing the tensioner, lift the chain to check its tension—it should be tight.*

8. With the engine positioned at TDC on its compression stroke, check and record the valve clearances as described in Chapter Three. If one or more of the clearances are incorrect, it will be necessary to install the appropriate size shims before reinstalling the camshaft holder. Checking the clearances now will allow you to obtain and install the correct size shims during assembly.

9. Loosen the cam chain tension as follows:

*NOTE*
*A stopper plate is required to turn and lock the tensioner in its retracted position. Fabricate the stopper plate from the dimensions shown in* **Figure 32**.

    a. On 2002-2003 models, remove the screw and O-ring from the tensioner housing.

b. On 2004-on models, remove the bolt and sealing washer from the tensioner housing.

c. Insert the small end of the stopper plate (**Figure 33**) into the tensioner and turn the pushrod clockwise until it stops. Then insert the stopper plate into one set of notches machined in the tensioner housing to lock the tensioner.

*NOTE*
*Figure 34 shows the tensioner assembly removed with the pushrod locked in its retracted position. Spring pressure should be felt when turning the stopper plate in substep c. If the tensioner turns easily, it is most likely damaged.*

10. If it is necessary to service the decompressor assembly mounted on the camshaft, loosen, but do not remove, the decompressor mounting bolt (**Figure 35**). If the engine turns over when attempting to loosen the bolt, hold the primary drive gear with the hex socket (**Figure 28**).

11. Remove the exposed cam sprocket bolt, then turn the crankshaft clockwise and remove the other cam sprocket bolt.

*NOTE*
*If the camshaft holder is being removed to adjust the valve clearance, do not remove the sprocket from the cam chain as described in Step 12. Instead, after removing the cam sprocket mounting bolts, allow the sprocket to rest against the chain guides (Figure 36).*

12. Disconnect the sprocket (C, **Figure 29**) from the camshaft and support the cam chain with a piece of wire.

13. Before removing the camshaft holder, note the following:

a. The camshaft is installed inside the camshaft holder. The camshaft holder and camshaft are removed as an assembly. Then, if necessary, the camshaft is removed from the camshaft holder.

b. Use a divided container to store the intake valve lifters and the four adjustment shims in their original mounting position.

c. The intake valve lifters will probably come out with the camshaft holder. The intake

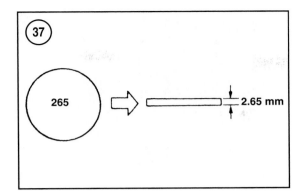

valve adjustment shims will either stay inside the valve lifters or remain in the spring seats at end of the valves. Remove the camshaft holder carefully so the shims do not dislodge and fall into the engine.

d. The exhaust valve adjustment shims should remain in the end of the exhaust valves as the camshaft holder is being removed.

e. Each adjustment shim was originally marked with a number indicating its thickness (**Figure 37**). If a shim number is indecipherable, measure the shim's thickness with a micrometer and record it to identify the shim with its original mounting position.

5

> *CAUTION*
> *Failure to loosen the camshaft holder mounting bolts in stages can cause damage to the camshaft holder.*

14. Remove the camshaft holder assembly as follows:

a. Make sure the piston is at TDC on its compression stroke (Step 7).

b. Loosen the camshaft holder mounting bolts (A, **Figure 38**) in a crossing pattern and in several steps. Remove the bolts.

c. Remove the camshaft holder assembly (B, **Figure 38**) and quickly turn it over.

d. Remove the intake valve lifters (**Figure 39**) and shims (if they are stuck inside the valve lifters). Store them in a divided container.

15. Remove the intake (A, **Figure 40**) and exhaust valve (B) shims and install them in a divided container.

16. To remove the camshaft from the holder and service the camshaft, camshaft holder and decompressor assembly, refer to *Camshaft Holder Service* in this chapter.

**Cleaning**

1. Clean the camshaft holder assembly in solvent and dry with compressed air. Lubricate the camshaft machined surfaces and bearings with engine oil. Make sure the oil passages in the camshaft holder are clear.

2. Clean the threads on the cam sprocket bolts (A, **Figure 41**) and in the camshaft sprocket flange (B) of all threadlock residue. Replace the bolts if damaged.

3. Clean and dry the camshaft holder mounting bolts (C, **Figure 41**). Replace the bolts if damaged.

4. Clean and dry the camshaft sprocket.

### Installation

1. Review *Crankshaft Timing Marks* in this section.

2. Set the engine at TDC by turning the crankshaft *clockwise* and aligning the TDC mark on the flywheel (A, **Figure 30**) with the index mark on the left crankcase cover (B). The engine must be held in this position when installing and timing the cam sprocket.

> *NOTE*
> *If you are using the timing marks on the primary drive gear and right crankcase cover, align the TDC mark on the primary drive gear with the index mark on the right crankcase cover (**Figure 25** or **Figure 26**).*

3. If removed, lubricate the valve adjustment shims with engine oil and install them into the spring seats (A and B, **Figure 40**). Install the shims in their original position. If one or more of the original shims are to be replaced for valve adjustment, install the new shims in their correct position in the spring seats.

4. Make sure the two dowels pins (D, **Figure 41**) are installed in the camshaft holder.

5. Apply molybdenum disulfide oil solution to the outer surface of each intake valve lifter. Then install the intake valve lifters into the camshaft holder in their original mounting position (**Figure 39**).

6. Turn the camshaft so the intake cam lobes face rearward (A, **Figure 42**) and install the camshaft holder into the cylinder head. Make sure the rocker arm pads (B, **Figure 42**) are resting over the exhaust valves. Seat the camshaft holder flush against the cylinder head and check that the camshaft can be moved slightly in both directions by hand.

> *CAUTION*
> *If the camshaft holder will not seat flush against the cylinder head, it is likely the camshaft was not positioned with its intake lobes facing rearward.*

7. Lubricate the camshaft holder bolt threads and flange seating surfaces with engine oil and install

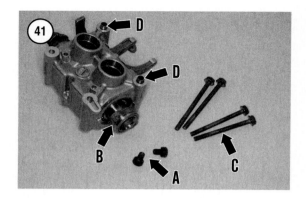

them. The front bolts (C, **Figure 42**) are longer than the rear (D) bolts. Tighten the camshaft holder mounting bolts in a crossing pattern and in two steps to 14 N•m (124 in.-lb.).

> *NOTE*
> *If the camshaft holder was removed only to adjust the valve clearance, recheck the valve clearance before installing the cam sprocket (Chapter Three). If a valve clearance is still incorrect, remove the camshaft holder and install the correct size shim. Repeat this sequence until the valve clearance is correct, then continue with Step 8 to install the cam sprocket and complete the installation procedure.*

8. Before installing the cam sprocket, note the following:

  a. Keep the front of the cam chain taut so there is no play in the chain with the sprocket installed.

  b. Make sure the cam chain tensioner pushrod is held in its retracted position with the stopper

plate. See Step 9 under *Camshaft Holder Removal* in this section.

9. Install and time the cam sprocket as follows:

   a. Align the cam sprocket with the cam chain so that its index line is visible and facing forward (A, **Figure 43**).

   b. Install the cam chain onto the cam sprocket and install the sprocket onto the camshaft flange. Check that the index line on the cam sprocket (A, **Figure 43**) aligns with the triangle mark on the cam holder (B) and the bolt holes in the sprocket align with the bolt holes in the camshaft flange.

   c. Apply a medium strength threadlock onto the cam sprocket bolt threads. Install the first bolt (C, **Figure 43**) finger-tight.

   d. Recheck the flywheel timing mark (A, **Figure 30**) set in Step 2 and the cam sprocket and cam holder marks (A and B, **Figure 43**). These marks must align.

> *CAUTION*
> *If the timing marks are not in these exact locations with the engine at TDC, cam timing will be incorrect. Excessive engine damage could occur if the camshaft is not properly installed.*

10. Turn the engine clockwise 360° and install the second cam sprocket bolt. Tighten this bolt to 20 N•m (15 ft.-lb.).

11. Turn the engine clockwise 360° and tighten the first cam sprocket bolt to 20 N•m (15 ft.-lb.).

12. Listen for an audible *snap* while watching the rear chain run at the cam sprocket, then remove the stopper plate (**Figure 33**) from the tensioner. The chain should tighten while the noise indicates that the tensioner pushrod has extended. If this noise did not occur, remove and inspect the tensioner.

13. Turn the crankshaft *clockwise* several times, then place it at TDC (**Figure 30**) on its compression stroke. Make sure the timing marks on the cam sprocket camshaft holder flange align (**Figure 43**). If not, the camshaft timing is incorrect.

14. Reinstall the cam chain tensioner sealing screw and O-ring (2002-2003) or sealing bolt and sealing washer (2004-on).

15. If the decompressor cam mounting bolt (**Figure 35**) is loose, hold the crankshaft with an Allen socket (**Figure 28**) and tighten the bolt to 24 N•m (18 ft.-lb.).

16. Check the decompressor clearance and adjust if necessary (Chapter Three).

17. Install and tighten the spark plug.

18. Install and tighten the ignition timing hole cap as specified in **Table 6**. On 2005 models, tighten the hole cap securely.

19. Lubricate the crankshaft hole cap threads with grease and tighten to 15 N•m (133 in.-lb.).

20. Install the cylinder head cover as described in this chapter.

21. Install the engine mounting plates at the cylinder head as described under *Engine Installation* in this chapter.

## CAMSHAFT HOLDER SERVICE

This section describes service for the camshaft, camshaft holder and decompressor cam assembly. Refer to **Figure 44**.

### Removal/Installation

Refer to *Camshaft Holder* in this chapter.

### Camshaft Holder Assembled Inspection

This section describes cleaning and inspection procedures without removing the camshaft from the camshaft holder.

1. Clean the camshaft holder assembly in solvent and dry with compressed air.

2. Check that the camshaft (A, **Figure 45**) turns freely and that the camshaft bearings do not exhibit any noticeable noise or roughness.

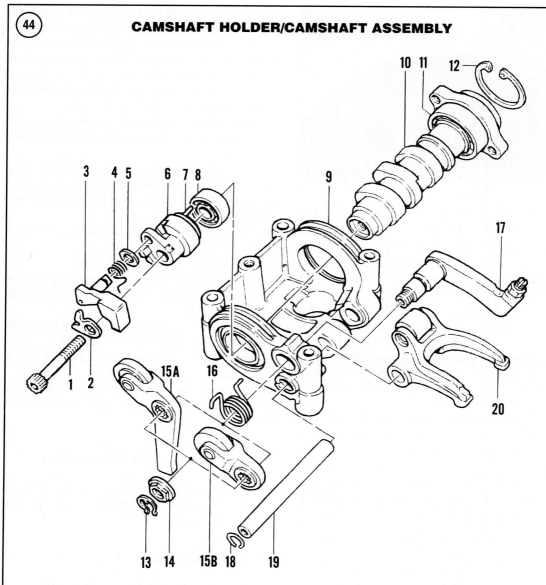

**CAMSHAFT HOLDER/CAMSHAFT ASSEMBLY**

1. Decompressor cam mounting bolt
2. Stopper washer
3. Balance weight
4. Spring
5. Washer
6. Decompressor cam assembly
7. Pin (press fit in decompressor cam assembly)
8. Right side bearing (press fit in camshaft holder)
9. Camshaft holder
10. Camshaft
11. Left side bearing (permanently installed on camshaft)
12. Snap ring
13. Clip
14. Decompressor arm mounting nut
15A. Decompressor lifter (2002-2003)
15B. Decompressor lifter (2004-on)
16. Spring
17. Decompressor arm
18. Clip
19. Rocker arm shaft
20. Rocker arm

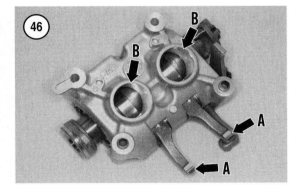

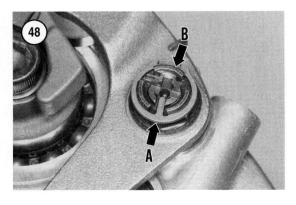

3. Inspect the machined surfaces on the camshaft for cracks or roughness.

4. Check that the rocker arm (B, **Figure 45**) pivots smoothly. Check the rocker arm contact surfaces (A, **Figure 46**) for uneven wear or damage.

5. Inspect the valve lifter bores (B, **Figure 46**) in the camshaft holder for cracks, score marks or other visible damage. The bore surfaces must be smooth for proper valve lifter operation. If there is any noticeable damage or wear, inspect the valve lifters for the same condition.

6. Perform the *Valve Lifter and Valve Lifter Bore Clearance Check* in this section to determine the condition of these parts.

7. Check the balance weight (A, **Figure 47**) and the decompressor arm (B) for any binding or roughness. Poor movement indicates seizure or wear problems. Check the spring on the decompressor lifter for damage.

8. If necessary, disassemble and service the camshaft holder assembly if there was any noticeable damage or operational wear with any component.

9. If further service is not required, lubricate the camshaft journals, bearings and rocker arm pivot surfaces with clean engine oil and store the assembly in a plastic bag until installation.

**Camshaft Holder Disassembly**

This section describes disassembly of the decompressor cam assembly (**Figure 44**) and camshaft removal.

*NOTE*
*This procedure shows the decompressor lifter (15A, Figure 44) used on 2002-2003 models. Part 15B in Figure 44 identifies the 2004-on decompressor lifter.*

1. Remove the clip (A, **Figure 48**) and the decompressor lifter mounting nut (B).

2. See **Figure 49** on how to mark the decompressor lifter installed position on the decompressor arm before separating them. This ensures proper alignment during assembly.

3. Remove the decompressor lifter (**Figure 50**) and spring.

4. Remove the decompressor arm (**Figure 51**).

5. Remove the clip (**Figure 52**) and discard it.

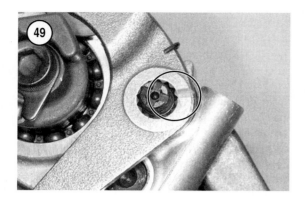

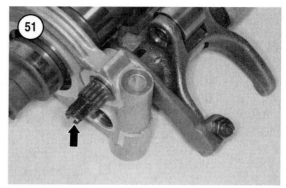

6. Thread a 6 mm screw (A, **Figure 53**) into the rocker arm shaft and remove the rocker arm shaft and rocker arm (B). Leave the screw in the shaft.

7. Remove the decompressor cam mounting bolt (A, **Figure 54**) (loosened under *Camshaft Holder Removal*), and the stopper washer (B).

8. Remove the decompressor cam assembly (A, **Figure 55**). The pin (B, **Figure 55**) is a press fit.

9. Remove the camshaft as follows:

   a. Remove the snap ring (**Figure 56**).

   b. Tap the camshaft holder to slide the left side bearing (A, **Figure 57**) from the bearing bore, then remove the camshaft (B). The camshaft cannot be removed until the left side bearing is free from its bore in the holder.

10. Inspect the camshaft, decompressor and camshaft holder assembly as described under *Component Inspection* in this section.

**Camshaft Holder Assembly**

Refer to **Figure 44**.

1. Clean and dry all parts before assembly.

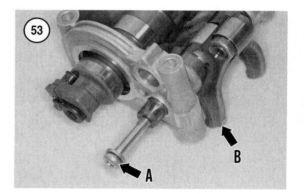

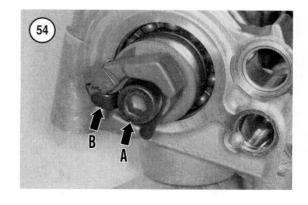

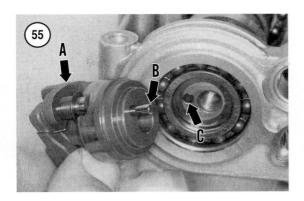

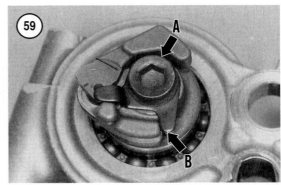

5

2. Install the camshaft (B, **Figure 57**) and left side bearing (A) into the camshaft holder and right side bearing. Fit the left side bearing in its bearing bore and install the snap ring (**Figure 56**) into the camshaft holder groove. Check that the camshaft spins freely in both bearings.

3. Install the decompressor cam assembly (A, **Figure 55**) by inserting the pin (B) into the hole (C) in the camshaft.

4. Install the stopper washer against the decompressor cam assembly as shown in **Figure 58**.

5. Lubricate the decompressor cam mounting bolt threads and seating surface with engine oil. Install the decompressor cam mounting bolt (A, **Figure 59**) and tighten hand-tight. Make sure the stopper washer (B, **Figure 59**) remains in its original position. The bolt will be tightened to its torque specification after the camshaft holder is installed on the engine. See Step 15 under *Camshaft Holder, Installation*.

6. Lubricate the rocker arm shaft and the rocker arm bore with engine oil (**Figure 60**).

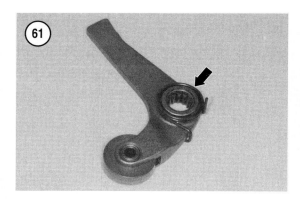

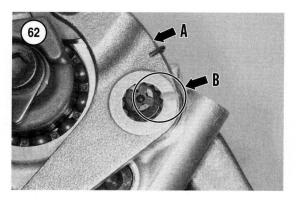

7. Install the rocker arm (B, **Figure 53**) and rocker arm shaft (A) into the camshaft holder. Remove the screw from the rocker arm shaft.

8. Install a new clip into the camshaft holder groove (**Figure 52**). Make sure the clip seats in the groove completely.

9. Lubricate the decompressor arm bearing surface with engine oil and install it into the camshaft holder (**Figure 51**).

10. If removed, install the spring onto the decompressor lifter as shown in **Figure 61**.

11. Install the decompressor lifter (A, **Figure 62**) by aligning the marks (B) made before removal. Then hook the spring against the tab on the camshaft holder as shown in **Figure 63**. See the decompressor lifter and decompressor arm alignment shown in **Figure 64**.

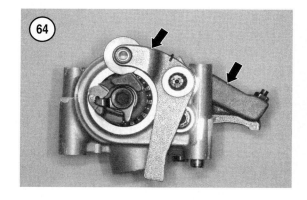

12. Lubricate the decompressor lifter mounting nut threads (B, **Figure 48**) with engine oil and tighten to 22 N•m (16 ft.-lb.).

13. Install the clip into the end of the decompressor arm and through a notch in the nut as shown in A, **Figure 48**.

14. Install the camshaft holder assembly as described in this chapter.

**Component Inspection**

This section describes inspection procedures for the camshaft, decompressor and camshaft holder assemblies (**Figure 44**). Replace parts that show obvious damage, or meet or exceed the service limits in **Table 2**.

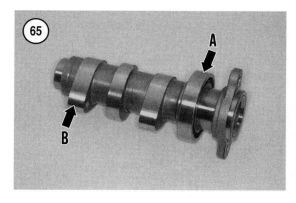

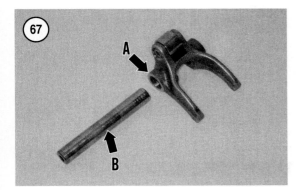

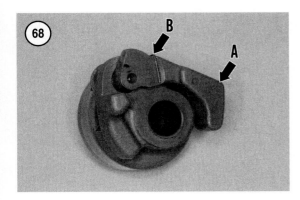

### Camshaft

1. Clean and dry the camshaft and left side bearing (**Figure 65**).

2. Spin the bearing (A, **Figure 65**) by hand and check for roughness and excessive play. If damaged, replace the camshaft assembly. This bearing cannot be replaced separately.

3. Inspect the cam lobes (B, **Figure 65**) for scoring or damage.

4. Measure each cam lobe height (**Figure 66**) with a micrometer.

### Rocker arm and shaft

1. Clean and dry the rocker arm and shaft. Inspect the rocker arm for a plugged oil hole.

2. Inspect the rocker arm (A, **Figure 67**) for wear and damage. If the camshaft contact surfaces on the rocker arm are damaged, inspect the valve adjustment shims and camshaft lobes for damage.

3. Measure the rocker arm inside diameter.

4. Inspect the rocker arm shaft (B, **Figure 67**) for any scoring or other damage. The shaft must be smooth.

5. Measure the rocker arm shaft outside diameter.

6. Subtract the rocker arm shaft outside diameter measurement (Step 5) from the rocker arm inside diameter (Step 3) to determine the rocker arm-to-shaft clearance. Replace the rocker arm and shaft if the clearance is too large.

### Decompressor cam assembly

1. Clean and dry the decompressor cam assembly. Refer to parts 3-7 in **Figure 44**.

2. Pivot the balance weight (A, **Figure 68**) by hand. It must move smoothly and return under spring pressure. Check the spring for fatigue and damage.

3. To rebuild the decompressor cam assembly:
   a. Remove the balance weight, spring and washer from the decompressor cam assembly.
   b. Replace the damaged part(s).
   c. Reassemble the balance weight as shown in **Figure 44** and **Figure 69**. Hook the spring over the balance weight as shown in **Figure 69** and B, **Figure 68**.

*Decompressor lifter and decompressor arm*

1. Clean and dry both parts (**Figure 70**).
2. Inspect the decompressor lifter (A, **Figure 70**) for:
   a. Weak or damaged spring.
   b. Seized or damaged roller.
   c. Damaged splines.
3. Inspect the decompressor arm (B, **Figure 70**) for:
   a. Damaged adjuster.
   b. Damaged splines or threads.
   c. Damaged bearing surface.

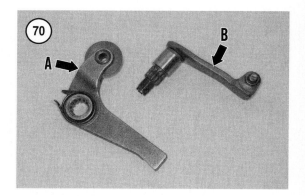

## Right Side Bearing Inspection/Replacement

The right side bearing is a press fit in the camshaft holder.
1. Clean and dry the bearing (**Figure 71**).
2. Check that the bearing is a tight fit in the camshaft holder bearing bore. Replace the camshaft holder and bearing if the bearing is a loose fit.
3. Spin the bearing inner race by hand and check for roughness and excessive play. If damaged, replace the bearing in Step 4.
4. Support the camshaft holder and press the bearing out of the bore. Inspect the bore for any cracks or other damage. If the bore is in good condition, press in the new bearing.

## Valve Lifter and Valve Lifter Bore Clearance Check

Replace the camshaft holder or valve lifters if they are obviously damaged, or not within specification.
1. Inspect the camshaft holder (A, **Figure 72**) for cracks or other damage.
2. Inspect the camshaft holder bores and valve lifters for scoring or other damage.
3. Measure each valve lifter bore inside diameter (B, **Figure 72**). See **Table 2** for specifications.
4. Measure each valve lifter (C, **Figure 72**) outside diameter (**Table 2**).

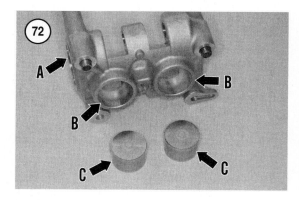

## CAM CHAIN TENSIONER, GUIDES AND CAM CHAIN

The engine is equipped with a cam chain tensioner mounted on the cylinder block, a front and rear chain guide and cam chain. The cam chain tensioner, cam chain and both guides can be replaced with the engine mounted in the frame.

## Cam Chain Tensioner Removal/Inspection/Installation

The cam chain tensioner controls cam chain tension with an adjustable spring-loaded pushrod. As the cam chain wears and stretches, the pushrod automatically adjusts to maintain the proper amount

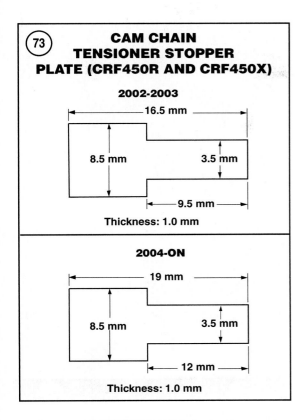

**CAM CHAIN TENSIONER STOPPER PLATE (CRF450R AND CRF450X)**

**2002-2003**

16.5 mm

8.5 mm          3.5 mm

9.5 mm

Thickness: 1.0 mm

**2004-ON**

19 mm

8.5 mm          3.5 mm

12 mm

Thickness: 1.0 mm

of cam chain tension. When a cam chain tensioner no longer provides the correct amount of tension against the chain, the chain free play can increase and allow the chain to jump one or more teeth on the camshaft sprocket. This will change the cam timing and possibly cause a loss of engine compression and engine damage.

1. Position the engine at TDC on its compression stroke as described under *Valve Adjustment* in Chapter Three. This step removes tension from the valve springs to help prevent camshaft movement and the cam chain jumping time.

2. Clean the area around the cam chain tensioner.

3. Retract the cam chain tensioner pushrod as follows:

*NOTE*
*A stopper plate is used to turn and lock the tensioner pushrod in its retracted position. Fabricate the stopper plate to the dimensions shown in **Figure 73**.*

a. On 2002-2003 models, remove the screw (**Figure 74**) and O-ring from the tensioner housing.

b. On 2004-on models, remove the bolt and sealing washer from the tensioner housing.

c. Insert the small end of the stopper plate (A, **Figure 75**) into the tensioner and turn the pushrod clockwise until it stops. Then insert the outer portion of the stopper plate into one set of notches machined in the tensioner housing to lock the tensioner.

4. Remove the mounting bolts (B, **Figure 75**) and the tensioner housing (C). Remove and discard the gasket.

*CAUTION*
*Do not turn the engine over once the cam chain tensioner has been removed.*

5. Remove the stopper plate (**Figure 76**). The pushrod should click and extend (**Figure 77**).

6. Inspect the cam chain tensioner as follows:

a. Inspect the pushrod and tensioner housing for damage.

b. With the pushrod extended (**Figure 77**), try to push the pushrod by hand. It should not move.

c. Use the stopper plate to turn the tensioner and retract the pushrod. It should move evenly under spring pressure. If the pushrod moves, but does not feel like it is under spring tension, the tensioner is most likely damaged.

d. The cam chain tensioner is available only as a unit assembly. Do not attempt to disassemble it. Replace the tensioner assembly if necessary.

7. Remove all gasket residue from the cam chain tensioner and cylinder block gasket surfaces.

*CAUTION*
*The cam chain tensioner must be installed with the pushrod locked in its retracted position.*

8. Turn and lock the pushrod in its retracted position as described in Step 3 (**Figure 76**).

9. Install a new gasket onto the tensioner.

10. Install the tensioner (C, **Figure 75**) and tighten its mounting bolts (B) to 12 N•m (106 in.-lb.).

11. Remove the stopper plate to allow the pushrod to extend.

*NOTE*
*The tensioner should click after removing the stopper plate, which indicates the pushrod has extended. If not, remove the tensioner and check pushrod operation.*

12A. On 2002-2003 models, install a new O-ring and tighten the screw (**Figure 74**).

12B. On 2004-on models, install a new sealing washer and tighten the bolt.

**Cam Chain Guides and Cam Chain Removal/Installation**

A continuous one-piece cam chain is used. Do not cut the chain as master links are not available.

1. Remove the cylinder head as described in this chapter.

2. Remove the front chain guide (**Figure 78**).

3. To remove the rear chain guide and cam chain:

a. Remove the flywheel (Chapter Ten).

b. Remove the bolt (B, **Figure 79**), washer, collar and rear chain guide (C).

c. Remove the cam chain (D, **Figure 79**).

4. Inspect the chain guides, cam chain (**Figure 80**) and sprockets as follows:

a. Check the chain fit on the cam and crankshaft sprockets. The chain should completely seat between the sprocket teeth and not have a tendency to slide up the teeth.

b. Inspect the crankshaft sprocket for wear or damage. The profile of each tooth should be symmetrical.

c. Check the chain for excessive play between the links, indicating worn rollers and pins.

d. Visually inspect the chain guides for excessive wear (grooves), cuts or other damage.

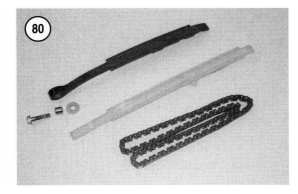

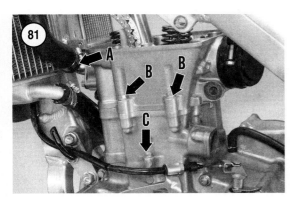

*NOTE*
*If there is damage with any of these parts, check the cam chain tensioner as described in this section.*

5. Install the cam chain (**D, Figure 79**) around the crankshaft sprocket.

6. Apply a medium strength threadlock onto the rear chain guide mounting bolt threads. Install the rear chain guide (C, **Figure 79**), collar, washer and tighten the bolt (B) to 12 N•m (106 in.-lb.).

7. Install the front cam chain guide (**Figure 78**). Seat the upper part of the guide into the cylinder notch and its lower end into the guide channel (A, **Figure 79**).

8. Install the flywheel (Chapter Ten).

9. Install the cylinder head as described in this chapter.

## CYLINDER HEAD

This section describes removal, inspection and installation of the cylinder head. After removing the cylinder head, refer to the appropriate sections in this chapter for further disassembly, inspection and assembly procedures. The cylinder head can be removed with the engine mounted in the frame.

**Removal**

1. Remove the upper engine mounting bolts, nut and collars.

2. Remove the engine hanger plates at the cylinder head as described under *Engine, Removal* in this chapter.

3. Drain the coolant (Chapter Three).

4. Remove the exhaust pipe as described in this chapter.

5. Remove the ignition coil (Chapter Ten).

6. Remove the carburetor (Chapter Nine).

7. Remove the cylinder head cover as described in this chapter.

8. Remove the camshaft holder as described in this chapter. Make sure to remove the valve adjustment shims when removing the camshaft holder.

9. Disconnect the coolant hose (A, **Figure 81**) at the cylinder head.

10. Remove the two cylinder head 6 mm mounting bolts (B, **Figure 81**).

11. Loosen the cylinder 6 mm mounting bolt (C, **Figure 81**).

12. Loosen the four cylinder head mounting nuts (**Figure 82**) in several stages and in a crossing pattern. Remove the nuts and washers.

13. Loosen the cylinder head by lightly tapping around its base with a soft mallet. Lift the head from the engine and remove it through the top of the frame.

14. Remove the head gasket (A, **Figure 83**) and the two dowel pins (B) from the cylinder.

15. Secure the cam chain with a piece of wire.

5

16. Cover the engine openings with clean shop rags to prevent debris from entering.

17. Inspect the cylinder head assembly as described in this chapter.

### Installation

1. Make sure to remove all gasket residue from the mating surfaces. All cylinder head and cylinder block surfaces must be clean and dry.

2. Check both cylinder head ports for loose parts.

3. Make sure the front chain guide is installed in the cylinder block (**Figure 78**).

4. Insert the two dowel pins (B, **Figure 83**) and a new cylinder head gasket (A) onto the cylinder.

5. Lower the cylinder head onto the engine, routing the cam chain through the head.

6. Lubricate the cylinder head washers, nuts and stud threads with engine oil.

7. Install the washers and nuts and tighten finger-tight.

8A. On CRF450R models, tighten the nuts (**Figure 82**) in two or three steps and in a crossing pattern to 59 N•m (43 ft.-lb.).

8B. On CRF450X models, tighten the nuts (**Figure 82**) in two or three steps and in a crossing pattern to 66 N•m (49 ft.-lb.).

9A. On 2002-2004 models, tighten the cylinder 6 mm mounting bolt (C, **Figure 81**) to 9.8 N•m (87 in.-lb.).

9B. On 2005 models, tighten the cylinder 6 mm mounting bolt securely.

10A. On 2002-2004 models, install and tighten the cylinder head 6 mm mounting bolts (B, **Figure 81**) to 9.8 N•m (87 in.-lb.).

10B. On 2005 models, install and tighten the cylinder head 6 mm mounting bolts (B, **Figure 81**) securely.

11. Reconnect the coolant hose (A, **Figure 81**) onto the cylinder head water pipe. Tighten the clamp securely.

12. Reverse Steps 1-8 under *Removal* to complete installation, while noting the following:

    a. Tighten the engine hanger plate bolts as described under *Engine, Installation* in this chapter.

    b. Check the valve clearance (Chapter Three).

    c. Refill and bleed the cooling system (Chapter Three).

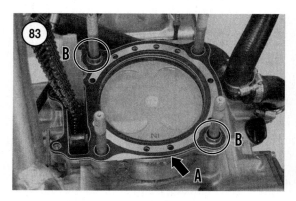

### Inspection

1. Test the valves for leakage by performing a solvent test as described under *Valves* in this chapter.

2. Remove all gasket residue from the cylinder head mating surfaces. Do not scratch or gouge the surfaces.

3. Remove all carbon deposits from the combustion chamber and valve ports (**Figure 84**). Use solvent and a fine wire brush or hardwood scraper. Do not use sharp-edged tools such as screwdrivers or putty knives.

> *CAUTION*
> *If the valves are removed from the head, the valve seats are exposed and can be damaged from careless cleaning. A damaged valve seat will not seal properly.*

4. Inspect the spark plug hole threads and note the following:

    a. If the threads are dirty or mildly damaged, use a spark plug thread tap to clean and straighten the threads. Use kerosene or aluminum tap-cutting fluid to lubricate the threads.

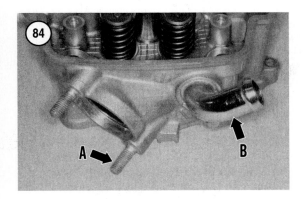

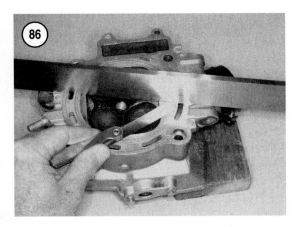

b. If the threads are galled, stripped or cross-threaded, repair with a steel thread insert (Heli-Coil).

*CAUTION*
*Prevent thread damage by applying antiseize compound to the spark plug threads before installation. Do not overtighten the spark plug.*

5. Inspect the exhaust pipe studs (A, **Figure 84**) for thread damage. Replace damaged studs as described in Chapter One.

6. Clean the entire cylinder head assembly in fresh solvent.

*CAUTION*
*If the head was bead-blasted, wash the entire assembly in hot soapy water to remove all blasting grit that is lodged in crevices and threads. Clean and chase all threads to ensure no grit remains. Grit that remains in the head will contaminate the engine oil and damage other parts of the engine.*

7. Inspect the cylinder head for cracks in the combustion chamber, water jackets and exhaust port (**Figure 85**). If there are cracks, have a dealership or machine shop determine if the cylinder head can be repaired.

8. Inspect the cylinder head for warp as follows:
   a. Place a straightedge across the cylinder head as shown in **Figure 86**.
   b. Attempt to insert a flat feeler gauge between the straightedge and the machined surface of the head. If clearance exists, record the measurement.
   c. Repeat substep a and substep b several times, laying the straightedge both across and diagonally on the head.

9. Compare the measurements in Step 8 to the warp service limit in **Table 2**. If the clearance is not within the service limit, have a dealership or machine shop inspect and possibly resurface the cylinder head. If the head warpage is minor, true the head as follows:
   a. Tape a sheet of 400-600 grit emery paper to a thick sheet of glass or surface plate.
   b. Place the head on the emery paper and move the head in a figure-eight pattern.
   c. Rotate the head at regular intervals so material is removed evenly.
   d. Check the progress often, measuring the clearance with the straightedge and feeler gauge. If clearance is excessive, or increases, stop the procedure and have a dealership or machine shop determine if the cylinder head can be repaired.
   e. Reclean the cylinder head.

10. Clean and inspect the cylinder head nuts and washers:

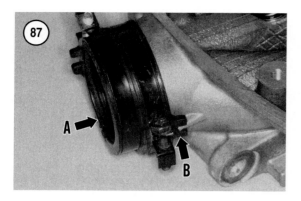

a. Check the stud threads for damage.

b. Check the washers for cracks and warp. The washers must be flat.

11. Check the intake tube (A, **Figure 87**) for damage. If there is any dirt on the inside of the tube, check the carburetor and air box. Install the intake tube by aligning its notch with the tab on the side of the cylinder head (B, **Figure 87**). Tighten the hose clamp securely.

## VALVES

*CAUTION*
*The intake valves are titanium and protected with a thin oxide coating. Handle these valves carefully during all cleaning and inspection procedures.*

### Solvent Test

Perform a solvent test with the valves installed in the cylinder head. The test can reveal if valves are fully seating, as well as expose undetected cracks in the cylinder head.

1. Remove the cylinder head as described in this chapter.

2. Make sure the combustion chamber is dry and the valves are seated.

3. Pour solvent or kerosene into the intake or exhaust port as shown in **Figure 88**.

4. Inspect the combustion chamber for leakage around the valve.

5. Clean and dry the combustion chamber and repeat Steps 3-5 for the other valves.

6. If there is leakage, inspect for:

a. A worn or damaged valve face.

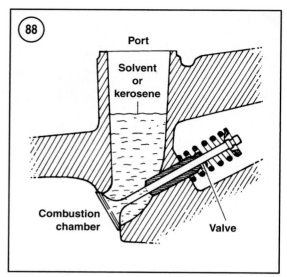

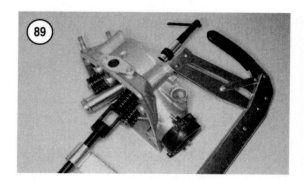

b. A worn or damaged valve seat.

c. A bent valve stem.

d. A crack in the combustion chamber.

### Valve Removal

1. Remove the cylinder head as described in this chapter.

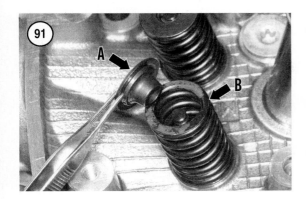

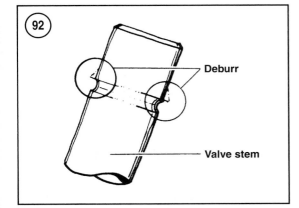

Deburr

Valve stem

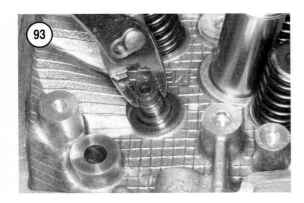

2. Perform a solvent test on the intake and exhaust valves as described in this section.

*NOTE*
*The Motion Pro Valve Spring Compressor (part No. 08-0247) is used to remove and install the valves in the following steps.*

3. Install a valve spring compressor over the valve assembly. Place one end of the tool squarely over

the valve head. Place the other end of the tool squarely on the spring seat (**Figure 89**).

*CAUTION*
*Do not overtighten the valve spring. This can cause a loss of valve spring tension.*

4. Tighten the compressor until the spring seat no longer holds the valve keepers in position. Remove the keepers (**Figure 90**) from the valve stem.

5. Slowly relieve the pressure on the valve spring and remove the valve compressor from the head.

6. Remove the upper spring seat (A, **Figure 91**) and spring (B).

7. Inspect the valve stem for sharp and flared metal around the groove (**Figure 92**). Deburr the valve stem before removing the valve from the head.

*CAUTION*
*Burrs on the valve stem can damage the valve guide.*

8. Remove the valve from the cylinder head.

9. Remove and discard the valve stem seal (**Figure 93**).

10. Remove the lower spring seat (**Figure 94**).

11. Store the valve parts (**Figure 95**, typical) in a divided container so they can be reinstalled in their original position.

*CAUTION*
*Do not intermix the valve components or poor valve seating may result.*

12. Repeat to remove the remaining valves.

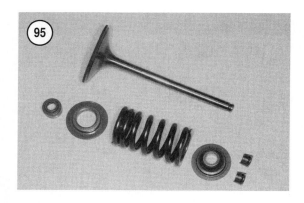

13. Inspect the valve components and cylinder head valve seats as described in this section.

*NOTE*
*Do not remove the valve guides unless they require replacement.*

**Valve Installation**

Perform the following procedure for each set of valve components.

1. Refer to your disassembly notes to identify the valve assemblies and install them in their original mounting position. Note the following:
   a. Refer to **Figure 96** to identify the upper spring seats.
   b. Refer to **Figure 97** to identify the valve keepers.
2. Clean the cylinder head in solvent and dry with compressed air.
3. Install the lower spring seat (**Figure 94**).
4. Coat the inside of a new valve stem seal with engine oil and push it squarely over the end of the valve guide until it snaps into the groove on the outside of the guide (**Figure 98**).
5. Coat the valve stem shaft with molybdenum oil solution.
6. Insert the appropriate valve into the cylinder head. Hold the top of the valve stem seal, then rotate the valve to pass it through the seal. Check that the seal remains seated in the valve guide groove.
7. Install the valve spring with the closely spaced coil pitch end (**Figure 99**) facing down (toward the cylinder head). See B, **Figure 91**.
8. Install the upper spring seat (A, **Figure 91**).
9. Install a valve spring compressor over the valve assembly. Place the tool squarely over the valve head and spring seat (**Figure 89**).

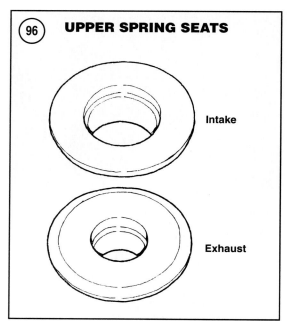

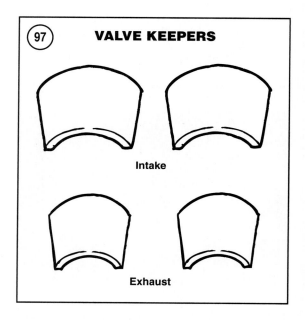

10. Tighten the compressor enough to install the valve keepers.

*CAUTION*
*Do not overtighten and compress the valve spring. This can cause a loss of valve spring tension.*

11. Insert the keepers around the groove in the valve stem (**Figure 100**), then slowly relieve the

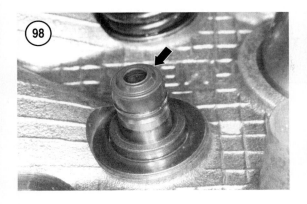

5

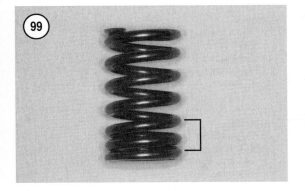

pressure on the valve spring and remove the compressor from the head.

12. Tap the end of the valve stem with a soft mallet to ensure that the keepers (**Figure 101**) are locked in the valve stem groove. See **Figure 102** (intake) and **Figure 103** (exhaust).

13. After installing all the valves, perform a solvent test as described in this chapter.

14. Install the cylinder head as described in this chapter.

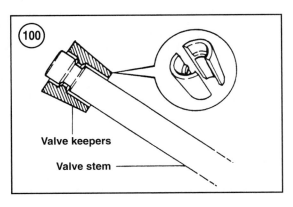

**Valve Inspection**

Refer to the troubleshooting chart in **Figure 104** when performing valve inspection procedures in this section. When measuring the valves and valve components, compare the actual measurements to the specifications in **Table 2**. Replace parts that are damaged or out of specification as described in this section. Maintain the alignment of the valve components as they must be reinstalled in their original position.

1. Soak the valves in solvent to soften the carbon deposits. Then clean and dry carefully. Do not damage the valve seating surface.

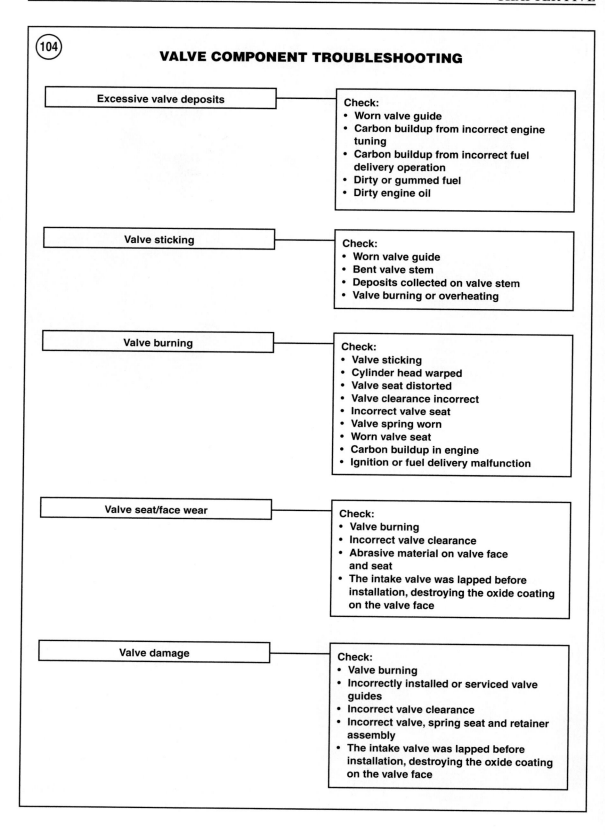

**VALVE COMPONENT TROUBLESHOOTING**

104

**Excessive valve deposits**

Check:
- Worn valve guide
- Carbon buildup from incorrect engine tuning
- Carbon buildup from incorrect fuel delivery operation
- Dirty or gummed fuel
- Dirty engine oil

**Valve sticking**

Check:
- Worn valve guide
- Bent valve stem
- Deposits collected on valve stem
- Valve burning or overheating

**Valve burning**

Check:
- Valve sticking
- Cylinder head warped
- Valve seat distorted
- Valve clearance incorrect
- Incorrect valve seat
- Valve spring worn
- Worn valve seat
- Carbon buildup in engine
- Ignition or fuel delivery malfunction

**Valve seat/face wear**

Check:
- Valve burning
- Incorrect valve clearance
- Abrasive material on valve face and seat
- The intake valve was lapped before installation, destroying the oxide coating on the valve face

**Valve damage**

Check:
- Valve burning
- Incorrectly installed or serviced valve guides
- Incorrect valve clearance
- Incorrect valve, spring seat and retainer assembly
- The intake valve was lapped before installation, destroying the oxide coating on the valve face

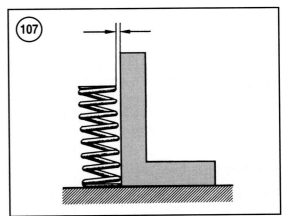

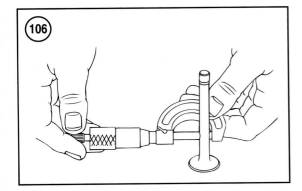

*valve guides with solvent to wash out all particles and dry with compressed air.*

5. Insert each valve into its respective valve guide and move it up and down by hand. The valve should move smoothly.

6. Measure each valve guide inside diameter with a small hole gauge and record the measurements. Note the following:

*NOTE*
*Because valve guides wear unevenly (oval shape), measure each guide at different positions. Use the largest diameter measurement when determining its size.*

  a. If a valve guide is out of specification, replace it as described in this section.

  b. If a valve guide is within specification, record the measurement so it can be used to determine the valve stem-to-guide clearance in Step 7.

7. Subtract the measurement made in Step 4 from the measurement made in Step 6 to determine the valve stem-to-guide clearance. Note the following:

  a. If the clearance is out of specification, determine if a new guide would bring the clearance within specification.

  b. If the clearance would be out of specification with a new guide, replace the valve and guide as a set.

8. Inspect the valve springs as follows:

  a. Inspect each spring for any cracks or other visual damage.

  b. Use a square and check the spring for distortion or tilt (**Figure 107**).

2. Inspect the valve face (**Figure 105**) for burning, pitting or other signs of wear. Unevenness of the valve face is an indication that the valve is not serviceable. If the wear on an exhaust valve is too extensive to be corrected by hand-lapping the valve into its seat, replace the valve. The titanium intake valves cannot be lapped. Replace these valves if defective.

3. Inspect the valve stems for wear and roughness. Check the valve keeper grooves for damage.

4. Measure each valve stem outside diameter with a micrometer (**Figure 106**). Note the following:

  a. If a valve stem is out of specification, discard the valve.

  b. If a valve stem is within specification, record the measurement so it can be used to determine the valve stem-to-guide clearance in Step 7.

*NOTE*
*Honda recommends reaming the valve guides to remove any carbon buildup before checking and measuring the guides. For the home mechanic it is more practical to remove carbon and varnish from the valve guides with a stiff spiral wire brush. Then clean the*

c. Measure the free length of each valve spring with a vernier caliper (**Figure 108**).

d. Replace defective springs.

9. Check the valve keepers. If they are in good condition, they may be reused; replace in pairs as necessary.

10. Inspect the spring seats for damage.

11. Inspect the valve seats as described under *Valve Seat Inspection* in this section.

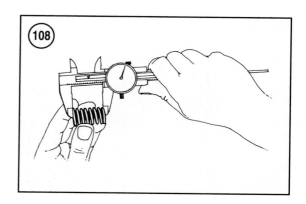

## Valve Seat Inspection

The most accurate method for checking the valve seal is to use a marking compound (machinist's dye), available from auto parts and tool stores. Marking compound is used to locate high or irregular spots when checking or making close fits. Follow the manufacturer's directions.

> *NOTE*
> *Because of the close operating tolerances within the valve assembly, the valve stem-to-guide clearance guide must be within specification; otherwise, the inspection results will be inaccurate.*

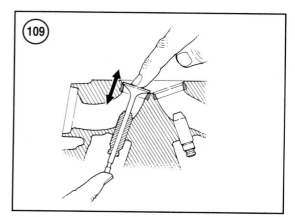

1. Remove, clean and inspect the valves as described in this chapter. The valve face must be in good condition for the inspection results to be accurate.

2. Clean the valve seat in the cylinder head and valve mating areas with contact cleaner.

3. Thoroughly clean all carbon deposits from the valve face with solvent and dry thoroughly.

4. Spread a thin layer of marking compound evenly on the valve face.

5. Slowly insert the valve into its guide and tap the valve against its seat several times (**Figure 109**) without spinning it.

6. Remove the valve and examine the impression left by the marking compound. If the impression (on the valve or in the cylinder head) is not even and continuous, and the valve seat width (**Figure 110**) is not within the specified tolerance listed in **Table 2**, the valve seat in the cylinder head must be reconditioned.

7. Closely examine the valve seat in the cylinder head (**Figure 111**). It should be smooth and even with a polished seating surface.

8. If the valve seat is not in good condition, recondition the valve seat as described in this section.

9. Repeat for the other valves.

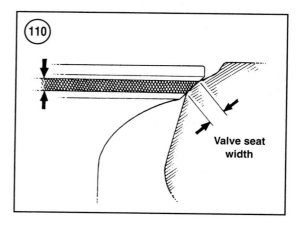

**Valve seat width**

## Valve Guide Replacement

Worn or damaged valve guides must be replaced. Special tools and considerable experience are required to properly replace the valve guides in the cylinder head. If these tools are unavailable, have a Honda dealership perform this procedure. Removing the cylinder head, then taking it to a dealership to replace the valve guides, can save a considerable

*NOTE*
*Flangeless valve guides are used. Step 3 confirms that the original guides were installed to the correct valve guide projection height specified in Table 2. If the projection height measurement is incorrect, the valve guide bore(s) in the cylinder head may have widened, allowing the guide to move.*

3. Measure the valve guide projection height above the cylinder head surface with a vernier caliper (**Figure 112**) and record for each valve guide. Compare to the valve guide projection height specification in **Table 2**. If a valve guide is positioned incorrectly, check its bore for damage.

4. Place the cylinder head on a hot plate and heat to a temperature of 130-140° C (266-284° F). Do not exceed 150° C (300° F). Monitor the temperature with heat sticks, available at welding supply stores, or use an infrared thermometer.

*WARNING*
*Wear welding gloves or similar insulated gloves when handling the cylinder head. It will be very hot.*

*CAUTION*
*Do not heat the cylinder head with a torch; never bring a flame into contact with the cylinder head or valve guide. The direct heat will destroy the case hardening of the valve guide and may warp the cylinder head.*

5. Remove the cylinder head from the hot plate and place on wooden blocks with the combustion chamber facing *up*.

6. From the combustion chamber side of the head, drive out the valve guide with the valve guide remover (**Figure 113**). Quickly repeat this step for each guide to be replaced. Reheat the head as required. Discard the valve guides after removing them.

*CAUTION*
*Because the valve guides are installed with an interference fit, do not attempt to remove them if the head is not hot enough. Doing so may damage (widen) the valve guide bore in the cylinder head and require replacement of the head.*

amount of money. When replacing a valve guide, also replace the valve.

Read the entire procedure before attempting valve guide replacement. When using heat in the following steps, it is necessary to work quickly and have the correct tools on hand.

*Tools*

See a Honda dealership for the correct valve guide and valve guide reamer.

*Procedure*

1. Remove all the valves and valve guide seals from the cylinder head.

2. Place the new valve guides in the freezer for approximately one hour prior to heating the cylinder head. Chilling them slightly reduces the outside diameter, while the cylinder is slightly larger due to heat expansion. This will make valve guide installation much easier. Remove the guides, one at a time, as needed.

7. Allow the cylinder head to cool.

8. Inspect and clean the valve guide bores. Check for cracks or any scoring along the bore wall.

9. Reheat the cylinder head as described in Step 4, then place onto wooden blocks with the valve spring side facing *up*.

10. Remove one new valve guide, either intake or exhaust, from the freezer.

11. Align the valve guide in the bore. Using the valve guide driver tool and a hammer, drive in the valve guide into the cylinder head until the valve guide projection height (**Figure 112**) is within the specification in **Table 2**.

12. Repeat to install the remaining valve guides.

13. Allow the cylinder head to cool to room temperature.

14. Ream each valve guide as follows:

   a. Place the cylinder head on wooden blocks with the combustion chamber facing *up*. The guides are reamed from this side.

   b. Coat the valve guide and valve guide reamer with cutting oil.

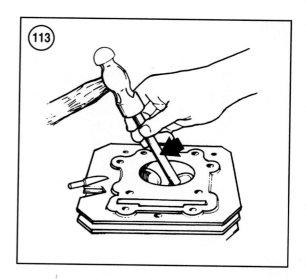

> *CAUTION*
> *Always rotate the reamer **clockwise** through the entire length of the guide, both when reaming the guide and when removing the reamer. Rotating the reamer counterclockwise will reverse cut and damage (enlarge) the valve guide bore.*

> *CAUTION*
> *Do not allow the reamer to tilt. Keep the tool square to the hole and apply even pressure and twisting motion during the entire operation.*

   c. Rotate the reamer clockwise into the valve guide (**Figure 114**).

   d. Slowly rotate the reamer through the guide, while periodically adding cutting oil.

   e. As the end of the reamer passes through the valve guide, maintain the clockwise motion and work the reamer back out of the guide while continuing to add cutting oil.

   f. Clean the reamer of all chips and relubricate with cutting oil before starting on the next guide. Repeat for each guide as required.

15. Thoroughly clean the cylinder head and all valve components in solvent, then with detergent

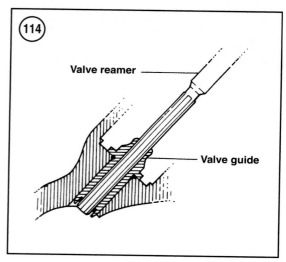

Valve reamer

Valve guide

and hot water to remove all cutting residue. Rinse in cold water and dry with compressed air.

16. Measure the valve guide inside diameter with a small hole gauge. The measurement must be within the specification listed in **Table 2**.

17. Apply engine oil to the valve guides to prevent rust.

18. Lubricate a valve stem with engine oil and pass it through its valve guide, verifying that it moves without any roughness or binding. Repeat for each valve and guide.

19. After installing a new valve guide, the valve seat must be refaced with a 45° seat cutter as described under *Valve Seat Reconditioning* in this chapter.

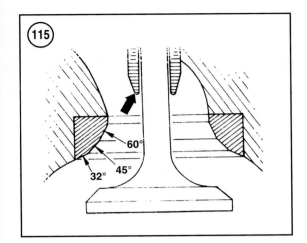

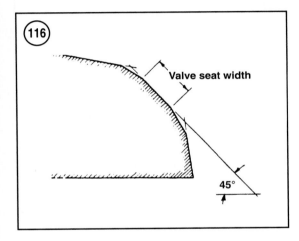

**Valve seat width**

**Valve Seat Reconditioning**

Before reconditioning the valve seats, inspect and measure them as described under *Valve Seat Inspection* in this chapter.

*Tools*

To cut the cylinder head valve seats, the following tools are required:

1. Valve seat cutters (**Figure 115**). See a Honda dealership.

2. Vernier caliper.

3. Gear-marking compound.

4. Valve lapping tool.

*Procedure*

If the intake valve seats must be cut, discard the original intake valves and use new intake valves during this procedure.

*NOTE*
*Follow the manufacturer's instructions when using valve facing equipment.*

1. Carefully rotate and insert the solid pilot into the valve guide. Make sure the pilot is correctly seated.
2. Install the 45° cutter and cutter holder onto the solid pilot.

*CAUTION*
*Work slowly and make light cuts during reconditioning. Overcutting the valve seats will recede the valves into the cylinder head, reducing the valve adjustment range. If cutting is excessive, the ability to set the valve adjustment may be lost. This condition requires cylinder head replacement.*

3. Using the 45° cutter (**Figure 116**), de-scale and clean the valve seat with one or two turns.
4. If the seat is still pitted or burned, turn the 45° cutter additional turns until the surface is clean. Avoid removing too much material from the cylinder head.
5. Measure the valve seat with a vernier caliper (**Figure 110**). Record the measurement to use as a reference point when performing the following.

*CAUTION*
*The 32° cutter removes material quickly. Work carefully and check the progress often.*

6. Install the 32° cutter onto the solid pilot and lightly cut the seat to remove 1/4 of the existing valve seat (**Figure 117**).
7. Install the 60° cutter onto the solid pilot and lightly cut the seat to remove 1/4 of the existing valve seat (**Figure 118**).
8. Measure the valve seat with a vernier caliper (**Figure 110**). Then fit the 45° cutter onto the solid pilot and cut the valve seat to the specified width (**Figure 116**) in **Table 2**.
9. When the valve seat width is correct, check valve seating as follows:
   a. Clean the valve seat with contact cleaner.

b. Spread a thin layer of marking compound evenly on the valve face.

c. Slowly insert the valve into its guide.

d. Support the valve with two fingers (**Figure 109**) and tap the valve up and down in the cylinder head several times. Do not rotate the valve or a false reading will result.

e. Remove the valve and examine the impression left by the marking compound (**Figure 119**).

f. Measure the valve seat width as shown in **Figure 110**. Refer to **Table 2** for specified valve seat width.

g. The valve contact should be approximately in the center of the valve seat area (**Figure 119**).

10. If the contact area is too high on the valve, or if it is too wide, use the 32° cutter and remove a portion of the top area of the valve seat material to lower and narrow the contact area on the valve (**Figure 119**).

11. If the contact area is too low on the valve, or too wide, use the 60° cutter and remove a portion of the lower area of the valve seat material to raise and narrow the contact area on the valve (**Figure 111**).

12. After obtaining the desired valve seat position and width, use the 45° cutter to lightly clean off any burrs that may have been caused by previous cuts.

13A. Exhaust valves—When the contact area is correct, lap the valve as described in this chapter.

13B. Intake valves—The titanium intake valves have a thin oxide coating on their face and must not be lapped. When new intake valve seats are cut in the cylinder head, install new intake valves without lapping them.

14. Repeat Steps 1-13B for all remaining valve seats.

15. Thoroughly clean the cylinder head and all valve components in solvent, then with detergent and hot water. Rinse in cold water and dry with compressed air. Apply a light coat of clean engine oil to all non-aluminum surfaces to prevent rust.

## Valve Lapping

### Intake valves

Do not lap the intake valves. These valves are titanium and have a thin oxide coating (approximately 1.0 micron thick) on their face. Lapping

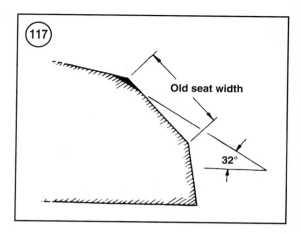

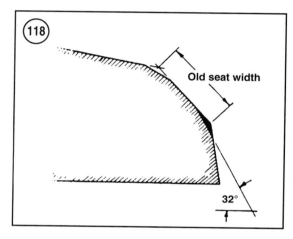

removes the oxide coating and causes the valve face to wear faster. This causes short valve and seat life and a significant power loss. When new intake valve seats are cut in the cylinder head, install new intake valves without lapping them.

### Exhaust valves

Valve lapping can restore the exhaust valve seat without machining if the amount of wear or distortion is not too great.

Perform this procedure after determining that the valve seat width and outside diameter are within specifications. A valve lapping tool and compound are required.

1. Smear a light coating of fine grade valve lapping compound on the valve face seating surface.

2. Insert the valve into the head.

3. Wet the suction cup of the lapping stick and stick it onto the head of the valve. Spin the tool in both di-

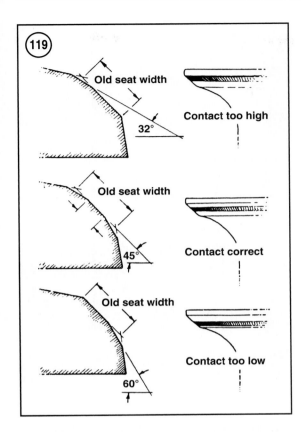

4. Closely examine the valve seat in the cylinder head (**Figure 110**). It should be smooth and even with a smooth, polished seating ring.

5. Repeat Steps 1-4 for the other exhaust valve.

6. Thoroughly clean the cylinder head and all valve components in solvent, then with detergent and hot water. Rinse in cold water and dry with compressed air. Apply a light coat of clean engine oil to all non-aluminum surfaces to prevent rust.

*CAUTION*
*Any compound left on the valves or in the cylinder head causes excessive wear to the engine components.*

7. Install the valve assemblies as described in this chapter.

8. After completing the lapping and reinstalling the valves are in the head, perform the *Solvent Test* described under *Valves* in this chapter. There should be no leakage past the seat. If leakage occurs, the combustion chamber will appear wet. If fluid leaks past any of the exhaust valve seats, disassemble that valve assembly and repeat the lapping procedure until there is no leakage. If fluid leaks past an intake valve seat, remove the valve and inspect the valve face and seat.

9. If the cylinder head and valve components are cleaned in detergent and hot water, apply a light coat of engine oil to all bare metal surfaces to prevent rust formation.

## CYLINDER

The cylinder and piston can be removed with the engine installed in the frame.

### Removal

*NOTE*
*Before removing the top end, clean the area above the cylinder so dirt and other abrasive material cannot fall into the engine.*

1. Remove the cylinder head as described in this chapter.

2. Remove the front chain guide (A, **Figure 121**).

3. Remove the 6 mm cylinder mounting bolt (B, **Figure 121**).

4. Loosen the cylinder by tapping around the base.

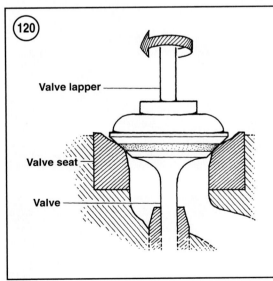

rections, while pressing it against the valve seat and lap the valve to the seat. Every 5 to 10 seconds, lift and rotate the valve 180° in the valve seat. Continue until the gasket surfaces on the valve and seat are smooth and equal in size. See **Figure 120**.

5. Remove the cylinder from the crankcase, routing the cam chain through the chain tunnel. Do not dislodge and drop the three dowel pins into the crankcase.

6. Remove the base gasket (A, **Figure 122**).

7. Remove the coolant passage dowel pin (B, **Figure 122**) and the two cylinder dowel pins (C).

8. Slide pieces of cut hose down the cylinder studs to protect the piston rings from damage.

9. Cover the cam chain tunnel and piston to prevent small parts from falling into the engine.

10. Check for damaged or broken piston rings. Check the piston as described under *Piston Inspection* in this chapter.

11. Clean and inspect the cylinder as described in this section.

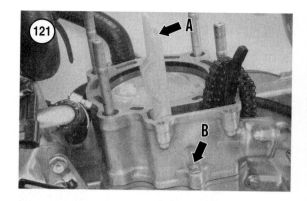

**Installation**

1. Clean the cylinder and crankcase gasket surfaces. Note the following:

   a. If the crankcase halves were reassembled, remove all protruding gasket material from the crankcase joint surfaces (A, **Figure 123**).

   b. Do not drop gasket material into the coolant passage (B, **Figure 123**).

   c. Do not drop gasket material into the engine oil passage (C, **Figure 123**). Doing so plugs the crankcase oil jet (**Figure 124**).

   d. Make sure the cylinder block oil passage is clear. This passage provides oil to the engine top end.

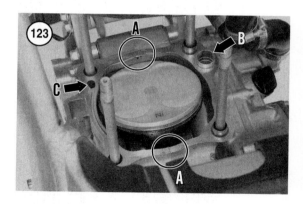

2. If used, remove the hoses from the cylinder studs.

3. Install the coolant passage dowel pin (B, **Figure 122**) and the two cylinder dowel pins (C).

*NOTE*
*The stock base gasket is equipped with two sealer pads (**Figure 125**) to help seal the crankcase mating areas.*

4. Install a new base gasket (A, **Figure 122**) onto the crankcase. Check that the gasket seats flush around the dowel pins.

5. Lubricate the following components with engine oil.

   a. Piston and rings.

   b. Piston pin and small end of connecting rod.

   c. Cylinder bore.

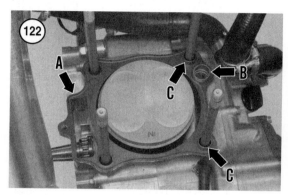

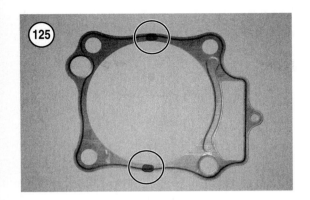

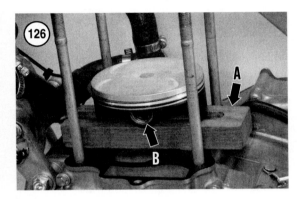

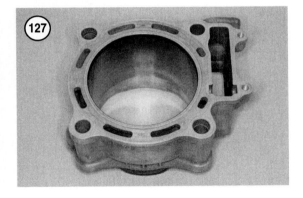

5

6. Rest the piston on a wooden holding fixture (A, **Figure 126**).

7. Make sure the piston circlips (B, **Figure 126**) are properly installed.

8. Stagger the piston ring gaps on the piston as shown under *Piston Installation* in this chapter.

*NOTE*
*If there is interference during cylinder installation, the cylinder may be contacting the coolant hose on the right side of the engine.*

9. Lower the cylinder over the piston, routing the cam chain and rear cam chain guide (if installed) through the chain tunnel. Compress each ring so it can enter the cylinder. When the bottom ring is in the cylinder, remove the holding fixture and lower the cylinder onto the crankcase. Secure the cam chain so it cannot fall into the engine.

10. Install the 6 mm cylinder mounting bolt (B, **Figure 121**) but do not tighten it. This bolt will be tightened during cylinder head installation.

11. Pull up on the cam chain so it cannot bind against the crankshaft sprocket and turn the engine over slowly by operating the kick pedal by hand. If there is any excessive noise or roughness, remove the cylinder and check for a broken piston ring.

12. Install the front chain guide (A, **Figure 121**).

13. Install the cylinder head as described in this chapter.

**Inspection**

1. Remove all gasket residue from the cylinder and crankcase surfaces. Use solvent and a soft scraper to remove residue. Do not use sharp-edge tools that can scratch surfaces. If necessary, soak the surfaces with a solvent-soaked rag to soften deposits.

2. Wash the cylinder in solvent and dry with compressed air. Clean all deposits from the water jacket.

3. Inspect the cylinder bore (**Figure 127**) for obvious scoring or gouges. If damage is evident, replace or resleeve the cylinder.

4. Measure and check the cylinder for wear, taper and out-of-round. Measure the inside diameter of the cylinder with a bore gauge or inside micrometer (**Figure 128**) as follows:

a. Measure the cylinder at three points along the bore axis (**Figure 129**). At each point, measure in line (X measurement) with the piston pin, and 90° to the pin (Y measurement). Record and identify the six measurements.

b. Cylinder wear—Use the largest measurement recorded (X or Y) and compare it to the specifications and service limit in **Table 3**. If the cylinder bore is not within the service limit, replace or resleeve the cylinder.

c. Cylinder out-of-round—Determine the largest Y measurement made in substep a. Determine the smallest X measurement made in substep a. Determine the difference between the two measurements. Compare the result to the service limit in **Table 3**. If the cylinder bore is not within the service limit, replace or resleeve the cylinder.

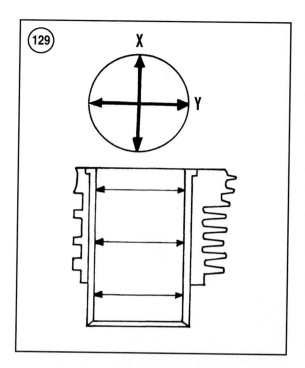

> *NOTE*
> *An out-of-round cylinder bore will cause ring scuffing, thus accelerating piston ring and bore wear.*

d. Cylinder taper—Determine the largest X or Y measurement made at the top of the cylinder. Determine the largest X or Y measurement made at the bottom of the cylinder. Determine the difference between the two measurements. Compare the result to the service limit in **Table 3**. If the cylinder bore is not within the service limit, replace or resleeve the cylinder.

> *NOTE*
> *If the cylinder bore is out of specification, either replace or resleeve the cylinder. When replacing the cylinder, install new piston and rings as a set. If the cylinder is resleeved, the machine shop will fit a new piston to the new cylinder.*

> *NOTE*
> *If the cylinder is within all service limits, and the current piston and rings are reusable, do not deglaze or hone the stock cylinder bore. This procedure may damage the hardened bore. If the cylinder has been resleeved, the cast iron bore can be deglazed. In all instances, do not remove the carbon ridge at the top of the cylinder bore.*

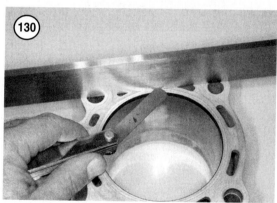

*Removing the buildup will promote oil consumption.*

5. Use a straightedge and feeler gauge set (**Figure 130**) and check the top of the cylinder for warp. Replace the cylinder if the warp exceeds the service limit in **Table 3**.

6. Wash the cylinder in hot, soapy water and rinse with clear water. Then check the cleanliness by passing a clean, white cloth over the bore. No residue should be evident. When the cylinder is thoroughly clean and dry, lightly coat the cylinder bore with oil and wrap it in plastic until reassembly.

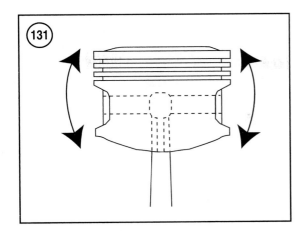

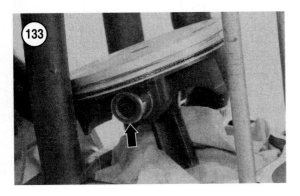

5

necting rod with a chrome-plated, steel piston pin. The pin is a precision fit in the piston and rod, and held in place with plain circlips.

While cleaning and measuring each component of the piston assembly, record and identify all measurements. Refer to the measurements and **Table 3** when calculating clearances and checking wear limits.

**Piston Removal**

*CAUTION*
*When it is necessary to rotate the crankshaft, pull up the cam chain so it cannot bind against the crankshaft sprocket. Guide and protect the piston so it will not be damaged when retracted into the crankcase.*

1. Remove the cylinder as described in this chapter.
2. Before removing the piston, hold the rod and try to rock the piston from side to side (**Figure 131**). A rocking (not sliding) motion indicates wear on either the piston pin, pin bore, rod bushing or a combination of all three parts. Careful inspection will be required to determine which parts require replacement.
3. Stuff shop rags around the connecting rod and in the cam chain tunnel to prevent debris and small parts from falling into the crankcase.
4. Slide a rubber hose over the front cylinder studs to protect the piston and rings.
5. Find the IN piston identification mark on the piston crown. If there is no mark, scribe an alignment mark on top of the piston.
6. Remove the circlips from the piston pin bore (**Figure 132**). Discard the circlips.

*NOTE*
*Install new circlips during assembly.*

7. Push the piston pin out of the piston by hand (**Figure 133**). If the pin is tight, use a pin puller (Motion Pro part No. 08-0068) or a homemade removal tool (**Figure 134**).

*CAUTION*
*Do not attempt to drive the pin out with a hammer and drift. The piston and connecting rod assembly may be damaged.*

*CAUTION*
*The cylinder must be washed in hot soapy water. Solvents will not remove the fine grit left in the cylinder. This grit will cause premature wear of the rings and cylinder.*

## PISTON AND PISTON RINGS

The piston is made of aluminum alloy and fitted with two rings. The piston is attached to the con-

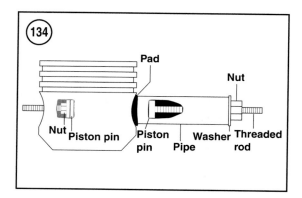

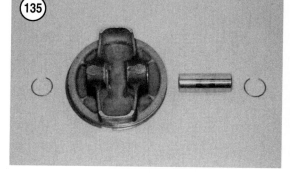

8. Lift the piston off the connecting rod.

9. Inspect the piston, piston rings and piston pin as described in this section.

**Piston Installation**

1. Install the piston rings onto the piston as described in this chapter.

2. Make sure all parts are clean and ready to install. Install new piston circlips (**Figure 135**).

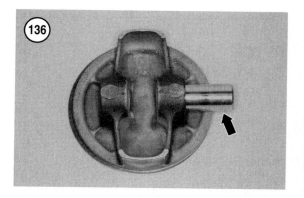

> *CAUTION*
> *Never install used circlips, although they appear reusable, as they fatigue and distort during removal. Engine damage will occur if a circlip pops out of its groove during engine operation.*

3. Install a new circlip into one side of the piston. Rotate the circlip in the groove until the end gap is facing down.

4. Lubricate the following components with molybdenum disulfide oil.

  a. Piston pin.

  b. Piston pin bores.

  c. Connecting rod bore.

5. Start the piston pin into the open piston pin bore (**Figure 136**). Place the piston over the connecting rod so the IN mark (**Figure 137**) faces the intake side of the engine. If the IN mark is unreadable, use the identification mark made before piston removal.

> *CAUTION*
> *The piston must be installed correctly to accommodate piston pin offset and prevent the valves from striking the piston. Failure to install the piston correctly can lead to engine damage.*

6. Align the piston with the rod and slide the pin through the piston and rod (**Figure 133**).

7. Install a wooden holding fixture under the piston to steady the piston when installing the circlip.

8. Install the second circlip into the piston groove (**Figure 132**). Rotate the circlip in the groove until the end gap is facing down.

9. Stagger the ring end gaps as shown in **Figure 138**.

10. Install the cylinder as described in this chapter.

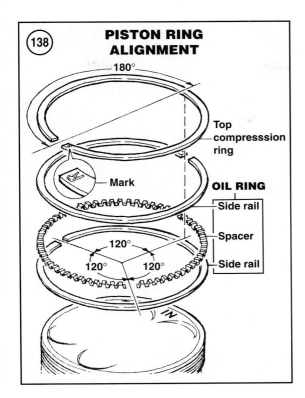

PISTON RING ALIGNMENT

Top compresssion ring

Mark

OIL RING

Side rail

Spacer

Side rail

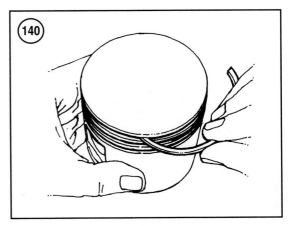

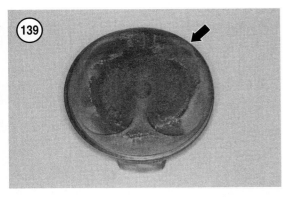

## Piston Inspection

The recommended piston replacement interval is every six races or after 15 hours of engine operation.

Inspect the used piston at this time interval to detect any possible engine or tuning problems that could damage the new piston.

1. Remove the piston rings as described in this section.

2. Slide a finger along the piston's intake skirt. The surface should feel smooth. If the surface feels coarse or grainy, dirt may be passing through the air filter. Check for a dirty or damaged air filter or leaking air box.

3. Check the piston crown (**Figure 139**) for wear or damage. If the piston crown is pitted, overheating is likely occurring. This can be caused by a lean fuel mixture and/or preignition. If damage is evident, perform the troubleshooting procedures as described in Chapter Two. Recheck the crown after cleaning it.

> *CAUTION*
> *If the piston crown was damaged by pre-ignition or other causes, inspect the connecting rod for damage. Heat passing through the piston may have weakened the rod. If there is any doubt, replace the crankshaft (this chapter).*

> *CAUTION*
> *Clean the piston carefully as tools can scratch or chip the valve pockets and damage the piston. This will cause hot spots on the piston when the engine is running.*

4. Soak the piston in solvent to soften the carbon buildup. Then clean the piston crown using a soft scraper. Do not use tools that can damage the surface. Clean the oil holes in the oil ring groove and at the top of the piston skirt, directly below the oil ring groove. Do not enlarge the holes.

5. Clean the piston pin bore, ring grooves and piston skirt. Clean the ring grooves with a soft brush, or use a broken piston ring (same shape and thickness as original ring [**Figure 140**]) to remove carbon and oil residue. Polish any mild galling or

discoloration off the piston skirt with fine emery cloth and oil.

*CAUTION*
*Do not wire brush piston skirts or ring lands. The wire brush removes aluminum and increases piston clearance. It also rounds the corners of the ring lands, which causes decreased support for the piston rings.*

6. Inspect the ring grooves for dents, nicks, cracks or other damage. The grooves should be square and uniform for the circumference of the piston. Particularly inspect the top compression ring groove. It is lubricated the least and is nearest the combustion chamber and higher operating temperatures. If the oil ring appears worn, or if the oil ring was difficult to remove, the piston has likely overheated and distorted. Replace the piston if any type of damage is detected.

7. Inspect the piston skirt (**Figure 141**). If the skirt shows excessive galling or partial seizure (bits of metal embedded in the skirt), replace the piston.

8. Inspect the interior of the piston. Check the crown, skirt, piston pin bores and bosses for cracks or other damage. Check the circlip grooves for cleanliness and damage. Replace the piston if necessary.

9. Measure the piston pin bore diameter (A, **Figure 142**) with a small hole gauge and micrometer. Measure each bore horizontally and vertically. Record the measurements. Compare the largest measurement to the specifications in **Table 3**. Record this measurement to determine the piston pin bore-to-piston pin clearance described in *Piston Pin and Connecting Rod Inspection* in this section.

10. Inspect the piston ring-to-ring groove clearance as described in *Piston Ring Inspection and Removal* in this section. This check will help locate a dented or damaged ring groove.

## Piston-to-Cylinder Clearance Check

Calculate the clearance between the piston and cylinder as follows:

1. Clean and dry the piston and cylinder before measuring.

2. Determine the cylinder inside diameter as described under *Cylinder Inspection* in this chapter. If the measurement exceeds the specification in **Table**

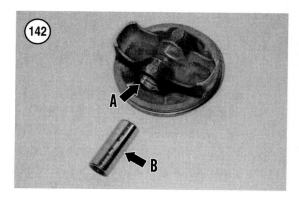

**3**, either install a new cylinder or resleeve the cylinder. If the cylinder bore is within specification, continue with Step 3.

3. Measure the piston skirt outside diameter at a position 90° to the direction of the piston pin (**Figure 143**), while measuring up from the bottom edge of the piston skirt the dimension specified in **Table 3**. Record the measurement. If the piston diameter is within specification, continue with Step 4. If the piston diameter is too small, install a new piston and ring set and perform Step 4.

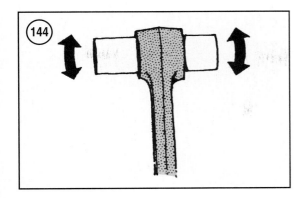

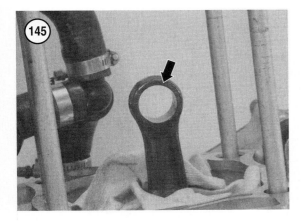

4. Determine the clearance by subtracting the piston measurement from the largest cylinder measurement. If the clearance is too large, either replace or resleeve the cylinder. When replacing the cylinder, install a new piston and ring set. If the cylinder is resleeved, the machine shop will fit a new piston to the new cylinder.

## Piston Pin and Connecting Rod Inspection

1. Clean and dry the piston pin.

2. Inspect the piston pin (B, **Figure 142**) for chrome flaking, wear or discoloration from overheating.

3. Inspect the piston pin bore in the connecting rod (**Figure 144**). Check for scoring, uneven wear, and discoloration from overheating or excessive wear.

4. Lubricate the piston pin and slide it into the connecting rod. The pin is a slip fit and should slide through the rod with no resistance. Slowly pivot the pin and check for radial play (**Figure 144**). If there is play, one or both of the parts are worn. Measure

the parts in the following steps to determine their condition and operating clearance.

5. Determine the connecting rod-to-piston pin clearance as follows:

    a. Measure the connecting rod small end inside diameter (**Figure 145**) and compare against the specifications in **Table 3**. If the inside diameter is too large, replace the crankshaft (this chapter).

    b. Measure the piston pin at its middle point (B, **Figure 142**). Replace the piston pin if the measurement exceeds the service limit in **Table 3**.

    c. If both parts are within specification, subtract the piston pin measurement from the connecting rod measurement. If the measurement exceeds the service limit and the connecting rod inside diameter is within specification, replace the piston pin.

*CAUTION*
*If the piston crown was damaged by pre-ignition or other causes, heat passing through the piston may have weakened the rod. If there is any doubt, replace the crankshaft (this chapter).*

6. Determine the piston pin bore-to-piston pin clearance as follows:

    a. Measure the piston pin at both ends (B, **Figure 142**). Record the measurements. Replace the pin if any measurement exceeds the service limit listed in **Table 3**.

    b. Subtract the smallest piston pin measurement from the piston pin bore measurement. This measurement is described under *Piston Inspection* in this chapter. Replace the piston and pin if they exceed the service limit in **Table 3**.

## Piston Ring Inspection and Removal

The recommended replacment interval for the piston rings is every six races or after 15 hours of engine operation. During these time intervals, the operational life of the piston rings depends greatly on periodic oil and filter changes and air filter service. Poor service and dirty oil shortens ring life and reduces engine performance.

5

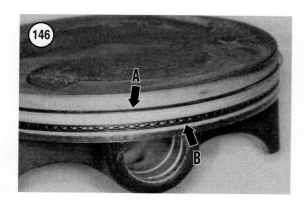

The ring assembly consists of a single compression ring (A, **Figure 146**) and an oil control ring assembly (B). The oil ring assembly consists of two side rails and a spacer. See **Figure 138**.

1. Check the piston ring sealing surfaces (**Figure 146**) for abrasive wear and scuffing. Vertical scratches on the rings indicates that dirt is passing through the air filter. Scuffing is usually caused by excessive engine temperatures or an out-of-round cylinder bore.

2. Check the compression piston ring-to-ring groove clearance as follows:

   a. Clean the ring and groove (A, **Figure 146**) so accurate measurements can be made with a flat feeler gauge.

   b. Press the top ring into the groove, so the ring is nearly flush with the piston.

   c. Insert a flat feeler gauge between the ring and groove (**Figure 147**). Record the measurement. Repeat this step at other points around the piston. Replace the ring if any measurement exceeds the service limit in **Table 3**. If excessive clearance remains after installing a new ring, replace the piston.

3. Spread the compression ring by hand (**Figure 148**) and remove it from the piston. Mark the topside of the ring if the original R mark is not visible. If the ring is to be reused, it must be installed facing in its original direction.

*CAUTION*
*Piston ring edges are sharp. Be careful when handling.*

*CAUTION*
*Piston rings are brittle. Do not overspread rings when removing.*

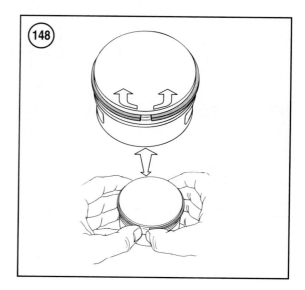

4. Remove the oil ring assembly by first removing the topside rail, followed by the bottom side rail. Remove the spacer last (**Figure 138**). Identify the side rails so they can be installed facing in their original position.

5. Clean and inspect the piston as described in *Piston Inspection* in this section.

6. Measure the piston ring end gap as follows:

*NOTE*
*When measuring the oil control ring, only measure the side rails. Do not measure the spacer.*

   a. Inspect the ring ends for any carbon buildup and remove with a fine-cut file. Do not remove metal from the ring ends.

   b. Place the ring into the middle of the cylinder and square it with the piston. The accuracy of

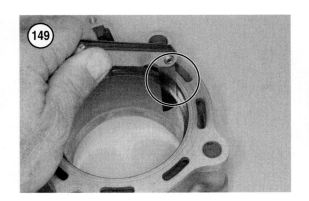

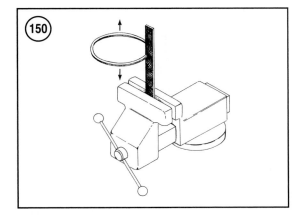

this measurement depends on how square the ring is in the cylinder.

c. Measure the ring gap with a flat feeler gauge (**Figure 149**). Record the measurement and compare to the specified gap in **Table 3**. Replace the rings as a set if any gap measurement exceeds the service limit in **Table 3**.

d. If new rings are installed, gap the new rings after the cylinder has been serviced. If the new ring gap is too small, carefully widen the gap using a fine-cut file as shown in **Figure 150**. Work slow and measure often.

7. Roll the compression ring around its piston groove and check for carbon and binding from a damaged ring groove. Remove carbon with a broken piston ring as described under *Piston Inspection* in this section. Repair minor damage with a fine-cut file. If damage is excessive, replace the piston and rings as a set.

### Piston Ring Installation

1. Check that the piston and rings are clean and dry.

*CAUTION*
*Install the rings by hand (**Figure 148**). Piston rings are brittle. Spread them only enough to clear the piston.*

*NOTE*
*If reusing the piston rings, refer to your identification marks to install them facing in their original direction.*

2. Install the oil control ring assembly (**Figure 138**) as follows:

a. New oil control rings are not marked. The side rails and spacer can be installed with either side facing up.

b. Install the oil control ring assembly into the bottom ring groove. Install the spacer first, then the lower and upper side rail. Make sure the ends of the spacer butt together. They must not overlap.

c. Squeeze the ring assembly by hand. Make sure the assembly compresses properly into the ring groove. If not, the spacer ends are overlapping.

3. Install the compression ring into the top ring groove with its manufacturer's R mark facing up.

### COUNTERSHAFT SEAL REPLACEMENT

A leaking countershaft seal (**Figure 151**) can be replaced with the engine assembled and installed in the frame. If oil is leaking from this seal, replace it as follows:

1. Support the bike on a stand.

2. Remove the drive sprocket cover and drive sprocket (Chapter Twelve).

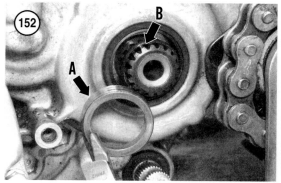

3. Clean the area around the seal. Do not force water past the damaged seal.

4. Remove the spacer (A, **Figure 152**) and O-ring (B) from the countershaft.

5. Remove the seal with a seal removal tool as shown in **Figure 153**. Place a rag between the tool and engine to prevent engine damage. If the seal is tight, apply pressure at alternate spots around the seal until it begins to move.

6. Clean the sealing area in the crankcase. Check the seal bore for cracks or other damage.

7. Check the spacer for excessive wear or other damage, especially where it operates against the seal. Remove burrs and smooth the spacer surface with a file. Then clean the spacer.

8. Pack the lip of the new seal with grease.

9. Install the seal over the countershaft and center it in the seal bore. Then push the seal squarely into the bore until its outer surface is 0.5-1.0 mm (0.02-0.04 in.) within the outer bore surface (**Figure 154**).

10. Lubricate a new O-ring with oil and slide it over the countershaft.

11. Install the spacer with its shoulder side facing the engine. Turn and push the spacer past the seal until it contacts the O-ring and bottoms against the countershaft bearing.

12. Install the drive sprocket and cover (Chapter Twelve).

13. Check the transmission oil level and refill as needed (Chapter Three).

## SHIFT SHAFT SEAL REPLACEMENT

A leaking shift shaft seal (**Figure 155**) can be replaced with the engine installed in the frame. If oil is leaking from this seal, replace it as follows:

1. Support the bike on a stand.

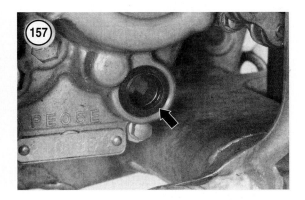

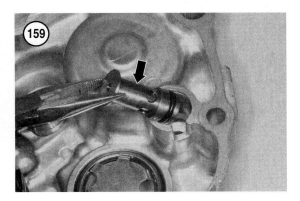

2. Clean the area around the seal. Do not force water past the damaged seal.

3. Remove the shift shaft assembly (Chapter Seven).

4. Remove the seal with a hooked tool and rag as shown in **Figure 156**. Make sure the end of the tool contacts the seal and not the seal bore.

5. Clean the seal bore in the crankcase. Check the seal bore for cracks or other damage.

6. Pack the lip of the new seal with grease.

7. Align the new seal with the seal bore and install it by hand until it is flush with the outer bore surface (**Figure 157**).

8. Inspect the shift shaft where it rides against the seal. The shaft must be smooth in this area. Remove any raised burrs with a file. However, do not remove material or reduce the shaft diameter as this will cause the new seal to leak. If there is a low spot on the shaft at the seal operating area, replace the shift shaft.

9. Install the shift shaft (Chapter Seven).

## OIL RELIEF VALVE, OIL PUMP DRIVE GEAR AND OIL STRAINER

This section covers lubrication system components that can be serviced with the engine installed in the frame.

> *NOTE*
> *Lubrication system components installed inside the engine are covered separately. Refer to **Oil Pump and One-Way Valve** in this chapter to service these components. To service the oil jet installed in the left crankcase, refer to **Inspection** under **Crankcase** in this chapter.*

### Oil Relief Valve
### Removal/Inspection/Installation

The oil relief valve is mounted inside the left crankcase cover.

1. Remove the left crankcase cover (Chapter Ten).

2. Remove the snap ring (**Figure 158**) and oil relief valve (**Figure 159**) from the left crankcase cover.

3. Before cleaning the oil relief valve (A, **Figure 160**), check it for clogging and other debris. The passage holes in the valve should be clear.

4. Discard the O-ring (B, **Figure 160**) and clean the valve in solvent. Dry thoroughly.

5. Replace the oil relief valve if damaged. Do not disassemble the valve as replacement parts are not available.

6. Clean the left crankcase cover oil passages as described under *Left Crankcase Cover* in Chapter Ten.

7. Lubricate a new O-ring and install it into the valve groove.

8. Lubricate the valve with engine oil and install it into the left crankcase cover. Install the snap ring with its flat side facing out.

9. Install the left crankcase cover (Chapter Ten).

10. Install a new oil filter and refill the engine with oil (Chapter Three).

### Oil Pump Drive Gear and Oil Strainer Removal/Inspection/Installation

These components are mounted behind the left crankcase cover.

1. Remove the flywheel (Chapter Ten).

2. Remove the balancer shaft (Chapter Seven).

3. Turn the oil pump drive gear (A, **Figure 161**) by hand. The shaft should turn freely. If there is any roughness, disassemble the crankcase and remove the oil pump shaft and rotors for inspection.

4. Remove the snap ring (B, **Figure 161**), oil pump drive gear (A) and pin (**Figure 162**) from the oil pump shaft. Discard the snap ring.

5. Remove the two mounting bolts (A and B, **Figure 163**), brackets and oil strainer assembly (C).

6. Oil pump drive gear (**Figure 164**):
   a. Clean and dry the oil pump drive gear and pin.
   b. Replace the gear and pin if damaged.
   c. If the pin is damaged, check the mating hole in the oil pump shaft for damage.

7. Oil strainer assembly:
   a. Remove the O-ring (A, **Figure 165**) and grommet (B) from the oil strainer. Discard the O-ring.
   b. Check the strainer for contamination and damage. Carefully pick large contaminants from the screen face (**Figure 166**). Then blow compressed air through the open end of the oil pipe (C, **Figure 165**). Do not blow air through the outside of the screen.
   c. After cleaning the screen, clean the oil strainer in clean solvent, then blow through

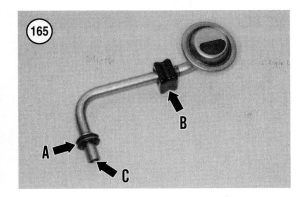

the oil pipe (C, **Figure 165**) a final time to clean the pipe and screen. Make sure the oil strainer is dry so that there is no solvent remaining in the strainer that could contaminate the engine oil.

   d. Discard the grommet (B, **Figure 165**) if damaged.

   e. Install the grommet over the oil pipe as shown in B, **Figure 165**.

   f. Lubricate a new O-ring with engine oil and install it onto the end of the oil pipe (A, **Figure 165**).

8. Install the oil strainer as shown in A, **Figure 167**. Seat the O-ring (B, **Figure 167**) into the crankcase oil passage and position the grommet (C) on the crankcase notch.

9. Install the brackets and bolts (A and B, **Figure 163**) and tighten securely.

10. Install the pin (A, **Figure 168**) through the hole in the oil pump shaft.

11. Install the oil pump drive gear by aligning the cutout in the backside of the gear (B, **Figure 168**) with the pin (A).

12. Install a new snap ring (B, **Figure 161**) into the groove in the end of the oil pump shaft. Install the snap ring with its flat side facing out, making sure it seats in the groove completely. Turn the gear to make sure the shaft turns smoothly.

13. Reverse Step 1 and Step 2 to complete installation.

## CRANKCASE

The following procedures detail the disassembly and reassembly of the crankcase. When the two halves of the crankcase are disassembled or split, the oil pump, one-way valve, oil jet, crankshaft and transmission assemblies can be removed.

The crankcase halves are made of cast aluminum alloy. Do not hammer or excessively pry on the crankcase. The case halves will fracture or break. The case halves are aligned and sealed at the joint by dowels and a gasket.

The crankshaft consists of two full-circle flywheels pressed onto the crankpin. The assembly is supported at each end by a ball bearing.

The oil pump, one-way valve and oil jet are mounted in the left crankcase.

5

## Special Tools

No special tools are required to disassemble and reassemble the crankcase halves, or to remove and install the crankshaft. However, special tools are required to replace the crankcase bearings.

Crankshaft overhaul requires the use of a hydraulic press and a number of special measuring tools.

## Disassembly

This procedure describes disassembly of the crankcase halves and removal of the crankshaft, internal shift mechanism, transmission, oil pump and one-way valve.

Identify parts or make written notes as required to help with reassembly. Note any damaged or worn parts.

*NOTE*
*References to the **right** and **left** side of the engine refer the engine as it sits in the frame, not as it sits on the workbench.*

1. Remove all exterior engine assemblies as follows:
   a. Cylinder head, cam chain and guides, cylinder, and piston (this chapter).
   b. Flywheel (Chapter Ten).
   c. Oil pump drive gear and oil strainer (this chapter).
   d. Drive sprocket (Chapter Twelve).
   e. Clutch, kickstarter, external shift linkage (Chapter Seven).
   f. Primary drive gear, balancer shaft assembly and starter clutch (CRF450X) (Chapter Seven).
2. Place the engine on wooden blocks with the left side facing up.

*NOTE*
*To ensure that the crankcase bolts are correctly located during assembly, make an outline of the left crankcase on a piece of cardboard. Punch holes in the cardboard at the same locations as the bolts. As each bolt is removed from the crankcase, place the bolt in its respective hole in the template (**Figure 169**).*

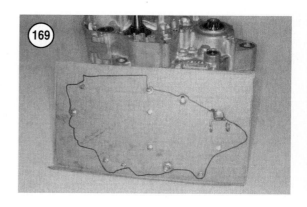

3. Remove the transmission drain bolt and washer (**Figure 170**).
4. Loosen each crankcase 6 mm bolt (**Figure 170**) 1/4 turn, working in a crossing pattern. Loosen the bolts in two or three steps until they can be removed by hand. Remove the bolts, along with the washers (where used).
5. Grasp both crankcase halves (so they cannot separate) and turn the engine over so the right side (**Figure 171**) faces up.
6. Lightly tap the right crankcase half and remove it. All the internal crankcase components will remain in the left case half. If necessary, alternately tap on the ends of the transmission shafts to prevent them from binding the right crankcase half.

*CAUTION*
*Do not hammer or pry on areas of the engine cases that are not reinforced. Do not pry on gasket surfaces.*

7. Immediately check for the outer washer installed on the countershaft (A, **Figure 172**). If the washer is not on the countershaft, remove it from the right case half and reinstall it.
8. Remove the one-way valve (B, **Figure 172**) and the oil pump rotors and shaft (C).
9. Reinstall the right crankcase half on the left case half. Then grasp both crankcase halves (so they cannot separate) and turn the engine over so the left side faces up. Remove the left case half (A, **Figure 173**).
10. Immediately check for the outer mainshaft (A, **Figure 174**) and countershaft (B) washers. If not installed on their respective shafts, remove them from the left case half and reinstall them.
11. Remove the two dowel pins (C, **Figure 174**) and crankcase gasket.

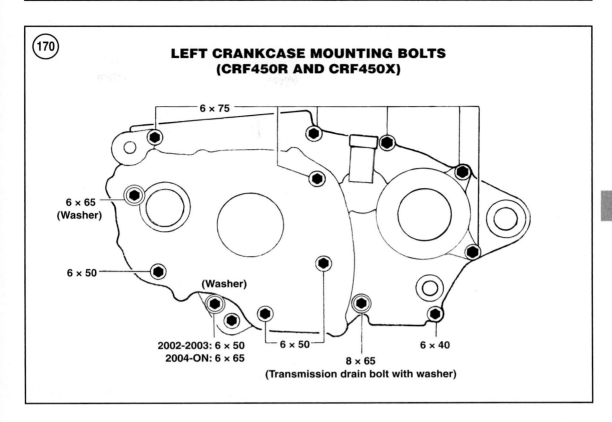

(170)

## LEFT CRANKCASE MOUNTING BOLTS
## (CRF450R AND CRF450X)

6 × 75

6 × 65
(Washer)

6 × 50

(Washer)

2002-2003: 6 × 50
2004-ON: 6 × 65

6 × 50

8 × 65
(Transmission drain bolt with washer)

6 × 40

5

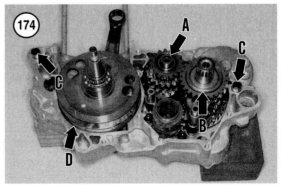

12. Remove the crankshaft (D, **Figure 174**).

13. Remove the transmission assembly (**Figure 175**) from the right case half as follows:

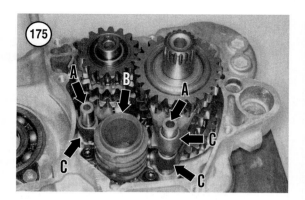

> *NOTE*
> *If the engine was experiencing shifting problems, examine the transmission assembly before removing it. Look for excessive wear or damaged parts. Spin the countershaft and turn the shift drum by hand to shift the transmission. Check the movement and operation of each shift fork and sliding gear. Look for hard shifting and incomplete gear dog engagement. Check also for seized gears and bushings.*

a. Remove the two shift fork shafts (A, **Figure 175**). Note any binding or roughness when removing the shafts.

b. Move the shift forks away from the shift drum, then remove the shift drum (B, **Figure 175**).

c. Remove the shift forks (C, **Figure 175**).

> *NOTE*
> *The transmission shafts (**Figure 176**) are removed at the same time.*

d. Position the right crankcase so the transmission shafts are parallel with the workbench. Then tap the shafts and remove them (**Figure 177**).

e. Inspect and service the transmission assembly as described in Chapter Eight.

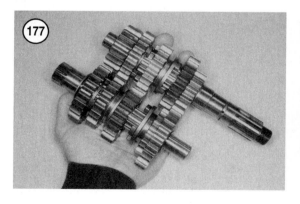

14. Inspect the crankshaft assembly as described in this chapter.

15. Inspect the oil pump as described in this chapter.

16. Clean and inspect the cases and bearings as described in this chapter.

**Assembly**

1. Before assembly:

a. Make sure a new center case gasket is on hand. Do not reuse the original gasket.

b. Lubricate the seal lips with grease.

c. Confirm that the transmission shafts are properly assembled (Chapter Eight). Then apply

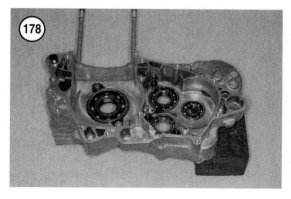

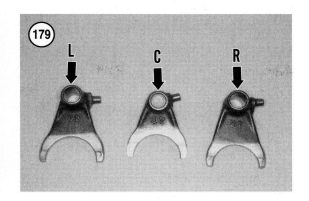

grease to the outer washers on each transmission shaft to help hold them in place.

   d. Lubricate the crankshaft, bearings and transmission sliding surfaces with engine oil.

2. Support the right crankcase assembly on wooden blocks (**Figure 178**).

3A. On CRF450R models, identify the shift forks by the letter cast on each fork. The left (L, **Figure 179**) and right (R) shift forks engage with the countershaft. The center (C, **Figure 179**) shift fork engages with the mainshaft.

3B. On CRF450X models, identify the shift forks by the letters cast on each fork. The left (L, **Figure 179**) and right (R) shift forks engage with the countershaft. The center (C, **Figure 179**) shift fork engages with the mainshaft.

*NOTE*
*For clarity, the CRF450X shift forks will be referred to as the L (left), C (center) and R (right) shift forks in Step 4.*

4. Install the transmission and internal shift mechanism as follows:

   a. Mesh the transmission shafts (**Figure 177**) and install them into the right crankcase at the same time. See **Figure 176**.

   b. Install the R shift fork into the countershaft fifth gear groove (A, **Figure 180**). The R mark should face up.

   c. Install the L shift fork into the countershaft fourth gear groove (B, **Figure 180**). The L mark should face up.

   d. Install the C shift fork into the mainshaft third gear groove (C, **Figure 180**). The C mark should face down.

   e. Install the shift drum (A, **Figure 181**) into the right case bearing.

   f. Install the R shift fork pin into the lower shift drum groove (B, **Figure 181**).

   g. Install the C shift fork pin into the center shift drum groove (C, **Figure 181**).

   h. Install the L shift fork pin into the upper shift drum groove (D, **Figure 181**).

   i. Lubricate the shift fork shafts with engine oil. Install the long shift fork shaft (A, **Figure 182**) through the L and R shift forks. Install the other shaft (B, **Figure 182**) through the C shift fork. Make sure both shafts bottom out in the right case half.

5

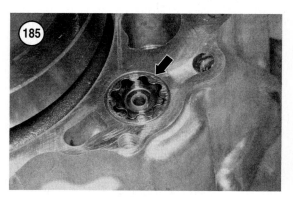

j. Spin the transmission shafts and turn the shift drum by hand to check transmission operation. Check that each shift fork travels through its operating groove in the shift drum and bottoms against both ends of the groove (**Figure 183**).

*NOTE*
*It is difficult to identify the different gear positions when turning the shift drum without the stopper lever installed on the engine. Substep j only determines if the shift forks can move through their complete operational range.*

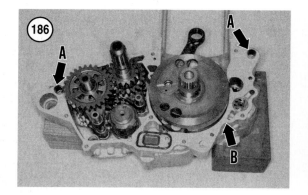

5. Install the crankshaft as shown in D, **Figure 174**.
6. Install both dowel pins (C, **Figure 174**).
7. Install the left case half (A, **Figure 173**) and seat it against the right case half. Check that the left crankshaft oil seal lip (B, **Figure 173**) is seated fully against the crankshaft. If there is a gap, part of the seal's lip folded over. If so, remove and reinstall the left case half.
8. Grasp both case halves so they cannot separate and turn the engine over so the right case half faces up. Then carefully remove the right case half. Immediately locate the outer countershaft washer (A, **Figure 172**) and reinstall it, if necessary.
9. Install the one-way valve into the left crankcase groove as shown in **Figure 184**.
10. Lubricate the oil pump rotors and shaft and install them into the left crankcase bore (**Figure 185**).
11. Install the dowel pins (A, **Figure 186**) and a new gasket (B).
12. Make sure the right crankcase gasket surface is clean and dry. Then install the right crankcase (**Figure 187**) onto the left crankcase. Tap the case to seat it flush against the gasket (**Figure 171**). Excessive

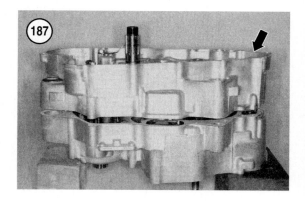

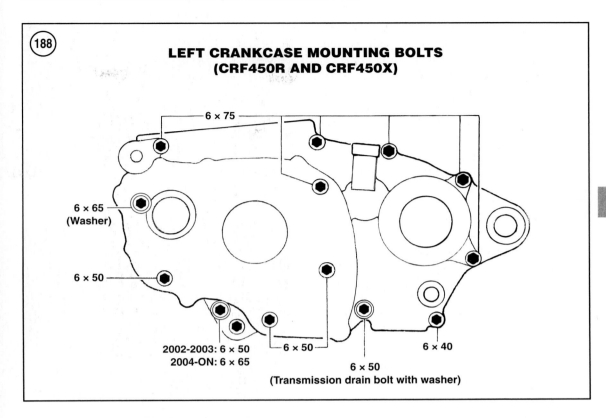

(188)

**LEFT CRANKCASE MOUNTING BOLTS
(CRF450R AND CRF450X)**

6 × 75

6 × 65
(Washer)

6 × 50

2002-2003: 6 × 50
2004-ON: 6 × 65

6 × 50

6 × 40

6 × 50
(Transmission drain bolt with washer)

5

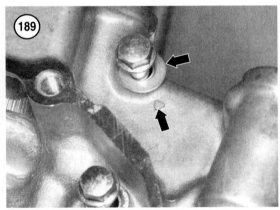

(189)

force should not be necessary as there are no press-fits between the crankshaft and its main bearings.

13. Grasp both case halves so they cannot separate and turn the engine over so the left case half faces up.

14. Install and tighten the crankcase mounting bolts as follows:

 a. Clean and dry the crankcase mounting bolts. Replace crushed or damaged washers.

 b. Install the crankcase mounting bolts into their original mounting position, using the template made during disassembly (**Figure 169**) and **Figure 188**.

 c. Triangle marks cast adjacent to a bolt hole indicate where a sealing washer must be used with the mounting bolt (**Figure 189**).

*CAUTION*
*If the crankcase bolts were not identified and stored in a cardboard template, identify the bolts as indicated in* ***Figure 188***. *Tightening a too long or short bolt will strip the crankcase threads.*

*CAUTION*
*Throughout the tightening process, occasionally turn the crankshaft and countershaft. If there is any binding, STOP. Take the case apart and find the trouble. Usually it is a gear installed backward or an incorrectly installed dowel pin.*

d. Tighten all crankcase bolts (**Figure 188**), working in a crossing pattern and in several steps until they are all tight.

e. Install a new washer on the transmission drain bolt and tighten to 22 N•m (16 ft.-lb.).

f. Turn the crankshaft and both transmission shafts. If there is binding, separate the cases to determine the cause.

g. Cover the crankcase opening.

15. Carefully trim the center case gasket at the cylinder base surface (**Figure 190**). Do not allow any of the gasket material to fall into the crankcase.

16. Check the transmission for proper shifting as follows:

a. Install the shift drum cam, small locating pin and mounting bolt (A, **Figure 191**). Then install the stopper lever (B, **Figure 191**) and its mounting bolt (C). The spring and washer used with the stopper lever is not required. Use fingers to engage the stopper lever with the shift drum cam when checking shifting.

*NOTE*
*If necessary, refer to Chapter Seven for additional information on installing the shift drum cam and stopper lever assembly.*

b. Turn the mainshaft while turning the shift drum cam and align its raised ramp with the stopper lever (D, **Figure 191**). This is the transmission's *neutral* position. The mainshaft and countershaft should turn independently of one another.

c. Turn the mainshaft while turning the shift drum cam *clockwise*. Stop when the stopper lever can seat between the ramps of the shift drum cam. This is the first gear position. The mainshaft and countershaft should be meshed together.

d. Turn the shift drum cam *counterclockwise*. Turn the shift drum cam past neutral, then place the stopper lever between the ramps to check the remaining gears for proper engagement. The mainshaft and countershaft should mesh whenever the transmission is in gear.

e. Remove the shift drum cam and stopper lever after completing the check. If the transmission did not engage properly, disassemble the crankcase and inspect the transmission for proper assembly or damaged parts.

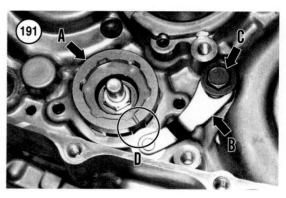

17. Reverse Step 1 under *Disassembly*.

**Inspection**

1. Remove the crankcase seals as described in this chapter.

2. Remove all gasket residue from the gasket surfaces.

3. Clean the crankcase halves in solvent.

4. Using clean solvent, flush each bearing. Make sure all gasket residue is removed from the bearings, oil passages and bolt holes.

5A. On CRF450R models, check the oil jet (**Figure 192**) installed in the left case half and clean with compressed air. If replacing the oil jet, tighten to 2.0 N•m (17 in.-lb.).

5B. On CRF450X models, service the oil jet as follows:

a. Remove the bolt and oil jet (**Figure 193**) from the left crankcase.

b. Check the oil jet and the oil passage in the left crankcase for debris and other contamination.

c. After cleaning the oil jet and left crankcase in solvent, blow dry with compressed air.

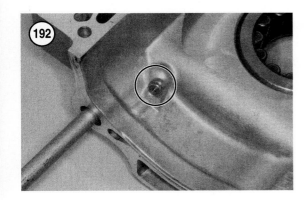

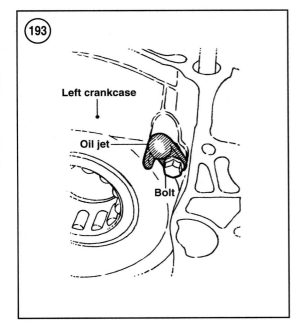

spin the bearing at excessive speed, possibly causing the bearing to destruct.

7. Blow through each oil passage with compressed air.

8. Lightly oil the engine bearings before inspecting their condition. A dry bearing exhibits more sound and looseness than a properly lubricated bearing.

9. Inspect the bearings for roughness, pitting, galling and play. Replace any bearing that is not in good condition. Always replace the opposite bearing at the same time. When inspecting the clutch release lever bearing, insert the release lever into the bearing and check for roughness.

10. Inspect the cases for fractures around all mounting and bearing bosses, stiffening ribs and threaded holes. If repair is required, have a dealership or machine shop inspect the cases.

11. Check all threaded holes for damage or buildup. Clean threads with the correct size metric tap. Lubricate the tap with kerosene or aluminum tap fluid.

12. Inspect the oil pump and one-way valve as described under *Oil Pump And One-Way Valve* in this chapter.

### CRANKCASE SEAL AND BEARING REPLACEMENT

Refer to *Basic Service Methods* in Chapter One for bearing removal and installation techniques. Also refer to *Interference Fit* if it is necessary to use heat for the removal and installation of the bearings in the housings.

Refer to this section for specific removal and installation techniques for bearings that are unique to this engine.

**Seal Replacement**

Replace all the crankcase seals during an engine overhaul.

> *CAUTION*
> *Do not allow the pry tool to contact the seal bore when removing the seal. It may gouge the bore and cause the new seal to leak.*

d. Install the oil jet into the left crankcase. Apply a medium strength threadlock onto the oil jet mounting bolt and tighten to 10 N•m (88 in.-lb.).

> *NOTE*
> *Depending on model year, different size oil jets have been used. Always confirm the oil jet size before installing a new jet.*

6. Dry the cases with compressed air.

> *WARNING*
> *When drying a bearing with compressed air, do not allow the inner bearing race to rotate. The air can*

1. Pry out the old seal with a seal puller or wide-blade screwdriver, as shown in **Figure 194**. Place a folded shop cloth under the tool to prevent damage to the case.

2. If installing a new bearing, replace the bearing before installing the new seal.

3. Inspect the seal bore. Sand or file any raised grooves in the bore surface, then clean thoroughly.

4. Pack grease into the lip of the new seal.

5. Place the seal in the bore, with the closed side of the seal facing out. The seal must be square to the bore.

6. Install the new seal with a seal driver (**Figure 195**) to the dimensions specified below. If a seal dimension is not identified, install the seal until its outer edge is even with the top of the bore.

   a. Left crankshaft seal (A, **Figure 196**): 0.5-1.5 mm (0.02-0.06 in.).

   b. On CRF450R models, right crankshaft seal (A, **Figure 197**): 0.5-1.5 mm (0.02-0.06 in.).

   c. On CRF450X models, right crankshaft seal (A, **Figure 197**): Flush with top of bore.

   d. On CRF450R models, countershaft seal (B, **Figure 196**): 0.5-1.5 mm (0.02-0.06 in.).

   e. On CRF450X models, countershaft seal (B, **Figure 196**): Flush with top of bore.

*CAUTION*
*When driving seals, the driver must fit at the perimeter of the seal. If the driver presses toward the center of the seal, the seal can distort and the internal garter spring can become dislodged, causing the seal to leak.*

## Crankcase Bearing Identification

1. When replacing crankcase bearings, note the following:

   a. Phillips screws and Allen head screws secure the crankcase bearing retainers. All these bearing retainer screws are secured with a threadlock and tightened securely. Heat the area around the screws with a heat gun before attempting to loosen them. Loosen Phillips screws (**Figure 198**, typical) with a hand-impact driver with the appropriate size Phillips bit. The cross-slot part of these screws strip easily, which makes removal difficult.

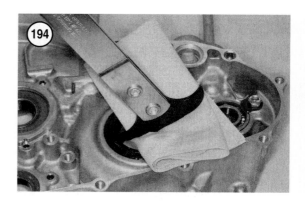

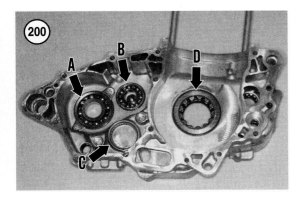

5

*NOTE*
*Refer to **Screwdrivers** in Chapter One for additional information on removing Phillips screws using ACR Phillips II screwdriver bits and tips on how to increase the grip of a Phillips bit.*

b. Before installing the bearing retainer screws, clean the screw threads and threaded holes of all threadlock residue. To ensure accurate torque readings, the screw threads must be clean and in good condition. Replace the screw if the driving part of the screw head is damaged.

c. Install bearing crankcase bearing retainer screws using threadlocking compound, such as ThreeBond TB1360, and tighten to 9.8 N•m (87 in.-lb.).

d. Identify and record the size code of each bearing before removing it from the case. This will eliminate confusion when installing the bearings in their correct bores.

e. Record the orientation of each bearing in its bore. Note if the size code faces toward the inside or outside of the case. Some bearings are also machined with a shoulder on one side to accept bearing retainer plates. If these bearings are installed backward, the retainer will not seat correctly against the bearing.

f. Use a hydraulic press or a set of bearing drivers to remove and install bearings. Bearings can also be removed and installed using heat, as described in Chapter One.

g. Bearings that are only accessible from one side of the case are removed with a blind bearing puller. The puller is fitted through the bearing, then expanded to grip the back-side of the bearing (**Figure 199**).

*NOTE*
*The tool shown in **Figure 199** is the Motion Pro Blind Bearing and Bushing Remover (part No. 08-0292). Refer to **www.motionpro.com** for a description of this tool.*

2. The following identifies the *left* crankcase bearings:

a. Countershaft bearing (A, **Figure 200**).

b. Mainshaft bearing (B, **Figure 200**). The side of the bearing that faces toward the left case half is sealed (**Figure 201**) to protect it from dirt and water that passes through the clutch release lever bore.

c. Shift drum bearing (C, **Figure 200**).

d. Crankshaft bearing (D, **Figure 200**).

e. Clutch release lever bearings (C, **Figure 196**).

f. Oil pump bearing (A, **Figure 202**).

g. Balancer shaft bearing (B, **Figure 202**). Remove the snap ring before removing the bearing. During installation, install the snap ring with its flat side facing out.

3. The following identifies the *right* crankcase bearings:

   a. Crankshaft bearing (A, **Figure 203**).
   b. Mainshaft bearing (B, **Figure 203**).
   c. Shift drum bearing (C, **Figure 203**).
   d. Countershaft bearing (D, **Figure 203**).
   e. Balancer shaft bearing (B, **Figure 197**).

## Crankcase Bearing Replacement

All crankcase bearings can be replaced during the following steps.

> *NOTE*
> *Before removing the bearings, refer to the **Crankcase earing Identification** section to determine if there is specific information related to the bearing being replaced.*

1. Place the new bearing(s) in a freezer and chill for at least one hour.
2. Remove the crankcase seal, if applicable.
3. Remove the snap ring from the bearing bore, if applicable. Discard the snap ring if weak, rusted or damaged.
4. Remove the bearing retainers, if applicable.
5. Make note of which side of the bearing is facing out.
6. Heat the crankcase as described in *Interference Fit* in Chapter One. Observe all safety and handling procedures when the case is heated.

> *CAUTION*
> *Do not heat the housing or bearing with a propane or acetylene torch. The direct heat will destroy the case hardening of the bearing and may warp the case.*

7. Support the heated crankcase on wooden blocks, allowing space for the bearing to fall from the bore.
8. Remove the bearing(s) from the bore, using a press, bearing-driver set or bearing puller. Discard the bearing(s).
9. Allow the case to cool.
10. Clean and inspect the bearing bore. Check that all oil holes (where applicable) are clean.
11. When the bearing(s) have chilled, reheat the crankcase.

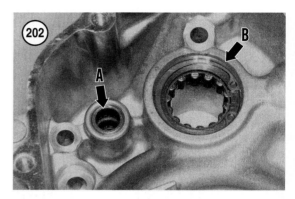

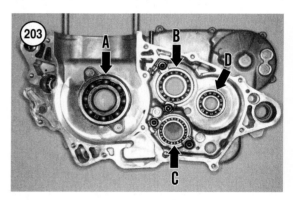

12. Support the heated crankcase on wooden blocks, checking that the case is supported directly below the bearing bore.

13. Place the bearing squarely over the bore and check that it is properly oriented as noted before removal and under *Crankcase Bearing Identification*. Center the bearing into the bore. If the bearing drops into the bore, carefully apply pressure to the bearing (Step 14) to make sure it bottoms correctly.

14. Press the bearing into place using a driver that fits on the outer bearing race.

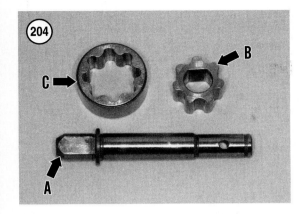

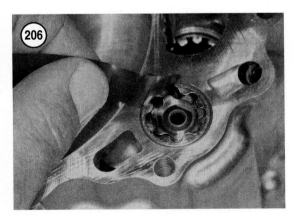

15. Install the seal (if applicable) as described in this chapter.

## OIL PUMP AND ONE-WAY VALVE

The oil pump and one-way valve are removed and installed during crankcase *Disassembly* and *Reassembly*.

### Inspection

The oil pump operates in a bore in the left crankcase. If the pump is badly worn, it cannot maintain oil pressure. While the oil pump components can be replaced separately, it is safer to replace all the parts (**Figure 204**) at the same time if there is any worn or damaged parts, or if the oil pump clearances in **Table 4** are excessive.

1. Clean all parts in fresh solvent. Blow dry with compressed air and place on a clean cloth.

2. Inspect the oil pump drive gear as described under *Oil Relief Valve, Oil Pump Drive Gear and Oil Strainer* in this chapter.

3. Inspect the oil pump shaft (A, **Figure 204**) for:
   a. Worn, scored or damaged surfaces.
   b. Damaged drive pin hole. Check for cracks leading from the hole on both sides of the shaft.
   c. Damaged inner rotor drive shoulder.
   d. Damaged snap ring groove.

4. Inspect the inner (B, **Figure 204**) and outer (C) rotors for:
   a. Scratches, scoring, wear grooves, flaking and other damage.
   b. Wear or damage on the rotor engagement teeth.
   c. Inner rotor shoulder for wear and damage.

5. Inspect the oil pump bore in the left crankcase (**Figure 205**) for scoring, cracks or other damage. If the bore is damaged, replace the left case half.

*NOTE*
*If there is no visible wear on the rotor or bore surfaces, continue with Step 6 to measure the oil pump operating clearances.*

6. Measure and record the oil pump operating clearances as follows. Refer to **Table 4** to determine if the measurements are within specification:
   a. Install the oil pump shaft, inner rotor and outer rotor into the left crankcase oil pump bore.
   b. Measure the tip clearance between the rotors as shown in **Figure 206**. If out of specification, replace both rotors and remeasure.
   c. Measure the side clearance (**Figure 207**). Measure at several places around the housing bore. If the clearance is excessive, repeat the measurement with a new outer rotor. If the

5

clearance is still excessive, replace the left case half.

d. Install the center case gasket on the left case half. Then place a straightedge across the pump housing and measure the rotor end clearance (**Figure 208**). If the clearance is excessive, replace the rotors and remeasure the clearance.

7. Remove the oil pump assembly from the case bore. Then clean and place in a plastic bag until assembly.

## One-Way Valve Inspection

1. The one-way valve (**Figure 209**) is not designed to be disassembled. Do not attempt to remove the screw (**Figure 209**) that secures the valve to the holder as the screw head may snap off. This screw is secured with threadlock.

2. Inspect the one-way valve plate (**Figure 210**) for bending or other damage. The plate should seat flush against its seat.

3. Replace the one-way valve if there is any detectable wear or damage.

## CRANKSHAFT

### Connecting Rod Big End
### Bearing Lubrication

Oil forced under pressure through a passageway in the left crankcase cover enters a hole in the left end of the crankshaft (**Figure 211**) and lubricates the connecting rod big end bearing assembly. A seal

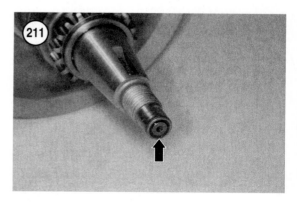

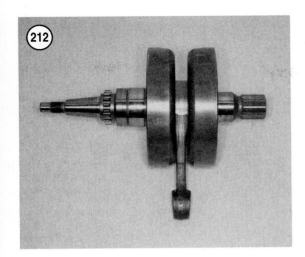

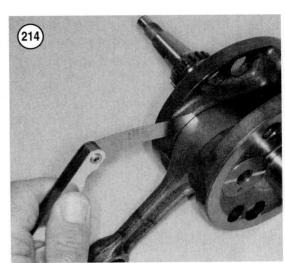

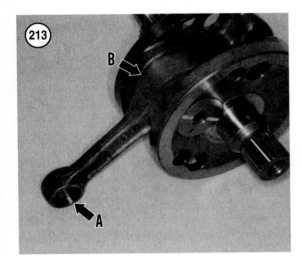

installed in the left crankcase cover seals the end of the crankshaft and the oil passageway. Refer to *Left Crankcase Cover* in Chapter Ten to service the oil seal and clean the cover oil passageway.

**Inspection**

Carefully handle the crankshaft assembly during inspection. Do not place the crankshaft where it could accidentally roll off the workbench. The crankshaft is an assembly-type, with its two halves joined by the crankpin. The crankpin is pressed into the flywheels and aligned, both vertically and horizontally, with calibrated equipment. If the crankshaft assembly shows signs of wear, or is out of alignment, have a dealership inspect the crankshaft.

While Honda does not sell OEM parts to rebuild the crankshaft, aftermarket overhaul kits are available.

Inspect the crankshaft assembly as follows:

1. Clean the crankshaft with solvent.

2. Dry the crankshaft with compressed air.

3. Blow through all oil passages with compressed air.

4. Inspect the crankshaft bearing surfaces (**Figure 212**) for scoring, heat discoloration or other damage. Repair minor damage with 320 grit carborundum cloth.

5. Inspect the splines, sprocket and shaft taper for wear or damage.

*NOTE*
*If the sprocket is damaged, check the cam chain, upper cam sprocket, chain guides and cam chain tensioner for damage.*

6. Inspect the connecting rod small end (A, **Figure 213**) as described under *Piston Pin and Connecting Rod Inspection* in this chapter.

7. Inspect the connecting rod big end bearing (B, **Figure 213**) as follows:

   a. Turn the rod and inspect the bottom bearing and rod for scoring, galling or heat damage. Roughness indicates a damaged bearing and rod.

   b. Slide the connecting rod to one side and measure the connecting rod side clearance with a flat feeler gauge (**Figure 214**). Refer to **Table 5** for service limits.

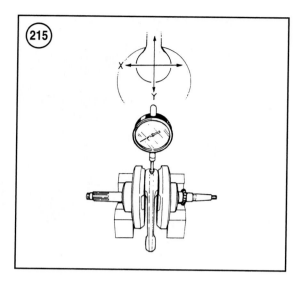

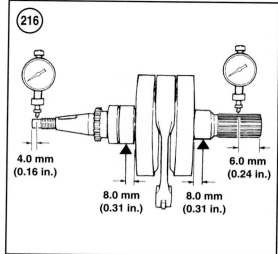

c. Support the crankshaft on a set of V-blocks and position the pointer of a dial indicator in the middle of the connecting rod lower end (**Figure 215**). Hold the crankshaft and then move the connecting rod as shown in **Figure 215**. Replace the crankshaft if the clearance exceeds the radial clearance service limit in **Table 5**.

8. Place the crankshaft on a set of V-blocks at the points indicated in **Figure 216**. Rotate the crankshaft two revolutions and measure crankshaft runout with a dial indicator at the two points indicated in **Figure 216**. If the runout exceeds the service limit in **Table 5**, have a dealership evaluate and possibly true the crankshaft.

### Table 1 ENGINE GENERAL SPECIFICATIONS (CRF450R AND CRF450X)

|  | Specification |
|---|---|
| Engine type | 4-stroke, single cylinder, liquid cooled, chain-driven OHC with rocker arm |
| Engine displacement | 449.4 cc (27.42 cu. in.) |
| Bore and stroke | 96.0 × 62.1 mm (3.78 × 2.44 in.) |
| Compression ratio |  |
| CRF450R |  |
| 2002-2003 | 11.5:1 |
| 2004 | 12.0:1 |
| CRF450X | 12.0:1 |
| Engine dry weight |  |
| CRF450R |  |
| 2002 | 29.5 kg (65.0 lbs.) |
| 2003 | 29.4 kg (64.8 lbs.) |
| 2004 | 28.9 kg (63.7 lbs.) |
| CRF450X | 32.3 kg (71.2 lbs.) |
| (continued) | |

**Table 1 ENGINE GENERAL SPECIFICATIONS (CRF450R AND CRF450X) (continued)**

| | Specification |
|---|---|
| Valve timing* | |
| CRF450R | |
| Intake valve opens | 15° BTDC |
| Intake valve closes | 50° ABDC |
| Exhaust valve opens | 55° BBDC |
| Exhaust valve closes | |
| 2002 | 25° ATDC |
| 2003-on | 15° ATDC |
| CRF450X | |
| Intake valve opens | 10° BTDC |
| Intake valve closes | 45° ABDC |
| Exhaust valve opens | 50° BBDC |
| Exhaust valve closes | 15° ATDC |
| *At 1 mm (0.04 in.) lift. | |

5

**Table 2 CYLINDER HEAD, CAMSHAFT AND VALVE SPECIFICATIONS (CRF450R AND CRF450X)**

| | New mm (in.) | Service limit mm (in.) |
|---|---|---|
| Cylinder head warp limit | – | 0.05 (0.002) |
| Camshaft | | |
| Lobe height | | |
| CRF450R | | |
| Intake | | |
| 2002 | 37.540-37.750 (1.4779-1.4862) | 37.39 (1.472) |
| 2003-on | 37.540-37.780 (1.4779-1.4874) | 37.39 (1.472) |
| Exhaust | | |
| 2002 | 35.452-35.692 (1.3957-1.4052) | 35.30 (1.390) |
| 2003-on | 35.187-35.427 (1.3853-1.3948) | 35.04 (1.380) |
| CRF450X | | |
| Intake | 36.890-37.130 (1.4524-1.4618) | 36.890 (1.4524) |
| Exhaust | 35.063-35.303 (1.3804-1.3899) | 35.063 (1.3804) |
| Rocker arm | | |
| Inside diameter | 12.000-12.018 (0.4724-0.4731) | 12.05 (0.474) |
| Rocker arm shaft outside diameter | 11.967-11.975 (0.4711-0.4715) | 11.92 (0.469) |
| Rocker arm-to-shaft clearance | 0.025-0.051 (0.001-0.002) | 0.10 (0.004) |
| Valves | | |
| Stem outside diameter | | |
| Intake | 5.475-5.490 (0.2156-0.2161) | – |
| Exhaust | 4.965-4.980 (0.1955-0.1961) | 4.96 (0.195) |
| Valve guide inside diameter | | |
| Intake | 5.500-5.512 (0.2166-0.2170) | 5.552 (0.2186) |
| Exhaust | 5.000-5.012 (0.1969-0.1973) | 5.052 (0.1989) |
| Valve seat width | | |
| Intake | 1.1-1.3 (0.043-0.051) | 2.0 (0.08) |
| Exhaust | 1.3-1.5 (0.051-0.059) | 2.0 (0.08) |
| Valve stem-to-guide clearance | | |
| Intake | 0.010-0.037 (0.0004-0.0015) | – |
| Exhaust | 0.020-0.047 (0.0008-0.0019) | – |
| Valve guide projection height | | |
| Intake | 16.1-16.3 (0.63-0.64) | – |
| Exhaust | 17.9-18.1 (0.70-0.71) | – |
| (continued) | | |

**Table 2 CYLINDER HEAD, CAMSHAFT AND VALVE SPECIFICATIONS**
**(CRF450R AND CRF450X) (continued)**

|  | New<br>mm (in.) | Service limit<br>mm (in.) |
|---|---|---|
| Valves (continued) |  |  |
| Valve spring free length |  |  |
| Intake | 40.68 (1.602) | 39.7 (1.56) |
| Exhaust |  |  |
| CRF450R | 43.16 (1.699) | 42.2 (1.66) |
| CRF450X | 42.82 (1.686) | 41.9 (1.65) |
| Valve lifter outside diameter | 25.978-25.993 (1.0228-1.0233) | 25.97 (1.022) |
| Valve lifter bore inside<br>diameter | 26.010-26.026 (1.0240-1.0246) | 26.04 (1.025) |

**Table 3 CYLINDER, PISTON AND PISTON RING SERVICE SPECIFICATIONS**
**(CRF450R AND CRF450X)**

|  | New<br>mm (in.) | Service limit<br>mm (in.) |
|---|---|---|
| Cylinder |  |  |
| Bore diameter | 96.000-96.015 (3.7795-3.7801) | 96.05 (3.781) |
| Out-of-round | – | 0.010 (0.0004) |
| Taper | – | 0.010 (0.0004) |
| Warp | – | 0.05 (0.002) |
| Piston-to-cylinder clearance | 0.020-0.045 (0.0008-0.0018) | 0.18 (0.007) |
| Piston and piston pin |  |  |
| Piston outside diameter | 95.970-95.980 (3.7783-3.7787) | 95.87 (3.774) |
| Piston pin bore inside diameter | 19.002-19.008 (0.7481-0.7483) | 19.03 (0.749) |
| Piston pin outside diameter | 18.994-19.000 (0.7478-0.7480) | 18.98 (0.747) |
| Piston pin bore-to-piston pin<br>clearance | 0.002-0.014 (0.0001-0.0006) | 0.04 (0.002) |
| Piston measuring point from<br>bottom of piston skirt |  |  |
| 2002-2003 | 7.0 (0.28) | – |
| 2004 | 5.0 (0.20) | – |
| Piston rings |  |  |
| Piston ring-to-ring groove<br>clearance |  |  |
| Top compression ring | 0.065-0.100 (0.0026-0.0039) | 0.115 (0.0045) |
| Oil ring | – |  |
| Ring end gap |  |  |
| Top compression ring | 0.25-0.31 (0.010-0.012) | 0.45 (0.018) |
| Oil ring side rails | 0.20-0.70 (0.008-0.028) | 0.90 (0.035) |
| Connecting rod |  |  |
| Small end inside diameter | 19.016-19.034 (0.7487-0.7494) | 19.04 (0.750) |
| Connecting rod-to-piston pin<br>clearance | 0.016-0.040 (0.0006-0.0016) | 0.06 (0.002) |

**Table 4 OIL PUMP SERVICE SPECIFICATIONS (CRF450R AND CRF450X)**

|  | New<br>mm (in.) | Service limit<br>mm (in.) |
|---|---|---|
| Body clearance | 0.15-0.21 (0.006-0.008) | – |
| Tip clearance | 0.15 (0.006) | 0.20 (0.008) |
| Side clearance | 0.05-0.13 (0.002-0.005) | – |

### Table 5 CRANKSHAFT SERVICE SPECIFICATIONS (CRF450R AND CRF450X)

| | New<br>mm (in.) | Service limit<br>mm (in.) |
|---|---|---|
| Connecting rod side clearance | | |
| CRF450R | 0.30-0.55 (0.012-0.022) | 0.6 (0.02) |
| CRF450X | 0.30-0.75 (0.012-0.030) | 0.75 (0.030) |
| Radial clearance | 0.006-0.018 (0.0002-0.0007) | 0.05 (0.002) |
| Runout | | |
| Left side | – | 0.05 (0.002) |
| Right side | – | 0.03 (0.001) |

### Table 6 ENGINE TORQUE SPECIFICATIONS (CRF450R AND CRF450X)

| | N·m | in.-lb. | ft.-lb. |
|---|---|---|---|
| Balancer shaft bearing set plate bolt[1] | 10 | 88 | – |
| Balancer shaft nut[2] | 44 | – | 33 |
| Cam chain tensioner housing mounting bolt | 12 | 106 | – |
| Cam chain tensioner guide mounting bolt[1] | 12 | 106 | – |
| Cam sprocket bolt[1] | 20 | – | 15 |
| Camshaft holder mounting bolt[2] | 14 | 124 | – |
| Countershaft bearing set plate screws | 9.8 | 87 | – |
| Crankshaft bearing retainer screws | 9.8 | 87 | – |
| Crankshaft hole cap[3] | 15 | 133 | – |
| Cylinder head cover bolt | 9.8 | 87 | – |
| Cylinder head mounting bolt (6 mm) | | | |
| 2002-2004 | 9.8 | 87 | – |
| 2005 | – | – | – |
| Cylinder head nut[2] | | | |
| CRF450R | 59 | – | 44 |
| CRF450X | 66 | – | 49 |
| Cylinder mounting bolt (6 mm) | | | |
| 2002-2004 | 9.8 | 87 | – |
| 2005 | – | – | – |
| Decompressor adjuster locknut | 9.8 | 87 | – |
| Decompressor cam mounting bolt[2] | 24 | – | 18 |
| Decompressor lifter mounting nut[2] | 22 | – | 16 |
| Drive sprocket bolt | | | |
| 2002-2004 | 26 | – | 19 |
| 2005 | 31 | – | 23 |
| Engine oil drain bolt | | | |
| 2002-2003 | 22 | – | 16 |
| 2004-on | 16 | 142 | – |
| Exhaust system | | | |
| CRF450R | | | |
| Exhaust pipe joint nuts | 21 | – | 15 |
| Muffler joint band bolt | 21 | – | 15 |
| Muffler mounting bolts | 22 | – | 16 |
| CRF450X | | | |
| Diffuser Torx screw | 11 | 97 | – |
| Exhaust pipe joint nuts | 21 | – | 15 |
| Muffler heat shield bolt | 12 | 106 | – |
| Muffler joint band bolt | 21 | – | 15 |
| Muffler mount bolts | 26 | – | 19 |
| Spark arrestor mounting bolts | 12 | 106 | – |

(continued)

**Table 6 ENGINE TORQUE SPECIFICATIONS (CRF450R AND CRF450X) (continued)**

|  | N•m | in.-lb. | ft.-lb. |
|---|---|---|---|
| Ignition timing hole cap |  |  |  |
| CRF450R |  |  |  |
| 2002-2003 | 9.9 | 87 | – |
| 2004 | 5.9 | 52 | – |
| 2005 | – | – | – |
| CRF450X | 10 | 88 | – |
| Kick pedal mounting bolt |  |  |  |
| 2002-2004 | 37 | – | 27 |
| 2005 | 38 | – | 28 |
| Mainshaft bearing set plate screws[2] | 10 | 88 | – |
| Oil jet[1] |  |  |  |
| CRF450R | 2 | 17 | – |
| CRF450X | 10 | 88 | – |
| Primary drive gear bolt[2] | 108 | – | 80 |
| Shift drum bearing set plate bolts[2] | 9.8 | 87 | – |
| Transmission oil check bolt |  |  |  |
| 2002-2004 | 9.8 | 87 | – |
| 2005 | – |  |  |
| Transmission oil drain bolt | 22 | – | 16 |

1. Apply medium strength threadlock to fastener threads.
2. Lubricate threads and seating surface with engine oil.
3. Lubricate threads with grease.

**Table 7 ENGINE MOUNT TORQUE SPECIFICATIONS (CRF450R AND CRF450X)**

|  | N•m | ft.-lb. |
|---|---|---|
| CRF450R |  |  |
| 2002-2004 |  |  |
| Front engine hanger plate nuts |  |  |
| Engine side | 54 | 40 |
| Frame side | 26 | 19 |
| Lower engine mount nut | 54 | 40 |
| Upper engine hanger plate nut |  |  |
| Engine side | 54 | 40 |
| Frame side |  |  |
| 2002 |  |  |
| Front | 26 | 19 |
| Rear | 29 | 21 |
| 2003-2004 | 26 | 19 |
| 2005 |  |  |
| Front engine mount nut | 59 | 44 |
| Lower engine mount nut | 59 | 44 |
| Upper engine hanger plate bolt | 26 | 19 |
| Upper engine hanger plate nut | 59 | 44 |
| Swing arm pivot shaft nut | 88 | 65 |
| Upper shock absorber mounting nut |  |  |
| 2005 | 44 | 33 |

CHAPTER SIX

# CLUTCH, PRIMARY DRIVE, STARTER CLUTCH, KICKSTARTER AND EXTERNAL SHIFT MECHANISM (CRF250R AND CRF250X)

This chapter describes service procedures for the components installed behind the right crankcase cover.

1. Right crankcase cover.
2. Clutch cover.
3. Clutch.
4. Clutch release lever.
5. Balancer and primary drive gears.
6. Starter clutch (CRF250X).
7. Kickstarter.
8. External shift mechanism.

Read this chapter before attempting repairs to the clutch and other components in the right crankcase cover. Become familiar with the procedures to understand the skill and equipment required. Refer to Chapter One for tool usage and service methods.

While the inspection procedures in this chapter help detect parts that are excessively worn or damaged, it is important to inspect the parts during their removal and disassembly, especially when troubleshooting a problem area. Look for loose fasteners, incorrect adjustments, binding, rough turning and abnormal wear marks or patterns.

Tables 1-3 are at the end of this chapter.

## RIGHT CRANKCASE COVER

The right crankcase cover can be removed without having to remove the water pump cover.

### Removal/Installation

1. Remove the right engine guard.
2. Drain the engine coolant (Chapter Three).
3. Drain the transmission oil (Chapter Three).
4. Remove the rear brake pedal (Chapter Fifteen).
5. Unbolt and remove the kick pedal (A, **Figure 1**). If the kick pedal is stuck, perform the following:
   a. Spray penetrating lubricant around the kick pedal splines. Give the lubricant time to dissolve some of the rust, then tap the pedal and slide it off the shaft.
   b. If the kick pedal is tight from corrosion or damaged splines, install the kick pedal bolt finger-tight, and then back it out two turns. Mount a small two-jaw puller across the kick

pedal boss, centering the pressure bolt against the mounting bolt, then operate the puller to remove the kick pedal.

*CAUTION*
*Do not pry the kick pedal off as this may damage the right crankcase cover.*

6. Loosen the hose clamp and disconnect the hose at the water pump (B, **Figure 1**).

*NOTE*
*Different length bolts secure the right crankcase cover to the engine. To ensure that the bolts are correctly located during assembly, make an outline of the right crankcase cover on a piece of cardboard. Punch holes in the cardboard at the same locations as the bolts. After removing each bolt from the cover, place the bolt in its respective hole in the template.*

7. Remove the bolts securing the right crankcase cover (C, **Figure 1**) to the engine. If necessary, lightly tap the cover to loosen it from the engine.

8. Locate the thrust washer and reinstall it onto the kickstarter (**Figure 2**).

9. Locate the washer and install it onto the water pump shaft (**Figure 3**).

10. Remove the gasket and cover dowel pins (**Figure 4**).

11. Remove the water by-pass pipe and O-ring (**Figure 5**).

12. To service the water pump, refer to Chapter Eleven.

13. Clean and inspect the right crankcase cover as follows:

   a. Clean and dry the cover.

*NOTE*
*If the water pump assembly is installed in the right crankcase cover, do not submerge the cover in solvent.*

   b. Inspect the cover for cracks and other damage.

   c. Inspect the kickstarter seal and replace if leaking or damaged. Install the new seal with its flat side facing out and lubricate the seal lip with grease.

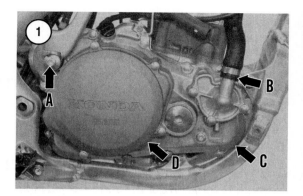

14. Installation is the reverse of removal. Note the following:

   a. Remove all gasket residue from the cover and crankcase mating surfaces.

   b. Make sure the kickstarter is properly installed with the correct amount of spring preload as described under *Kickstarter and Kick Idle Gear* in this chapter.

   c. Install a new gasket.

   d. Install a new water by-pass O-ring (**Figure 5**), if necessary.

e. Lubricate the kickstarter oil seal lip with grease.

f. When installing the crankcase cover, turn the water pump shaft to align its gear with the balancer shaft gear, then seat the cover into place.

g. Tighten the right crankcase cover mounting bolts in two or three steps and in a crossing pattern.

h. Tighten the kick pedal mounting bolt (A, **Figure 1**) to 37 N·m (27 ft.-lb.).

i. Refill the cooling system (Chapter Three).

j. Refill the transmission with oil (Chapter Three.

k. Check for oil and coolant leaks after starting the engine.

## CLUTCH COVER

The clutch cover is a separate cover mounted on the right crankcase cover assembly. On CRF250R

models, the clutch plates and clutch hub can be serviced through the clutch cover opening. To service the clutch housing, the right crankcase cover must be removed. On CRF250X models, the clutch plate assembly and clutch housing can be serviced through the clutch cover opening.

### Removal/Installation

1. Remove the rear brake pedal (Chapter Fifteen).
2. Unbolt and remove the clutch cover and its O-ring (D, **Figure 1**).
3. Installation is the reverse of removal. Note the following:
   a. Replace the clutch cover O-ring if leaking or damaged.
   b. Tighten the clutch cover mounting bolts in two or three steps and in a crossing pattern.

## CLUTCH

The clutch is a multi-plate type that operates immersed in the transmission oil supply. The clutch assembly consists of a clutch hub and clutch housing. Clutch plates are alternately locked to the two parts. The gear-driven clutch housing is mounted on the transmission mainshaft. The housing receives power from the primary drive gear mounted on the crankshaft. The housing then transfers the power via its plates to the plates locked to the clutch hub. The clutch hub is splined to the mainshaft and powers the transmission. The clutch plates are engaged by springs and disengaged by a cable-actuated release lever and pushrod assembly.

### Component Identification

Some clutch parts have two or more names. To prevent confusion, the following list provides the component names used in this manual and common synonyms:

1. Drive plate (9A, 9B and 11, **Figure 6**)—Clutch disc, clutch plate, friction disc, outer plate and friction plate. The tabs on the drive plates engage with slots in the clutch housing.

2. Driven plate (10A and 10B, **Figure 6**)—Aluminum plate, clutch disc, clutch plate, inner plate and steel plate. The inner teeth on the driven plates engage with the raised splines on the clutch hub.

6

## CLUTCH (CRF250R AND CRF250X)

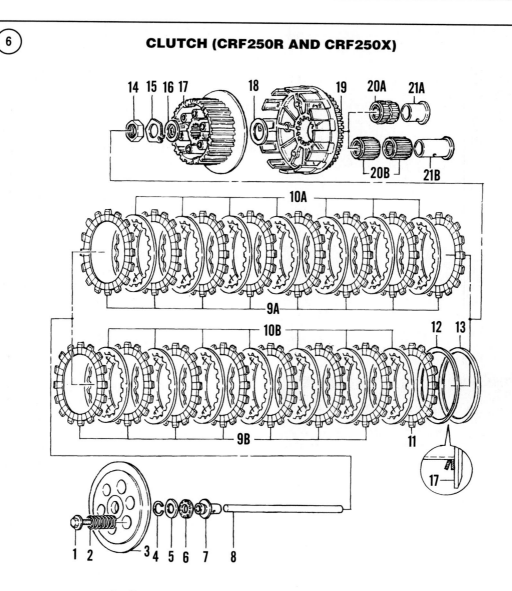

1. Clutch spring bolt
2. Clutch spring
3. Pressure plate
4. Clip
5. Thrust washer
6. Thrust bearing
7. Clutch lifter
8. Pushrod
9A. Drive plate (CRF250R)
9B. Drive plate A (CRF250X)
10A. Driven plate (CRF250R)
10B. Driven plate (CRF250X)
11. Drive plate B (CRF250X)
12. Friction spring (CRF250X)
13. Spring seat (CRF250X)
14. Clutch locknut
15. Lockwasher
16. Thrust washer
17. Clutch hub
18. Thrust washer
19. Clutch housing
20A. Needle bearing (CRF250R)
20B. Needle bearings (CRF250X)
21A. Bushing (CRF250R)
21B. Bushing (CRF250X)

*NOTE*
*The terms drive and driven plates are given to these parts, depending on where they are installed in the clutch assembly. The drive plates operate in the clutch housing, which is driven by the engine. The drive plates are always spinning, no matter if the clutch is engaged or disengaged. The driven plates operate on the clutch hub, which is connected to the transmission mainshaft. When the clutch is disengaged, the clutch hub and driven plates stop spinning.*

3. Clutch plates—When clutch plates are used in the text, it refers to both the drive and driven plates as an assembly.

4. Clutch hub (17, **Figure 6**)—Clutch boss, clutch center and inner hub.

5. Clutch housing (19, **Figure 6**)—Clutch basket, clutch outer, outer clutch hub and primary driven gear basket.

**Special Tools**

A clutch holder is required to hold the clutch hub when loosening and tightening the clutch locknut. This tool is described in the service procedure.

**Removal**

Refer to **Figure 6**.
1A. CRF250R:
    a. If only servicing the clutch plates, remove the clutch cover as described in this chapter.
    b. If the clutch housing must be removed, remove the right crankcase cover as described in this chapter.
1B. CRF250X—Remove the clutch cover as described in this chapter.
2. Loosen the clutch cable at the handlebar adjuster.
3. Loosen the clutch spring bolts (A, **Figure 7**) in a crisscross pattern and in several stages to relieve pressure on the bolts. Remove the bolts and springs from the clutch.
4. Remove the pressure plate (B, **Figure 7**).
5. Remove the clutch lifter assembly (A, **Figure 8**) and pushrod (B).

*NOTE*
*On CRF250X models, the first drive plate installed in the clutch plate assembly (11, **Figure 6**) has a larger inside diameter than other drive plates (9B).*

6. Remove the clutch plates (**Figure 9**) from the clutch housing.
7. CRF250X—Remove the friction spring (12, **Figure 6**) and spring seat (13) from the clutch hub.

6

8. Remove the clutch locknut, lockwasher and thrust washer as follows:

    a. Pry the lockwasher tabs (**Figure 10**) away from the clutch locknut.

> *CAUTION*
> *The spline area on the clutch hub is very thin and can easily break when being held with a clutch holding tool. Do not overtighten the tool.*

    b. Mount a clutch holder onto the clutch hub as shown in A, **Figure 11**. Position the tool so its arms engage as much of the clutch hub splines as possible. Tighten the tool so the arms are secure and cannot slip when the clutch locknut is loosened. However, overtightening the arms may also damage the clutch hub.

    c. While grasping the holder tool, loosen the clutch locknut (B, **Figure 11**) with a socket and breaker bar.

    d. Remove the clutch locknut and lockwasher.

    e. Remove the clutch holder.

9. Remove the thrust washer (A, **Figure 12**) and clutch hub (B).

10. Remove the thrust washer (A, **Figure 13**) and clutch housing (B).

11. Remove the needle bearing(s) and bushing (**Figure 14**) from the mainshaft.

> *NOTE*
> *CRF250R models use one needle bearing, while CRF250X models use two; see 20A and 20B, **Figure 6**.*

12. Inspect the clutch assembly as described in this chapter.

13. If necessary, service the clutch release lever as described in this chapter.

## Installation

1. The following parts must be installed before installing the clutch:

    a. Balancer and primary drive gears.

    b. CRF250X—Starter clutch.

    c. Kickstarter and idle gear.

    d. External shift mechanism.

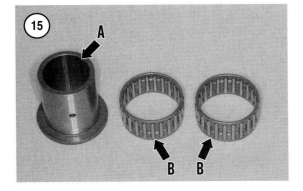

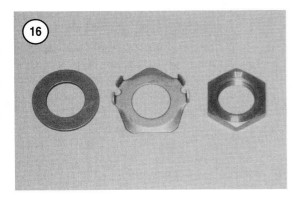

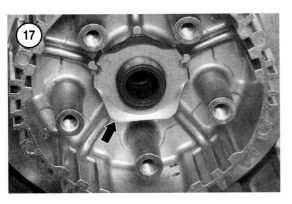

*NOTE*
*If the kickstarter was not removed, make sure its return spring is mounted correctly in the crankcase. The spring may have been dislodged when the right crankcase cover was removed.*

2. If removed, install the clutch release lever and reconnect the clutch cable as described in this chapter.

3. Lubricate the bushing's inner bore (A, **Figure 15**) with molybdenum oil solution. Lubricate the needle bearing(s) (B, **Figure 15**) with transmission oil.

*NOTE*
*Molybdenum oil solution is a 50:50 mixture of transmission oil and molybdenum grease.*

4. Install the bushing and needle bearing(s) onto the mainshaft (**Figure 14**).

5. Install the clutch housing (B, **Figure 13**) over the mainshaft. Mesh the primary driven gear on the backside of the clutch housing with the primary drive gear.

6. Lubricate the thrust washer (A, **Figure 13**) with transmission oil and seat it against the clutch housing.

7. Install the clutch hub (B, **Figure 12**) over the mainshaft splines and seat it against the thrust washer.

8. Install and tighten the clutch locknut assembly (**Figure 16**) as follows:

  a. Lubricate the thrust washer (A, **Figure 12**) with transmission oil and seat it against the clutch hub.

  b. Install a new lockwasher by seating it against the thrust washer and engaging it with raised tabs on the clutch hub (**Figure 17**, typical).

*NOTE*
*Figure 17 shows the lockwasher used on CRF250X models. The lockwasher used on CRF250R models is similar.*

  c. Lubricate the mainshaft threads with transmission oil.

  d. Lubricate the clutch locknut threads with transmission oil and thread onto the mainshaft until it seats flush against the lockwasher (B, **Figure 11**). Make sure the lockwasher remains locked against the clutch hub.

e. Mount the clutch holder (A, **Figure 11**) onto the clutch hub. Position the tool so its arms engage as much of the clutch hub splines as possible. Tighten the tool so the arms are secure and will not slip when the clutch locknut is tightened. However, do not overtighten the arms, as this may damage the clutch hub.

f. While grasping the holder tool, tighten the clutch locknut to the torque specification in **Table 3**. Remove the tool.

g. Hold the clutch housing and spin the clutch hub by hand. It must turn freely.

*NOTE*
*If the clutch hub is locked or turns roughly, check for a missing thrust washer.*

h. Bend the lockwasher tabs against the clutch locknut (**Figure 10**, typical).

*CAUTION*
*Do not bend the lockwasher more than once in the same spot. Doing so weakens the lockwasher and prevents it from securing the locknut. Install a new lockwasher when necessary.*

9. Identify the clutch plates, while noting the following:

a. On CRF250R models, all the drive plates (9A, **Figure 6**) are identical.

b. On CRF250X models, the first drive plate installed (11, **Figure 6**) has a larger inside diameter than the other drive plates (9B) because it must fit around the friction spring and spring seat without interference. See **Figure 18**.

c. The driven plates (10A and 10B, **Figure 6**) are stamped during manufacturing and have one flat side and one chamfered side. Install all the driven plates with their flat side facing in the same direction (either in or out).

10. Install the clutch plate assembly as follows:

a. Refer to Step 9 to identify the clutch plates.

b. Lubricate all the drive and driven plates with transmission oil. When installing new drive plates, soak them in clean transmission oil for a few minutes before installation.

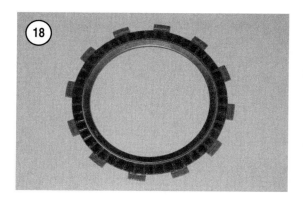

c. On CRF250X models, install the spring seat (A, **Figure 19**) and friction spring (B) onto the clutch hub. The cupped side of the friction spring must face out. When the spring seat and friction spring are properly installed, there will be a gap between them as shown in **Figure 20**.

d. Install the clutch plate assembly in the order shown in **Figure 6**. On CRF250X models, install the drive plate with the larger inside diameter first (11, **Figure 6**).

11. Lubricate both ends of the pushrod (B, **Figure 8**) with transmission oil and install it into the mainshaft.

12. Lubricate the clutch lifter assembly with transmission oil and install it over the end of the pushrod (**Figure 21**).

13. Apply pressure against the clutch lifter assembly with your finger, then operate the clutch lever at the handlebar to make sure the pushrod moves in and out. If it does not, the pushrod is not properly seated against the clutch release lever. Check clutch release lever installation as described in this chapter.

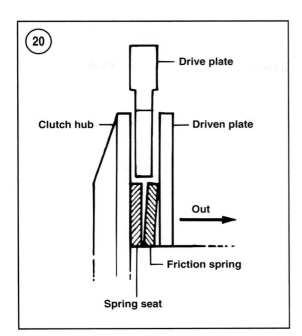

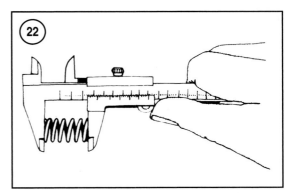

6

14. Align the pressure plate and clutch hub splines and install the pressure plate (B, **Figure 7**). Make sure it seats flush against the outer drive plate.

15. Install the clutch springs and clutch spring bolts (A, **Figure 7**). Tighten the clutch spring bolts securely in two or three steps and in a crossing pattern to the torque specification in **Table 3**.

16. Adjust the clutch (Chapter Three), then operate the clutch lever at the handlebar. Make sure the pressure plate releases the clutch plates when the clutch lever is applied.

17. Install the clutch cover or right crankcase cover as described in this chapter.

18. Shift the transmission into neutral and start the engine. After the engine warms up, pull the clutch lever in and shift the transmission into first gear. Note the following:

   a. If the clutch makes a loud grinding and spinning noise immediately after the engine is started, either the transmission oil level is too low or the new drive plates were not lubricated with oil.

   b. If the motorcycle jumps forwards and stalls, or creeps with the transmission in gear and the clutch lever is pulled in, recheck the clutch adjustment. If the clutch will not adjust properly, either the clutch cable or the drive plates are excessively worn. Replace them.

   c. If the clutch adjustment, clutch cable and clutch release lever seem to be working correctly, the clutch may have been assembled incorrectly or a broken part is in the clutch. Disassemble the clutch as described in this section and inspect the parts.

**Inspection**

Always replace drive plates, driven plates or clutch springs as a set if individual components do not meet specifications (**Table 1**). If parts show other signs of wear or damage, replace them, regardless of their specifications.

1. Clean and dry all parts.

2. Inspect the clutch springs for cracks and blue discoloration (heat damage).

3. Measure the free length of each clutch spring (**Figure 22**). Replace the springs as a set if any one spring is too short.

4. Inspect each drive plate (9A, 9B and 11, **Figure 6**) as follows:

   a. Inspect the friction material for excessive or uneven wear, cracks and other damage.

b. Inspect the tabs for cracks, grooves and noticeable wear. The tabs must be smooth so the drive plates can slide in the clutch housing grooves when the clutch is released.

*NOTE*
*If the drive plate tabs are damaged, inspect the clutch housing grooves for damage as described in this section.*

c. Measure the thickness of each drive plate (**Figure 23**) at different locations around the plate.

5. Inspect each driven plate (10A and 10B, **Figure 6**) as follows:

a. Inspect the driven plates for cracks, damage or color change. Overheated driven plates will have a blue discoloration.

b. After washing the driven plates in solvent, check them for an oil glaze buildup. Remove it by lightly sanding both sides of each plate with 400-grit sandpaper placed on a surface plate or piece of glass.

c. Inspect the inner teeth for wear, grooves and other damage. The teeth must be able to slide smoothly on the clutch hub when the clutch is released.

d. Check each driven plate for warp by placing it on a flat surface and measuring any gap around its perimeter with a feeler gauge (**Figure 24**).

6. CRF250X—Check the friction spring and spring seat for cracks and damage. Place both parts on a flat surface and check for warp. A damaged friction spring (12, **Figure 6**) causes unequal clutch plate contact. A damaged or warped spring seat (13, **Figure 6**) prevents the friction spring from apply-

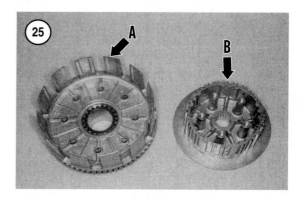

ing equal pressure against the clutch plates. Either condition can cause clutch slippage.

7. Check the clutch housing (A, **Figure 25**) as follows:

a. Inspect the clutch housing slots (**Figure 26**) for notches, grooves or other damage. Repair minor damage with a fine-cut file. If damage is excessive, replace the clutch housing. The slots must be smooth so the drive plates can move when the clutch is released.

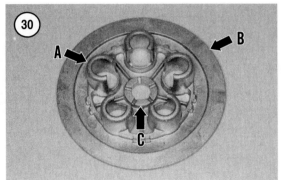

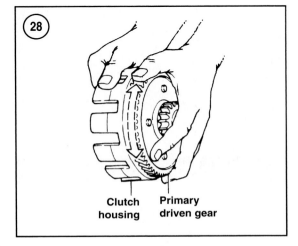

**Clutch housing**    **Primary driven gear**

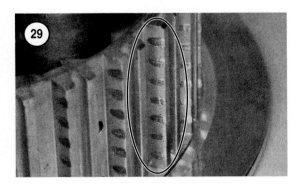

*NOTE*
*Filing the clutch housing slots is only a temporary fix as removing metal from the sides of the slots provides more room for the plates to move around and start wearing new grooves.*

b. Check the clutch housing bore (A, **Figure 25**) for scoring, cracks, pitting or other damage. If

there is damage, inspect the needle bearing(s) and bushing for similar damage.

c. Check the clutch housing gears (A and B, **Figure 27**) for excessive wear, pitting, chipped gear teeth or other damage.

d. Hold the clutch housing and turn the primary driven gear (**Figure 28**). Replace the clutch housing if there is any free play.

8. Inspect the bushing and needle bearing assembly (**Figure 15**) as follows:

a. Check the bushing for grooves, cracks and other damage. The inner and outer diameters must be smooth.

b. Inspect the needle bearing(s). The rollers should be smooth and polished with no flat spots, burrs or other damage. Inspect the bearing cage for cracks or other damage. Replace the bearing(s) if necessary.

9. Inspect the clutch hub (B, **Figure 25**) as follows:

a. Inspect the outer splines (**Figure 29**) for rough spots, grooves or other damage. Repair minor damage with a file or oil stone. If the damage is excessive, replace the clutch hub. The splines must be smooth so the driven plates can move when the clutch is released.

b. Check for damaged spring towers and threads.

10. Check the pressure plate (**Figure 30**) as follows:

a. Inspect for damaged spring towers (A, **Figure 30**).

b. Inspect the plate surface area (B, **Figure 30**) for cracks, grooves and other damage.

c. Check the clutch lifter operating area (C, **Figure 30**) in the center of the plate for cracks or damage.

11. Separate the thrust bearing parts installed on the clutch lifter and inspect it for damage (**Figure 31**). If there is any visual damage, or if further inspection is required, service the assembly as follows:

   a. Remove the clip and disassemble the clutch lifter/thrust bearing assembly (**Figure 32**). Discard the clip.
   b. Inspect the clutch lifter for scoring, roughness and other damage.
   c. Inspect the thrust bearing for cracks and damaged needles. The needles must be smooth and polished with no flat spots.
   d. Inspect the thrust washer for scoring, cracks and other damage.
   e. Assemble the clutch lifter/thrust bearing assembly in the order shown in **Figure 32**. Install a new clip into the clutch lifter groove.

12. Inspect the pushrod for bending and other damage. Check both pushrod ends for wear and roughness.

### CLUTCH RELEASE LEVER

The clutch release lever is installed on the left side of the engine. Operating the clutch lever moves the clutch release lever, which then moves the pushrod to release the pressure plate against the clutch plates.

### Removal/Installation

1. Remove the pressure plate as described under *Clutch Removal* in this chapter. Make sure there is no tension applied against the clutch lifter or pushrod.

2. Disconnect the clutch cable at the clutch release lever.

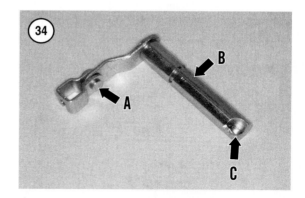

3. Remove the mounting bolt (A, **Figure 33**), mounting bracket (B) and clutch release lever (C) from the engine.

4. Inspect the clutch release lever (**Figure 34**) for the following:

   a. Damaged cable connector and rivet (A, **Figure 34**).
   b. Worn or damaged shaft, especially in the seal operating area (B, **Figure 34**).
   c. Damaged pushrod operating end (C, **Figure 34**).

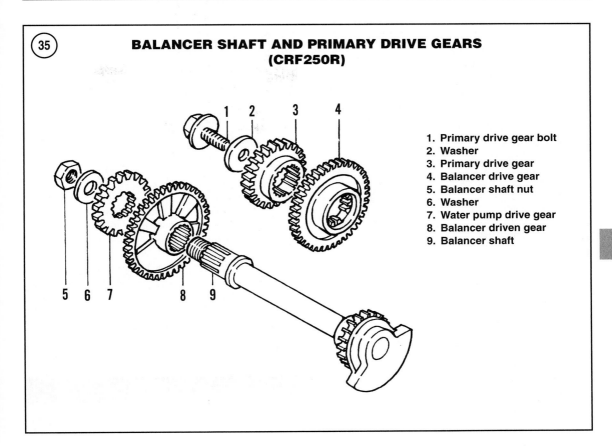

**(35)**

## BALANCER SHAFT AND PRIMARY DRIVE GEARS (CRF250R)

1. Primary drive gear bolt
2. Washer
3. Primary drive gear
4. Balancer drive gear
5. Balancer shaft nut
6. Washer
7. Water pump drive gear
8. Balancer driven gear
9. Balancer shaft

5. Inspect the release lever seal in the left case half and replace if damaged. Install the seal with its closed side facing out.

6. Lubricate the release lever seal lips with molybdenum disulfide grease.

7. Lubricate the release lever shaft with molybdenum disulfide grease and install it into the crankcase (C, **Figure 33**).

8. Install the hooked part of the mounting bracket (B, **Figure 33**) into the lever's groove and tighten the mounting bolt (A) securely.

9. Reconnect the clutch cable at the release lever.

10. Apply pressure against the clutch lifter assembly (**Figure 21**) and operate the clutch lever at the handlebar to make sure the pushrod/clutch lever assembly is properly engaged. If not, reposition the clutch release lever so its flat end contacts the pushrod.

11. Install the pressure plate as described under *Clutch Installation* in this chapter.

12. Adjust the clutch (Chapter Three).

## BALANCER SHAFT AND PRIMARY DRIVE GEAR ASSEMBLY(CRF250R)

### Tools

A gear holder is required to lock the gears and their shafts when loosening and tightening the primary drive gear bolt and the balancer shaft nut. The following options are available:

1. Use the Honda gear holder, M2.5 (part No. 07724-001A100).

2. Lock the crankshaft by holding the flywheel with a strap-type holding tool.

3. Make a gear holder from a discarded gear as described under *Balancer Shaft and Primary Drive Gear Assembly (CRF450R)* in Chapter Seven.

### Removal

1. Refer to **Figure 35** to identify the following components:

    a. Primary drive gear bolt.

    b. Primary drive gear.

**6**

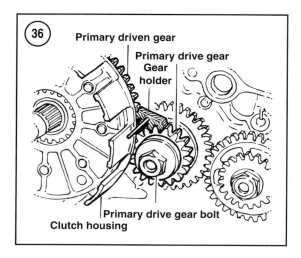

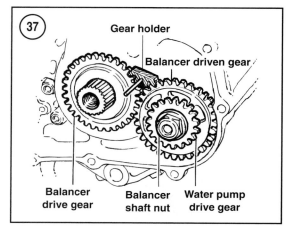

c. Balancer drive gear.
d. Balancer shaft nut.
e. Water pump gear.
f. Balancer driven gear.
g. Primary driven gear (A, **Figure 27**).
2. Remove the right crankcase cover as described in this chapter.
3. Remove the clutch as described in this chapter.

*CAUTION*
*If the cam chain is not connected to the camshaft, lift the chain so it does not bind on the crankshaft sprocket when turning the crankshaft and loosening the fasteners in this section.*

4. Remove the flywheel (Chapter Ten).
5. Temporarily install the bushing, needle bearing and clutch housing (**Figure 36**) onto the mainshaft.
6. Mesh the gear holder between the primary drive and driven gears (**Figure 36**) to lock them. Then remove the primary drive gear bolt (**Figure 36**) and washer.
7. Remove the gear holder, clutch housing, needle bearing and bushing from the mainshaft.
8. Mesh the gear holder between the balancer drive gear and balancer driven gear (**Figure 37**) to lock them. Then remove the balancer shaft nut (**Figure 37**) and washer.
9. Remove the gear holder (**Figure 37**).
10. Remove the water pump drive gear, balancer drive gear and balancer driven gear (**Figure 37**).
11. Turn the balancer shaft so its counterweight faces in the direction shown in **Figure 38** and remove it from the engine.

12. Clean and inspect the parts as described in this section.

**Installation**

The timing marks on the primary drive and balancer gear components must be properly aligned during installation.

*CAUTION*
*If the cam chain is not connected to the camshaft, lift the chain so it does not bind on the crankshaft sprocket when turning the crankshaft and tightening the fasteners in this section.*

1. Lubricate the machined surfaces on the balancer shaft with transmission oil.
2. Align the balancer shaft counterweight as shown in **Figure 38** and install it into the engine. Mesh the balancer shaft gear with the oil pump driven gear.

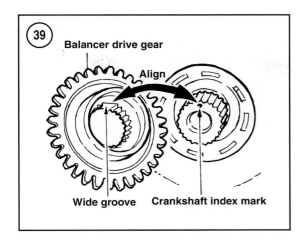

**39**
Balancer drive gear
Align
Wide groove    Crankshaft index mark

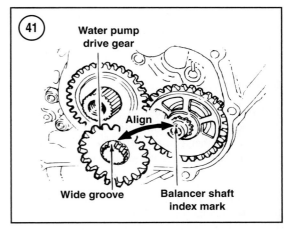

**41**
Water pump drive gear
Align
Wide groove    Balancer shaft index mark

6

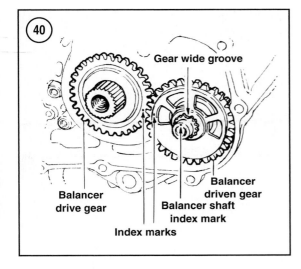

**40**
Gear wide groove
Balancer drive gear    Balancer shaft index mark    Balancer driven gear
Index marks

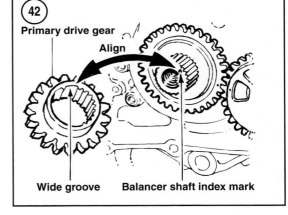

**42**
Primary drive gear
Align
Wide groove    Balancer shaft index mark

3. Lubricate the balancer drive gear shoulder with grease.

4. Install the balancer drive gear by aligning its wide groove with the index mark on the end of the crankshaft (**Figure 39**). Push the gear's shoulder through the seal until it bottoms.

5. Install the balancer driven gear by aligning its wide groove with the index mark on the end of the balancer shaft (**Figure 40**).

6. Install the water pump drive gear by aligning its wide groove with the index mark on the end of the balancer shaft (**Figure 41**).

7. Lubricate the balancer shaft washer and nut threads with transmission oil. Then install the washer and nut (**Figure 37**) and tighten finger-tight.

8. Mesh the gear holder between the balancer drive gear and balancer driven gear (at the bottom of the gears) to lock them. Then tighten the balancer shaft nut to 44 N•m (33 ft.-lb.).

9. Remove the gear holder.

10. Install the primary drive gear by aligning its wide groove with the index mark on the crankshaft (**Figure 42**).

11. Lubricate the primary drive gear washer and bolt threads with transmission oil. Then install the washer and bolt and tighten finger-tight (**Figure 36**).

12. Temporarily install the bushing, needle bearing and clutch housing (**Figure 36**) onto the mainshaft.

13. Mesh the gear holder between the primary drive and driven gears (at the bottom of the gears) to lock them and tighten the primary drive gear bolt to 108 N•m (80 ft.-lb.).

14. Remove the gear holder.

15. Remove the clutch housing assembly.

16. Install the clutch as described in this chapter.

17. Install the flywheel (Chapter Ten).

18. Install the right crankcase cover as described in this chapter.

### Inspection

1. Clean and dry all parts.

2. Inspect the gear teeth and splines for pitting, cracks and other damage. If there is damage, replace the mating gears at the same time.

> *NOTE*
> *If there is wear in Step 2, also check the primary driven gear mounted on the clutch housing for the same defects. Refer to **Clutch** in this chapter.*

3. Inspect the balancer shaft bearing surface, splines and threads for pitting, cracks and other damage. Replace if necessary.

### STARTER CLUTCH, BALANCER SHAFT AND PRIMARY DRIVE GEAR ASSEMBLY (CRF250X)

#### Tools

The Honda universal holder (part No. 07725-0030000) or equivalent (A, **Figure 43**) is required to hold the starter clutch when loosening and tightening the primary drive gear bolt and the balancer shaft nut.

> *NOTE*
> *When working alone, use a wooden block (B, **Figure 43**) to secure the universal holder when loosening and tightening the fasteners in this section. It is very difficult to hold the starter clutch when attempting to loosen or tighten the fasteners at the same time.*

#### Removal

1. Refer to **Figure 44** to identify the following components:
   a. Starter gear holder assembly (A, **Figure 44**).
   b. Primary drive gear bolt (B, **Figure 44**).
   c. Primary drive gear (C, **Figure 44**).
   d. Starter clutch (D, **Figure 44**).
   e. Balancer shaft nut (E, **Figure 44**).

   f. Water pump drive gear (F, **Figure 44**).
   g. Balancer driven gear (G, **Figure 44**).
   h. Primary driven gear.

> *NOTE*
> *The balancer drive gear is installed on the crankshaft, behind the starter clutch.*

2. Remove the right crankcase cover as described in this chapter.

3. Remove the clutch as described in this chapter.

*CAUTION*
*If the cam chain is not connected to the camshaft, lift the chain so it does not bind on the crankshaft sprocket when turning the crankshaft and loosening the fasteners in this section.*

4. Remove the flywheel (Chapter Ten).

5. Hold the starter clutch with the universal holder (A, **Figure 43**) and loosen the balancer shaft nut (E, **Figure 44**) and the primary drive gear bolt (B).

6. Remove the universal holder.

7. Remove the balancer shaft nut (E, **Figure 44**), washer, water pump drive gear (F) and collar.

8. Remove the primary drive gear bolt (B, **Figure 44**) and primary drive gear (C).

9. Remove the starter clutch (D, **Figure 44**).

10. Remove the balancer drive gear (A, **Figure 45**) and balancer driven gear (B, **Figure 45**).

11. Turn the balancer shaft so its counterweight faces in the direction shown in **Figure 46** and remove it from the engine.

12. Remove the bolts and the starter gear holder assembly (A, **Figure 44**) and its locating pin (**Figure 47**).

13. Clean and inspect the parts as described in this section.

**Installation**

A balancer shaft is used with the full-circle crankshaft to correct any primary imbalance caused by the top end components during engine operation. Installing the components in this section times the balancer shaft to the crankshaft.

Timing is accomplished by aligning the wide groove in the spline of each gear with a master spline (a uniquely shaped spline) machined on the crankshaft and balancer shaft. The master spline aligns with an index mark on the end of its shaft. If a gear does not slide on its shaft, do not force it. Reposition the gear and try to install it again. If the timing marks are properly aligned but the gear does not slide on, check for and remove any burrs from the splines with a fine-tooth file.

*CAUTION*
*If the cam chain is not connected to the camshaft, lift the chain so it does not bind on the crankshaft sprocket when turning the crankshaft and tightening the fasteners in this section.*

1. Install the starter gear holder locating pin (**Figure 47**), starter gear holder (A, **Figure 44**) and tighten its mounting bolts to 22 N•m (16 ft.-lb.).

2. Lubricate the machined surfaces on the balancer shaft with transmission oil.

3. Align the balancer shaft counterweight as shown in **Figure 46** and install it into the engine. Mesh the balancer shaft gear with the oil pump driven gear.

4. Lubricate the balancer drive gear shoulder with grease.

5. Install the balancer drive gear by aligning its wide groove (A, **Figure 48**) with the index mark (B)

6

on the end of the crankshaft. Push the gear's shoulder through the seal until it bottoms (A, **Figure 45**).

6. Initially install the balancer driven gear by aligning its wide groove (A, **Figure 49**) with the index mark (B) on the balancer shaft. Then turn the balancer shaft to align the index marks on the drive and driven gears (C, **Figure 45**) and push the driven gear all the way onto the balancer shaft.

7. Install the starter clutch by aligning its wide groove with the index mark on the end of the crankshaft (**Figure 50**).

8. Install the primary drive gear with its timing mark (A, **Figure 51**) facing out, and then align the wide groove in the gear (B) with the index mark on the end of the crankshaft (C).

9. Lubricate the primary drive gear washer and bolt threads with transmission oil. Then install the washer and bolt and tighten finger-tight (B, **Figure 44**).

10. Hold the starter clutch with the universal holder (A, **Figure 43**) and tighten the primary drive gear bolt (B, **Figure 44**) to 108 N•m (80 ft.-lb.).

11. Install the collar (A, **Figure 52**) onto the balancer shaft.

12. Install the water pump drive gear by aligning its wide groove (B, **Figure 52**) with the index mark on the end of the balancer shaft (C).

13. Lubricate the balancer shaft washer and nut threads with transmission oil. Then install the washer and nut and tighten finger-tight (E, **Figure 44**).

14. Hold the starter clutch with the universal holder (A, **Figure 43**) and tighten the balancer shaft nut (E, **Figure 44**) to 44 N•m (33 ft.-lb.).

15. Install the clutch as described in this chapter.

16. Install the flywheel (Chapter Ten).

17. Install the right crankcase cover as described in this chapter.

### Inspection

1. Clean and dry all parts.

2. Inspect the gear teeth and splines (**Figure 53**, typical) for pitting, cracks and other damage. If there is damage, replace the mating gears at the same time.

*NOTE*
*If there is wear in Step 2, also check the primary driven gear mounted on*

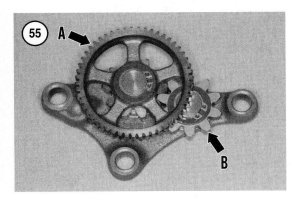

*the clutch housing for the same defects. Refer to **Clutch** in this chapter.*

3. Inspect the balancer shaft (**Figure 54**) bearing surface, splines and threads for pitting, cracks and other damage. Replace if necessary.

### Reduction Gear and Idle Gear Assembly Inspection/Disassembly/Reassembly

Replace parts that are out of specification (**Table 2**) or show damage as described in this section.

1. Clean and dry the reduction gear and idle gear assembly.

2. Inspect the reduction gear (A, **Figure 55**) and idle gear teeth (B) for pitting, cracks and tooth damage.

3. Spin the reduction gear by hand. Both gears should turn smoothly. If there is any roughness, remove the gears (Step 4) and check for damage.

4. Remove the snap rings, washers and gears (**Figure 56**). Discard the snap rings.

5. Check the gear bores and mating shafts for any damage. Both surfaces must be smooth. The shafts must fit tightly in the holder assembly.

6. Measure the starter reduction gear (A, **Figure 56**) and idle gear (B) inside diameters.

7. Measure the outside diameter of both starter gear shafts (C, **Figure 56**).

8. Check the washers for cracks, cupping and other damage. The washers must be flat.

9. Lubricate the shafts and gear bores with transmission oil and install the gears, washers and new snap rings. Install the snap rings with their flat side facing away from the gears. Make sure the snap rings seat in their grooves completely.

### Starter Clutch Inspection/Disassembly/Reassembly

Refer to **Figure 57** when servicing the starter clutch assembly. Replace parts that are out of specification (**Table 2**) or show damage as described in this section.

1. Clean and dry the starter clutch assembly.

2. Check the one-way clutch operation as follows:

 a. Place the starter clutch on the workbench with the starter driven gear facing up as shown in **Figure 58**.

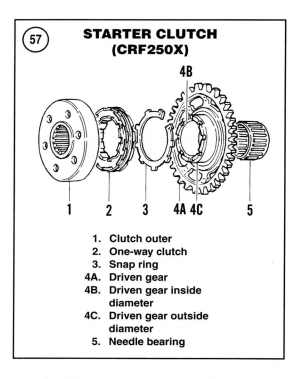

**STARTER CLUTCH (CRF250X)**

1. Clutch outer
2. One-way clutch
3. Snap ring
4A. Driven gear
4B. Driven gear inside diameter
4C. Driven gear outside diameter
5. Needle bearing

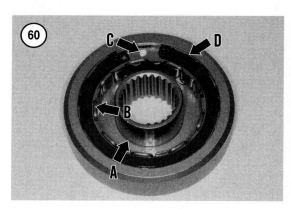

b. Hold the clutch outer and try to turn the starter driven gear clockwise and then counterclockwise. The starter driven gear should only turn clockwise as viewed in **Figure 58**.

3. Remove the starter driven gear and needle bearing (**Figure 59**) from the one-way clutch assembly.

4. Inspect the starter driven gear (**Figure 59**) for the following conditions:

a. Worn or damaged gear teeth.

b. Worn or damaged inside and outside bearing shoulder surfaces. Both surfaces must be smooth.

c. Measure the inside (4B, **Figure 57**) and outside (4C) diameters of the starter driven gear bearing shoulder and refer to **Table 2**.

5. Inspect the needle bearing (**Figure 59**). The rollers should be smooth and polished with no flat spots, burrs or other damage. Inspect the bearing cage for cracks or other damage. Replace the bearing if necessary.

6. Inspect the one-way clutch (**Figure 60**) for the following conditions:

a. Worn or damaged bearing shoulder (A, **Figure 60**).

b. Worn or damaged one-way clutch rollers (B).

7. Replace the one-way clutch (**Figure 60**) as follows:

*NOTE*
*If the one-way clutch is difficult to remove, see **One-Way Clutch Removal/Installation** in Chapter Seven.*

a. Locate the paint mark at the top of the one-way clutch (C, **Figure 60**). The new one-way clutch must be installed with its paint mark facing out.

b. Remove the snap ring (D, **Figure 60**) and remove the one-way clutch (B).

c. Clean the clutch outer and inspect its bore surface for damage. The bore must be smooth.

6

d. Install the new one-way clutch into the clutch outer with its paint mark facing out (C, **Figure 60**).

e. Install the snap ring (D, **Figure 60**) and seat it into the groove in the clutch outer.

## KICKSTARTER AND KICK IDLE GEAR

### Kickstarter Removal

*NOTE*
*If troubleshooting the kickstarter, examine its mounting position in the engine before removing it. Make sure the return spring has sufficient preload and is hooked in the crankcase hole.*

1. Remove the right crankcase cover and clutch as described in this chapter.

2. Remove the idle gear (**Figure 61**) as follows:

  a. On CRF250R models, remove the idle gear and washer.

  b. On CRF250X models, remove the snap ring, thrust washer, idle gear and thrust washer (**Figure 62**). Both thrust washers are identical.

*WARNING*
*Wear safety glasses when disconnecting the return spring in Step 3.*

3. While preventing the kickstarter from coming out of the engine case, unhook the return spring (A, **Figure 63**) and slowly allow the spring to unwind. Then turn the kickstarter assembly counterclockwise until the starter ratchet clears the kick guide and remove the kickstarter assembly (B, **Figure 63**). Locate the ratchet spring (A, **Figure 64**) installed on the inner part of the kick axle.

*NOTE*
*After removing the kickstarter, hold the assembly together as parts can slide off both ends of the axle.*

4. If necessary, service the kickstarter as described in this section.

### Kickstarter Installation

1. Check that the kick guide (A, **Figure 65**) and oil guide plate (B) are properly indexed and tightened securely in the right crankcase. If necessary, apply a

medium strength threadlock onto the bolt threads and tighten securely.

2. Check that the kickstarter is assembled correctly as described under *Assembly* in this section.

3. Lubricate the kick axle (B, **Figure 64**) and its operating bore (C) with molybdenum disulfide oil solution.

4. Install the kickstarter by inserting the arm on the starter ratchet (D, **Figure 64**) behind the kick guide (E), then install the kick axle into the crankcase bore.

*WARNING*
*Wear safety glasses when hooking the return spring and checking kick-starter operation in Step 5 and Step 6.*

5. Hold the kickstarter (B, **Figure 63**), then turn the return spring clockwise and hook it into the hole in the crankcase (A, **Figure 63**).

6. Install the thrust washer (D, **Figure 63**) onto the kick axle.

7. Check the kickstarter operation as follows:
   a. With the kickstarter in its rest position, the kick gear (C, **Figure 63**) should spin freely.
   b. Install the kick pedal onto the kick axle. Then hold the kickstarter assembly and turn the kick pedal counterclockwise. Check that the kick gear is now locked to the kick axle. If not, remove the kickstarter and check the ratchet and kick axle index marks as described under *Kickstarter Assembly* in this section.
   c. Carefully remove the kick pedal without disturbing the kickstarter and its return spring installation positions.

8. Install the idle gear as follows:
   a. Locate the shoulder (**Figure 66**) on the idle gear. This side of the gear faces toward the engine.
   b. Lubricate the idle gear bore and countershaft with molybdenum disulfide oil solution.
   c. On CRF250R models, install the idle gear and washer (**Figure 61**).
   d. On CRF250X models, install the thrust washer, idle gear, thrust washer and snap ring (**Figure 61**). Both thrust washers are identical. Make sure the snap ring seats in the countershaft groove completely.

9. Install the clutch and right crankcase cover as described in this chapter.

**Kickstarter Disassembly**

1. Hold the kickstarter to prevent the parts from sliding off, then dip the assembly in solvent and dry with compressed air.

2. Disassemble the kickstarter in the order shown in **Figure 67**.

3. Discard the snap ring.

4. Inspect the kickstarter assembly as described in this section.

**Kickstarter Assembly**

*NOTE*
*The thrust washers (1, 5 and 7, **Figure 67**) used on the kickstarter assembly are identical.*

1. Lubricate all sliding surfaces with transmission oil.

2. Install the kick gear assembly (**Figure 68**) as follows:

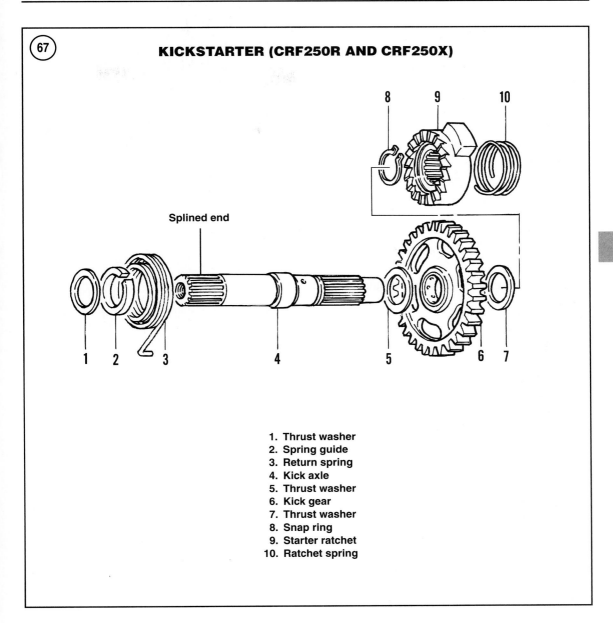

**KICKSTARTER (CRF250R AND CRF250X)**

Splined end

1. Thrust washer
2. Spring guide
3. Return spring
4. Kick axle
5. Thrust washer
6. Kick gear
7. Thrust washer
8. Snap ring
9. Starter ratchet
10. Ratchet spring

a. Lubricate the kick gear bushing with molybdenum oil solution.

b. Install the thrust washer (5, **Figure 67**) and seat it against the shoulder on the kick axle, opposite the splined end.

c. Install the kick gear (6, **Figure 67**) with its ratchet teeth facing away from the splined end. Refer to **Figure 69**.

d. Install the thrust washer (7, **Figure 67**) and seat it against the kick gear.

e. Install a new snap ring (8, **Figure 67**) with its sharp edge facing away from the kick gear. Make sure the snap ring seats in the kick axle groove completely.

f. Spin the kick gear, making sure it turns smoothly.

3. Install the starter ratchet (9, **Figure 67**) by aligning the starter ratchet and kick axle index marks (**Figure 70**).

> *NOTE*
> *The kickstarter will not work if the index marks in **Figure 70** are not properly aligned.*

4. Install the ratchet spring (**Figure 71**) and seat it against the starter ratchet.

5. Install the return spring assembly (**Figure 72**) as follows:

a. Hook the end of the return spring into the hole in the kick axle (A, **Figure 73**). Make sure the other end of the spring faces toward the kick gear.

b. Install the spring guide by aligning its slot with the spring end (B, **Figure 73**).

c. Install the thrust washer (C, **Figure 73**) onto the kick axle.

6. **Figure 74** shows a properly assembled kickstarter assembly.

## Kickstarter and Idle Gear Inspection

Refer to **Figure 67** when servicing the kickstarter assembly. Replace parts that are out of specification (**Table 1**) or show damage as described in this section.

1. Check the kick gear (A, **Figure 75**) for:

a. Chipped or missing gear teeth.

b. Worn, damaged or rounded ratchet teeth (B, **Figure 75**).

c. Worn or damaged gear bore.

d. Measure the kick gear inside diameter (C, **Figure 75**).

2. Inspect the kick axle (D, **Figure 75**) for:

a. Heat discoloration, scored or cracked operating surfaces.

b. Measure the kick axle outside diameter at the kick gear's operating position (E, **Figure 75**).

c. Check both sets of splines for twisting, cracks and other damage. The starter ratchet must

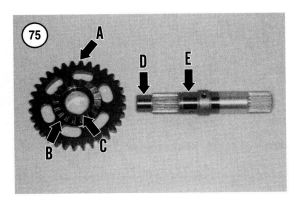

slide freely on the inner kick axle splines. If the outer splines are damaged, the kick pedal may slip when under use.

   d. Elongation of the return spring hole.

   e. Damaged snap ring groove.

3. Check the starter ratchet (9, **Figure 67**) for:

   a. Cracks or other damage.

   b. Worn, damaged or rounded-off ratchet teeth.

   c. Worn or damaged splines.

*CAUTION*
*Check the ratchet teeth on the kick gear and starter ratchet. When the two parts are mated, the ratchet teeth must smoothly slip in one direction and positively lock in the other direction. Worn or damaged ratchet teeth will cause the kickstarter to slip when under use.*

4. Inspect the return spring (3, **Figure 67**) and ratchet spring (10) for cracks or other visible damage. Check both return spring ends for damage.

5. Check the spring guide for excessive wear or damage.

6. Inspect the thrust washers for burrs, excessive thrust wear and other damage.

7. Measure the countershaft outside diameter at the idle gear's operating position (**Figure 76**). If out of specification, disassemble the engine (Chapter Four) and replace the countershaft (Chapter Eight).

8. Inspect the idle gear (**Figure 62**) for:

   a. Chipped or missing gear teeth.

   b. Worn or damaged gear bore.

   c. Measure the idle gear inside diameter.

**Kick Guide Inspection**

The kick guide (A, **Figure 65**), mounted on the crankcase, prevents the starter ratchet from engaging the kick gear when the kickstarter is at rest. When the kickstarter is operated, the arm on the starter ratchet slips from behind the kick guide. The ratchet spring then moves the starter ratchet against the kick gear. The teeth on the starter ratchet and kick gear lock, which locks the kick gear to the kick axle. Make sure the kick guide is in good condition and tightly secured to the crankcase. If the bolt is loose, apply a medium strength threadlock onto its threads and tighten securely.

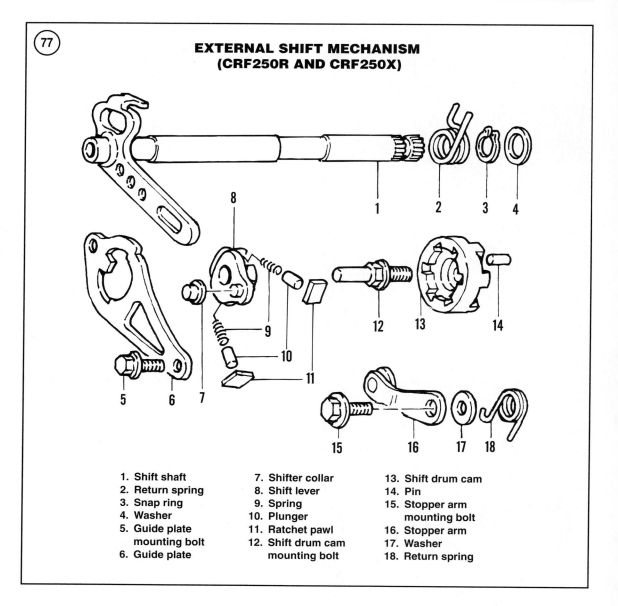

**EXERNAL SHIFT MECHANISM (CRF250R AND CRF250X)**

1. Shift shaft
2. Return spring
3. Snap ring
4. Washer
5. Guide plate mounting bolt
6. Guide plate
7. Shifter collar
8. Shift lever
9. Spring
10. Plunger
11. Ratchet pawl
12. Shift drum cam mounting bolt
13. Shift drum cam
14. Pin
15. Stopper arm mounting bolt
16. Stopper arm
17. Washer
18. Return spring

## Kick Pedal
## Disassembly/Reassembly

If the kick pedal fails to lock in place after returning it to its closed position, service the kick pedal assembly as described under *Kickstarter and Kick Idle Gear* in Chapter Seven.

## EXTERNAL SHIFT MECHANISM

The external shift mechanism consists of the shift shaft and pedal, stopper arm assembly and shift drum cam assembly (**Figure 77**). These parts can be removed with the engine mounted in the frame. Repair of the shift drum and forks requires engine removal and crankcase separation (Chapter Four).

### Removal

1. Remove the right crankcase cover and clutch as described in this chapter.
2. On CRF250X models, remove the starter clutch as described in this chapter.
3. Remove the pinch bolt and shift pedal.

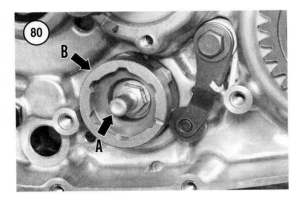

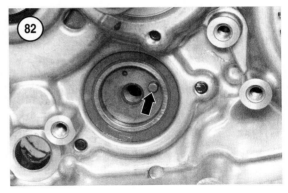

*NOTE*
*If the shift pedal is tight, check the splines for bending or other damage. Insert a screwdriver into the slot in the pedal, then spread the slot and remove the pedal.*

4. Remove the shift shaft (A, **Figure 78**) and its washer.

5. Remove the shifter collar (A, **Figure 79**) from the pin on the shift lever.

*NOTE*
*The shift lever assembly consists of parts 5-11 in **Figure 77**. After removing the guide plate mounting bolts (5), remove the shift lever assembly with the guide plate (6). The plungers (10) and ratchet pawls (11) are spring-loaded and can eject as the shift lever (8) is removed from the shift drum cam. When removing the shift lever assembly, try to hold the ratchet pawls in position.*

6. Remove the guide plate bolts (B, **Figure 79**). Then remove guide plate (C, **Figure 79**) and shift lever assembly (D) at the same time.

7. Turn the bolt (A, **Figure 80**) and shift drum cam (B) counterclockwise until they stop. Then loosen and remove the bolt and shift drum cam.

8. Remove the stopper arm mounting bolt (A, **Figure 81**), stopper arm (B), washer and return spring.

9. Remove the pin (**Figure 82**) from the shift drum.

10. Inspect the parts as described in this section.

## Installation

It is easier to install the stopper arm assembly first, then the shift drum cam.

1. Install the pin (**Figure 82**) into the shift drum.

2. Install the stopper arm assembly (**Figure 83**) as follows:

    a. Assemble the stopper arm as shown in **Figure 84**.

    b. Install the stopper arm as shown in B, **Figure 81**. Finger-tighten the stopper arm mounting bolt. Make sure the spring is aligned around the bolt and against the crankcase as shown in **Figure 81**.

    c. Using a screwdriver, push the stopper arm down and release it to make sure it moves under spring tension. If the stopper arm does not move, it is pinched under the mounting bolt. Loosen the bolt and center the stopper arm on the bolt's shoulder, then retighten the bolt.

    d. When the stopper arm moves correctly, tighten the stopper arm mounting bolt (A, **Figure 81**) to 12 N•m (106 in.-lb.).

3. Install the shift drum cam as follows:

    a. Apply a medium strength threadlock onto the shift drum cam mounting bolt threads (12, **Figure 77**). Set the bolt aside until it is to be installed.

    b. Pry the stopper arm assembly away from the shift drum with a screwdriver. Align the slot in the shift drum cam (A, **Figure 85**) with the dowel pin (B), and install the shift drum cam. Hold the shift drum cam firmly and release the screwdriver to allow the stopper arm to rest against the cam.

    c. Install the shift drum cam mounting bolt (A, **Figure 80**) and tighten until the shift drum is sitting flush against the shift drum and you can release your hand without the cam slipping or moving out of position.

    d. Turn the shift drum cam mounting bolt (A, **Figure 80**) clockwise to lock the shift drum cam, then tighten the bolt to 22 N•m (16 ft.-lb.).

4. Install the shift lever assembly (parts 5-11, **Figure 77**) as follows:

    a. Lubricate the shift drum cam mounting bolt shoulder (A, **Figure 80**) with transmission oil.

    b. Insert the springs, plungers and ratchet pawls (**Figure 86**) into the shift lever. The notch in

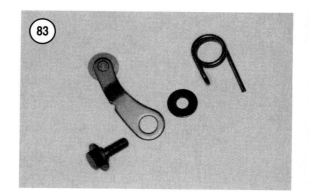

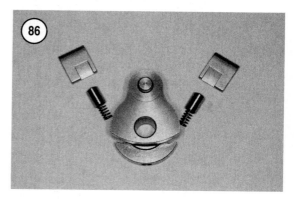

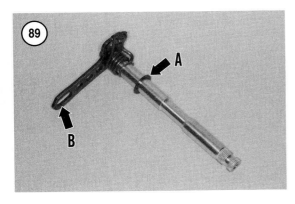

the ratchet pawls must face in the direction shown in **Figure 87**, and the rounded ends of the ratchet pawls must seat against the shift lever (**Figure 88**).

c. Slide the guide plate over the shift lever assembly. Position the plate to hold the pawls in place.

*NOTE*
*C, Figure 79 shows how the guide plate aligns and fits over the shift lever. The UP mark on the guide plate should be facing up.*

d. Slide the hole in the shift lever (D, **Figure 79**) over the shift drum cam mounting bolt while feeding the pawls into the shift drum cam. Hold the shift lever in position and align the guide plate (C, **Figure 79**), then install the mounting bolts (B).

e. Tighten the guide plate mounting bolts (B, **Figure 79**) to 12 N•m (106 in.-lb.).

5. Install the shifter collar (A, **Figure 79**) onto the shift lever pin.

6. Install the shift shaft as follows:

a. Wipe the shift shaft oil seal with a rag, then lubricate the seal lips with grease. If the seal is damaged or was previously leaking oil, replace it as described under *Shift Shaft Seal Replacement* in Chapter Four.

b. Lubricate the shift shaft with transmission oil.

c. Install the washer (A, **Figure 89**) onto the shift shaft.

d. Slide the shaft slowly through the engine, then engage the return spring with the spring pin (B, **Figure 78**) while aligning the shift shaft pawl with the shifter collar (C).

7. Install the shift pedal and tighten its pinch bolt to 12 N•m (106 in.-lb.).

8. Support the motorcycle with the rear wheel off the ground and check the shifting as follows:

a. Mount an aluminum plate across the crankcase to hold the shift shaft in position (**Figure 90**).

b. Slowly turn the rear wheel and shift the transmission into first gear, then shift to neutral and the remaining forward gears.

*NOTE*
*Note in Figure 91 the stopper arms engagement with the raised ramp on*

*the shift drum. This is the shift drum's
neutral position.*

c. If the shift shaft moves and then locks in
place, the return spring may not be centered
on the spring pin (B, **Figure 78**).

d. If the transmission over-shifts, check for an
incorrectly assembled stopper arm assembly.

e. If the transmission does not shift properly,
check for an incorrectly installed shift shaft
return spring (**Figure 92**). Then check the
shift lever assembly.

f. Remove the bolt and aluminum plate.

9. Install the clutch and right crankcase cover as
described in this chapter.

**Inspection**

Worn or damaged external shift linkage components causes missed shifts and wear to the transmission gears, shift forks and shift drum. Replace parts
that show excessive wear or damage.

1. Clean and dry the parts. Remove all threadlock
residue from the shift drum cam mounting bolt
threads.

2. Inspect the shift shaft assembly (**Figure 89**) as
follows:

a. Inspect the splines for damage.

b. Inspect the shaft for straightness.

c. Inspect the return spring (**Figure 92**) for
cracks and other damage.

d. Inspect the shift pawl (B, **Figure 89**) for excessive wear or damage.

e. Make sure the return spring seats in the shift
pawl grooves.

3. Check the stopper arm (**Figure 83**) assembly
for:

a. Weak or damaged spring. Check spring for
cracks.

b. Bent, cracked or damaged stopper arm.
Check roller for flat spots.

c. Damaged stopper arm mounting bolt.

4. Check the shift drum cam assembly (13, **Figure
77**) as follows:

a. Inspect the detents in the face of the cam. The
detents must not be worn or shifting will be
rough.

b. Inspect the ramps in the rear side of the cam
for wear or damage. If the sides of the ramps
are rounded or damaged, the stopper arm

roller can slip and the transmission will jump
out of gear.

c. Inspect the bolt (12, **Figure 77**) for scoring or
gouges that would prevent the shift lever (8)
from operating correctly.

5. Check the shift lever assembly (parts 5-11, **Figure 77**) as follows:

a. Inspect the shift lever for cracks and other
damage.

b. The guide plate controls the movement of the
ratchet pawls during shifting. Inspect the

guide plate for bending and other damage. Inspect the guide plate where the ratchet pawls operate. This area must be smooth.

c. Inspect the pawls for wear at their round edge.

d. Inspect the springs and plungers for cracks and damage.

e. Inspect the shifter collar for damage.

6. Inspect the shift shaft return spring pin bolt (B, **Figure 78**) for looseness and damage. Replace the bolt if its shoulder is damaged.

7. Tighten the shift shaft return spring pin bolt to 22 N•m (16 ft.-lb.).

## CLUTCH CABLE REPLACEMENT

1. Before disconnecting or removing the clutch cable, make a drawing of the cable routing from the handlebar and around the left side of the frame to the clutch release lever at the engine. Replace the cable exactly as it was, avoiding any sharp turns.

2. Loosen the clutch cable adjuster locknut and adjuster at the handlebar, then disconnect the clutch cable.

3. Disconnect the clutch cable at the clutch release lever (**Figure 93**).

4. Remove the cable.

5. Lubricate the new clutch cable before reconnecting it. Refer to Chapter Three.

6. Install the new clutch cable by reversing these removal steps. Make sure it is correctly routed with no sharp turns. Adjust the clutch cable as described in Chapter Three.

**Table 1 CLUTCH AND KICKSTARTER SERVICE SPECIFICATIONS (CRF250R AND CRF250X)**

|  | New<br>mm (in.) | Service limit<br>mm (in.) |
|---|---|---|
| Drive plate thickness | 2.92-3.08 (0.115-0.121) | 2.85 (0.112) |
| Driven plate warp | – | 0.10 (0.004) |
| Clutch spring free length |  |  |
| CRF250R |  |  |
| 2004 | 37.1 (1.46) | 36.3 (1.43) |
| 2005 | 38.0 (1.50) | 37.2 (1.46) |
| CRF250X | 38.8 (1.53) | 38.0 (1.50) |
| Countershaft outside diameter |  |  |
| at idle gear operating area | 16.983-16.994 (0.6686-0.6691) | 16.97 (0.668) |
| Idle gear inside diameter | 17.016-17.034 (0.6699-0.6706) | 17.06 (0.672) |
| Kick axle outside diameter | 16.466-16.484 (0.6483-0.6490) | 16.46 (0.648) |
| Kick gear inside diameter | 16.516-16.534 (0.6502-0.6509) | 16.55 (0.652) |

**Table 2 STARTER CLUTCH SERVICE SPECIFICATIONS (CRF250X)**

|  | New<br>mm (in.) | Service limit<br>mm (in.) |
|---|---|---|
| Starter driven gear bearing |  |  |
| shoulder |  |  |
| Inside diameter | 35.009-35.034 (1.3783-1.3793) | 35.07 (1.381) |
| Outside diameter | 45.660-45.673 (1.7976-1.7982) | 45.64 (1.797) |
| Starter gear shaft outside |  |  |
| diameter | 11.983-11.994 (0.4718-0.4722) | 11.98 (0.472) |
| Starter idle gear inside diameter | 12.016-12.034 (0.4731-0.4738) | 12.05 (0.474) |
| Starter reduction gear inside |  |  |
| diameter | 12.016-12.034 (0.4731-0.4738) | 12.05 (0.474) |

**Table 3 CLUTCH TORQUE SPECIFICATIONS (CRF250R AND CRF250X)**

|                                       | N•m  | in.-lb. | ft.-lb. |
|---------------------------------------|------|---------|---------|
| Balancer shaft nut[1]                 | 44   | –       | 33      |
| Clutch locknut[1]                     |      |         |         |
|   CRF250R                             | 69   | –       | 51      |
|   CRF250X                             | 80   | –       | 59      |
| Clutch spring bolt                    |      |         |         |
|   CRF250R                             | 9.8  | 87      | –       |
|   CRF250X                             | 12   | 106     | –       |
| Guide plate bolt                      | 12   | 106     | –       |
| Kick pedal bolt                       | 37   | –       | 27      |
| Primary drive gear bolt[1]            | 108  | –       | 80      |
| Shift drum cam mounting bolt[2]       | 22   | –       | 16      |
| Shift pedal pinch bolt                | 12   | 106     | –       |
| Shift shaft return spring pin bolt    | 22   | –       | 16      |
| Starter gear holding bolt             |      |         |         |
|   CRF250X                             | 22   | –       | 16      |
| Stopper arm mounting bolt             | 12   | 106     | –       |

1. Lubricate threads and seating surface with transmission oil.
2. Apply medium strength threadlock to fastener threads.

# CHAPTER SEVEN

# CLUTCH, PRIMARY DRIVE, KICKSTARTER AND EXTERNAL SHIFT MECHANISM (CRF450R AND CRF450X)

This chapter describes service procedures for the components installed behind the right crankcase cover.

1. Right crankcase cover.
2. Clutch cover.
3. Clutch.
4. Clutch release lever.
5. Balancer and primary drive gears.
6. Starter clutch (CRF450X).
7. Kickstarter.
8. External shift mechanism.

Read this chapter before attempting repairs to the clutch and other components in the right crankcase cover. Become familiar with the procedures to understand the skill and equipment required. Refer to Chapter One for tool usage and service methods.

While the inspection procedures in this chapter help detect parts that are excessively worn or damaged, it is important to inspect the parts during their removal and disassembly, especially when troubleshooting a problem area. Look for loose fasteners, incorrect adjustments, binding, rough turning and abnormal wear marks or patterns.

**Tables 1-3** are at the end of this chapter.

## RIGHT CRANKCASE COVER

The right crankcase cover can be removed without having to remove the water pump cover.

### Removal/Installation

1. Remove the right engine guard.
2. Drain the engine coolant (Chapter Three).
3. Drain the transmission oil (Chapter Three).
4. Remove the rear brake pedal (A, **Figure 1** [Chapter Fifteen]).
5. Unbolt and remove the kick pedal (B, **Figure 1**). If the kick pedal is stuck, perform the following:
   a. Spray penetrating lubricant around the kick pedal splines. Give the lubricant time to dis-

solve some of the rust, then tap the pedal and slide it off the shaft.

b. If the kick pedal is tight from corrosion or damaged splines, install the kick pedal bolt finger-tight, and then back it out two turns. Mount a small two-jaw puller across the kick pedal boss, centering the pressure bolt against the mounting bolt, then operate the puller to remove the kick pedal.

*CAUTION*
*Do not pry the kick pedal off as this may damage the right crankcase cover.*

6A. On CRF450R models, loosen the hose clamp and disconnect the hose at the water pump (C, **Figure 1**).
6B. On CRF450X models, remove the bolts, water hose joint and O-ring from the top of the water pump housing (**Figure 2**).

*NOTE*
*Different length bolts secure the right crankcase cover to the engine. To ensure that the bolts are correctly located during assembly, make an outline of the right crankcase cover on a piece of cardboard. Punch holes in the cardboard at the same locations as the bolts. After removing each bolt from the cover, place the bolt in its respective hole in the template.*

7. Remove the bolts securing the right crankcase cover (D, **Figure 1**) to the engine. If necessary, lightly tap the cover to loosen it from the engine.
8. Remove the gasket and cover dowel pins (**Figure 3**).
9. Remove the water by-pass pipe and O-ring (**Figure 4**).
10. To service the water pump, refer to Chapter Eleven.
11. Clean and inspect the right crankcase cover as follows:
a. Clean and dry the cover.

*NOTE*
*If the water pump assembly is installed in the right crankcase cover, do not submerge the cover in solvent.*

b. Inspect the cover for cracks and other damage.

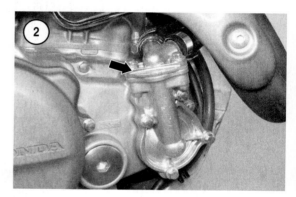

c. Inspect the kickstarter seal (**Figure 5**) and replace if leaking or damaged. Install the new seal with its flat side facing out and lubricate the seal lip with grease.

12. Installation is the reverse of removal. Note the following:

a. Remove all gasket residue from the cover and case half mating surfaces.

b. Make sure the kickstarter is properly installed with the correct amount of spring preload as

described under *Kickstarter and Kick Idle Gear* in this chapter.

c. Install a new gasket.

d. Install a new water by-pass O-ring (**Figure 4**), if necessary.

e. Lubricate the kickstarter oil seal lip with grease.

f. When installing the crankcase cover on CRF450R models, align the flat surface on the end of the water pump shaft with the

groove in the balancer shaft, then seat the cover into place.

g. When installing the crankcase cover on CRF450X models, align the slot in the end of the water pump shaft with the shoulder on the end of the balancer shaft, then seat the cover in place.

h. On 2002-2004 models, tighten the right crankcase cover mounting bolts securely in two or three steps and in a crossing pattern.

i. On 2005 models, tighten the right crankcase cover mounting bolts in two or three steps and in a crossing pattern to 10 N•m (88 in.-lb.).

j. Tighten the kick pedal mounting bolt (B, **Figure 1**) to the torque specification in **Table 2**.

k. On CRF450X models, replace the water joint O-ring if leaking or damaged. Then reconnect the hose joint onto the water pump cover and tighten the mounting bolts (**Figure 2**) securely.

l. Refill the cooling system (Chapter Three).

m. Refill the transmission with oil (Chapter Three).

n. Check for oil and coolant leaks after starting the engine.

## CLUTCH COVER

The clutch cover is a separate cover mounted on the right crankcase cover assembly. The clutch cover can be removed to disassemble and inspect the clutch components (**Figure 6**). The right crankcase cover must be removed to service the clutch housing assembly.

**Removal/Installation**

1. Remove the rear brake pedal (A, **Figure 1** [Chapter Fifteen]).
2. Unbolt and remove the clutch cover and its O-ring (E, **Figure 1**).
3. Installation is the reverse of removal. Note the following:

a. Replace the clutch cover O-ring if leaking or damaged.

b. The bolt identified in F, **Figure 1** is longer (6 × 65 mm) than the other clutch cover mounting bolts (6 × 25 mm). Make sure all of the bolts stick out of the cover equally before tightening them.

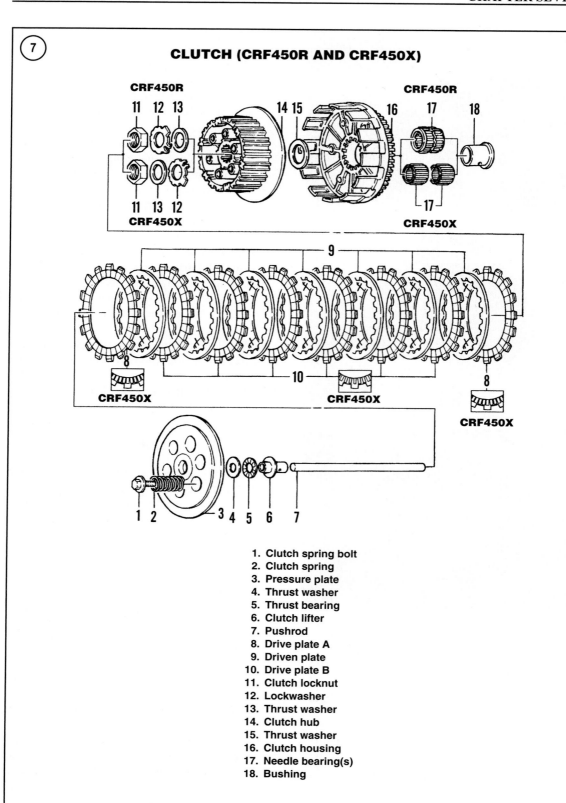

**CLUTCH (CRF450R AND CRF450X)**

1. Clutch spring bolt
2. Clutch spring
3. Pressure plate
4. Thrust washer
5. Thrust bearing
6. Clutch lifter
7. Pushrod
8. Drive plate A
9. Driven plate
10. Drive plate B
11. Clutch locknut
12. Lockwasher
13. Thrust washer
14. Clutch hub
15. Thrust washer
16. Clutch housing
17. Needle bearing(s)
18. Bushing

c. On 2002-2004 models, tighten the clutch cover mounting bolts securely in two or three steps and in a crossing pattern.

d. 2005-on models, tighten the clutch cover mounting bolts in two or three steps and in a crossing pattern to 10 N•m (88 in.-lb.).

## CLUTCH

The clutch is a multi-plate type that operates immersed in the transmission oil supply. The clutch assembly consists of a clutch hub and clutch housing. Clutch plates are alternately locked to the two parts. The gear-driven clutch housing is mounted on the transmission mainshaft. The housing receives power from the primary drive gear mounted on the crankshaft. The housing then transfers the power via its plates to the plates locked to the clutch hub. The clutch hub is splined to the mainshaft and powers the transmission. The clutch plates are engaged by springs and disengaged by a cable-actuated release lever and pushrod assembly.

### Component Identification

Some clutch parts have two or more names. To prevent confusion, the following list provides the component names used in this manual and common synonyms:

1. Drive plate (8 and 10, **Figure 7**)—Clutch disc, clutch plate, friction disc, outer plate and friction plate. The tabs on the drive plates engage with slots in the clutch housing.

2. Driven plate (9, **Figure 7**)—Aluminum plate, clutch disc, clutch plate, inner plate and steel plate. The inner teeth on the driven plates engage with the raised splines on the clutch hub.

*NOTE*
*The terms drive and driven plates are given to these parts, depending on where they are installed in the clutch assembly. The drive plates operate in the clutch housing, which is driven by the engine. The drive plates are always spinning, no matter if the clutch is engaged or disengaged. The driven plates operate on the clutch hub, which is connected to the transmission mainshaft. When the clutch is*

*disengaged, the clutch hub and driven plates stop spinning.*

3. Clutch plates—When clutch plates are used in the text, it refers to both the drive and driven plates as an assembly.

4. Clutch hub (14, **Figure 7**)—Clutch boss, clutch center and inner hub.

5. Clutch housing (16, **Figure 7**)—Clutch basket, clutch outer, outer clutch hub and primary driven gear basket.

### Tools

A clutch holder is required to hold the clutch hub when loosening and tightening the clutch locknut. This tool is described in the service procedure.

7

### Removal

Refer to **Figure 7**.

1A. If only servicing the clutch plates, remove the clutch cover as described in this chapter.

1B. If the clutch housing must be removed, remove the right crankcase cover as described in this chapter.

*NOTE*
*When troubleshooting the clutch, visually inspect the clutch and its operation before removing it. Pull the clutch lever while watching the clutch. Make sure the pressure plate opens and releases the plates. If not, check for a damaged pressure plate. Because the plates are soaked with oil, they may not automatically move out when the pressure plate is released. Have an assistant pull and hold the clutch lever. Then grasp the outer plate at two places opposite each other and attempt to move it. Check for any roughness or binding.*

2. Loosen the clutch cable at the handlebar adjuster.

3. Loosen the clutch spring bolts (A, **Figure 8**) in a crisscross pattern and in several stages to relieve pressure on the bolts. Remove the bolts and springs from the clutch.

4. Remove the pressure plate (B, **Figure 8**).

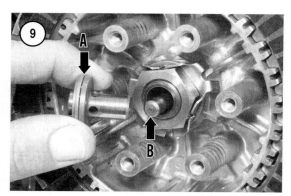

5. Remove the thrust washer, thrust bearing and clutch lifter assembly (A, **Figure 9**).

6. Remove the pushrod (B, **Figure 9**).

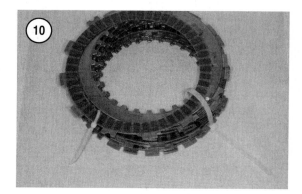

*NOTE*
*Different drive plates are used in the clutch (8 and 10, **Figure 7**). Use different color plastic ties to identify these plates and to keep them in order after removing them (**Figure 10**).*

7. Remove the clutch plates (**Figure 11**) from the clutch housing.

8. Remove the clutch locknut assembly as follows:

   a. Pry the lockwasher tabs (**Figure 12**) away from the clutch locknut.

*CAUTION*
*The spline area on the clutch hub is very thin and can easily break when being held with a clutch holding tool. Do not overtighten the tool.*

   b. Mount a clutch holder onto the clutch hub as shown in A, **Figure 13**. Position the tool so its arms engage as much of the clutch hub splines as possible. Tighten the tool so the arms are secure and cannot slip when the clutch locknut is loosened. However, overtightening the arms may also damage the clutch hub.

   c. While grasping the holder tool, loosen the clutch locknut (B, **Figure 13**) with a socket and breaker bar.

   d. On CRF450R models, remove the clutch locknut, lockwasher and thrust washer.

   e. On CRF450X models, remove the clutch locknut, thrust washer and lockwasher.

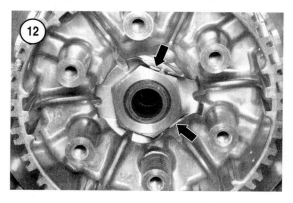

9. Remove the clutch holder and clutch hub (C, **Figure 13**).

10. Remove the thrust washer (A, **Figure 14**) and clutch housing (B).

11A. On CRF450R models, remove the needle bearing and bushing (**Figure 15**) from the mainshaft.

11B. On CRF450X models, remove the two needle bearings and bushing (**Figure 7**) from the mainshaft.

12. Inspect the clutch assembly as described in this chapter.

13. If necessary, service the clutch release lever as described in this chapter.

**Installation**

1. The following parts must be installed before installing the clutch:
   a. Balancer and primary drive gears.
   b. Starter clutch assembly (CRF450X).
   c. Kickstarter and idle gear.
   d. External shift mechanism.

> *NOTE*
> *If the kickstarter was not removed, make sure its return spring is mounted correctly in the crankcase. The spring may have been dislodged when the right crankcase cover was removed.*

2. If removed, install the clutch release lever and reconnect the clutch cable as described in this chapter.

3. Lubricate the needle bearing(s) and bushing (**Figure 16**) with molybdenum oil solution and install them onto the mainshaft (**Figure 15**). The CRF450R uses one needle bearing. The CRF450X uses two needle bearings. See **Figure 7**.

> *NOTE*
> *Molybdenum oil solution is a 50:50 mixture of transmission oil and molybdenum grease.*

4. Install the clutch housing (B, **Figure 14**) over the mainshaft. Mesh the primary driven gear on the backside of the clutch housing with the primary drive gear.

5. Lubricate the thrust washer with transmission oil and seat it against the clutch housing (A, **Figure 14**).

6. Install the clutch hub (C, **Figure 13**) over the mainshaft splines and seat it against the thrust washer.

7A. On CRF450R models, perform the following:

   a. Lubricate the thrust washer with transmission oil and seat it against the clutch hub.

   b. Install a new lockwasher by aligning its two sets of bent arms with the two ribs on the clutch hub (**Figure 17**).

7B. On CRF450X models, perform the following:

   a. Install a new lockwasher by aligning its two sets of bent arms with the two ribs on the clutch hub (**Figure 17**).

   b. Lubricate the thrust washer with transmission oil and seat it against the lockwasher.

8. Install and tighten the clutch locknut as follows:

   a. Lubricate the mainshaft threads with transmission oil.

   b. Lubricate the clutch locknut threads with transmission oil and thread onto the mainshaft until it seats flush against the lockwasher (CRF450R) or thrust washer (CRF450X). Make sure the lockwasher remains locked against the clutch hub.

   c. Mount the clutch holder (A, **Figure 13**) onto the clutch hub. Position the tool so that its arms engage as much of the clutch hub splines as possible. Tighten the tool so the arms are secure and will not slip when the clutch locknut is tightened.

   d. Hold the clutch holder tool and tighten the clutch locknut to 80 N•m (59 ft.-lb.). Remove the tool.

   e. Hold the clutch housing and turn the clutch hub by hand. It must turn freely.

*NOTE*
*If the clutch hub is locked or turns roughly, check for a missing thrust washer.*

   f. Bend the lockwasher tabs (**Figure 12**) against the clutch locknut.

*CAUTION*
*Do not bend the lockwasher more than once in the same spot. Doing so weakens the lockwasher and prevents it from securing the locknut. Install a new lockwasher when necessary.*

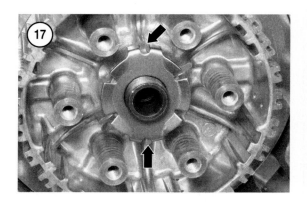

9A. On CRF450R models, refer to **Figure 7** to identify the drive plates, while noting the following:

   a. The two outer drive plates (8, **Figure 7**) are not marked.

   b. On 2002-3003 models, the inner drive plate set (10, **Figure 7**) is not marked.

   c. On 2004-on models, the inner drive plate set (10, **Figure 7**) can be identified by a yellow paint mark on one of the plate tabs.

   d. If reinstalling the original drive plates, refer to the identification marks made during disassembly.

9B. On CRF450X models, refer to **Figure 7** to identify the drive plates, while noting the following:

   a. The two outer drive plates (8, **Figure 7**) are different from the six inner drive plates (10, **Figure 7**). Referring to the insert box in **Figure 7**, the grooves on the outer (8) and inner (10) drive plates are different.

   b. If reinstalling the original drive plates, refer to the identification marks made during disassembly.

10. Install the clutch plate assembly as follows:

   a. Lubricate all of the drive and driven plates with transmission oil. Before installing new drive plates, soak them in clean transmission oil.

*NOTE*
*The driven plates (9, **Figure 7**) are stamped during manufacturing and have one flat side and one chamfered side. Install all of the driven plates with their flat side facing in the same direction (either in or out).*

   b. Install the clutch plate assembly in the order shown in **Figure 7**. Refer to Step 9 to identify the drive plates.

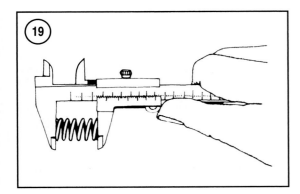

17. Install the clutch cover or right crankcase cover as described in this chapter.

18. Shift the transmission into neutral and start the engine. After the engine warms up, pull the clutch lever in and shift the transmission into first gear. Note the following:

   a. If the clutch makes a loud grinding and spinning noise immediately after starting the engine, either the transmission oil level is low or the new drive plates were not lubricated with oil.

   b. If the motorcycle jumps forward and stalls, or creeps with the transmission in gear and the clutch lever pulled in, recheck the clutch adjustment. If the clutch will not adjust properly, either the clutch cable or the drive plates are excessively worn. Replace them.

   c. If the clutch adjustment, clutch cable and clutch release lever seem to be working correctly, the clutch may have been assembled incorrectly or there is a broken part is in the clutch. Disassemble the clutch as described in this section and inspect the parts.

**Inspection**

Always replace drive plates, driven plates or clutch springs as a set if individual components do not meet specifications (**Table 1**). If parts show other signs of wear or damage, replace them, regardless of their specifications.

1. Clean and dry all parts.

2. Inspect the clutch springs for cracks and blue discoloration (heat damage).

3. Measure the free length of each clutch spring (**Figure 19**). Replace the springs as a set if any one spring is too short.

4. Inspect each drive plate (8 and 10, **Figure 7**) as follows:

   a. Inspect the friction material for excessive or uneven wear, cracks and other damage.

   b. Inspect the tabs for cracks, grooves and noticeable wear. The tabs must be smooth so the drive plates can slide in the clutch housing grooves when the clutch is released.

11. Lubricate both ends of the pushrod (B, **Figure 9**) and install it into the mainshaft.

12. Lubricate the clutch lifter, thrust bearing and thrust washer assembly (**Figure 18**) with transmission oil and install them in the order shown in **Figure 7**. Slide the clutch lifter over the end of the pushrod (A, **Figure 9**).

13. Apply pressure against the clutch lifter assembly with a finger, then operate the clutch lever at the handlebar to make sure the pushrod moves in and out. If it does not, the pushrod is not properly seated against the clutch release lever. Check clutch release lever installation as described in this chapter.

14. Align the pressure plate and clutch hub splines and install the pressure plate (B, **Figure 8**). Make sure it seats flush against the outer drive plate.

15. Install the clutch springs and clutch spring bolts (A, **Figure 8**). Tighten the clutch spring bolts securely in two or three steps and in a crossing pattern to 12 N•m (106 in.-lb.).

16. Adjust the clutch (Chapter Three), then operate the clutch lever at the handlebar. Make sure the pressure plate releases the clutch plates when the clutch lever is applied.

*NOTE*
*If the drive plate tabs are damaged, inspect the clutch housing grooves for damage as described in this section.*

c. Measure the thickness of each drive plate (**Figure 20**) at different locations around the plate.

5. Inspect each driven plate (9, **Figure 7**) as follows:

a. Inspect the driven plates for cracks, damage or color change. Overheated driven plates will have a blue discoloration.

b. After washing the driven plates in solvent, check them for an oil glaze buildup. Remove by lightly sanding both sides of each plate with 400-grit sandpaper placed on a surface plate or piece of glass.

c. Inspect the inner teeth for wear, grooves and other damage. The teeth must be able to slide smoothly on the clutch hub when the clutch is released.

d. Check each driven plate for warpage by placing it on a flat surface and measuring any gap around its perimeter with a feeler gauge (**Figure 21**).

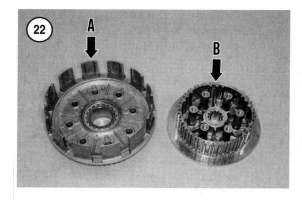

6. Check the clutch housing (A, **Figure 22**) as follows:

a. Inspect the clutch housing slots (**Figure 23**) for notches, grooves or other damage. Repair minor damage with a file. If damage is excessive, replace the clutch housing. The slots must be smooth so the drive plates can move when the clutch is released.

*NOTE*
*Filing the clutch housing slots is only a temporary fix as removing metal from the sides of the slots provides more room for the plates to move around and start wearing new grooves.*

b. Check the clutch housing bore (A, **Figure 22**) for scoring, cracks, pitting or other damage. If there is damage, inspect the needle bearing(s) and bushing for similar damage.

c. Check the clutch housing gears (A and B, **Figure 24**) for excessive wear, pitting, chipped gear teeth or other damage.

d. Hold the clutch housing and turn the primary driven gear (**Figure 25**). Replace the clutch housing if there is any free play.

7. Inspect the bushing and needle bearing assembly (**Figure 16**) as follows:

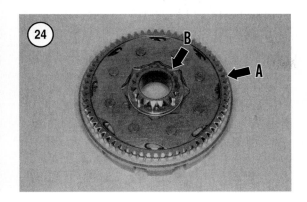

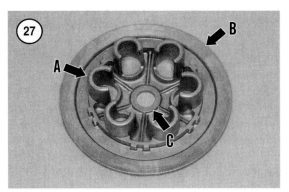

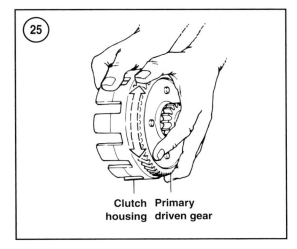

Clutch Primary
housing driven gear

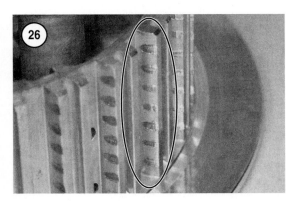

a. Check the bushing for grooves, cracks and other damage. The inner and outer diameters must be smooth.

b. Inspect the needle bearing(s). The rollers should be smooth and polished with no flat spots, burrs or other damage. Inspect the bearing cage for cracks or other damage. Replace the bearing(s) if necessary.

8. Inspect the clutch hub (B, **Figure 22**) as follows:

   a. Inspect the outer splines (**Figure 26**) for rough spots, grooves or other damage. Repair minor damage with a file or oil stone. If the damage is excessive, replace the clutch hub. The splines must smooth so the driven plates can move when the clutch is released.

   b. Check for damaged spring towers and threads.

9. Check the pressure plate (**Figure 27**) as follows:

   a. Inspect for damaged spring towers (A, **Figure 27**).

   b. Inspect the plate surface area (B, **Figure 27**) for cracks, grooves and other damage.

   c. Check the clutch lifter/thrust bearing operating area (C, **Figure 27**) in the center of the plate for cracks or damage.

10. Inspect the clutch lifter/thrust bearing assembly (**Figure 18**) as follows:

   a. Inspect the clutch lifter for scoring, roughness and other damage.

   b. Inspect the needle bearing for cracks and damaged needles.

   c. Inspect the thrust washer for scoring, cracks and other damage.

11. Inspect the pushrod for bending and other damage. Check both pushrod ends for wear and roughness.

## CLUTCH RELEASE LEVER

The clutch release lever is installed on the left side of the engine. Operating the clutch lever moves the clutch release lever, which then moves the pushrod to release the pressure plate against the clutch plates.

**Removal/Installation**

1. Remove the pressure plate as described under *Clutch Removal* in this chapter. Make sure there is no tension applied against the clutch lifter or pushrod.

2. Disconnect the clutch cable at the clutch release lever.

3. Remove the mounting bolt (A, **Figure 28**), mounting bracket (B) and clutch release lever (C) from the engine.

4. Inspect the clutch release lever (**Figure 29**) for the following:

    a. Damaged cable connector and rivet (A, **Figure 29**).

    b. Worn or damaged shaft, especially in the seal operating area (B, **Figure 29**).

    c. Damaged pushrod operating end (C, **Figure 29**).

5. Inspect the release lever seal (**Figure 30**) in the left case half and replace if damaged. Install the seal with its closed side facing out.

6. Lubricate the release lever seal lips with molybdenum disulfide grease.

7. Lubricate the release lever shaft with molybdenum disulfide grease and install it into the into the crankcase (C, **Figure 28**).

8. Install the hooked part of the mounting bracket (B, **Figure 28**) into the lever's groove and tighten the mounting bolt (A) securely.

9. Reconnect the clutch cable at the release lever.

10. Apply pressure against the clutch lifter assembly (**Figure 31**) and operate the clutch lever at the handlebar to make sure the pushrod/clutch lever assembly is properly engaged. If not, reposition the clutch release lever so that its flat end contacts the pushrod.

11. Install the pressure plate as described under *Clutch Installation* in this chapter.

12. Adjust the clutch (Chapter Three).

## BALANCER SHAFT AND PRIMARY DRIVE GEAR ASSEMBLY (CRF450R)

**Tools**

The following tools are required in this procedure:

1. Honda locknut wrench, 20 × 24 mm (part No. 07716-0020100) or equivalent. See A, **Figure 32**.

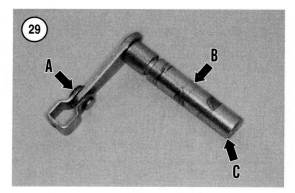

This wrench is required to loosen and tighten the balancer shaft nut.

2. Honda gear holder, M2.5 (part No. 07724-001A100). This tool is a small section of gear teeth that is placed between two separate sets of gears to lock them and their shafts together. A gear holder can be made by cutting a section of gear teeth (B, **Figure 32**) from a discarded gear, using a small hand grinder and cut-off wheel as follows:

    a. If possible, select a gear with a large inside diameter (**Figure 32**). This will reduce the amount of material that must be cut through the gear.

    b. Small cut-off wheels wear rapidly, especially when cutting gears and other hardened material. Purchase a sufficient amount of cut-off wheels for the job.

    c. Mark the number of gear teeth to be removed, then mount the gear in a vise.

*WARNING*
*Using a cut-off wheel and hand grinder as described in this procedure will cause flying particles. Do not operate a grinding tool without proper eye protection.*

    d. Cut through the gear with a hand grinder and cut-off wheel (**Figure 33**) at the marks made in substep C. If the gear holder is too long after cutting it, shorten it with a bench grinder.

*WARNING*
*The gear holder and gear will be hot. Allow them to cool before handling them.*

**Removal**

1. Refer to **Figure 34** to identify the following components:

    a. Primary drive gear bolt (A, **Figure 34**).

    b. Primary drive gear (B, **Figure 34**).

    c. Balancer drive gear (C, **Figure 34**).

    d. Balancer shaft nut (D, **Figure 34**).

    e. Balancer weight (E, **Figure 34**).

    f. Balancer driven gear (F, **Figure 34**).

    g. Primary driven gear. (A, **Figure 24**).

2. Remove the right crankcase cover as described in this chapter.

3. Remove the clutch as described in this chapter.

*CAUTION*
*If the cam chain is not connected to the camshaft, lift the chain so it does not bind on the crankshaft sprocket when turning the crankshaft and loosening the fasteners in this section.*

4. Remove the flywheel (Chapter Ten).

5. Temporarily install the bushing, needle bearing and clutch housing (A, **Figure 35**) onto the mainshaft.

6. Mesh the gear holder (B, **Figure 35**) between the primary drive and driven gears to lock them. Then

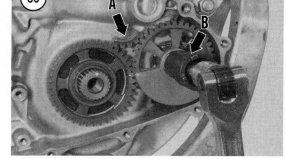

remove the primary drive gear bolt (C, **Figure 35**) and washer.

7. Remove the gear holder, clutch housing, needle bearing and bushing from the mainshaft.

8. Mesh the gear holder between the balancer drive gear and balancer driven gear (A, **Figure 36**) to lock them. Then remove the balancer shaft nut with the Honda locknut wrench (B, **Figure 36**). Remove the washer.

9. Remove the gear holder (A, **Figure 36**).

10. Remove the balancer weight (E, **Figure 34**), balancer driven gear (F) and balancer drive gear (C).

11. Turn the balancer shaft so its counterweight faces in the direction shown in **Figure 37** and remove it from the engine.

12. Clean and inspect the parts as described in this section.

### Installation

Index marks on the primary drive and balancer gear components must be properly aligned during installation to prevent engine vibration and damage.

> *CAUTION*
> *If the cam chain is not connected to the camshaft, lift the chain so it does not bind on the crankshaft sprocket when turning the crankshaft and tightening the fasteners in this section.*

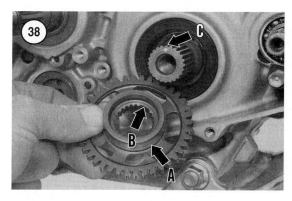

1. Lubricate the machined surfaces on the balancer shaft with transmission oil.

2. Align the balancer shaft counterweight as shown in **Figure 37** and install it into the engine. Mesh the balancer shaft gear with the oil pump driven gear.

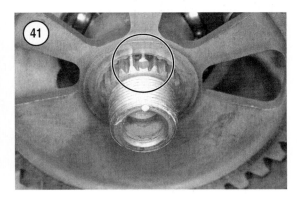

3. Lubricate the balancer drive gear shoulder (A, **Figure 38**) with grease.

4. Install the balancer drive gear by aligning its wide groove (B, **Figure 38**) with the flat tooth (C) on the crankshaft. See **Figure 39**. Push the gear's shoulder through the seal until it bottoms.

5. Install the balancer driven gear by aligning the outer index marks on both balancer gears (A, **Figure 40**), while at the same time aligning the inner mark on the balancer driven gear with the flat tooth on the balancer shaft (B). See **Figure 41**.

6. Install the balancer weight by aligning the wide groove in the balancer weight with the flat tooth on the balancer shaft (A, **Figure 42**). Then check that the index mark on the balancer weight aligns with the timing mark on the balancer drive gear (B, **Figure 42**).

7. Lubricate the balancer shaft washer and nut threads with transmission oil. Then install the washer and nut (A, **Figure 43**) and tighten finger-tight.

8. Mesh the gear holder (B, **Figure 43**) between the balancer drive gear and balancer driven gear to lock them. Then tighten the balancer shaft nut (A, **Figure 43**) with the Honda locknut wrench to 44 N•m (33 ft.-lb.).

9. Remove the gear holder.

10. Install the primary drive gear with its index mark (A, **Figure 44**) facing out, and then aligning the wide groove in the gear (A, **Figure 45**) with the flat tooth on the crankshaft (B, **Figure 45**). Then check that the index mark on the primary drive gear (A, **Figure 44**) aligns with the index marks on the balancer drive gear and the balancer weight (B).

11. Lubricate the primary drive gear washer and bolt threads with transmission oil. Then install the

washer and bolt (A, **Figure 46**) and tighten fin-ger-tight.

12. Temporarily install the bushing, needle bearing and clutch housing (B, **Figure 46**) onto the mainshaft.

13. Mesh the gear holder (C, **Figure 46**) between the primary drive and driven gears to lock them and tighten the primary drive gear bolt to 108 N•m (80 ft.-lb.).

14. Remove the gear holder.

15. Remove the clutch housing assembly.

16. Install the clutch as described in this chapter.

17. Install the flywheel (Chapter Ten).

18. Install the right crankcase cover as described in this chapter.

### Inspection

1. Clean and dry all parts.

2. Inspect the gear teeth and splines (**Figure 47**) for pitting, cracks and other damage. If there is damage, replace mating gears at the same time.

> *NOTE*
> *If wear is found in Step 2, also check the primary driven gear mounted on the clutch housing for the same de-fects. See **Clutch** in this chapter.*

3. Inspect the balancer shaft bearing surface, splines and threads (**Figure 48**) for pitting, cracks and other damage. Replace if necessary.

### STARTER CLUTCH, BALANCER SHAFT AND PRIMARY DRIVE GEAR ASSEMBLY(CRF450X)

#### Tools

The same holding tools used to service the CRF450R are required. Refer to *Tools* under *Balancer Shaft and Primary Drive Gear Assembly (CRF450R)* in this chapter.

#### Removal

1. Refer to **Figure 49** to identify the following components:

    a. Gear holder assembly (A, **Figure 49**).

    b. Reduction gear B (B, **Figure 49**).

    c. Primary drive gear bolt (C, **Figure 49**).

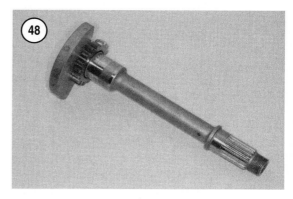

d. Primary drive gear (D, **Figure 49**).

e. Starter clutch (E, **Figure 49**).

f. Balancer shaft nut (F, **Figure 49**).

g. Balancer driven gear (G, **Figure 49**).

h. Primary driven gear.

*NOTE*
*The balancer drive gear is installed on the crankshaft, behind the starter clutch.*

2. Remove the right crankcase cover as described in this chapter.

3. Remove the clutch as described in this chapter.

*NOTE*
*If the cam chain is not connected to the camshaft, lift the chain so that it does not bind on the crankshaft sprocket when turning the crankshaft and loosening the fasteners in this section.*

4. If the balancer shaft will be removed, remove the flywheel as described in Chapter Ten.

*NOTE*
*If the balancer shaft will not be removed, it is unnecessary to remove the left crankcase cover, which requires the engine oil to be first drained. However, if the balancer drive gear will be removed in this procedure, first drain the engine oil as described in Chapter Three. The shoulder on the balancer drive gear seals tightly against the crankshaft oil seal. Because the oil level in the crankcase is higher than the lowest point on the seal, oil will drain past this seal once the balancer drive gear is removed.*

5. Remove the shaft and reduction gear B (B, **Figure 49**). If reduction gear B is difficult to remove, rotate the crankshaft clockwise to move reduction gear B (**Figure 50**) away from the idler gear, then remove it.

6. Temporarily install the bushing, needle bearings and clutch housing (A, **Figure 51**) onto the mainshaft.

7. Mesh the gear holder between the primary drive and driven gears (B, **Figure 51**) to lock them. Then remove the primary drive gear bolt (C, **Figure 51**) and washer.

8. Remove the gear holder, clutch housing, needle bearings and bushing from the mainshaft.

9. Remove the primary drive gear (D, **Figure 51**) and the starter clutch (E) from the crankshaft.

10. Remove the gear holder (B, **Figure 51**).

11. Mesh the gear holder between the balancer drive gear and balancer driven gear (A, **Figure 52**) to lock them. Then remove the balancer shaft nut

7

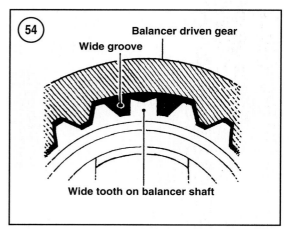

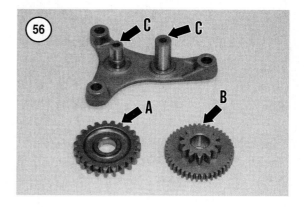

with the Honda locknut wrench (B, **Figure 52**). Remove the washer.

12. Remove the balancer drive gear (C, **Figure 52**) and balancer driven gear (D).

13. Turn the balancer shaft so that its counterweight faces in the direction shown in **Figure 37** and remove it from the engine.

14. Clean and inspect the parts as described in this section.

### Installation

A balancer shaft is used with the full-circle crankshaft to correct any primary imbalance caused by the top end components during engine operation. Installing the components described in this section times the balancer shaft to the crankshaft.

Timing is accomplished by aligning the wide groove in the spline of each gear with a master spline (a uniquely shaped spline) machined on the crankshaft and balancer shaft. The master spline aligns with an index mark on the end of its shaft and is easy to locate. If a gear will not slide on its shaft, do not force it. Reposition the gear and try to install

it again. If the timing marks are properly aligned but the gear will not slide on, check for and remove any burrs from the splines with a fine-tooth file.

*NOTE*
*If the cam chain is not connected to the camshaft, lift the chain so that it does not bind on the crankshaft sprocket when turning the crankshaft*

*and tightening the fasteners in this section.*

1. Lubricate the machined surfaces on the balancer shaft with transmission oil.

2. Align the balancer shaft counterweight as shown in **Figure 37** and install it into the engine. Mesh the balancer shaft gear with the oil pump driven gear.

3. Lubricate the balancer drive gear shoulder with grease.

4. Install the balancer drive gear (A, **Figure 53**) by aligning its wide groove with the index mark (B) on the end of the crankshaft. Push the gear's shoulder through the seal until it bottoms.

5. Initially install the balancer driven gear (C, **Figure 53**) by aligning its wide groove with the wide spline tooth on the balancer shaft (**Figure 54**). Then turn the balancer shaft to align the index marks on the drive and driven gears (D, **Figure 53**) and push the driven gear all the way onto the balancer shaft. Recheck the timing mark alignment (D, **Figure 53**).

6. Lubricate the balancer shaft washer and nut threads with transmission oil. Then install the washer and nut (E, **Figure 53**) and tighten finger-tight.

7. Mesh the gear holder (A, **Figure 55**) between the balancer drive gear and balancer driven gear to lock them. Then tighten the balancer shaft nut with the Honda locknut wrench (B, **Figure 55**) to 44 N•m (33 ft.-lb.). Remove the gear holder.

8. Install the gear holder assembly as follows:

   a. Lubricate shafts and gear bores (**Figure 56**) with transmission oil.

   b. Install the idle gear (A, **Figure 57**) and reduction gear (B) onto the gear holder.

   c. Install the gear holder by meshing the reduction gear with the starter motor (A, **Figure 58**).

*NOTE*
*One bolt (B, **Figure 58**) is longer than the other bolts (C).*

   d. Install the mounting bolts (B and C, **Figure 58**) and tighten securely.

9. Install the starter clutch (**Figure 59**).

*NOTE*
*Install the primary drive gear with its punch mark (A, **Figure 60**) facing out.*

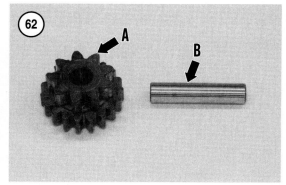

10. Install the primary drive gear by aligning its index hole (B, **Figure 60**) with the index mark on the end of the crankshaft (C).

11. Lubricate the primary drive gear washer and bolt threads with transmission oil. Then install the washer and bolt and tighten finger-tight.

12. Temporarily install the bushing, needle bearings and clutch housing onto the mainshaft.

13. Mesh the gear holder between the primary drive and driven gears to lock them and tighten the primary drive gear bolt to 108 N•m (80 ft.-lb.). Remove the gear holder.

14. Remove the clutch housing assembly.

15. Install the clutch as described in this chapter.

16. Install reduction gear B and its shaft (**Figure 61**).

17. Install the flywheel (Chapter Ten).

18. Install the right crankcase cover as described in this chapter.

**Inspection**

1. Clean and dry all parts.

2. Inspect the gear teeth and splines for pitting, cracks and other damage. If damage is noted, replace mating gears at the same time.

> *NOTE*
> *If wear is found in Step 2, also check the primary driven gear mounted on the clutch housing for the same defects. See* ***Clutch*** *in this chapter.*

3. Inspect the balancer shaft (**Figure 48**) bearing surface, splines and threads for pitting, cracks and other damage. Replace if necessary.

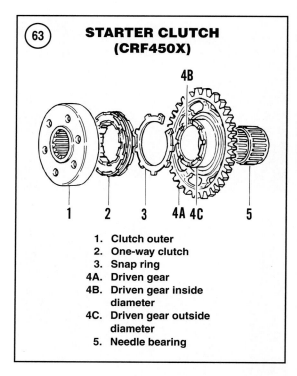

**STARTER CLUTCH
(CRF450X)**

1. Clutch outer
2. One-way clutch
3. Snap ring
4A. Driven gear
4B. Driven gear inside diameter
4C. Driven gear outside diameter
5. Needle bearing

**Reduction Gear and Idle Gear Assembly
Inspection/Disassembly/Reassembly**

Replace parts that are out of specification (**Table 2**) or show damage as described in this section.

1. Clean and dry the reduction gear and idle gear assembly.

2. Inspect the idle gear (A, **Figure 56**) and reduction idle gear (B) gear teeth for pitting, cracks and tooth damage. Measure both gear inside diameters and compare to **Table 2**.

3. Inspect the shafts on the gear holder (C, **Figure 56**) for scoring and other damage. Measure both

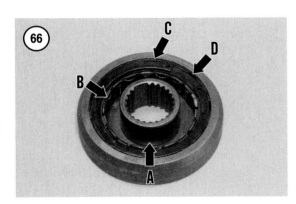

and the shaft outside diameter and compare to **Table 2**.

### Starter Clutch
### Inspection

Refer to **Figure 63** when servicing the starter clutch assembly. Replace parts that are out of specification (**Table 2**) or show damage as described in this section.

1. Clean and dry the starter clutch assembly.

2. Check the one-way clutch operation as follows:

   a. Place the starter clutch on the workbench with the starter driven gear facing up as shown in **Figure 64**.

   b. Hold the housing and try to turn the starter driven gear clockwise and then counterclockwise. The starter driven gear should only turn clockwise as viewed in **Figure 64**.

3. Remove the starter driven gear and needle bearing (**Figure 65**) from the one-way clutch assembly.

4. Inspect the starter driven gear (**Figure 65**) for the following conditions:

   a. Worn or damaged gear teeth.

   b. Worn or damaged inside and outside bearing shoulder surfaces. Both surfaces must be smooth.

   c. Measure the starter driven gear inside (4B, **Figure 63**) and outside (4C) diameters and refer to **Table 2**.

5. Inspect the needle bearing (**Figure 65**). The rollers should be smooth and polished with no flat spots, burrs or other damage. Inspect the bearing cage for cracks or other damage. Replace the bearing if necessary.

6. Inspect the one-way clutch (**Figure 66**) for the following conditions:

   a. Severely worn or damaged bearing shoulder (A, **Figure 66**).

   b. Severely worn or damaged one-way clutch rollers (B, **Figure 66**).

7. If the one-way clutch is damaged or requires further inspection, go to *One-Way Clutch Removal/Installation* in this section.

gear holder shaft outside diameters and compare to **Table 2**.

4. Lubricate the gear holder shafts, reduction gear A and the idle gear shafts and gear bores with transmission oil and install the gears as shown in **Figure 57**.

5. Inspect the reduction gear B (A, **Figure 62**) gear teeth for pitting, cracks and tooth damage. Inspect the shaft (B, **Figure 62**) for scoring and other damage. Measure the reduction gear B inside diameter

**One-Way Clutch**
**Removal/Installation**

> *NOTE*
> *A snap ring (C, **Figure 66**) secures the one-way clutch (B) inside the housing. After removing this snap ring, the two snap rings (A, **Figure 67**) that hold the one-way clutch together must slide past by the snap ring groove (B) machined inside the housing. However, small tabs on the outside of these snap rings may catch in the snap ring groove, making removal of the one-way clutch difficult. If this happens, follow the suggestions in the text to prevent from damaging the snap ring groove in the housing.*

> *NOTE*
> *The one-way clutch rollers are held in place by a metal spring band. If the one-way clutch is dropped or mishandled, the rollers can fall out of the one-way clutch assembly. If this happens, the rollers must be reinstalled facing in their correct position for the one-way clutch to be operational.*

1. Locate the paint mark at the top of the one-way clutch (D, **Figure 66**). The one-way clutch must be installed with this paint mark facing out.
2. Remove the snap ring (C, **Figure 66**) and remove the one-way clutch. See **Figure 67**. If the upper snap ring on the one-way clutch is binding in the housing's snap ring groove, perform the following:

> *NOTE*
> ***Figure 68*** *and **Figure 69** shows the housing placed horizontally on the workbench. However, when compressing the snap rings in this procedure, it will be necessary to support the housing vertically so that the backside of the housing can be tapped to move the one-way clutch out of the housing. If possible, have an assistant support the housing when removing the one-way clutch.*

a. Use snap ring pliers to compress the outer snap ring (**Figure 68**) securing the one-way clutch assembly. Then tap the backside of the housing to move the one-way clutch outward. When the outer snap ring is free of the hous-

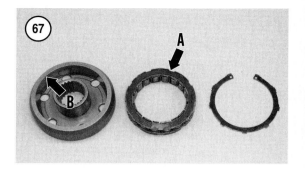

ing, release it so that the one-way clutch cannot fall apart.

b. With half of the one-way clutch free of the housing, try and remove the one-way clutch completely. If the lower snap ring is now binding in the snap ring groove, locate where the snap ring is caught in the snap ring groove. Then carefully pry the snap ring inward with a screwdriver (**Figure 69**) while tapping the housing. It may be necessary to repeat this at several places around the one-way clutch. When the one-way clutch is free of the housing, check the lower snap ring to make sure it is seated correctly in the one-way clutch roller holder grooves.

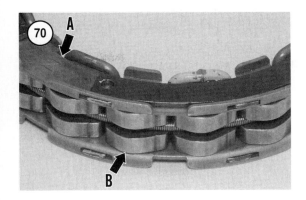

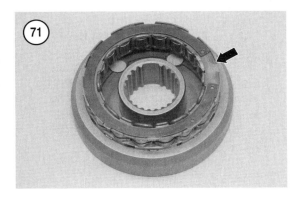

3. Clean the clutch housing and inspect its bore surface for damage. The bore must be smooth.

4. Inspect the one-way clutch rollers (**Figure 70**) for scoring, flat spots and other damage. If any damage is noted, replace the one-way clutch assembly.

5. If the one-way clutch assembly fell apart, position the roller holder with its paint mark (A, **Figure 70**) facing up. Then install the rollers facing in the direction shown in B, **Figure 70**.

6. Install the new one-way clutch into the clutch housing with its paint mark facing out (**Figure 71**). If the snap rings on the one-way clutch catch in the clutch outer snap ring groove, use the techniques described in Step 2 to partially compress the snap rings during installation.

7. When the one-way clutch is fully seated in the housing, install the snap ring (D, **Figure 66**) into the housing snap ring groove. Make sure the snap ring seats in the groove completely.

8. Reassemble the starter clutch and check its operation as described under *Starter Clutch Inspection* in this chapter.

## KICKSTARTER AND KICK IDLE GEAR

This section services the following components:
1. Kickstarter.
2. Idle gear.
3. Kick guide.
4. Kick pedal.

### Kickstarter Removal

*NOTE*
*If troubleshooting the kickstarter, examine its mounting position in the engine before removing it. Make sure the return spring has sufficient preload and is hooked in the crankcase hole.*

1. Remove the right crankcase cover and clutch as described in this chapter.

2A. On CRF450R models, remove the idle gear and bushing (**Figure 72**).

2B. On CRF450X models, remove the snap ring, thrust washer, idle gear and bushing (**Figure 73**).

*WARNING*
*Wear safety glasses when disconnecting the return spring in Step 3.*

3. While preventing the kickstarter from coming out of the engine case, unhook the return spring (A, **Figure 74**) and slowly allow the spring to unwind. Then turn the kickstarter assembly counterclockwise until the starter ratchet clears the kick guide and remove the kickstarter assembly (B, **Figure 74**). Locate the ratchet spring (A, **Figure 75**) installed on the inner part of the kick axle.

> *NOTE*
> *After removing the kickstarter, hold the assembly together as parts can slide off both ends of the axle.*

4. If necessary, service the kickstarter as described in this section.

## Kickstarter Installation

1. Check that the kick guide (A, **Figure 76**) and oil guide plate (B) are properly indexed and tightened securely in the right crankcase. If necessary, apply a medium strength threadlock onto the bolt threads and tighten securely.

2. Check that the kickstarter is assembled correctly as described under *Kickstarter Assembly* in this section.

3. Lubricate the kick axle (B, **Figure 75**) and its operating bore (C) with molybdenum disulfide oil solution.

4. Install the kickstarter by inserting the arm on the starter ratchet (A, **Figure 77**) behind the kick guide plate (B), then install the kick axle into the crankcase bore.

> *WARNING*
> *Wear safety glasses when hooking the return spring and checking kickstarter operation in Step 5 and Step 6.*

5. Hold the kickstarter (B, **Figure 74**), then turn the return spring clockwise and hook it into the hole in the crankcase (A, **Figure 74**).

6. Check the kickstarter operation as follows:
   a. With the kickstarter in its rest position, the kick gear (C, **Figure 74**) should spin freely.
   b. Install the kick pedal onto the kick axle. Then hold the kickstarter assembly and turn the kick pedal counterclockwise. Check that the kick gear (**Figure 78**) is now locked to the kick axle. If not, remove the kickstarter and check the ratchet and kick axle index marks

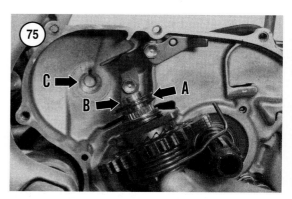

as described under *Kickstarter Assembly* in this section.

   c. Carefully remove the kick pedal without disturbing the kickstarter and its return spring installation positions.

7. Install the idle gear and bushing assembly as follows:

   a. Locate the shoulder (A, **Figure 79**) on the idle gear. This side of the gear faces toward the engine.

b. Lubricate the idle gear bushing with molybdenum disulfide oil solution and install it into the backside of the idle gear (B, **Figure 79**).

c. Install the bushing and idle gear onto the countershaft. See **Figure 72** (CRF450R) or **Figure 73** (CRF450X).

d. On CRF450X models, install the thrust washer and snap ring (**Figure 73**). Make sure the snap ring seats in the groove completely.

8. Install the clutch and right crankcase cover as described in this chapter.

## Kickstarter
## Disassembly

1. Hold the kickstarter to prevent the parts from sliding off, then dip the assembly in solvent and dry with compressed air.
2. Disassemble the kickstarter in the order shown in **Figure 80**.
3. Discard the snap ring.

## Kickstarter and Idle Gear
## Inspection

Refer to **Figure 80** when servicing the kickstarter assembly. Replace parts that are out of specification (**Table 1**) or show damage as described in this section.

1. Inspect the kick axle (A, **Figure 81**) for:
   a. Heat discoloration, scored or cracked operating surfaces.
   b. Measure the kick axle outside diameter at the kick gear's operating position (B, **Figure 81**).

*NOTE*
*On 2004-on models, a bushing is used between the kick gear and kick axle (**Figure 80**). Measure the kick axle at the bushing's operating position.*

   c. Check both sets of splines for twisting, cracks and other damage. The starter ratchet must slide freely on the inner kick axle splines. If the outer splines are damaged, the kick pedal may slip when under use.
   d. Elongation of the return spring hole.
   e. Damaged snap ring groove.
2. On 2004-on models, measure the kick gear bushing (5, **Figure 80**) inside and outside diameters.
3. Check the kick gear (C, **Figure 81**) for:
   a. Chipped or missing gear teeth.
   b. Worn, damaged or rounded ratchet teeth (D, **Figure 81**).
   c. Worn or damaged gear bore.
   d. Measure the kick gear inside diameter (E, **Figure 81**).
4. Check the starter ratchet (9, **Figure 80**) for:
   a. Cracks or other damage.
   b. Worn, damaged or rounded-off ratchet teeth.

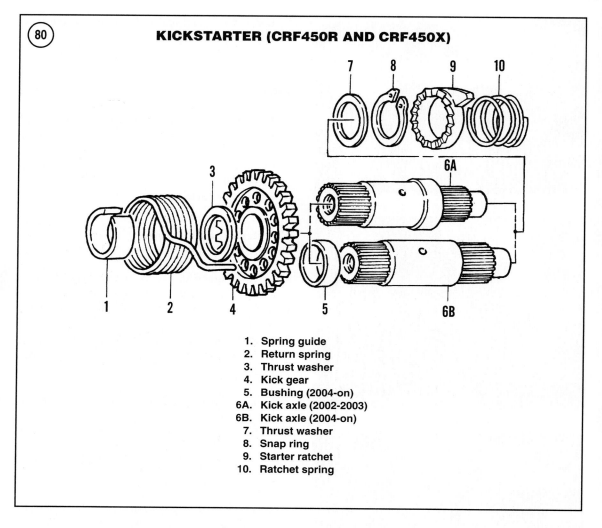

**KICKSTARTER (CRF450R AND CRF450X)**

1. Spring guide
2. Return spring
3. Thrust washer
4. Kick gear
5. Bushing (2004-on)
6A. Kick axle (2002-2003)
6B. Kick axle (2004-on)
7. Thrust washer
8. Snap ring
9. Starter ratchet
10. Ratchet spring

c. Worn or damaged splines.

*NOTE*
*Check the ratchet teeth on the kick gear (E, Figure 81) and starter ratchet (9, Figure 80). When the two parts are mated, the ratchet teeth must smoothly slip in one direction and positively lock in the other direction. Worn or damaged ratchet teeth will cause the kickstarter to slip when under use.*

5. Inspect the return spring (2, **Figure 80**) and ratchet spring (10) for cracks or other visible damage. Check both return spring ends for damage.

6. Check the spring guide for excessive wear or damage.

7. Inspect the washers for burrs, excessive thrust wear and other damage.

8. Measure the countershaft outside diameter at the idle gear's operating position (**Figure 82**). If out of specification, disassemble the engine (Chapter Five) and replace the countershaft (Chapter Eight).

9. Inspect the idle gear (A, **Figure 83**) for:

  a. Chipped or missing gear teeth.

  b. Worn or damaged gear bore.

  c. Measure the idle gear inside diameter (B, **Figure 83**).

10. Inspect the idle gear bushing (C, **Figure 83**) for:

  a. Cracks, scoring and other damage.

  b. Measure the idle gear bushing inside and outside diameters.

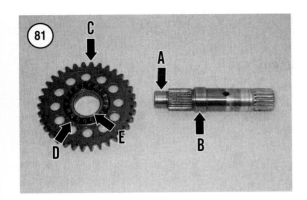

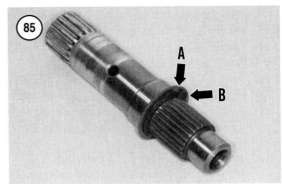

7

## Kickstarter Assembly

1. Lubricate all sliding surfaces with transmission oil.

2. Install the inner components (**Figure 84**) onto the kick axle as follows:

> *NOTE*
> *On all models, install the snap ring so that its sharp edge will face away from the kick gear.*

a. On 2002-2003 models, install the thrust washer (A, **Figure 84**) and seat it against the axle's shoulder (A, **Figure 85**). Then install the snap ring into the groove next to the thrust washer.

b. On 2004 models, install the snap ring and seat it into the kick axle groove.

c. Install the starter ratchet (C, **Figure 84**) by aligning the starter ratchet and kick axle index marks (**Figure 86**).

> *NOTE*
> *The kickstarter will not work if the index marks in **Figure 86** are not properly aligned.*

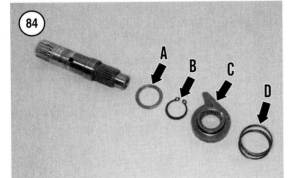

d. Install the ratchet spring (D, **Figure 84**) and seat it against the starter ratchet.

3. Install the outer components (**Figure 87**) onto the kick axle as follows:

    a. On 2004 models, install the thrust washer (7, **Figure 80**) and seat it against the snap ring.

    b. On 2004 models, install the kick gear bushing (5, **Figure 80**) and seat it against the thrust washer.

    c. Install the kick gear (A, **Figure 87**) with its ratchet teeth facing the starter ratchet. On 2004-on models, seat the gear over the bushing.

    d. Install the thrust washer (B, **Figure 87**) and seat it against the kick gear.

    e. Install return spring (C, **Figure 87**) by hooking the end of the spring into the hole in the kick axle (A, **Figure 88**). Make sure the other end of the spring faces toward the inner side of the kick axle.

    f. Install the spring guide (D, **Figure 87**) by aligning its slot with the spring end (B, **Figure 88**).

4. **Figure 89** shows a properly assembled kick-starter assembly.

### Kick Guide Inspection

The kick guide (A, **Figure 76**), mounted on the crankcase, prevents the starter ratchet from engaging the kick gear when the kickstarter is at rest. When the kickstarter is operated, the arm on the starter ratchet slips from behind the kick guide. The ratchet spring then moves the starter ratchet against the kick gear. The teeth on the starter ratchet and kick gear lock, which locks the kick gear to the kick axle. Make sure the kick guide is in good condition and tightly secured to the crankcase. If the bolt is loose, apply a medium strength threadlock onto its threads and tighten securely.

### Kick Pedal
### Disassembly/Reassembly

If the kick pedal fails to lock in place after returning it to its closed position, service the kick pedal assembly as follows:

1. Remove the screw (A, **Figure 90**) and kick boss (B, **Figure 90**) from the kick pedal.

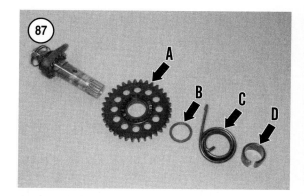

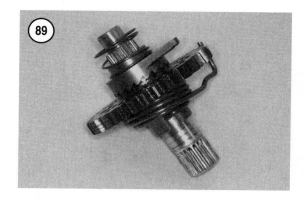

2. Remove the ball, spring and seal from the kick boss (**Figure 91**).

3. Clean and dry all parts.

4. Inspect and replace damaged parts.

5. Lubricate the lips of a new seal with grease and install it onto the kick boss (A, **Figure 92**).

6. Lubricate the spring and ball with grease. Install the spring and ball (B, **Figure 92**) into the hole in the kick boss.

7. Lubricate the kick boss shoulder with grease, then install the kick boss (B, **Figure 90**) into the

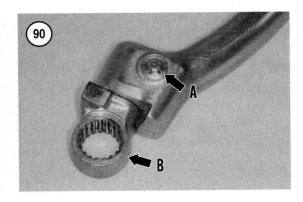

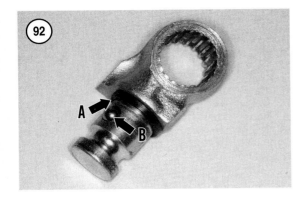

kick pedal. Install and tighten the screw (A) securely.

8. Operate the kick pedal by hand.

## EXTERNAL SHIFT MECHANISM

The external shift mechanism consists of the shift shaft and pedal, stopper arm assembly and shift drum cam assembly (**Figure 93**). These parts can be removed with the engine mounted in the frame. Re-

pair of the shift drum and forks requires engine removal and crankcase separation (Chapter Five).

### Removal

1. Remove the right crankcase cover and clutch as described in this chapter.

2. Remove the pinch bolt and shift pedal.

> *NOTE*
> *If the shift pedal is tight, check the splines for bending or other damage. Insert a screwdriver into the slot in the pedal, then spread the slot and remove the pedal.*

3. Remove the shift shaft (A, **Figure 94**) and its washer.

4. Remove the shifter collar (A, **Figure 95**) from the pin on the shift lever.

> *NOTE*
> *The shift lever assembly consists of parts 5-11 in **Figure 93**. After removing the guide plate mounting bolts (5), the shift lever assembly is removed with the guide plate (6). The plungers (10) and ratchet pawls (11) are spring-loaded and can eject while removing the shift lever (8) from the shift drum cam. When removing the shift lever assembly, try to hold the ratchet pawls in position.*

5. Remove the guide plate bolts (B, **Figure 95**). Then remove the guide plate (C) and shift lever assembly (D) at the same time.

6. Turn the bolt (A, **Figure 96**) and shift drum cam (B) counterclockwise until they stop. Then loosen and remove the bolt and shift drum cam.

7. Remove the stopper arm mounting bolt (A, **Figure 97**), stopper arm (B), washer and return spring.

8. Remove the pin (C, **Figure 97**) from the shift drum.

9. Inspect the parts as described in this section.

### Installation

It is easier to install the stopper arm assembly first, then the shift drum cam.

1. Install the pin (C, **Figure 97**) into the shift drum.

7

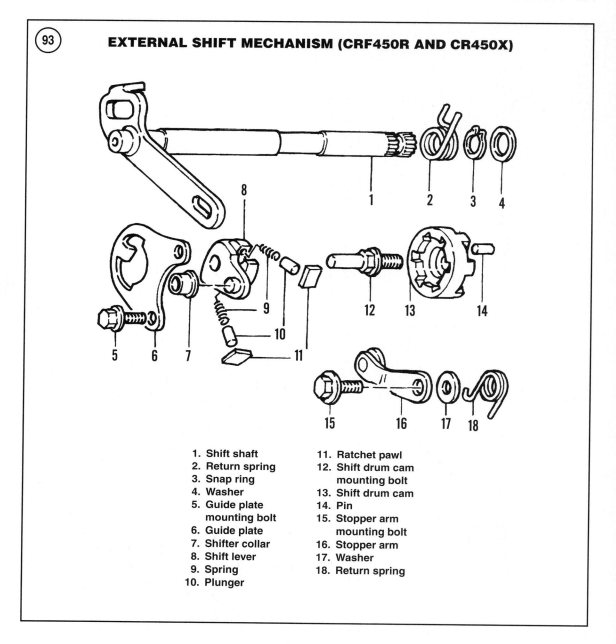

**EXTERNAL SHIFT MECHANISM (CRF450R AND CR450X)**

1. Shift shaft
2. Return spring
3. Snap ring
4. Washer
5. Guide plate mounting bolt
6. Guide plate
7. Shifter collar
8. Shift lever
9. Spring
10. Plunger
11. Ratchet pawl
12. Shift drum cam mounting bolt
13. Shift drum cam
14. Pin
15. Stopper arm mounting bolt
16. Stopper arm
17. Washer
18. Return spring

2. Install the stopper arm assembly (**Figure 98**) as follows:

a. Assemble the stopper arm as shown in **Figure 99**.

b. Install the stopper arm as shown in B, **Figure 97**. Finger-tighten the stopper arm mounting bolt. Make sure the spring is aligned around the bolt and against the crankcase as shown in **Figure 97**.

c. Using a screwdriver, push the stopper arm down and release it to make sure it moves under spring tension (**Figure 100**). If the stopper arm will not move, it is pinched under the mounting bolt. Loosen the bolt and center the stopper arm on the bolt's shoulder, then retighten the bolt.

d. When the stopper arm moves correctly, tighten the stopper arm mounting bolt (A, **Figure 97**) to 12 N•m (106 in.-lb.).

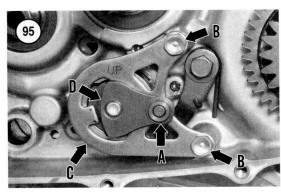

3. Install the shift drum cam as follows:

a. Apply a medium strength threadlock onto the shift drum cam mounting bolt threads (12, **Figure 93**). Set the bolt aside until it is to be installed.

b. Pry the stopper arm assembly away from the shift drum with a screwdriver. Align the slot in the shift drum cam (A, **Figure 101**) with the dowel pin (B), and install the shift drum cam. Hold the shift drum cam firmly and release the screwdriver to allow the stopper arm to rest against the cam.

c. Install the shift drum cam mounting bolt (A, **Figure 96**) and tighten until the shift drum is sitting flush against the shift drum and you can release your hand without the cam slipping or moving out of position.

d. Turn the shift drum cam mounting bolt (A, **Figure 96**) clockwise to lock the shift drum cam, then tighten the bolt to 22 N•m (16 ft.-lb.).

4. Install the shift lever assembly (parts 5-11, **Figure 93**) as follows:

a. Lubricate the shift drum cam mounting bolt shoulder (A, **Figure 96**) with transmission oil.

b. Insert the springs, plungers and ratchet pawls (**Figure 102**) into the shift lever. The notch in the ratchet pawls must face in the direction shown in **Figure 103**, and the rounded ends of the ratchet pawls must seat against the shift lever (**Figure 104**).

c. Slide the guide plate over the shift lever assembly. Position the plate to hold the pawls in place.

*NOTE*
*C, **Figure 95** shows how the guide plate aligns and fits over the shift lever.*

d. Slide the hole in the shift lever (D, **Figure 95**) over the shift drum cam mounting bolt while feeding the pawls into the shift drum cam. Hold the shift lever in position and align the guide plate (C, **Figure 95**), then install the mounting bolts (B).

e. Tighten the guide plate mounting bolts (B, **Figure 95**) securely.

5. Install the shifter collar (A, **Figure 95**) onto the shift lever pin.

6. Install the shift shaft as follows:

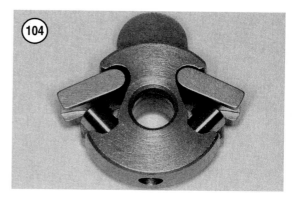

a. Wipe the shift shaft oil seal with a rag, then lubricate the seal lips with grease. If the seal is damaged or was previously leaking oil, replace it as described under *Shift Shaft Seal Replacement* in Chapter Five.

b. Lubricate the shift shaft with transmission oil.

c. Install the washer (A, **Figure 105**) onto the shift shaft.

d. Slide the shaft slowly through the engine, then engage the return spring with the spring

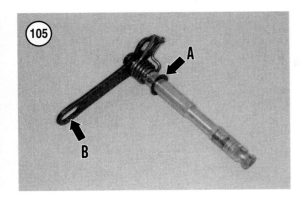

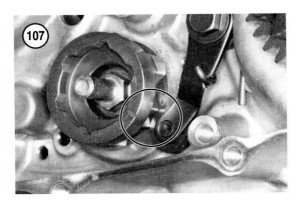

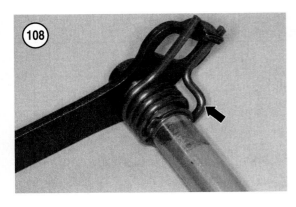

pin (B, **Figure 94**) while aligning the shift shaft pawl with the shifter collar (C).

7. Install the shift pedal and tighten its pinch bolt to 12 N•m (106 in.-lb.).

8. Support the motorcycle with the rear wheel off the ground and check the shifting as follows:

    a. Mount an aluminum plate across the crankcase to hold the shift shaft in position (**Figure 106**).

    b. Slowly turn the rear wheel and shift the transmission into first gear, then shift to neutral and the remaining forward gears.

*NOTE*
*Note in **Figure 107** the stopper arm's engagement with the raised ramp on the shift drum. This is the shift drum's neutral position.*

    c. If the shift shaft moves and then locks in place, the return spring may not be centered on the spring pin (D, **Figure 94**).

    d. If the transmission over-shifts, check for an incorrectly assembled stopper arm assembly.

    e. If the transmission does not shift properly, check for an incorrectly installed shift shaft return spring (**Figure 108**). Then check the shift lever assembly.

    f. Remove the bolt and aluminum plate.

9. Install the clutch and right crankcase cover as described in this chapter.

**Inspection**

Worn or damaged external shift linkage components will cause missed shifts and wear to the transmission gears, shift forks and shift drum. Replace parts that show excessive wear or damage.

1. Clean and dry the parts. Remove all threadlock residue from the shift drum cam mounting bolt threads.

2. Inspect the shift shaft assembly (**Figure 105**) as follows:

    a. Inspect the splines for damage.

    b. Inspect the shaft for straightness.

    c. Inspect the return spring (**Figure 108**) for cracks and other damage.

    d. Inspect the shift pawls (11, **Figure 93**) for excessive wear or damage.

    e. Make sure the return spring seats in the shift pawl grooves (**Figure 108**).

3. Check the stopper arm (**Figure 98**) assembly for:

   a. Weak or damaged spring. Check spring for cracks.

   b. Bent, cracked or damaged stopper arm. Check roller for flat spots.

   c. Damaged stopper arm mounting bolt.

4. Check the shift drum cam assembly (13, **Figure 93**) as follows:

   a. Inspect the detents in the face of the cam. The detents must not be worn or shifting will be rough.

   b. Inspect the ramps in the rear side of the cam for wear or damage. If the sides of the ramps are rounded or damaged, the stopper arm roller can slip and the transmission will jump out of gear.

   c. Inspect the bolt (12, **Figure 93**) for scoring or gouges that would prevent the shift lever (8, **Figure 93**) from operating correctly.

5. Check the shift lever assembly (parts 5-11, **Figure 93**) as follows:

   a. Inspect the shift lever for cracks and other damage.

   b. The guide plate controls the movement of the ratchet pawls during shifting. Inspect the guide plate for bending and other damage. Inspect the guide plate where the ratchet pawls operate. This area must be smooth.

   c. Inspect the pawls for wear at their round edge.

   d. Inspect the springs and plungers for cracks and damage.

   e. Inspect the shifter collar for damage.

6. Inspect the shift shaft return spring pin bolt (D, **Figure 94**) for looseness and damage. Replace the bolt if its shoulder is damaged.

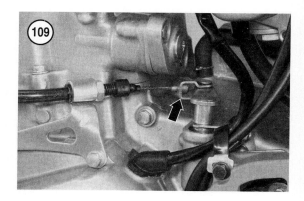

7. Tighten the shift shaft return spring pin bolt to 22 N•m (16 ft.-lb.).

## CLUTCH CABLE REPLACEMENT

1. Before disconnecting or removing the clutch cable, make a drawing of the cable routing from the handlebar and around the left side of the frame to the clutch release lever at the engine. Replace the cable exactly as it was, avoiding any sharp turns.

2. Loosen the clutch cable adjuster locknut and adjuster at the handlebar, then disconnect the clutch cable.

3. Disconnect the clutch cable at the clutch release lever (**Figure 109**).

4. Remove the cable.

5. Lubricate the new clutch cable before reconnecting it. Refer to Chapter Three.

6. Install the new clutch cable by reversing these removal steps. Make sure it is correctly routed with no sharp turns. Adjust the clutch cable as described in Chapter Three.

**Table 1 CLUTCH AND KICKSTARTER SERVICE SPECIFICATIONS
(CRF450R AND CRF450X)**

|  | New mm (in.) | Service limit mm (in.) |
|---|---|---|
| Drive plate thickness | 2.92-3.08 (0.115-0.121) | 2.85 (0.112) |
| Driven plate warp | – | 0.15 (0.006) |
| Clutch spring free length |  |  |
|   2002-2003 | 45.7 (1.80) | 44.7 (1.76) |
|   2004-on | 44.7 (1.76) | 43.7 (1.72) |
| Countershaft outside diameter |  |  |
|   at idle gear operating area | 16.966-16.984 (0.6680-0.6687) | 16.95 (0.667) |
| | *(continued)* | |

**Table 1 CLUTCH AND KICKSTARTER SERVICE SPECIFICATIONS (CRF450R AND CRF450X) (continued)**

|  | New mm (in.) | Service limit mm (in.) |
|---|---|---|
| Idle gear bushing | | |
|   Inside diameter | 17.000-17.018 (0.6693-0.6700) | 17.04 (0.671) |
|   Outside diameter | 19.979-20.000 (0.7866-0.7874) | 19.96 (0.786) |
| Idle gear inside diameter | 20.020-20.041 (0.7882-0.7890) | 20.07 (0.790) |
| Kick axle outside diameter | | |
|   2002-2003 | 21.959-21.980 (0.8645-0.8654) | 21.95 (0.864) |
|   2004-on | 19.980-19.993 (0.7866-0.7871) | 19.97 (0.786) |
| Kick gear bushing | | |
|   2002-2003 | – | |
|   2004-on | | |
|     Inside diameter | 20.000-20.021 (0.7874-0.7882) | 20.04 (0.789) |
|     Outside diameter | 21.979-22.000 (0.8653-0.8661) | 21.96 (0.865) |
| Kick gear inside diameter | 22.007-22.028 (0.8664-0.8672) | 22.05 (0.868) |

7

**Table 2 STARTER CLUTCH SERVICE SPECIFICATIONS (CRF450X)**

|  | New mm (in.) | Service limit mm (in.) |
|---|---|---|
| Idle gear inside diameter | 12.010-12.050 (0.4728-0.4744) | 12.050 (0.4744) |
| Gear holder shafts outside diameter | 11.989-12.000 (0.4720-0.4724) | 11.989 (0.4720) |
| Reduction gear A inside diameter | 12.010-12.050 (0.4728-0.4744) | 12.050 (0.4744) |
| Reduction gear B inside diameter | 10.045-10.085 (0.3955-0.3970) | 10.085 (0.3970) |
| Reduction gear shaft outside diameter | 9.980-0.995 (0.3929-0.3935) | 0.980 (0.3929) |
| Starter driven gear | | |
|   Inside diameter | 36.009-36.034 (1.4177-0.1.4187) | 36.034 (1.4187) |
|   Outside diameter | 45.660-45.673 (1.7976-1.7981) | 45.660 (1.7976) |

**Table 3 CLUTCH TORQUE SPECIFICATIONS (CRF450R AND CRF450X)**

|  | N•m | in.-lb. | ft.-lb. |
|---|---|---|---|
| Balancer shaft nut[1] | 44 | – | 33 |
| Clutch cover mounting bolt | | | |
|   2002-2004 | – | – | – |
|   2005 | 10 | 88 | – |
| Clutch locknut[1] | 80 | – | 59 |
| Clutch spring bolt | 12 | 106 | – |
| Kick pedal bolt | | | |
|   CRF450R | 37 | – | 27 |
|   CRF450X | 38 | – | 28 |
| Primary drive gear bolt[1] | 108 | – | 80 |

(continued)

**Table 3 CLUTCH TORQUE SPECIFICATIONS (CRF450R AND CRF450X) (continued)**

| | N•m | in.-lb. | ft.-lb. |
|---|---|---|---|
| **Right crankcase cover mounting bolt** | | | |
| 2002-2004 | – | – | – |
| 2005 | 10 | 88 | – |
| Shift drum cam mounting bolt$^2$ | 22 | – | 16 |
| Shift pedal pinch bolt | 12 | 106 | – |
| Shift shaft return spring pin bolt | 22 | – | 16 |
| Stopper arm mounting bolt | 12 | 106 | – |

1. Lubricate threads and seating surface with transmission oil.
2. Apply medium strength threadlock to fastener threads.

# CHAPTER EIGHT

# TRANSMISSION AND INTERNAL SHIFT MECHANISM

This chapter describes disassembly and reassembly of the transmission shafts and internal shift mechanism. Remove the engine and separate the crankcase halves to service these components as described in Chapter Four or Chapter Five.

Read this chapter before attempting repairs to the transmission and shift mechanism. It is important to become familiar with the procedures and to understand the skill and equipment required. Refer to Chapter One for tool usage and techniques.

**Table 1** lists transmission gear ratios. **Tables 2-4** list transmission and shift fork service specifications. **Tables 1-4** are located at the end of this chapter.

## TRANSMISSION OPERATION

The transmission is a five-speed constant-mesh. The gears on the mainshaft (A, **Figure 1**) mesh with the gears on the countershaft (B). Each pair of meshed gears represents one gear ratio. For each pair of gears, one of the gears is splined to its shaft, while the other gear freewheels on its shaft. Next to each freewheeling gear is another gear that is splined to the same shaft. This locked gear can move laterally on its splines and against the freewheeling gear. The splined gear and the freewheeling gear have mating dogs and slots that allow the two gears to lock together, thus locking the free-

wheeling gear to the shaft. Any time the transmission is *in gear* a pair of meshed gears are locked to their shafts, and that gear ratio is selected. All other meshed gears have one freewheeling gear.

To engage and disengage the various gear ratios, the splined gears are moved by the shift forks (C, **Figure 1**). Each fork fits in a groove at the side of one of the splined gears. The guide pin, at the opposite end of each fork, fits in one of the grooves of the shift drum (D, **Figure 1**). As the transmission is shifted, the shift drum rotates and guides the forks to engage and disengage pairs of gears on the transmission shafts. The grooves are curved, to guide the forks to the selected gears by cam-action.

## TRANSMISSION OVERHAUL (CRF250R AND CRF250X)

The CRF250R and CRF250X transmission gear ratios are different. However, procedures for servicing the transmission shafts are nearly identical. Where differences occur, they are described. Refer to **Table 1** for gear ratio specifications.

### Preliminary Inspection

1. Clean and dry the transmission shafts before servicing them.

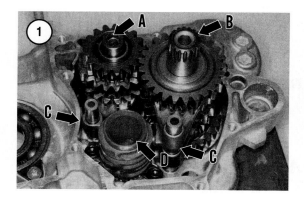

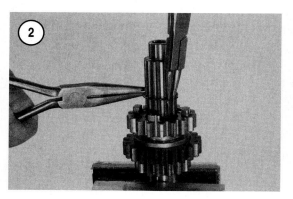

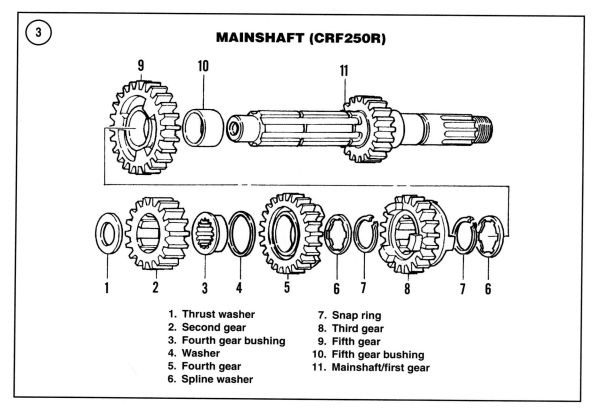

**MAINSHAFT (CRF250R)**

1. Thrust washer
2. Second gear
3. Fourth gear bushing
4. Washer
5. Fourth gear
6. Spline washer
7. Snap ring
8. Third gear
9. Fifth gear
10. Fifth gear bushing
11. Mainshaft/first gear

2. Before disassembling the transmission shafts, perform the following:

   a. Rotate each fixed gear and slide each grooved gear on its shaft. Any roughness or binding may indicate a problem with a gear bore, bushing or shaft.

   b. Hold each transmission shaft, one at a time, and lock each sliding gear against its fixed gear. Visually check the engagement between the gear dogs on both gears. The dogs should be pointed.

3. Parts with two different sides, such as gears, snap rings and shift forks, can be installed backward. To maintain the correct alignment and position of the parts during disassembly, store each part in order and in a divided container.

4. Before removing the snap rings, try to turn them without spreading them. If they can turn, the thrust washer installed beside the snap ring is probably worn.

5. Because snap rings fatigue and distort during their removal, do not reuse them, although they may

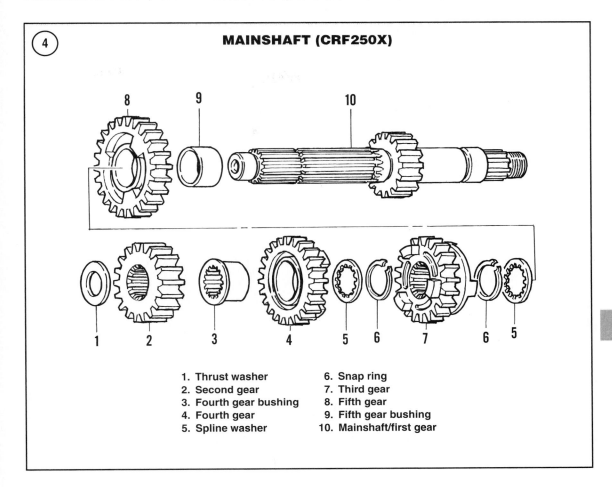

**MAINSHAFT (CRF250X)**

1. Thrust washer
2. Second gear
3. Fourth gear bushing
4. Fourth gear
5. Spline washer
6. Snap ring
7. Third gear
8. Fifth gear
9. Fifth gear bushing
10. Mainshaft/first gear

appear to be in good condition. Install *new* snap rings during reassembly.

6. To install new snap rings without distorting them, open the new snap ring with a pair of snap ring pliers while holding the back of the snap ring with a pair of pliers (**Figure 2**). Slide the snap ring down the shaft and seat it into its correct groove. This technique can also be used to remove snap rings from a shaft once they are free from their grooves.

### Mainshaft Disassembly

Remove the parts from the mainshaft in the order below. Mark the parts (**Figure 3** or **Figure 4**) with a grease pencil or metal marking pen so they can be installed facing in their original operating position.

1. Hold the mainshaft to keep the parts from sliding off, then clean in solvent and dry with compressed air.

2. Remove the thrust washer.

*NOTE*
*Before removing second gear, examine both sides of the gear. If the sides are symmetrical, mark the side of the gear facing away from fourth gear so it can be installed facing in its original direction. If one side of the second gear is machined with a groove, this side will face away from fourth gear.*

3. Identify second gear's installed position and then remove it.

4A. On CRF250R models, remove the fourth gear bushing, washer and fourth gear.

4B. On CRF250X models, remove the fourth gear bushing and fourth gear.

5. Remove the spline washer and snap ring.

6. Remove third gear.

7. Remove the snap ring and spline washer.

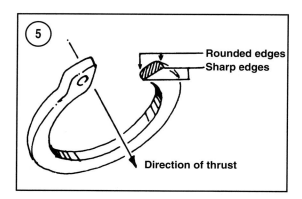

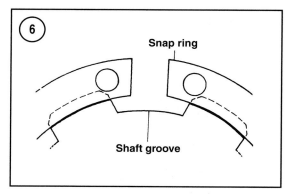

8. Remove fifth gear and the fifth gear bushing.

*NOTE*
*Mainshaft first gear is an integral part of the mainshaft.*

9. Inspect the mainshaft assembly as described under *Transmission Inspection* in this chapter.

**Mainshaft Assembly**

Refer to **Figure 3** or **Figure 4**.

1. Before beginning assembly, note the following:
   a. Have two new snap rings on hand. Both snap rings have the same part number.
   b. Install the snap rings with their chamfered edge facing *away* from the thrust load. See **Figure 5**.
   c. Align the snap ring end gaps with the transmission shaft grooves (**Figure 6**).
   d. Throughout the procedure, the orientation of many parts is made in relationship to first gear (A, **Figure 7**).

2. Lubricate all sliding surfaces with engine oil.

3. Install the fifth gear bushing (B, **Figure 7**) and seat it against first gear.

4. Install fifth gear (A, **Figure 8**) with its gear dogs facing away from first gear.

5. Install the spline washer and snap ring (B, **Figure 8**). Seat the snap ring in the groove next to fifth gear.

6. Install third gear with its shift fork groove (**Figure 9**) facing toward fifth gear.

7. Install the snap ring (A, **Figure 10**) in the mainshaft groove.

8. Install the thrust washer (B, **Figure 10**) and seat it against the snap ring.

9. Install fourth gear as follows:

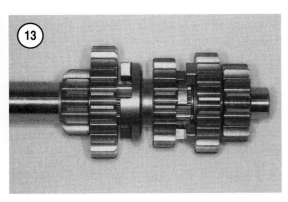

a. On CRF250R models, install fourth gear (5, **Figure 3**) with its gear dogs facing toward third gear. Then install the thrust washer (4, **Figure 3**) over the bushing (3) and install the bushing through fourth gear.

b. On CRF250X models, install fourth gear (A, **Figure 11**) with its gear dogs facing toward third gear. Install the bushing (B, **Figure 11**) through fourth gear.

10. Install second gear (A, **Figure 12**) as follows:

a. If the sides of the gear are symmetrical, install the gear according to the marks made on the gear during disassembly. When installing a new second gear and both sides are symmetrical, either side can face out.

b. If the gear is machined with a shoulder or groove on one side, install the gear with the grooved side facing away from fourth gear.

11. Install the thrust washer (B, **Figure 12**) and seat it against second.

12. Compare the assembled transmission assembly with **Figure 13**.

**Countershaft Disassembly**

Remove the parts from the countershaft in the order below, while noting in **Figure 14** that the parts are removed from both sides of the countershaft. Mark the parts with a grease pencil or metal marking pen so they can be installed facing in their original operating position.

1. Hold the countershaft to keep the parts from sliding off, then clean in solvent and dry with compressed air.

2. Remove the following parts from the countershaft's splined end:

a. Thrust washer.

b. Second gear bushing and second gear.

c. Thrust washer.

d. Fourth gear.

3. Thrust washer, first gear, first gear bushing and thrust washer.

4. Fifth gear.

5. Snap ring and spline washer.

6. Third gear and third gear bushing.

7. Thrust washer.

8. Inspect the countershaft assembly as described under *Transmission Inspection* in this chapter.

8

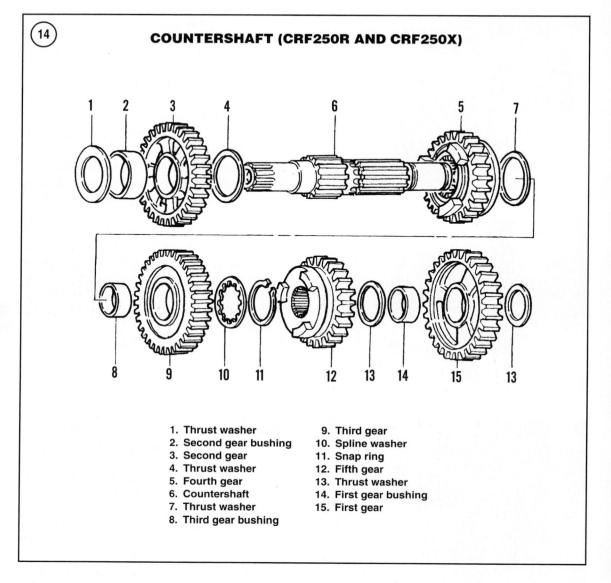

**COUNTERSHAFT (CRF250R AND CRF250X)**

1. Thrust washer
2. Second gear bushing
3. Second gear
4. Thrust washer
5. Fourth gear
6. Countershaft
7. Thrust washer
8. Third gear bushing
9. Third gear
10. Spline washer
11. Snap ring
12. Fifth gear
13. Thrust washer
14. First gear bushing
15. First gear

**Countershaft Assembly**

Refer to **Figure 14**.

1. Before beginning assembly, note the following:
   a. Have one new snap ring on hand.
   b. Install the snap ring with its chamfered edge facing *away* from the thrust load (**Figure 5**).
   c. Align the snap ring end gaps with the transmission shaft grooves (**Figure 6**).
   d. Throughout the procedure, the orientation of many parts is made in relationship to the splined end of the countershaft (A, **Figure 15**), on which the drive sprocket is mounted.

2. Lubricate all parts with molybdenum disulfide oil.

3. Install the thrust washer (7, **Figure 14**) onto the countershaft, opposite the splined end. See B, **Figure 15**).

4. Install the third gear bushing (C, **Figure 15**) onto the countershaft and seat it against the thrust washer.

5. Install third gear (A, **Figure 16**) so the shift dogs face away from the splined end.

6. Install the thrust washer (B, **Figure 16**) and seat it against third gear.

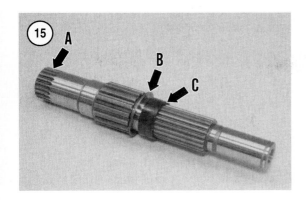

8

7. Install the snap ring and seat it into the groove next to the thrust washer (**Figure 17**).

8. Install fifth gear with its shift groove (A, **Figure 18**) facing toward third gear.

9. Install the thrust washer (B, **Figure 18**) and the first gear bushing (C).

10. Install first gear (A, **Figure 19**) with its shift dogs facing toward fifth gear.

11. Install the thrust washer (B, **Figure 19**) and seat it against first gear.

12. Turn the shaft around and install the remaining parts from the splined end.

13. Install fourth gear with its shift fork groove (**Figure 20**) facing toward third gear.

14. Install the thrust washer (A, **Figure 21**) and the second gear bushing (B).

15. Install second gear (A, **Figure 22**) with its shift dogs facing toward fourth gear.

*NOTE*
*When second gear is properly in-stalled, the large chamfer on the edge of the gear teeth will face **away** from fifth gear as shown in **Figure 23**.*

16. Install the thrust washer (B, **Figure 22**).

17. Compare the assembled transmission assembly with **Figure 24**.

## TRANSMISSION OVERHAUL
## (CRF450R AND CRF450X)

### Preliminary Inspection

1. Clean and dry the transmission shafts before servicing them.

2. Before disassembling the transmission shafts, perform the following:

    a. Rotate each fixed gear and slide each grooved gear on its shaft. Any roughness or binding may indicate a problem with a gear bore, bushing or shaft.

    b. Hold each transmission shaft, one at a time, and lock each sliding gear against its fixed gear. Visually check the engagement between the gear dogs on both gears. The dogs should be pointed.

3. Parts with two different sides, such as gears, snap rings and shift forks, can be installed backward. To maintain the correct alignment and position of the parts during disassembly, store each part in order and in a divided container.

4. Before removing the snap rings, try to turn them without spreading them. If they can turn, the thrust washer installed beside the snap ring is probably worn.

5. Because snap rings fatigue and distort during their removal, do not reuse them, although they may appear to be in good condition. Install *new* snap rings during reassembly.

6. To install new snap rings without distorting them, open the new snap ring with a pair of snap ring pliers while holding the back of the snap ring with a pair of pliers (**Figure 2**). Slide the snap ring down the shaft and seat it into its correct groove. This technique can also be used to remove snap rings from a shaft once they are free from their grooves.

### Mainshaft Disassembly

Remove the parts from the mainshaft in the order below. Mark the parts (**Figure 25**) with a grease

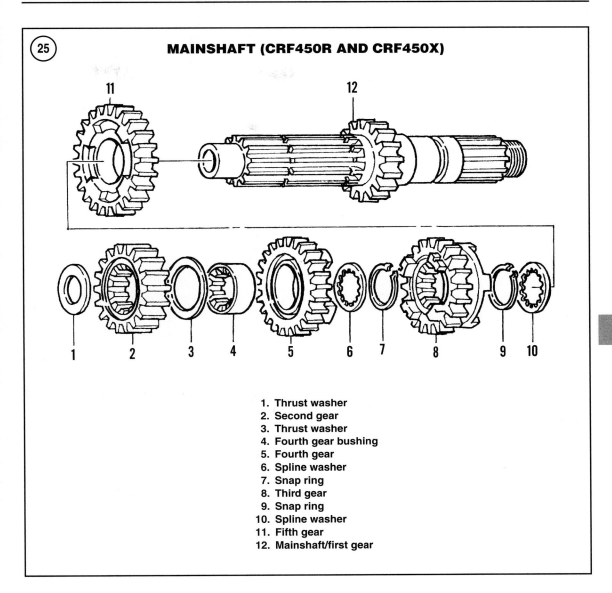

**25**

**MAINSHAFT (CRF450R AND CRF450X)**

1. Thrust washer
2. Second gear
3. Thrust washer
4. Fourth gear bushing
5. Fourth gear
6. Spline washer
7. Snap ring
8. Third gear
9. Snap ring
10. Spline washer
11. Fifth gear
12. Mainshaft/first gear

8

pencil or metal marking pen so they can be installed facing in their original operating position.

1. Hold the mainshaft to keep the parts from sliding off, then clean in solvent and dry with compressed air.

2. Remove the thrust washer and second gear.

3. Remove the thrust washer, fourth gear and the fourth gear bushing.

4. Remove the spline washer and the snap ring.

5. Remove third gear.

6. Remove the snap ring and spline washer.

7. Remove fifth gear.

*NOTE*
*Mainshaft first gear is an integral part of the mainshaft.*

8. Inspect the mainshaft assembly as described under *Transmission Inspection* in this chapter.

**Mainshaft Assembly**

Refer to **Figure 25**.

1. Before beginning assembly, note the following:
   a. Have two new snap rings on hand. Both snap rings have the same part number.

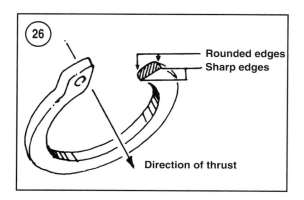

Rounded edges
Sharp edges

Direction of thrust

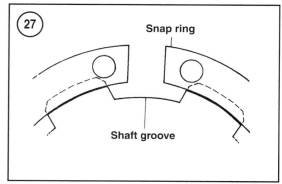

Snap ring

Shaft groove

b. Install the snap rings with their chamfered edge facing *away* from the thrust load. See **Figure 26**.

c. Align the snap ring end gaps with the transmission shaft grooves (**Figure 27**).

d. Throughout the procedure, the orientation of many parts is made in relationship to first gear (A, **Figure 28**).

2. Lubricate all sliding surfaces with engine oil.

3. Install fifth gear (B, **Figure 28**) with its gear dogs facing away from first gear.

4. Install the spline washer and snap ring (**Figure 29**). Seat the snap ring in the groove next to fifth gear.

5. Install third gear with its shift fork groove (**Figure 30**) facing toward fifth gear.

6. Install the snap ring (A, **Figure 31**).

7. Install the thrust washer (B, **Figure 31**) and seat it against the snap ring.

8. Install the fourth gear bushing (C, **Figure 31**).

9. Install fourth gear with its gear dogs (A, **Figure 32**) facing toward third gear.

10. Install the thrust washer (B, **Figure 32**).

11. Install second gear (A, **Figure 33**) with its shoulder facing away from fourth gear.

12. Install the thrust washer (B, **Figure 33**) and seat it against second gear.

13. Compare the assembled transmission assembly with **Figure 34**.

## Countershaft Disassembly

Remove the parts from the countershaft in the order below, while noting in **Figure 35** that the parts are removed from both sides of the countershaft. Mark the parts with a grease pencil or metal mark-

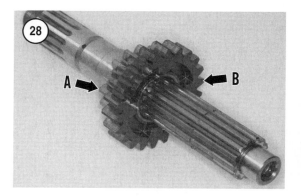

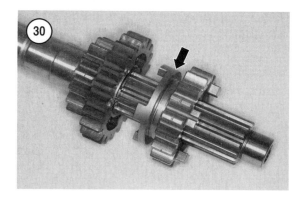

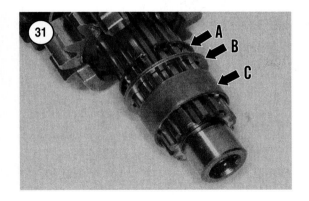

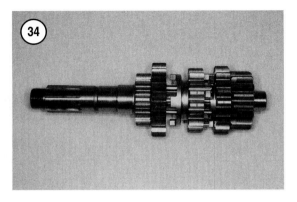

ing pen so they can be installed facing in their original operating position.

1. Hold the countershaft to keep the parts from sliding off, then clean in solvent and dry with compressed air.

2. Remove the following parts from the countershaft's splined end:

    a. Thrust washer.

    b. Second gear bushing and second gear.

    c. Thrust washer.

    d. Fourth gear.

3A. On 2002-2004 models, thrust washer, first gear, first gear bushing and thrust washer.

3B. On 2005 models, thrust washer, first gear, first gear needle bearing and thrust washer.

4. Fifth gear.

5. Snap ring and spline washer.

6. Third gear.

7. Thrust washer.

8. Inspect the countershaft assembly as described under *Transmission Inspection* in this chapter.

**Countershaft Assembly**

Refer to **Figure 35**.

1. Before beginning assembly, note the following:

    a. Have one new snap ring on hand.

    b. Install the snap ring with its chamfered edge facing *away* from the thrust load (**Figure 26**).

    c. Align the snap ring end gaps with the transmission shaft grooves (**Figure 27**).

    d. Throughout the procedure, the orientation of many parts is made in relationship to the splined end of the countershaft (A, **Figure 36**), on which the drive sprocket is mounted.

2. Lubricate all parts with molybdenum disulfide oil.

3. Install fourth gear onto the countershaft with its shift fork groove (B, **Figure 36**) facing away from the splined end.

4. Install the thrust washer (7, **Figure 35**) onto the countershaft, opposite the splined end. See A, **Figure 37**).

5. Install third gear with its shift dogs (B, **Figure 37**) facing away from the splined end.

6. Install the thrust washer (A, **Figure 38**) and seat it against third gear.

7. Install the snap ring and seat it into the groove next to the thrust washer (B, **Figure 38**).

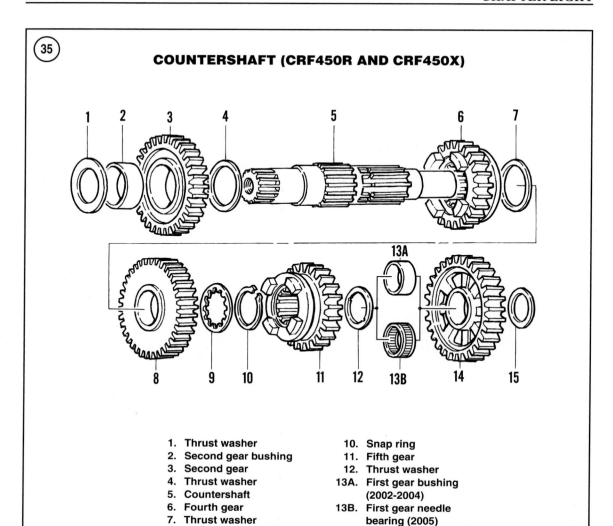

**COUNTERSHAFT (CRF450R AND CRF450X)**

1. Thrust washer
2. Second gear bushing
3. Second gear
4. Thrust washer
5. Countershaft
6. Fourth gear
7. Thrust washer
8. Third gear
9. Spline washer
10. Snap ring
11. Fifth gear
12. Thrust washer
13A. First gear bushing (2002-2004)
13B. First gear needle bearing (2005)
14. First gear
15. Thrust washer

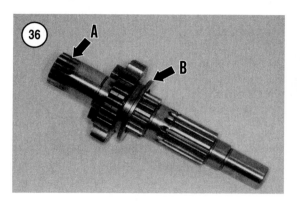

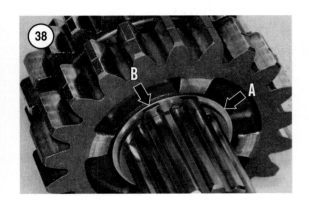

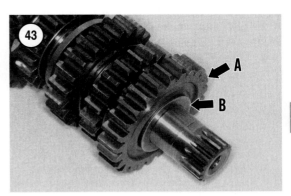

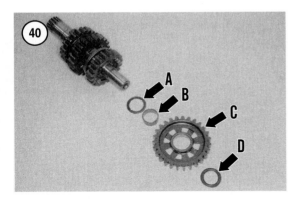

8

8. Install fifth gear with its shift groove (**Figure 39**) facing toward third gear.

9A. On 2002-2004 models, install the thrust washer (A, **Figure 40**) and the first gear bushing (B).

9B. On 2005 models, install the thrust washer (A, **Figure 40**) and the first gear needle bearing (13B, **Figure 35**).

10. Install first gear (C, **Figure 40**) with its shift dogs facing toward fifth gear. See A, **Figure 41**.

11. Install the thrust washer (D, **Figure 40**) and seat it against first gear. See B, **Figure 41**.

12. Turn the shaft around and install the remaining parts from the splined end.

13. Install the thrust washer (A, **Figure 42**) and the second gear bushing (B).

14. Install second gear (C, **Figure 42**) with its shift dogs facing toward fourth gear. See A, **Figure 43**.

15. Install the thrust washer (C, **Figure 42**). See B, **Figure 43**.

16. Compare the assembled transmission assembly with **Figure 44**.

## TRANSMISSION INSPECTION

Refer to **Table 2** or **Table 3** when measuring the transmission components and calculating clearances in this section. Replace parts that are out of specification or show damage as described in this section.

*NOTE*
*Maintain the alignment of the transmission components when cleaning and inspecting the parts in this section.*

1. Inspect the mainshaft (**Figure 45**) and countershaft (**Figure 46**) for:
   a. Worn or damaged splines.
   b. Missing, broken or chipped first gear teeth (mainshaft).
   c. Worn or damaged bearing surfaces.
   d. Cracked or rounded snap ring grooves.

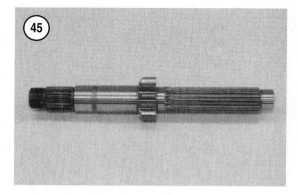

*NOTE*
*Refer to the exploded view drawings under **Transmission Overhaul** in this chapter to identify the gear/shaft positions called out in the following steps.*

2. Measure the mainshaft outside diameter at its fifth gear operating position.
3. Measure the countershaft outside diameter at the following gear operating positions:
   a. First gear.
   b. Second gear.
   c. Third gear.
4. Check each gear for excessive wear, burrs, pitting, or chipped or missing teeth. Check the splines on sliding gears and the bore on stationary gears for excessive wear or damage.
5. To check stationary gears for wear, install the gear and its bushing (if used) on their correct shaft and in their original operating position. If necessary, use the old snap rings to secure them in place. Then spin the gear by hand. The gear should turn smoothly. A rough turning gear indicates heat damage. Check for a dark blue color or galling on the operating surfaces. Rocking indicates excessive wear, either to the gear, bushing or shaft.
6. To check the sliding gears, install them on their correct shaft and in their original operating position.

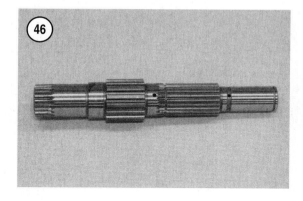

The gear should slide back and forth without any binding or excessive play.

7. Check the dogs and dog slots on the gears (**Figure 47**, typical) for rounded or damaged engagement edges. Any wear on the dogs and mating recesses should be uniform. If the dogs are not worn evenly, the remaining dogs will be overstressed and possibly fail. Check the engagement of the dogs by placing the gears at their appropriate positions on their shaft, then twist the gears together. Check for positive engagement in both directions. If damage

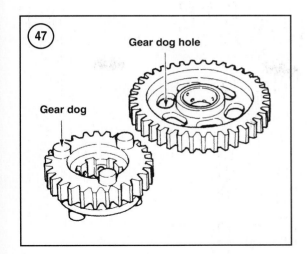

Gear dog hole

Gear dog

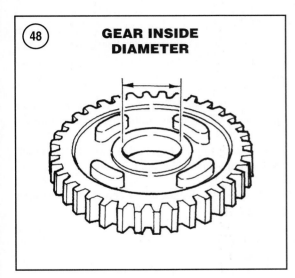

## GEAR INSIDE DIAMETER

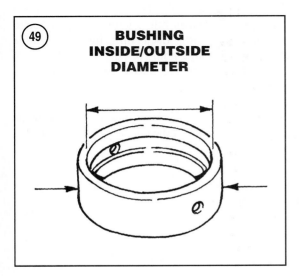

## BUSHING INSIDE/OUTSIDE DIAMETER

is evident, also check the condition of the shift forks, as described in this chapter.

*NOTE*
*The side of the gear dogs that carries the engine load will wear and eventually become rounded. The unloaded side of the dogs will remain unworn. Rounded dogs will cause the transmission to jump out of gear.*

8. Check for worn or damaged shift fork grooves. Check the gear groove and its mating shift fork.

9. Measure the mainshaft and countershaft gear inside diameters (**Figure 48**) specified in **Table 2** or **Table 3**.

10. Check the bushings for:
   a. Worn or damaged bearing surface.
   b. Worn or damaged splines.
   c. Cracked or scored gear bore.

11. Measure the mainshaft and countershaft bushing inside and outside diameters (**Figure 49**) specified in **Table 2** or **Table 3**.

12. Using the measurements recorded in the previous steps, determine the bushing-to-shaft and gear-to-bushing clearances specified in **Table 2** or **Table 3**. Replace worn parts to correct any clearance not within specification.

*NOTE*
*Replace defective gears and their mating gear at the same time, though they may not show equal wear or damage.*

13. Inspect the spline washers. The teeth in the washer should be uniform, and the washers should not be loose on the shaft.

14. Inspect the thrust washers for damage. While it is normal for the thrust washers to show wear, replace them when their thickness has been reduced.

15. On 2005 models, inspect the countershaft first gear needle bearing (13B, **Figure 35**). The rollers should be smooth and polished with no flat spots, burrs or other damage. Inspect the bearing cage for cracks or other damage. Replace the needle bearing if necessary.

## INTERNAL SHIFT MECHANISM

As the transmission is upshifted and downshifted, the shift drum and fork assembly engages and disengages pairs of gears on the transmission shafts. Gear shifting is controlled by the shift forks, which are guided by cam grooves in the shift drum.

8

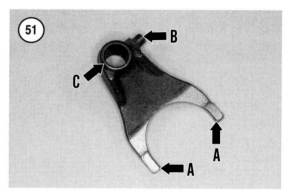

It is important that the shift drum grooves, shift forks and mating gear grooves be in good condition. Too much wear between the parts causes unreliable and poor engagement of the gears. This can lead to premature wear of the gear dogs and other parts.

## Shift Drum Inspection

1. Clean and dry the shift drum.
2. Check the shift drum (**Figure 50**) for wear and damage as follows:
   a. The shift drum grooves (A, **Figure 50**) should be a uniform width. Worn grooves can prevent complete gear engagement, which can cause rough shifting and allow the transmission to disengage.
   b. The shift drum cam (B, **Figure 50**) inner and outer surfaces should be uniform in appearance. Check the ramp surfaces for uneven wear and damage.
   c. The bearing surfaces must not be worn or show overheating discoloration due to lack of lubrication.

## Shift Fork and Shaft Inspection

**Table 4** lists new and service limit specifications for the shift forks and shift fork shaft. Replace the

shift forks and shafts if out of specification or if they show damage as described in this section.

1. Inspect each shift fork (**Figure 51**) for wear or damage. Examine the shift forks where they contact the slider gear (A, **Figure 51**). These surfaces must be smooth with no signs of excessive wear, bending, cracks, heat discoloration or other damage.

2. Check each shift fork for arc-shaped wear or burn marks. These marks indicate a bent shift fork.

3. The guide pin (B, **Figure 51**) should be symmetrical and not flat on the sides.

4. Measure the thickness of each shift fork finger (A, **Figure 51**).

5. Measure the inside diameter (C, **Figure 51**) of each shift fork.

6. Check the shift fork shafts for bending or other damage. Install each shift fork on its shaft and slide it back and forth. Each shift fork must slide smoothly with no binding or tight spots. If there is any noticeable binding, check for a bent shift fork shaft.

7. Inspect the shift fork shafts for wear and damage. Measure each at the operating locations of the shift forks.

**Table 1 TRANSMISSION GEAR RATIOS**

| | |
|---|---|
| Transmission type | 5-speed constant mesh |
| Primary reduction | |
|   Type | Gear |
|   Ratio | |
|     CRF250R | 3.166 (57/18) |
|     CRF250X | 3.611 (65/18) |
|     CRF450R and CRF450X | 2.739 (63/23) |
| Secondary reduction | |
|   Type | Chain and sprockets |
|   Ratio | |
|     CRF250R | 3.923 (51/13) |
|     CRF250X | 3.786 (53/14) |
|     CRF450R | |
|       2002-2003 | 3.846 (50/13) |
|       2004-on | 3.692 (48/13) |
|     CRF450X | 3.923 (51/13) |
| Gear ratios | |
|   CRF250R | |
|     First | 2.142 (30/14) |
|     Second | 1.750 (28/16) |
|     Third | 1.450 (29/20) |
|     Fourth | 1.227 (27/22) |
|     Fifth | 1.041 (25/24) |
|   CRF250X | |
|     First | 2.384 (31/13) |
|     Second | 1.750 (28/16) |
|     Third | 1.333 (28/21) |
|     Fourth | 1.042 (25/24) |
|     Fifth | 0.815 (22/27) |
|   CRF450R | |
|     First | 1.800 (27/15) |
|     Second | 1.471 (25/17) |
|     Third | 1.235 (21/17) |
|     Fourth | 1.050 (21/20) |
|     Fifth | 0.909 (20/22) |
|   CRF450X | |
|     First | 2.231 (29/13) |
|     Second | 1.625 (26/16) |
|     Third | 1.235 (21/17) |
|     Fourth | 1.000 (19/19) |
|     Fifth | 0.826 (19/23) |
| Gearshift pattern | 1-N-2-3-4-5 |

**8**

**Table 2 TRANSMISSION SERVICE SPECIFICATIONS (CRF250R AND CRF250X)**

| | New<br>mm (in.) | Service limit<br>mm (in.) |
|---|---|---|
| Bushing inside diameter | | |
|   Countershaft first gear | 17.000-17.018 (0.6693-0.6700) | 17.04 (0.671) |
|   Countershaft second gear | 24.000-24.021 (0.9449-0.9457) | 24.04 (0.946) |
|   Countershaft third gear | 22.000-22.021 (0.8661-0.8670) | 22.04 (0.868) |
|   Mainshaft fifth gear | 20.000-20.021 (0.7874-0.7882) | 20.04 (0.789) |

(continued)

**Table 2 TRANSMISSION SERVICE SPECIFICATIONS (CRF250R AND CRF250X) (continued)**

|  | New<br>mm (in.) | Service limit<br>mm (in.) |
|---|---|---|
| Bushing outside diameter |  |  |
| Countershaft first gear | 19.979-20.000 (0.7866-0.7874) | 19.95 (0.785) |
| Countershaft second gear | 26.979-27.000 (1.0622-1.0630) | 26.95 (1.061) |
| Countershaft third gear | 24.979-25.000 (0.9834-0.9843) | 24.96 (0.983) |
| Mainshaft fourth and fifth |  |  |
| gears | 22.979-23.000 (0.9047-0.9055) | 22.96 (0.904) |
| Bushing-to-shaft clearance |  |  |
| Countershaft first gear | 0.006-0.035 (0.0002-0.0014) | 0.07 (0.003) |
| Countershaft second and third |  |  |
| gears | 0.020-0.062 (0.0008-0.0024) | 0.12 (0.005) |
| Mainshaft fifth gear | 0.020-0.062 (0.0008-0.0024) | 0.12 (0.005) |
| Countershaft outside diameter |  |  |
| At first gear | 16.983-16.994 (0.6686-0.6691) | 16.97 (0.668) |
| At second gear | 23.959-23.980 (0.9433-0.9441) | 23.94 (0.943) |
| At third gear | 21.959-21.980 (0.8645-0.8654) | 21.94 (0.864) |
| Gear inside diameter |  |  |
| Countershaft first gear | 20.020-20.041 (0.7882-0.7890) | 20.07 (0.790) |
| Countershaft second gear | 27.020-27.041 (1.0638-1.0646) | 27.07 (1.066) |
| Countershaft third gear | 25.020-25.041 (0.9850-0.9859) | 25.07 (0.987) |
| Mainshaft fourth and fifth |  |  |
| gears | 23.020-23.041 (0.9063-0.9071) | 23.07 (0.908) |
| Gear-to-bushing clearance |  |  |
| All | 0.020-0.062 (0.0008-0.0024) | 0.12 (0.005) |
| Mainshaft outside diameter |  |  |
| At fifth gear bushing | 19.959-19.980 (0.7858-0.7866) | 19.94 (0.785) |

**Table 3 TRANSMISSION SERVICE SPECIFICATIONS (CRF450R AND CRF450X)**

|  | New<br>mm (in.) | Service limit<br>mm (in.) |
|---|---|---|
| Bushing inside diameter |  |  |
| Countershaft first gear |  |  |
| 2002-2004 | 19.000-19.021 (0.7480-0.7489) | 19.04 (0.750) |
| 2005 | – |  |
| Countershaft second gear | 27.000-27.021 (1.0630-1.0638) | 27.04 (1.064) |
| Bushing outside diameter |  |  |
| Countershaft first gear |  |  |
| 2002-2004 | 21.979-22.000 (0.8653-0.8661) | 21.95 (0.864) |
| 2005 | – |  |
| Countershaft second gear | 29.979-30.000 (1.1802-1.1811) | 29.95 (1.179) |
| Mainshaft fourth gear | 27.959-27.980 (1.1007-1.1015) | 27.94 (1.100) |
| Bushing-to-shaft clearance |  |  |
| Countershaft first gear |  |  |
| 2002-2004 | 0.020-0.062 (0.0008-0.0024) | 0.12 (0.005) |
| 2005 | – |  |
| Countershaft second gear | 0.020-0.062 (0.0008-0.0024) | 0.12 (0.005) |
| Countershaft outside diameter |  |  |
| First gear position |  |  |
| CRF450R | 18.959-18.980 (0.7464-0.7472) | 18.94 (0.746) |
| CRF450X | 18.987-19.000 (0.7475-0.7480) | 18.94 (0.746) |
| Second gear position | 26.959-26.980 (1.0614-1.0622) | 26.94 (1.061) |
| Third gear position |  |  |
| CRF450R | 24.959-24.979 (0.9826-0.9834) | 24.96 (0.983) |
| CRF450X | 24.959-24.980 (0.9826-0.9835) | 24.96 (0.983) |

(continued)

**Table 3 TRANSMISSION SERVICE SPECIFICATIONS (CRF450R AND CRF450X) (continued)**

| | New mm (in.) | Service limit mm (in.) |
|---|---|---|
| Gear inside diameter | | |
| Countershaft first gear | | |
| CRF450R | | |
| 2002-2004 | 22.020-22.041 (0.8669-0.8678) | 22.07 (0.869) |
| 2005 | 22.000-22.021 (0.8661-0.8670) | 22.04 (0.868) |
| CRF450X | 22.007-22.028 (0.8664-0.8672) | 22.04 (0.868) |
| Countershaft second gear | 30.020-30.041 (1.1819-1.1827) | 30.07 (1.184) |
| Countershaft third gear | 25.020-25.041 (0.9850-0.9859) | 25.07 (0.987) |
| Mainshaft fourth gear | 28.007-28.028 (1.1026-1.1035) | 28.05 (1.104) |
| Mainshaft fifth gear | 25.020-25.041 (0.9850-0.9859) | 25.07 (0.987) |
| Gear-to-bushing clearance | | |
| Countershaft first gear | | |
| 2002-2004 | 0.020-0.062 (0.0008-0.0024) | 0.12 (0.005) |
| 2005 | – | |
| Countershaft second gear | 0.020-0.062 (0.0008-0.0024) | 0.12 (0.005) |
| Mainshaft fourth gear | 0.027-0.069 (0.0011-0.0027) | 0.11 (0.004) |
| Gear-to-shaft clearance | | |
| Countershaft third gear | | |
| CRF450X | 0.040-0.082 (0.0016-0.0032) | 0.082 (0.0032) |
| CRF450R | 0.041-0.082 (0.0016-0.0032) | 0.11 (0.004) |
| Mainshaft fifth gear | 0.040-0.082 (0.0016-0.0032) | 0.13 (0.005) |
| Mainshaft outside diameter | | |
| Mainshaft fifth gear | 24.959-24.980 (0.9826-0.9835) | 24.94 (0.982) |

**Table 4 SHIFT FORK AND SHIFT FORK SHAFT SERVICE SPECIFICATIONS**

| | New mm (in.) | Service limit mm (in.) |
|---|---|---|
| Shift fork finger thickness | 4.93-5.00 (0.194-0.197) | 4.8 (0.19) |
| Shift fork inside diameter | | |
| Center | | |
| CRF450X | 10.989-11.011 (0.4326-0.4335) | 11.011 (0.4335) |
| All other models | 11.003-11.024 (0.4332-0.4340) | 11.04 (0.435) |
| Right and left | 12.035-12.056 (0.4738-0.4746) | 12.07 (0.475) |
| Shift fork shaft outside diameter | | |
| Center | | |
| CRF450X | 10.969-10.980 (0.4319-0.4323) | 10.969 (0.4319) |
| All other models | 10.983-10.994 (0.4324-0.4328) | 10.97 (0.432) |
| Right and left | 11.966-11.984 (0.4711-0.4718) | 11.95 (0.470) |

8

# CHAPTER NINE

# FUEL AND EMISSION CONTROL SYSTEMS

This chapter describes service procedures for the fuel and emission control (CRF250X and CRF450X California models) systems.

**Tables 1-5** list fuel tank and carburetor specifications. **Tables 6-13** list carburetor tuning information. **Tables 1-14** are found at the end of the chapter.

## FUEL SYSTEM SAFETY

When working on the fuel system, observe the following safety practices:

*WARNING*
*Gasoline and most cleaning solvents are extremely flammable. Do not smoke or use electrical tools in the work area. Turn off heating appliances, and those with a pilot light. If gasoline can be smelled in the work area, a potential hazard exists.*

1. Turn the fuel valve off.
2. Work very carefully when the engine is hot.
3. Wipe up fuel and solvent spills immediately.
4. Work in a well-ventilated area.

5. Wear eye protection when using compressed air and when using solvents and degreasers.
6. Keep a fire extinguisher in the shop, rated for class B (fuel) and class C (electrical) fires.

## FUEL TANK

**Table 1** lists fuel tank capacities.

### Removal/Installation

*WARNING*
*Some fuel may spill from the fuel hose or carburetor when performing this procedure. Because gasoline is an extremely flammable and explosive petroleum, perform this procedure away from all open flames (including pilot lights) and sparks. Do not smoke or allow someone who is smoking in the work area. Always work in a well-ventilated area. Wipe up any spills immediately.*

1. Support the motorcycle on a workstand.
2. Remove the seat (Chapter Sixteen).

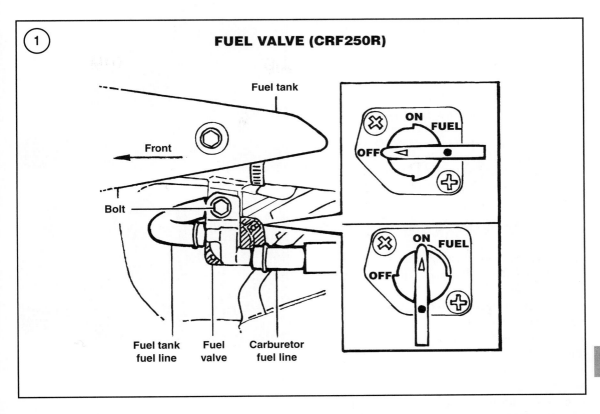

**1**

**FUEL VALVE (CRF250R)**

Fuel tank

Front

Bolt

Fuel tank fuel line

Fuel valve

Carburetor fuel line

ON FUEL

OFF

ON FUEL

OFF

**9**

**2**

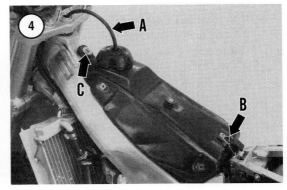

**4**

A

C

B

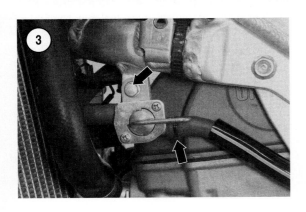

**3**

3. Remove the radiator shrouds (Chapter Sixteen).
4. Turn the fuel valve off and disconnect the carburetor fuel line at the fuel valve. Do not disconnect the fuel tank fuel line when the fuel tank has fuel in it.

    a. **Figure 1** (CRF250R).
    b. **Figure 2** (CRF250X and CRF450X).
    c. **Figure 3** (CRF450R).

5. Remove the bolt securing the fuel shutoff valve to the frame. See **Figure 1**, **2** or **3**.
6. Pull the fuel fill cap vent tube (A, **Figure 4**) free from the steering head area.

7. Unhook the strap at the back of the fuel tank (B, **Figure 4**).

8. Remove the bolt and washer (C, **Figure 4**) securing the fuel tank to the frame.

*CAUTION*
*The fuel shutoff valve is attached to a hose connected to the fuel tank. When removing the fuel tank, guide the fuel shutoff valve carefully through the frame so its lever does not catch and turn on and flood the work area with fuel.*

9. Remove the fuel tank and fuel valve from the frame.

10. Check for loose, missing or damaged fuel tank brackets and rubber dampers. Tighten or replace parts as required.

11. Inspect the fuel hoses for cracks, leaks, soft spots and deterioration.

12. Service the fuel shutoff valve as described in this chapter.

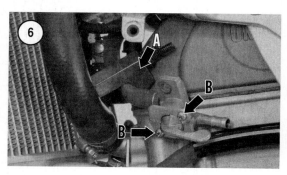

13. Reverse these steps to install the fuel tank, plus the following:

    a. Make sure the fuel tank is secured properly to the frame.

    b. If so equipped, fit the air filter case cover over the fuel tank, then reconnect the rubber strap (**Figure 5**).

    c. Reconnect the fuel hose and secure each end with a clamp.

    d. Turn the fuel valve on and check the fuel hose for leaks.

## FUEL SHUTOFF VALVE AND FUEL FILTER

The fuel shutoff valve and fuel filter are mounted in separate housings. The fuel filter is mounted onto the bottom of the fuel tank. The fuel shutoff valve is mounted between the fuel filter and carburetor with two separate hoses.

### Fuel Shutoff Valve
### Removal/Installation

Repair parts for the fuel shutoff valve are not available. However, the cover and lever assembly can be removed from the valve to allow cleaning

and inspection of the valve passage and seal assembly.

*WARNING*
*Some fuel will spill when performing this procedure. Because gasoline is an extremely flammable and explosive petroleum, perform this procedure away from all open flames (including pilot lights) and sparks. Do not smoke or allow someone who is smoking in the work area. Always work in a well-ventilated area. Wipe up any spills immediately.*

1. Turn the fuel valve off and disconnect the carburetor fuel line at the fuel valve. Do not disconnect the fuel tank fuel line when the fuel tank has fuel in it.

    a. **Figure 1** (CRF250R).

    b. **Figure 2** (CRF250X and CRF450X).

    c. **Figure 3** (CRF450R).

2. Remove the bolt securing the fuel shutoff valve to the frame. See **Figure 1, 2** or **3**.

3A. To remove the fuel shutoff valve with the fuel tank mounted on the motorcycle:

    a. Pinch the fuel hose between the fuel tank and fuel shutoff valve with a fuel hose clamp (A, **Figure 6**). On CRF250X and CRF450X mod-

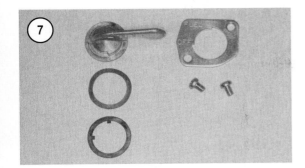

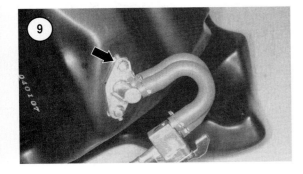

els, pinch both hoses with separate clamps. If this tool is not available, either drain the fuel tank with the tank mounted on the motorcycle or remove the fuel tank and drain it later.

b. Disconnect the fuel tank hose at the fuel shutoff valve and remove the valve.

3B. To remove the fuel shutoff and fuel tank, remove the fuel tank as described in this section. Pinch the fuel hose(s) with a hose clamp (described in Step 3A) or drain the fuel into an approved fuel storage can.

4. Disconnect the fuel hose(s) from the fuel shutoff and remove the fuel shutoff valve assembly.

5. To partially disassemble and inspect the fuel shutoff valve assembly:

*NOTE*
*Because the fuel shutoff valve lever is mounted inside toward the engine on CRF250R models, it will be necessary to remove the fuel shutoff valve if the fuel tank is mounted on the motorcycle.*

*NOTE*
*Make a diagram of the parts after removing each one from the fuel shutoff valve so they can be assembled correctly.*

a. Remove the two screws (B, **Figure 6**), outer cover, notched washer, wave washer and lever from the housing. See **Figure 7**.

b. Inspect the passages (**Figure 8**) for clogging, contamination and damage. If any damage is noted, replace the fuel shutoff valve assembly.

c. If the parts are in good condition, clean the fuel shutoff valve assembly and reassemble it.

6. Installation is the reverse of these steps. Remove the hose clamps from the fuel hose(s) if used. Then turn the fuel valve on and check for leaks.

**Fuel Filter**
**Removal/Installation**

The fuel filter is mounted in the bottom of the fuel tank.

*WARNING*
*Some fuel will spill when performing this procedure and fuel vapors remain in an empty tank. Because gasoline is extremely flammable and explosive, perform this procedure away from all open flames (including pilot lights) and sparks. Do not smoke or allow someone who is smoking in the work area. Always work in a well-ventilated area. Wipe up any spills immediately.*

1. Remove the fuel tank as described in this chapter.
2. Drain the fuel into a fuel storage container.
3. Remove the screws and the fuel filter housing assembly (**Figure 9**, typical).
4A. On CRF250X and CRF450X models, inspect the fuel filter screen for contamination or damage.

9

Remove and clean the screen if contaminated. The screen can be replaced separately (**Figure 10**).

4B. On CRF250R and CRF450R models, inspect the fuel filter screen for contamination or damage. If the screen cannot be thoroughly cleaned, or if it is damaged, replace the fuel filter housing assembly. The filter screen cannot be replaced separately (**Figure 11**).

> *CAUTION*
> *Do not overtighten the fuel filter housing mounting bolts. Doing so may cause the threaded inserts in the fuel tank to turn and damage their mounting hole. This will prevent the bolts from being properly loosened or tightened later.*

5. Install the fuel filter housing using a new O-ring and tighten the bolts securely.

6. After connecting the fuel shutoff valve to the fuel filter, add a small amount of fuel to the tank and check the fuel filter housing for leaks.

7. Reinstall the fuel tank as described in this chapter.

## AIR BOX

### Removal/Installation

#### CRF250R and CRF450R

1. Remove the subframe (Chapter Sixteen).
2. Remove the mud guard from the subframe.
3. Unbolt and remove the rear fender from the subframe.
4. Unbolt and remove the air box from the subframe.
5. Check the air filter for proper installation and sealing, then remove it.
6. Check the carburetor boot where it is attached to the air box for loose or missing screws or nuts or a damaged clamp. Check the boot for cracks and other damage. Check the boot plate to make sure it is positioned flush against the boot.
7. Check the carburetor boot to make sure the boot is sealing properly and no dirt is passing by the air filter. If there is dirt inside the boot, check for a damaged boot or air filter.
8. If necessary, remove and reseal the carburetor boot as described in this section.

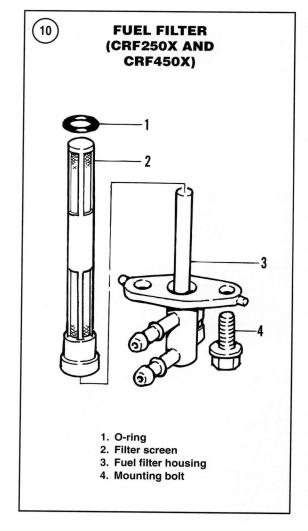

**10**　　　**FUEL FILTER (CRF250X AND CRF450X)**

1. O-ring
2. Filter screen
3. Fuel filter housing
4. Mounting bolt

9. Install the air box by reversing these removal steps.

#### CRF250X and CRF450X

1. Raise and lock the subframe as described in Chapter Sixteen.
2. On California models, disconnect the air suction hose at the air box. See **Figure 12** (CRF250X) or A, **Figure 13** (CRF450X).
3. Disconnect the breather hose at the air box. See A, **Figure 14** (CRF250X) or B, **Figure 13** (CRF450X).
4. Remove the bolt, clamp and collar at the air box.
5. Remove the bolts and collars securing the air box to the subframe and remove the air box.

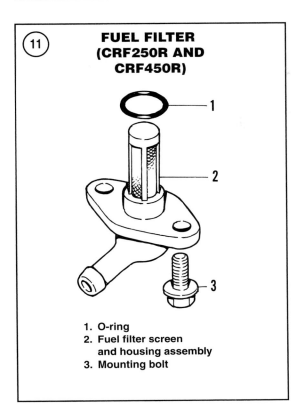

**FUEL FILTER (CRF250R AND CRF450R)**

1. O-ring
2. Fuel filter screen and housing assembly
3. Mounting bolt

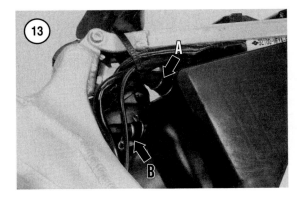

6. Remove the mud guard from the air box.

7. Check the air filter for proper installation and sealing, then remove it.

8. Check the carburetor boot where it is attached to the air box for loose or missing screws or nuts or a damaged clamp. Check the boot for cracks and other damage. Check the plate to make sure it is positioned flush against the boot.

9. Check the carburetor boot to make sure the boot is sealing properly and no dirt is passing by the air filter. If there is dirt inside the boot, check for a damaged boot or air filter.

10. If necessary, remove and reseal the carburetor boot as described in this section.

11. Install the air box by reversing these removal steps.

**Carburetor Boot Resealing**

Use a fuel resistant weatherstrip adhesive to seal the carburetor boot to the air box.

1. Remove the air box from the subframe as described in this section.

2. Clean the air box thoroughly.

3. Remove the screws or nuts securing the carburetor boot to the air box. Then remove the boot plate, boot and the filter holder inside the air box.

4. On CRF250X and CRF450X models, a rubber seal is used between the front side cover and the air box. See **Figure 15** (CRF250X) or **Figure 16** (CRF450X). If dirt is leaking between the front side cover and air box, remove the screws and front side cover and replace the rubber seal.

5. Inspect the filter holder and replace if damaged.

6. Clean the boot and air box mating surfaces of all old sealant residue.

7. Inspect the carburetor boot for damage and replace if necessary.

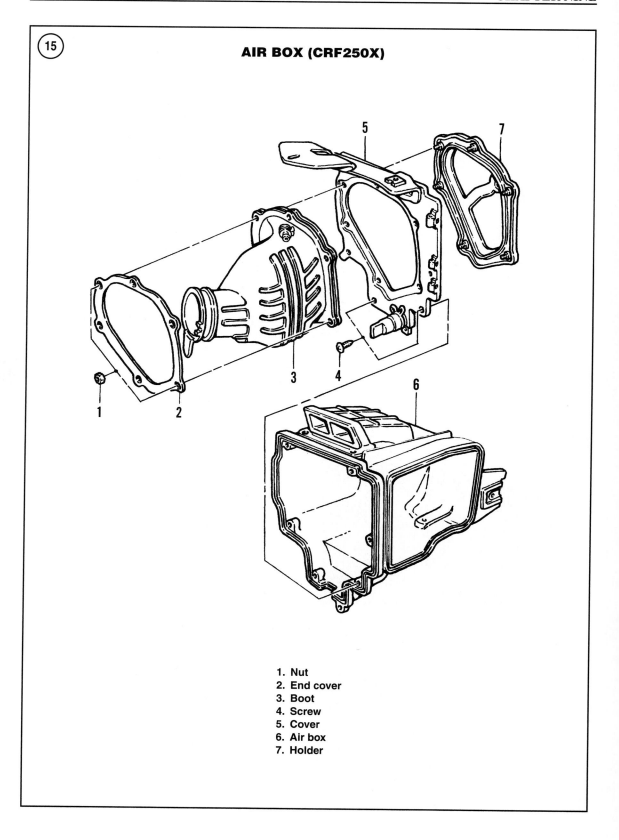

(15) **AIR BOX (CRF250X)**

1. Nut
2. End cover
3. Boot
4. Screw
5. Cover
6. Air box
7. Holder

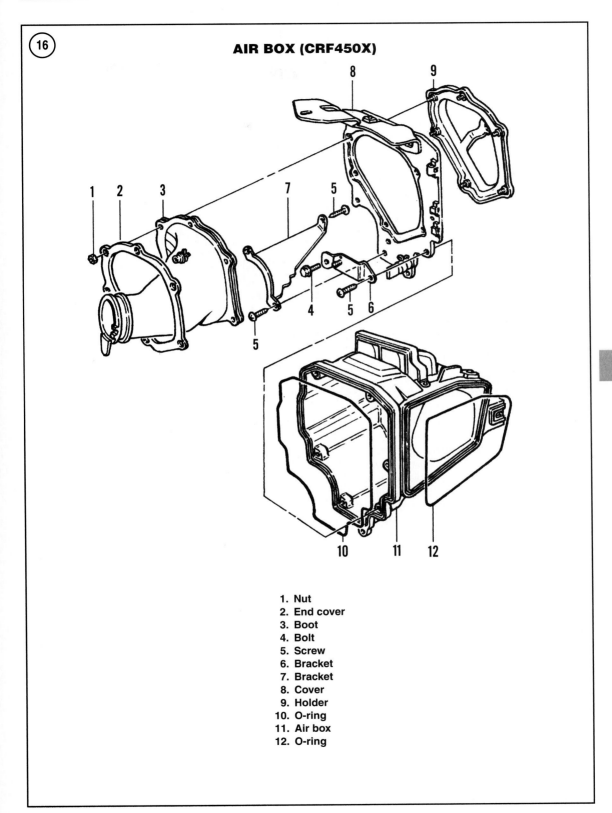

## AIR BOX (CRF450X)

1. Nut
2. End cover
3. Boot
4. Bolt
5. Screw
6. Bracket
7. Bracket
8. Cover
9. Holder
10. O-ring
11. Air box
12. O-ring

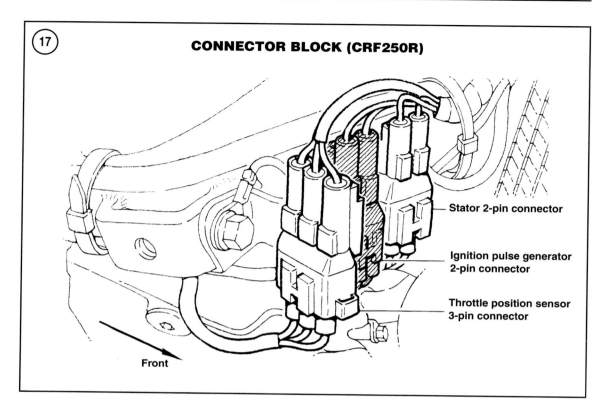

**CONNECTOR BLOCK (CRF250R)**

(17)

— Stator 2-pin connector

— Ignition pulse generator
2-pin connector

— Throttle position sensor
3-pin connector

Front

8. Replace the boot plate if damaged.

*WARNING*
*Adequate ventilation must be pro-*
*vided when using a weatherstrip ad-*
*hesive in Step 10. Do not use where*
*there are sparks or any open flames.*
*Vapors can cause flash fires, as well*
*as dizziness and headaches. Follow*
*the manufacturer's directions and*
*safety information.*

9. Install the filter holder inside the air box. Make sure all holes align.

10. Apply a weatherstrip adhesive to the boot sealing edge on the air box.

11. Install the carburetor boot, boot plate and secure with the screws or nuts.

12. Reinstall the air box as described in this section.

## CARBURETOR

This section describes service procedures for removing and installing the carburetor.

**Removal**
**(CRF250R and CRF250X)**

1. Support the motorcycle on a workstand.

2. Clean the area around the carburetor to prevent dirt from entering the cylinder head and carburetor air boot.

3. Remove the seat (Chapter Sixteen).

4. Remove the fuel tank (this chapter).

5A. On CRF250R models, remove the subframe (Chapter Sixteen).

5B. On CRF250X models, raise and lock the subframe (Chapter Sixteen). Then disconnect the breather hose (A, **Figure 14**) at the air box to provide room when removing the upper shock absorber nut and bolt.

6. Remove the upper shock absorber mounting nut and bolt (B, **Figure 14**, typical). Then pull and tie the shock absorber back to provide room behind the carburetor.

7. Disconnect the throttle position sensor connector. See **Figure 17** (CRF250R) or **Figure 18** (CRF250X).

8. Disconnect the carburetor side fuel hose at the fuel valve.

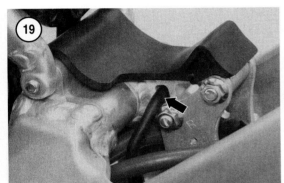

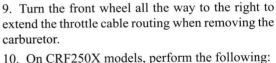

9. Turn the front wheel all the way to the right to extend the throttle cable routing when removing the carburetor.

10. On CRF250X models, perform the following:

   a. Remove the air vent hose from the hole in the top of the frame (**Figure 19**). The opposite end of this hose is attached to the carburetor.

   b. Disconnect the clamp (A, **Figure 20**) securing the carburetor vent hoses to the alternator wire harness.

11. Note the carburetor overflow and vent hose routing, then pull the hoses free so they can be removed with the carburetor (**Figure 21**).

12. Loosen the front carburetor hose clamp (B, **Figure 20**). Then pull/twist the carburetor out of the manifold (**Figure 22**).

13. Loosen the hot start valve nut (**Figure 23**) and remove the hot start valve (**Figure 24**) from the carburetor. If necessary, disconnect the hot start valve and spring from the cable.

14. Cover the intake tube with a rubber plug.

15. Remove the bolt (A, **Figure 25**) and throttle drum cover (B).

16. Loosen the locknut and throttle cable adjusters at the carburetor. Disconnect the pull cable (A, **Figure 26**), then the return cable (B).

17. Remove the carburetor between the right side of the frame and the rear shock absorber (**Figure 27**).

18. Service the carburetor as described in this chapter.

## Installation
## (CRF250R and CRF250X)

1. Install the vent hoses onto the carburetor, if removed. See *Carburetor Service* in this chapter.

2. Turn the front wheel all the way to the right.

3. Install the carburetor (**Figure 27**) through the right side of the frame, in front of the rear shock absorber.

4. Reconnect the return cable (A, **Figure 28**), then the pull cable (B) onto the carburetor. When the cables and adjusters are positioned correctly (**Figure 26**), adjust the throttle cables as described in Chapter Three.

*NOTE*
*The throttle cable adjustment will be checked after installing the carburetors into the intake tube.*

5. Install the throttle drum cover (B, **Figure 25**) and tighten the mounting bolt to 3.9 N•m (34.5 in.-lb.).

6. If removed, install the spring over the end of the hot start cable and compress it by hand. Then connect the hot start valve to the cable end and release the spring so it tensions and holds the valve in place (**Figure 24**).

*NOTE*
*The hot start valve locknut is plastic and its threads can strip easily if they are not properly aligned when tightening the locknut.*

7. Wipe the hot start valve off with a clean rag, then install it into the carburetor bore. Thread the locknut into the carburetor and tighten securely (**Figure 23**).

8. Remove the plug from the intake tube.

9. Install the carburetor by aligning the tab on the carburetor with the groove in the intake tube (C, **Figure 20**).

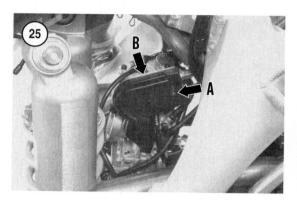

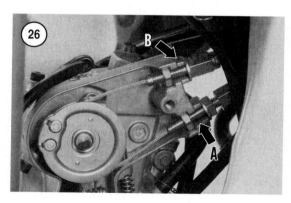

10. Tighten the intake tube hose clamp securely (B, **Figure 20**).

11. Route the carburetor overflow and vent hoses following the notes made during removal.

12. On CRF250X models, perform the following:

a. Reconnect the clamp (A, **Figure 20**) securing the carburetor vent hoses to the alternator wire harness.

b. Install the air vent hose through the hole in the top of the frame (**Figure 19**).

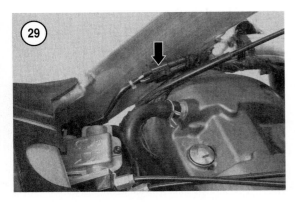

13. Adjust the following as described in Chapter Three:

a. Throttle cables.

b. Hot start cable.

14. Reconnect the fuel hose at the fuel valve. Secure the hose with a clamp.

15. Apply dielectric grease to the throttle position sensor connector halves. Then reconnect the connectors. See **Figure 17** (CRF250R) or **Figure 18** (CRF250X).

16. Reinstall the upper shock absorber mounting bolt from the right side. Install the nut (B, **Figure 14**) and tighten to 44 N•m (33 ft.-lb.).

17A. On CRF250R models, install the subframe (Chapter Sixteen).

17B. On CRF250X models, perform the following:

a. Reconnect the breather hose (A, **Figure 14**) at the air box.

b. Lower and secure the subframe (Chapter Sixteen).

18. Install the fuel tank (this chapter). Turn the fuel valve on and check for leaks at the fuel valve and at the carburetor overflow hose.

19. Install the seat (Chapter Sixteen).

*WARNING*
*Do not ride the motorcycle until the throttle cables are adjusted properly and the throttle opens and returns smoothly.*

**Removal**
**(CRF450R and CRF450X)**

1. Support the motorcycle on a workstand.

2. Clean the area around the carburetor to prevent dirt from entering the cylinder head and carburetor air boot.

3. Remove the seat (Chapter Sixteen).

4. Remove the fuel tank (this chapter).

5A. On CRF450R models, remove the subframe (Chapter Sixteen).

5B. On CRF450X models, perform the following:

a. Raise and lock the subframe (Chapter Sixteen).

b. Remove the upper shock absorber mounting nut and bolt (B, **Figure 14**, typical). Then pull and tie the shock absorber back to provide room behind the carburetor.

6. Disconnect the throttle position sensor connector (**Figure 29**).

7. Disconnect the carburetor side fuel hose at the fuel valve.

8. Turn the front wheel all the way to the right to extend the throttle cable routing when removing the carburetor.

9. Note the carburetor overflow and vent hose routing, then pull the hoses free so they can be removed with the carburetor.

10. Loosen the front carburetor hose clamp (A, **Figure 30**). Then pull/twist the carburetor out of the intake tube and place on top of the frame (**Figure 31**).

11. Cover the intake tube with a rubber plug.

12. Loosen the hot start valve nut (**Figure 32**) and remove the hot start valve (**Figure 33**) from the carburetor. If necessary, disconnect the hot start valve and spring from the cable.

13. Remove the bolt (A, **Figure 34**) and throttle drum cover (B).

14. Loosen the locknut and throttle cable adjusters at the carburetor. Disconnect the pull cable (A, **Figure 35**), then the return cable (B).

15. Service the carburetor as described in this chapter.

### Installation
### (CRF450R and CRF450X)

1. Install the vent hoses onto the carburetor, if removed. See *Carburetor Service* in this chapter.

2. Turn the front wheel all the way to the right.

3. Reconnect the return cable (B, **Figure 35**), then the pull cable (A) onto the carburetor. When the cables and adjusters are positioned correctly, adjust the throttle cables as described in Chapter Three.

> *NOTE*
> *The throttle cable adjustment will be checked after installing the carburetors into the intake tube.*

4. Install the throttle drum cover (B, **Figure 34**) and tighten the mounting bolt to 3.9 N•m (34.5 in.-lb.).

5. If removed, install the spring over the end of the hot start cable and compress it by hand. Then connect the hot start valve to the cable end and release the spring so it tensions and holds the valve in place (**Figure 33**).

> *NOTE*
> *The hot start valve locknut is plastic and its threads can strip easily if they are not properly aligned when tightening the locknut.*

6. Wipe the hot start valve off with a clean rag, then install it into the carburetor bore. Thread the locknut into the carburetor and tighten securely (**Figure 32**).

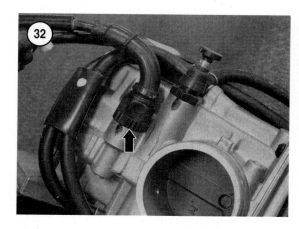

7. Remove the plug from the intake tube.

8. Install the carburetor by aligning the tab on the carburetor with the groove in the intake tube (B, **Figure 30**).

9A. On 2002-2004 CRF450R and CRF450X models, tighten the intake tube hose clamp securely (A, **Figure 30**).

9B. On 2005 CRF450R models, tighten the intake tube hose clamp so the distance between the clamp ends is 11-13 mm (7/16-1/2 in).

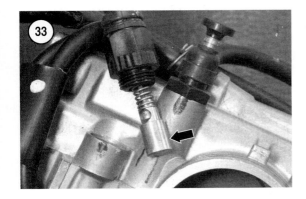

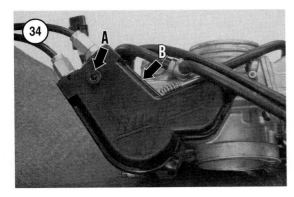

10. Route the carburetor overflow and vent hoses following the notes made during removal.

11. Adjust the following as described in Chapter Three:

    a. Throttle cables.

    b. Hot start cable.

12. Reconnect the fuel hose at the fuel valve. Secure the hose with a clamp.

13. Apply dielectric grease to the throttle position sensor connector halves. Then reconnect the connectors (**Figure 29**).

14A. On CRF450R models, install the subframe (Chapter Sixteen).

14B. On CRF450X models, perform the following:

    a. Reinstall the upper shock absorber mounting bolt from the right side. Then install the nut (B, **Figure 14**, typical) and tighten to 44 N•m (33 ft.-lb.).

    b. Lower and secure the subframe (Chapter Sixteen).

15. Install the fuel tank (this chapter). Turn the fuel valve on and check for leaks at the fuel valve and at the carburetor overflow hose.

16. Install the seat (Chapter Sixteen).

> *WARNING*
> *Do not ride the motorcycle until the throttle cables are adjusted properly and the throttle opens and returns smoothly.*

## CARBURETOR SERVICE

### Disassembly

Refer to **Figure 36**.

1. Disconnect and label the carburetor vent and drain hoses (**Figure 37**, typical).

> *NOTE*
> *Do not loosen or remove the throttle position sensor (TPS) from the carburetor unless it is necessary to adjust or replace the sensor (**Figure 38**). Refer to* ***Throttle Position Sensor*** *in this chapter.*

2. Remove the screws from the top cover, and then remove the cover and O-ring. See **Figure 39** (CRF250R and CRF250X) or **Figure 40** (CRF450R and CRF450X).

3. Remove the jet needle holder (**Figure 41**) and jet needle (**Figure 42**).

4. Remove the throttle shaft screw (**Figure 43**). Then turn the throttle shaft to raise and remove the throttle valve assembly (**Figure 44**).

> *CAUTION*
> *One roller (A, **Figure 45**) and the throttle valve plate (B) can be removed from the throttle valve. The other three rollers are fixed to the throttle valve. Before removing the*

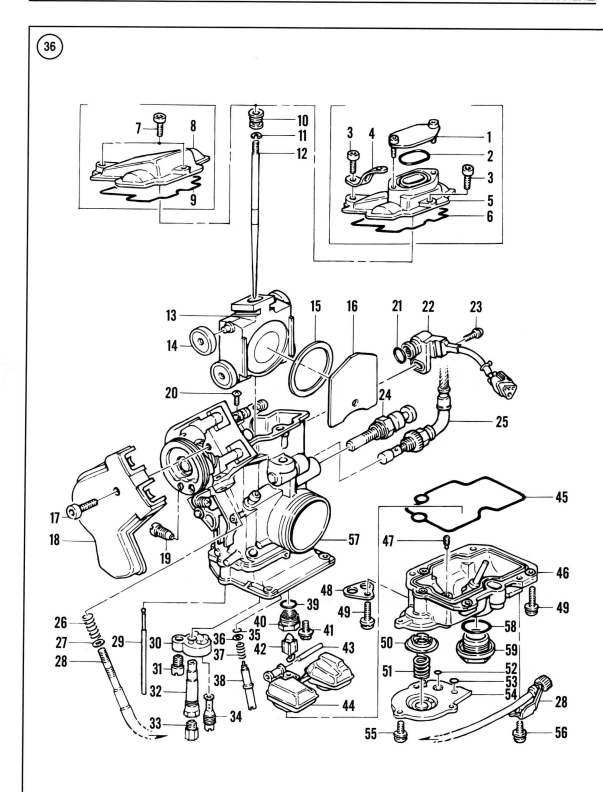

## CARBURETOR

1. Access cover/screw assembly
2. O-ring
3. Bolt
4. Clamp
5. Top cover
6. O-ring
7. Bolt
8. Top cover
9. O-ring
10. Jet needle holder
11. Clip
12. Jet needle
13. Throttle valve
14. Roller
15. Ring
16. Throttle valve plate
17. Bolt
18. Throttle drum cover
19. Pilot air jet
20. Throttle shaft screw
21. O-ring
22. Throttle position sensor (TPS)
23. Screw
24. Choke
25. Hot start valve and cable assembly
26. Spring
27. Washer
28. Throttle stop screw adjuster
29. Accelerator pump rod
30. Baffle plate
31. Starter jet
32. Needle jet
33. Main jet
34. Pilot jet
35. O-ring
36. Washer
37. Spring
38. Pilot screw
39. O-ring (2002-2003 CRF40R only)
40. Float valve seat (2002-2003 CRF40R only)
41. Screw
42. Float valve
43. Float pin
44. Float
45. O-ring
46. Float bowl
47. Leak jet
48. Hose guide
49. Screw
50. Accelerator pump diaphragm
51. Spring
52. O-ring or D-ring
53. O-ring
54. Accelerator pump cover
55. Screw
56. Throttle stop screw
57. Carburetor body
58. O-ring
59. Drain bolt

9

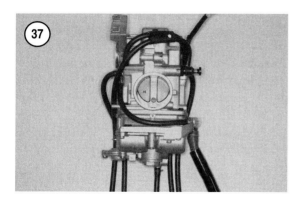

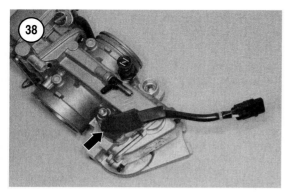

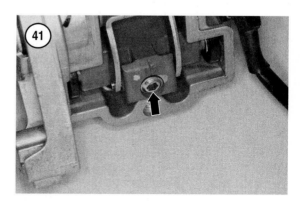

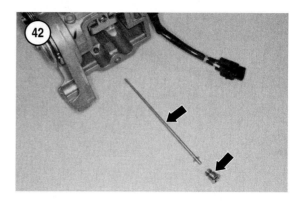

throttle valve plate (B, **Figure 45**) from the throttle valve, note the plate's installed position. If the plate is installed incorrectly, the motorcycle will experience driveability problems. The plate is installed correctly when the hole in the plate is facing down and its rubber ring seats into the round groove in the throttle valve.

5. Unscrew the locknut and remove the choke assembly (**Figure 46**).

> *NOTE*
> *On some carburetors, the O-ring installed in the accelerator pump cover is actually a D-ring with one flat side. The flat side faces toward the accelerator pump cover.*

6. Remove the accelerator pump cover (**Figure 47**), and then remove the two O-rings, spring and diaphragm (**Figure 48**).

7. Remove the float bowl as follows:

    a. Remove the screw and the throttle stop screw mounting bracket (A, **Figure 49**).

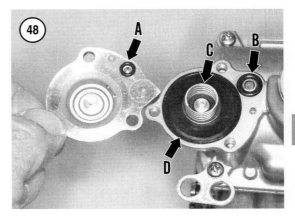

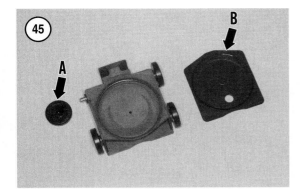

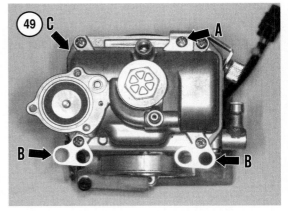

**9**

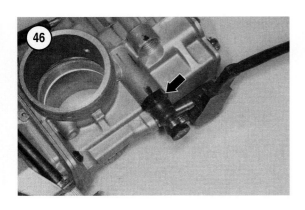

b. Note the position of the hose guides (B, **Figure 49**) before removing them.

c. Remove the screws and float bowl (C, **Figure 49**).

8. Push the link lever (A, **Figure 50**) up, then pull the accelerator pump rod (B) to disconnect it from the link lever.

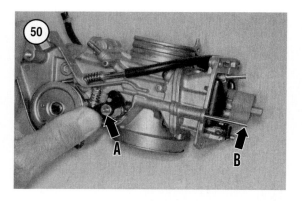

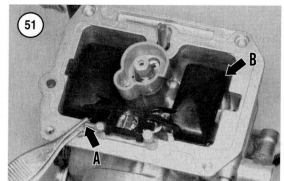

9. Remove the float pin (A, **Figure 51**), float (B) and float valve (**Figure 52**).

> *CAUTION*
> *On 2002-2003 CRF450R models, the float valve seat can be removed from the carburetor. However, the O-ring used to seal the seat can make it difficult to remove the float valve seat. When removing the float valve seat, do not use excessive force as this may damage the float valve seat or carburetor housing.*

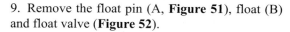

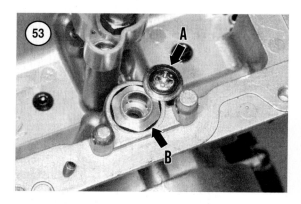

10. On 2002-2003 CRF450R models, remove the screw (A, **Figure 53**) and float valve seat (B).

11. Remove the pilot screw (A, **Figure 54**) as follows:

  a. Accurately count the number of turns required to *lightly* seat the pilot screw into the carburetor.

  b. Record the number of turns.

  c. Remove the pilot screw, spring, washer and O-ring (**Figure 55**).

> *NOTE*
> *If the O-ring did not come off with the screw, remove it from the pilot screw bore with a piece of wire.*

12. Remove the main jet (B, **Figure 54**), needle jet and baffle plate (C). See **Figure 56**.

13. Remove the pilot jet (A, **Figure 57**).

14. Remove the starter jet (B, **Figure 57**).

15. Remove the pilot air jet (**Figure 58**).

16. Remove the leak jet (**Figure 59**) from the float bowl.

17. Clean and inspect the parts as described in this section.

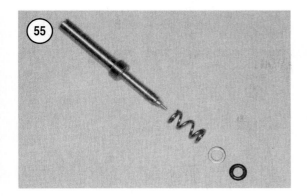

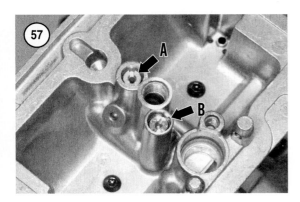

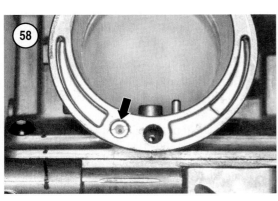

## Assembly

Refer to **Figure 36**.

1. Install and tighten the leak jet (**Figure 59**).
2. Install and tighten the pilot air jet (**Figure 58**).
3. Install and tighten the starter jet (B, **Figure 57**).
4. Install and tighten the pilot jet (A, **Figure 57**).
5. Install the baffle plate (C, **Figure 54**) and the needle jet. Tighten the needle jet securely.
6. Install and tighten the main jet (B, **Figure 54**).
7. Install the pilot screw assembly (**Figure 55**) as follows:
   a. Install the spring, washer and a new O-ring onto the pilot screw (**Figure 60**).
   b. Install and *lightly* seat the pilot screw assembly (A, **Figure 54**). Then turn it out the number of turns recorded during disassembly. If the number of turns is not known, refer to **Tables 2-5** at the end of this chapter for the standard setting.
8. On 2002-2003 CRF450R models, install a new O-ring onto the float valve seat if necessary. Then install the float valve seat (B, **Figure 53**) and secure it with its screw (A).
9. Install the float assembly as follows:

a. Hook the float valve (**Figure 52**) onto the float.

b. Place the float (B, **Figure 51**) and float valve assembly into the carburetor, seating the valve into the seat.

c. Install the float pin (A, **Figure 51**).

d. Check the float height as described in this chapter.

10. Push the round accelerator pump rod end (A, **Figure 61**) into the slot (B) in the link lever. See **Figure 50**.

11. Install the float bowl as follows:

a. If removed, install the O-ring into the float bowl groove (**Figure 62**).

b. Align the passage in the float bowl with the accelerator pump rod and install the float bowl (C, **Figure 49**).

c. Install the hose guides (B, **Figure 49**) and the float bowl mounting screws. Tighten the screw securely.

d. Install the throttle stop screw mounting bracket (A, **Figure 49**) and tighten the mounting screw securely.

12. Install the accelerator pump assembly as follows:

*NOTE*
*On some carburetors, the O-ring (A, **Figure 48**) installed in the accelerator pump cover is actually a D-ring with one flat side.*

a. Install the O-ring or D-ring into the accelerator pump cover (A, **Figure 48**). If a D-ring is used, install it with its flat side facing toward the accelerator pump cover.

b. Install the larger O-ring (B, **Figure 48**) into the carburetor body groove.

c. Install the diaphragm (D, **Figure 48**) with its shoulder side facing up.

d. Install and center the spring (C, **Figure 48**) into the diaphragm.

e. Install the cover (**Figure 47**) and tighten the screws securely.

13. Install and tighten the choke assembly (**Figure 46**). Operate the choke knob to make sure the valve opens and closes.

14. Install the roller (A, **Figure 45**) onto the throttle valve.

15. Install the throttle valve plate (B, **Figure 45**) onto the throttle valve with its hole (**Figure 63**) fac-

ing down. The rubber ring on the throttle valve plate must seat into the round groove on the throttle valve.

16. Install the throttle valve assembly as follows:

a. Turn the throttle shaft so the valve lever rollers are at the top of the carburetor (A, **Figure 64**).

b. Insert the throttle valve into the carburetor in the direction shown in B, **Figure 64**. The side of the throttle valve with the plate (16, **Figure 36**) must face toward the front side of the carburetor (engine side).

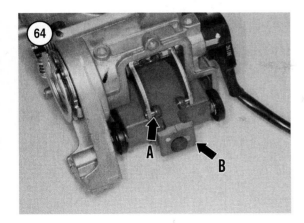

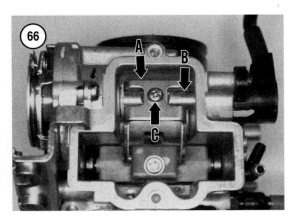

c. Engage the throttle valve with the valve lever rollers (**Figure 65**).

d. Align the valve lever (A, **Figure 66**) with the throttle shaft (B). Apply a threadlock onto the throttle shaft screw. Install the screw (C, **Figure 66**) through the valve lever and thread into the throttle shaft. Tighten the screw securely.

e. Operate the throttle to check the throttle valve for proper operation.

17. If removed, install the jet needle and the jet needle holder (**Figure 42**). Tighten the jet needle holder (**Figure 41**) securely.

18. Install the O-ring into the top cover groove.

19. Install the top cover and secure with the mounting screws (**Figure 40**).

20. Connect the carburetor hoses.

21. If necessary, service the throttle position sensor as described in this chapter.

22. Install the carburetor as described in this chapter.

23. Adjust the carburetor as described in this chapter.

**Cleaning and Inspection**

> *CAUTION*
> *Do not attempt to clean the jet orifices or seats with drill bits. These items can scratch the surfaces and alter flow rates, or cause leaking.*

1. Clean all the parts in carburetor cleaner. Remove all sediment from the float bowl surfaces, and clean all carburetor passages and hoses with compressed air.

> *CAUTION*
> *Do not submerge the throttle position sensor or wiring harness in solvent. Only wipe the outside of the unit and wiring harness with a shop cloth.*

2. Inspect all the brass jets. Check that all holes, in the ends and sides, are clean and undamaged.

3. Inspect the pilot screw assembly (**Figure 55**). Inspect the tip for dents or bends. Replace the O-ring if worn or damaged.

4. Inspect the accelerator pump (**Figure 67**) assembly for wear and damage. Inspect the diaphragm for cracks, tears or brittleness. Check the spring for weakness or damage. Check the passages in the cover and carburetor body for clogging. Replace the O-rings (and D-ring if used) if worn or damaged.

5. Inspect the float and float valve assembly:

a. Inspect the tip of the float valve (A, **Figure 68**) and replace if it is stepped or dented.

b. Lightly press on the spring-loaded pin (B, **Figure 68**) in the float valve. The pin should easily move in and out of the valve. Replace the float valve if the pin is varnished with fuel residue and does not move correctly.

c. On 2002-2003 CRF450R models, inspect the float valve seat (C, **Figure 68**). The seat should be clean and scratch-free. If it is not, the float valve will not seat properly and the carburetor will overflow. Replace the seat and float valve.

d. On all other models, the float seat is an integral part of the carburetor body. Inspect the seat as described in sub-step c. If the damage is severe, it will be necessary to replace the carburetor.

e. On 2002-2003 CRF450R models, inspect the screen (D, **Figure 68**) on the float valve seat. If necessary, clean with solvent and compressed air.

f. On 2002-2003 CRF450R models, replace the O-ring (E, **Figure 68**) on the float valve seat if damaged.

g. Submerge the float in water and check for leakage. Replace the float if water or fuel is inside the float.

6. Inspect the choke valve (**Figure 69**) for wear or damage. Hold the housing and operate the knob by hand. If there is any sticking or binding, check for a bent shaft. Check the spring for damage.

7. Inspect the throttle valve assembly (**Figure 70**) as follows:

a. Remove the needle holder, spring, collar and jet needle.

b. The jet needle must be smooth and evenly tapered. If it is stepped, dented, worn or bent, replace the jet needle.

c. Check the throttle valve plate for cracks or other damage.

d. Check that the rollers on the throttle valve turn freely.

e. Inspect the fit of the throttle valve assembly in the carburetor body. The assembly should fit snugly, but easily slide through the bore. If drag or binding is felt, inspect the bore and throttle valve for excessive wear, roughness and other damage.

f. Install the jet needle, spring and jet needle holder.

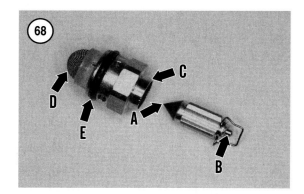

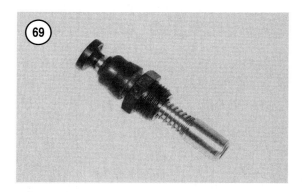

8. Replace the float bowl O-ring (**Figure 62**) if leaking or damaged.

## FLOAT HEIGHT ADJUSTMENT

The float and float valve maintain a constant fuel level in the float bowl. As fuel is used, the float lowers and allows more fuel past the valve. As the fuel level rises, the float closes the valve when the required fuel level is reached. If the float is out of adjustment, the fuel level will be too high or low. A low fuel level will result in lean fuel mixture—at

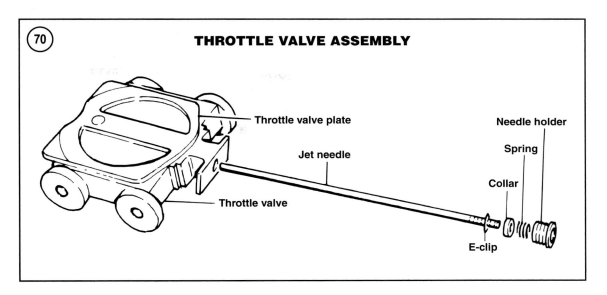

**⑦⓪ THROTTLE VALVE ASSEMBLY**

Throttle valve plate

Jet needle

Throttle valve

Needle holder

Spring

Collar

E-clip

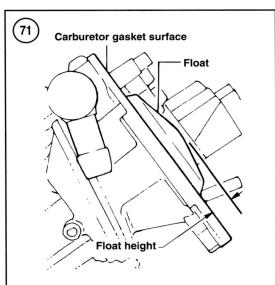

**⑦① Carburetor gasket surface**

Float

Float height

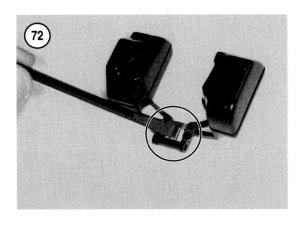

**⑦②**

high rpm the engine will act like it is running out of fuel. A high fuel level will richen the fuel mixture—the engine will hesitate and run roughly, especially on deceleration.

1. Remove the carburetor as described in this chapter.

2. Remove the float bowl as described in this chapter.

3. Lightly touch the float to ensure the float valve is seated.

4. Hold the carburetor so the float valve remains seated, but the spring-loaded pin in the valve is not being compressed by the tab on the float. The tab should only touch the pin.

5. Measure the distance from the carburetor gasket surface to the highest point on the float (**Figure 71**). Refer to **Tables 2-5** for float height specifications.

6. If the float height is incorrect, remove the float from the carburetor and bend the float tab (**Figure 72**) in the appropriate direction to raise or lower the float. Recheck the height after adjusting the float.

7. Install the float bowl as described in this chapter.

8. Install the carburetor as described in this chapter.

### CARBURETOR ADJUSTMENT AND REJETTING (CRF250R AND CRF450R)

The performance of the carburetor is affected by altitude, temperature, humidity and riding conditions. If the motorcycle is not running or performing to expectations, check the following before adjusting or rejetting the carburetor:

1. Throttle cables. Make sure the throttle cables are not dragging and are correctly adjusted.

2. Make sure the air filter is clean.

3. Make sure the fuel flow is adequate from the fuel tank to the carburetor.

4. Make sure the ignition timing is correct and the throttle position sensor is operating correctly.

5. Make sure the muffler is not restricted.

6. Make sure the brakes are not dragging.

7. Before disassembling the carburetor, understand the function of the pilot, jet needle and main jet systems. When evaluating or troubleshooting these systems, keep in mind that their operating ranges overlap one another during the transition from closed to fully open throttle.

## Carburetor Settings

The standard carburetor jetting has been set for an unmodified engine operating at sea level at an ambient temperature of 59-80° F (15-27° C). When operating the motorcycle under different altitude and temperature conditions, the carburetor may require rejetting or other adjustments. **Tables 6-11** list information for tuning the carburetor at different temperature and altitude conditions. Before adjusting the carburetor, note the following:

1. Check for the following conditions. Clean, repair or replace the component(s) as required.

   a. Old or contaminated fuel.

   b. Dirty or damaged air filter.

   c. Plugged or restricted carburetor jets, caused by dirt in the fuel or carburetor.

   d. Engine air leaks. The engine must be sealed, starting at the carburetor and ending at the exhaust system. Check for leaks at the exhaust pipe, spark plug, intake pipe (at the cylinder head), carburetor and air box.

   e. Incorrect float height. Remove the carburetor and check the level. The problem may be due to dirt that has entered the fuel valve seat and is preventing the fuel valve from closing.

   f. Fouled or improper heat range spark plug. Refer to Chapter Three for the correct heat range spark plug.

   g. Incorrect ignition timing (indicates a problem in the ignition system). Refer to Chapter Two and Chapter Ten.

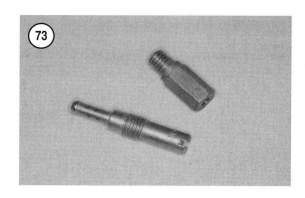

   h. Low engine compression. If the engine compression is low, check for a faulty auto-decompression system or worn or damaged top end components.

2. After using the information in **Tables 6-11** to rejet the carburetor, it should not be necessary to make additional jet changes by more than one jet size, either richer or leaner. If a larger jet change is needed, check for a problem with the engine or exhaust system. Recheck the items described in Step 1.

3. Always adjust the main jet before adjusting the jet needle. This will prevent engine damage if the new jet needle is too lean.

4. When in doubt about a main jet change, always install the next richer jet size to prevent engine damage. Only install a leaner main jet when it is determined that after test riding the motorcycle that the main jet circuit is too rich.

5. As shown in **Tables 6-11**, note how weather and altitude conditions affect the air/fuel mixture. Note the following:

   a. Cold temperatures cause a leaner mixture. Adjust the carburetor richer.

   b. Dry air (low humidity) causes a leaner mixture. Adjust the carburetor richer.

   c. Higher altitudes cause a richer mixture. Adjust the carburetor leaner.

   d. Higher humidity cause a richer mixture. Adjust the carburetor leaner.

   e. Warm ambient temperatures cause a richer mixture. Adjust the carburetor leaner.

6. Track conditions can also dictate a main jet change. Increase the main jet by one size when one or more of the following track conditions are present:

   a. The track is muddy.

   b. The track is mostly sand.

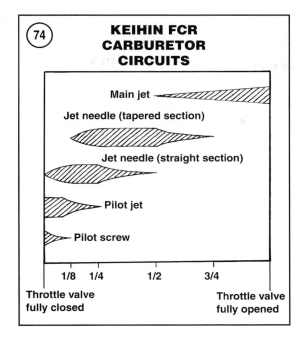

**KEIHIN FCR CARBURETOR CIRCUITS**

Main jet

Jet needle (tapered section)

Jet needle (straight section)

Pilot jet

Pilot screw

1/8    1/4        1/2        3/4

Throttle valve fully closed

Throttle valve fully opened

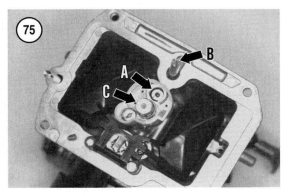

c. The track has a very long uphill section or a long straightway.

7. When in doubt about a jetting change, return the carburetor to the standard jetting and adjustment numbers and start again.

## Carburetor Jets

The main jets and pilot jets (**Figure 73**) are identified with a jet size number and are available from Honda in increments of 2, 2.5 or 3 sizes, depending on the model year. It is important to note that the numbering system used on the Honda jets does *not* match the numbering system of any other FCR flat side carburetor installed on a different manufacturer's motorcycle. When rejetting a carburetor in-

stalled on a CRF model covered in this manual, use only Honda main and pilot jets.

## Carburetor Circuits

**Figure 74** identifies the main carburetor circuits and how they overlap at different throttle valve positions. The main circuits are described in the following sections:

### Pilot jet and pilot screw

The main pilot system components are the pilot jet (A, **Figure 75**), pilot screw (B) and pilot air jet (**Figure 58**). The pilot system controls the air/fuel mixture from closed throttle to 1/4 throttle. The pilot jet draws fuel from the float bowl and mixes it with air from the pilot air jet. The atomized air/fuel mixture then passes to the pilot screw, where it is regulated and discharged into the airstream in the throat of the carburetor. Turning the pilot screw in will *lean* the mixture flow to the engine at low speeds, while turning the screw out will *richen* the flow.

The pilot jet is interchangeable with jets that provide a leaner or richer air/fuel mixture. Replacing the standard pilot jet with a larger numbered jet will make the mixture *richer*. Pilot jets with a smaller number will make the mixture *leaner*.

Note the following before adjusting the pilot system:

1. The pilot screw must be adjusted within one to three turns out from a *lightly* seated position. If the pilot screw can be adjusted within this range, the pilot jet size installed in the carburetor is correct. However, if the pilot screw requires an adjustment of less than one turn out, the next smaller pilot jet is required. If the pilot screw adjustment exceeds three turns out, the next larger pilot jet is required. See **Table 2** or **Table 4** for the standard pilot jet sizes.

2. Pilot screw adjustment is critical when attempting to adjust or improve off-idle performance. Note the following:

    a. If the engine surges when exiting a corner, the pilot screw adjustment is too lean. Turn the pilot screw out to richen the mixture.

    b. If the engine stumbles or is slow to accelerate when exiting a corner, the pilot adjustment is

9

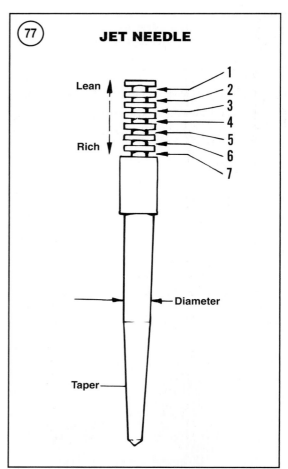

too rich. Turn the pilot screw in to lean the mixture.

### Jet needle

The jet needle is connected to the throttle valve (**Figure 76**) and controls the mixture from closed throttle to 3/4 throttle. The jet needle operates inside the needle jet, and regulates the air/fuel mixture from the jet to the carburetor throat. The jet needle used in the Keihin FCR carburetor regulates fuel by its taper, diameter and clip position (**Figure 77**). In the closed throttle position, the tapered needle shuts off flow from the needle jet. As the throttle opens, the needle allows fuel to pass by the taper, and between the straight portion of the needle and needle jet wall. The diameter of the straight section affects throttle response from closed throttle while tapering off at approximately 1/2 throttle.

The position of the needle in the jet can be adjusted by removing the needle clip and positioning it on a higher or lower groove in the needle. Raising the clip will lower the needle into the jet, creating a *lean* condition. Lowering the clip will raise the needle, creating a *rich* condition.

Adjust the needle if it is determined the engine will perform better for the loads or climate in which it is operated. Do not adjust the needle in an attempt to correct other problems that may exist with the carburetor. Engine damage can occur if riding conditions do not warrant an overly rich or lean fuel mixture.

The clip position on the standard jet needle can be changed to improve mid-range performance for most riding, weather and altitude conditions. However, when a condition occurs that requires a jet needle change, different needles are available that

provide a leaner or richer air/fuel mixture. Replacement needles all have the same starting point for the tapers. The difference in the needles is the taper angle and the diameter and length of the straight portion. See **Table 12** (CRF250R) or **Table 13** (CRF450R) for a description of the optional jet needle sizes.

### Main jet

The main jet (C, **Figure 75**) is mounted in the bottom of the needle jet and controls the mixture from approximately 1/2 to full throttle. The main jet is numbered and is interchangeable with Honda jets that will provide a leaner or richer air/fuel mixture. Replacing the standard jet with a larger numbered jet make the mixture *richer*. Jets with a smaller number will make the mixture *leaner*.

*Leak jet*

The leak jet (**Figure 59**) is mounted in the bottom of the float bowl and adjusts the flow of fuel discharged by the accelerator pump. Because the accelerator pump only operates when the throttle is opened, the leak jet adjusts the fuel mixture ratio for optimum throttle response, especially when the throttle is opened quickly. Replacing the standard leak jet with a smaller numbered jet will make the mixture *richer*. Leak jets with larger numbers will make the mixture *leaner*. Honda does not recommend or provide different size leak jets.

**Pilot Screw Adjustment**

The pilot screw is preset and routine adjustment should not be necessary unless the pilot screw is replaced or the motorcycle is operating under different temperature and altitude conditions. Refer to *Carburetor Settings* in this section for a description of the altitude and temperature charts found in **Tables 6-11**.

This procedure can be performed to adjust the pilot screw to its standard setting or to one of the adjustment settings in **Tables 6-11**.

A tachometer capable of reading rpm readings of 50 rpm or less is required to accurately adjust the pilot screw.

1. The engine must be in good running condition. Refer to *Carburetor Settings* in this section.

2A. To set the pilot screw to its standard setting, *lightly* seat the pilot screw (A, **Figure 78**), then back it out the number of turns in **Table 2** or **Table 4**.

2B. To adjust the pilot screw to a different setting, *lightly* seat the pilot screw (A, **Figure 78**), then back it out the number of turns listed under the appropriate temperature and altitude setting in **Tables 6-11**.

3. Start and allow the engine to reach operating temperature. Then ride the motorcycle for ten minutes and turn the engine off.

4. Attach a tachometer to the engine following the manufacturer's directions.

5. Start the engine and adjust the idle speed with the throttle stop screw (B, **Figure 78**) to 1600-1800 rpm.

6. Start the engine and test ride the motorcycle. If throttle response is poor and the carburetor was adjusted to its standard setting, different temperature and altitude conditions may require a different adjustment as described in Step 2B.

**Main Jet, Pilot Jet and Needle Jet Replacement and Adjustment**

This section describes how to rejet the carburetor by changing the main jet, pilot jet and/or needle jet. The main jet, pilot jet and jet needle can be replaced with the carburetor mounted on the motorcycle. Before rejetting the carburetor, note the following:

1. Read the information at the beginning of this section.

2. Record all settings/clip position of the part being removed.

3. Make sure that the pilot system is adjusted correctly before changing the main jet or jet needle.

4. Start and warm up the engine.

5. Test ride the motorcycle with the standard jetting, or make the appropriate changes specified in the tuning charts in **Tables 6-11**. During the test ride, note the throttle response and acceleration at the different throttle valve operating positions. To check the main jet, run the bike at full throttle in an open area. Shut off the engine while it is running at full throttle, then pull in the clutch and coast to a stop. If necessary, remove the spark plug and check its firing end as described in Chapter Three.

6. If a jetting change is required, perform the following steps in this section on how to change the main jet, pilot jet and the jet needle.

*Main jet and pilot jet*

1. Refer to *Carburetor Jets* in this section.

9

2. If necessary, adjust the pilot screw to either its standard setting or to one of the temperature/altitude adjustment settings listed in **Tables 6-11**. Refer to *Pilot Screw Adjustment* in this section.

3. Turn the fuel valve off and disconnect the fuel line at the fuel valve.

4. Loosen the plug (C, **Figure 78**) at the bottom of the float bowl while the carburetor is still held tightly with both clamps.

5. Loosen the carburetor hose clamps and pivot the carburetor float bowl toward the left side. Do not remove the carburetor from the intake pipe or air box boot as this allows dirt to enter the carburetor.

6. Remove the plug loosened in Step 2. Any fuel remaining in the float bowl will drain out.

7. Replace the pilot jet (A, **Figure 79**) or main jet (B) with the correct size Honda jet.

8. Install the plug and its O-ring into the bottom of the float bowl and tighten hand-tight.

9. Pivot the carburetor and center the tab on the side of the carburetor between the two tabs on the intake tube (**Figure 80**). Tighten both hose clamps securely.

10. Tighten the plug (C, **Figure 78**) securely.

11. Reconnect the fuel line at the fuel valve.

12. Turn the fuel valve on and check for leaks at the plug.

13. Start and ride the motorcycle to recheck the jetting and engine performance. Make plug readings as previously described to make sure the engine is not running lean. Rejet the pilot or main jet as required.

*Jet needle*

1. Remove the fuel tank as described in this chapter.

2. On CRF250R models, loosen the carburetor hose clamps and pivot the top of the carburetor toward the left side. Do not remove the carburetor from the intake pipe or air box boot as this allows dirt to enter the carburetor.

3A. On CRF250R models, remove the access cover and its O-ring (**Figure 81**).

3B. On CRF450R models, remove the top cover and its O-ring (**Figure 82**).

4. Loosen and remove the jet needle holder (**Figure 83**, typical).

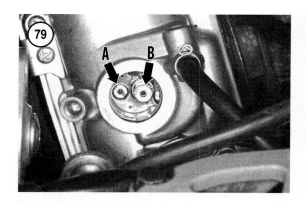

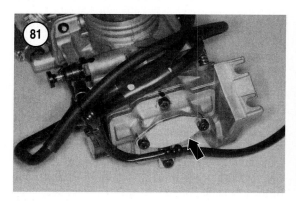

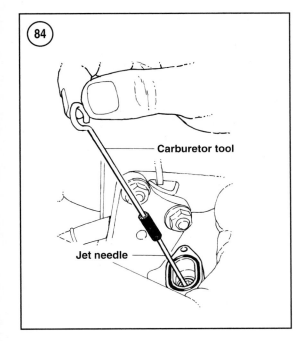

Carburetor tool

Jet needle

5A. On CRF250R models, insert the carburetor maintenance tool through the opening in the top cover and remove the jet needle (**Figure 84**).

5B. On CRF450R models, remove the jet needle through the top of the carburetor with a pair of needle nose pliers (**Figure 85**).

6. Change the standard jet needle's clip position or replace the jet needle as described under *Carburetor Circuits* in this section.

7. Reinstall the O-ring and the access cover or top cover and tighten securely.

8. On CRF250R models, pivot the carburetor and center the tab on the side of the carburetor between the two tabs on the intake tube (**Figure 80**). Tighten both hose clamps securely.

9. Install the fuel tank as described in this chapter.

10. Start and test ride the motorcycle.

## CARBURETOR ADJUSTMENT
## (CRF250X AND CRF450X)

This section describes carburetor adjustments for the CRF250X and CRF450X. Honda does not recommende different needle jet, pilot jet or main jet sizes for the carburetor installed on these models. However, except for the carburetor tuning and jet needle replacement charts listed for the CRF250R and CRF450R models, much of the information under *Carburetor Adjustment and Rejetting (CRF250R and CRF450R)* in this chapter can be used to understand the operating circuits used on the CRF250X and CRF450X carburetors.

### Pilot Screw Adjustment
### (49-State and Canada Models)

The pilot screw is preset and routine adjustment should not be necessary unless the pilot screw is replaced.

A tachometer capable of reading rpm readings of 50 rpm or less is required to accurately adjust the pilot screw.

1. The engine must be in good running condition.

*CAUTION*
*Seat the pilot screw **lightly** in Step 2 or the screw tip can break off into the pilot screw bore.*

2. To set the pilot screw to its standard setting, *lightly* seat the pilot screw (A, **Figure 86**), then back it out the number of turns in **Table 3** or **Table 5**.

9

3. Start and allow the engine to reach operating temperature. Then ride the motorcycle for ten minutes and turn the engine off.

4. Attach a tachometer to the engine following the manufacturer's directions.

5. Start the engine and adjust the idle speed with the throttle stop screw (B, **Figure 86**) to 1600-1800 rpm.

6. Start the engine and test ride the motorcycle.

### Pilot Screw Adjustment
### (Idle Drop Procedure)
### (California Models)

The pilot screw is preset and routine adjustment should not be necessary unless the pilot screw is replaced.

A tachometer that can register a change of 50 rpm or less, a pilot screw wrench and a vacuum pump are required to adjust the pilot screw.

1. The engine must be in good running condition. Refer to *Carburetor Settings* in this chapter.

> *CAUTION*
> *Seat the pilot screw **lightly** in Step 2 or the screw tip can break off into the pilot screw bore.*

2. To set the pilot screw to its standard setting, *lightly* seat the pilot screw (A, **Figure 86**), then back it out the number of turns in **Table 3** or **Table 5**.

3. Start and allow the engine to reach operating temperature. Then ride the motorcycle for ten minutes and turn the engine off.

4. Attach a tachometer to the engine following the manufacturer's directions.

5. Perform the following at the PAIR control valve (A, **Figure 87** [CRF250X] or A, **Figure 88** [CRF450X]) installed on the right side of the motorcycle:

   a. Disconnect the vacuum hose at the PAIR control valve (B, **Figure 87** or B, **Figure 88**). Plug the hose to prevent air from entering.

   b. Connect a vacuum pump to the PAIR control valve vacuum hose joint (B, **Figure 87** or B, **Figure 88**) in place of the vacuum hose.

6. Apply 56 kPa (16.5 in. Hg) of vacuum to the PAIR control valve.

7. Start the engine and turn the throttle stop screw (B, **Figure 86**) in or out to achieve an idle speed of 1600-1800 rpm.

8. Turn the pilot screw (A, **Figure 86**) in or out slowly to obtain the highest engine idle speed possible.

9. Operate the throttle slowly two or three times, then turn the throttle stop screw (B, **Figure 86**) and reset the idle speed to 1600-1800 rpm.

10. While reading the tachometer scale, turn the pilot screw in (clockwise) until the idle speed drops 50 rpm. Then turn the pilot screw 1/2 turn out (counterclockwise).

11. Turn the engine off, remove the plug from the vacuum hose and disconnect the vacuum pump. Reconnect the vacuum hose onto the PAIR control valve (B, **Figure 87** or B, **Figure 88**).

12. Start the engine and allow it to idle. Turn the throttle stop screw (B, **Figure 86**) to obtain an idle speed of 1600-1800 rpm.

13. Turn the engine off and disconnect the portable tachometer.

14. Test ride the motorcycle. Throttle response from idle should be rapid and without any hesitation.

## High Elevation Adjustment

### CRF250X

If the motorcycle is going to be ridden for any sustained period at high elevation (1500 m/500 ft.), the carburetor should be readjusted to improve performance and decrease emissions.

1. Remove the carburetor as described in this chapter.

*NOTE*
*Refer to* **Carburetor Disassembly and Reassembly** *in this chapter when replacing the main jet and removing the needle jet.*

2. Remove the float bowl and replace the standard main jet with a No. 128 Honda main jet. Reinstall the float bowl.

3. Remove the jet needle and move the clip to the No. 1 position. Refer to *Jet Needle* under *Carburetor Adjustment and Rejetting (CRF250R and CRF450R)* in this chapter.

4. Reassemble and install the carburetor onto the motorcycle as described in this chapter.

5. Start the engine and allow to idle for three minutes.

6. Turn the pilot screw (A, **Figure 86**) 1/4 out (clockwise) from the standard position.

7. Turn the throttle stop screw (B, **Figure 86**) to obtain an idle speed of 1600-1800 rpm.

8. When the motorcycle is returned to elevations below 1500 m (5000 ft.), adjust the pilot screw to its original position and reset the idle speed as described in this section.

### CRF450X

Honda does not provide a high elevation adjustment procedure for the CRF450X.

## THROTTLE POSITION SENSOR

A throttle position sensor (TPS) is installed on the carburetor to provide the ignition control module (ICM) with an electronic signal that coincides with the throttle valve position (A, **Figure 89**). This varying signal is analyzed by the ICM, along with the engine speed signal from the stator coil. The ICM then adjusts ignition timing for the immediate engine load. The TPS unit must be accurately adjusted so the signal represents the actual throttle position.

*CAUTION*
*Do not loosen the TPS sensor screws, except to adjust or replace the sensor. If the screw(s) are loosened, the TPS must be readjusted as described in this section. Failing to adjust the TPS unit will reduce engine performance.*

### Resistance Test

The carburetor does not have to be removed from the motorcycle to check the TPS resistance.

1. Remove the fuel tank as described in this chapter.

2. Disconnect the TPS connector. See **Figure 90** (CRF250R), **Figure 91** (CRF250X), **Figure 92** (CRF450R) or **Figure 93** (CRF450X).

*NOTE*
*The TPS must be at room temperature (approximately 68° F/20° C) when*

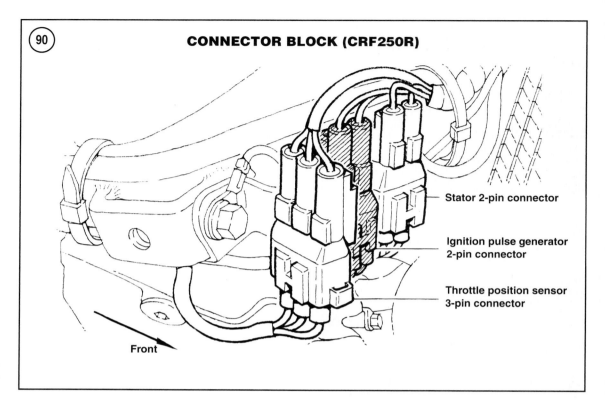

**CONNECTOR BLOCK (CRF250R)**

90

Stator 2-pin connector

Ignition pulse generator
2-pin connector

Throttle position sensor
3-pin connector

Front

*performing the tests in Step 3 and Step 4. If the engine was just turned off or if it is hot, allow the sensor to cool before testing it.*

*CAUTION*
*Do not insert the ohmmeter test leads too far into the TPS connector. Doing so may damage the waterproof material in the connector. If necessary, insert thin electrical conductors into the TPS connector, then attach the meter leads to them.*

3. Check the TPS coil resistance as follows:

   a. Connect the ohmmeter between the blue and black TPS connector terminals (**Figure 94**).

   b. The ohmmeter should read 4000-6000 ohms.

4. Check the TPS coil variable resistance as follows:

   a. Connect the ohmmeter between the yellow and black TPS terminals (**Figure 94**).

   b. Note the reading with the throttle valve fully closed.

   c. Slowly open the throttle valve and watch the resistance reading on the meter. The resistance should increase.

   d. Slowly close the throttle valve and watch the resistance reading on the meter. The resistance should decrease.

5. If the resistance is not within specifications in Step 3 or the resistance does not increase and decrease as described in Step 4, check the integrity of the wires to the sensor, and for loose or damaged connector pins. If the wiring and connector pins are good, and the tests are still incorrect, replace the TPS as described in this chapter.

6. If the TPS passes all checks, reattach the connectors and install the fuel tank.

**Throttle Position Sensor**
**Replacement and Adjustment**

1. Start the engine and adjust the idle speed as described in Chapter Three. Turn the engine off.

2. Partially remove the carburetor until the TPS unit is accessible. See *Carburetor Removal* in this chapter.

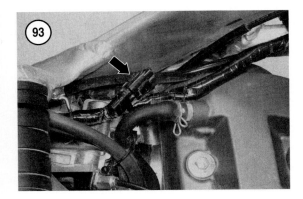

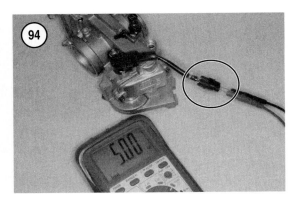

*NOTE*
*A tamper resistant T-25 bit is required to loosen and tighten the TPS Torx screw.*

3. Remove the Torx screw securing the TPS (B, **Figure 89**, typical) to the carburetor. Remove the unit.

4. Install the new TPS by aligning the tabs on the TPS with the flat side of the throttle valve shaft. Apply a medium strength threadlock onto the Torx screw threads and install the screw finger-tight.

*CAUTION*
*Do not insert the ohmmeter test leads too far into the TPS connector. Doing so may damage the waterproof material in the connector. If necessary, insert thin electrical conductors into the TPS connector, then attach the meter leads to them.*

5. Determine the TPS coil resistance as follows:
   a. Connect the ohmmeter between the blue and black TPS terminals (**Figure 94**).
   b. The ohmmeter should read 4000-6000 ohms. Record the actual reading.

6. Determine the idle speed variable coil resistance and adjust the TPS as follows:
   a. Calculate the required idle speed variable coil resistance by multiplying the actual measured coil resistance determined in Step 4 by 0.13 and 0.15. For example, if the measured coil resistance is 4000 ohms, the required variable coil resistance is 520 to 600 ohms at idle speed ($4000 \times 0.13 = 520$; $4000 \times 0.15 = 600$ ohms).
   b. Connect the ohmmeter to the yellow and black TPS connector terminals (**Figure 94**).
   c. Loosen the screw (B, **Figure 89**) and turn the TPS until the required reading determined in substep a is achieved for the throttle shaft idle speed position. Tighten the screws and recheck the measurement.

## THROTTLE CABLE REPLACEMENT

1. Remove the fuel tank as described in this chapter.

2. Note the throttle cable routing from the handlebar to the carburetor. Also note the position of any cable clamps and guides.

9

3. Partially remove the carburetor to access the throttle cables, then disconnect the throttle cables as described under *Carburetor Removal* in this chapter. See **Figure 95** (CRF250R and CRF250X) or **Figure 96** (CRF450R and CRF450X).

4. Disconnect the throttle cables at the throttle housing as described in Chapter Thirteen. See **Figure 97**, typical.

5. Remove the throttle cables.

6. Route the new cables from the throttle control to the carburetor.

7. Lubricate the ends of the cable with lithium grease, then insert the ends into the throttle control.

8. Reconnect the throttle cables and secure the throttle assembly to the handlebar as described in Chapter Thirteen.

9. Reconnect the throttle cables at the carburetor and install the carburetor as described in this chapter.

10. Adjust the throttle cables as described in Chapter Three.

11. Install the fuel tank as described in this chapter.

*WARNING*
*Do not ride the motorcycle until the throttle cables are installed and adjusted properly and the throttle opens and returns smoothly.*

## HOT START CABLE REPLACEMENT

1. Remove the fuel tank as described in this chapter.

*NOTE*
*Before removing the cable, make a drawing of the cable routing through the frame. Replace the cable exactly as it was, avoiding any sharp turns.*

2. Disconnect the hot start cable (**Figure 98**) at the handlebar.

3. Partially remove the carburetor to access the end of the cable. Refer to *Carburetor Removal* in this chapter.

4. Loosen the hot start valve nut (**Figure 99**) and remove the hot start valve (**Figure 100**) from the carburetor. Disconnect the hot start valve and spring from the cable and install them on the new cable.

5. Pull the cable out of any retaining clips on the frame.

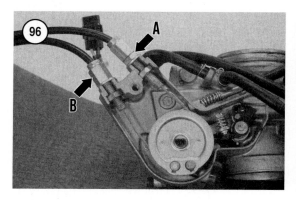

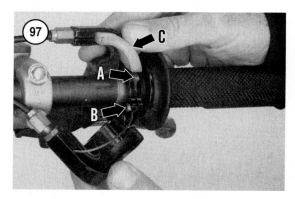

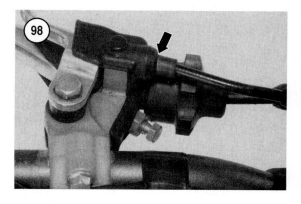

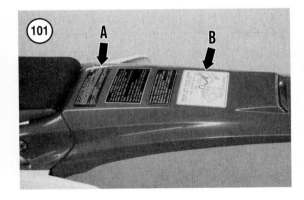

6. Remove the cable.

7. Before installing the new cable, service it as follows:

    a. Lubricate the cable as described in Chapter Three. Wipe off any residue from the lower end of the cable.

    b. Install the spring and the hot start valve onto the lower end of the new cable (**Figure 100**).

    c. Lightly lubricate the upper cable end with lithium grease.

8. Install the new hot start cable by reversing these removal steps. Make sure the cable is correctly routed with no sharp turns.

9. Adjust the hot start cable as described in Chapter Three.

### EMISSION CONTROL LABELS (CRF250X AND CRF450X CALIFORNIA MODELS)

Emission control labels are attached to the rear fender. The vehicle emission control information label (A, **Figure 101**) lists tune-up information. The vacuum hose routing diagram label (B, **Figure 101**) shows a schematic of the emission control system. This information is useful when identifying hoses used in the emission control system.

### CRANKCASE BREATHER SYSTEM (CRF250X AND CRF450X CALIFORNIA MODELS)

The engine is equipped with a closed crankcase breather system (**Figure 102**). The system draws blow-by gasses from the crankcase and recirculates them into the combustion chamber to be burned.

Liquid residues collect in the crankcase breather drain tube. These must be emptied at periodic intervals. See *Crankcase Breather Inspection* in Chapter Three for service intervals and procedures.

### PULSE SECONDARY AIR INJECTION SYSTEM (CRF250X AND CRF450X CALIFORNIA MODELS)

The pulse secondary air injection (PAIR) control valve supplies filtered air into the exhaust gasses in the exhaust port (**Figure 103**). The introduction of air raises the exhaust temperature, which consumes some of the unburned fuel in the exhaust and changes most of the hydrocarbons and carbon monoxide into carbon dioxide and water vapor, which lowers emission output. A reed valve installed inside the PAIR control valve prevents a reverse flow of air though the system during engine deceleration, thus preventing backfiring or afterburn in the exhaust system.

No adjustments are provided for or required for the secondary air supply system. However, inspect the system at the intervals listed in Chapter Three.

9

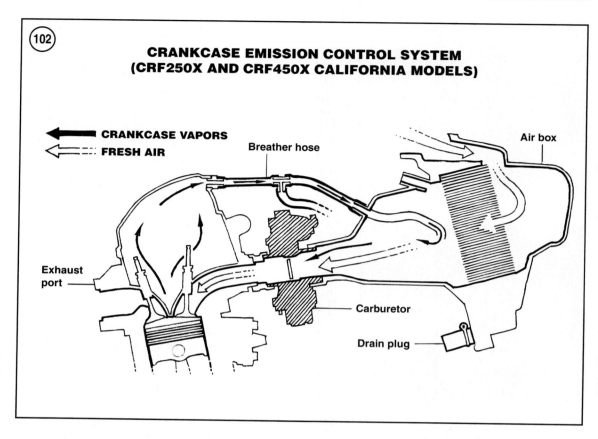

**102**

## CRANKCASE EMISSION CONTROL SYSTEM
### (CRF250X AND CRF450X CALIFORNIA MODELS)

➡ **CRANKCASE VAPORS**

⇨ **FRESH AIR**

Breather hose

Air box

Exhaust port

Carburetor

Drain plug

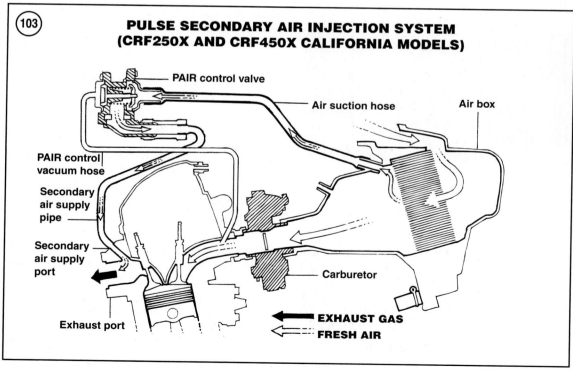

**103**

## PULSE SECONDARY AIR INJECTION SYSTEM
### (CRF250X AND CRF450X CALIFORNIA MODELS)

PAIR control valve

Air suction hose

Air box

PAIR control vacuum hose

Secondary air supply pipe

Secondary air supply port

Carburetor

Exhaust port

➡ **EXHAUST GAS**

⇨ **FRESH AIR**

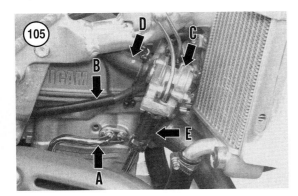

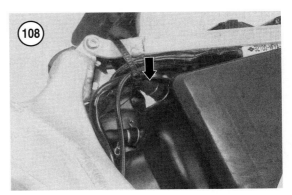

**System Inspection**

1. Remove the bolt and the secondary air supply pipe at the cylinder head. See **Figure 104** (CRF250X) or A, **Figure 105** (CRF450X). Remove any carbon deposits from the secondary air intake port. Replace the O-ring on the end of the pipe if leaking or damaged. Reinstall the pipe and O-ring and tighten the mounting bolt securely.

2. Start and warm up the engine to normal operating temperature, then turn it off.

3. Remove the seat (Chapter Sixteen).

4. Disconnect the PAIR control vacuum hose and plug the end of the hose. See A, **Figure 106** (CRF250X) or B, **Figure 105** (CRF450X).

5. Connect a vacuum pump to the PAIR control valve where the vacuum hose was disconnected in Step 4. See B, **Figure 106** (CRF250X) or C, **Figure 105** (CRF450X).

6. Disconnect the air suction hose at the air box. See **Figure 107** (CRF250X) or **Figure 108** (CRF450X).

7. Start the engine and open the throttle slightly. Place a thumb across the air suction hose end and check that air is being sucked through the hose. If not, turn the engine off and disconnect the opposite end of the hose at the PAIR control valve. See C, **Figure 106** or D, **Figure 105** (CRF450X). Check the hose for blockage. Reconnect the hose and repeat the test. If there is still no suction, remove the PAIR control valve and inspect the reed valve as described in this section. If there is suction at the hose, reconnect the hose at the PAIR control valve and continue with Step 8.

8. Start the engine and slowly apply vacuum to the PAIR control valve until the gauge on the vacuum pump reads 56 kPa (16.5 in. Hg). Check that the air suction hose stops drawing air and the amount of

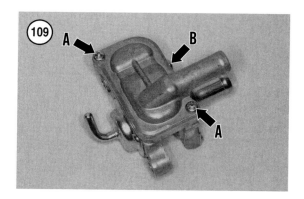

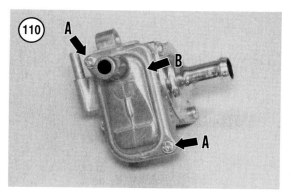

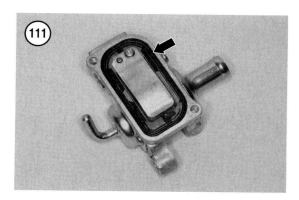

vacuum shown on the gauge is maintained. Note the following:

    a. If the test is correct, the PAIR control valve is in good condition.

    b. If air is still being drawn into the air suction hose and/or the specified amount of vacuum does not hold, replace the PAIR control valve as described in this section.

9. Turn the engine off.

10. Disconnect the vacuum pump. Then remove the plug from the end of the PAIR control vacuum hose and reconnect it at the PAIR control valve. See A, **Figure 106** (CRF250X) or B, **Figure 105** (CRF450X).

11. Reconnect the air suction hose at the air box. See **Figure 107** (CRF250X) or **Figure 108** (CRF450X).

12. Reinstall the seat (Chapter Sixteen).

### PAIR Control Valve
### Removal/Installation

#### *CRF250X*

1. Remove the right radiator shroud (Chapter Sixteen).

2. Disconnect the following hoses at the PAIR control valve:

    a. Vacuum hose (A, **Figure 106**).

    b. Air suction hose (C, **Figure 106**).

    c. Air supply hose (D, **Figure 106**).

3. Remove the bolts, nuts and the PAIR control valve (E, **Figure 106**).

4. Installation is the reverse of removal.

#### *CRF450X*

1. Remove the right radiator shroud (Chapter Sixteen).

2. Disconnect the following hoses at the PAIR control valve:

    a. Vacuum hose (B, **Figure 105**).

    b. Air suction hose (D, **Figure 105**).

    c. Air supply hose (E, **Figure 105**).

3. Remove the bolts, nuts and the PAIR control valve (C, **Figure 105**).

4. Installation is the reverse of removal.

### PAIR Check Valve
### Removal/Inspection/Installation

1. Remove the PAIR control valve as described in this section.

2. Remove the screws and the PAIR reed valve cover. See A and B, **Figure 109** (CRF250X) or A and B, **Figure 110** (CRF450X).

3. Remove the reed valve. See **Figure 111** (CRF250X) or **Figure 112** (CRF450X).

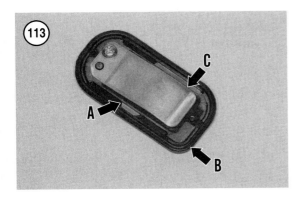

4. Check the reed valve assembly and replace if any of the following conditions are present:

*NOTE*
*The reed valve must not be serviced or disassembled. Do not try to bend the stopper. If any part of the valve is defective, replace the PAIR control valve as an assembly.*

a. Damaged reed valve (A, **Figure 113**, typical). Check for cracks and splitting.

b. Clearance between the reed valve and its seat.

c. Check the reed valve seat (B, **Figure 113**, typical) for cracks, separation and other damage.

d. Loose or damaged stopper (C, **Figure 113**, typical).

e. If any part of the reed valve is damaged, replace the PAIR reed valve assembly. The reed valve is not available separately.

5. Check inside the PAIR reed valve housing for excessive carbon buildup or other damage.

6. Installation is the reverse of these steps.

**Air Supply Pipe**
**Removal/Inspection/Installation**

1A. On CRF250X models, remove both radiator shrouds (Chapter Sixteen).

1B. On CRF450X models, remove the right radiator shroud (Chapter Sixteen).

2. Disconnect the air supply hose at the PAIR control valve. See D, **Figure 106** (CRF250X) or E, **Figure 105** (CRF450X).

3. Remove the bolt and the secondary air supply pipe at the cylinder head. See **Figure 104** (CRF250X) or A, **Figure 105** (CRF450X).

4. Remove the air supply pipe assembly.

5. Inspect the pipe assembly for any blockage or other damage. Check the metal pipe for cracks or creases. Inspect the rubber hose for softness, cracks and other damage. Replace damaged parts as required.

6. Replace the O-ring on the end of the pipe if leaking or damaged.

7. Installation is the reverse of these steps. On CRF250X models, install the air supply pipe so that the clutch cable is routed behind it (**Figure 114**).

**Tables 1-14 are on the following pages.**

## Table 1 FUEL TANK CAPACITY

| Model | Liter | U.S. gal. |
|---|---|---|
| CRF250R | 7.3 | 1.93 |
| CRF250X | | |
| Capacity | 8.3 | 2.20 |
| Reserve | 1.5 | 0.40 |
| CRF450R | | |
| 2002-2004 | 7.4 | 1.95 |
| 2005 | 7.2 | 1.90 |
| CRF450X | | |
| Capacity | 8.6 | 2.27 |
| Reserve | 1.4 | 0.37 |

## Table 2 CARBURETOR SPECIFICATIONS (CRF250R)

| | |
|---|---|
| Manufacturer/type | Keihin/FCR-MX37 |
| I.D. mark | |
| 2004 | FCR01A |
| 2005 | FCR01B |
| Float level | 8.0 mm (0.31 in.) |
| Idle speed | 1600-1800 rpm |
| Jet needle/clip position | |
| 2004 | NCYR/4th |
| 2005 | NCYQ/3rd |
| Main jet | |
| 2004 | 160 |
| 2005 | 172 |
| Pilot jet | |
| 2004 | 40 |
| 2005 | 42 |
| Pilot screw initial opening | |
| 2004 | 2 1/4 turns out |
| 2005 | 1 3/4 turns out |
| Throttle position sensor resistance* | 4000-6000 ohms |

*Measurement taken at 20° C (68° F).

## Table 3 CARBURETOR SPECIFICATIONS (CRF250X)

| | |
|---|---|
| Manufacturer/type | Keihin/FCR-MX37 |
| I.D. mark | |
| 2004 | |
| 49-state and Canada | FCR02A |
| California | FCR03A |
| 2005 | FCR02A |
| Float level | 8.0 mm (0.31 in.) |
| Idle speed | 1600-1800 rpm |
| Jet needle/clip position | |
| 2004 | |
| 49-state and Canada | NCVT/3rd |
| California | NCYU/2nd |
| 2005 | |
| 49-state and Canada | NCVT/3rd |
| California | NCYV/2nd |
| Main jet | 130 |

(continued)

### Table 3 CARBURETOR SPECIFICATIONS (CRF250X) (continued)

| | |
|---|---|
| Pilot jet | 40 |
| Pilot screw initial opening | |
| 2004-on | |
| 49-state and Canada | 2 1/4 turns out |
| California | 2 turns out |
| Throttle position sensor | |
| resistance* | 4000-6000 ohms |

*Measurement taken at 20° C (68° F).

### Table 4 CARBURETOR SPECIFICATIONS (CRF450R)

| | |
|---|---|
| Manufacturer/type | Keihin/FCR-MX40 |
| I.D. mark | |
| 2002 | FCR00A |
| 2003 | FCR00B |
| 2004 | FCR00C |
| 2005 | FCR00D |
| Float height | 8.0 mm (0.31 in.) |
| Idle speed | 1600-1800 rpm |
| Jet needle/clip position | |
| 2002 | OBEKR/4th |
| 2003 | OBELR/5th |
| 2004 | NCYR/4th |
| 2005 | NGGQ/4th |
| Main jet | |
| 2002 | 175 |
| 2003 | 170 |
| 2004 | 170 |
| 2005 | 168 |
| Pilot jet | |
| 2002 | 45 |
| 2003-on | 42 |
| Pilot screw initial opening | |
| 2002 | 1 1/4 turns out |
| 2003-2004 | 1 1/2 turns out |
| 2005 | 1 7/8 turns out |
| Throttle position sensor resistance* | 4000-6000 ohms |

*Measurement taken at 20° C (68° F).

### Table 5 CARBURETOR SPECIFICATIONS (CRF450X)

| | |
|---|---|
| Manufacturer | Keihin |
| Venturi diameter | 40 mm (1.6 in.) |
| I.D. mark | FCR04A |
| Float height | 8.0 mm (0.31 in.) |
| Idle speed | 1600-1800 rpm |
| Jet needle/clip position | NCVU/2nd |
| Main jet | 142 |
| Pilot jet | 45 |
| Pilot screw initial opening | 1 1/4 turns out |
| Throttle position sensor resistance* | 4000-6000 ohms |

*Measurement taken at 20° C (68° F).

9

## Table 6 CARBURETOR TUNING SPECIFICATIONS (2004 CRF250R)[1]

| | | -21°↔0° F / 30°↔17° C | -1°↔20° F / -18°↔-6° C | 19°↔40° F / -7°↔5° C | 39°↔60° F / -4°↔16° C | 59°↔80° F / 15°↔27° C | 79°↔100° F / 26°↔38° C | 99°↔120° F / 37°↔49° C |
|---|---|---|---|---|---|---|---|---|
| 10,000 ft. ↑ 7500 ft. | Pilot screw: Pilot jet: Jet needle: Main jet: | 2 1/4 40 NCYR/4th 160 | 2 1/4 40 NCYR/4th 158 | 2 40 NCYR/3rd 158 | 2 40 NCYR/3rd 155 | 2 40 NCYR/3rd 155 | 1 3/4 40 NCYR/3rd 152 | 1 3/4 40 NCYR/3rd 152 |
| 7499 ft. ↑ 5000 ft. | Pilot screw: Pilot jet: Jet needle: Main jet: | 2 1/4 40 NCYR/4th 162 | 2 1/4 40 NCYR/4th 160 | 2 1/4 40 NCYR/4th 158 | 2 40 NCYR/3rd 158 | 2 40 NCYR/3rd 155 | 2 40 NCYR/3rd 155 | 2 40 NCYR/3rd 152 |
| 4999 ft. ↑ 2500 ft. | Pilot screw: Pilot jet: Jet needle: Main jet: | 2 1/2 40 NCYR/4th 162 | 2 1/4 40 NCYR/4th 162 | 2 1/4 40 NCYR/4th 160 | 2 1/4 40 NCYR/4th 158 | 2 40 NCYR/3rd 158 | 2 40 NCYR/3rd 155 | 2 40 NCYR/3rd 155 |
| 2499 ft. ↑ 1000 ft. | Pilot screw: Pilot jet: Jet needle: Main jet: | 2 1/2 40 NCYR/5th 165 | 2 1/2 40 NCYR/4th 162 | 2 1/4 40 NCYR/4th 162 | 2 1/4 40 NCYR/4th 160 | 2 1/4 40 NCYR/4th 158 | 2 40 NCYR/3rd 158 | 2 40 NCYR/3rd 155 |
| 999 ft. ↑ Sea level | Pilot screw: Pilot jet: Jet needle: Main jet: | 2 1/2 40 NCYR/5th 165 | 2 1/2 40 NCYR/5th 165 | 2 1/2 40 NCYR/4th 162 | 2 1/4 40 NCYR/4th 162 | *2 1/4*[2] *40* *NCYR/4th* *160* | 2 1/4 40 NCYR/4th 158 | 2 40 NCYR/3rd 158 |

1. See text for information on how to use table and tuning for special conditions.
2. Original equipment carburetor settings italicized.

## Table 7 CARBURETOR TUNING SPECIFICATIONS (2005 CRF250R)[1]

| | | -21°↔0° F / 30°↔17° C | -1°↔20° F / -18°↔-6° C | 19°↔40° F / -7°↔5° C | 39°↔60° F / -4°↔16° C | 59°↔80° F / 15°↔27° C | 79°↔100° F / 26°↔38° C | 99°↔120° F / 37°↔49° C |
|---|---|---|---|---|---|---|---|---|
| 10,000 ft. ↑ 7500 ft. | Pilot screw: Pilot jet: Jet needle: Main jet: | 1 3/4 42 NCYQ/3rd 172 | 1 3/4 42 NCYQ/3rd 170 | 1 1/2 42 NCYQ/2nd 170 | 1 1/2 42 NCYQ/2nd 168 | 1 1/2 42 NCYQ/2nd 168 | 1 1/4 42 NCYQ/2nd 165 | 1 1/4 42 NCYQ/2nd 165 |
| 7499 ft. ↑ 5000 ft. | Pilot screw: Pilot jet: Jet needle: Main jet: | 1 3/4 42 NCYQ/3rd 175 | 1 3/4 42 NCYQ/3rd 172 | 1 3/4 42 NCYQ/3rd 170 | 1 1/2 42 NCYQ/2nd 170 | 1 1/2 42 NCYQ/2nd 168 | 1 1/2 42 NCYQ/2nd 168 | 1 1/4 42 NCYQ/2nd 165 |
| 4999 ft. ↑ 2500 ft. | Pilot screw: Pilot jet: Jet needle: Main jet: | 2.0 42 NCYQ/4th 175 | 1 3/4 42 NCYQ/3rd 175 | 1 3/4 42 NCYQ/3rd 172 | 1 3/4 42 NCYQ/3rd 170 | 1 1/2 42 NCYQ/2nd 170 | 1 1/2 42 NCYQ/2nd 168 | 1 1/2 42 NCYQ/2nd 168 |
| 2499 ft. ↑ 1000 ft. | Pilot screw: Pilot jet: Jet needle: Main jet: | 2.0 42 NCYQ/4th 178 | 2.0 42 NCYQ/4th 175 | 1 3/4 42 NCYQ/3rd 175 | 1 3/4 42 NCYQ/3rd 172 | 1 3/4 42 NCYQ/3rd 170 | 1 1/2 42 NCYQ/2nd 170 | 1 1/2 42 NCYQ/2nd 168 |
| 999 ft. ↑ Sea level | Pilot screw: Pilot jet: Jet needle: Main jet: | 2.0 42 NCYQ/4th 178 | 2.0 42 NCYQ/4th 178 | 2.0 42 NCYQ/4th 175 | 1 3/4 42 NCYQ/3rd 172 | *1 3/4*[2] *42* *NCYQ/3rd* *172* | 1 3/4 42 NCYQ/3rd 170 | 1 1/2 42 NCYQ/2nd 170 |

1. See text for information on how to use table and tuning for special conditions.
2. Original equipment carburetor settings italicized.

## Table 8 CARBURETOR TUNING SPECIFICATIONS (2002 CRF450R)[1]

| | | -21°↔0° F | -1°↔20° F | 19°↔40° F | 39°↔60° F | 59°↔80° F | 79°↔100° F | 99°↔120° F |
| --- | --- | --- | --- | --- | --- | --- | --- | --- |
| | | 30°↔17° C | -18°↔-6° C | -7°↔5° C | -4°↔16° C | 15°↔27° C | 26°↔38° C | 37°↔49° C |
| 10,000 ft. ↑ 7500 ft. | Pilot screw: Pilot jet: Jet needle: Main jet: | 1 1/4 45 OBEKR/4th 175 | 1 1/4 45 OBEKR/4th 172 | 1 45 OBEKR/3rd 172 | 1 42 OBEKR/3rd 170 | 3/4 42 OBEKR/3rd 170 | 3/4 42 OBEKR/3rd 168 | 3/4 40 OBEKR/3rd 168 |
| 7499 ft. ↑ 5000 ft. | Pilot screw: Pilot jet: Jet needle: Main jet: | 1 1/4 45 OBEKR/4th 178 | 1 1/4 45 OBEKR/4th 175 | 1 1/4 45 OBEKR/4th 172 | 1 45 OBEKR/3rd 172 | 1 42 OBEKR/3rd 170 | 3/4 42 OBEKR/3rd 170 | 3/4 42 OBEKR/3rd 168 |
| 4999 ft. ↑ 2500 ft. | Pilot screw: Pilot jet: Jet needle: Main jet: | 1 1/2 45 OBEKR/5th 178 | 1 1/4 45 OBEKR/4th 178 | 1 1/4 45 OBEKR/4th 175 | 1 1/4 45 OBEKR/4th 172 | 1 45 OBEKR/3rd 172 | 1 42 OBEKR/3rd 170 | 3/4 42 OBEKR/3rd 170 |
| 2499 ft. ↑ 1000 ft. | Pilot screw: Pilot jet: Jet needle: Main jet: | 1 1/2 48 OBEKR/5th 180 | 1 1/2 45 OBEKR/5th 178 | 1 1/4 45 OBEKR/4th 178 | 1 1/4 45 OBEKR/4th 175 | 1 1/4 45 OBEKR/4th 172 | 1 45 OBEKR/3rd 172 | 1 42 OBEKR/3rd 170 |
| 999 ft. ↑ Sea level | Pilot screw: Pilot jet: Jet needle: Main jet: | 1 3/4 48 OBEKR/5th 180 | 1 1/2 48 OBEKR/5th 180 | 1 1/2 45 OBEKR/5th 178 | 1 1/4 45 OBEKR/4th 178 | 1 1/4[2] 45 OBEKR/4th 175 | 1 1/4 45 OBEKR/4th 172 | 1 45 OBEKR/3rd 172 |

1. See text for information on how to use table and tuning for special conditions.
2. Original equipment carburetor settings italicized.

9

## Table 9 CARBURETOR TUNING SPECIFICATIONS (2003 CRF450R)[1]

| | | -21°↔0° F | -1°↔20° F | 19°↔40° F | 39°↔60° F | 59°↔80° F | 79°↔100° F | 99°↔120° F |
| --- | --- | --- | --- | --- | --- | --- | --- | --- |
| | | 30°↔17° C | -18°↔-6° C | -7°↔5° C | -4°↔16° C | 15°↔27° C | 26°↔38° C | 37°↔49° C |
| 10,000 ft. ↑ 7500 ft. | Pilot screw: Pilot jet: Jet needle: Main jet: | 1 1/2 42 OBELR/5th 170 | 1 1/2 42 OBELR/5th 168 | 1 1/4 42 OBELR/4th 168 | 1 1/4 42 OBELR/4th 165 | 1 1/4 40 OBELR/4th 165 | 1 40 OBELR/4th 162 | 1 40 OBELR/4th 162 |
| 7499 ft. ↑ 5000 ft. | Pilot screw: Pilot jet: Jet needle: Main jet: | 1 1/2 42 OBELR/5th 172 | 1 1/2 42 OBELR/5th 170 | 1 1/2 42 OBELR/5th 168 | 1 1/4 42 OBELR/4th 168 | 1 1/4 42 OBELR/4th 165 | 1 1/4 40 OBELR/4th 165 | 1 40 OBELR/4th 162 |
| 4999 ft. ↑ 2500 ft. | Pilot screw: Pilot jet: Jet needle: Main jet: | 1 3/4 42 OBELR/6th 172 | 1 1/2 42 OBELR/5th 172 | 1 1/2 42 OBELR/5th 170 | 1 1/2 42 OBELR/5th 168 | 1 1/4 42 OBELR/4th 168 | 1 1/4 42 OBELR/4th 165 | 1 1/4 42 OBELR/4th 165 |
| 2499 ft. ↑ 1000 ft. | Pilot screw: Pilot jet: Jet needle: Main jet: | 1 3/4 45 OBELR/6th 175 | 1 3/4 42 OBELR/6th 172 | 1 1/2 42 OBELR/5th 172 | 1 1/2 42 OBELR/5th 170 | 1 1/2 42 OBELR/5th 168 | 1 1/4 42 OBELR/4th 168 | 1 1/4 42 OBELR/4th 165 |
| 999 ft. ↑ Sea level | Pilot screw: Pilot jet: Jet needle: Main jet: | 1 3/4 45 OBELR/6th 175 | 1 3/4 45 OBELR/6th 175 | 1 3/4 42 OBELR/6th 172 | 1 1/2 42 OBELR/5th 172 | 1 1/2[2] 42 OBELR/5th 170 | 1 1/2 42 OBELR/5th 168 | 1 1/4 42 OBELR/4th 168 |

1. See text for information on how to use table and tuning for special conditions.
2. Original equipment carburetor settings italicized.

## Table 10 CARBURETOR TUNING SPECIFICATIONS (2004 CRF450R)[1]

| | | -21°↔0° F / 30°↔17° C | -1°↔20° F / -18°↔-6° C | 19°↔40° F / -7°↔5° C | 39°↔60° F / -4°↔16° C | 59°↔80° F / 15°↔27° C | 79°↔100° F / 26°↔38° C | 99°↔120° F / 37°↔49° C |
|---|---|---|---|---|---|---|---|---|
| 10,000 ft. ↑ 7500 ft. | Pilot screw:<br>Pilot jet:<br>Jet needle:<br>Main jet: | 1 1/2<br>42<br>NCYR/4th<br>165 | 1 1/2<br>42<br>NCYR/4th<br>162 | 1 1/4<br>43<br>NCYR/3rd<br>162 | 1 1/4<br>42<br>NCYR/3rd<br>160 | 1 1/4<br>40<br>NCYR/3rd<br>160 | 1<br>40<br>NCYR/3rd<br>158 | 1<br>40<br>NCYR/3rd<br>158 |
| 7499 ft. ↑ 5000 ft. | Pilot screw:<br>Pilot jet:<br>Jet needle:<br>Main jet: | 1 1/2<br>42<br>NCYR/4th<br>168 | 1 1/2<br>42<br>NCYR/4th<br>165 | 1 1/2<br>42<br>NCYR/4th<br>162 | 1 1/4<br>42<br>NCYR/3rd<br>162 | 1 1/4<br>42<br>NCYR/3rd<br>160 | 1 1/4<br>40<br>NCYR/3rd<br>160 | 1<br>40<br>NCYR/3rd<br>158 |
| 4999 ft. ↑ 2500 ft. | Pilot screw:<br>Pilot jet:<br>Jet needle:<br>Main jet: | 1 3/4<br>42<br>NCYR/5th<br>168 | 1 1/2<br>42<br>NCYR/4th<br>168 | 1 1/2<br>42<br>NCYR/4th<br>165 | 1 1/2<br>42<br>NCYR/4th<br>162 | 1 1/4<br>42<br>NCYR/3rd<br>162 | 1 1/4<br>42<br>NCYR/3rd<br>160 | 1 1/4<br>42<br>NCYR/3rd<br>160 |
| 2499 ft. ↑ 1000 ft. | Pilot screw:<br>Pilot jet:<br>Jet needle:<br>Main jet: | 1 3/4<br>45<br>NCYR/5th<br>170 | 1 3/4<br>42<br>NCYR/5th<br>168 | 1 1/2<br>42<br>NCYR/4th<br>168 | 1 1/2<br>42<br>NCYR/4th<br>165 | 1 1/2<br>42<br>NCYR/4th<br>162 | 1 1/4<br>42<br>NCYR/3rd<br>162 | 1 1/4<br>42<br>NCYR/3rd<br>160 |
| 999 ft. ↑ Sea level | Pilot screw:<br>Pilot jet:<br>Jet needle:<br>Main jet: | 1 3/4<br>45<br>NCYR/5th<br>170 | 1 3/4<br>45<br>NCYR/5th<br>170 | 1 3/4<br>42<br>NCYR/5th<br>168 | 1 1/2<br>42<br>NCYR/4th<br>168 | *1 3/8[2]<br>42<br>NCYR/4th<br>165* | 1 1/2<br>42<br>NCYR/4th<br>162 | 1 1/4<br>42<br>NCYR/3rd<br>162 |

1. See text for information on how to use table and tuning for special conditions.
2. Original equipment carburetor settings italicized.

## Table 11 CARBURETOR TUNING SPECIFICATIONS (2005 CRF450R)[1]

| | | -21°↔0° F / 30°↔17° C | -1°↔20° F / -18°↔-6° C | 19°↔40° F / -7°↔5° C | 39°↔60° F / -4°↔16° C | 59°↔80° F / 15°↔27° C | 79°↔100° F / 26°↔38° C | 99°↔120° F / 37°↔49° C |
|---|---|---|---|---|---|---|---|---|
| 10,000 ft. ↑ 7500 ft. | Pilot screw:<br>Pilot jet:<br>Jet needle:<br>Main jet: | 1 7/8<br>42<br>NGGQ/4th<br>168 | 1 7/8<br>42<br>NGGQ/4th<br>165 | 1 5/8<br>42<br>NGGQ/3rd<br>165 | 1 5/8<br>42<br>NGGQ/3rd<br>162 | 1 5/8<br>40<br>NGGQ/3rd<br>160 | 1 3/8<br>40<br>NGGQ/3rd<br>160 | 1 3/8<br>40<br>NGGQ/3rd<br>160 |
| 7499 ft. ↑ 5000 ft. | Pilot screw:<br>Pilot jet:<br>Jet needle:<br>Main jet: | 1 7/8<br>42<br>NGGQ/4th<br>170 | 1 7/8<br>42<br>NGGQ/4th<br>168 | 1 7/8<br>42<br>NGGQ/4th<br>165 | 1 5/8<br>42<br>NGGQ/3rd<br>165 | 1 5/8<br>42<br>NGGQ/3rd<br>162 | 1 5/8<br>40<br>NGGQ/3rd<br>162 | 1 3/8<br>40<br>NGGQ/3rd<br>160 |
| 4999 ft. ↑ 2500 ft. | Pilot screw:<br>Pilot jet:<br>Jet needle:<br>Main jet: | 2 1/8<br>42<br>NGGQ/5th<br>170 | 1 7/8<br>42<br>NGGQ/4th<br>170 | 1 7/8<br>42<br>NGGQ/4th<br>168 | 1 7/8<br>42<br>NGGQ/4th<br>165 | 1 5/8<br>42<br>NGGQ/3rd<br>165 | 1 5/8<br>42<br>NGGQ/3rd<br>162 | 1 5/8<br>42<br>NGGQ/3rd<br>162 |
| 2499 ft. ↑ 1000 ft. | Pilot screw:<br>Pilot jet:<br>Jet needle:<br>Main jet: | 2 1/8<br>45<br>NGGQ/5th<br>172 | 2 1/8<br>42<br>NGGQ/5th<br>170 | 1 7/8<br>42<br>NGGQ/4th<br>170 | 1 7/8<br>42<br>NGGQ/4th<br>168 | 1 7/8<br>42<br>NGGQ/4th<br>165 | 1 5/8<br>42<br>NGGQ/3rd<br>165 | 1 5/8<br>42<br>NGGQ/3rd<br>162 |
| 999 ft. ↑ Sea level | Pilot screw:<br>Pilot jet:<br>Jet needle:<br>Main jet: | 2 1/8<br>45<br>NGGQ/5th<br>172 | 2 1/8<br>45<br>NGGQ/5th<br>172 | 2 1/8<br>45<br>NGGQ/5th<br>170 | 1 7/8<br>45<br>NGGQ/5th<br>172 | *1 7/8[2]<br>45<br>NGGQ/5th<br>168* | 1 7/8<br>45<br>NGGQ/5th<br>165 | 1 5/8<br>45<br>NGGQ/3rd<br>172 |

1. See text for information on how to use table and tuning for special conditions.
2. Original equipment carburetor settings italicized.

### Table 12 OPTIONAL JET NEEDLES (CRF250R)

| Year/rich-lean | Standard series* jet needle diameter | Leaner series* jet needle diameter |
|---|---|---|
| | 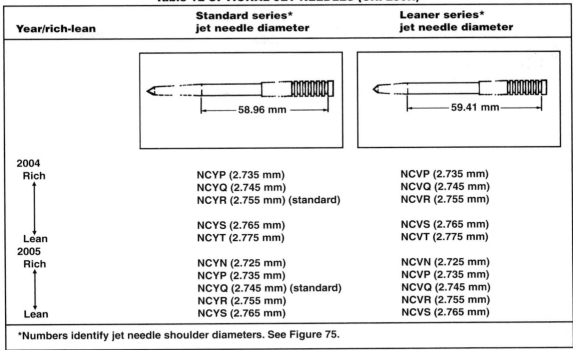 | |
| **2004** Rich ↑ ↓ Lean | NCYP (2.735 mm)<br>NCYQ (2.745 mm)<br>NCYR (2.755 mm) (standard)<br><br>NCYS (2.765 mm)<br>NCYT (2.775 mm) | NCVP (2.735 mm)<br>NCVQ (2.745 mm)<br>NCVR (2.755 mm)<br><br>NCVS (2.765 mm)<br>NCVT (2.775 mm) |
| **2005** Rich ↑ ↓ Lean | NCYN (2.725 mm)<br>NCYP (2.735 mm)<br>NCYQ (2.745 mm) (standard)<br>NCYR (2.755 mm)<br>NCYS (2.765 mm) | NCVN (2.725 mm)<br>NCVP (2.735 mm)<br>NCVQ (2.745 mm)<br>NCVR (2.755 mm)<br>NCVS (2.765 mm) |

*Numbers identify jet needle shoulder diameters. See Figure 75.

### Table 13 OPTIONAL JET NEEDLES (CRF450R)

| Year/rich-lean | Standard series* jet needle diameter | Leaner series* jet needle diameter |
|---|---|---|
| **2002** | 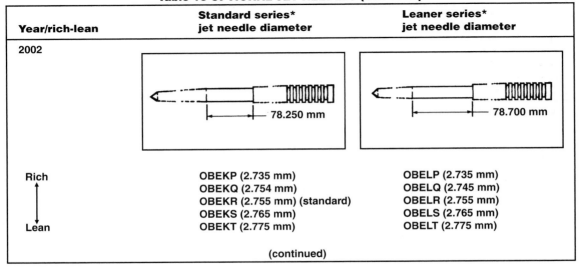 | |
| Rich ↑ ↓ Lean | OBEKP (2.735 mm)<br>OBEKQ (2.754 mm)<br>OBEKR (2.755 mm) (standard)<br>OBEKS (2.765 mm)<br>OBEKT (2.775 mm) | OBELP (2.735 mm)<br>OBELQ (2.745 mm)<br>OBELR (2.755 mm)<br>OBELS (2.765 mm)<br>OBELT (2.775 mm) |

(continued)

**Table 13 OPTIONAL JET NEEDLES (CRF450R) (continued)**

| Year/rich-lean | Standard series*<br>jet needle diameter | Leaner series*<br>jet needle diameter |
|---|---|---|
| 2003 | <br>78.700 mm | <br>78.250 mm |
| Rich ↑<br><br>Lean ↓ | OBELP (2.735 mm)<br>OBELQ (2.745 mm)<br>OBELR (2.755 mm) (standard)<br>OBELS (2.765 mm)<br>OBELT (2.775 mm) | OBEKP (2.735 mm)<br>OBEKQ (2.745 mm)<br>OBEKR (2.755 mm)<br>OBEKS (2.765 mm)<br>OBEKT (2.775 mm) |
| 2004 | <br>58.96 mm | <br>59.41 mm |
| Rich ↑<br><br>Lean ↓ | NCYP (2.735 mm)<br>NCYQ (2.745 mm)<br>NCYR (2.755 mm) (standard)<br>NCYS (2.765 mm)<br>NCYT (2.775 mm) | NCVP (2.735 mm)<br>NCVQ (2.745 mm)<br>NCVR (2.755 mm)<br>NCVS (2.765 mm)<br>NCVT (2.775 mm) |
| 2005 | <br>60.16 mm | <br>60.61 mm |
| Rich ↑<br><br>Lean ↓ | NGGN (2.725 mm)<br>NGGP (2.735 mm)<br>NGGQ (2.745 mm) (standard)<br>NGGR (2.755 mm)<br>NGGS (2.765 mm) | NGJN (2.725 mm)<br>NGJP (2.735 mm)<br>NGJQ (2.745 mm)<br>NGJR (2.755 mm)<br>NGJS (2.765 mm) |

*Numbers identify jet needle shoulder diameters. See Figure 77.

**Table 14 FUEL SYSTEM TORQUE SPECIFICATIONS**

|  | N•m | in.-lb. | ft.-lb. |
|---|---|---|---|
| Throttle drum cover bolt | 3.9 | 34.5 | – |
| Shock absorber upper mounting nut | 44 | – | 33 |

# CHAPTER TEN

# ELECTRICAL SYSTEM

This chapter describes service procedures for the ignition, lighting and electric starting systems (CRF250X and CRF450X models).

Refer to Chapter Three for spark plug data. Refer to Chapter Two for troubleshooting information.

**Tables 1-6** are at the end of this chapter.

## ELECTRICAL CONNECTORS

Refer to the wiring diagrams at the end of this manual to help identify the connectors and wire terminal color codes called out in this chapter. Note that the position of the connectors may have been changed during previous repairs. Always confirm the wire colors to and from the connector and follow the wiring harness to the various components when performing tests.

*CAUTION*
*Connector terminals are easily damaged and dislodged, which may cause a malfunction. Use care when handling or testing the connectors.*

Under normal operating conditions, the connectors are weather-tight. However, the connectors and their locking mechanisms become worn from abuse, age and heat deterioration. To help prevent contamination from water and other contaminants, pack the connectors with dielectric grease. Do not use a substitute that may interfere with current flow. Dielectric grease is specifically formulated to seal the connector and not increase current resistance. For best results, the compound should fill the entire inner area of the connector. It is recommended that each time a connector is unplugged, that it be cleaned and sealed with dielectric grease.

The ground connections are often overlooked when troubleshooting. Make sure they are tight and corrosion free. Apply dielectric grease to the terminals before reconnecting them.

## LEFT CRANKCASE COVER

### Removal

1. Remove the left engine guard.

2. Remove the shift pedal.

3. Remove the fuel tank (Chapter Nine).

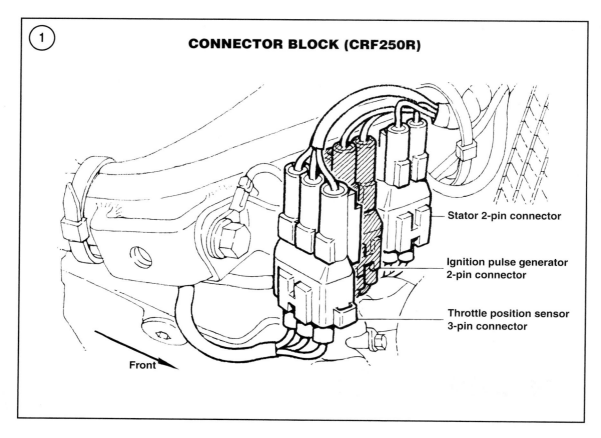

**CONNECTOR BLOCK (CRF250R)**

Stator 2-pin connector

Ignition pulse generator
2-pin connector

Throttle position sensor
3-pin connector

Front

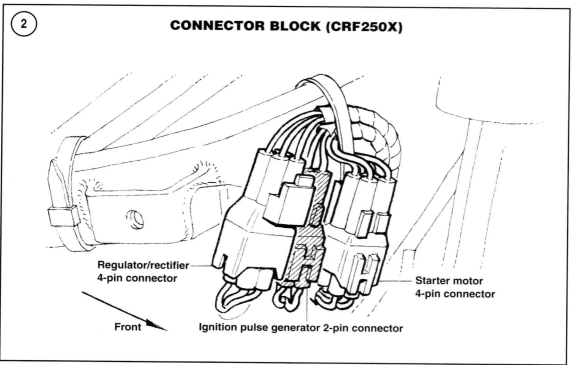

**CONNECTOR BLOCK (CRF250X)**

Regulator/rectifier
4-pin connector

Starter motor
4-pin connector

Front    Ignition pulse generator 2-pin connector

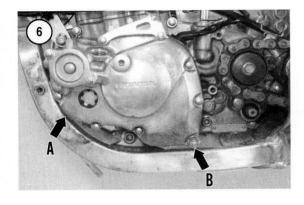

4. Drain the engine oil (Chapter Three). On CRF450R and CRF450X models, do not reinstall the engine oil drain bolt.

*NOTE*
*The left crankcase cover can be removed without having to remove the oil filter cover and oil filter. However, if the left crankcase cover will be cleaned or serviced, remove the oil filter as described in Chapter Three.*

5. Note the alternator wire harness routing.

6A. On CRF250R models, disconnect the stator coil and ignition pulse generator 2-pin connectors (**Figure 1**).

6B. On CRF250X models, disconnect the regulator/rectifier 4-pin connector and the ignition pulse generator 2-pin connector (**Figure 2**).

6C. On 2002-2004 CRF450R models, disconnect the alternator and ignition pulse generator connectors (**Figure 3**).

6D. On 2005 CRF450R models, disconnect the 2-pin exciter coil and 2-pin pulse generator connectors mounted on the left side of the frame between the left radiator and the fuel shutoff valve.

6E. On CRF450X models, disconnect the 4-pin alternator (A, **Figure 4**) and 2-pin pulse generator (B) connectors.

7. Remove the crankcase cover mounting bolts and the clutch cable holder if used. Lightly tap the cover and remove it from the engine while guiding the alternator wiring harness through the frame. Remove and discard the gasket. See **Figure 5** (CRF250R and CRF250X) or A, **Figure 6** (CRF450R and CRF450X).

8. Remove the two dowel pins. See **Figure 7** (CRF250R and CRF250X) or **Figure 8** (CRF450R and CRF450X).

10

9. On CRF250R and CRF250X models, remove and clean the oil strainer (**Figure 9**).

10. If there is no further service required with the cover or the coils, store the cover in a plastic bag to prevent contamination from entering the oil passages in the cover.

11. If necessary, service the stator and ignition pulse generator coils as described under *Stator and Ignition Pulse Generator* in this chapter.

12. If necessary, service the crankshaft oil passage seal installed in the left crankcase cover as described under *Stator and Ignition Pulse Generator* in this chapter.

13. If necessary, service the oil relief valve as described under *Lubrication System Components* in Chapter Four or Chapter Five.

## Installation

1. On CRF250R and CRF250X models, install the oil strainer (**Figure 9**), if removed.

2. If the wire harness grommet (A, **Figure 10**) is loose, clean it of all sealer residue. Then reseal the grommet with RTV. Allow the sealer to set for fifteen minutes before installing the gasket and cover. See A, **Figure 10** (CRF250R and CRF250X) or A, **Figure 11** (CRF450R and CRF450X).

3. Install the dowel pins and a new gasket. See **Figure 7** (CRF250R and CRF250X) or **Figure 8** (CRF450R and CRF450X).

4. Install the left crankcase cover and the clutch cable holder (if used). Make sure the cover seats flush against the gasket. See **Figure 5** (CRF250R and CRF250X) or A, **Figure 6** (CRF450R and CRF450X).

*CAUTION*
*Different length cover bolts are used. Check that each one sticks out approximately the same amount before tightening them.*

5A. On CRF250R models, tighten the left crankcase mounting bolts securely in a crossing pattern and in two or three steps.

5B. On CRF250X and CRF450R models, tighten the left crankcase mounting bolts in a crossing pattern and in two or three steps to the torque specification in **Table 6**. On CRF450R models, install a new washer on the engine oil drain bolt (B, **Figure 6**) and tighten to the torque specification in **Table 6**.

5C. On CRF450X models, tighten the left crankcase bolts in the following order:

a. Tighten bolt No. 1 (**Figure 12**) finger-tight.

b. Tighten bolts No. 2-9 (**Figure 12**) securely and in numerical order.

c. Install a new washer on the engine oil drain bolt (10, **Figure 12**) and tighten to 16 N•m (12 ft.-lb.).

6. Route the alternator wiring harness through the frame following its original path. Clean the connec-

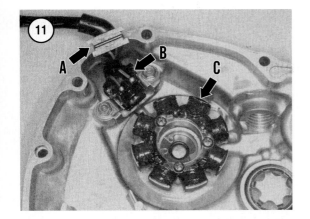

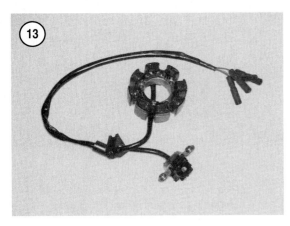

## STATOR AND IGNITION PULSE GENERATOR

The ignition pulse generator (B, **Figure 10**) and stator (C) coil assemblies are mounted inside the left crankcase cover. This section also covers the crankshaft oil passage seal (D, **Figure 10**) installed in the left crankcase cover.

### Removal/Installation

Refer to **Figure 10** (CRF250R and CRF250X) or **Figure 11** (CRF450R and CRF450X).

1. Remove the left crankcase cover as described in this chapter.

> *CAUTION*
> *The Phillips screws used to secure the stator coil are secured with a threadlock. Use a hand impact driver with the correct size Phillips bit when loosening and tightening the screws to avoid damaging the screw heads. A threadlock is also used on the ignition pulse generator mounting bolt threads.*

2. Remove the bolts, wire clamps and screws securing the ignition pulse generator (B, **Figure 11**) and stator coil (C) assemblies to the left crankcase cover. Remove both coils and the wiring harness as an assembly (**Figure 13**).

3. If necessary, service the crankshaft oil passage seal as described in this section.

4. Clean the cover in solvent and dry thoroughly. Remove all threadlock residue from the bolt holes in the cover. Flush the oil hole passage and dry with compressed air.

5. Remove all threadlock from the coil bolts and screws. Replace damaged fasteners.

6. Installation is the reverse of removal. Note the following:

   a. Apply a medium strength threadlock onto the bolt and screw threads.

   b. Tighten the stator coil mounting screws (C, **Figure 11**) to the torque specification in **Table 6**.

   c. Tighten the ignition pulse generator coil mounting bolts (B, **Figure 11**) to the torque specification in **Table 6**.

tors and pack them with dielectric grease, then reconnect them.

7. Refill the engine with the correct type and quantity oil (Chapter Three).

8. Install the fuel tank (Chapter Nine).

9. Install the shift pedal.

10. Install the left engine guard.

**10**

## Crankshaft Oil Passage Seal Replacement

1. Remove the ignition pulse generator and stator coil assembly as described in this section.

2. Remove the snap ring (**Figure 14**) and washer (if used).

3. Support a hooked tool with a rag and pry the seal out of its mounting bore (**Figure 15**). Discard the seal.

4. Clean the cover and oil passage in solvent and dry with compressed air.

5. Lubricate the lip of a new seal with engine oil. Then press the seal into its mounting bore with its closed side facing up (**Figure 14**).

6. Install the washer (if used).

7. Install the snap ring (**Figure 14**) into the cover groove. Make sure the snap ring seats in the groove completely.

8. Install the ignition pulse generator and stator coil assembly as described in this section.

## FLYWHEEL

The flywheel fits over the crankshaft with a taper fit. A Woodruff key aligns the flywheel with the crankshaft for proper ignition timing. When the flywheel nut is tightened, it effectively forces the tapers together, locking the flywheel to the crankshaft. A puller is required to remove the flywheel.

## Tools

The following is required to remove the flywheel from the crankshaft:

1. A 24 mm × 1.5 right-hand internal thread flywheel puller.

   a. Motion Pro flywheel puller (A, **Figure 16**): part No. 08-0257. This set includes both the flywheel puller and a shaft protector cap that fits over the crankshaft to protect the oil hole in the end of the crankshaft.

   b. Honda flywheel puller: part No. 07AMC-MEBA100.

   c. Honda flywheel puller adapter: part No. 07943-MF50200.

2. Strap type flywheel holder (B, **Figure 16**).

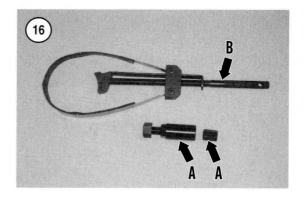

*CAUTION*
*Do not attempt to remove the flywheel without an appropriate flywheel puller. Do not pry or hammer on the flywheel to remove it. Damage to the flywheel and crankshaft will likely occur.*

## Removal

1. Place the bike on a workstand.

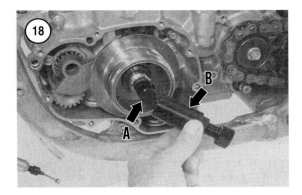

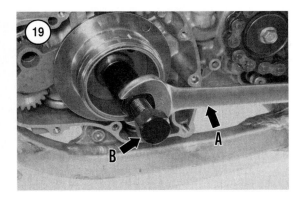

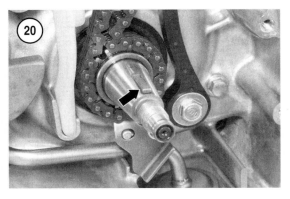

2. Remove the left crankcase cover as described in this chapter.

*NOTE*
*If troubleshooting an ignition problem, check the tightness of the flywheel and flywheel nut before loosening the nut. If these parts are loose, check the flywheel and crankshaft Woodruff key alignment.*

3. Hold the flywheel with the holding tool (A, **Figure 17**), then loosen and remove the flywheel nut and washer (B). Remove the tool from the flywheel.

*CAUTION*
*Do not use excessive force to remove the flywheel. Forcing the puller may strip the threads in the flywheel. Take the engine to a Honda dealership and have them remove the flywheel.*

4. Install the protective cap (A, **Figure 18**) over the end of the crankshaft. Apply grease onto the outer end of the protective cap that will contact the flywheel puller center bolt.

*CAUTION*
*The protective cap prevents the flywheel puller from damaging the oil hole in the end of the crankshaft. Removing the flywheel without the protective cap may cause permanent crankshaft damage.*

5. Thread the flywheel puller (B, **Figure 18**) onto the flywheel until it bottoms, then back it out half a turn.

6. Hold the puller body with a wrench (A, **Figure 19**), then turn the center bolt (B) until the flywheel pops free from the crankshaft taper.

7. Remove the flywheel, then remove the puller from the flywheel. Remove the protective cap from the end of the crankshaft.

8. If necessary, remove the Woodruff key (**Figure 20**) from the crankshaft groove.

9. Inspect the parts as described in this section.

**Inspection**

The flywheel is permanently magnetized and cannot be tested. Installing a flywheel that is known to be good is the only way of determining if the fly-

**10**

wheel is the cause of performance problems. A flywheel can lose magnetism from sharp blows. A defective flywheel must be replaced; it cannot be re-magnetized.

1. Clean and dry the flywheel.

2. Check the flywheel (**Figure 21**) carefully for cracks or breaks and replace if damaged. Do not attempt to repair a cracked or damaged flywheel.

3. Inspect the bore taper and keyway for damage.

*WARNING*
*Always replace a cracked or chipped flywheel. A damaged flywheel can fly apart at high engine speeds, throwing metal fragments and damaging the stator coils. Do not repair a damaged flywheel.*

4. Check the flywheel for rust or other contamination, and clean with sandpaper and solvent.

5. Check the flywheel for abrasions from contact with the stator coils. If abrasions are evident, inspect the crankshaft bearing.

6. Inspect the flywheel nut and washer and replace if damaged.

7. Check the flywheel tapered bore, keyway and the crankshaft taper for cracks or other abnormal conditions.

8. Inspect the Woodruff key for damage. Replace the key if the edges are not square.

**Installation**

1. Before installing the flywheel, inspect its magnets (**Figure 21**) for metal shavings and parts that may be attached to the magnets.

*CAUTION*
*Installing a flywheel with a washer or other metal part magnetized inside of it will damage the stator coil when the engine is turned over.*

2. Rotate the crankshaft so the keyway points upward.

3. If removed, align and lightly tap the Woodruff key into the crankshaft keyway (**Figure 20**). The Woodruff key must fit snugly in the keyway. Position the straight edge of the key parallel with the crankshaft to allow easy installation of the flywheel.

4. Clean the crankshaft and flywheel tapers with contact cleaner and allow to dry before installing the flywheel. These surfaces must be dry and free of oil.

5. Lubricate the flywheel nut threads and its seating surface with engine oil.

6. Align the flywheel keyway with the Woodruff key and install the flywheel onto the crankshaft. Make sure the Woodruff key remains in place.

7. Hold the flywheel in place and install the washer and flywheel nut.

8. Secure the flywheel with a holding tool (A, **Figure 17**) and tighten the flywheel nut (B) to 64 N•m (47 ft.-lb.). Remove the holding tool.

9. Install the left crankcase cover as described in this chapter.

*NOTE*
*If the flywheel, stator plate or ICM unit were replaced, check the ignition timing as described in this chapter.*

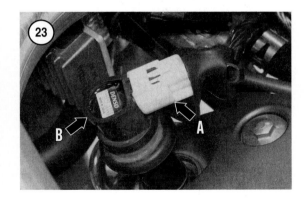

## IGNITION COIL
## (CRF250R AND CRF250X)

These models use a direct ignition coil where the ignition coil is in the spark plug cap (**Figure 22**), eliminating the secondary spark plug wire. Refer to *Ignition System Testing* in this chapter to test the ignition coil.

### Removal/Installation

1. Remove the fuel tank (Chapter Nine).

2. Grasp the ignition coil (**Figure 22**) and twist it slightly to break it loose, then pull it from the spark plug.

3. Pull the rubber cover off the ignition coil to expose the electrical connector. Then disconnect the electrical connector (A, **Figure 23**) and remove the ignition coil (B).

4. Check the electrical connector for contamination or damage contacts.

5. Check the ignition coil assembly for hairline cracks, terminal contamination and other damage.

6. Test the ignition coil as described under *Ignition System Testing* in this chapter.

7. Installation is the reverse of removal.

## IGNITION COIL
## (CRF450R AND CRF450X)

The ignition coil is mounted on the main frame front downtube and centered between both radiators.

### Removal/Installation

1. Place the bike on a work stand.

2. Remove the fuel tank (Chapter Nine).

3. On CRF450X models, remove the left radiator shroud (Chapter Sixteen).

4. Disconnect the spark plug lead at the spark plug.

5. Disconnect the primary connector at the ignition coil (A, **Figure 24**).

6. Remove the bolts securing the ignition coil (B, **Figure 24**) to the frame and remove the coil. On CRF450X models, remove the bolt and mounting bracket (**Figure 25**). Note the ground wire connection mounted on either the upper or lower mounting bolt.

7. Inspect the ignition coil (A, **Figure 26**) for cracks and other damage.

8. Check the secondary wire (B, **Figure 26**) for brittleness, cracks and worn insulation. The secondary wire is permanently attached to the ignition coil. Do not attempt to remove this wire as doing so will damage the ignition coil.

9. Check both ends the spark plug cap (C, **Figure 26**) for tears and other damage.

10. Check the primary wire and connector for dirty or loose connections. Check for a broken wire, brittleness or frayed insulation.

**10**

11. Install by reversing these removal steps. Note the following:

    a. Make sure all electrical connectors are tight and free of corrosion. Make sure the ground wire connection point on the coil is free of corrosion.

    b. Pack the electrical connectors with dielectric grease.

### Spark Plug Cap
### Removal/Installation

The spark plug cap can be replaced with the ignition coil mounted on the motorcycle. Hold the secondary wire and unscrew the plug cap to remove it (**Figure 27**). Do not pull the cap off the secondary wire as this will damage the wire ends in the end of the secondary wire. Clean the cap terminal and secondary wire ends. To install the cap, thread it tightly onto the secondary coil wire, making sure it seals tightly against the wire (**Figure 26**).

> *NOTE*
> *Water leaking into a damaged or loose-fitting spark plug cap is a common cause of ignition misfire.*

### IGNITION CONTROL MODULE (ICM)

On CRF250R and CRF450R models, the ICM unit is mounted on the steering neck, behind the number plate. On CRF250X models, the ICM is mounted behind the right side cover. On CRF450X models, the ICM is mounted behind the left side cover.

Refer to the appropriate wiring diagram at the end of this manual for a visual description of the ICM wires and connectors.

### Removal/Installation
### (CRF250R and CRF450R)

1. Remove the number plate.
2. Disconnect the ICM connector(s) (A, **Figure 28**) at the ICM unit.
3. Remove the ICM (B, **Figure 28**) from its rubber case.
4. Check the connectors for dirty or loose connections. Check for a broken wire or frayed insulation.

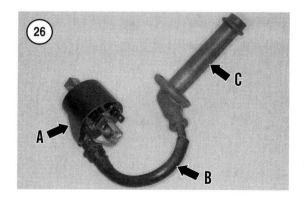

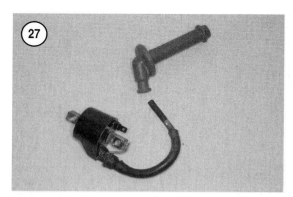

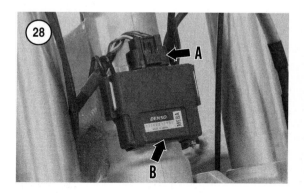

5. Install by reversing these removal steps. Note the following:

    a. Clean the ICM connectors with contact cleaner and pack them with dielectric grease.

    b. If a new ICM was installed, check the ignition timing as described in this chapter.

### Removal/Installation
### (CRF250X)

1. Remove the left and right side covers (Chapter Sixteen).

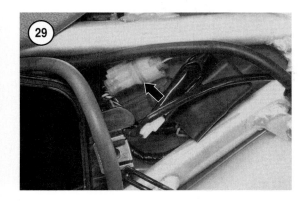

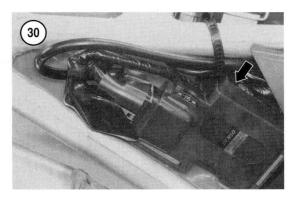

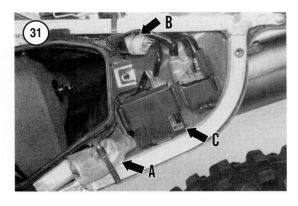

2. Remove the battery as described in this chapter.

3. Disconnect the two ICM connectors (**Figure 29**) located behind the left side cover.

4. Note the ICM wire harness routing across the rear fender, then remove the wiring harness.

5. Remove the ICM (**Figure 30**) from its rubber case.

6. Check the connectors for dirty or loose connections. Check for a broken wire or frayed insulation.

7. Install by reversing these removal steps. Note the following:

    a. Clean the ICM connectors with contact cleaner and pack them with dielectric grease.

    b. If a new ICM was installed, check the ignition timing as described in this chapter.

### Removal/Installation (CRF450X)

1. Remove the left side cover (Chapter Sixteen).

2. Disconnect the two ICM connectors (A and B, **Figure 31**).

3. Remove the ICM (C, **Figure 31**) from its rubber case.

4. Check the connectors for dirty or loose connections. Check for a broken wire or frayed insulation.

5. Install by reversing these removal steps. Note the following:

    a. Clean the ICM connectors with contact cleaner and pack them with dielectric grease.

    b. If a new ICM was installed, check the ignition timing as described in this chapter.

### IGNITION SYSTEM TESTING

All models are equipped with a solid state capacitor discharge ignition (CDI) system.

Alternating current from the magneto is rectified and used to charge the capacitor. As the piston approaches the firing position, a pulse from the ignition pulse generator triggers the silicon controlled rectifier. This causes the capacitor to discharge into the primary side of the high-voltage ignition coil where the charge is amplified to a high enough voltage to jump the spark plug gap.

Refer to *Electrical Connectors* in this chapter when disconnecting and reconnecting the electrical connectors in this section.

### CDI Precautions

When servicing the CDI system, note the following:

1. Keep all electrical connections clean and secure.

2. Never disconnect any of the electrical connections while the engine is running, or excessive voltage may damage the ignition control module (ICM).

3. When kicking the engine over with the spark plug removed, make sure the spark plug or a spark checker is installed in the plug cap and grounded

10

against the cylinder head. If not, excessive resistance may damage the ICM. See *Spark Test* in Chapter Two.

4. The ICM is mounted inside a thick rubber case to protect it from vibration (**Figure 30**, typical). Make sure the ICM is mounted correctly. Handle the ICM carefully when removing and installing it in the frame. The ICM is a sealed unit. Do not attempt to open it as this will cause permanent damage.

## Resistance Testing

Resistance tests are performed after disconnecting the component from the main wiring harness. It is not necessary to remove the part to test it. Instead, locate and disconnect the part's wiring connectors.

When using an ohmmeter, follow the manufacturer's instructions, while keeping the following guidelines in mind:

1. Make sure the test leads are connected properly.

2. Take all ohmmeter readings when the engine is cold (ambient temperature of 20° C [68° F]). Readings taken on a hot engine will show increased resistance caused by engine heat and may lead to unnecessary parts replacement.

> *NOTE*
> *With the exception of certain semiconductors, the resistance of a conductor increases as its temperature increases. In general, the resistance of a conductor rises 10 ohms per each degree of temperature change. The opposite is true if the temperature drops. Test specifications are based on testing done at 20° C (68° F).*

3. When using an analog ohmmeter and switching between ohmmeter scales, always cross the test leads and zero the needle to ensure a correct reading.

### *Ignition coil*
### *CRF250R and CRF250X*

> *NOTE*
> *A defective coil may pass a resistance test. If the ignition coil fails one or all of the following tests, take the coil to a Honda dealership and have them make an operational spark test to see*

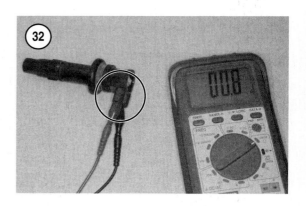

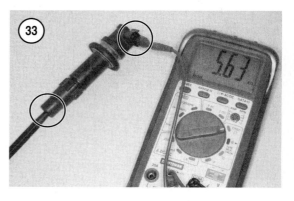

*if the coil is producing an adequate spark under operating conditions.*

1. Remove the ignition coil as described in this chapter.

2. Check the primary coil resistance as follows:
   a. Connect the ohmmeter between the two primary terminals shown in **Figure 32**.
   b. Refer to **Table 1** for the primary winding resistance specification.
   c. Replace the ignition coil if the resistance is out of specification.

3. Check the secondary coil resistance as follows:
   a. Connect the ohmmeter leads between primary and secondary terminals shown in **Figure 33**.
   b. Refer to **Table 1** for the secondary winding resistance specification.
   c. Replace the ignition coil if the resistance is out of specification.

4. Reinstall the ignition coil as described in this chapter.

5. Perform a spark test (Chapter Two) to make sure the ignition coil is plugged into its connector correctly.

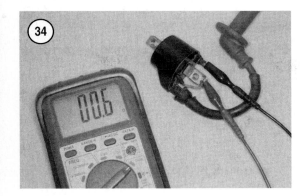

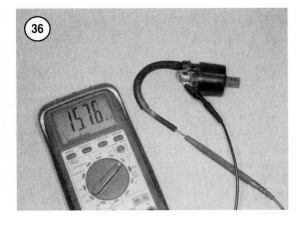

**Ignition coil
CRF450R**

*NOTE*
*A defective coil may pass a resistance test. If the ignition coil fails one or all of the following tests, take the coil to a Honda dealership and have them make an operational spark test to see if the coil is producing an adequate spark under operating conditions.*

*NOTE*
*The ignition coil can be tested while mounted on the frame. The following tests show the coil removed for clarity.*

1. Disconnect the primary electrical connector (A, **Figure 24**, typical) at the ignition coil and the spark plug cap at the spark plug.

2. Check the primary coil resistance as follows:
   a. Connect the ohmmeter to the primary terminal and its body ground as shown in **Figure 34**.
   b. Refer to **Table 1** for the primary winding resistance specification.
   c. Replace the ignition coil if the resistance is out of specification.

3. Check the secondary coil resistance with the plug cap as follows:
   a. Connect the ohmmeter to the primary terminal and the spark plug terminal as shown in **Figure 35**.
   b. Refer to **Table 1** for the secondary winding resistance (with plug cap) specification.
   c. Replace the ignition coil if the resistance is out of specification.

4. Check the secondary coil resistance without the plug cap as follows:
   a. Unscrew the spark plug cap (**Figure 27**) from the secondary wire.
   b. Connect the ohmmeter to the primary terminal and the secondary wire terminal (**Figure 36**).
   c. Refer to **Table 1** for the secondary winding resistance (without plug cap) specification.
   d. Replace the ignition coil if the resistance is out of specification.

*NOTE*
*If the test result without the plug cap is correct, but incorrect with the plug cap, the plug cap is probably faulty. Replace the plug cap and retest.*

   e. Before installing the spark plug cap, clean the cap terminal and secondary wire ends.

5. Reconnect the primary coil electrical connector (A, **Figure 24**, typical) and the spark plug cap at the spark plug.

6. Perform a spark test (Chapter Two) to make sure the plug cap is correctly installed onto the secondary wire.

**10**

## Exciter coil
## (CRF450R and CRF450X)

The exciter coil (C, **Figure 11**) is mounted inside the left crankcase cover. The exciter coil can be tested with the left crankcase cover mounted on the engine.

1A. On 2002-2003 CRF450R models, disconnect the connector at the ICM as described under *Ignition Control Module (ICM)* in this chapter.

1B. On 2004-on CRF450R models, disconnect the 4-pin connector at the ICM as described under *Ignition Control Module (ICM)* in this chapter.

1C. On CRF450X models, remove the left radiator shroud (Chapter Sixteen). Then disconnect the alternator 5-pin connector (A, **Figure 4**).

2. Refer to **Table 1** for the resistance specification.

3A. On 2002-2003 CRF450R models, connect the ohmmeter between the blue and white wire terminals in the ICM harness side connector.

3B. On 2004-on CRF450R models, connect the ohmmeter between the blue and white wire terminals in the ICM 4-pin harness side connector.

3C. On CRF450X models, connect the ohmmeter between the black/red and blue wire terminals in the alternator 4-pin harness side connector.

4. If the resistance is not within specifications, disconnect the connectors closest to the exciter coil and repeat the resistance test at the exciter coil connectors. If the resistance is still out of specification, the exciter coil is faulty. If the resistance is now correct, the wiring harness and/or connectors installed between the exciter coil and the ICM unit are contaminated or damaged. Clean/repair the wiring harness and connectors and repeat the test. If the exciter coil is damaged, replace the stator coil assembly as described in this chapter. The exciter coil cannot be replaced separately.

5. Reverse these steps to reconnect the connector(s).

## Ignition pulse generator
## (CRF450R and CRF450X)

The ignition pulse generator (B, **Figure 10**) is mounted inside the left crankcase cover. The ignition pulse generator can be tested with the left crankcase cover mounted on the engine.

1A. On 2002-2003 models, disconnect the connector at the ICM as described under *Ignition Control Module (ICM)* in this chapter.

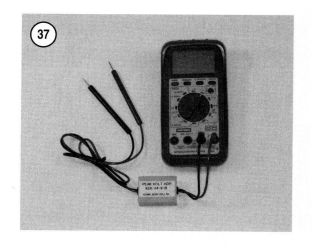

1B. On 2004-on models, disconnect the 6-pin connector at the ICM as described under *Ignition Control Module (ICM)* in this chapter.

1C. On CRF450X models, disconnect the clear 6-pin connector at the ICM as described under *Ignition Control Module* in this chapter.

2. Refer to **Table 1** for the resistance specification.

3A. On 2002-2003 CRF450R models, connect the ohmmeter between the blue/yellow and green wire terminals in the ICM harness side connector.

3B. On 2004-on CRF450R and CRF450X models, connect the ohmmeter between the blue/yellow and green/white wire terminals in the ICM 6-pin harness side connector.

4. If the resistance is not within specifications, disconnect the connectors closest to the ignition pulse generator and repeat the resistance test at the ignition pulse generator connectors. On 2002-2003 CRF450R models, connect the ohmmeter between the blue/yellow and green/white wire terminals. On 2004-on CRF450R and CRF450X models, connect the ohmmeter to the same color code wires specified in Step 3B. If the resistance is still out of specification, the ignition pulse generator is faulty. If the resistance is now correct, the wiring harness and/or connectors installed between the ignition pulse generator and the ICM unit are contaminated or damaged. Clean and repair the wiring harness and connectors and repeat the test. If the ignition pulse generator is damaged, replace the stator coil assembly as described in this chapter. The ignition pulse generator cannot be replaced separately.

5. Reverse these steps to reconnect the connector(s).

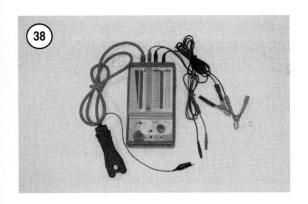

## Peak Voltage Testing and Equipment

> *WARNING*
> *High voltage is present during igni-*
> *tion system operation. Do not touch*
> *ignition system components, wires or*
> *test leads while cranking or running*
> *the engine.*

The following tests describe ignition system troubleshooting using a peak voltage tester. Peak voltage tests are designed to check the voltage output of the ignition coil, exciter coil and pulse generator coil at normal cranking speed. These tests make it possible to accurately test the voltage output under operating conditions.

The peak voltage specifications listed in **Table 1** are minimum values. If the measured voltage meets or exceeds the specification, the test results are satisfactory. In some cases, the voltage may greatly exceed the minimum specification.

To check peak voltage, a peak voltage tester is required. One of the following testers or an equivalent can be used to perform peak voltage tests described in this chapter. Refer to the manufacturer's instructions when using these tools.

1. Kowa Seiki Peak Voltage Adapter (part No. KEK-54-9B). This tool must be used in combination with a digital multimeter with an minimum impedance of 10M ohms/DCV (10-megaohm). The Kowa Seiki peak voltage adapter plugs into the digital multimeter and displays the peak voltage readings directly off the multimeter. A meter with a lower impedance does not display accurate measurements. Refer to **Figure 37**.

2. IgnitionMate Peak Voltage Ignition Tester (Motion Pro part No. 08-0193 [**Figure 38**]). This tester reads and displays the test results without the need of a multimeter. The adapters included with this tester make it easy to connect to different types of connectors and wire terminals.

### Preliminary checks

Before testing the ignition system, make the following checks:

1. On CRF250X and CRF450X models, when using the starter in these tests, make sure the battery is fully charged and in good condition. A weak battery will result in a slow engine cranking speed.

2. Perform the *Spark Test* in Chapter Two. If there is a crisp, blue spark, the ignition system is working correctly. If there is no spark, check for a disconnected or contaminated connector or a damaged engine stop switch. Also check for a fouled or damaged spark plug, loose spark plug cap/direct ignition coil or water in the spark plug cap/direct ignition coil. If the problem was not found and the inspected parts are in good working order, perform the peak voltage tests in this section to locate the damaged component.

### Ignition coil

Refer to **Figure 39** for test results.

1. On CRF250X and CRF450X models, check the battery to make sure it is fully charged and in good condition. A weak battery causes a slow engine cranking speed and inaccurate peak voltage tests results.

2. Remove the fuel tank (Chapter Nine).

3. Check engine compression as described in Chapter Three. If the compression is low, the following test results will be inaccurate.

4. Check each ignition component electrical connector and the wiring harness. Make sure the connectors are clean and properly connected. Use the correct wiring diagram at the end of this manual to identify the different connectors.

5. Shift the transmission into neutral.

6A. On CRF250R and CRF250X models, perform the following:

   a. Pull the rubber cover off the ignition coil and disconnect the electrical connector (A, **Figure 23**).

   b. Connect the tester's positive test lead to the ignition coil connector black/yellow terminal

(39)

# IGNITION COIL PRIMARY PEAK VOLTAGE TROUBLESHOOTING

| No peak voltage. |
| --- |

Check the following in order:
1. Incorrect peak voltage adapter connections.
2. Damaged engine stop switch.
3. Open circuit in the engine stop switch wiring harness.
4. Poorly connected connectors or an open circuit in the ignition coil circuit.
5. Loose or contaminated ICM connector(s).
6. Damaged ignition pulse generator. Check peak voltage at ignition pulse generator as described in this chapter.
7. Damaged exciter coil. Check peak voltage at exciter coil as described in this chapter.
8. Damaged ignition control module (ICM) when all of the above are normal.

| Peak voltage reading is normal, but there is no spark. |
| --- |

Check the following in order:
1. Open circuit in the ignition coil ground circuit.
2. Damaged ignition coil or direct ignition coil.
3. Loose spark plug cap or direct ignition coil.
4. Damaged spark plug wire or direct ignition coil harness.

| Low peak voltage. |
| --- |

Check the following in order:
1. Incorrect peak voltage adapter connections.
2. The multimeter impedance is too low.
3. Cranking speed is too low.
4. Poorly connected connectors or an open in the ignition system.
5. The test sampling and measured pulse were not synchronizing. If measured voltage is over the minimum voltage at least once, the system is normal.
6. Damaged ignition coil.
7. Damaged exciter coil. Check peak voltage at exciter coil as described in this chapter.
8. Damaged ignition control module (ICM) when all of the above are normal.

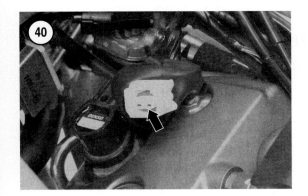

and the negative test lead to the green terminal. See **Figure 40**.

6B. On CRF450R and CRF450X models, perform the following:

a. Disconnect the spark plug cap. Then connect a new spark plug to the plug cap and ground the plug (**Figure 41**). Do not remove the spark plug installed in the cylinder head.

*NOTE*
*Do not disconnect the primary wire (A, Figure 24) from the ignition coil. This wire must remain connected to the ignition coil during the test.*

b. Connect the tester's positive test lead to the ignition coil primary coil terminal (A, **Figure 24**) and the negative test lead to ground.

*WARNING*
*High voltage is present during ignition system operation. Do not touch the spark plug, ignition components, connectors or test leads while cranking the engine.*

7. Kick the engine over with the kickstarter or use the starter (CRF250X and CRF450X) while reading the tester and note the following:

a. Refer to the minimum ignition coil peak voltage reading in **Table 1**.

b. If there is no peak voltage reading, check for an open circuit in the black/yellow and green wire (CRF250X) and green/black (CRF450X) between the ignition coil and the ICM. Check the connectors and wire terminals for corrosion or damage. If the wires and connectors are good, follow the troubleshooting procedure in **Figure 39**.

c. If the peak voltage reading is too low, follow the troubleshooting procedures in **Figure 39**.

d. If the peak voltage reading is correct, continue with Step 8.

8. Disconnect the test leads.

9. Reverse the disassembly steps.

***Exciter coil (CRF250R, CRF250X and CRF450R)***

Refer to **Figure 42** for test results.

1A. On CRF250R models, disconnect the 4-pin connector at the ICM as described under I*gnition Control Module (ICM)* in this chapter.

1B. On CRF250X models, disconnect the 6-pin connector at the ICM as described under *Ignition Control Module (ICM)* in this chapter.

1C. On 2002-2003 CRF450R models, disconnect the connector at the ICM as described under *Ignition Control Module (ICM)* in this chapter.

1D. On 2004-on CRF450R models, disconnect the 6-pin connector at the ICM as described under *Ignition Control Module (ICM)* in this chapter.

2. On CRF250X models, check the battery to make sure it is fully charged and in good condition. A weak battery results in a slow engine cranking speed and inaccurate peak voltage tests results.

3. Check all of the ignition component electrical connectors and wiring harnesses. Make sure the connectors are clean and properly connected. Use the correct wiring diagram at the end of this manual to identify the different connectors.

4. Shift the transmission into neutral.

5A. On CRF250X models, connect the tester's positive test lead to the blue/white terminal in the 6-pin ICM wire harness connector and the negative test lead to the white terminal in the same connector.

**10**

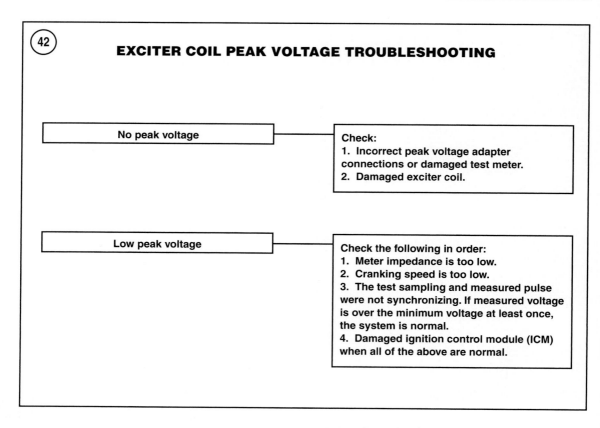

42

**EXCITER COIL PEAK VOLTAGE TROUBLESHOOTING**

| No peak voltage |
|---|

**Check:**
1. **Incorrect peak voltage adapter connections or damaged test meter.**
2. **Damaged exciter coil.**

| Low peak voltage |
|---|

**Check the following in order:**
1. **Meter impedance is too low.**
2. **Cranking speed is too low.**
3. **The test sampling and measured pulse were not synchronizing. If measured voltage is over the minimum voltage at least once, the system is normal.**
4. **Damaged ignition control module (ICM) when all of the above are normal.**

5B. On CRF250R and CR450R models, connect the tester's positive test lead to the blue terminal in the ICM wire harness connector and the negative test lead to the white terminal in the same connector. See **Figure 43**.

> *WARNING*
> *High voltage is present during ignition system operation. Do not touch the spark plug, ignition components, connectors or test leads while cranking the engine.*

6. Kick the engine over with the kickstarter or use the starter motor (CRF250X) while reading the tester and note the following:
   a. Refer to the minimum exciter coil peak voltage reading in **Table 1**.
   b. If there is no peak voltage reading, check for an open circuit in the blue/white and white wires (CRF250X) or in the blue and white wires (CRF250R and CRF450R) between the exciter coil and the ICM. Check the connectors and wire terminals for corrosion or damage. If the wires and connectors are good,

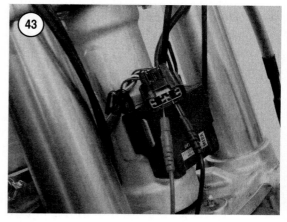

43

follow the troubleshooting procedure in **Figure 42**.
   c. If the peak voltage reading is too low, following the troubleshooting procedures in **Figure 42**.
   d. If the peak voltage reading is correct, continue with Step 7.
7. Disconnect the test leads.
8. Reverse the disassembly steps.

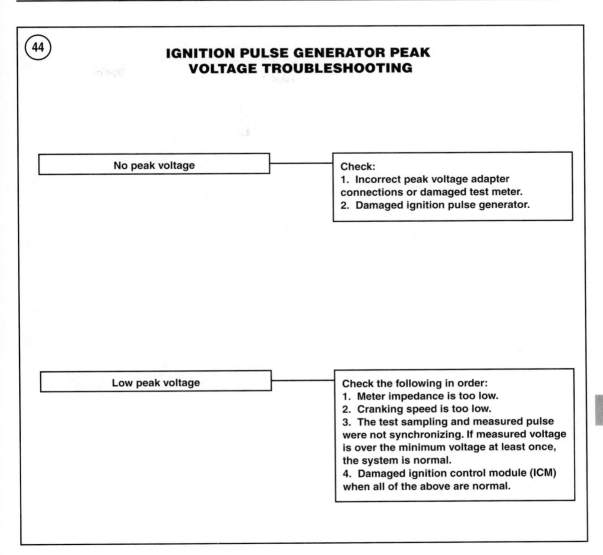

Ignition pulse generator

Refer to **Figure 44** for test results.

1A. On CRF250R models, disconnect the 6-pin connector at the ICM as described under *Ignition Control Module (ICM)* in this chapter.

1B. On CRF250X models, disconnect the 6-pin connector at the ICM as described under (Ignition Control Module (ICM) in this chapter.

1C. On 2002-2003 CRF450R models, disconnect the connector at the ICM as described under *Ignition Control Module (ICM)* in this chapter.

1D. On 2004-on CRF450R and CRF450X models, disconnect the 6-pin connector at the ICM as described under *Ignition Control Module (ICM)* in this chapter.

2. On CRF250X and CRF450X models, check the battery to make sure it is fully charged and in good condition. A weak battery results in a slow engine cranking speed and inaccurate peak voltage test results.

3. Check each ignition component electrical connector and wiring harness. Make sure the connectors are clean and properly connected. Use the correct wiring diagram at the end of this manual to identify the different connectors.

4. Shift the transmission into neutral.

5A. On CRF250X models, connect the tester's positive test lead to the blue/yellow terminal in the 6-pin ICM wire harness connector and the negative test lead to the green/white terminal in the same connector.

5B. On CRF250R models, connect the tester's positive test lead to the blue/yellow terminal in the 6-pin ICM wire harness connector and the negative test lead to the green/white terminal in the same connector.

5C. On 2002-2003 CRF450R models, connect the tester's positive test lead to the blue/yellow terminal in the 6-pin ICM wire harness connector and the negative test lead to the green terminal in the same connector.

5D. On 2004-on CRF450R and CRF450X, connect the tester's positive test lead to the blue/yellow terminal in the 6-pin ICM wire harness connector and the negative test lead to the green/white terminal in the same connector.

> *WARNING*
> *High voltage is present during ignition system operation. Do not touch the spark plug, ignition components, connectors or test leads while cranking the engine.*

6. Kick the engine over with the kickstarter or use the starter motor (CRF250X and CRF450X) while reading the tester and note the following:

a. Refer to the minimum ignition pulse generator peak voltage reading in **Table 1**.

b. If there is no battery voltage check for an open circuit in the blue/yellow and green wires (2002-2003 CRF450R) or in the blue/yellow and green/white wires (all other models) between the ICM and the ignition pulse generator. Check the connectors and wire terminals for corrosion or damage. If the wires and connectors are good, follow the troubleshooting procedure in **Figure 44**.

c. If the peak voltage reading is too low, following the troubleshooting procedures in **Figure 44**.

c. If the peak voltage reading is correct, continue with Step 7.

7. Disconnect the test leads.

8. Reverse the disassembly steps.

## IGNITION TIMING

All models are equipped with a capacitor discharge ignition (CDI), which has no provision for

adjusting the timing. However, checking the ignition timing can be used as a troubleshooting aid. If the ignition timing is incorrect, there is a defective component in the ignition system.

> *WARNING*
> *Never start and run the motorcycle in a closed area. The exhaust gasses contain carbon monoxide, a colorless, odorless, poisonous gas. Carbon monoxide levels build quickly in enclosed areas and can cause unconsciousness and death in a short time. When running the engine, always do so in a well-ventilated area.*

> *NOTE*
> *On CRF250R and CRF450R models, a 12-volt battery is required to operate the timing light.*

1. Start the engine and warm to normal operating temperature. Turn the engine off.

2. Place the bike on a workstand.

3. Remove the ignition timing hole cap (**Figure 45**) from the left crankcase cover.

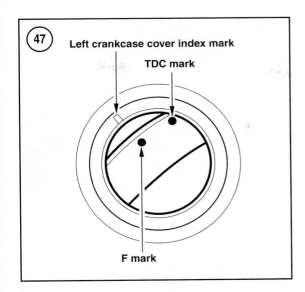

(47) Left crankcase cover index mark

TDC mark

F mark

4. Connect a tachometer to the engine following the manufacturer's directions.

5. On CRF250R and CRF450R models, connect the timing light battery leads to a separate 12-volt battery. On CRF250X and CRF450X models, connect the timing light to the battery terminals on the motorcycle. Connect the timing light inductive lead to the spark plug wire. Route the wire so it does not contact the exhaust pipe.

*NOTE*
*When checking the ignition timing, hot oil will spray through the timing hole in the left crankcase cover. Make sure the motorcycle is positioned upright. Place a sheet of plastic underneath the left side of the motorcycle (**Figure 46**) to help catch some of the oil.*

6. Start and run the engine at 1600-1800 rpm.

7. Point the timing light at the crankcase cover timing hole (**Figure 45**). The ignition timing is correct when the *F* mark on the flywheel aligns with the index notch on the left crankcase cover (**Figure 47**). Turn the engine off.

8. If the ignition timing is correct, the ignition system is working correctly. If the ignition timing is incorrect, one or more components in the ignition system are defective. To find the defective component(s), perform the *Ignition System Troubleshooting* procedure in Chapter Two.

9. Disconnect the timing light leads from the spark plug and battery.

10. Lubricate the ignition timing hole cap threads (**Figure 45**) with grease and tighten to the torque specification in **Table 6**.

11. Wipe up oil sprayed on the left crankcase cover and other engine components.

12. Recheck the oil level and top off as required. See Chapter Three.

### BATTERY
### (CRF250X and CRF450X)

The CRF250X and CRF450X uses a sealed, maintenance-free battery. The battery electrolyte level cannot be serviced. When replacing the battery, use a sealed type; do not install a non-sealed battery. Never attempt to remove the sealing cap from the top of the battery. See **Table 2** for battery specifications.

To prevent accidental shorts when working on the electrical system, always disconnect the negative battery cable from the battery.

*WARNING*
*Although the battery is a sealed type, protect your eyes, skin and clothing; electrolyte is corrosive and can cause severe burns and permanent injury. The battery case may be cracked and leaking electrolyte. If electrolyte gets into your eyes, flush your eyes thoroughly with clean, running water and get immediate medical attention. Always wear safety goggles when servicing the battery.*

*WARNING*
*While batteries are being charged, highly explosive hydrogen gas forms in each cell. Some of this gas escapes through a vent opening and may form an explosive atmosphere in and around the battery. This condition can persist for several hours. Sparks, an open flame or a lighted cigarette can ignite the gas, causing an internal battery explosion and possible serious injury.*

*NOTE*
*Recycle the old battery. When replacing the old battery, be sure to turn in the old battery at that time. The lead plates and the plastic case can be recycled. Most*

10

*motorcycle dealerships accept old bat-
teries in trade when purchasing a new
one. Never place an old battery in
household trash; it is illegal, in most
states, to place any acid or lead (heavy
metal) contents in landfills.*

## Safety Precautions

Take the following precautions to prevent an explosion:

1. Do not smoke or permit any open flame near any battery being charged or which has been recently charged.
2. Do not disconnect live circuits at the battery. A spark usually occurs when a live circuit is broken.
3. Take care when connecting or disconnecting a battery charger. Make sure the power switch is *off* before making or breaking connections. Poor connections are a common cause of electrical arcs, which cause explosions.
4. Keep children and pets away from the charging equipment and battery.

## Removal/Installation

The battery is installed in the battery box, underneath the seat.

1. Read *Safety Precautions* in this section.
2. Remove the seat (Chapter Sixteen).

*NOTE*
***Figure 48*** *shows the battery for the
CRF250X. The battery/terminal mount-
ing position for the CRF450X is the
same. The only difference is that the
CRF450X uses a wider holding strap.*

3. Remove the battery holder (A, **Figure 48**).
4. Disconnect the negative battery cable (B, **Figure 48**), then the positive cable (C) from the battery terminals and remove the battery.
5. After servicing the battery, install it by reversing these removal steps while noting the following:
   a. Always connect the positive cable first, then the negative cable.

*CAUTION*
*Make sure the battery cables are con-
nected to their proper terminals. Connecting the battery backward reverses
the polarity and damages components*

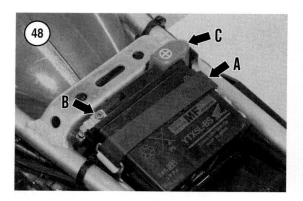

*in the electrical system. When install-
ing a replacement battery, confirm the
battery terminal positions on the
battery.*

   b. Coat the battery leads with dielectric grease or petroleum jelly.

## Cleaning/Inspection

The battery electrolyte level cannot be serviced. *Never* attempt to remove the sealing cap from the top of the battery (**Figure 49**). The battery does not require periodic electrolyte inspection or refilling.

1. Read *Safety Precautions* in this section.
2. Remove the battery from the motorcycle as described in this section. Do not clean the battery while it is mounted in the motorcycle.
3. Inspect the physical condition of the battery. Look for bulges or cracks in the case, leaking electrolyte or corrosion buildup.
4. Check the battery terminal bolts, spacers and nuts for corrosion and damage. Clean parts with a solution of baking soda and water and rinse thoroughly. Replace if damaged.

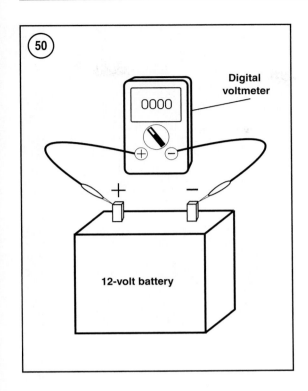

**50**

Digital voltmeter

0000

+ −

+ −

**12-volt battery**

5. Check the battery cable clamps for corrosion and damage. If corrosion is minor, clean the battery cable clamps with a stiff brush. Replace excessively worn or damaged cables.

**Voltage Test**

Use a digital voltmeter to test the battery while it is mounted on the motorcycle. See **Table 2** and **Table 3** for battery voltage readings.

1. Read *Safety Precautions* in this section.

> *NOTE*
> *To prevent false test readings, do not test the battery if the battery terminals are corroded. Remove and clean the battery and terminals as described in this section, then reinstall it.*

2. Connect a digital voltmeter between the battery negative and positive leads (**Figure 50**). Then locate the voltage reading in **Table 3** to determine the battery state of charge. Note the following:

a. If the battery voltage is 12.8-13.0 volts, the battery is fully charged.

b. If the battery voltage is below 12.3-12.5 volts, the battery is undercharged and requires charging.

3. If the battery is undercharged, recharge it as described in this section. Then test the charging system as described under *Charging System* in this chapter.

**Load Test**

A battery load test or capacity test performed with a load tester is the most accurate way to determine battery condition. A battery load test places an electrical load on the battery to determine if it can provide current while maintaining the minimum required voltage.

A battery load test procedure will vary depending on the type of tester. Use the following guidelines to supplement the manufacturer's instructions:

1. Remove the battery as described in this chapter.

2. Inspect the battery case for any leaks or damage. Do not test the battery if the case is damaged.

3. Clean the battery terminals.

4. Perform the *Voltage Test* in this section. Charge the battery if the reading is below 12.3 volts.

5. Connect the load tester to the battery terminals—red lead to the positive terminal, and the black lead to the negative terminal.

6. Determine the correct amount of load to apply to the battery. Refer to the manufacturer's instructions, plus the following:

a. Refer to **Table 2** for battery capacity. CRF250X models use a 12 volt, 4 amp hour battery. CRF450X models use a 12 volt, 6 amp hour battery.

b. The amount of load to apply to the battery is determined by the original capacity of the battery. This is measured in cold cranking amperes (CCA) or in the amp/hour rating. The correct load to apply is three times the amp/hour rating (4 amps × 3 = 12 amps for CRF250X and 6 amps × 3 = 18 amps for CRF450X).

7. Test the battery and determine the results following the manufacturer's instructions.

8. It the battery fails the load test, recharge the battery and retest. If the battery fails the load test again, replace the battery.

**10**

## Charging

Refer to *New Battery Setup* in this chapter if the battery is new.

To recharge a maintenance-free battery, a digital voltmeter and a charger (**Figure 51**) with an adjustable or automatically variable amperage output are required. If this equipment is not available, have the battery charged by a shop with the proper equipment. Excessive voltage and amperage from an unregulated charger can damage the battery and shorten service life.

The battery should only self-discharge approximately one percent of its given capacity each day. If a battery not in use, without any loads connected, loses its charge within one week after charging, the battery is defective.

If the motorcycle is not used for long periods, an automatic battery charger with variable voltage and amperage outputs is recommended for optimum battery service life.

> *WARNING*
> *During the charging process, highly explosive hydrogen gas is released from the battery. Charge the battery only in a well-ventilated area away from any open flames (including pilot lights on home gas appliances). Do not allow any smoking in the area. Never check the charge of the battery by connecting screwdriver blades or other metal objects between the terminals; the resulting spark can ignite the hydrogen gas.*

> *CAUTION*
> *Always remove the battery from the motorcycle before connecting the battery charger. Never recharge a battery in the frame; corrosive gasses emitted during the charging process will damage surfaces.*

1. Remove the battery as described in this section.
2. Measure the battery voltage as described under *Voltage Test* in this section. Locate the voltage reading in **Table 3** to determine the battery state of charge.

> *NOTE*
> *If the voltage reading is 11.5 volts or less, internal resistance in the battery may prevent it from recovering when following normal charging attempts. When a battery's state of charge is 25*

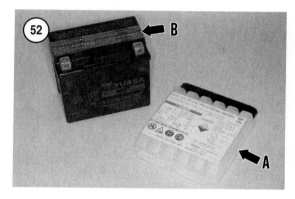

*percent or less (**Table 3**), it is necessary to increase the charging voltage of the battery by applying a low current rate to allow the battery to recover. This requires an adjustable battery charger with a separate amp and voltmeter. However, some battery chargers can do this automatically. The OptiMate III battery charger (**Figure 51**) can automatically diagnose and recover deep-discharged batteries. The OptiMate III can also be used to charge and maintain batteries during all normal battery service without overcharging or overheating the battery. Refer to the charger manufacturer's instructions and specifications for making this test.*

3. Clean the battery terminals and case.

4. Connect the positive charger lead to the positive battery terminal and the negative charger lead to the negative battery terminal.

5. Charge the battery following the manufacturer's instructions. Set the charger at 12 volts and switch it on. Charge the battery at a slow charge rate of 1/10 its given capacity. To determine the current output in

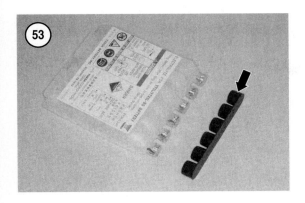

amps, divide the battery amp/hour rating by 10. See **Table 2**.

> *NOTE*
> *When using an adjustable battery charger, follow the manufacturer's instructions. Do not use a larger output battery charger or increase the charge rate on an adjustable battery charger to reduce charging time. Doing so can cause permanent battery damage.*

6. After the battery has been charged for 4-5 hours, turn the charger off, disconnect the leads and allow the battery to set for a minimum of 30 minutes. Then check the battery with a digital voltmeter. A fully charged battery will read 12.8 volts or higher 30 minutes after taken off the charger. If the battery reading is between 12.5 and 12.8 volts, it may require charging again.

## Storage

When the motorcycle is ridden infrequently or put in storage for an extended amount of time, the battery must be periodically charged to ensure it will be capable of working correctly when returned to service. Use an automatic battery charger with variable voltage and amperage outputs (**Figure 51**).

1. Remove the battery as described in this chapter.
2. Clean the battery and terminals with a solution of baking soda and water.
3. Inspect the battery case for any cracks, leaks or bulging. Replace the battery if the case is leaking or damaged.
4. Clean the battery box in the motorcycle.
5A. If the motorcycle will be used infrequently, install the battery into the motorcycle but do not connect

the battery terminals. Check the battery every two weeks and charge as necessary.

5B. When storing the motorcycle longer than one month, charge the battery to 100 percent. Then store the battery in a cool dry place. Continue to charge the battery once a month when stored in temperatures below 60° F (16° C) and every two weeks when stored in temperatures above 60° F (16° C).

## New Battery Setup

When installing a new battery, it will be necessary to fill and charge the battery. Follow the battery manufacturer's instructions while observing the following guidelines when activating a new battery:

> *WARNING*
> *Wear safety goggles when servicing and handling the battery in this section.*

> *CAUTION*
> *A new battery must be fully charged before installation. Failure to do so reduces the life of the battery. Using a new battery without an initial charge causes permanent battery damage. That is, the battery will never be able to hold more than an 80 percent charge. Charging a new battery after it has been used will not bring its charge to 100 percent. When purchasing a new battery from a dealership or parts store, verify its charge status. If necessary, have them perform the initial or booster charge before accepting the battery.*

1. Use only the electrolyte supplied with the battery (A, **Figure 52**). Do not use electrolyte from a common container, as its specific gravity reading may be incompatible with the new battery.
2. Remove the aluminum tape (B, **Figure 52**) placed across the filler holes and discard it.

> *CAUTION*
> *When removing the plastic cap in Step 3, do not puncture the aluminum seals installed over the electrolyte containers.*

3. Carefully remove the sealing cap (**Figure 53**) installed across the electrolyte container, but do not dis-

card it. This cap will be used to seal the battery after filling it.

4. Align the electrolyte container with the battery filler holes and push it squarely into the battery (**Figure 54**). Posts inside the filler holes will break the aluminum seals and allow the electrolyte to drain and fill the battery cells. Do not remove the electrolyte container until *all* the electrolyte has drained into the battery.

5. Remove the electrolyte container and allow the battery to sit for a minimum of 30 minutes. This allows the plates to absorb the electrolyte for optimum performance.

6. Loosely install the sealing cap over the battery filling holes.

7. Charge the battery following the manufacturer's instructions. Wait 30 minutes and test the battery as described under *Voltage Test* in this section. If the battery charge is 12.8 volts or higher, the battery is considered fully charged. If the battery charge reads 12.7 volts or less, repeat the charging process. When the battery charge reads 12.8 volts 30 minutes after charging, go to Step 8.

8. Press the sealing cap firmly to seal each of the battery filler holes. Make sure the cap seats flush into the battery. See **Figure 49**.

> *CAUTION*
> *Never remove the sealing cap or add electrolyte to the battery.*

## CHARGING SYSTEM (CRF250X AND CRF450X)

The charging system supplies power to operate the engine and electrical system components and keeps the battery charged. The charging system consists of the battery, alternator and a voltage regulator/rectifier. A 15-amp fuse protects the circuit. Refer to the appropriate wiring diagram at the end of this manual.

Alternating current generated by the alternator is rectified to direct current. The voltage regulator maintains constant voltage to the battery and additional electrical loads (such as lights or ignition) despite variations in engine speed and load.

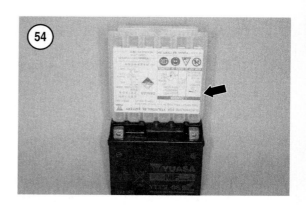

### Troubleshooting

Because the charging system is not equipped with an indicator system (light or gauge), slow cranking or short headlight bulb life may be the first indicator of a charging system problem.

1. A fully charged battery is required to accurately test the charging system. Perform the battery load test described in this chapter. If the battery is damaged or discharged, the charging system may not be at fault.

2. Use the correct wiring diagram at the end of this manual to identify and locate the appropriate connectors.

3. After making a repair, repeat the *Charging Voltage Test* in this section to confirm the charging system is working correctly.

### *Battery discharging*

If the battery is dead or the regulated voltage reading recorded in the *Charging Voltage Test* in this section was too low, perform the steps in the order listed below.

1. Check all the connections. Make sure they are tight and free of corrosion.

2. Perform the battery load test described in this chapter. Note the following:

   a. If the battery is good, continue with Step 2.

   b. If the battery is faulty, install a new battery and repeat the *Charging Voltage Test* in this section. If the charging voltage is incorrect, go to Step 7.

3. Perform the *Current Draw Test* as described this in this section. Note the following:

   a. If the current draw rate is correct, go to Step 5.

b. If the current draw rate is incorrect, continue with Step 4.

4. Disconnect the 4-pin regulator/rectifier connector as described under *Regulator/Rectifier Removal/Installation* in this section. Then repeat the *Current Draw Test* described in Step 3. Note the following:

a. If the current draw rate is now correct, the regulator/rectifier is faulty. Replace the regulator/rectifier as described in this section and retest.

b. If the current draw rate is still incorrect, the problem is probably caused by a short in the wiring or the main relay (CRF250X) is faulty. Check for a short circuit in the charging system by disconnecting the connectors one at a time while repeating the current draw test performed in Step 3. (Reconnect the connector before disconnecting another connector.) If the current draw returns to normal when a connector is disconnected, that circuit is shorting to ground. If a short circuit cannot be located on CRF250X models, perform the test under *Main Relay (CRF250X)* in this chapter.

5. Test the alternator charge coil as described under *Alternator Charge Coil Resistance Test* in this section. Note the following:

a. If the test results are correct, continue with Step 6.

b. If the test results are incorrect, the charge coil is faulty. Replace the stator coil assembly as described in this chapter and retest.

6. Perform the *Charging Voltage Test* in this section. Note the following:

a. If the regulated voltage reading is correct, the battery is faulty. Replace the battery and retest.

b. If the regulated voltage reading is incorrect, continue with Step 7.

7. Test the regulator/rectifier circuits as described under *Regulator/Rectifier System Test* in this section. Note the following:

a. If all of the readings are correct, the regulator/rectifier is faulty. Replace the regulator/rectifier and retest.

b. If one or more readings are incorrect, check the wires in the circuit that tested incorrectly for an open circuit and for dirty or damaged connector terminals.

### Battery overcharging

If the regulated voltage is too high, perform this test in the order listed below.

1. Perform the *Charging Voltage Test* in this section. Note the following:

a. If the regulated voltage reading is correct, replace the battery and retest.

b. If the regulated voltage reading is too high, go to Step 2.

2. Perform the ground circuit test as described under *Regulator/Rectifier System Test* in this section. Note the following:

a. If there is continuity, check the regulator/rectifier connector for dirty or loose-fitting terminals. If the battery continues to overcharge after cleaning or repairing these connectors, replace the regulator/rectifier.

b. If there is no continuity, check for dirty or loose-fitting terminals. Then check for an open circuit in the wiring harness.

### Current Draw Test

A short circuit can increase current draw and drain the battery. Perform this test before troubleshooting the charging system or performing the charging voltage test.

*NOTE*
*When installing electrical accessories, do not wire them into a live circuit where they stay on all the time. Refer to the manufacturer's instructions.*

1. Remove the seat (Chapter Sixteen).

2. Disconnect the negative battery cable (B, **Figure 48**) at the battery.

*CAUTION*
*Before connecting the ammeter into the circuit, set the meter to its highest amperage scale. This prevents a large current flow from damaging the meter or blowing the meter's fuse.*

3. Connect the ammeter positive lead to the negative battery cable and the ammeter negative lead to the negative battery terminal (**Figure 55**).

4. Switch the ammeter to its lowest scale and note the reading. The maximum current draw is 0.1 mA

**10**

or less. A current draw that exceeds 0.1 mA will drain the battery.

5. If the current draw is excessive, consider the following probable causes:

   a. Damaged battery.

   b. Faulty regulator/rectifier.

   c. Short circuit in the system.

   d. Loose, dirty or faulty electrical connectors.

   e. Aftermarket electrical accessories added to the electrical system.

6. To find the short circuit that is causing the excessive current draw, refer to the wiring diagram at the end of this manual. Then disconnect different electrical connectors one by one while monitoring the ammeter. When the current draw returns to an acceptable level, the faulty circuit is indicated. Test the circuit further to find the problem.

7. Disconnect the ammeter.

8. Reconnect the negative battery cable and install the seat.

### Charging Voltage Test

This procedure tests charging system operation. It does not measure maximum charging system output.

To obtain accurate test results, the battery must be fully charged (13.0-13.2 volts).

1. Start and run the engine until it reaches normal operating temperature, then turn the engine off.

2. Connect a digital voltmeter to the battery terminals as shown in **Figure 50** and record the voltage reading. To prevent a short, make sure the voltmeter leads attach firmly to the battery terminals.

> *CAUTION*
> *Do not disconnect either battery cable when making this test. Doing so may damage the voltmeter or electrical accessories.*

3. Start the engine and allow it to idle. Gradually increase engine speed to 5000 rpm and read the voltage indicated on the voltmeter. The voltmeter should show a reading greater than the measured battery voltage recorded in Step 2 and less than 15.5 volts.

> *NOTE*
> *If the battery is often discharged, but the charging voltage tested normal*

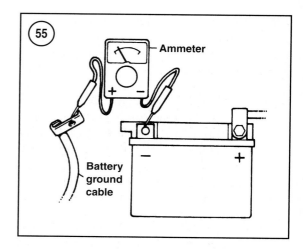

*during Step 3, the battery may be damaged. Perform a battery load test as described in this chapter.*

4. If the charging voltage reading is incorrect, perform the *Regulator/Rectifier System Test* in this section, while noting the following:

   a. If the charging voltage is too low, check for an open or short circuit in the charging system wiring harness, an open or short in the stator, or a damaged regulator/rectifier.

   b. If the charging voltage is too high, check for a poor regulator/rectifier ground, damaged regulator/rectifier or a damaged battery.

### Alternator Charge Coil Resistance Test

1A. On CRF250X models, perform the following:

   a. Remove the right radiator shroud (Chapter Sixteen).

   b. Disconnect the black 4-pin alternator charge coil connector from the connector block

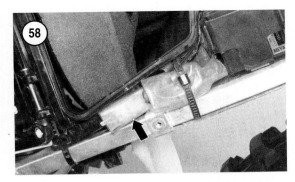

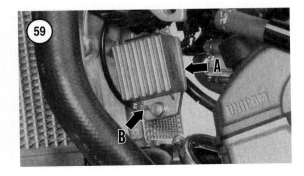

tor charge coil side connector and not on the wiring harness side connector:

    a. Yellow terminal and ground.

    b. On CRF250X, blue terminal and ground.

    c. On CRF450X, white terminal and ground.

4. Continuity must be recorded during each test. If either test is incorrect, replace the stator assembly as described in this chapter.

5. Reconnect the connectors and install the radiator shroud.

### Regulator/Rectifier System Test

This procedure tests the integrity of the wires and connectors attached to the regulator/rectifier.

1A. On CRF250X models, perform the following:

    a. Remove the right radiator shroud (Chapter Sixteen).

    b. Disconnect the white 4-pin regulator/rectifier connector from the connector block shown in B, **Figure 56**. The wire colors in this connector are blue, green, red/white and yellow.

1B. On CRF450X models, perform the following:

    a. Remove the left side cover (Chapter Sixteen).

    b. Disconnect the regulator/rectifier electrical connector (**Figure 58**).

2. Check for loose or corroded terminals in the regulator/rectifier and wiring harness side connectors.

*NOTE*
*Perform the tests on the wiring harness connector side, not on the regulator/rectifier connector side.*

3. Check the battery charge circuit as follows:

    a. Connect a voltmeter between the red/white wire and a good engine ground.

    b. The voltmeter should read battery voltage.

    c. If there is no voltage, check the red/white wire between the regulator/rectifier and the starter relay switch for an open circuit.

    d. Disconnect the voltmeter leads.

4. Check the ground circuit as follows:

    a. Connect the ohmmeter between the green wire and a good engine ground.

    b. The ohmmeter should read continuity.

    c. If there is no continuity, check the green wire for on an open circuit. On CRF250X models, also check the green wire connector (A, **Figure 59**) at the regulator/rectifier for corrosion.

shown in A, **Figure 56**. The wire colors in this connector are blue, blue/white, white and yellow.

1B. On CRF450X models, perform the following:

    a. Remove the left radiator shroud (Chapter Sixteen).

    b. Disconnect the black 4-pin alternator connector (**Figure 57**). The wire colors in this connector are black/red, blue, white and yellow.

2. Check for loose or corroded terminals in the alternator charge coil and wiring harness side connectors.

3. Check for continuity between the following wire terminals and ground. Make the test on the alterna-

**10**

5. Check the alternator charge coil circuit as described under *Alternator Charge Coil Resistance Test* in this section.

6. Reconnect the connector and install the radiator shroud (CRF250X) or side cover (CRF450X).

### Regulator/Rectifier
### Removal/Installation

#### *CRF250X*

1. Remove the fuel tank (Chapter Nine).
2. Trace the wiring harness from the regulator/rectifier (A, **Figure 59**) to the connector block on the right side of the engine and disconnect the regulator/rectifier white 4-pin connector (B, **Figure 56**).
3. Remove the mounting bolts and remove the regulator/rectifier unit (A, **Figure 59**).
4. Installation is the reverse of removal. Note the following:
   a. Route the wiring harness along its original path.
   b. Clean the ground wire terminal (B, **Figure 59**) of all dirt and corrosion.
   c. Reconnect the ground wire terminal and tighten both mounting bolts securely.

#### *CRF450X*

1. Remove the left side cover (Chapter Sixteen).
2. Remove the wire band (A, **Figure 60**) securing the wiring harness to the subframe.
3. Disconnect the regulator/rectifier white 4-pin connector (**Figure 58**).
4. Remove the nut and the regulator/rectifier (B, **Figure 60**).
5. Installation is the reverse or removal. Note the following:
   a. Route the wiring harness along its original path.
   b. Align the locating pin on the regulator/rectifier with the hole on the mounting bracket.

### STARTING SYSTEM TESTING
### (CRF250X AND CRF450X)

The starting system consists of the battery, starter, starter relay switch, starter button, starter drive mechanism and related wiring.

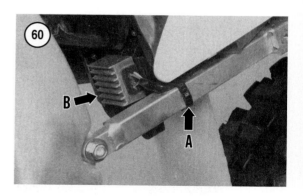

When the clutch lever is pulled in and the starter button is pushed, current is transmitted from the battery to the starter relay switch. When the relay is activated, it activates the starter relay switch that mechanically engages the starter with the engine.

A starting system problem may be electrical or mechanical. The *Engine Will Not Start* procedure in Chapter Two lists general troubleshooting procedures to help isolate starting problems.

1. If troubleshooting a starting system problem, check the following before proceeding with more in-depth testing:
   a. Make sure the battery is fully charged and has passed a battery load test.
   b. Make sure the battery cables are the proper size and length. Replace damaged or undersized cables.
   c. Make sure all electrical connections are clean and tight. High resistance caused from dirty or loose connections can affect voltage and current levels.
   d. Make sure the wiring harness is in good condition, with no worn or frayed insulation or lose harness sockets.
   e. Make sure the fuel tank is filled with an adequate supply of fresh gasoline.
   f. Make sure the spark plug is in good condition.
   g. Make sure the ignition system is working correctly.
2. Perform these quick tests to isolate the starter problem:
   a. Check the fuse as described under *Fuse* in this chapter. If the fuse is good, check the battery.
   b. Pull the clutch lever in and push the starter button to start the engine. The starter relay switch should click. If not, the problem is in

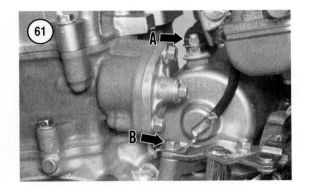

the wiring to the starter relay switch, starter switch or the starter relay switch is faulty.

c. If the starter relay switch did click but the starter did not turn the engine over, the problem may be due to excessive voltage drop in the starter circuit or the starter is damaged. This could be due to worn brushes or a shorted commutator. The problem can also be in the starter drive system or engine.

3. If the problem is traced to the starter circuit, refer to *Starter Circuit Testing* in this section and perform the procedure that matches the starting problem.

**Starter Circuit Testing**

The symptom related problems described in this section are:

1. Starter spins slowly.
2. Starter relay switch clicks but engine does not turn over.
3. Starter operates but engine does not turn over.
4. Starter does not spin.

> *CAUTION*
> *Never operate the starter for more than 5 seconds at a time. Allow the starter to cool 10 seconds before reusing it. Failing to allow the starter to cool after continuous starting attempts can damage the starter.*

**Starter spins slowly**

If the starter operates but does not turn the engine over at normal speed, check the following:

1. Test the battery as described in this chapter.
2. Check for the following:
   a. Loose or corroded battery terminals.

b. Loose or corroded battery ground cable.
   c. Loose starter cable.
3. If the battery is fully charged and passes a load test, and the cables are in good condition, the starter may be faulty. Remove, disassemble and bench test the starter as described in this chapter.

**Starter relay switch clicks but engine does not turn over**

1. Test the battery as described in this chapter.
2. Crankshaft cannot turn over because of mechanical failure.

**Starter operates but engine does not turn over**

1. If the starter was just overhauled, it may have been assembled incorrectly and is turning backward.
2. On CRX450X, remove and ground the spark plug and check the starter again. If the engine now turns over, the decompressor clearance is excessive. Adjust the decompressor clearance (Chapter Three).
3. Check for a damaged starter clutch or starter drive system as described in Chapter Six (CRF250X) or Chapter Seven (CRF450X).

**Starter does not spin**

1. Check the fuse as described in this chapter. If the fuse is good, continue with Step 2.
2. Test the battery as described in this chapter. If the battery is good, continue with Step 3.
3. Pull the clutch lever in and push the starter button to start the engine. The starter relay switch should click.
   a. If the starter relay clicked, continue with Step 4.
   b. If the starter relay did not click, go to Step 5.

> *CAUTION*
> *Because of the large amount of current that flows from the battery to the starter in Step 4, use large diameter cables when making the connection. To avoid damaging the starter, do not leave the battery connected for more than 5 seconds.*

4. Shift the transmission into neutral. Use a separate battery and apply battery voltage directly to the starter motor. Connect the positive lead to the starter motor terminal (A, **Figure 61**) and the negative lead

**10**

to ground (B, **Figure 61**). The starter should turn when battery voltage is directly applied.

   a. If the starter did not turn, disassemble and inspect the starter as described in this chapter. Test the starter components and replace worn or damaged parts as required.

   b. If the starter turned, check for loose or damaged starter cables. If the cables are good, remove and test the starter relay switch as described in this chapter.

5. Check the starter relay switch ground circuit for continuity as described under *Starter Relay Switch (CRF250X and CRF450X)* in this chapter. There should be continuity.

   a. If there is continuity, continue with Step 6.

   b. If there is no continuity, check for a loose or damaged connector or an open circuit in the wiring harness.

6. Check the starter relay switch power input circuit for continuity as described under *Starter Relay Switch (CRF250X and CRF450X)* in this chapter. There should be continuity.

   a. If there is continuity, continue with Step 7.

   b. If there is no continuity, check for a loose or damaged connector or an open circuit in the wiring harness. If the wire harness is good, check for a faulty clutch switch and a faulty engine start switch as described in this chapter.

7. Check the starter relay switch continuity circuit as described under *Starter Relay Switch (CRF250X and CRF450X)* in this chapter. There should be continuity.

   a. If there is continuity, check the starter relay switch for loose or damaged connectors or poor wire contact.

   b. If there is no continuity, the starter relay switch is faulty. Replace the switch and retest.

### STARTER (CRF250X AND CRF450X)

*CAUTION*
*Do not operate the starter for more than five seconds at a time. Wait approximately 10 seconds between starting attempts.*

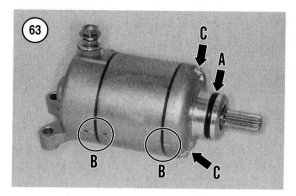

### Removal/Installation

1. Disconnect the negative battery cable at the battery as described in this chapter.

2. Remove the cylinder as described in Chapter Four or Chapter Five.

*NOTE*
*Step 3 describes how to hold the lower starter terminal nut to prevent the terminal bolt from turning and damaging the insulator plate installed inside the starter motor. The insulator plate cannot be purchased separately. If the insulator plate is damaged, the starter motor must be replaced or rebuilt with a part removed from a discarded starter.*

3. Hold the lower nut (A, **Figure 62**, typical) at the starter motor terminal, then remove the upper nut (B) and disconnect the starter motor cable.

4. Remove the two starter mounting bolts (C, **Figure 62**). On CRF250X models, disconnect the ground cable.

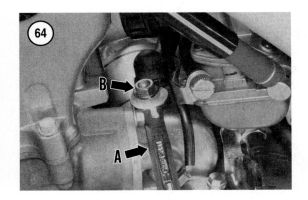

5. On CRF250X models, remove the clutch cable mounting bracket (D, **Figure 62**) out of the way. It is not necessary to disconnect the clutch cable.

6. Pull the starter to the left side of the engine and remove it from the engine (**Figure 62**).

7. Replace the starter motor O-ring (A, **Figure 63**, typical) if damaged. Lubricate with engine oil.

8. Install the starter motor into the engine.

9. On CRF250X models, install the clutch cable mounting bracket (D, **Figure 62**) and ground cable.

10. Install the starter motor mounting bolts (C, **Figure 62**) and tighten securely.

11. Reconnect the starter motor cable onto the starter and install the upper nut (B, **Figure 62**) finger-tight.

*NOTE*
*Do not tighten the upper nut (B, **Figure 62**) until after the carburetor is installed on the engine.*

12. Install the cylinder as described in Chapter Four or Chapter Five.

13. With the carburetor installed on the engine, check the starter motor cable routing around the carburetor. Then hold the lower nut (A, **Figure 64**) and tighten the upper starter motor cable nut (B) securely. Pull the rubber cover over the starter motor cable.

14. Reconnect the negative battery cable as described in this chapter.

15. Pull the clutch lever in and operate the starter button to make sure the starter works correctly.

**Disassembly
(CRF250X)**

Refer to **Figure 65** for this procedure.

1. Find the alignment marks across the armature housing and both end covers (B, **Figure 63**).

2. Remove the bolts and O-ring (C, **Figure 63**).

*NOTE*
*The number of shims and washers used in each starter varies. The shims and washers must be reinstalled in their correct order and number. Failing to install the correct number of shims and washers may increase armature end play and cause the starter motor to draw excessive current. Record the thickness and alignment of each shim and washer removed during disassembly.*

3. Remove the front cover (A, **Figure 66**) and the lockwasher (B).

4. Remove the insulated washer (C, **Figure 66**) from the armature shaft.

5. Remove the steel shim(s) (D, **Figure 66**) from the armature shaft.

6. Remove the rear cover (A, **Figure 67**) and shim(s) (B).

*NOTE*
*Do not remove the seal from the front cover. It is not available as a replacement part.*

7. Remove the armature (A, **Figure 68**) from the housing.

8. Before removing the brush holder, test the brushes and terminal bolt as follows:

a. Check for continuity between the starter terminal and the positive brush (**Figure 69**). There should be continuity. If there is no continuity, replace the terminal bolt during reassembly.

b. Check for continuity between the terminal bolt and armature housing (**Figure 70**). There should be no continuity. If there is continuity, check for a damaged insulator plate (15, **Figure 65**) or damaged, missing or improperly installed insulators on the terminal bolt (positive brush).

9. Remove the lower nut and remove the steel washer, insulators and O-ring (**Figure 71**).

10. Remove the brush holder (A, **Figure 72**), terminal bolt and insulator plate from the rear cover. See **Figure 73**.

10

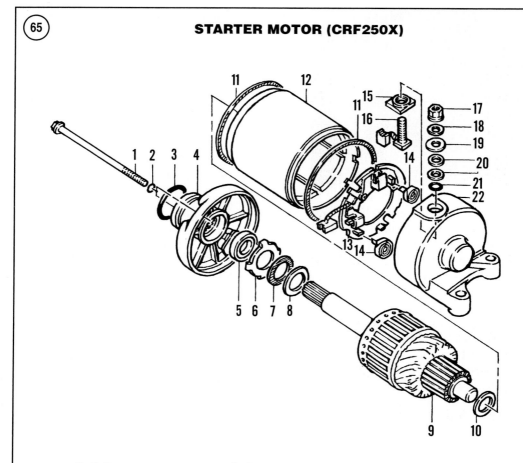

**STARTER MOTOR (CRF250X)**

1. Bolt
2. O-ring
3. O-ring
4. Front cover
5. Seal
6. Lockwasher
7. Insulated washer
8. Steel shim

9. Armature
10. Shim
11. O-ring
12. Armature housing
13. Brush holder
(negative brush)
14. Spring
15. Insulator plate

16. Terminal bolt
(positive brush)
17. Nut
18. Steel washer
19. Large insulated washer
20. Small insulated washers
21. O-ring
22. Rear cover

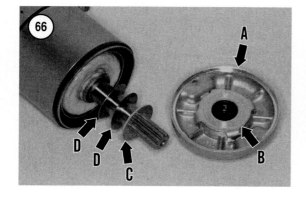

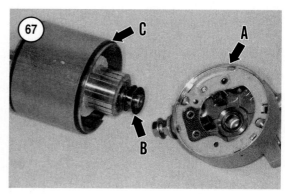

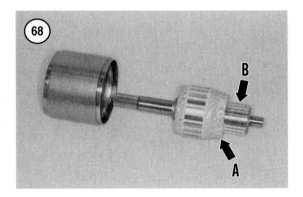

10

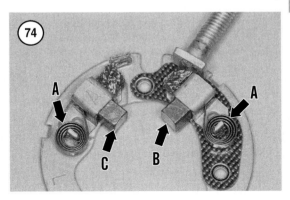

11. Clean and inspect the starter assembly as described under *Inspection* in this section.

**Assembly
(CRF250X)**

Refer to **Figure 65**.

1. Assemble the springs and brushes onto the brush holder as follows:

   a. Set the springs onto the posts on the brush holder as shown in A, **Figure 74**. The end of

the spring that contacts the brush should be positioned through the slot in the brush holder.

b. Install the terminal bolt (positive brush) assembly onto the brush holder as shown in B, **Figure 74**.

c. Make sure both brushes are positioned in their brush holder with the end of the springs contacting the brushes (**Figure 74**).

2. Slide the insulator plate (**Figure 73**) over the terminal bolt with its shoulder facing away from the brush holder. The shoulder on the insulator plate must seat in the hole in the rear cover.

*CAUTION*
*If the insulator plate is installed incorrectly, it may crack when the nuts on the terminal bolt are tightened.*

3. Install the brush holder (A, **Figure 72**) by aligning the tab on the brush holder with the groove in the rear cover (B, **Figure 72**). The two bolts holes in the rear cover should align with the two holes in the brush holder (C, **Figure 72**). Then position the insulator plate so its shoulder fits into the hole in the rear cover.

*NOTE*
*In the next step, reinstall all parts (**Figure 71**) in the order described. This is essential to insulate the terminal bolt (positive brush) from the starter.*

4. Install the O-ring (21, **Figure 65**), two small insulators (20), large insulator (19), steel washer (18) and nut (17) to secure the terminal bolt to the rear cover. Tighten the nut securely.

5. Perform the two continuity checks described in Step 8 of *Disassembly* in this section to check the terminal bolt (positive brush) for proper installation.

6. Install the commutator into the rear cover (**Figure 75**) as follows:

a. Install the shim(s) onto the armature shaft (**Figure 75**).

b. Hold the armature with the shims facing up, then install the rear cover over the commutator, while at the same time, compressing the brushes into their holder (**Figure 76**).

c. Hold the rear cover and turn the armature by hand. The armature should turn under ten-

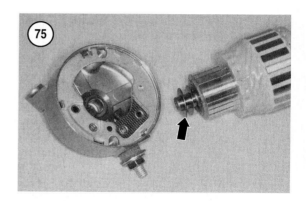

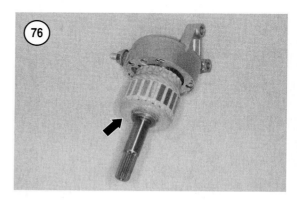

sion, indicating that the brushes are contacting the commutator.

7. Install the O-rings (A, **Figure 77**) onto the armature housing grooves.

*NOTE*
*In Step 8, magnetic force pulls the armature against the coils inside the armature housing. Hold the armature tightly to prevent it from being pulled away from the rear cover and possibly damaging the coils or brushes.*

8. Hold the armature into the rear cover and install the armature housing (B, **Figure 77**). Seat the armature housing against the rear cover while aligning the rear cover and armature housing alignment marks (B, **Figure 63**). Make sure the O-ring is seated evenly between the cover and housing.

9. Install the steel shim(s) (D, **Figure 66**) and insulated washer (C, **Figure 66**) onto the armature shaft.

10. Lightly lubricate the oil seal lip in the front cover with grease.

11. Install the lockwasher (B, **Figure 66**) into the front cover.

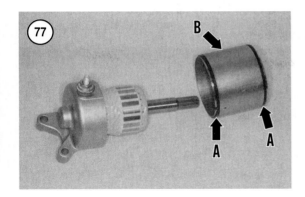

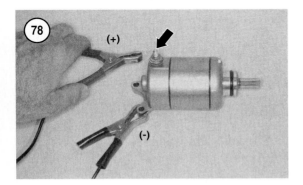

starter should turn when battery voltage is directly applied. If the starter does not turn, disassemble and inspect the starter as described in this section.

**Disassembly**
**(CRF450X)**

Refer to **Figure 79**.
1. Remove the O-ring (A, **Figure 80**).
2. Remove the bolt (B, **Figure 80**) and locate the alignment marks (**Figure 81**) previously hidden by the bolt. Highlight these marks with a pen if necessary.
3. Remove the second bolt (C, **Figure 80**).

> *NOTE*
> *The number of shims and washers used in each starter varies. The shims and washers must be reinstalled in their correct order and number. Failing to install the correct number of shims and washers may increase armature end play and cause the starter to draw excessive current. Record the thickness and alignment of each shim and washer removed during disassembly.*

4. Remove the front cover (A, **Figure 82**) and the lockwasher (B).

> *NOTE*
> *Do not remove the seal from the front cover. It is not available as a replacement part.*

5. Remove the insulated washer (C, **Figure 82**) from the armature shaft.
6. Remove the steel shim(s) (D, **Figure 82**) from the armature shaft.
7. Remove the rear cover (**Figure 83**) from the housing.
8. Remove the two O-rings (A, **Figure 84**) from the housing.
9. Remove the armature (B, **Figure 84**) through the housing's rear cover end. See the directional arrow in **Figure 84**.

> *NOTE*
> *A shoulder inside the housing bore prevents armature removal from the front side.*

12. Install the front cover over the armature shaft, making sure not to damage the oil seal with the splines on the armature shaft. Seat the front cover against the armature housing while aligning the cover and housing alignment marks (B, **Figure 63**). Make sure the O-ring is seated evenly between the cover and housing.
13. Install the starter bolts (C, **Figure 63**) and tighten securely.

> *NOTE*
> *If one or both bolts will not pass through the starter, the end covers and/or brush holder are installed incorrectly.*

14. Lubricate the O-ring with grease and install it into the front cover groove (A, **Figure 63**).
15. Hold the starter and turn the armature shaft by hand. The armature should turn with some resistance, but should not bind or lock up. If the armature does not turn properly, disassemble the starter and check the shim(s), insulated washer and lockwasher alignment.
16. Momentarily, apply battery voltage (12-volts) directly to the starter as shown in **Figure 78**. The

**10**

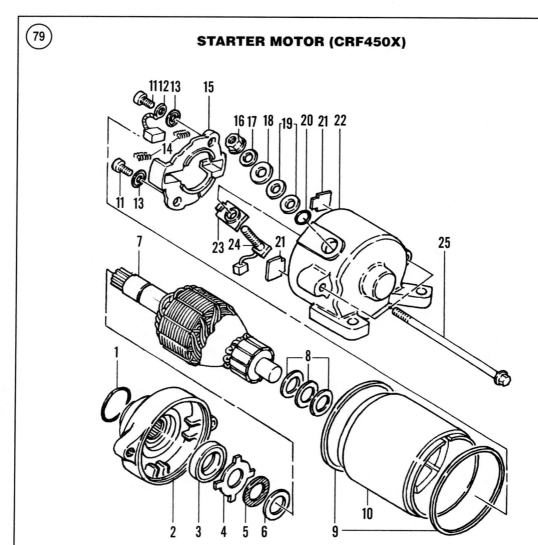

(79)

**STARTER MOTOR (CRF450X)**

1. O-ring
2. Front cover
3. Dust seal
4. Lockwasher
5. Insulated washer
6. Steel washer
7. Armature housing
8. Shim(s)
9. O-ring
10. Housing
11. Screw
12. Negative brush
13. Washer
14. Spring
15. Brush holder
16. Nut
17. Steel washer
18. Inuslated washer (large)
19. Insulated washer (small)
20. O-ring
21. Insulator plate
22. Rear cover
23. Insulator plate
24. Positive brush
25. Bolts

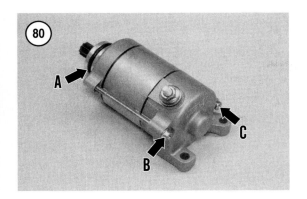

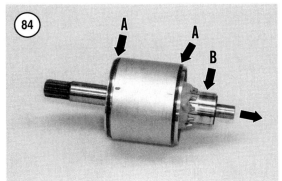

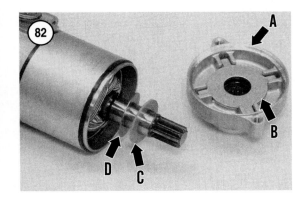

10. Remove the brush springs (A, **Figure 85**) from the guides in the brush holder.

11. Remove the shim(s) (B, **Figure 85**).

12. Before removing the brush holder, test the brushes and terminal bolt as follows:

    a. Check for continuity between the starter terminal and the positive brush (**Figure 86**). There should be continuity. If there is no continuity, replace the terminal bolt during reassembly.

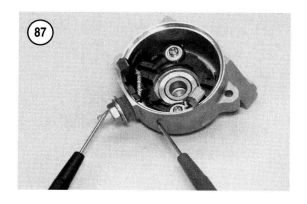

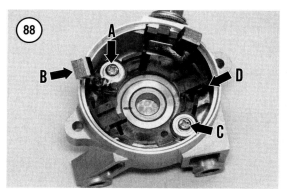

b. Check for continuity between the terminal bolt and armature housing (**Figure 87**). There should be no continuity. If there is continuity, check for a damaged brush holder (15, **Figure 79**) or damaged, missing or improperly installed insulators on the terminal bolt (positive brush).

13. Remove the screw (A, **Figure 88**), washer and negative brush (B).

14. Remove the screw (C, **Figure 88**), washer and brush holder (D).

15. Remove the insulator plates (**Figure 89**) from the rear cover.

16. Remove the lower nut (A, **Figure 90**), steel washer, insulators and O-ring. See **Figure 91**.

17. Remove the terminal bolt and insulator plate (B, **Figure 90**) from the rear cover.

18. Clean and inspect the starter assembly as described under *Inspection* in this section.

## Assembly
## (CRF450X)

Refer to **Figure 79**.

1. Install the insulator plate onto the terminal bolt. The tab on the insulator plate must be facing toward the brush. Then, install the terminal bolt assembly so that the insulator tab and brush are facing up (**Figure 92**).

> *NOTE*
> *In the next step, reinstall all parts (**Figure 91**) in the order described. This is essential to insulate the terminal bolt (positive brush) from the starter.*

2. Install the O-ring (20, **Figure 79**), two small insulators (19), large insulator (18), steel washer (17) and nut (16) to secure the terminal bolt to the rear cover. Tighten the nut (A, **Figure 90**) securely.

3. Perform the two continuity checks described in Step 12 of *Disassembly* in this section to check the terminal bolt (positive brush) for proper installation.

4. Install the insulator plates (**Figure 89**).

5. Install the brush holder into the rear cover as shown in D, **Figure 88**.

6. Install the negative brush (B, **Figure 88**) and secure it with the washer and screw (A). Then install the second washer and screw (C, **Figure 88**). Tighten both screws securely.

7. Install the brush springs, brushes and armature as follows:

*NOTE*
*Having to compress the brushes and springs and install the armature at the same time without an assistant can be difficult. If an assistant is unavailable, the text shows how to use a small clamp to hold one of the brushes. In addition, snap ring pliers will be required to hold the brushes in position when installing the armature.*

10

a. Apply a light film of grease onto the shims (8, **Figure 79**) and slide them onto the armature (**Figure 93**). The grease will prevent the shims from sliding off the armature during its installation. Set the armature aside until installation.

b. Use screws to secure the rear cover to a wooden block as shown in **Figure 94**, then clamp the block to the workbench. This will stabilize the rear cover when compressing the brushes and installing the armature. If necessary, grind the screw heads to provide clearance beside the rear cover before installing them. The area between the cover and its two bolt holes is very small.

*NOTE*
***Figure 95*** *shows how the brushes and wires should be installed and routed in the brush holder.*

c. Align and install a brush spring (**Figure 96**) into one of the holders. The brush springs are

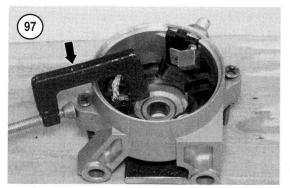

irregular shaped and will only fit one way. Then align and install the appropriate brush so that it compresses the spring. Have an assistant hold this brush and spring in place with a small screwdriver, then install the other spring and brush. If an assistant is unavailable, secure the brush in place with a small clamp (**Figure 97**).

d. When both springs and brushes are properly installed, hold them in place with a pair of snap ring pliers as shown in **Figure 98**.

e. Install the armature (with the shims in place) into the rear cover until its shaft bottoms, then release the brushes. See **Figure 99**.

f. Inspect the rear cover to make sure the shims did not fall off the armature and that both brushes seat flush against the commutator.

g. Remove the screws and rear cover from the wooden block.

8. Install the housing over the armature as follows:

*NOTE*
*Magnetic force will pull the armature hard against the coils inside the armature housing. When installing the housing, hold the armature tightly to prevent it from being pulled out of the rear cover and possibly damaging the coils or brushes.*

a. Install an O-ring (A, **Figure 100**) onto the end of the housing with the notch (B). This side faces the rear cover.

b. Install the housing by aligning the notch in the housing (B, **Figure 100**) with the raised tab on the insulator plate (C). Make sure the O-ring is seated evenly between the rear cover and housing.

9. Install the O-ring into the end of the housing facing the front cover (D, **Figure 100**).

10. Install the steel shim(s) (D, **Figure 82**) and insulated washer (C, **Figure 82**) onto the armature shaft. Make sure the insulated washer faces out.

11. Lightly lubricate the oil seal lip in the front cover with grease.

12. Install the lockwasher (B, **Figure 82**) into the front cover. The tabs on the lockwasher must fit into the slots in the front cover.

13. Install the front cover over the armature shaft, making sure not to damage the oil seal with the splines on the armature shaft. Seat the front cover against the armature housing while aligning the cover and housing alignment marks (**Figure 81**). Make sure the O-ring is seated evenly between the cover and housing.

14. Install the starter bolts (B and C, **Figure 80**) and tighten securely.

15. Lubricate the O-ring with grease and install it into the front cover groove (A, **Figure 80**).

16. Hold the starter and turn the armature shaft by hand. The armature should turn with some resistance, but should not bind or lockup. If the armature

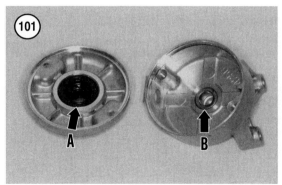

10

does not turn properly, disassemble the starter and check the shim(s), insulated washer and lockwasher alignment.

17. Momentarily apply battery voltage (12-volts) directly to the starter as shown in **Figure 78**. The starter should turn when battery voltage is directly applied. If the starter does not turn, disassemble and inspect the starter as described in this section.

## Inspection
## (All Models)

If any starter component (other than O-rings and brush sets) are severely worn or damaged, the starter must be replaced as an assembly. Individual replacement parts are not available.

*NOTE*
*Before purchasing a new starter, try to find a replacement starter through a motorcycle wrecking yard. If an identical starter cannot be located, look for a starter that is similar in design. The internal part needed may be*
*useable, either directly or after modification.*

1. The internal parts in a used starter are often contaminated with carbon and copper dust released from the brushes and commutator. Because a starter motor can be damaged from improper cleaning, note the following:
   a. Clean all parts (except the armature, armature housing and insulated washers in solvent. Use a rag lightly damped with solvent to wipe off the armature, insulated washers and the armature housing (inside and outside).
   b. Use fine grade sandpaper to clean the brushes. Do not use emery cloth as its fibers may insulate the brushes.
   c. Use only crocus cloth to clean the commutator. Do not use emery cloth or sandpaper. Any abrasive material left on or embedded in the commutator may cause excessive brush wear. Do not leave any debris on or between the commutator bars.

2. Replace the armature housing O-rings if damaged.
3. Inspect the seal and needle bearing (A, **Figure 101**, typical) in the front cover for damage. Do not remove the seal to check the bearing.
4. Inspect the bushing (B, **Figure 101**) in the rear cover for excessive wear or damage.

*NOTE*
*The bushing, seal and bearing used in the end covers are not available separately.*

5. Check the lockwasher, shims and insulated washers for damage.
6. On CRF250X models, inspect the brushes (A and B, **Figure 74**) as follows:

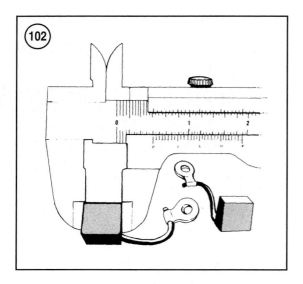

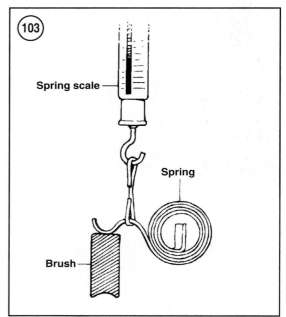

a. Inspect each brush for cracks and other damage.

b. Inspect the insulation plate (**Figure 73**) installed on the terminal bolt for looseness, wear or damage.

c. Check the negative brush wire (C, **Figure 74**) to make sure it is fixed securely to the brush holder.

d. Push and release each brush where it is fixed to its holder (A or B, **Figure 74**). It should move and return under spring tension.

e. Measure the length of each brush (**Figure 102**). If one brush is too short (**Table 4**), replace both brushes (**Figure 74**) as a set. The negative brush (B, **Figure 74**) is permanently fixed to the brush holder. The positive brush (A, **Figure 74**) is permanently fixed to the terminal bolt. Soldering is not required when replacing brushes.

7. On CRF250X models, inspect the brush springs (C, **Figure 74**) for weakness or damage. Even though a spring tension measurement is not available, compare spring tension using a spring scale as follows:

a. Support the brush holder in a vise with soft jaws.

b. Hook a spring scale to the exposed part of the spring as shown in **Figure 103**.

c. Pull the spring scale and record the spring tension measurement the moment the spring lifts off the brush.

d. Repeat for the other spring. If there is any noticeable difference in tension measurements, replace both springs (C, **Figure 74**) as a set.

8. On CRF450X models, inspect the brushes and springs as follows:

a. Check the brushes (**Figure 104**) for damage. If any one brush is damaged, replace both as a set.

b. Measure the length of each brush (**Figure 102**). If one brush is too short (**Table 4**), replace both brushes (**Figure 104**) as a set.

c. Check the springs for stretched or damaged coils. Compare the springs and replace if the spring length is different. Replace both springs as a set.

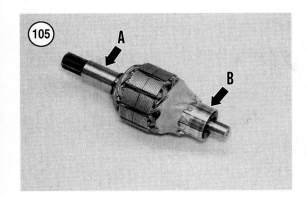

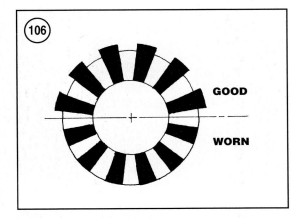

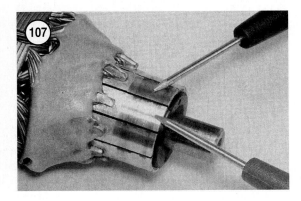

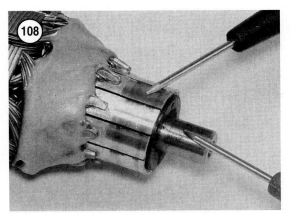

10. Inspect the commutator (B, **Figure 105**):

   a. Inspect the commutator bars for visual damage.

   b. Clean the commutator surface as described in Step 1.

   c. The mica must be below the surface of the copper bars. On a worn commutator, the mica and copper bars may be worn to the same level (**Figure 106**).

   d. If the mica level is too high or if its shape is too narrow or V-shaped, undercut the mica with a hacksaw blade.

   e. Inspect the commutator copper bars for discoloration. If a pair of bars are discolored, grounded armature coils are indicated.

   f. Check for continuity across all adjacent pairs of commutator bars (**Figure 107**). There should be continuity across all pairs of bars. If an open circuit exists between a pair of bars, replace the starter motor.

   g. Check for continuity between the armature shaft and each commutator bar (**Figure 108**). There should be no continuity. If there is continuity, replace the starter.

   h. Check for continuity between the armature coil core and each commutator bar. There should be no continuity. If there is continuity, replace the starter.

11. Inspect the armature housing for cracks or other damage. Then inspect for loose, chipped or damaged magnets.

   d. Inspect the brush holder (15, **Figure 79**) and insulators (21, **Figure 79**) for damage.

9. Inspect the armature (A, **Figure 105**):

   a. Inspect the shafts for scoring and other damage.

   b. Inspect the windings for obvious damage.

   c. To check the armature for a short circuit, have it tested on a growler. Refer this service to a Honda dealership or an automotive electrical repair shop.

## STARTER RELAY SWITCH
## (CRF250X AND CRF450X)

On CRF250X models, the starter relay switch is mounted behind the right side cover (**Figure 109**). On CRF450X models, it is behind the left side cover (**Figure 110**). A 15-amp fuse is located in the connector holder plugged into the starter relay switch.

### Testing

1. Refer to *Starting System Testing* in this chapter to test the starting circuit. If the problem has been isolated to the starter relay switch, perform the following test.

2. Remove the seat and the left or right side cover (Chapter Sixteen).

3. Shift the transmission into neutral.

4. Pull the clutch lever in and push the starter button to start the engine. The starter relay switch should click.

    a. Yes. The starter relay switch is working correctly.

    b. No. Continue with Step 5.

5. Remove the starter relay switch from its rubber case. See **Figure 109** (CRF250X) or **Figure 110** (CRF450X).

6. Disconnect the starter relay switch electrical connector (**Figure 111**, typical). Repair any dirty, loose fitting or damaged terminals. If the wiring is in good condition, leave the connector disconnected and continue with Step 7.

7. Ground circuit test: Shift the transmission into neutral. Check for continuity between the starter relay switch connector green wire and ground. There should be continuity. Repeat the test with the clutch lever pulled in. There should be continuity.

    a. Continuity: Go to Step 8.

    b. No continuity: Repair the open circuit in the green starter relay switch wire.

8. Power circuit test: Reconnect the starter relay switch electrical connector (**Figure 111**). Shift the transmission into neutral. Pull the clutch lever in and measure voltage between the starter relay switch yellow/red wire at the starter relay switch connector (**Figure 111**) and ground when pressing the starter button. There should be battery voltage.

    a. Battery voltage: Go to Step 9.

    b. No battery voltage: Repair the open in the yellow/red wire between the starter/relay switch connector and the starter switch connector.

9. Continuity circuit test. Perform the following:

    a. Shift the transmission into neutral.

    b. Make sure the battery leads are connected. Connect the ohmmeter test leads across the two large leads on the starter relay switch (**Figure 112**). Pull the clutch lever in and check for continuity when pressing the starter

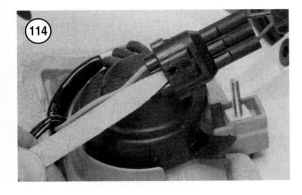

button. There should be continuity. If there is no continuity, the starter relay switch is faulty.

   c. Disconnect the negative battery lead at the battery and repeat substep b. There should be no continuity. If there is continuity, the starter relay switch is faulty.

10. Install all parts previously removed.

**Removal/Installation**

1. Remove the seat and the left (CRF450X) or right (CRF250X) side cover (Chapter Sixteen).

2. Disconnect the negative battery lead at the battery as described in this chapter.

3. Remove the starter relay switch from its rubber case. See **Figure 109** (CRF250X) or **Figure 110** (CRF450X).

4. Disconnect the starter relay switch electrical connector (**Figure 111**, typical).

5. Label and then disconnect the battery and starter cable leads (**Figure 112**, typical) at the starter relay switch.

6. Installation is the reverse of removal. Note the following:

   a. Clean the battery and starter cable leads before connecting them to the relay.

   b. Make sure to install the cover firmly over the two cable leads at the starter relay switch.

   c. Install the 15-amp fuse into the new starter relay switch socket.

### LIGHTING SYSTEM (CRF250X AND CRF450X)

   See **Table 5** for headlight bulb specifications. Always use the correct wattage headlight bulb. Using the wrong size bulb gives a dim light or causes the bulb to burn out prematurely. An LED is used in the taillight.

**10**

**Headlight Bulb Replacement**

> *WARNING*
> *If the headlight has just burned out or just turned off, it will be hot. Allow the bulb to cool before removal.*

> *CAUTION*
> *A quartz-halogen bulb is used. Do not touch the bulb glass. Traces of oil on the bulb drastically reduce the life of the bulb. Clean all traces of oil from the bulb glass with a cloth moistened in alcohol or lacquer thinner.*

1. Remove the front visor (Chapter Sixteen) and rest it on the front fender.

2. Remove the headlight bulb wiring harness from the clamp (**Figure 113**).

3. Insert a small wooden stick between the connector halves (**Figure 114**) and lift/pry the connector tab to unlock the connectors, then disconnect them.

4. Remove the dust cover (A, **Figure 115**) from around the bulb and slide it up the wiring harness.

5. Push the bulb socket (**Figure 116**) in while turning it counterclockwise to disconnect it from the headlight bulb holder.

6. Remove the bulb (**Figure 117**).

7. Test the bulb with an ohmmeter connected across each of the bulb terminals. The meter should read continuity.

8. Install the new bulb by aligning the tabs on the bulb with the notches in the bulb holder.

9. Install the dust cover with its TOP mark (B, **Figure 115**) facing up. Make sure the cover fits tightly against the bulb housing.

10. Reconnect the headlight bulb connector securely to the wire harness with the clamp (**Figure 113**).

11. Install the front visor (Chapter Sixteen).

12. Start the engine and check headlight operation.

13. If necessary, adjust the headlight as described in Chapter Three.

## Headlight Housing
## Removal/Installation

1. Remove the front visor (Chapter Sixteen) and rest it on the front fender.

2. Remove the headlight bulb wiring harness from the clamp (**Figure 113**).

3. Insert a small wooden stick between the connector halves (**Figure 114**) and lift/pry the connector tab to unlock the connectors, then disconnect them.

4. Measure the headlight adjuster screw's exposed length (A, **Figure 118**) and record it for installation. Then remove the adjuster screw, nut (B, **Figure 118**) and spring (C).

5. Remove the two mounting screws (C, **Figure 115**) and the headlight housing.

6. Installation is the reverse of these steps. Note the following:

    a. Reinstall the adjuster screw to the dimensions recorded in Step 4.

    b. After installing the front visor, check and adjust the headlight as described in Chapter Three.

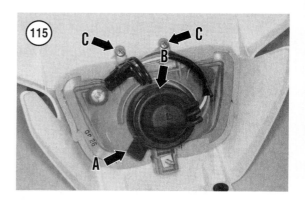

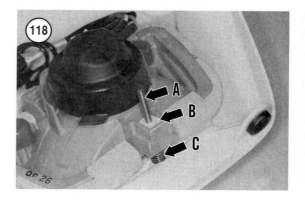

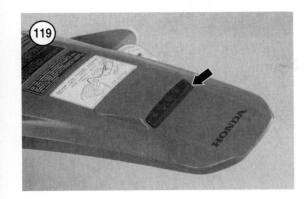

**Taillight LED**
**(Inspection and Replacement)**

1. Start the engine and allow to idle. If any LED does not light, replace the taillight assembly (**Figure 119**).

2. Remove the seat and both side covers (Chapter Sixteen).

3. Disconnect the taillight 2-pin connector from the connector pouch (**Figure 120**, typical) located on the left side of the motorcycle.

4. Remove the bolt, washer, screws and clamps securing the wiring harness to the rear fender.

5. Remove the bolts and bracket securing the LED unit to the rear fender.

6. Installation is the reverse of these steps. Tighten the rear fender mounting bolt to 13 N•m (115 in.-lb.).

7. Start the engine and check the LED operation.

## SWITCHES

### Switch Testing

Before performing any of the tests in this section, note the following:

1. All tests are performed with an ohmmeter.

2. When using an analog ohmmeter and switching between ohmmeter scales, always cross the test leads and zero the needle to ensure a correct reading.

3. Refer to the wiring diagram at the back of the manual as needed.

4. When reassembling the connections, apply dielectric grease to all connectors to prevent the entry of moisture and dirt.

5. When testing parts at the connectors, check that the wire connections being tested actually lead to the part being checked.

### Engine Stop Switch
### Testing/Removal/Installation

The engine stop switch (**Figure 121**, typical) is mounted on the left side of the handlebar.

1A. On CRF250R and CRF450R models, remove the fuel tank (Chapter Nine).

1B. On CRF250X and CRF450X models, remove the front visor (Chapter Sixteen).

2A. On CRF250R and CRF450R models, disconnect the engine stop switch connectors.

2B. On CRF250X and CRF450X models, disconnect the engine stop switch 3-pin connector (A, **Figure 122**).

3. On CRF250R and CRF450R models, connect an ohmmeter to the two engine stop switch connector terminals. On CRF250X and CRF450X models, connect the ohmmeter between the black/white and black/green terminals. There should be continuity with the stop switch button pressed and no continuity with the button released.

10

4. Replace the engine stop switch if it did not test as described in Step 4.

5. Unscrew the engine stop switch clamp screw (**Figure 123**) at the handlebar and remove the switch.

6. Check the engine stop switch wires and connector for dirty or loose connections. Check for a broken wire or frayed insulation.

*CAUTION*
*The engine stop switch wiring harness can be damaged from tie-downs when transporting the motorcycle.*

7. Install by reversing these removal steps. Note the following:

a. Route the switch wiring harness through the frame and onto the handlebar.

b. Align the switch clamp mating halves with the punch or paint mark on the handlebar (**Figure 123**).

c. Make sure all electrical connectors are tight and free of corrosion.

d. Apply dielectric grease to the electrical connectors.

e. Start the engine and operate the switch to make sure it shuts off the engine.

**Starter Switch**
**Testing/Removal/Installation**
**(CRF250X and CRF450X)**

The starter switch (**Figure 124**) is mounted on the right side of the handlebar.

1. Remove the front visor (Chapter Sixteen).

2. Disconnect the starter switch 2-pin connector (B, **Figure 122**).

3. Check for continuity between the two starter switch connector terminals. There should be continuity with the starter switch button pressed and no continuity with the button released.

4. Replace the starter switch if it did not test as specified in Step 4.

5. Remove the wire bands (A, **Figure 125**) from the handlebar. Then remove the screws and the starter switch housing (B, **Figure 125**).

6. Install the starter switch housing by aligning the groove in the switch housing with the arm on the throttle housing (**Figure 126**). Tighten the screws securely. Then secure the wiring harness to the handlebar (**Figure 125**).

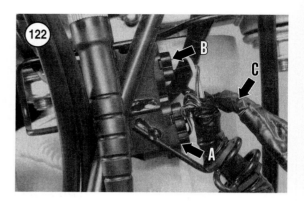

7. Reconnect the starter switch 2-pin connector (B, **Figure 122**).

*NOTE*
*The starter switch wiring harness can be damaged from tie-downs when transporting the motorcycle.*

8. Install by reversing these removal steps. Note the following:

a. Route the switch wiring harness through the frame and onto the handlebar.

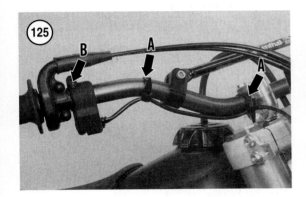

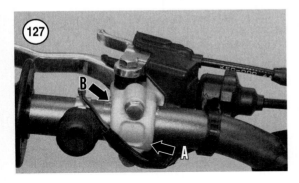

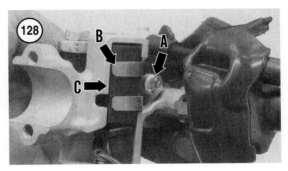

b. Make sure all electrical connectors are tight and free of corrosion.

c. Apply dielectric grease to the electrical connectors.

d. Pull the clutch lever in and push the starter switch to make sure it operates the starter motor.

**Clutch Switch
Testing/Replacement
(CRF250X and CRF450X)**

The clutch switch is a normally open switch that prevents the starter from operating when the starter button is pushed and the clutch lever is not pulled in. Pulling the clutch lever in closes the clutch switch. The starter button can then be pushed to operate the starter.

1. Remove the front visor (Chapter Sixteen) and rest it on the front fender.

2. Disconnect the engine stop switch 3-pin connector (A, **Figure 122**).

3. Disconnect the single-pin clutch switch wire connector taped around the headlight wiring harness (C, **Figure 122**).

*NOTE*
*In Step 5, make the test on the switch side of the clutch switch and engine stop switch connectors, not on the harness side connectors.*

4. Check for continuity between the black/red terminal in the clutch switch connector and the black/brown terminal in the engine stop switch 3-pin connector. There should be continuity with the clutch lever pulled in and no continuity with the clutch lever released.

5. Replace the clutch switch if it did not test as specified in Step 4.

6. Remove the clutch lever holder (A, **Figure 127**) mounting bolts and remove the holder and clutch cable from the handlebar.

7. Slide the rubber boot away from the clutch lever holder.

8. Remove the screw (A, **Figure 128**), mounting bracket (B) and clutch switch (C).

9. Disconnect the two connectors (**Figure 129**) at the clutch switch and test the switch at its contacts. The switch should have continuity when the button is pressed, and no continuity when the button is released. Note the following:

a. Replace the clutch switch if faulty.

10

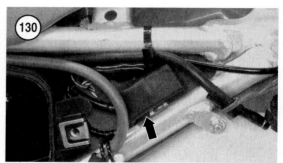

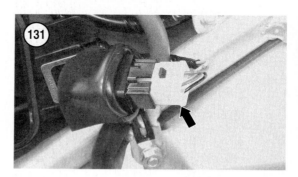

b. If the clutch switch operates correctly, check for a short in the wiring between the clutch switch and the starter relay switch and between the clutch switch and the engine stop switch.

10. Installation is the reverse of these steps. Note the following:

a. Make sure the electrical connectors are tight and free of corrosion.

b. Apply dielectric grease to the electrical connectors.

c. Align the clamp surface on the clutch lever holder with the punch or paint mark on the handlebar (B, **Figure 127**). Install the clutch lever holder and tighten the upper bolt, then the lower bolt to 8.8 N•m (78 in.-lb.).

*NOTE*
*On models with Renthal aluminum handlebars, a strip of plastic was originally wrapped around the handlebar underneath the clutch lever holder. The plastic allows the clutch lever holder to be tightened fully, while allowing the holder to rotate in a fall without damaging the handle bar.*

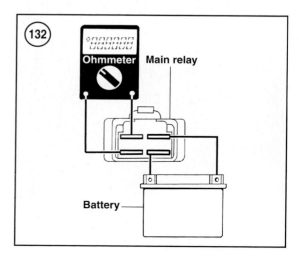

## MAIN RELAY
### (CRF250X)

The main relay is mounted on the left side of the motorcycle, directly above the coolant reserve tank.

## Testing/Replacement

1. Remove the left side cover (Chapter Sixteen).
2. Push the main relay and its connector (**Figure 130**) to disconnect its rubber boot from the frame

bracket. Then disconnect the connector (**Figure 131**) and remove the main relay.

3. Bench test the main relay as follows:

a. Clean the main relay electrical contacts.

b. Check for continuity across the two main relay terminals identified in **Figure 132**. There should be no continuity.

c. If there is continuity, replace the main relay.

d. If there is no continuity, leave the ohmmeter connected to the main relay and continue with substep e.

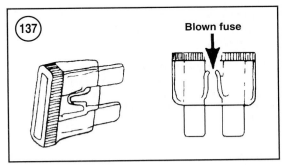

trouble is a short circuit in the wiring. Worn-through insulation may cause this or a short from a disconnected wire to ground.

A 15-amp plastic encapsulated fuse is mounted next to the starter relay switch.

1. Remove the left (CRF450X) or right (CRF250X) side cover (Chapter Sixteen).

2. Pull the starter relay switch from its rubber case. See **Figure 133** (CRF250X) or **Figure 134** (CRF450X).

3. Disconnect the starter relay switch electrical connector (**Figure 135**, typical). Repair any dirty, loose fitting or damaged terminals.

4. Remove the fuse (**Figure 136**, typical). Replace the fuse if blown (**Figure 137**).

5. Install by reversing these steps.

*NOTE*
*Always carry a spare 15-amp fuse.*

e. Connect the positive lead, then the negative lead from a fully charged 12-volt battery to the main relay terminals identified in **Figure 132**. There should be continuity.

f. If there is no continuity, replace the main relay.

g. If there is continuity, the main relay is operational.

4. Reverse Step 1 and Step 2 to complete installation.

## FUSE
### (CRF250X AND CRF450X)

Whenever the fuse blows, find out the reason for the failure before replacing the fuse. Usually, the

## WIRING DIAGRAMS

Wiring diagrams for all models are located at the end of this manual.

10

### Table 1 IGNITION SYSTEM SPECIFICATIONS

| | |
|---|---|
| Alternator exciter coil peak voltage | |
| CRF250R, CRF250X and CRF450R | 50 volts minimum |
| CRF450X | – |
| Alternator exciter coil resistance* | |
| CRF450R | 9-25 ohms |
| CRF450F | 9-28 ohms |
| Direct ignition coil peak voltage | |
| CRF250R | 100 volts minimum |
| CRF250X | 200 volts minimum |
| Ignition coil peak voltage | |
| CRF450R and CRF450X | 100 volts minimum |
| Ignition coil resistance* | |
| Primary | |
| CRF250R and CRF250X | 0.07-0.10 ohms |
| CRF450R and CRF450X | 0.1-0.3 ohms |
| Secondary | |
| CRF250R and CRF250X | 4.6-4.8 k ohms |
| CRF450R and CRF450X (with plug cap) | 9-16 k ohms |
| CRF450R and CRF450X (without plug cap) | 4-8 k ohms |
| Ignition pulse generator peak voltage | 0.7 volts minimum |
| Ignition pulse generator resistance* | |
| CRF450R and CRF450X | 180-280 ohms |
| All other models | – |
| Ignition timing | |
| CRF250R and CRF250X | 6-8° BTDC at 1700 rpm |
| CRF450R | 6-8° BTDC at 1500 rpm |
| CRF450X | 6-8° BTDC at 1800 rpm |

*Test must be made at an ambient temperature of 20° C (68° F). Do not test when the engine or component is hot.

### Table 2 BATTERY AND CHARGING SYSTEM SPECIFICATIONS (CRF250X AND CRF450X)

| | |
|---|---|
| Alternator capacity | |
| CRF250X | 64.4 watts at 5000 rpm |
| CRF450X | 76 watts at 5000 rpm |
| Battery | |
| Type | Maintenance-free (sealed) |
| Capacity | |
| CRF250X | 12 volts, 4 amp hour |
| CRF450X | 12 volts, 6 amp hour |
| Battery charging current | |
| Normal charge | 0.5 amps at 5-10 hours |
| Quick charge | |
| CRF250X | 5.0 amps at 30 minutes |
| CRF450X | 3.0 amps at 1 hour |
| Current leakage test | 0.1 mA (maximum) |
| Voltage (at 20° C [68° F]) | |
| Fully charged | 13.0-13.2 volts |
| Requires charging | Below 12.3 volts |

### Table 3 MAINTENANCE-FREE BATTERY STATE OF CHARGE (CRF250X AND CRF450X)

| Voltage reading | State of charge |
|---|---|
| 12.8-13.0 | 100% |
| 12.5-12.8 | 75-100% |
| | (continued) |

### Table 3 MAINTENANCE-FREE BATTERY STATE OF CHARGE (CRF250X AND CRF450X) (continued)

| Voltage reading | State of charge |
|---|---|
| 12.0-12.5 | 50-75% |
| 11.5-12.0 | 25-50% |
| 11.5 volts or less | 0-25% |

### Table 4 STARTER BRUSH SPECIFICATIONS (CRF250X AND CRF450X)

| Starter motor brush length | |
|---|---|
| Standard | 10.25 mm (0.404 in.) |
| Service limit | 6.75 mm (0.266 in.) |

### Table 5 REPLACEMENT BULBS AND MAIN FUSE (CRF250X AND CRF450X)

| | |
|---|---|
| Headlight | 12 volt, 35 watt |
| Taillight | LED |
| Main fuse | 15 amp |

### Table 6 ELECTRICAL SYSTEM TORQUE SPECIFICATIONS

| | N•m | in.-lb. | ft.-lb. |
|---|---|---|---|
| Clutch lever holder mounting bolts | 8.8 | 78 | – |
| Engine oil drain bolt | | | |
|   CRF250R and CRF250X | 22 | – | 16 |
|   CRF450R | | | |
|     2002-2003 | 22 | – | 16 |
|     2004-on | 16 | – | 12 |
|   CRF450X | 16 | – | 12 |
| Flywheel nut[1] | 64 | – | 47 |
| Ignition pulse generator mounting bolt[2] | | | |
|   CRF250R and CRF250X | 5.2 | 46 | – |
|   CRF450R | | | |
|     2002-2004 | 5.4 | 48 | – |
|     2005 | 5.2 | 46 | – |
|   CRF450X | 5.2 | 46 | |
| Left crankcase cover mounting bolts | | | |
|   CRF250R | – | – | – |
|   CRF250X | 12 | 106 | – |
|   CRF450R | | | |
|     2002-2004 | 9.8 | 87 | – |
|     2005 | 12 | 106 | – |
|   CRF450X | see text | – | – |
| Rear fender mounting bolt | | | |
|   CRF250X | 13 | 115 | – |
|   All other models | – | – | – |
| Stator mounting screw[2] | | | |
|   CRF250R and CRF250X | 2.5 | 22 | – |
|   CRF450R | | | |
|     2002-2003 | 2.0 | 18 | – |
|     2004-on | 2.6 | 23 | – |
|   CRF450X | 2.6 | 23 | – |

(continued)

10

**Table 6 ELECTRICAL SYSTEM TORQUE SPECIFICATIONS (continued)**

|                            | N•m  | in.-lb. | ft.-lb. |
|----------------------------|------|---------|---------|
| Ignition timing hole cap[3] |      |         |         |
| CRF250R and CRF250X        | 5.9  | 52      | –       |
| CRF450R                    |      |         |         |
| 2002-2003                  | 9.9  | 87      | –       |
| 2004                       | 5.9  | 52      | –       |
| 2005                       | 6.0  | 53      | –       |
| CRF450X                    | 10   | 88      | –       |

1. Lubricate the flywheel nut threads and seating surface with engine oil.
2. Apply medium strength threadlock onto fastener threads.
3. Lubricate threads with grease.

# CHAPTER ELEVEN

# COOLING SYSTEM

The cooling system consists of two radiators, a radiator cap, water pump and hoses. A coolant reserve tank is used on CRF250X and CRF450X models. An optional electric cooling fan can be installed on CRF250X models and is covered in this chapter. During operation, the coolant heats up and expands, thus pressurizing the system. The radiator cap seals the system. A water and antifreeze mixture, cooled in the radiator, circulates through the radiator and into the cylinder head, where it passes through the cylinder water jackets and back into the radiator.

The water pump requires no routine maintenance; it can be serviced after first removing the right crankcase cover. There is no thermostat or cooling fan (except for the optional CRF250X cooling fan) and the cooling system can be serviced with the engine mounted in the frame.

This chapter describes repair and replacement of cooling system components. Cooling system maintenance procedures are in Chapter Three.

Cooling system specifications are in **Tables 1-3** and at the end of this chapter.

## COOLING SYSTEM SAFETY PRECAUTIONS

*WARNING*
*Do not remove the radiator cap (A, Figure 1, typical), coolant drain plug or disconnect any coolant hose immediately after or during engine operation. Scalding fluid and steam may be blown out under pressure and cause injury.*

When removing the radiator cap, first place a rag over the cap and stand to one side of the radiator. Slowly turn the radiator cap counterclockwise to its safety stop position to allow pressure in the system to escape. Then push the cap down and turn it counterclockwise to remove it from the radiator. On CRF250R and CRF450R models, check the coolant level in the radiator *before* the first ride of the day when the engine is cold. On CRF250X and CRF450X models, check the coolant level in the coolant reserve tank.

11

To protect the engine and cooling systems, drain and flush the cooling system at the intervals specified in Chapter Three. Refer to the *Coolant Change* in Chapter Three.

Always handle coolant in a safe manner. Do not store coolant in open containers where it is accessible to children or pets. Dispose of coolant in an appropriate manner.

> *CAUTION*
> *Never operate the cooling system with water only, even in climates where antifreeze protection is not required. Antifreeze protects the engine and cooling system internal surfaces while acting as a lubricant.*

## COOLING SYSTEM INSPECTION

1. Check the radiators for clogged or damaged fins.
2. Flush each radiator with a low-pressure stream of water from a garden hose. Spray the front and back of the radiators to remove all dirt and debris. Carefully use a whiskbroom or stiff paintbrush to remove any stubborn dirt.
3. Check each radiator for loose or missing mounting bolts.
4. Check all coolant hoses for cracks or damage. Replace any questionable parts. Make sure the hose clamps are tight, but not so tight that they cut the hoses. Note the direction of the hose clamps before removing them.
5. Make sure the overflow tube (CRF250R and CRF450R) or siphon tube (CRF250X and CRF450X) is connected to the radiator (B, **Figure 1**) and is not clogged or damaged.
6. To check the cooling system for leaks, pressure test it as described in this chapter.
7. If coolant loss is evident, check the cooling system hoses, water pump and water jackets (cylinder and cylinder head) carefully. Coolant stains around hoses and other parts in the cooling system may indicate a leak.

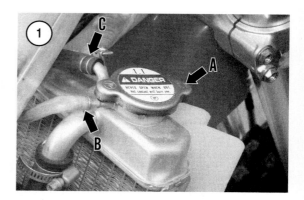

seals are damaged and the water pump should be rebuilt. Refer to *Water Pump* in this chapter.

## WATER PUMP SEAL INSPECTION

Check for signs of coolant or coolant stains from the inspection hole in the bottom of the right crankcase cover. See **Figure 2** (CRF250R and CRF250X) or **Figure 3** (CRF450R and CRF450X). If there is leakage, one or both of the water pump

## COOLING SYSTEM PRESSURE TEST

Perform the following test whenever troubleshooting the cooling system. Perform this test when the engine is cold. Use a hand pump tester to pressurize the system.

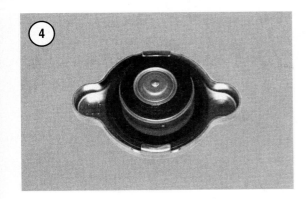

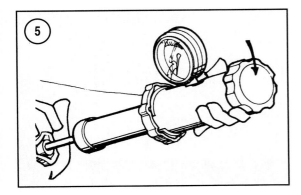

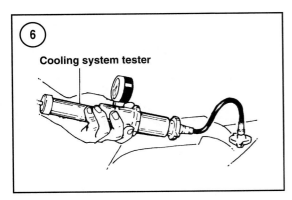

Cooling system tester

*WARNING*
*Never remove the radiator cap (A, Figure 1), coolant drain plug or disconnect any coolant hose while the engine and radiator are hot. Scalding fluid and steam may be blown out under pressure and cause serious injury.*

1. With the engine cold, remove the radiator cap (A, **Figure 1**).

2. Add coolant to the radiator to bring the level up to the filler neck.

3. Check the rubber washers on the radiator cap (**Figure 4**). Replace the cap if the washers show signs of deterioration, cracking or other damage. If the radiator cap is good, perform Step 4.

*CAUTION*
*Do not exceed the maximum pressure test specification in Table 1 or the cooling system components may be damaged.*

4. Lubricate the rubber washer on the bottom of the radiator cap with coolant and install it on a cooling system pressure tester (**Figure 5**). Apply the amount of pressure specified in **Table 1** and check for a pressure drop. Replace the cap if it cannot hold this pressure.

5. Mount the pressure tester onto the radiator filler neck (**Figure 6**) and pressure test the cooling system to the specification listed in **Table 1**. If the system cannot hold this pressure, check for a coolant leak:

   a. Radiator cap. If the radiator cap passed the pressure test in Step 4, but is now leaking, inspect the radiator filler neck and cap mounting flange for damage.

   b. Leaking or damaged coolant hoses.

   c. Damaged water pump mechanical seal.

   d. Water pump leakage.

   e. Loose coolant drain bolt.

   f. Warped cylinder head or cylinder mating surfaces.

*NOTE*
*If the test pressure drops rapidly, but there are no visible coolant leaks, coolant may be leaking into the cylinder head. Perform a leakdown test as described in Chapter Two.*

6. Check all cooling system hoses for damage or deterioration. Replace any questionable hose. Make sure all hose clamps are tight.

7. Remove the tester and install the radiator cap.

## RADIATORS

The radiators are linked with hoses at the top and bottom tanks. Heated water from the engine returns to the radiator by the upper hose. The water is cooled as it circulates to the bottom of the radiators,

11

where the cooled water then returns to the engine by the lower hose.

### Removal/Installation

1. Place the bike on a workstand.
2. Remove the seat (Chapter Sixteen).
3. Remove the fuel tank (Chapter Nine).
4. Drain the cooling system as described in Chapter Three.
5. On CRF250X models, if the optional cooling fan is installed, disconnect the single pin connector at the fan motor switch and the 2-pin black connector at the fan motor.
6. Remove aftermarket radiator guards, if so equipped.
7. Remove the radiator shrouds.
8. Remove the radiator grills (**Figure 7**, typical). Check for cracked or broken mounting tabs on the radiator grills.
9. Check the cooling system (hoses, radiators and water pump) for coolant stains (green or white residue), loose hose clamps and damage before removing parts. To confirm a leak, pressure test the system as described in this chapter.

> *CAUTION*
> *Take care in removing each hose from its fitting. Fittings are fragile and easily damaged. **Carefully** twist the hose to break its bond from the fitting. If the hose is seized, insert a small screwdriver between the hose and fitting, then use a spray lubricant, like WD-40, to loosen the hose. Another option is to heat the hose end with a heat gun, then twist the hose. After heating the hose, wear thick work or*

> *welding gloves when removing the hose as it will be hot! Thoroughly clean the fitting. Replace damaged hoses. See **Removing Hoses** in Chapter One.*

> *NOTE*
> *Before removing preformed hoses, note the hose routing and direction. These hoses must be reinstalled correctly.*

10. Disconnect the overflow (CRF250R and CRF450R) or siphon (CRF250X and CRF450X) hose at the radiator (B, **Figure 1**, typical).

> *NOTE*
> *Note the direction of the hose clamps before removing them.*

11. Loosen the hose clamps and disconnect the hoses from the radiator:
   a. CRF250R and CRF250X: See **Figure 8**, **Figure 9** and **Figure 10**.
   b. CRF450R and CRF450X: See C, **Figure 1**, **Figure 11** and **Figure 12**.

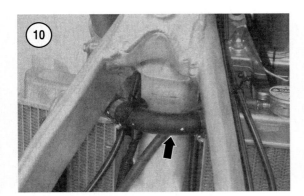

12. Perform the *Inspection* procedures in this section.

13. Install the radiators by reversing the removal steps while noting the following:

*CAUTION*
*When installing aftermarket radiator guards, make sure the mounting bolts are of the correct length. Check the placement of each bolt to avoid damaging the bolt or frame.*

  a. Replace missing or damaged bushings.
  b. If removed, make sure to install all collars within the rubber mounting bushings.
  c. When installing the radiators, do not pinch the wiring harnesses between the radiators and frame. Check both radiators.
  d. Install the clamps so they only clamp the hose and do not contact surrounding parts. Do not overtighten the clamps. Position the clamps so they can be easily accessed when checking their tightness with a screwdriver or socket.
  e. Do not tighten the radiator mounting bolts until the hoses are connected at both ends. Then

check the hose routing to make they are not twisted. Tighten the radiator mounting bolts securely.

  f. Add engine coolant and bleed the cooling system as described in Chapter Three. Check for leaks.

**Inspection**

Air must be allowed to pass through the radiators to dissipate heat from the coolant, to the radiator fins and then into the air. Clogged, bent and damaged radiator fins reduce the cooling efficiency and can cause engine overheating.

1. Flush off the exterior of the radiator with a low-pressure stream of water from a garden hose. Spray the front and back of the radiator to remove all dirt and debris. Carefully use a whiskbroom or a stiff paintbrush to remove any stubborn dirt.

*CAUTION*
*Do not damage the cooling fins and tubes.*

2. Examine the radiator's cooling surface for damage. If the radiator is slightly damaged and is repairable, refer service to a radiator repair shop.

3. Carefully straighten out any bent cooling fins with a wide-blade screwdriver. Replace the radiator if it is damaged across 20 percent or more of its frontal area.

4. Check for cracks or leakage (usually a moss green colored residue) at the filler neck, the inlet and outlet hose fittings and the tank seams.

5. Check for missing or damaged radiator mounting bushings and collars. Replace them if necessary.

6. Check the sealing surface in the top of the right radiator where the radiator cap pressure seal oper-

11

ates (**Figure 13**). This surface must be smooth and clean. Check the sealing surface if the radiator has been damaged in this area.

7. Inspect the radiator cap (**Figure 4**) and seal for damage. Check for a bent or distorted cap. Raise the vacuum valve and rubber seal and rinse the cap with water to flush away any loose rust or dirt particles. If the condition of the radiator cap is in doubt, pressure-check it as described in this chapter.

8. Replace hoses that are hard, cracked or show signs of deterioration. Hold each hose and flex it in several directions to check for damage.

9. Clean the hose clamps with solvent. Replace damaged or corroded hose clamps.

10. On CRF250X models, if used, service the optional cooling fan assembly as described in this chapter.

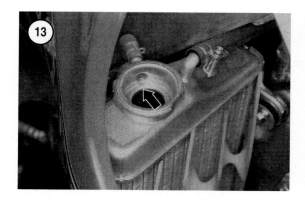

## COOLANT RESERVE TANK (CRF250X AND CRF450X)

The coolant reserve tank, mounted behind the left side cover, helps to keep the radiator full of coolant at all times. A siphon hose connects the coolant reserve tank to the right side radiator.

In operation, the coolant reserve tank is partially filled with coolant. Upper and lower level lines on the tank indicate the correct coolant level. As the coolant heats up, it expands and flows through the radiator cap and into the reserve tank. As the engine nears its operating temperature, a vacuum valve in the radiator cap closes and seals the cooling system. When the engine stops running and the coolant temperature begins to drop, a vacuum is created in the radiator. The vacuum opens the vacuum valve in the radiator cap and draws coolant from the reserve tank, through the valve in the radiator cap and into the radiator to refill it.

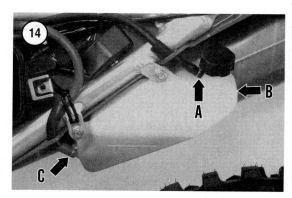

### Removal/Installation

1A. On CRF250X models, perform the following:

    a. Remove the left side cover (Chapter Sixteen).

    b. Disconnect the breather hose (A, **Figure 14**) at the tank.

    c. Unbolt and remove the coolant reserve tank (B, **Figure 14**). Note the hose clamp used on the front mounting bolt.

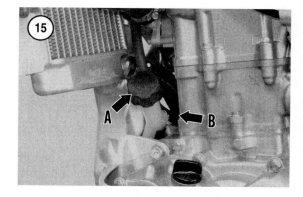

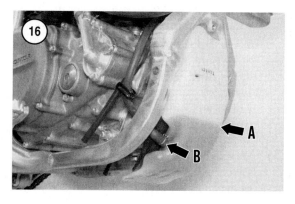

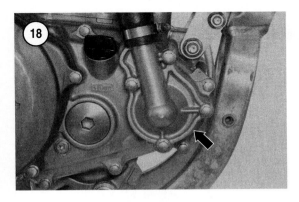

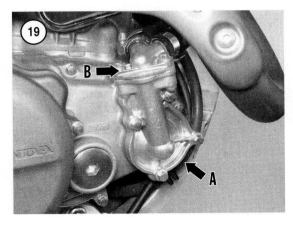

d. Disconnect the siphon hose (C, **Figure 14**) and drain the coolant into a clean container. Plug the siphon hose.

1B. On CRF450X models, perform the following:

a. Remove the right engine guard and center engine guard (Chapter Sixteen).

b. Remove the fill cap (A, **Figure 15**) and remove the coolant reserve tank (A, **Figure 16**) from the frame.

c. Remove the breather (B, **Figure 15**) and siphon (B, **Figure 16**) hoses at the tank. Plug the siphon hose.

2. Drain the coolant into a clean container.

3. Check the tank for damage. Coolant stain marks on the outside of the tank may indicate a leaking cap or damaged tank.

4. Reverse this procedure to install the coolant reserve tank. Note the following:

a. Check the breather and siphon hose routing at the tank.

b. Fill the tank so the coolant level is between the two level marks on the tank. Start the engine and allow it to warm up for a few minutes.

c. With the engine running at idle speed, support the machine in an upright position. Do not support it on its sidestand. The coolant level must be between the level marks on the tank.

d. Turn the engine off. Add coolant to the tank if necessary.

## WATER PUMP

The water pump is mounted inside the right crankcase cover, and is gear driven by the crankshaft. The water pump bearing is mounted in the right crankcase cover and is lubricated by engine oil. The water pump uses two different types of seals. An oil seal prevents oil from leaking into the coolant passage, and a water seal prevents coolant from leaking into the oil.

The integrity of the pump seals can be made by examining the inspection hole (**Figure 2** or **Figure 3**) in the bottom of the right crankcase cover and the condition of the engine oil. If there is leakage from the hole, the oil or water seal is damaged. Coolant discoloration or milky engine oil is an indication of seal and water pump damage. In both instances, the water pump must be rebuilt. A general inspection of the water pump impeller can be made by removing the water pump cover as described in this section.

### Water Pump Cover
### Removal/Installation

The water pump cover can be removed with the right crankcase cover installed on the engine. See **Figure 17** (CRF250R and CRF250X), **Figure 18** (CRF450R) or A, **Figure 19** (CRF450X).

11

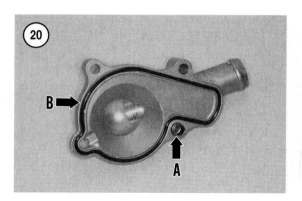

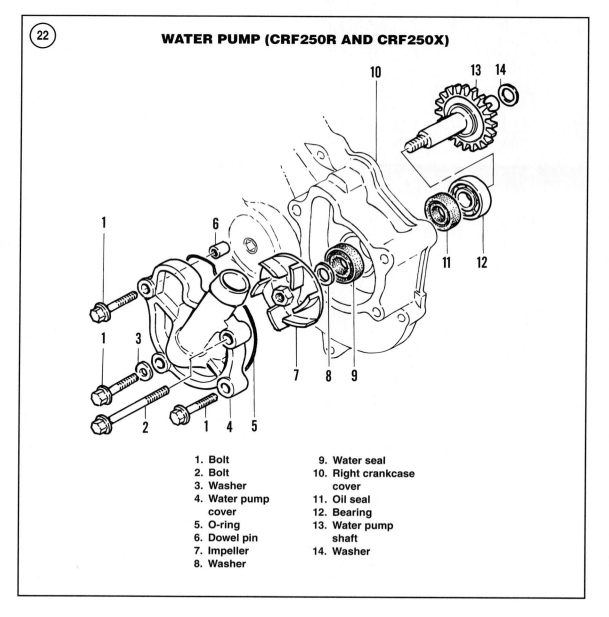

**WATER PUMP (CRF250R AND CRF250X)**

1. Bolt
2. Bolt
3. Washer
4. Water pump
   cover
5. O-ring
6. Dowel pin
7. Impeller
8. Washer
9. Water seal
10. Right crankcase
    cover
11. Oil seal
12. Bearing
13. Water pump
    shaft
14. Washer

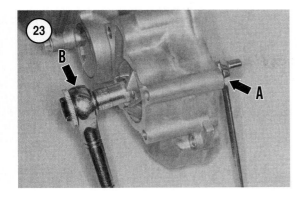

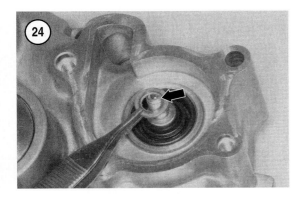

1. Drain the cooling system as described under *Coolant Change* in Chapter Three.

2A. On CRF450X models, remove the bolts, water hose joint and O-ring from the top of the water pump housing (B, **Figure 19**).

2B. All other models, loosen the hose clamps and disconnect the coolant hose from the water pump cover.

> *NOTE*
> *Different length cover bolts are used. Note their location so they can be reinstalled in the correct location.*

3. Loosen and remove the water pump cover mounting bolts in a crossing pattern. Do not lose the washer on the coolant drain bolt.

4. Remove the water pump cover and O-ring.

5. Locate the dowel pin (A, **Figure 20**, typical) and remove if necessary.

6. Clean the cover and replace the O-ring (B, **Figure 20**, typical) if leaking or damaged.

7. Inspect the impeller (**Figure 21**, typical) for damage. If necessary, replace the impeller as described in this section.

> *NOTE*
> *The impeller can be replaced with the right crankcase cover mounted on the engine. Refer to the water pump procedure later in this section.*

8. Installation is the reverse of these steps. Note the following:

a. Lightly lubricate the O-ring with grease and install it into the groove in the cover (B, **Figure 20**, typical).

b. On CRF250R, CRF250X and 2002-2004 CRF450R models, tighten the water pump cover mounting bolts to 12 N•m (106 in.-lb.).

c. On 2005 CRF450R and CRF450X models, tighten the water pump cover mounting bolts securely.

d. On CRF450X models, replace the water joint O-ring if leaking or damaged. Then reconnect the hose joint onto the water pump cover and tighten the mounting bolts (B, **Figure 19**) securely.

e. Refill and bleed the cooling system as described in Chapter Three. Check for coolant leaks.

**Water Pump Removal/Installation
(CRF250R and CRF250X)**

Refer to **Figure 22**.

1. Remove the water pump cover as previously described.

2. Remove the right crankcase cover as described in Chapter Six.

> *NOTE*
> *The impeller uses left-hand threads.*

3. Hold the water pump shaft with a wrench (**Figure 23**), then turn the impeller *clockwise* to remove it. Remove the washer (**Figure 24**) installed behind the impeller.

> *CAUTION*
> *When removing the water pump shaft in Step 4, pull the shaft straight up and out of the crankcase cover to avoid tearing the seals.*

4. Remove the water pump shaft from the right crankcase (**Figure 25**).

5. Inspect the seals and bearing as described in this section. If necessary, replace the seals and bearing as described under *Bearing and Seal Replacement* in this chapter.

6. Lightly lubricate the water pump shaft and the water seal lip (9, **Figure 22**) with grease.

*CAUTION*
*If there are any nicks or burrs on the water pump shaft, remove them with a fine-grade sandpaper or crocus cloth. The shaft must be smooth to avoid damaging the oil and water seals.*

7. Install the shaft through the bearing from inside the crankcase cover (**Figure 25**). Then turn the shaft to pass it through both seals. Do not force the shaft as this may tear the seals.

8. Install the washer onto the water pump shaft (**Figure 24**).

*NOTE*
*The impeller uses left-hand threads.*

9. Turn the impeller *counterclockwise* to install it onto the water pump shaft. Hold the water pump shaft with a wrench and tighten the impeller (**Figure 23**) to 12 N•m (106 in.-lb.). Turn the water pump shaft by hand. It should turn under slight resistance.

10. Install the right crankcase cover (Chapter Six).

11. Install the water pump cover as described in this chapter.

**Water Pump Removal/Installation (CRF450R and CRF450X)**

Refer to **Figure 26** (CRF450R) or **Figure 27** (CRF450X).

1. Remove the water pump cover as previously described.

2. Remove the right crankcase cover as described in Chapter Seven.

*CAUTION*
*When removing the water pump shaft in Step 3, pull the shaft straight up and out of the crankcase cover to prevent tearing the seals.*

3A. On CRF450R models, perform the following:

a. Hold the water pump shaft with a wrench (**Figure 28**), then loosen and remove the impeller (**Figure 29**).

b. Remove the washer (**Figure 30**).

c. Remove the water pump shaft from the right crankcase.

3B. On CRF450X models, perform the following:

*NOTE*
*To prevent rounding the hex shoulders on the impeller, loosen it with a 6-point socket.*

a. Hold the water pump shaft with a tapered punch (**Figure 31**), then loosen and remove the impeller (**Figure 32**).

b. Remove the washer (**Figure 30**).

c. Remove the water pump shaft.

d. Note the seal assembly installed in the impeller (**Figure 33**).

4. Inspect the seals and bearing as described in this section. If necessary, replace the seals and bearing as described under *Bearing and Seal Replacement* in this chapter.

5. Lightly lubricate the water pump shaft and the water seal lip with grease.

*CAUTION*
*If there are any nicks or burrs on the water pump shaft, remove them with a fine-grade sandpaper or crocus cloth. The shaft must be smooth to prevent from damaging the oil and water seals.*

6. Install the shaft through the bearing from inside the crankcase cover. Then turn the shaft to pass it through both seals. Do not force the shaft as this may tear the seals.

㉖ **WATER PUMP (CRF450R)**

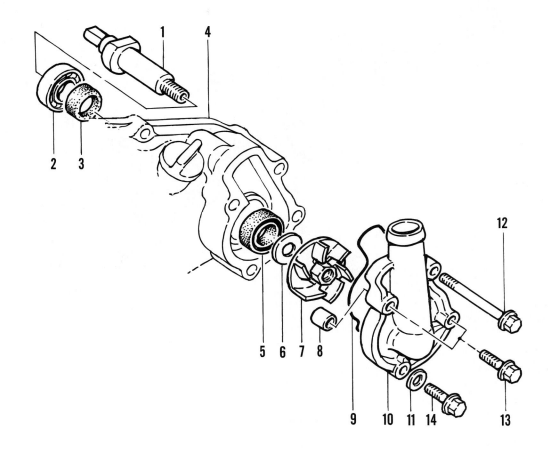

1. Water pump shaft
2. Bearing
3. Oil seal
4. Right crankcase cover
5. Water seal
6. Washer
7. Impeller
8. Dowel pin
9. O-ring
10. Water pump cover
11. Washer
12. Bolt
13. Bolt
14. Bolt

11

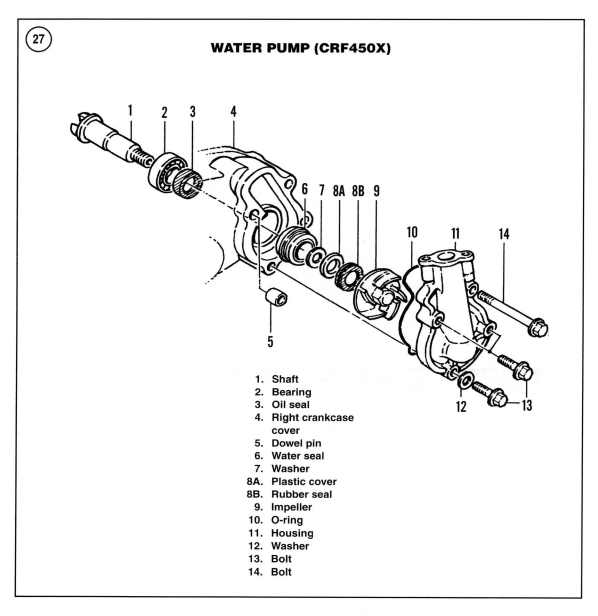

**(27)**

**WATER PUMP (CRF450X)**

1. Shaft
2. Bearing
3. Oil seal
4. Right crankcase
   cover
5. Dowel pin
6. Water seal
7. Washer
8A. Plastic cover
8B. Rubber seal
9. Impeller
10. O-ring
11. Housing
12. Washer
13. Bolt
14. Bolt

**(28)**

**(29)**

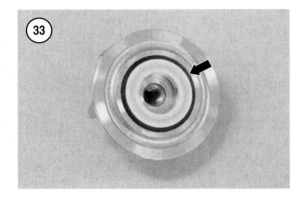

7. Install the washer onto the water pump shaft (**Figure 30**).

8. On CRF450X models, lubricate the impeller's plastic washer (where it contacts the seal) (**Figure 33**) with coolant.

9. Thread the impeller onto the water pump shaft. Hold the water pump shaft (**Figure 28** or **Figure 31**) and tighten the impeller to 12 N•m (106 in.-lb.). Turn the water pump shaft by hand. On CRF450R models, it should turn under slight resistance and have some end play. On CRF450X models, the shaft should turn with noticeable resistance and have no end play.

10. Install the right crankcase cover (Chapter Seven).

11. Install the water pump cover as described in this chapter.

**Water Pump Inspection (All Models)**

1. Clean and dry all parts.

2. Inspect the impeller blades for cracks and corrosion.

3. On CRF250R and CRF250X models, inspect the water pump shaft gear for broken or missing teeth.

4. Inspect the water pump shaft for burrs, excessive wear or damage. Check the areas on the shaft that contact the seals for wear. Replace the water pump shaft if there is any wear or scoring in these areas.

5. Inspect the water seal for tearing and other damage. See **Figure 34** (CRF450X) or **Figure 35** (all other models).

6. Turn the water pump shaft bearing (**Figure 36**) inner race by hand. The bearing race should turn smoothly. Replace the bearing and both seals if the bearing is damaged.

11

458                                                        CHAPTER ELEVEN

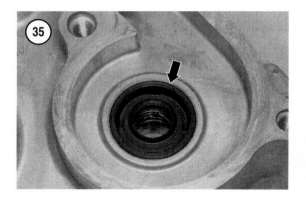

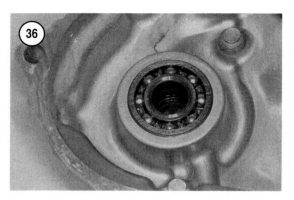

7. On CRF450X models, inspect the impeller seal assembly (**Figure 33**). Check the outer plastic piece for cracks, excessive wear and other damage. If damaged, replace both the impeller seal assembly (**Figure 33**) and the water seal (**Figure 34**) at the same time.

8. If there are signs of coolant leakage from the inspection hole in the bottom of the right crankcase cover, replace both seals and bearing as described in this section.

### Water Pump Bearing and Seal (All Models)

*Removal*

Refer to **Figure 22** (CRF250R and CRF250X), **Figure 26** (CRF450R) or **Figure 27** (CRF450X).

*CAUTION*
*When removing the seals, avoid damaging the mounting bore.*

1. Before removing the bearing, record the direction the manufacturer's marks face for proper rein-

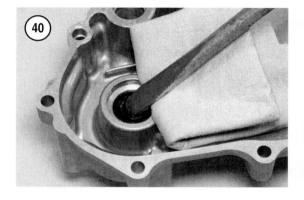

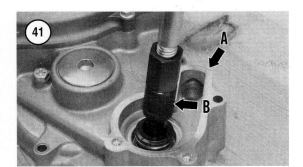

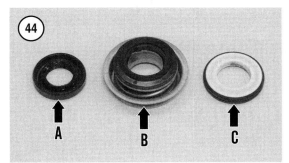

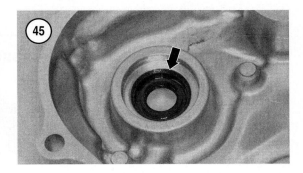

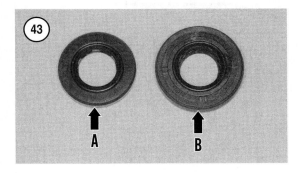

b. Have an assistant hold the right crankcase (A, **Figure 41**) cover firmly against a flat piece of wood or rubber mat. Then remove the water seal with a blind bearing removal tool (B, **Figure 41**). See **Figure 42**.

4. Clean and dry the mounting bore. On CRF450X models, remove all sealer residue from the cover's water seal mounting bore. This sealer was originally applied to the seal.

5. Inspect the bore for burrs or nicks that could cause the seals to leak.

*Installation*

Refer to the following illustrations when installing the seals and bearing in this section:

   a. **Figure 22** and **Figure 43** (CRF250R and CRF250X).

   b. **Figure 26** and **Figure 43** (CRF450R).

   c. **Figure 27** and **Figure 44** (CRF450X).

1. Install the oil seal (A, **Figure 43** or A, **Figure 44**) as follows:

   a. Support the right crankcase cover on wooden blocks with the inner surface facing up.

   b. Pack the lip of the new seal with grease.

   c. Position the seal in its bore with its open side facing up (**Figure 45**).

stallation. Install the seals in the direction specified in the text.

2. Remove the bearing with a blind bearing removal tool (**Figure 37**).

3A. On CRF250R, CRF250X and CRF450R models, remove the seals as follows:

   a. With the cover's outer surface facing up, carefully pry the water seal (**Figure 38**) from its mounting bore.

   b. Insert a socket through the opening in the cover and remove the oil seal as shown in **Figure 39**.

3B. On CRF450X models, remove the seals as follows:

   a. Carefully pry the oil seal (**Figure 40**) from its mounting bore.

11

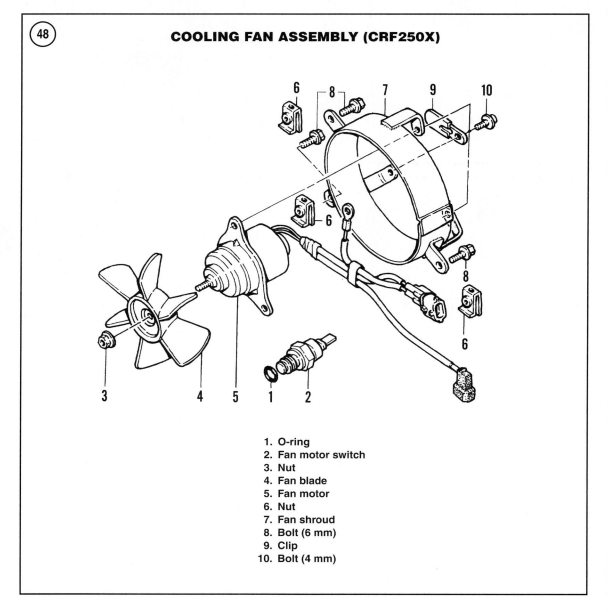

**COOLING FAN ASSEMBLY (CRF250X)**

1. O-ring
2. Fan motor switch
3. Nut
4. Fan blade
5. Fan motor
6. Nut
7. Fan shroud
8. Bolt (6 mm)
9. Clip
10. Bolt (4 mm)

d. Select a seal driver and drive the seal into the bore until it bottoms (**Figure 46**).
2. Install the bearing as follows:
 a. Support the right crankcase on wooden blocks with the inner surface facing up.
 b. Chill the bearing in a freezer before installing it.
 c. Place the new bearing squarely into the bore opening with its manufacturer's marks facing out.

*CAUTION*
*Applying pressure to the bearing's inner race will damage the bearing.*

 d. Place a bearing driver or socket on the bearing's outer race and drive the bearing into the bore until it bottoms. See **Figure 36**.
 e. Rotate the inner race by hand and check for smooth bearing rotation.
3A. On CRF250R, CRF250X and CRF450R models, install the water seal (B, **Figure 43**) as follows:
 a. Support the right crankcase cover on wooden blocks with the outer surface facing up.
 b. Pack the lip of the new seal with grease.
 c. Position the seal with its open side facing up and place it squarely against the bore opening.
 d. Select a seal driver and drive the seal into the bore until it is flush with the bearing bore surface (**Figure 35**).
3B. On CRF450X models, install the water seal (B, **Figure 44**) as follows:
 a. Support the right crankcase cover on wooden blocks with the outer surface facing up.

*NOTE*
*A sealer has been pre-applied to the metal part of the seal (B, **Figure 44**). Do not remove it.*

 b. Center the seal's metal shoulder into the bore.
 c. Select a driver that seats against the metal shoulder. The inside of the driver should be large enough to fit over the seal without damaging the top of the seal. Drive the seal squarely into the bore until its shoulder bottoms against the top of the seal bore (**Figure 34**).

4. On CRF450X models, install the impeller seal (C, **Figure 44**) so that the plastic part of the seal faces out (away from the impeller). See **Figure 33**.

**COOLING FAN
(CRF250X)**

An optional electric cooling fan (**Figure 48**) can be installed on the right radiator. The fan pulls air through the radiator to reduce the engine coolant temperature and is designed for use on CRF250X models used in competition. A fan motor switch installed in place of the plug in the right radiator, turns the fan motor on and off by sensing engine coolant temperature. The fan motor 2-pin connector plugs into a black 2-pin connector installed in the main wiring harness. A single pin connector wired into the fan motor switch plugs into the fan motor switch.

11

**Table 1 COOLING SYSTEM SPECIFICATIONS**

| | |
|---|---|
| Coolant | Pro Honda HP or equivalent ethylene glycol antifreeze* with non-abrasive corrosion inhibitors |
| Mixture | 50/50 mix of distilled water and antifreeze |
| Radiator cap relief pressure | |
| CRF250R and CRF250X | 93-123 kPa (13.5-17.8 psi) |
| CRF450R and CRF450X | 108-137 kPa (16-20 psi) |
| *Pro Honda HP coolant is premixed. Do not add water. | |

**Table 2 COOLANT CAPACITY**

|  | Liters | U.S. qt. |
|---|---|---|
| **Coolant change** | | |
| CRF205R | 0.93 | 0.98 |
| CRF250X | 1.13 | 1.19 |
| CRF450R | | |
| 2002-2004 | 1.03 | 1.09 |
| 2005 | 1.11 | 1.17 |
| CRF450X | 1.11 | 1.17 |
| **Engine disassembly** | | |
| CRF250R | 1.00 | 1.06 |
| CRF250X | 1.20 | 1.27 |
| CRF450R | | |
| 2002-2004 | 1.12 | 1.18 |
| 2005 | 1.20 | 1.27 |
| CRF450X | 1.20 | 1.27 |

**Table 3 COOLING SYSTEM TORQUE SPECIFICATIONS**

|  | N•m | in.-lb. |
|---|---|---|
| **Coolant drain bolt** | | |
| CRF250R, 2005 CRF450R and | | |
| CRF450X | – | – |
| All other models | 9.8 | 87 |
| **Water pump cover bolt** | | |
| CRF250R, CRF250X and | | |
| 2002-2004 CRF450R | 12 | 106 |
| 2005 CRF450R and CRF450X | – | – |
| **Water pump impeller** | 12 | 106 |

# CHAPTER TWELVE

# WHEELS, TIRES AND DRIVE CHAIN

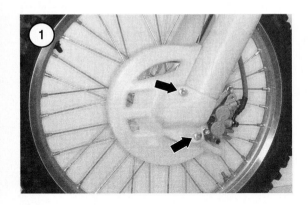

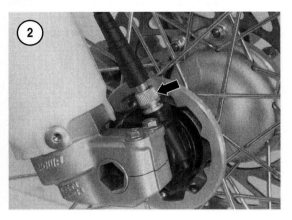

This chapter describes repair and maintenance for the front and rear wheels, hubs, drive chain, sprockets and tires. Routine maintenance procedures for these components are found in Chapter Three.

**Tables 1-3** are at the end of this chapter.

## FRONT WHEEL

### Removal

1. Support the motorcycle with the front wheel off the ground.
2. Remove the brake disc cover (**Figure 1**).
3. On CRF250X and CRF450X models, if necessary, disconnect the tripmeter cable (**Figure 2**). The tripmeter cable can be left onto the tripmeter gear unit when removing the front wheel.
4. Remove the axle nut (A, **Figure 3**).
5. Loosen the axle pinch bolts at both ends of the axle (B, **Figure 3** and **Figure 4**).
6. Remove the front axle from the right side and roll the wheel forward.
7. Remove the left side collar (**Figure 5**).
8A. On CRF250R and CRF450R models, remove the right side collar and dust seal (**Figure 6**).

8B. On CRF250X and CRF450X, remove the trip-meter gear unit (**Figure 7**).

*NOTE*
*Do not operate the front brake lever*
*whith the wheel removed. Insert a*
*spacer block between the pads until*
*the wheel is installed. This prevents*
*the caliper pistons from extending if*
*the lever is operated.*

9. Inspect the front wheel as described in this section.

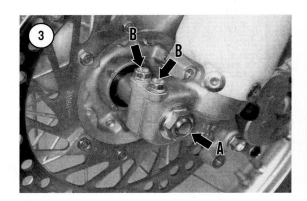

**Installation**

1. Clean the axle bearing surfaces on the fork tube and axle holders.
2. Remove the spacer block from between the brake pads.
3A. On CRF250R and CRF450R models, apply grease to both seal lips.
3B. On CRF250X and CRF450X models, lubricate the seal lips in the tripmeter gear unit and the left side seal with grease. Then lubricate the bore and the plastic gear in the tripmeter gear unit with grease.
4. Lubricate the axle with grease. Do not lubricate the threads on the axle or axle nut. These threads must remain free of oil and grease when the nut is tightened.
5. Install the left collar with its shoulder side facing out (**Figure 5**).
6A. On CRF250R and CRF450R models, install the right collar with its dust cover facing out (**Figure 6**).
6B. On CRF250X and CRF450X models, install the tripmeter gear unit by aligning its two arms (A, **Figure 7**) with the grooves (B) in the hub.
7. Carefully insert the disc between the brake pads, then install the front axle from the left side.
8. On CRF250X and CRF450X models, check that the arm on the tripmeter gear unit (**Figure 8**) fits over the axle holder on the fork tube. Reconnect the tripmeter cable and tighten its knurled nut (**Figure 2**) securely.
9. Tighten the axle nut finger-tight.

*CAUTION*
*The front axle and pinch bolt tighten-*
*ing sequence in Steps 10-13 correctly*
*seats the front axle so that both sliders*

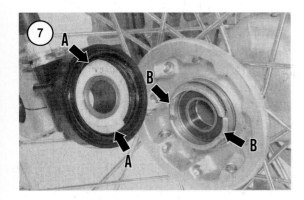

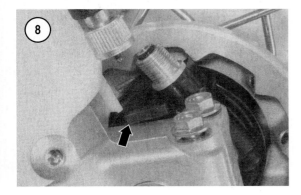

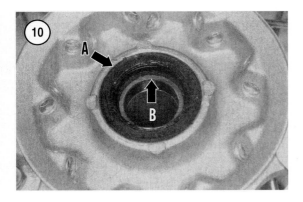

*are positioned parallel with each other. Fork misalignment can cause premature fork seal and bushing wear, increased wear against the slider and reduced fork performance and operation.*

10. Hold the axle with a 19 mm spark plug tool (Motion Pro 08-0239 [**Figure 9**]) and tighten the front axle nut (A, **Figure 3**) to 88 N•m (65 ft.-lb.).

11. Tighten the left axle pinch bolts (B, **Figure 3**) to 20 N•m (15 ft.-lb.).

12. Remove the motorcycle from the stand so the front wheel is on the ground. Apply the front brake, then compress and release the front suspension several times to reposition the pads against the disc and center the axle in the slider axle bores. Compress the fork as far as possible. Check that the fork legs are parallel.

13. Tighten the right axle pinch bolts (**Figure 4**) to 20 N•m (15 ft.-lb.).

14. Check that the wheel spins freely and the brake operates properly.

15. Install the brake disc cover bolts (with threadlock on threads) and tighten to 13 N•m (115 in.-lb.).

**Inspection**

1. Inspect the seal(s) (A, **Figure 10**) for wear, hardness, cracks or other damage. If necessary, replace the seals as described under *Front and Rear Hubs* in this chapter.

2. Inspect the bearings on both sides of the wheel for:

    a. Roughness. Turn each bearing inner race (B, **Figure 10**) by hand and check for smooth and quiet operation.

    b. Radial and lateral play (**Figure 11**). Try to push the bearing in and out to check for lateral play. Slight play is normal. Try to push the bearing up and down to check for radial play. Any radial play should be difficult to feel. If play is easily felt, the bearing is worn out. If necessary, replace both bearings as a set as described under *Front and Rear Hubs* in this chapter.

3. Clean the axle and collars in solvent to remove all grease and dirt. Make sure the axle contact surfaces are clean.

12

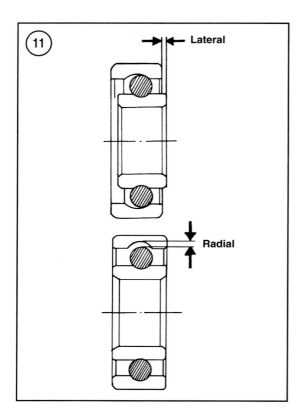

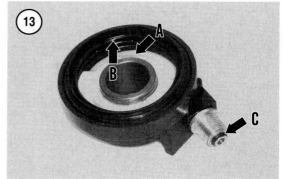

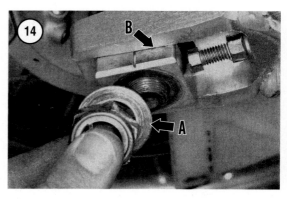

4. Check the axle for straightness with a set of V-blocks and dial indicator (**Figure 12**). Refer to **Table 1** for maximum axle runout. Actual runout is one-half of the gauge reading. Do not attempt to straighten a bent axle.

5. Check the brake disc bolts for tightness. To service the brake disc, refer to Chapter Fifteen.

6. On CRF250X and CRF450X models, check the speedometer gear unit. Inspect the plastic gear (A, **Figure 13**) for damage. Inspect the seal (B, **Figure 13**) for hardness, cracks and other damage. Replace the O-ring (C, **Figure 13**) if damaged.

7. Refer to *Wheel Service* in this chapter to inspect and true the rim.

## REAR WHEEL

### Removal

1. Support the motorcycle on a workstand with the rear wheel off the ground.

2. Loosen the rear axle nut. Then remove the axle nut, washer (A, **Figure 14**) and adjusting block (B) from the axle.

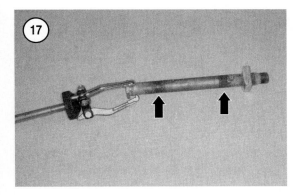

3. Move the rear wheel forward and slip the drive chain off the sprocket.

4. Remove the rear axle (A, **Figure 15**) and adjusting block (B, **Figure 15**) from the left side.

*NOTE*
*When an axle is not routinely lubricated with grease, water that enters along the axle may cause rust to form, seizing the rear axle to the rear wheel bearings. If the axle is stuck, spray a penetrating fluid (WD-40) along both sides of the wheel at the most accessible axle points. Allow time for the fluid to penetrate along the axle, then reinstall the axle nut and tap the axle with a plastic hammer to break it loose. If the axle is still tight, try to drive it far enough where a knock puller can be installed on its left side shoulder (**Figure 16**). Then remove the axle nut and operate the puller to remove the axle. When an axle must be removed this way, the wheel bearings may be damaged and should be inspected as described in this section. In addition, the axle surfaces that originally aligned with the wheel bearings may be corroded and damaged (**Figure 17**).*

5. Roll the rear wheel out of the swing arm, and remove the left (**Figure 18**) and right (**Figure 19**) collars.

**12**

*NOTE*
*The left and right collars are identical.*

6. If removed, reinstall the brake caliper mounting bracket onto the swing arm (**Figure 20**).

*NOTE*
*Do not operate the rear brake pedal with the wheel removed. Insert a spacer block between the pads until the wheel is installed. This prevents the caliper piston from extending if the pedal is operated.*

7. Inspect the rear wheel as described in this section.

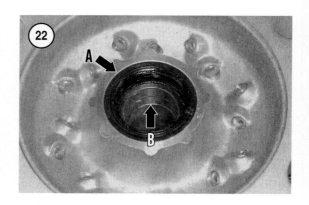

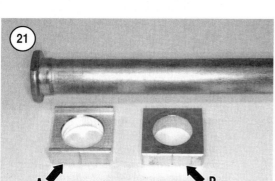

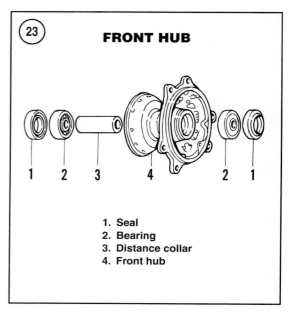

**FRONT HUB**

1. Seal
2. Bearing
3. Distance collar
4. Front hub

## Installation

1. Clean the axle, nut, adjust blocks and swing arm axle surfaces.

2. Apply grease to the axle and both seal lips. Do not lubricate the threads on the axle and axle nut. These threads must be free of oil and grease when the nut is tightened.

3. Install the left (**Figure 18**) and right (**Figure 19**) collars.

4. Remove the spacer block from between the brake pads.

5. If removed, install the brake caliper mounting bracket onto the swing arm (**Figure 20**).

6. Position the rear wheel between the swing arm.

> *NOTE*
> *Install the adjusting blocks with their index marks (B, **Figure 15**) facing the marks on the swing arm. The left adjusting block (A, **Figure 21**) is machined with a groove to hold the shoulder surfaces on the left side of the axle. The right adjusting block (B, **Figure 21**) is flat on both sides.*

7. Install the left adjusting block (B, **Figure 15**) onto the axle.

8. Lift the wheel and install the axle (A, **Figure 15**) from the left side. Make sure the axle passes through the caliper mounting bracket.

9. Slip the drive chain over the driven sprocket.

10. Remove any grease from the axle threads.

11. Install the right adjusting block (B, **Figure 14**), washer (A) and axle nut.

12. Adjust the drive chain as described in Chapter Three. Tighten the rear axle nut (**Figure 14**) to 127 N•m (94 ft.-lb.).

13. Rotate the wheel several times while applying the rear brake to reposition the rear brake pads and to make sure the wheel rotates freely. Make sure the brake operates properly.

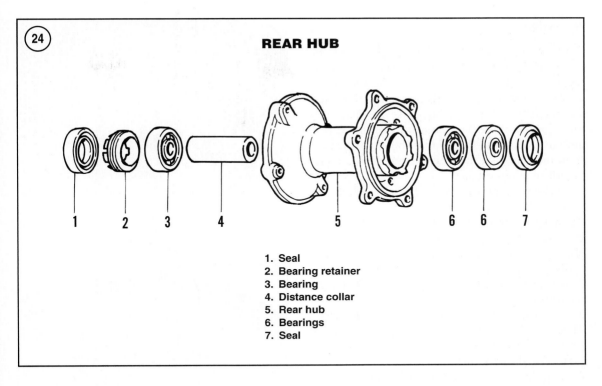

(24)  **REAR HUB**

1. Seal
2. Bearing retainer
3. Bearing
4. Distance collar
5. Rear hub
6. Bearings
7. Seal

## Inspection

1. Inspect the seals (A, **Figure 22**) for excessive wear, hardness, cracks or other damage. If necessary, replace seals as described under *Front and Rear Hubs* in this chapter.

2. Inspect the bearings on both sides of the wheel for:

    a. Roughness. Turn each bearing inner race (B, **Figure 22**) by hand and check for smooth and quiet operation.

    b. Radial and lateral play (**Figure 11**). Try to push the bearing in and out to check for lateral play. Slight play is normal. Try to push the bearing up and down to check for radial play. Any radial play should be difficult to feel. If play is easily felt, the bearing is worn out. If necessary, replace the three bearings as a set as described under *Front and Rear Hubs* in this chapter.

3. Clean the axle and collars in solvent to remove all grease and dirt. Make sure all axle contact surfaces are clean.

4. Check the axle for straightness with a set of V-blocks and dial indicator. Refer to **Table 1** for maximum axle runout. Actual runout is one-half of the gauge reading. Do not attempt to straighten a bent axle.

5. Check the brake disc bolts for tightness. To service the brake disc, refer to Chapter Fifteen.

6. Check the driven sprocket nuts for tightness. If loose, hold the Allen bolts and tighten the driven sprocket nuts to 32 N•m (24 ft.-lb.).

7. Refer to *Wheel Service* in this chapter to inspect and true the rim.

## FRONT AND REAR HUBS

The front and rear hubs contain the seals, wheel bearings and a distance collar. A brake disc is mounted onto each hub and the driven sprocket is mounted onto the rear hub. A retainer is used to secure the right wheel bearing in the rear hub. Refer to **Figure 23** (front) or **Figure 24** (rear) when servicing the front and rear hubs in this section.

Procedures for servicing the front and rear hubs are essentially the same. Where differences occur, they are described in the procedure.

12

**Inspection**

The bearings can be inspected with the wheels installed on the motorcycle. With the wheels installed, leverage can be applied to the bearings to detect wear. In addition, the wheels can be spun to listen for roughness in the bearings. Use the following procedure to check the bearings while the wheels are installed. If the wheels must be removed, perform the checks in the wheel removal procedures described in this chapter.

1. Support the motorcycle with the wheel off the ground. The axle nut must be tight.

2. Grasp the wheel with both hands, 180° apart. Rock the wheel up and down, and side to side, to check for radial and lateral play. Have an assistant apply the brake while the test is repeated. Play will be detected in severely worn bearings, even though the wheel is locked.

3. Push the front or rear brake caliper in by hand. This forces the caliper piston(s) away from the pads so that the wheel can spin without the brake pads contacting the brake disc.

4. Spin the wheel and listen for bearing noise. A grinding or catching noise indicates worn bearings.

*NOTE*
*If the disc brake drags and the bearing cannot be heard, remove the wheel and support it on a truing stand.*

5. If damage is evident, replace the bearings as a set. Always install new seals.

*CAUTION*
*Do not remove the wheel bearings to check their condition. If the bearings are removed, they must be replaced.*

6. Apply the front and rear brakes to reposition the brake pads against the brake disc.

**Seal Replacement**

Seals protect the bearings from dirt and moisture contamination. Always install new seals when replacing bearings.

*CAUTION*
*In the following procedure, do not set the wheel on the brake disc. Support the wheel on wooden blocks.*

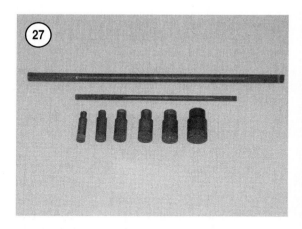

1. Pry the seals out of the hub with a seal puller, tire iron or wide-blade screwdriver (**Figure 25**). Place a shop cloth under the tool to protect the hub from damage.

*NOTE*
*If new bearings will be fitted, replace the bearings before installing the seals.*

2. Clean the seal bore.

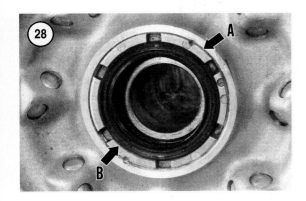

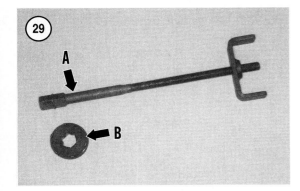

3. Inspect unshielded bearings for proper lubrication. If necessary, clean and repack the bearings while installed in the hub.

*NOTE*
*Unshielded bearings were not originally installed in the hubs. If so equipped, a previous owner installed them.*

4. Pack grease into the lip of the new seal.

5. Place the seal in the bore with the closed side of the seal facing out. The seal must be square in the bore.

6. Use a seal driver or socket (**Figure 26**) to install the seal in the bore. Install the seal so it is flush with the top of the hub bore surface. See A, **Figure 22**, typical.

*CAUTION*
*When driving seals, the edge of the driver must fit at the perimeter of the seal. If the driver outside diameter is appreciably smaller than that of the seal, the driver will press against the center of the seal and damage it.*

## Wheel Bearing Replacement

Wheel bearings are installed with a slight press fit and are not generally difficult to remove when the seals have been properly serviced. However, when damaged seals are not replaced, corrosion caused by water entering through the seals can seize or etch the bearings into the hub bore, making removal very difficult. Work carefully to avoid damaging the hub when replacing the bearings. Discard the bearings after removing them.

### *Tools*

This section lists various tool possibilities to remove the front and rear wheel bearings and the bearing retainer installed in the rear hub.

Two methods for removing the front and rear wheel bearings are provided:
1. Expanding wheel bearing collets (**Figure 27**)—Collets and driver rods can be purchased as a set or individually. A 20 mm (front hub) and 25 mm (rear hub) expanding collets and large driver rod are required. Bearing collets are available from Motion Pro.
2. Use one of the following tools to remove the bearing retainer (A, **Figure 28**) installed in the rear hub:
   a. Honda retainer wrench body (Honda part No. 07710-0010401 [A, **Figure 29**]) and Honda retainer wrench 48 × 15 (Honda part No. 07HMA-KS70100 [B, **Figure 29**]).
   b. Motion Pro CR Seal/Bearing Retainer Tool (Motion Pro part No. 08-0256 [A, **Figure 30**]).

12

3. Common shop tools—The wheel bearings can also be removed with a propane torch, drift and hammer.

### Removal

> *CAUTION*
> *In the following procedure, do not allow the wheel to rest on the brake disc. Support the wheel with wooden blocks.*

1. Remove the seals (B, **Figure 28**) as described in this section.

2. Examine the wheel bearings for excessive damage, especially the inner race. If the inner race of one bearing is damaged, remove the opposite bearing first. If both bearings are damaged, select the bearing with the least amount of damage and remove it first. On rusted and damaged bearings, applying pressure against the inner race can cause the inner race to pop out, leaving the outer race pressed in the hub. Refer to *Damaged Bearings* in this section.

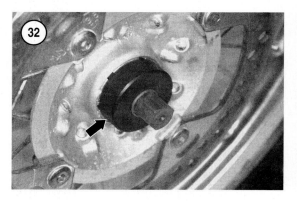

3. On rear wheels, remove the bearing retainer (B, **Figure 30**) with one of the tools described under *Tools*. Check that the tabs on the removal tool engage with the notches in the bearing retainer. **Figure 31** and **Figure 32** show how the Honda tools are assembled through the hub and onto the retainer.

> *WARNING*
> *Wear safety glasses when removing the bearings in the following steps.*

4A. Remove the wheel bearings with expanding collets (**Figure 33**):

  a. Select the correct size collet (**Figure 34**) and insert it into one of the hub bearings.

> *NOTE*
> *Two bearings are installed in the left side of the rear hub. Insert the collet through both bearings and try to remove them at the same time. If this is not possible, remove the outer and inner bearings separately.*

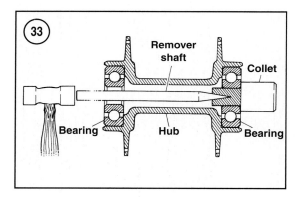

  b. From the opposite side of the hub, insert the remover shaft into the slot in the backside of the collet (**Figure 35**). Position the hub with the collet tool resting against a solid surface

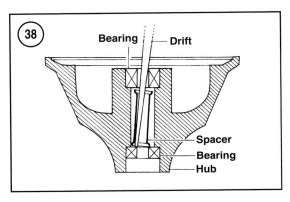

**38**

Bearing ┊ ┊ ─ Drift

── Spacer

── Bearing

── Hub

and strike the remover shaft so it wedges firmly into the collet.

c. Position the hub so the remover head is free to move. Strike the end of the remover shaft, forcing the bearing (**Figure 36**) out of the hub. Remove the bearing and tool. Release the collet from the bearing. Discard the bearing.

d. Remove the distance collar from the hub.

e. Repeat the procedure to remove the remaining bearing(s). See **Figure 37**.

4B. Remove the wheel bearings with a hammer, drift and propane torch as follows:

> *WARNING*
> *When using a propane torch to heat the hub, work in a well-ventilated area away from combustible materials. Wear protective clothing, including eye protection and insulated gloves. For additional information, refer to **Interference Fit** in Chapter One.*

a. Clean all lubricants from the wheel.

b. Heat the hub around the bearing to be removed. Work the torch in a circular motion around the hub, taking care not to hold the torch in one area. Turn the wheel over and remove the bearing as described in the following steps.

c. Tilt the distance collar away from one side of the bearing with a long driver (**Figure 38**).

> *CAUTION*
> *Do not damage the distance collar when removing the bearing. If necessary, grind a clearance groove in the drift to enable it to contact the bearing while clearing the distance collar.*

d. Tap around the inner bearing race. Make several passes until the bearing is removed from the hub.

e. Remove the distance collar from the hub.

f. Turn the hub over and heat the opposite side.

g. Drive out the opposite bearing using a large socket or bearing driver inserted through the hub.

h. Inspect the distance collar for burrs created during removal. Remove burrs with a file.

5. Clean and dry the hub and distance collar.

**12**

6. Check the hub mounting bore for cracks or other damage. If the bearings were a loose fit in the hub, the hub mounting bore and hub may be damaged.

7. Inspect the distance collar for flared ends. Check the ends for cracks or other damage. Do not try to repair the distance collar by cutting or grinding its end surfaces as this will shorten the distance collar. Replace the distance collar if one or both ends are damaged.

> *CAUTION*
> *The distance collar operates against the wheel bearing inner races to prevent them from moving inward when the axle is tightened. If a distance collar is too short, or if it is not installed, the inner bearing races will move inward and bind on the axle, causing bearing damage and seizure.*

### Installation

1. Before installing the new bearings and seals, note the following:
   a. Install bearings with their closed side (A, **Figure 39**) facing out. If a bearing is sealed on both sides, install the bearing with its manufacturer's marks facing out. If a shield is installed on one side of the bearing, the shield side must face out.
   b. Apply grease (NLGI No. 2) to bearings that are open on one or both sides (B, **Figure 39**). Work the grease into the cavities between the balls and races.
   c. Support the bottom side of the hub, near the bore, when installing bearings.
   d. At the front hub, install the left bearing first, then the right bearing.
   e. At the rear hub, install the right bearing first, then the left inner and outer bearings.

> *NOTE*
> *High-quality wheel bearing rebuild kits are available from Pivot Works (**Figure 40**). Each kit includes bearings and seals for one wheel assembly. Bearings are rubber sealed on each side. A new bearing retainer is included in the rear wheel bearing set. See a dealership or contact Pivot Works at **www.pivotworks.com**.*

2. Heat the hub evenly around the bearing bore.

3. Place the first bearing squarely against the bore opening with its closed side facing out. Select a driver with an outside diameter slightly smaller than the bearing's outside diameter. Then drive the bearing into the bore until it bottoms (**Figure 41**).

4. Turn the hub over. Install the distance collar and center it against the center race.

5. Position the opposite bearing squarely against the bore opening with its closed side facing out. Drive the bearing partway into the bearing bore. Make sure the distance collar is centered in the hub. If not, install the axle through the hub to align the distance collar with the bearing. Then remove the axle and continue installing the bearing until it bottoms. On the rear hub, seat the left outer bearing against the inner bearing (**Figure 42**).

6. Insert the axle though the hub and turn it by hand. Check for any roughness or binding, indicating bearing damage.

> *NOTE*
> *If the axle does not go in, the distance collar is not aligned correctly with one of the bearings.*

7.  Install the rear wheel bearing retainer (B, **Figure 30**) and tighten to 44 N•m (33 ft.-lb.). Peen the edge of the retainer against the hub in two places.

8.  Install the seals as previously described.

### *Damaged bearings*

If damaged wheel bearings remain in use, the inner race can break apart, leaving the outer race pressed in the hub. Removal is difficult because only a small part of the race is accessible above the hub's shoulder, leaving little material to drive against. To remove a bearing's outer race under these conditions, first heat the hub evenly with a propane torch. Drive out the outer race with a drift and hammer. It may be necessary to grind a clearance tip on the end of the drift, to avoid damaging the hub bore. Remove the race evenly by applying force at different points around the race. Do not allow the race to bind in its bore. After removing the race, inspect the hub mounting bore for cracks or other damage.

## WHEEL SERVICE

To prevent wheel failure, inspect the wheels, bearings and tires at the intervals specified in Chapter Three.

### Component Condition

Wheels used on motocross and off-road motorcycles receive a lot of abuse. It is important to inspect the wheel regularly for lateral (side-to-side) and radial (up-and-down) runout, spoke tension, and rim damage. When a wheel has a noticeable wobble, it is out of true. This is usually caused by loose spokes, but it can be caused by an impact-damaged rim.

Truing a wheel corrects the lateral and radial runout to bring the wheel back into specification.

The condition of the individual wheel components will affect the ability to successfully true the wheel. Note the following:

1.  Spoke condition: Do not attempt to true a wheel with bent or damaged spokes. Doing so places an excessive amount of tension on the spoke, hub and rim. Overtightening the spoke may damage the spoke nipple hole in the hub or rim. Inspect for and replace damaged spokes.

*NOTE*
*When a properly trued wheel hits a sharp object, all the torque or wheel impact is equally divided or transferred among all of the wheel's spokes. The spokes are able to bend or bow slightly, thus absorbing the shock and preventing the rim and hub from damage. When the spokes are overtightened, they are unable to flex, causing all the impact to be absorbed by the hub or rim. When the spokes are too loose, the torque or wheel impact is divided unequally between the spokes, with the tighter spokes receiving most of the torque and isolating the impact in one area along the rim and hub. This eventually causes a cracked or broken hub or rim.*

2.  Nipple condition: When truing the wheels the nipples must turn freely on the spokes. However, corroded and rusted spoke threads are common and difficult to adjust. Spray a penetrating liquid onto

12

the nipples and allow sufficient time for it to penetrate before trying to turn the nipples. Turn the spoke wrench in both directions and continue to apply penetrating liquid. If the spoke wrench rounds off the nipple, it is necessary to remove the tire from the rim, cut the spokes out of the wheel and install new spokes.

3. Rim condition: Minor rim runout can be corrected by truing the wheel; however, overtightening the spokes to correct a damaged rim may damage the hub and rim. Inspect the rims for cracks, flat spots or dents (**Figure 43**). Check the spoke holes for cracks or enlargement. Replace excessively damaged rims.

## Wheel Truing Preliminaries

Before checking the runout and truing the wheel, note the following:

1. Clean the rim and spoke nipples.

2. Make sure the wheel bearings are in good condition. Refer to the front and rear wheel inspection procedures in this chapter.

3. Inspect the spoke holes in the rim for cracks, hole elongation and other damage. Replace the rim if damaged.

4. A small amount of wheel runout is acceptable. Attempting to true the wheel to a zero reading may damage the rim and hub from overtightened spokes. Also, considering the environment off-road motorcycles operate in, minor rim and spoke damage may make it more difficult to accurately true the wheel.

5. Check runout by mounting a pointer against the fork or swing arm and slowly rotating the wheel. When checking the rear wheel, it will be easier if the chain is first removed from the driven sprocket. If the wheel needs major tuning, remove the tire and mount the wheel on a truing stand (**Figure 44**). An adjustable pointer or dial indicator can then be mounted next to the rim to measure runout in both directions **Figure 45**.

> *NOTE*
> *A solid pointer works better than a dial indicator when truing rims with deep scratches, dents and other contact wear.*

6. Use the correct size spoke wrench (**Figure 46**). Using the wrong type of tool or incorrect size spoke

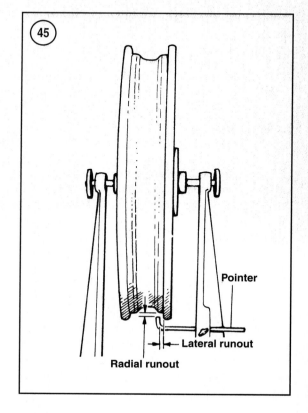

Pointer

Lateral runout

Radial runout

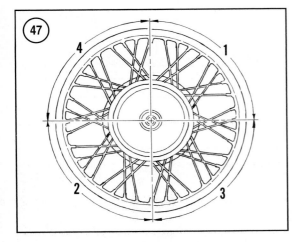

b. Hand check: Grasp and squeeze two spokes where they cross. Loose spokes can be flexed by hand. Tight spokes feel stiff with little noticeable movement. Tighten the spokes until the tension between the different spoke groups feels the same.

c. Spoke tone: Tapping a spoke causes it to vibrate and produce sound waves. Loose and tight spokes produce different sounds or tones. A tight spoke will ring. A loose spoke has a soft or dull ring. Tap each spoke with a spoke wrench or screwdriver to identify loose spokes.

3. Check the spokes using one of the methods described in Step 2. If there are loose spokes, spin the wheel and note the following:

a. If the wheel is running true, continue with Step 4 to tighten the loose spokes.

b. If the wheel is running out of true, go to *Wheel Truing Procedure* to measure runout and true the wheel.

4. Use tape and divide the rim into four equally spaced sections. Number the sections as shown in **Figure 47**.

5. Start by tightening the loose spokes in Section 1, then in sections 2, 3 and 4. Do not turn each spoke more than a fourth to a half turn at a time as this overtightens the spokes and bring the wheel out of true. Work slowly while checking spoke tightness. Continue until all of the spokes are tightened evenly.

*NOTE*
*If the spokes are hard to turn, spray penetrating oil into the top of the nipple. Wipe excess oil from the rim.*

6. When all the spokes are tightened evenly, spin the wheel. If there is any noticeable runout, true the wheel as described in the following procedure.

### Wheel Truing Procedure

**Table 1** lists lateral (side-to-side) and radial (up-and-down) runout specifications.

1. Clean the rim, spokes and nipples.

2. Position a pointer against the rim as shown in **Figure 45**. If the tire is mounted on the rim, position the pointer as shown in **Figure 44**.

wrench may round off the spoke nipples, making adjustment difficult.

### Tightening Loose Spokes

This section describes steps for checking and tightening loose spokes without effecting the wheel runout. When many spokes are loose and the wheel is running out of true, refer to *Wheel Truing Procedure* in this section.

1. Support the wheel so that it can turn freely. If the rear wheel is being checked while on the motorcycle, remove the chain from the driven sprocket.

2. Spokes can be checked for looseness by one of three ways:

a. Spoke torque: Spoke torque wrenches are available from different tool companies. When using a spoke torque wrench, the correct torque specification is 3.7 N•m (33 in.-lb.).

3. Spin the wheel slowly and check the lateral and radial runout. If the rim is out of adjustment, continue with Step 4.

*NOTE*
*It is normal for the rim to jump at the point where the rim was welded together. Also small cuts and dings in the rim will affect the runout reading, especially when using a dial indicator.*

4. Spray penetrating oil into the top of each nipple. Wipe excess oil from the rim.

*NOTE*
*If the runout is minimal, the tire can be left on the rim. However, if the runout is excessive, or if the rim must be centered with the hub (Step 5), remove the tire from the rim.*

5. If there are a large number of loose spokes, or if some or all of the spokes were replaced, measure the hub to rim offset as shown in **Figure 48** (front) or **Figure 49** (rear) and compare to the specifications in **Table 1**. If necessary, reposition the hub before truing the wheel.

6. Lateral runout adjustment: If the side-to-side runout is out of specification, adjust the wheel. For example, to pull the rim to the left side (**Figure 50**), tighten the spokes on the left side of the hub (at the runout point) and loosen the adjacent spokes on the right side of the hub. Always loosen and tighten the spokes in equal number of turns.

*NOTE*
*Determining the number of spokes to loosen and tighten depends on how far the runout is out of adjustment. Loosen two or three spokes, then tighten the opposite two or three spokes. If the runout is excessive and affects a greater area along the rim, loosen and tighten a greater number of spokes.*

7. Radial runout adjustment: If the up and down runout is out of specification, the hub is not centered in the rim. Draw the high point of the rim toward the centerline of the wheel by tightening the spokes in the area of the high point, and loosening the spokes on the side opposite the high point (**Fig-**

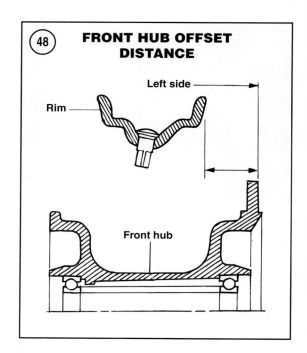

**(48) FRONT HUB OFFSET DISTANCE**

Left side

Rim

Front hub

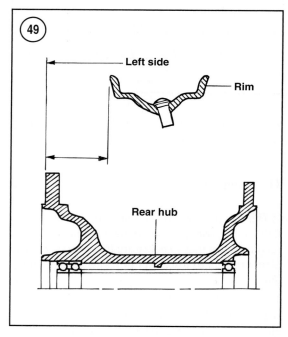

**(49)**

Left side

Rim

Rear hub

**ure 51**). Tighten the spokes in equal amounts to prevent distortion.

*NOTE*
*Alternate between checking and adjusting lateral and radial runout. Remember, changing spoke tension on*

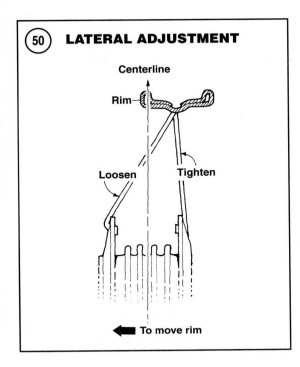

**50 LATERAL ADJUSTMENT**

Centerline

Rim

Loosen    Tighten

◀ To move rim

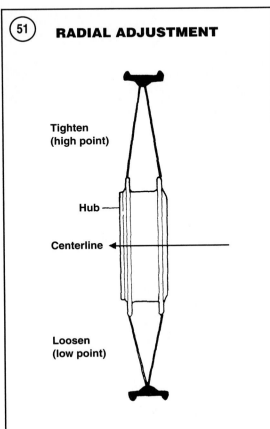

**51 RADIAL ADJUSTMENT**

Tighten
(high point)

Hub

Centerline ◀

Loosen
(low point)

**52**

one side of the rim will affect the tension on the other side of the rim.

8. After truing the wheel, seat each spoke in the
hub by tapping it with a flat nose punch and hammer. Then recheck the spoke tension and wheel runout. Readjust if necessary as described under
*Tightening Loose Spokes* in this section.

9. Check the ends of the spokes where they are
threaded in the nipples. Grind off any ends that protrude through the nipples to prevent them from
puncturing the tube.

## DRIVE CHAIN

Refer to **Table 2** for drive chain specifications.
Refer to *Drive Chain* in Chapter Three for routine
drive chain inspection, adjustment and lubrication
procedures.

When checking the condition of the chain, also
check the condition of the sprockets, as described in
Chapter Three. If either the chain or sprockets are
worn, replace all drive components at the same
time. Using new sprockets with a worn chain, or a
new chain on worn sprockets will shorten the life of
the new part.

### Removal/Installation
### (CRF250R and CRF450R)

1. Support the motorcycle on a workstand with its
rear wheel off the ground and shift the transmission
into neutral.

2. Find the master link on the chain. Remove the
spring clip (**Figure 52**) with a pair of pliers, then remove the link from the chain (**Figure 53**).

3. Remove the drive chain.

**12**

4. Clean and inspect the chain (Chapter Three).

5. Clean the drive and driven sprockets.

6. Check the drive chain rollers, slider and guide for worn or damaged parts (Chapter Three).

7. Reverse this procedure to install the chain. Note the following:

    a. Install the chain and reassemble a new master link (**Figure 53**).

    b. Install the spring clip on the master link with the closed end of the clip pointing toward the direction of travel (**Figure 54**).

    c. Adjust the chain (Chapter Three).

**Removal/Installation**
**(CRF250X and CRF450X)**

The CRF250X and CRF450X models are equipped with a DID 520MXV T-ring chain. This particular drive chain is 1.6 mm (0.063 in.) narrower than a comparable 520 O-ring chain and was specifically designed for use with the narrower engine cases used on the 250X models. When replacing the drive chain, use *only* the DID 520MXV drive chain. A standard 520 O-ring drive chain may contact and damage the engine cases. If selecting a different drive chain, confirm through a Honda dealership that it can be used on a CRF250X or CRF450X model.

The drive chain uses a staked master link (**Figure 55**) and can be removed/replaced with the swing arm mounted on the motorcycle by breaking the chain at the master link. The following section describes chain removal and installation using the Motion Pro Jumbo Chain Tool (part no. 08-0135 [**Figure 56**]). The Jumbo Chain Tool can be used to break roller chains up to No. 630 and can be used to rivet chain sizes up to No. 530. Always follow the tool manufacturer's instructions provided with the tool. Use the following steps to supplement the instructions provided with the chain tool.

1. Support the motorcycle with the rear wheel off the ground.

2. Loosen the rear axle nut and the chain adjuster bolts. Push the rear wheel forward until maximum chain slack is obtained.

3. Assemble the extractor bolt onto the body bolt. Then turn the extractor bolt until its pin is withdrawn into the pin guide chain tool, following the manufacturer's instructions.

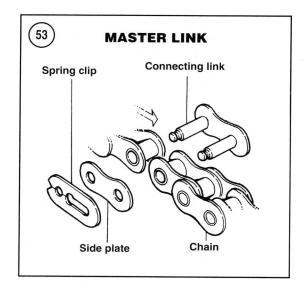

(53) **MASTER LINK**

Spring clip          Connecting link

Side plate          Chain

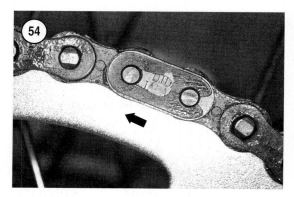

(54)

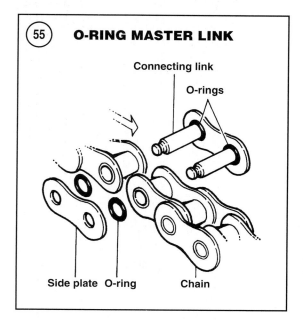

(55) **O-RING MASTER LINK**

Connecting link

O-rings

Side plate   O-ring      Chain

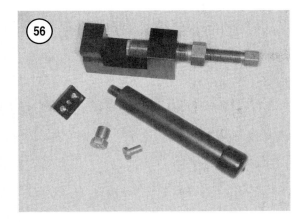

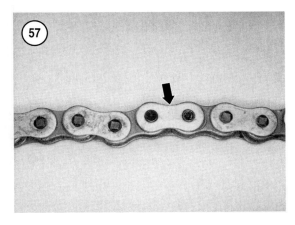

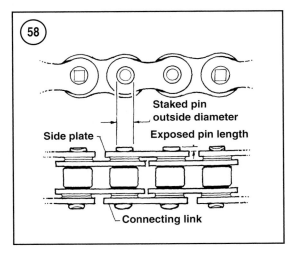

Staked pin
outside diameter

Side plate ⌐              Exposed pin length

Connecting link

4. Turn the chain to locate the crimped pin ends (**Figure 57**) on the master link. Break the chain at this point.

5. Install the chain tool across the master link, then operate the tool and push the connecting link out of

the side plate to break the chain. Remove the side plate, connecting link and O-rings (**Figure 55**) and discard them.

> *WARNING*
> *Discard the connecting link, side plate and O-rings after removing them. Never reuse these parts as they could break and cause the chain to separate. Reusing a staked master link may cause the chain to come apart and lock the rear wheel, causing a serious accident.*

6. If installing a new drive chain, count the links of the new chain, and if necessary, cut the chain to length as described under *Cutting A Drive Chain to Length* in this section. See **Table 2** for the original equipment chain sizes and lengths.

7. Install the chain around the drive sprocket, swing arm and driven sprocket.

> *NOTE*
> *Always install the drive chain around the swing arm before connecting and staking the master link.*

8. Assemble the new master link as follows:
   a. Install an O-ring on each connecting link pin (**Figure 55**).
   b. Insert the connecting link through the inside of the chain and connect both chain ends together.
   c. Install the remaining two O-rings (**Figure 55**) onto the connecting link pins.
   d. Install the side plate (**Figure 55**) with its identification mark facing out (away from chain).

9. Stake each connecting link pin as follows:

> *NOTE*
> *The master link service specifications referred to in the following steps and listed in **Table 2** are for the original equipment DID drive chain installed on the CRF250X and CRF450X.*

   a. Measure the height of the connecting link from the outer side plate surface to the top of the connecting link (**Figure 58**). The specified height measurement is 1.15-1.55 mm (0.45-0.061 in.). If the height measurement is incorrect, confirm that the correct master link is being installed. If so, readjust the side plate's height position on the connecting link.

b. Assemble the chain tool onto the master link and carefully stake each connecting link pin until its outside diameter (**Figure 58**) measures 5.50-5.80 mm (0.217-0.228 in.). Work carefully and do not exceed the specified outside diameter measurement. Measure with a vernier caliper (**Figure 59**) in two places on each pin, 90° apart.

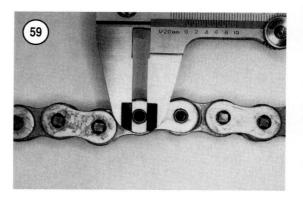

> *NOTE*
> *If the diameter of one pin end is out of specification, remove and discard the master link. Then install a new master link assembly.*

10. Remove the chain tool and inspect the master link for any cracks or other damage. Check the staked area for cracks (**Figure 60**). Then make sure the master link O-rings were not crushed. If there are cracks on the staked link surfaces or other damage, remove the master link and install a new one.

11. If there are no cracks, pivot the chain ends where they hook onto the master link. Each chain end must pivot freely. Compare by pivoting other links of the chain. If one or both drive chain ends cannot pivot on the master link, the chain is too tight. Remove and install a *new* master link assembly.

> *WARNING*
> *An incorrectly installed master link may cause the chain to come apart and lock the rear wheel, causing a serious accident. If the tools to safely rivet the chain together are not available, take it to a Honda dealership. Do not ride the motorcycle unless absolutely certain the master link is installed correctly.*

12. Adjust the drive chain and tighten the rear axle nut as described in Chapter Three.

## Cutting A Drive Chain To Length

**Table 2** lists the correct number of chain links required for original equipment gearing. If the replacement drive chain is too long, cut it to length as follows.

1. Stretch the new chain on a workbench.

2. If installing a new chain over stock gearing, refer to **Table 2** for the correct number of links for the new chain. If sprocket sizes were changed, install

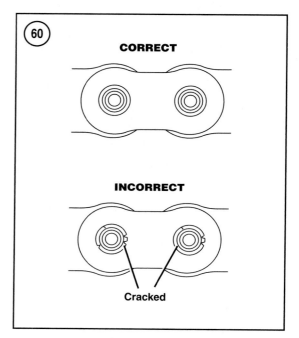

the new chain over both sprockets, with the rear wheel moved forward, to determine the correct number of links to remove (**Figure 61**). Make a chalk mark on the two chain pins to cut. Count the chain links one more time or check the chain length before cutting. Include the master link when counting the drive chain links.

> *WARNING*
> *Using a hand or bench grinder as described in Step 3 will cause flying particles. Do not operate a grinding tool without proper eye protection.*

3A. If using a chain breaker, use it to break the drive chain.

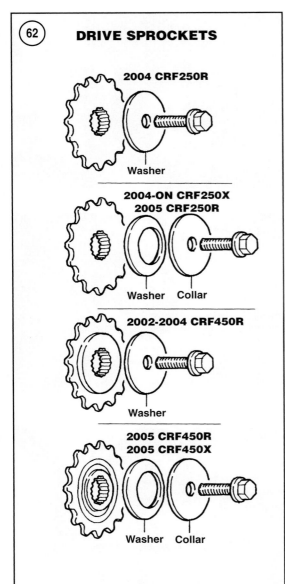

**DRIVE SPROCKETS**

2004 CRF250R

Washer

2004-ON CRF250X
2005 CRF250R

Washer    Collar

2002-2004 CRF450R

Washer

2005 CRF450R
2005 CRF450X

Washer    Collar

3B. To break the drive chain with a grinder, perform the following:

   a. Grind the head of two pins flush with the face of the side plate with a grinder or suitable grinding tool.

   b. Press the side plate out of the chain with a chain breaker; support the chain carefully while doing this. If the pins are still tight, grind more material from the end of the pins and then try again.

   c. Remove the side plate and push out the connecting link.

4. Install the new drive chain as described in this chapter.

**Service and Inspection**

For routine service and inspection of the drive chain, refer to *Drive Chain* in Chapter Three.

## SPROCKET REPLACEMENT

This section describes service procedures on replacing the drive (front) and driven (rear) sprockets. See **Table 2** for sprocket sizes.

After replacing the chain and sprockets, check the drive chain rollers, slider and guide for worn or damaged parts (Chapter Three).

**Drive Sprocket
Removal/Installation**

Refer to **Figure 62**.

1. Remove the sprocket cover (**Figure 63**) and case saver.

2. Shift the transmission into fifth gear and have an assistant apply the rear brake. Then loosen the drive sprocket bolt (**Figure 64**). If the drive chain is not installed on the motorcycle, hold the sprocket with a holding tool (**Figure 65**).

*NOTE*
*Identify the drive sprocket so it can be installed facing in its original direction.*

3. Remove the bolt, collar (if used), washer and drive sprocket as shown in **Figure 62**.

12

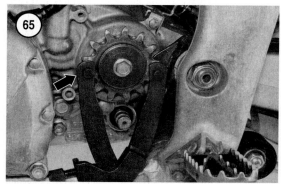

*NOTE*
*If the drive sprocket cannot be re-moved because the drive chain is too tight, loosen the rear axle nut and loosen the chain adjusters.*

4. Remove the collar (**Figure 66**) and its O-ring (**Figure 67**), if necessary.

5. Clean and inspect the parts.

6. Lubricate a new O-ring with grease and install it into the collar (**Figure 67**).

7. Lubricate the collar's outside diameter with grease. Install the collar over the countershaft and seat it against the countershaft bearing (**Figure 66**).

8. Install the drive sprocket as follows (**Figure 62**):

   a. On CRF250R and CRF250X models, install the drive sprocket with its flat side facing out.

   b. On 2002-2004 CRF450R models, install the drive sprocket as shown in **Figure 68**.

   c. On 2005 CRF450R and CRF450X models, install the drive sprocket with its grooved side facing out.

9. Install the washer and collar (if used) with its OUTSIDE mark facing out (**Figure 62**).

10. Install the bolt and tighten finger-tight.

11. Use the same method to prevent the drive sprocket from turning and tighten the drive sprocket mounting bolt to the torque specification in **Table 3**.

12. Install the case saver and drive sprocket cover.

## Driven Sprocket
## Removal and Installation

*NOTE*
*The driven sprocket is attached to the rear hub with Allen bolts and nuts. Do not loosen these fasteners by turning*

2. Have an assistant apply the rear brake, then hold the Allen bolts and loosen the nuts.

3. Remove the rear wheel as described in this chapter.

4. Remove the nuts, washers, Allen bolts and driven sprocket (**Figure 69**) from the rear hub.

5. Check the sprocket mounting tabs for cracks or other damage. Replace the hub if damaged.

6. Clean and dry the sprocket fasteners. Replace damaged fasteners.

7. Install the new sprocket onto the rear hub with its marked or stamped side facing out.

8. Install the Allen bolts, washers, and nuts and tighten finger-tight.

9. Install the rear wheel as described in this chapter.

10. Hold the Allen bolts and tighten the nuts in two or three steps and in a crossing pattern to 32 N•m (24 ft.-lb.).

12

*NOTE*
*The Motion Pro Torque Adapter (part No. 08-0134) can be used with a torque wrench to access and torque the nuts (Figure 70). Refer to* ***Torque Adapters*** *in Chapter One for additional information.*

11. Adjust the drive chain and tighten the rear axle nut as described in Chapter Three.

## TIRE CHANGING

### Removal

*the Allen bolt. Instead, hold the Allen bolt and loosen the nut to avoid rounding out the Allen bolt heads.*

1. Support the motorcycle on a workstand with the rear wheel off the ground.

1. Remove the valve core and deflate the tire.

2. Loosen the rim lock nut(s) (**Figure 71**).

3. Press the entire bead on both sides of the tire into the center of the rim.

4. Lubricate the beads with soapy water.

> *CAUTION*
> *Use tire irons without sharp edges. If necessary, file the ends of the tire irons to remove any rough edges.*

5. Insert the tire iron under the bead next to the valve stem (**Figure 72**). Force the bead on the opposite side of the tire into the center of the rim, then pry the bead over the rim with the tire iron.

6. Insert a second tire iron next to the first to hold the bead over the rim (**Figure 73**). While holding the tire with one iron, work around the tire with the second iron, prying the tire over the rim. Be careful not to pinch the inner tube with the tire irons.

7. Remove the inner tube from the tire (**Figure 74**). If necessary, reach inside the tire and remove the valve from the hole in the rim.

8. Remove the nut and washer and remove the rim lock(s) from the rim.

9. Stand the tire upright and pry the second tire bead (**Figure 75**) over the rim.

## Inspection

1. Inspect the tire for any damage.

2. Fill the tube with air to check for leaks.

3. Check the rim locks and replace if damaged.

4. Make sure the spoke ends do not protrude above the nipple heads and into the center of the rim. Grind or file off any protruding spoke ends.

> *NOTE*
> *If water and dirt are entering the rim, discard the rubber rim band. Wrap the center of the rim with two separate revolutions of duct tape. Punch holes through the tape at the rim lock and valve stem hole positions.*

## Installation

> *NOTE*
> *Installation will be easier if the tire is pliable. This can be achieved by warming the tire in the sun or in an enclosed vehicle.*

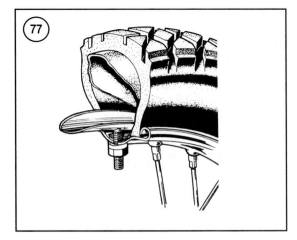

1. Sprinkle talcum powder around the interior of the tire casing. Distribute the powder so it is on all surfaces that will touch the inner tube. The powder minimizes chafing and helps the tube distribute itself when inflated.

*NOTE*
*Depending on the make and type of tire installed, check the sidewall and*

*determine if it must be installed in a specific direction. A direction arrow is often embossed in the sidewall.*

2. If a rubber rim band is used, make sure the band is in place with the rough side toward the rim. Align the holes in the band with the holes in the rim.

3. Lubricate one bead and push it onto the rim (**Figure 76**). When necessary, work the tire from the opposite side of the rim.

4. Install the rim lock, lockwasher and nut. Do not tighten at this time. The rim lock must be over the edge of both tire beads when installation is completed (**Figure 77**).

5. Install the core into the valve stem, then insert the tube into the tire. Check that the tube is not twisted as it is tucked into the tire. Put the locknut on the upper end of the valve stem to prevent the stem from falling out of the hole.

6. Inflate the tube until it is rounded and no longer wrinkled. Too much air makes tire installation difficult and too little air increases the chance of pinching the tube.

7. Lubricate the second tire bead, then start installation opposite the valve stem. Fit the rim lock over the tire bead, then work around the rim, hand-fitting as much of the tire as possible. If necessary, relubricate the bead. Before final installation, check that the valve stem is straight and the inner tube is not pinched. Use the tire irons to pry the remaining section of bead onto the rim (**Figure 78**).

8. Check the bead for uniform fit, on both sides of the tire.

*WARNING*
*If the tire does not seat at the recommended pressure, do not continue to overinflate the tire. Deflate the tire and reinflate to the recommended seating pressure. Relubricate the beads, if necessary.*

9. Lubricate both beads and inflate the tire to seat the beads onto the rim. Inflate the tire to 25-30 psi (172-207 kPa).

10. Tighten the rim lock nut(s) securely.

11. Bleed the tire pressure to the specification in **Table 1**.

12. Finger-tighten the valve stem locknut and install the cap.

12

**Table 1 FRONT AND REAR WHEEL SPECIFICATIONS**

| | |
|---|---|
| Axle runout limit | 0.20 mm (0.008 in.) |
| Front tire size | 80/100-21 51M and M/C 51M |
| Rear tire size | |
| CRF250R | 100/90-19 57M and M/C 57M |
| CRF250X | 100/100-18 59M and M/C 59M |
| CRF450R | 110/90-19 62M and M/C 62M |
| CRF450X | 110/100-18 64M |
| Rim size | |
| CRF250R | |
| Front | 1.60 x 21 |
| | 1.85 x 20* |
| Rear | 1.85 x 19 |
| CRF250X | |
| Front | 1.60 x 21 |
| Rear | 2.15 x 18 |
| CRF450R | |
| Front | 21 x 1.60 |
| | 20 x 1.85* |
| Rear | 19 x 2.15 |
| CRF450X | |
| Front | |
| Rear | |
| Tire brand | |
| CRF250R and CRF250X | |
| Front | Dunlop D742F |
| Rear | Dunlop D756 |
| CRF450R | |
| 2002-2003 | |
| Front | Dunlop K490G |
| Rear | Dunlop K695 |
| 2004 | |
| Front | Dunlop D745F |
| Rear | Dunlop D756 |
| 2005 | |
| Front | Dunlop D742F |
| Rear | Dunlop D756 |
| CRF450X | |
| Front | Dunlop D742 |
| Rear | Dunlop D756 |
| Tire pressure | |
| CRF250R | 98 kPa (14.2 psi) |
| CRF250X | 100 kPa (14.5 psi) |
| CRF450R | |
| 2002-2004 | 100 kPa (14.5 psi) |
| 2005 | 98 kPa (14.2 psi) |
| CRF450X | 100 kPa (14.5 psi) |
| Wheel hub-to-rim offset distance | |
| CRF250R | |
| Front | 25.0-27.0 mm (0.98-1.06 in.) |
| Rear | 47.75-49.75 mm (1.880-1.958 in.) |
| CRF250X | |
| Front | 27.0-29.0 mm (1.06-1.14 in.) |
| Rear | 44.5-46.5 mm (1.75-1.83 in.) |
| CRF450R | |
| Front | |
| 2002-2003 | 27.25 mm (1.07 in.) |
| 2004 | 28.0 mm (1.10 in.) |
| Rear | 45.5 mm (1.79 in.) |

(continued)

### Table 1 FRONT AND REAR WHEEL SPECIFICATIONS (continued)

| | |
|---|---|
| Wheel hub-to-rim offset distance (continued) | |
| CRF450X | |
|    Front | 27.0-29.0 mm (1.06-1.14 in.) |
|    Rear | 44.5-46.5 mm (1.75-1.83 in.) |
| Wheel rim runout | |
|    Radial and lateral | 2.0 mm (0.08 in.) |

*Optional front wheel assembly available through Honda dealerships.

### Table 2 DRIVE CHAIN AND SPROCKET SPECIFICATIONS

| | |
|---|---|
| Drive chain length wear limit (17 pins) | |
|    CRF250R and CRF450R | 259 mm (10.2 in.) |
|    CRF250X and CRF450X | – |
| Drive chain width wear limit | |
|    CRF250R and CRF450R | – |
|    CRF250X and CRF450X | 13.4 mm (0.53 in.) |
| Drive chain slack | 25-35 mm (1.0-1.4 in.) |
| Drive chain staked master link specifications | |
|    CRF250X and CRF450X | |
|       Connecting link staked outside diameter | 5.50-5.80 mm (0.217-0.228 in.) |
|       Master link pin length | 1.15-1.55 mm (0.045-0.061 in.) |
| Drive chain type | |
|    CRF250R | DID 520DMA2 |
|    CRF250X | DID 520MXV (T-ring type) |
|    CRF450R | DID 520MA2 |
|    CRF450X | DID 520MXV (T-ring type) |
| Number of links | |
|    CRF250R | 114 |
|    CRF250X | 116 |
|    CRF450R and CRF450X | 114 |
| Stock sprocket sizes (front/rear teeth number) | |
|    CRF250R | 13/51 |
|    CRF250X | 14/53 |
|    CRF450R | |
|       2002-2003 | 13/50 |
|       2004-on | 13/48 |
|    CRF450X | 13/51 |

12

### Table 3 FRONT AND REAR WHEEL TORQUE SPECIFICATIONS

| | N•m | in.-lb. | ft.-lb. |
|---|---|---|---|
| Brake disc nut | 16 | – | 12 |
| Drive sprocket bolt | | | |
|    CRF250R and CRF250X | 31 | – | 23 |
|    CRF450R | | | |
|       2002-2004 | 26 | – | 19 |
|       2005 | 31 | – | 23 |
|    CRF450X | 32 | – | 24 |
| Driven sprocket nut | 32 | – | 24 |
| Front axle nut | 88 | – | 65 |
| Front axle pinch bolt | 20 | – | 15 |
| Front brake disc cover bolt* | 13 | 115 | – |
| Rear axle nut | 127 | – | 94 |
| Rear wheel bearing retainer | 44 | – | 33 |
| Rim lock | 13 | 115 | – |
| Spoke nipple | 3.7 | 33 | – |

*Apply medium strength threadlock to fastener threads.

# CHAPTER THIRTEEN

# FRONT SUSPENSION AND STEERING

This chapter describes service procedures for the handlebar, steering stem and front fork. **Table 1** lists front suspension and steering specifications. **Tables 1-9** are at the end of the chapter.

## HANDLEBAR

*NOTE*
*This section describes service to the original equipment handlebar. When installing an aftermarket handlebar and/or handlebar holders, refer to the manufacturer's instructions for additional information.*

### Handlebar Removal

1. Support the motorcycle on a workstand.

*NOTE*
*If the handlebar appears bent, first make sure the rubber dampers (cones) installed in the upper fork bridge are not the cause of the misalignment.*

2. Remove the pad from the handlebar crossbar.

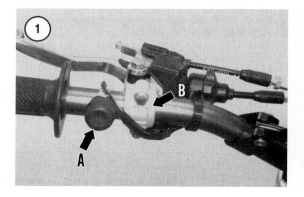

3. Remove the clamp securing the engine stop switch wiring harness to the handlebar and remove the switch (A, **Figure 1**).

*NOTE*
*Inspect the engine stop switch while it is off the handlebar. Check for damage that could cause the switch to ground against the handlebar and cause a no-spark condition.*

4. Remove the clutch lever holder (B, **Figure 1**) mounting bolts and remove the holder and clutch cable from the handlebar. Do not disconnect the cable unless necessary.

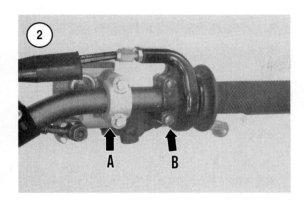

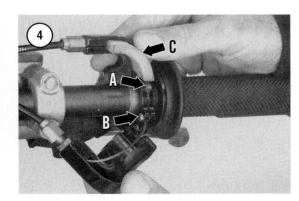

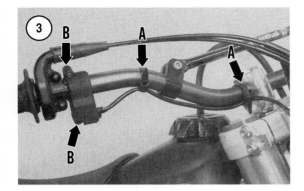

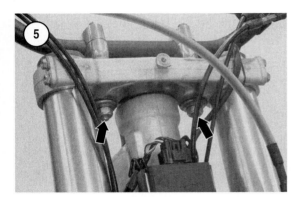

5. Remove the two bolts, clamp and master cylinder (A, **Figure 2**). Support the master cylinder upright so air does not enter the port holes in the master cylinder. Do not disconnect the brake hose unless necessary.

6. On CRF250X and CRF450X models, remove the wire bands (A, **Figure 3**) from the handlebar. Then remove the screws and the starter switch housing (B, **Figure 3**).

7. If necessary, replace the left handlebar grip as described in this section.

*NOTE*
*The handlebar can be removed without having to disassemble the throttle housing.*

8A. If the throttle housing will not be disassembled, loosen, but do not remove, the throttle housing bolts (B, **Figure 2**). Slide the housing off when removing the handlebar.

8B. If the throttle housing will be disassembled, perform the following:

    a. Slide the dust cover off the throttle housing.

    b. Remove the throttle housing bolts (B, **Figure 2**) and separate the housing.

    c. Disconnect the throttle cables from the throttle tube (**Figure 4**).

    d. Remove the throttle tube and grip from the handlebar.

9. If the lower handlebar holders are going to be removed or adjusted, loosen their mounting nuts (**Figure 5**) before removing the handlebar.

10. Remove the upper handlebar holder bolts and the upper holders (**Figure 6**). Remove the handlebar while sliding the throttle housing off the handlebar (if still assembled).

13

## Handlebar Inspection

1. Do not clean the handlebars with any cleaner that will leave an oil residue. When cleaning the clamp area and holders, use solvent or an electrical contact cleaner.

2. Inspect the handlebar for scores or cracks, especially at the handlebar, throttle and operating lever clamp mounting areas (**Figure 7**) on aluminum handlebars. If *any* damage is found, replace the handlebar. Cracks and scoring of the metal in these areas may cause the handlebar to break.

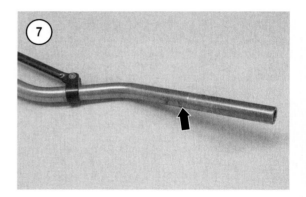

> *WARNING*
> *Never attempt to repair a damaged handlebar. These attempts can weaken the handlebar and may cause it to break while under stress or during a crash.*

3. If the throttle housing, brake or clutch holder clamps scored the handlebar, radius the clamp edges with a file (**Figure 8**) to remove any sharp edges. Do not remove a lot of material.

4. Inspect the handlebar mounting bolts for bending and damaged threads. Check the threaded holes in the lower holders for the same conditions. Clean the threads to remove all dirt and grease residue. Replace damaged bolts.

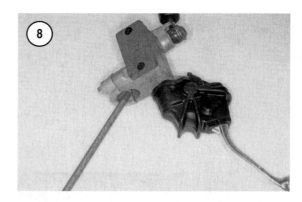

5. Clean the upper and lower handlebar holders with a stiff brush and solvent or electrical contact cleaner. Clean the clamp area on aluminum handlebars with solvent or contact cleaner and a soft brush. Clean the knurled clamp area on steel handlebars with a brush and solvent or contact cleaner.

## Lower Handlebar Holder
## Adjustment/Removal/Installation

This section describes handlebar adjustment for the handlebar holders. When adjusting the holders on aftermarket handlebar holders and upper fork brackets, follow the manufacturer's instructions.

1. The handlebar position can be moved forward 3 mm or 6 mm from the standard position (**Figure 9**):

   a. To move the handlebar forward 3 mm, install the optional handlebar holder set.

   b. To move the handlebar forward 6 mm, loosen and rotate the stock holders (**Figure 10**) 180°.

2. To replace the handlebar holders, remove the nuts (**Figure 11**), washers and handlebar holders.

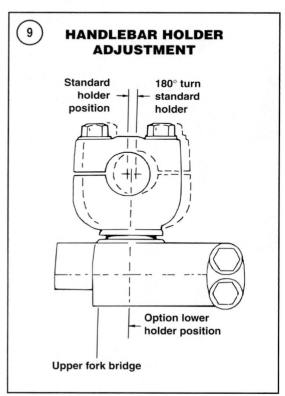

**HANDLEBAR HOLDER ADJUSTMENT**

Standard holder position

180° turn standard holder

Option lower holder position

Upper fork bridge

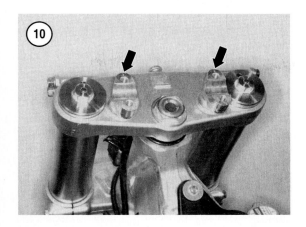

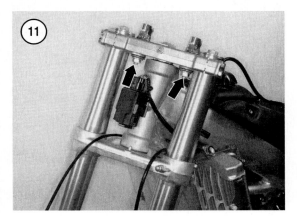

3. Install the handlebar holders, making sure they are both facing in the same direction.

4. Temporarily install the handlebar and the upper holders.

5. Tighten the lower holder nuts (**Figure 11**) to 44 N•m (33 ft.-lb.).

6. Adjust the handlebar and tighten the upper holder bolts as described in this section.

## Handlebar Holder Bushing Replacement

When increased handlebar movement or flex is noticeable, remove the lower handlebar holders and inspect the rubber bushings (cones) for deterioration, cracks, hardness and other damage (**Figure 12**). Replace all four bushings as a set.

## Replacement Handlebars

Before installing an aftermarket handlebar, refer to the manufacturer's instructions, while noting the following:

1. Carefully remove the stickers from the handlebar with solvent. Do not nick or damage the handlebar.

2. When installing aluminum bars, radius the handlebar holder and both clutch and master cylinder clamp edges with a file (**Figure 8**). Remove the sharp edges from each hole opening. Do not remove a lot of material.

3. The handlebar width can be adjusted by cutting the ends off with a hacksaw. When doing so, cut small, equal amounts from both ends until the desired width is achieved. To ensure a straight cut, wrap a strip of electrical tap of tape around the handlebar and use one edge as a cutting guide. Chamfer the edges to remove any burrs or roughness that could damage the left grip or interfere with throttle operation.

## Handlebar Installation

1. If the throttle housing was not disassembled, slide the throttle housing over the handlebar, then position the handlebar in the lower holders and install the upper holders (**Figure 6**) and the mounting bolts. Install the upper holders with their punch mark (A, **Figure 13**) facing *forward*.

### NOTE
*The handlebar marks identified in the following steps are for original equipment handlebars.*

13

2. Align the lower clamp surface with the handle-bar punch mark (B, **Figure 13**). Install the four handlebar mounting bolts and lightly tighten the front mounting bolts to hold the handlebar in place, then check the handlebar position while sitting and standing on the pegs. The handlebar should be comfortable in both positions. These positions can be confirmed when test riding the motorcycle.

3. Tighten the front handlebar bolts first, then tighten the rear bolts to 22 N•m (16 ft.-lb.). Check that the gap between the upper holders is at the back (**Figure 14**).

*WARNING*
*Do not ride the motorcycle until the handlebar clamps are mounted and tightened correctly. Improper mounting may cause the bars to slip, causing a loss of control.*

4. Lightly lubricate the right side of the handlebar where the throttle tube operates with a light-weight oil. Do not lubricate the area under the throttle housing clamp.

5. If the throttle housing was disassembled, perform the following:

   a. Lightly grease the end of the throttle cable ends.

   b. Reconnect the return (A) and pull (B) throttle cables as shown in **Figure 4**. Route the return cable (A, **Figure 4**) into the front groove in the cable guide and position the cable guide into the outer throttle housing (C).

   c. Install the inner throttle housing cover while routing the pull cable along the rear groove in the cable guide as shown in **Figure 15**. Mate both housing covers together and install the mounting bolts finger-tight.

   d. Slide the dust cover along the throttle cables and over the throttle housing.

6. Align the clamp mating surface on the throttle housing with the punch mark on the handlebar. Tighten the throttle housing bolts (B, **Figure 2**) to 8.8 N•m (80 in.-lb.). Open and release the throttle grip, making sure it returns smoothly. Then turn the handlebar and check the throttle operation in both lock positions.

7. On CRF250X and CRF450X models, install the starter switch housing by aligning the groove in the switch housing with the arm on the throttle housing (**Figure 16**). Tighten the screws securely. Then se-

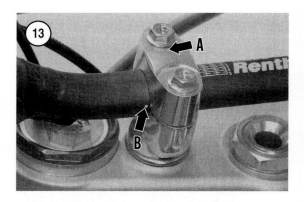

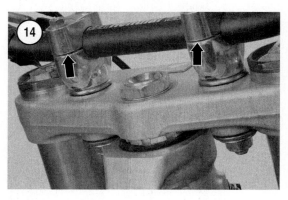

cure the wiring harness to the handlebar (A, **Figure 3**).

8. Install the master cylinder holder (A, **Figure 2**) with the UP mark on the holder facing up. Align the edge of the master cylinder clamp surface with the punch mark on the handlebar.

9. Install and tighten the master cylinder clamp bolts (A, **Figure 2**). Tighten the upper bolt first, then the lower mounting bolt to 9.8 N•m (87 in.-lb.).

10. To install the clutch lever holder, align the clamp surface on the clutch lever holder with the punch or paint mark on the handlebar (**Figure 17**). Install the clutch lever holder and tighten the upper bolt, then the lower bolt to 8.8 N•m (78 in.-lb.).

*NOTE*
*On models with original equipment Renthal aluminum handlebars, a strip of plastic was originally wrapped around the handlebar underneath the clutch lever holder (**Figure 17**). The plastic allows the clutch lever holder to be tightened fully, while allowing the holder to rotate in a fall without damaging the handlebar.*

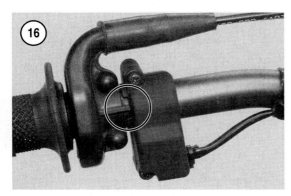

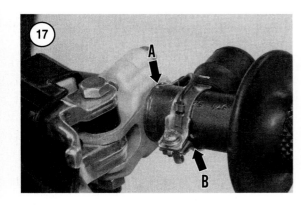

a. Position the control levers and engine stop switch so they can be operated when seated and standing.

b. Turn the handlebar from side-to-side to check the cables for binding.

## HANDLEBAR GRIP REPLACEMENT

Depending on the condition of the handlebar grips, different removal methods are available. Use contact cleaner and compressed air to remove the grips if they are to be reused. If the grips are torn and damaged, it may be possible to slide them off by hand. This section lists some different ways on removing grips. While some riders cut the grips off, the tool used in this method can score the throttle tube or the aluminum handlebar (if used), so use caution if using this method. Replace the grips with the handlebar installed on the motorcycle.

*NOTE*
*When removing handlebar grips that are in good condition, it is best to use a technique that pushes or slides them off the handlebar. Trying to pull a grip off the handlebar stretches the grip and tightens it against the handlebar.*

1. If the grips are to be reused, note any alignment marks on the grips or make your own.

2. If the grips are torn and damaged, grab the inner grip flange and pull it off the handlebar or throttle tube, inside out.

3. If cutting the grips, carefully cut through the grip flange and pull it back to expose the handlebar or throttle tube. Continue to pull the grip away from the handlebar or throttle pipe while cutting it lengthwise. Pulling the grip helps prevent the blade from contacting the handlebar or throttle pipe. After cutting the grip, spread it and pull it off, inside out.

4. To remove the left grip so it can be reused, insert a thin screwdriver between the grip and handlebar. Work carefully to prevent tearing the grip or gouging the handlebar. Then squirt contact cleaner into the open area under the grip (**Figure 18**). Immediately remove the screwdriver and turn the grip by hand to break the adhesive bond between the grip and handlebar, then push or slide the grip off. If necessary, repeat this step at different points around the grip until it slides off.

11. To install the engine stop switch, align the end of the switch bracket with the punch or paint mark on the handlebar (B, **Figure 17**). Tighten the bracket screw securely.

*CAUTION*
*Route the engine stop switch wire so it cannot be pinched by tie-downs.*

12. Sit on the motorcycle and recheck the riding position. Adjust the handlebar and controls, if necessary. Note the following:

13

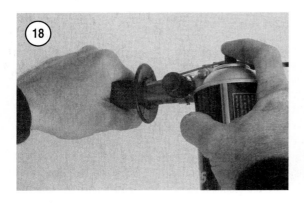

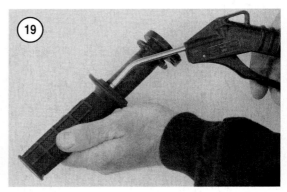

5. To remove the right grip from the throttle tube so it can be reused:

    a. Make sure the grip is in good condition. This technique does not work on cut or damaged grips.

    b. Disconnect the throttle cables and remove the throttle tube as described under *Handlebar Removal* in this chapter.

    c. Insert the nozzle from an air gun between the grip and throttle tube and carefully blow the grip slowly off the throttle pipe (**Figure 19**).

6. Remove grip adhesive from the handlebar and throttle tube with solvent or WD-40. Then clean with contact cleaner to remove any oil residue.

7. Inspect the throttle tube for any cracks and damage and replace if necessary.

*CAUTION*
*Do not install a new grip over a damaged or broken throttle tube. The glue will leak through and stick to the handlebar and the inner throttle tube surfaces.*

8. Inspect the handlebar ends for scoring, grooves and other damage. Sand or file until the surface is smooth.

9. Reinstall the throttle tube (without the new grip) and the throttle cables as described under *Handlebar Installation* in this chapter.

10A. If installing original equipment Honda grips, note the following:

    a. Align the index mark on the throttle grip flange with the edge of the throttle tube (**Figure 20**).

    b. Align the index mark on the left grip flange with the punch or paint mark on the handlebar (**Figure 20**).

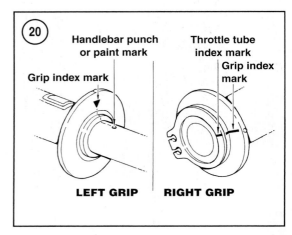

10B. On aftermarket grips, some are directional as to how they mount on the handlebar and throttle tube. Check the grips and manufacturer's instructions before installing them.

11. Recheck the riding position and adjust the handlebar, if necessary.

12. Identify the left and right (throttle tube) grips.

*NOTE*
*Make sure the grip cement is applicable for the grips being installed. ThreeBond GRIPLOCK (1501C) and Honda Hand Grip Cement can be used on most grips. However, a specific cement may be required when installing Gel grips and other soft compound grips. Use Renthal Grip Glue when installing soft or medium-compound Renthal grips. Always refer to the manufacturer's instructions for application and drying time.*

13. Install the grips as follows:

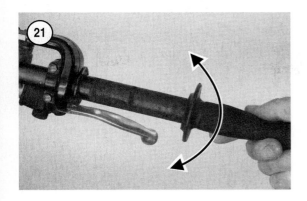

**21**

a. Cover the hole in the end of the throttle tube with duct tape to prevent the cement from contacting the handlebar and inner throttle tube surface.

b. If hidden end caps are to be used, install them into the handlebar ends before installing the grips.

c. Apply grip cement to the inside surface of the grip and to the grip contact surface on the left side of the handlebar or on the throttle tube.

d. Install the grip with a twisting motion (**Figure 21**) to spread the cement evenly. Then quickly align the grip with the handlebar or throttle tube. Squeeze the outer end of the left grip to make sure it contacts the end of the handlebar. For the right grip, make sure there is a small gap between the grip and the throttle housing, and the grip contacts the end of the throttle pipe.

14. Observe the grip cement manufacturer's drying time before riding the motorcycle.

## STEERING HEAD

The steering head (**Figure 22**) pivots on tapered roller bearings. The bearing inner races (mounted in the frame) and the lower bearing (mounted on the steering stem) should not be removed unless they require replacement.

Remove the steering stem and lubricate the bearings at the intervals specified in Chapter Three.

### Special Tools

1. A Motion Pro T-stem Nut Wrench and Bearing Adjustment Spanner (Honda part No. 08-0232) is used to loosen and tighten the steering stem nut and the steering adjust nut. See **Figure 23**. This tool can also be used to adjust the steering assembly when the front fork is installed on the motorcycle.

2. Honda steering stem socket (part No. 07916-3710101) or a spanner wrench that can be used as a torque adapter.

### Disassembly

> *NOTE*
> *When troubleshooting a steering complaint, check the steering adjust-*

---

**22** **STEERING HEAD**

1 — 1
2 — 2
3
4
5
6
7
8
9
10
11

1. Steering stem nut
2. Washer
3. Upper fork bridge
4. Steering adjust nut
5. Dust seal
6. Upper bearing
7. Upper bearing race
8. Lower bearing race
9. Lower bearing
10. Dust seal
11. Steering stem

**13**

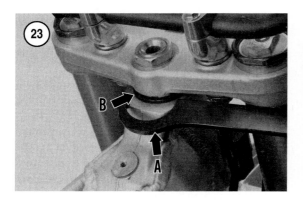

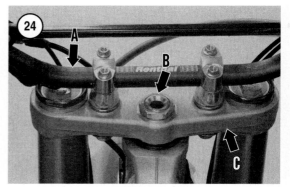

*ment before removing the front forks and steering assembly.*

1. Note the cable and wiring harness routing before removing them in the following steps.

2A. On CRF250R and CRF450R models, remove the number plate.

2B. On CRF250X and CRF450X models, remove the front visor and the trip meter (Chapter Sixteen).

3. Remove the front wheel (Chapter Twelve).

4. Remove the front fender.

5. Remove the handlebar (A, **Figure 24**) as described in this chapter.

6. Loosen the steering stem nut (B, **Figure 24**).

7. Remove the front forks as described in this chapter.

8. Remove the steering stem nut and washer (B, **Figure 24**).

9. Remove the upper fork bridge (C, **Figure 24**).

10. Loosen the steering adjust nut (**Figure 25**) with a spanner wrench.

11. Remove the steering adjust nut (A, **Figure 26**), dust seal (B) and upper bearing (**Figure 27**).

12. Remove the steering stem (**Figure 28**).

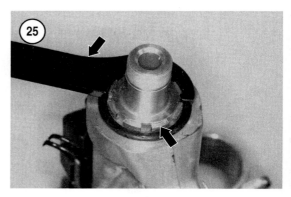

## Inspection

Replace worn or damaged parts as described in this chapter. If there is sufficient damage with any steering component, have a Honda dealership check the frame, steering stem and upper fork bridge.

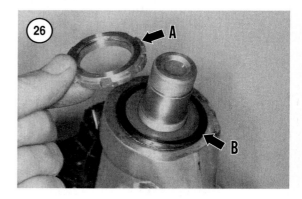

> *CAUTION*
> *Steering bearings are usually damaged from a lack of lubrication and incorrect adjustment. A loose steering adjustment increases clearance between bearings and races. High shock*

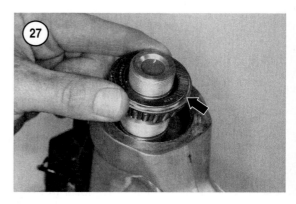

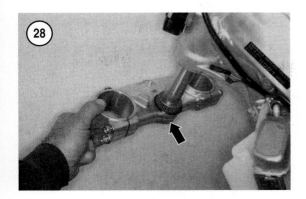

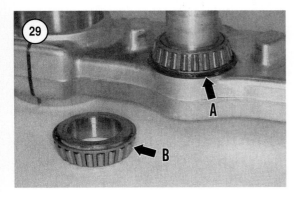

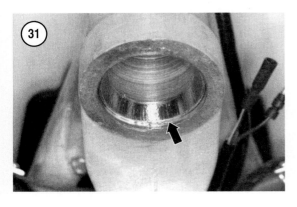

loads received from competition and off-road use pounds the bearings into the races and damages them. Over-tightening the bearing adjustment will also damage the bearings and races.

*NOTE*
*Do not remove the lower bearing (A, **Figure 29**) for cleaning or lubrication. If the bearing can be reused, service it while it is mounted on the steering stem. Remove the bearing only to replace it.*

1. Clean the bearings and races in solvent.

2. Clean the steering stem, steering adjust nut and steering stem nut threads thoroughly to ensure accurate torque readings and steering adjustment during reassembly.

3. Check the steering head frame welds for cracks and fractures. Refer repair to a qualified frame shop or welding service.

4. Check the steering stem nut and steering adjust nut for damage.

5. Check the steering stem and upper fork bridge for cracks and damage. Check the steering stem for straightness.

6. Check the bearing races (**Figure 30** and **Figure 31**) in the frame for dimples, pitting, galling and impact damage. If a race is worn or damaged, replace both races and bearings as described under *Steering Head Bearing Races* in this chapter.

7. Check the tapered roller bearings (**Figure 29**) for flat spots, pitting, wear and other damage. If a bearing is damaged, replace both races and bearings as described in this chapter.

8. When reusing bearings, clean them thoroughly with a degreaser. Pack the bearings with waterproof bearing grease.

**Assembly and Steering Adjustment**

Refer to **Figure 22**.

1. Make sure the upper (**Figure 30**) and lower (**Figure 31**) bearing races are properly seated in the frame.

2. Lubricate the bearings and races with a waterproof bearing grease.

3. Install the steering stem (**Figure 28**) through the bottom of the frame and hold it in place.

13

4. Install the upper bearing (**Figure 27**) over the steering stem and seat it into its race.

5. Install the dust seal (B, **Figure 26**) and the steering adjust nut (A). Tighten the nut finger-tight.

*NOTE*
*Two methods are provided for adjusting the steering stem bearings when assembling the steering assembly. Step 6A requires special tools and Step 6B does not.*

6A. To seat the bearings using a torque adapter and torque wrench, perform the following:

   a. Tighten the steering adjust nut (**Figure 32**) to 6.9 N•m (61 in.-lb.).

   b. Turn the steering stem (**Figure 33**) from lock-to-lock several times to seat the bearings.

   c. Retighten the steering adjust nut (**Figure 32**) to 6.9 N•m (61 in.-lb.).

   d. Check bearing play by turning the steering stem from lock-to-lock several times. The steering stem must pivot smoothly with no binding or roughness.

6B. If the tools described in Step 6A are not available, tighten the steering adjust nut as follows:

   a. Tighten the steering adjust nut (**Figure 34**) to seat the bearings. Turn the steering stem (**Figure 33**) several times to seat the bearings, then tighten the nut again.

   b. Tighten the steering adjust nut while checking bearing play.

*NOTE*
*In Step 6A and Step 6B, the steering adjust nut must be tight enough to remove play, both horizontal and vertical, yet loose enough so the steering assembly will turn to both lock positions without any excessive play.*

7. Install the upper fork bridge (C, **Figure 24**).

8. Install the washer and the steering stem nut (B, **Figure 24**). Tighten the nut finger-tight.

9. Slide both fork tubes into position and tighten the upper and lower fork tube pinch bolts so the forks cannot slide out.

10. Tighten the steering stem nut (**Figure 35**) to 108 N•m (80 ft.-lb.).

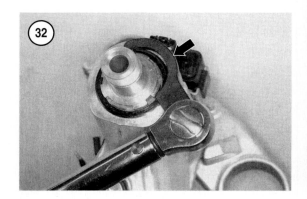

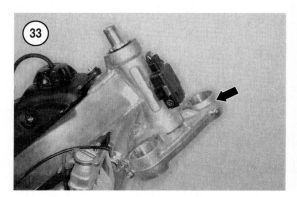

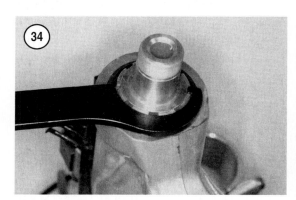

*NOTE*
*Because tightening the steering stem nut affects the steering bearing preload, it may be necessary to repeat these steps several times until the steering adjustment is correct.*

11. Check bearing play by turning the steering stem from side to side. The steering stem must pivot smoothly. If the steering stem adjustment is incorrect, readjust the bearing play as follows:

   a. Loosen the steering stem nut (A, **Figure 36**).

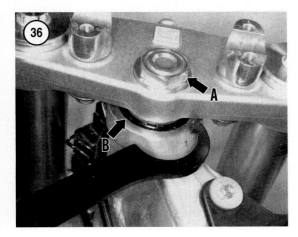

15. Install the front wheel (Chapter Twelve).

16A. On CRF250R and CRF450R models, install the number plate.

16B. On CRF250X and CRF450X models, install the trip meter and front visor (Chapter Sixteen).

17. After 30 minutes to 1 hour of riding time, check the steering adjustment. If necessary, adjust as described under *Steering Play Check and Adjustment* in this chapter.

## STEERING PLAY CHECK AND ADJUSTMENT

Steering adjustment takes up any slack in the steering stem and bearings and allows the steering stem to operate with free rotation. Any excessive play or roughness in the steering stem will make the steering imprecise and difficult and cause bearing damage. Improper bearing lubrication or an incorrect steering adjustment (too loose or tight) usually causes these conditions. Incorrect clutch and throttle cable routing can also effect steering operation.

*NOTE*
*The Motion Pro T-stem Nut Wrench and Bearing Adjustment Spanner (part No. 08-0232) is used to loosen and tighten the steering stem nut and the steering adjust nut in this section.*

b. Loosen or tighten the steering adjust nut (B, **Figure 36**) as required to adjust the steering play.

c. Retighten the steering stem nut (A, **Figure 36**) to 108 N•m (80 ft.-lb.).

d. Recheck bearing play by turning the steering stem from side to side. If the play feels correct, turn the steering stem so the front fork is facing straight ahead. While an assistant steadies the motorcycle, grasp the fork tubes, and try to move them front to back. If there is play and the bearing adjustment feels correct, the bearings and races are probably worn and require replacement.

12. Position the fork tubes and tighten the fork tube pinch bolts as described in this chapter.

13. Install the handlebar as described in this chapter.

14. Install the front fender.

1. Support the motorcycle with the front wheel off the ground.

2. Turn the handlebar from side to side. The steering stem should move freely and without any binding or roughness. If it feels like the bearings are catching, the bearing races are probably damaged.

3. Turn the handlebar so the front wheel points straight ahead. Alternately push (slightly) one end of the handlebar and then the other. The front end should turn to each side from the center under its own weight. Note the following:

a. If the steering stem moved roughly or stopped before hitting the frame stop, check the clutch and throttle cable routing. Reroute the cable(s) if necessary.

b. If the cable routing is correct and the steering is tight, the steering adjustment is too tight or the bearings require lubrication or replacement.

13

c. If the steering stem moved from side to side correctly, perform Step 4 to check for excessive looseness.

*NOTE*
*When checking for excessive steering play in Step 4, have an assistant steady the motorcycle.*

4. Grasp the fork tubes firmly (near the axle) and attempt to move the wheel front to back. Note the following:
 a. If movement can be felt at the steering stem, the steering adjustment is probably loose. Go to Step 5 to adjust the steering.
 b. If there is no movement and the front end turns correctly as described in Steps 2-4, the steering adjustment is correct.
5. Loosen the steering stem nut (**Figure 37**).
6. Adjust the steering adjust nut (B, **Figure 36**) as follows:
 a. If the steering is too loose, tighten the steering adjust nut.
 b. If the steering is too tight, loosen the steering adjust nut.
7. Tighten the steering stem nut (**Figure 38**) to 108 N•m (80 ft.-lb.).
8. Recheck the steering adjustment as described in this procedure.

*NOTE*
*Because tightening the steering stem nut affects the steering bearing preload, it may be necessary to repeat Steps 5-8 a few times until the steering adjustment is correct. If the steering adjustment cannot be corrected, the steering bearings may require lubrication or are damaged. Remove the steering stem and inspect the bearings as described in this chapter.*

## STEERING HEAD BEARING RACES

The steering head bearing races (**Figure 30** and **Figure 31**) are pressed into the frame's steering neck. Do not remove the bearing races unless they require replacement.

Due to the aluminum frame, Honda specifies the use of a number of special tools to remove and install the steering head bearing races. Due to the expense of these tools, it may be more worthwhile to have the

service work performed at a Honda dealership. Attempting to replace the bearing races without the special tools may damage the bearing race mounting bores in the frame. This may cause a variety of handling problems that cannot be corrected by normal adjustment methods. Depending on the degree of damage, frame repair or replacement may be required.

*NOTE*
*A steering bearing kit is available from Pivot Works (**Figure 39**). Each kit includes upper and lower bearing assemblies and seals for rebuilding the steering assembly. Pivot Works bearing kits can be ordered through motorcycle dealerships or contact them at **www.pivotworks.com**.*

**Special Tools**

The following Honda special tools are required to replace the bearing races:

1. Ball race remover: 07946-3710500.

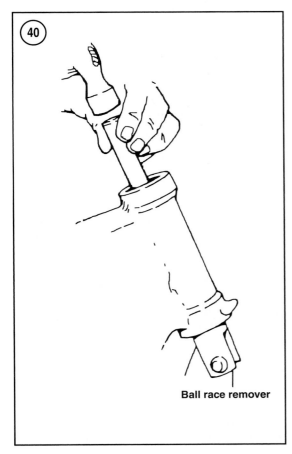

**Ball race remover**

2. Bearing race installer (two required): 07VMF-KZ30100.

3. Installer shaft: 07VMF-KZ30200.

**Outer Bearing Race Replacement**

Replace both bearing races and bearings at the same time.

*NOTE*
*The following procedure describes bearing removal with special tools to protect the frame from damage that may occur from using different tools and procedures that can bind the bearing races when removing and installing them.*

*CAUTION*
*If binding occurs when removing or installing the bearing races, stop and release tension from the bearing race. Check the tool alignment to make sure the bearing race is moving evenly in its mounting bore. Otherwise, the bearing race may gouge the frame mounting bore and cause permanent damage.*

1. Mount the ball race remover (**Figure 40**) onto the lower bearing. Make sure it is mounted squarely onto the race so the race will be driven squarely out of the frame.

2. Drive the lower race out from the inside (**Figure 40**).

3. Repeat for the upper race.

4. Clean the steering neck mounting bore and check for cracks and other damage.

5. Place the new lower race squarely into the mounting bore opening with its tapered side facing out.

6. Assemble the Honda tools as shown in **Figure 41**. Hold the installer shaft and tighten the nut to draw the race into the frame tube. Continue until the race bottoms out in its mounting bore. Remove the puller assembly and inspect the bearing race. It must seat fully and squarely in the steering neck (**Figure 41**).

*CAUTION*
*Do not allow the installer shaft to contact the bearing race.*

7. Reverse the tool (**Figure 42**) and repeat Step 5 and Step 6 to install the upper race.

8. Lubricate the upper and lower bearing races with grease.

**13**

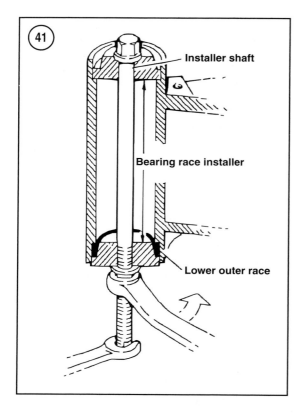

41

Installer shaft

Bearing race installer

Lower outer race

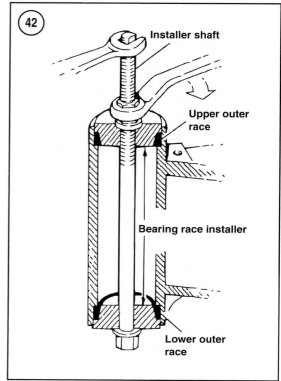

42

Installer shaft

Upper outer race

Bearing race installer

Lower outer race

## Steering Stem Bearing Replacement

Perform the following steps to replace the steering stem bearing (**Figure 43**).

1. Thread the steering stem nut onto the steering stem (**Figure 44**).

> *WARNING*
> *Wear safety glasses while removing the steering stem bearing in Step 2.*

2. Remove the steering stem bearing and dust seal with a hammer and chisel as shown in **Figure 44**. Strike at different spots underneath the bearing to prevent it from binding on the steering stem.

3. Clean the steering stem with solvent and dry thoroughly.

4. Inspect the steering stem and bearing mounting surface for damage.

5. Lubricate the new dust seal lip (10, **Figure 22**) with grease and slide it over the steering stem.

6. Pack the new bearing with a waterproof bearing grease.

43

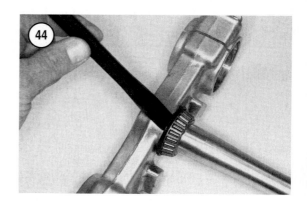

44

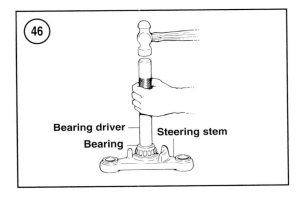

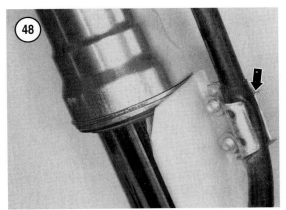

7. Position the new bearing with the tapered side facing up and slide it onto the steering stem until it stops.

8A. To install the new bearing with a press, perform the following:

    a. Install the steering stem and the new bearing in a press and support it with two bearing drivers as shown in **Figure 45**. Make sure the lower bearing driver seats against the inner bearing race and does not contact the bearing rollers.

    b. Press the bearing onto the steering stem until it bottoms out (**Figure 43**).

8B. To install the new bearing with a bearing driver, perform the following:

    a. Slide a bearing driver over the steering stem until it seats against the bearing's inner race (**Figure 46**). Make sure the driver does not contact the bearing rollers.

    b. Drive the bearing onto the steering stem until it bottoms out (**Figure 43**).

## FRONT FORK

### Removal

1. Remove the front wheel as described in Chapter Twelve.

2. Insert a plastic or wooden spacer block between the brake pads.

> *NOTE*
> *The spacer prevents the piston from being forced out of the caliper if the brake lever is applied with the disc removed. If a piston is forced out, the caliper must be disassembled to reseat the piston.*

3. On CRF250X and CRF450X models, perform the following:

    a. Remove the front visor (Chapter Sixteen).

    b. Note the trip meter cable routing around the right fork tube, then remove it (**Figure 47**).

4. Remove the brake hose clamp (**Figure 48**) from the left fork tube.

13

5. Remove the brake caliper mounting bolts and remove the brake caliper (**Figure 49**). Support the brake caliper with a piece of stiff wire.

*CAUTION*
*Do not allow the brake caliper to hang from its brake hose.*

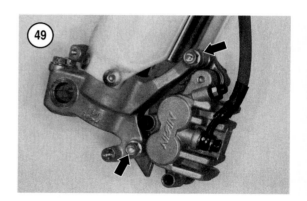

6. Remove the fork protectors.
7. If the fork tube is going to be disassembled, perform the following:
   a. Remove the holder mounting bolts, holder and reposition the handlebar away from the fork caps.
   b. Slowly loosen the air release screw (A, **Figure 50**) on the fork cap to release air inside the fork, then tighten the screw.

*NOTE*
*In substep c, only loosen the fork damper (50 mm). Do not loosen the fork cap (32 mm).*

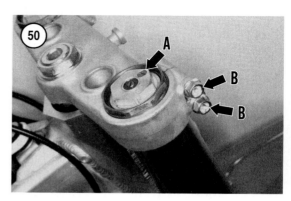

   c. Loosen the fork damper with a 50 mm locknut wrench (**Figure 51**). See *Fork Service* in this chapter for a description of the locknut wrench.

8. Note the position of the rebound adjuster and air release screw on the fork cap in relation to the upper fork bridge.
9. Loosen the upper (B, **Figure 50**) and lower (**Figure 52**, typical) fork tube pinch bolts and remove the fork tube.
10. Clean the fork tubes, both fork bridges and steering stem clamping surfaces.
11. Remove, clean and inspect the fork tube pinch bolts. Replace damaged bolts.

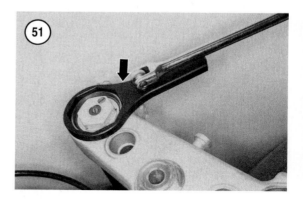

**Installation**

*CAUTION*
*Do not overtighten the fork tube pinch bolts in the following steps. Excessive tightening can permanently deform the fork tube.*

*NOTE*
*When tightening the fork damper with a 50 mm locknut wrench, mount the wrench at a 90° angle on the torque wrench (**Figure 53**). Because this mounting position does not increase the leverage of the torque wrench, the*

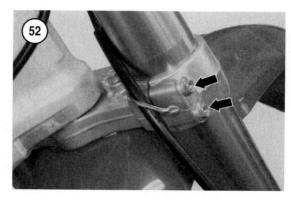

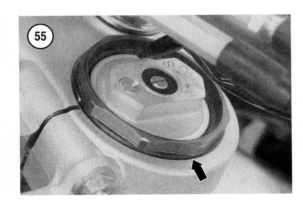

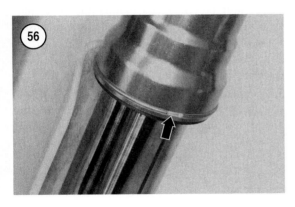

*torque setting does not have to be recalibrated. See **Torque Adapters** in Chapter One for more information.*

1. Install the left fork tube (with the brake caliper mount) into the steering stem. If the fork damper was loosened, temporarily tighten the lower fork tube pinch bolts and tighten the fork damper with a 50 mm locknut wrench (**Figure 53**) to 34 N•m (25 ft.-lb.).

2. Position and tighten the fork tube as follows:
   a. Loosen the lower fork tube pinch bolts and turn the fork tube so the air release screw (A, **Figure 50**) faces to the front.
   b. On CRF250R and CRF450R models, position the fork tube with its index mark aligned with the top fork bridge surface (**Figure 54**).
   c. On CRF250X and CRF450X models, align the fork cap surface with the top fork bridge surface (**Figure 55**).
   d. Tighten the lower fork tube pinch bolts (**Figure 52**, typical) to the torque specification in **Table 9**.
   e. Tighten the upper fork tube pinch bolts (B, **Figure 50**) to the torque specifications in **Table 9**.

3. Repeat Step 1 and Step 2 for the right fork tube.

4. Turn each wear ring with its end gap facing rearward (**Figure 56**).

5. Install the brake caliper as follows:
   a. Apply a medium strength threadlock onto the brake caliper mounting bolts.
   b. Position the brake caliper against the left fork tube bracket and secure it with the mounting bolts. Tighten the brake caliper mounting bolts (**Figure 49**) to 30 N•m (22 ft.-lb.).

6. Install the fork protectors. Apply a threadlock onto the fork protector mounting bolt threads and tighten the bolts to 6.9 N•m (61 in.-lb.).

7. Route the front brake hose around the inside of the fork tube and secure it with the clamp. Tighten the front brake hose guide bolts to 6.9 N•m (61 in.-lb.).

8. On CRF250X and CRF450X models, route the trip meter cable around the right fork tube as shown in **Figure 47**. Secure the cable into the right clamp shown in **Figure 52**.

9. Install the front wheel as described in Chapter Twelve. Turn the front wheel and squeeze the front brake lever a few times to reposition the pistons in

13

the caliper. If the brake lever feels spongy, bleed the front brake (Chapter Fifteen).

> *NOTE*
> *If the fork seals were leaking, inspect the front brake pads and caliper for oil contamination. Service the brakes as described in Chapter Fifteen.*

10. If necessary, adjust the front fork compression and rebound adjusters as described in this chapter.

## FORK SERVICE

Showa 47 mm inverted twin-chamber cartridge fork legs with compression and rebound damping adjusters are used on all models. Sealed damper cartridges use separate air and oil chambers to prevent aeration.

While the front fork is typically trouble-free, it does require periodic service to replace the fork oil, inspect the bushings and check for spring fatigue and slider out-of-round. Fork adjustment problems can typically be traced to infrequent oil changes and sagged or incorrect weight fork springs.

### Fork Tools

The following special tools are required to disassemble and reassemble the fork tubes:
1. A 47 mm split fork seal driver (A, **Figure 57**) to install the fork seal and slider bushing. Motion Pro part No. (08-0138).
2. A 50 mm locknut wrench to loosen and tighten the fork cap and fork damper. Adjustable or open-end wrenches are not recommended, as they will not adequately grip the damper and will round the hex-surfaces. Two types of wrenches are shown in **Figure 57**:
   a. Motion Pro locknut wrench (B) (part No. 08-0236).
   b. Honda locknut wrench (C) (part No. 07WMA-KZ30200).
3. Stopper plate tool (D, **Figure 57**) to hold the piston rod locknut when loosening and tightening the center bolt at the bottom of the slider. Make the tool from a 1 mm (0.039 in.) steel plate to the dimensions shown in **Figure 58**. Do not make or use a wooden tool as the high fork spring pressure exerted against the tool when under use may cause it to break apart.

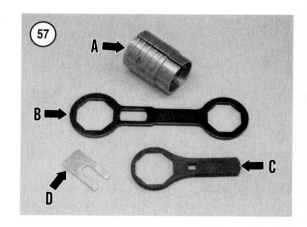

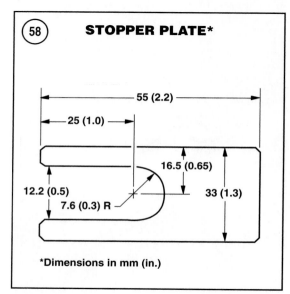

**58 STOPPER PLATE\***

55 (2.2)

25 (1.0)

16.5 (0.65)

12.2 (0.5)

33 (1.3)

7.6 (0.3) R

*Dimensions in mm (in.)*

### Disassembly

Refer to **Figure 59**.

1. Clean the fork assembly and the bottom of the center bolt before disassembling the fork tube. Carefully check the fork tube and slider for visual damage.
2. Open the air release screw (A, **Figure 60**) to release any pressure from the fork assembly.
3. Turn the compression adjuster (B, **Figure 60**) counterclockwise to its softest setting. Count and record the number of clicks from its original position.
4. Turn the rebound adjuster (**Figure 61**) counterclockwise to its softest setting. Count and record the number of clicks from its original position.

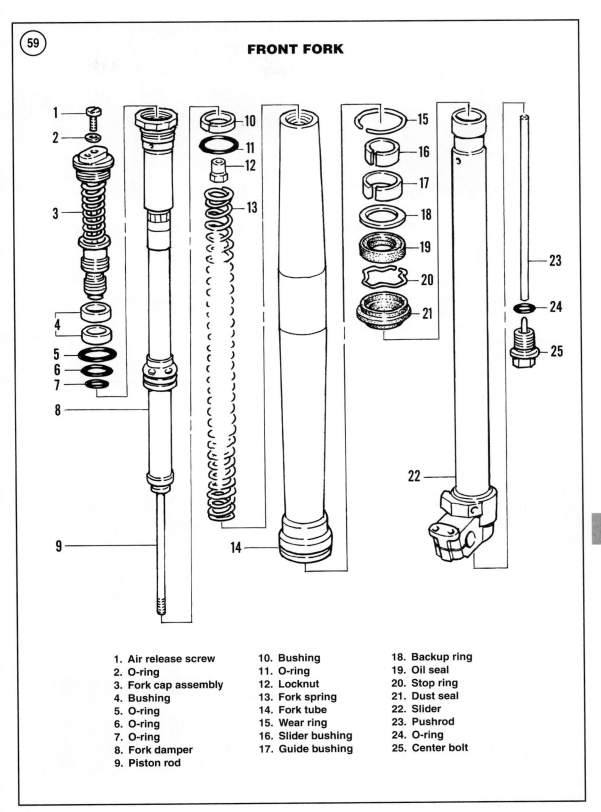

FRONT FORK

59

1. Air release screw
2. O-ring
3. Fork cap assembly
4. Bushing
5. O-ring
6. O-ring
7. O-ring
8. Fork damper
9. Piston rod

10. Bushing
11. O-ring
12. Locknut
13. Fork spring
14. Fork tube
15. Wear ring
16. Slider bushing
17. Guide bushing

18. Backup ring
19. Oil seal
20. Stop ring
21. Dust seal
22. Slider
23. Pushrod
24. O-ring
25. Center bolt

13

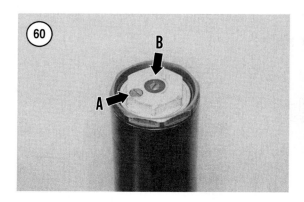

5. Measure and record the length between the axle holder and the fork tube (not dust seal) surfaces shown in **Figure 62**.

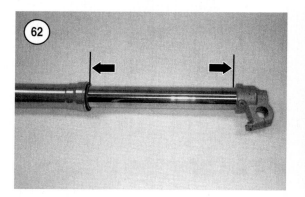

*NOTE*
*The standard length measurement is 315-319 mm (12.40-12.56 in.). If the measured length is longer than this measurement, the center bolt and locknut were installed incorrectly.*

6. Hold the fork tube vertically and remove the fork damper with the 50 mm locknut wrench (**Figure 63**). Then slowly lower the fork tube until the dust seal bottoms against the slider.

7. Hold the slider and pump the fork tube to drain fork oil from the fork tube (A, **Figure 64**) and through the hole in the fork damper (B).

8. Temporarily install the fork damper into the fork tube (**Figure 65**) and tighten hand-tight.

9. Lock the axle holder in a vise fitted with soft jaws (A, **Figure 66**).

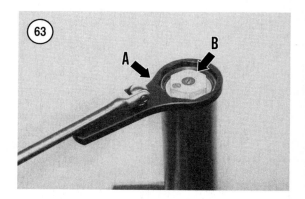

*CAUTION*
*Do not overtighten the vise.*

10. Loosen the center bolt (B, **Figure 66**) so that it is free from the slider.

*NOTE*
*Because the spring pressure applied against the center bolt is quite large, have an assistant push on the fork cap while the stopper plate is installed in Step 11.*

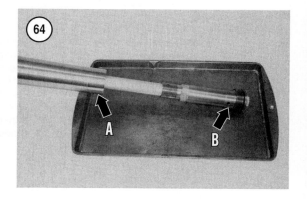

11. Push on the fork cap to extend the center bolt (A, **Figure 67**) and piston rod from the axle holder, then install the stopper plate (B) between the axle holder and the locknut (C). Slowly release the pis-

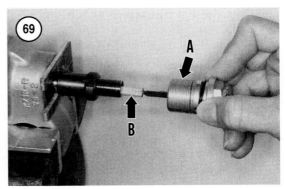

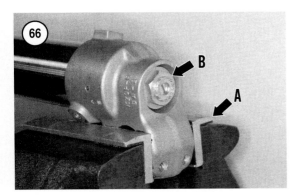

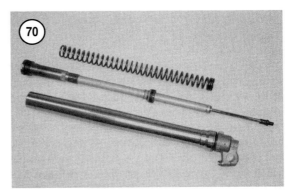

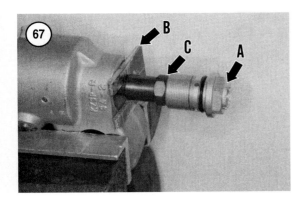

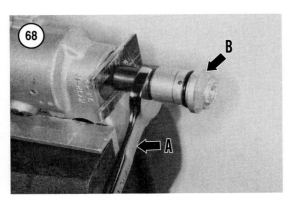

ton rod/center bolt assembly until the stopper plate is held tightly between the parts.

12. Hold the locknut with a wrench (A, **Figure 68**) and loosen the center bolt (B).

13. Remove the center bolt (A, **Figure 69**) and the pushrod (B).

14. Push on the fork damper and remove the stopper plate.

15. Remove the fork damper and fork spring from the slider. Then remove the slider from the vise. See **Figure 70**.

*NOTE*
*If servicing the fork to only change the fork oil capacity, stop at this point and go to **Fork Oil Refilling and Fork Assembly** in this section. If the oil in the fork damper is to be replaced, continue with Step 16. Steps 17-23 describe removing the oil seals and bushings and completing fork disassembly.*

16. Remove the fork cap assembly from the fork damper as follows:

13

a. Hold the fork damper across its flats in a vise with soft jaws.

b. Hold the fork damper with the 50 mm locknut wrench (A, **Figure 71**) to help steady the assembly, then loosen the fork cap (B, **Figure 71**) with a 6-point, 32 mm socket.

c. Remove the fork cap assembly from the fork damper (**Figure 72**).

d. Remove the fork damper from the vise and pump the piston rod (mounted on the bottom of the fork damper) to drain oil from the fork damper.

17. Carefully pry the dust seal (A, **Figure 73**) out of the fork tube.

18. Pry the stop ring (B, **Figure 73**) out of the groove in the fork tube.

19. Hold the fork tube and slowly move the slider up and down and check for roughness and binding. If the action is not smooth, inspect the slider and fork tube for damage.

20. There is an interference fit between the slider and guide bushings. To separate the fork tube from the slider, hold the fork tube and pull hard on the slider using quick in and out strokes (**Figure 74**). Repeat as necessary to separate the parts (**Figure 75**).

21. Carefully pry the slot in the slider bushing (A, **Figure 76**) to spread and remove it. Do not pry the opening more than necessary.

22. Remove the following parts from the slider:
a. Slider bushing.
b. Backup ring.
c. Oil seal.
d. Stop ring.
e. Dust seal.

23. Clean and inspect the fork assembly as described under *Inspection* in this section.

## Inspection

Replace parts that are out of specification or show damage as described in this section.

*NOTE*
*Handle the fork cap bushings and fork bushing carefully when cleaning them in Step 1. Harsh cleaning can remove or damage their coating material.*

1. Clean all of the fork parts, except the fork damper, in solvent, first making sure the solvent

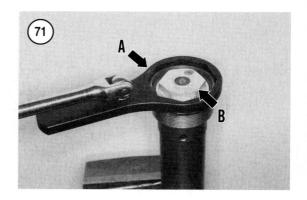

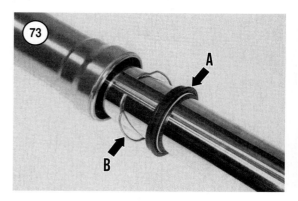

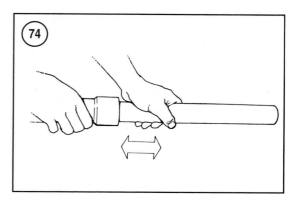

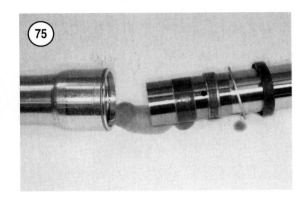

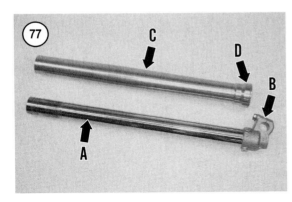

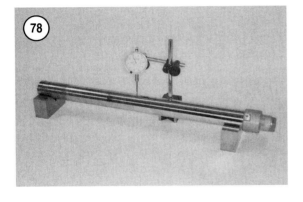

will not damage the fork bushings or rubber parts. Then clean with soap and water and rinse with plain water. Remove all threadlock residue from the center bolt threads. Dry with compressed air.

*NOTE*
*Because it is difficult to remove solvent and other cleaning liquids from the fork damper, clean the fork damper with new fork oil.*

2. Inspect the slider for:
   a. Nicks, rust, chrome flaking or creasing along the length of the slider (A, **Figure 77**). These conditions damage the dust and oil seals. Repair minor roughness with 600 grit sandpaper and solvent. Replace the slider if necessary.
   b. Stress cracks and other damage at the axle holder (B, **Figure 77**).
   c. Check the axle holder bore inner diameter for dents or burrs that could damage the center bolt O-ring when removing and installing the bolt. Remove burrs with a fine grit sandpaper or a fine-cut file.
   d. Runout. Place the slider on a set of V-blocks (**Figure 78**) and measure runout with a dial indicator. Compare with the service limit in **Table 1**. The actual runout is half of the indicator reading.
3. Inspect the fork tube for:
   a. Damage and wear, particularly at the bushing and seal operating areas (C, **Figure 77**).
   b. Damaged threads.
   c. Wear ring condition (D, **Figure 77**). Replace the wear ring when it is within 1.5 mm (0.06 in.) of the fork tube (**Figure 79**). The wear ring prevents the fork protector from contacting the fork tube during fork movement.
4. Check the fork cap assembly for:
   a. Check the hex edges on the fork cap for rounding and other damage.
   b. Damaged threads.
   c. Worn or damaged bushings (A, **Figure 80**). Replace the bushings if necessary.
   d. Operation of the compression adjuster. If the adjuster does not click when adjusting it, replace the fork cap assembly.
   e. Spring fatigue or damage (B, **Figure 80**).
   f. Worn or damaged O-rings (C, **Figure 80**, typical). Replace the O-rings if necessary. All the

**13**

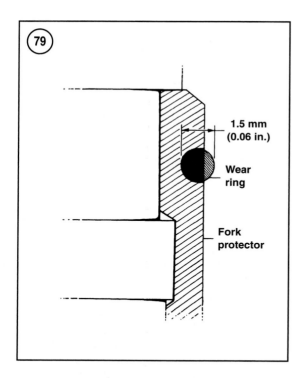

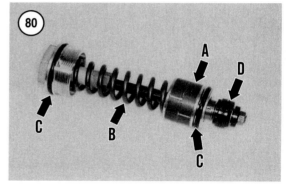

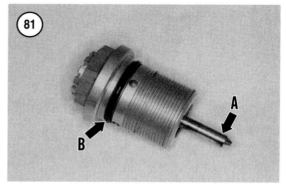

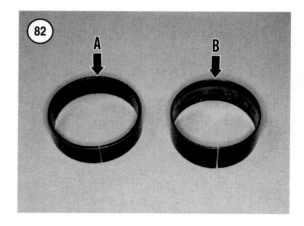

O-rings installed on the fork cap assembly can be replaced.

g. Debris buildup on the piston and shim assembly (D, **Figure 80**).

*CAUTION*
*Do not disassemble the fork cap assembly. Refer service or adjustment to a qualified suspension specialist.*

5. Inspect the fork center bolt and adjuster rod for:
   a. Damaged and debris buildup.
   b. Damaged adjuster rod (A, **Figure 81**). The shoulders on the adjuster rod must be square for proper engagement with the pushrod.
   c. Rebound adjuster operation.
   d. Damaged threads.
   e. Replace the O-ring (B, **Figure 81**) if damaged.

*NOTE*
*Do not attempt to disassemble and service the center bolt. If damaged, replace it as a complete assembly.*

6. Check the guide (A, **Figure 82**) and slider (B) bushings for scoring, scratches and excessive wear. Excessive wear is indicated when the bushings are discolored or when the coating is worn through and the metal is visible.

7. Inspect the backup ring and replace if it is distorted on its inner edge.

8. Measure the fork spring free length with a tape measure (**Figure 83**) and compare to the service limit in **Table 1**. Replace the fork spring if it is too short. Replace the fork spring in both fork tubes at the same time.

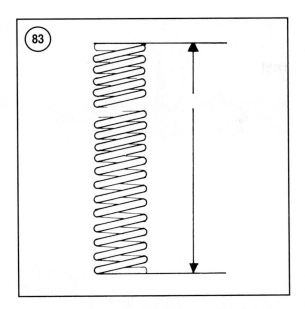

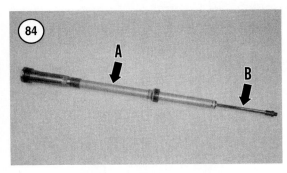

*NOTE*
*Refer to the information under **Fork Oil Refilling and Fork Assembly** in this chapter on how to identify the fork springs.*

9. Inspect the fork damper (A, **Figure 84**) and piston rod (B) for bending and other damage. Hold the fork damper and pump the piston rod and check for

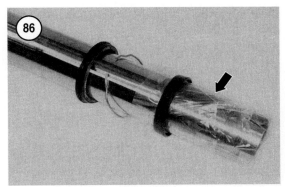

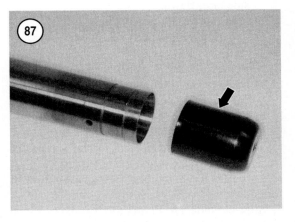

smooth operation. If the operation is not smooth, fill the damper with fork oil and repeat the check. If the operation is questionable, inspect the fork damper further during fork assembly when the fork damper is filled with oil and bled of air. Refer to *Assembly* in this section.

**13**

### Assembly

Lubricate the fork components with the same fork oil used to refill the fork. See **Table 1** for the specified fork oil.

Refer to **Figure 59**.

1. Before assembly, make sure all worn or defective parts have been repaired or replaced. Clean all parts before assembly.

2. Install the wear ring into the fork tube groove (**Figure 85**).

3. Cover the end of the fork tube with thin plastic (**Figure 86**) or use the 47 mm Motion Pro Fork Seal Bullet (part No. 08-0278 [**Figure 87**]). The plastic cover fits over the bushing groove in the top of the

slider to prevent the groove from tearing the seals during installation.

*NOTE*
*The Motion Pro Fork Seal Bullets are available in a set of seven sizes, or each can be purchased individually (36 mm, 41 mm, 43 mm, 45 mm, 46 mm, 47 mm and 48 mm).*

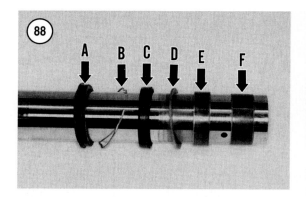

4. Lubricate the cover used in Step 3 with fork oil.
5. Install the following parts on the slider:
   a. Dust seal (A, **Figure 88**). Install so the closed side faces down.
   b. Stop ring (B, **Figure 88**).
   c. Oil seal (C, **Figure 88**). Install with the manufacturer's marks (closed side) facing down. Remove the cover from the slider.
   d. Backup ring (D, **Figure 88**). Install with the flat side facing down.
   e. Guide bushing (E, **Figure 88**).
   f. Slider bushing (F, **Figure 88**). Spread the bushing only far enough to slip it over the slider. Seat the bushing into the groove.
6. Lubricate the guide and slider bushings with fork oil.

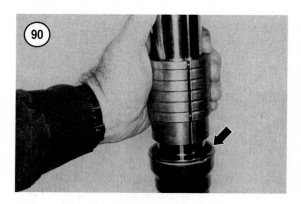

7. Slide the slider (A, **Figure 89**) into the fork tube and stand the fork assembly upright with the axle holder facing up.
8. Install the guide bushing and backup ring as follows:
   a. Slide the guide bushing (B, **Figure 89**) into the fork tube. When it is sitting flush in the tube, slide the backup ring (C, **Figure 89**) down the slider and sit it on top of the guide bushing.
   b. Assemble a split-type 47 mm fork seal driver over the slider. The narrow end of the driver should be facing the fork tube. Support the open end of the fork tube over a wooden block while holding the slider up with one hand. Then use the seal driver like a slide hammer to drive the guide bushing into the fork tube (**Figure 90**). When the sound of the seal driver changes, it indicates the backup ring is contacting the shoulder inside the fork tube and the bushing is fully installed. Turn the fork over and slide the backup ring away from the guide bushing to confirm that the bushing is positioned below the shoulder in the fork tube.

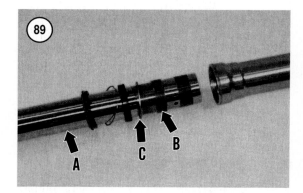

9. Install the oil seal as follows:
   a. Support the slider so its bottom end is facing up and slide the backup ring against the guide bushing.
   b. Slide the oil seal down the slider until it enters the fork tube. Check that the seal is seated squarely into the bore.
   c. Use the fork seal driver like a slide hammer (**Figure 90**) and drive the oil seal into the fork tube until the stop ring groove is visible above the seal.

10. Install and seat the stop ring (B, **Figure 73**) in the groove.

*NOTE*
*If the stop ring does not seat completely in its groove, the oil seal is not installed deep enough into the slider. Remove the stop ring and repeat Step 9.*

11. Slide the dust seal (A, **Figure 73**) down the slider and seat it into the top of the fork tube. See **Figure 91**.

12. Refer to *Fork Oil Refilling and Fork Assembly* in this section to fill the fork tube and complete assembly.

**Fork Oil Refilling and Fork Assembly**

Use the following procedure to refill the fork tubes with oil, either after rebuilding the tubes, during a routine fork oil change or when changing the front fork oil capacity. This procedure also completes fork tube assembly.

1. Note the following:

a. Fork oil is added to the fork assembly in two separate places: fork damper and fork tube.

b. **Table 1** lists the recommended fork oil.

c. **Table 3** lists the fork oil capacity for the fork damper.

d. **Table 4** lists the fork oil level for the fork damper.

e. **Table 5** lists fork oil capacity specifications for the fork tube. Three oil capacity specifications are listed for the different fork springs (standard, softer and stiffer) available from Honda. Select the minimum, standard or maximum oil capacity for the fork springs installed (**Table 5**). All models were originally equipped with standard fork springs. When working on a used or unfamiliar motorcycle, the standard fork spring may have been replaced with a softer or stiffer spring. To identify the Honda springs, check the identification mark(s) (or no mark) found on the end of the springs with the information in **Table 6**.

*NOTE*
*If the fork damper was not disassembled, go to Step 12B to fill the fork tube with oil and complete fork assembly.*

2. Check the fork damper and fork cap for cleanliness. The threads must be clean in both parts (**Figure 92**).

3. Support the damper so it is vertical and the piston rod can be fully extended (**Figure 93**).

4. Pour the recommended quantity of fork oil into the fork damper (**Figure 94**). See Step 1 for specifications and spring identification.

5. Slowly pump the piston rod (**Figure 95**) by hand several times to bleed air from the damper. On the last stroke, fully extend the piston rod (**Figure 93**).

6. Check and set the oil level. The oil level is the distance from the top of the oil to the top of the shoulder inside the fork damper. See **Figure 96** and **Figure 97**.

7. Lubricate the fork cap bushings and O-ring (**Figure 98**) with fork oil, then carefully install the assembly into the damper. Thread the cap into the fork damper by hand.

*NOTE*
*If the fork cap is difficult to install, the oil level in the fork damper may be too high. Recheck the oil level.*

**13**

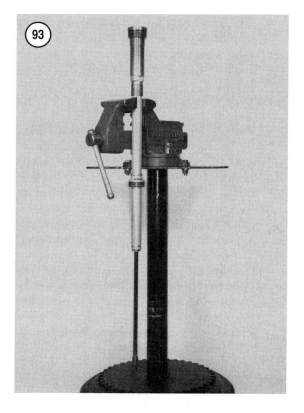

8. Tighten the fork cap as follows:
   a. Support the fork damper in a vise (**Figure 93**).
   b. Hold the top of the fork damper with a 50 mm locknut wrench (A, **Figure 99**) and tighten the fork cap (B) with a socket to 29 N•m (21 ft.-lb.).

9. With the fork damper held in a vise (**Figure 93**), slowly pump the piston rod a distance of 100 mm (3.9 in.) (**Figure 95**) several times. Do not bottom the piston rod when pumping it.

10. Remove excess oil from the fork damper spring chamber as follows:
   a. Turn the locknut (**Figure 100**) so it is fully seated on the piston rod.
   b. Check that the compression and rebound adjusters are positioned at their softest position (both turned fully counterclockwise).
   c. Lubricate the piston rod with fork oil.
   d. Hold the fork damper so the locknut on the piston rod straddles a hole drilled in a block of wood (**Figure 101**). Do not allow the end of the piston rod to contact the wood. All of the pressure should be on the sides of the locknut.

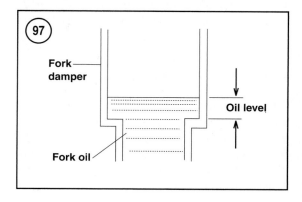

Fork damper

Oil level

Fork oil

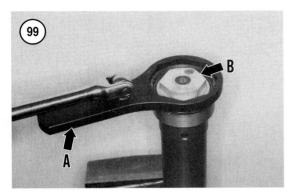

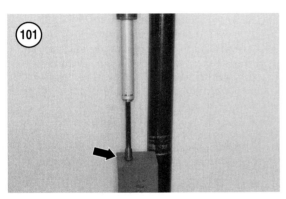

13

e. Carefully pump the piston rod in a vertical motion, and for its full length. Make sure the piston rod remains straight, or it may be bent.

f. Place the fork damper on a flat surface and drain the excess oil from the hole in the damper (**Figure 102**).

g. Use compressed air to blow excess oil from the damper (**Figure 103**). If compressed air is not available, remove the air release screw (**Figure 104**) and invert the fork damper for 10 minutes, until all oil has drained. Reinstall and tighten the screw.

11. Check the fork damper for proper operation as follows:

a. Lubricate the piston rod with fork oil.

b. Check for smooth operation. Hold the damper so the locknut on the piston rod straddles a hole in a block of wood (**Figure 101**). Do not allow the end of the piston rod to contact the wood. All of the pressure should be on the sides of the locknut. Carefully pump the fork damper in a vertical motion, and for its full length. If binding is evident, check the piston rod for bending, scoring and other damage.

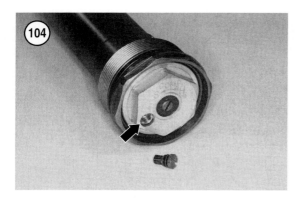

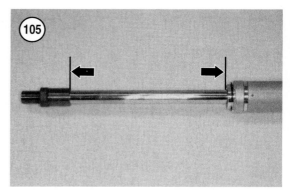

c. Check for piston rod extension. Place the damper on a flat surface. Carefully compress the piston rod in a horizontal motion, and for its full length (**Figure 105**). Release the piston rod when it is fully compressed. If the rod does not fully extend, air is in the damper. Bleed the damper again as described in this section.

d. Check for leakage. Wipe the piston rod clean, then lock the fork damper in a vise with soft jaws (**Figure 106**). Grip the wrench flats on the side of the fork damper. Do not overtighten the vise. Position the fork damper so the locknut on the piston rod straddles a hole in a block of wood (**Figure 101**). Do not allow the end of the piston rod to contact the wood. All of the pressure should be on the sides of the locknut. Carefully compress the piston rod 200-250 mm (7.9-9.8 in.). Do not allow the piston rod to move from vertical, or it may be bent. Add shims below the block of wood so the piston rod can be held in this position for 10 minutes. If leakage is evident, replace the fork damper assembly.

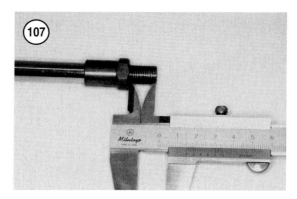

*NOTE*
*The fork oil level cannot be measured on the inverted twin-chamber cartridge fork serviced in this manual. Instead, these fork tubes are filled with a specific fork oil capacity. To ensure that both fork tubes are filled with the same amount of oil, the oil capacity must be carefully measured. If the fork tubes were not disassembled and cleaned, the amount of oil remaining inside the fork tubes must also be considered when determining the total oil capacity. Step 12A and*

*Step 12B describes how to drain oil from the tubes, while determining the approximate amount of oil that remains in the tubes after draining them. If the fork tubes were completely disassembled and cleaned of all oil, continue with Step 13.*

*NOTE*
*To determine the amount of oil that remains in the fork assembly after its initial draining during disassembly, the fork assembly will be inverted for*

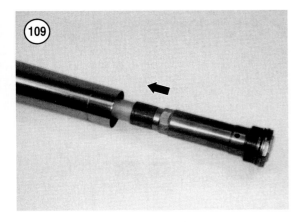

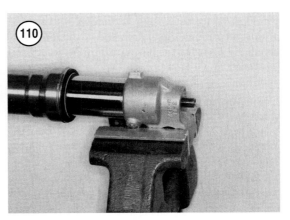

chart in **Table 8** shows that approximately 12 ml of oil will be left in the fork tube when it has been draining for 20 minutes at 20° C (68°).

13. Check that the locknut is seated on the piston rod, then measure the length of the exposed threads on the rod (**Figure 107**) for the model year being worked on:

    a. 2002: 15-17 mm (0.59-0.67 in.).

    b. 2003-on: 11-13 mm (0.43-0.51 in.).

14. Before installing the fork spring, check the spring ends for a scribe mark(s) or no scribe mark. Then refer to **Table 6** to identify the spring as to whether it is a standard, softer or stiffer rate spring. The spring rate must be known because it determines the amount of oil to add to the fork tube. Record the spring rate.

15. Install the spring (completely dry of all oil) into the fork tube (**Figure 108**).

16. Install the fork damper into the fork tube (**Figure 109**).

17. Lock the axle holder in a vise with soft jaws (**Figure 110**).

*CAUTION*
*Do not overtighten the vise.*

18. Thread the fork damper into the fork tube. Do not tighten the fork damper at this time.

*NOTE*
*In the following step, installing the stopper plate will be easier if an assistant can pull on the locknut and piston rod, while the fork leg is compressed. This also helps to minimize the chance of damaging the parts.*

*a measured time period. At the same time, consider the ambient temperature in the work area as it will affect how much oil actually drains from the inverted fork tubes in a measured time period; see **Table 7** and **Table 8**. After reading through Step 12A and Step 12B, select a drain time specified in **Table 7** or **Table 8** for draining the fork tubes. Then cross-reference the ambient temperature to determine the approximate amount of oil that remains in the fork tube.*

12A. If the fork damper *was* removed from the fork assembly, but the fork slider and fork tube were not disassembled, turn the fork assembly upside down to drain oil from the outer tube. For example, the chart in **Table 7** shows that approximately 7 ml of oil will be left in the fork tube when it has been draining for 20 minutes at 20° C (68°).

12B. If the fork damper *was not* removed from the fork assembly, turn the fork assembly upside down to drain oil from the outer tube. For example, the

13

19. Push on the fork cap to extend the locknut and piston rod through the bottom end of the fork, then install the stopper plate between the axle holder and locknut (**Figure 111**).

20. Remeasure the exposed threads on the piston rod as described in Step 13 to make sure the locknut did not turn when the stopper plate was installed in Step 19. If necessary, turn the locknut until the length of the exposed threads is the same as that specified in Step 13.

21. Install the pushrod (A, **Figure 112**) into the piston rod until it stops, then turn and engage it with the adjuster in the fork damper.

22. Install the center bolt (B, **Figure 112**) by aligning its adjusting rod with the pushrod. Then tighten the center bolt onto the locknut by hand until it stops (**Figure 113**).

23. Measure the gap between the center bolt and locknut (**Figure 113**). The gap must be 1.5-2.0 mm (0.06-0.08 in.). If the clearance is incorrect, the locknut, center bolt or pushrod were incorrectly installed. Remove and reinstall the parts until the gap is correct.

24. Tighten the locknut (A, **Figure 114**) until it contacts the center bolt (B, **Figure 114**). Then hold the center bolt and tighten the locknut to 22 N•m (16 ft.-lb.).

25. Remove the stopper plate from between the axle holder and locknut.

26. Thread the center bolt (**Figure 115**) into the axle holder and tighten to 69 N•m (51 ft.-lb.).

27. Remove the fork tube from the vise and lay it on a flat surface. Measure the length from the axle holder to the fork tube (not the dust seal) as shown in **Figure 116**. Compare the measurement with the one recorded during disassembly. The measurements should be the same (315-319 mm [12.40-12.56 in.]). If the lengths are different, check the installation of the center bolt and locknut.

28. Add the correct amount of fork oil to the fork tube as follows:

    a. Loosen the fork damper and lower the slider away from the fork damper (**Figure 117**).

    b. Cross-reference the spring rate number identified in Step 14 with the information in **Table 5** to determine the amount of oil to add to the fork tube. If Step 12A or Step 12B was performed, subtract the amount of oil determined to be remaining in the fork tube from the total amount of oil to be added to the fork. Slowly

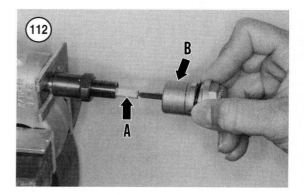

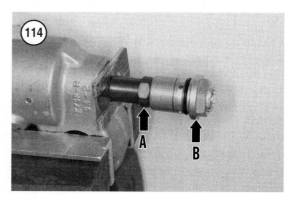

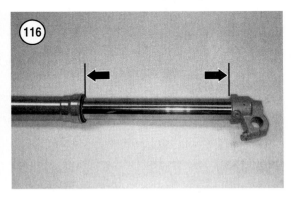

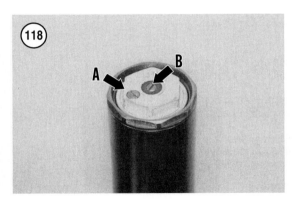

pour the recommended type and quantity of fork oil into the fork assembly.

29. Pull the fork tube up and hold it stationary, then thread the fork damper into the fork tube. Tighten the fork damper hand-tight.

30. Install the fork tube onto the motorcycle and tighten the fork damper as described under *Front Fork, Installation* in this chapter.

31. Reset the compression and rebound adjusters to the settings recorded during disassembly. If new settings are desired, adjust the fork as described in this chapter.

## FRONT FORK ADJUSTMENT

The front fork can be adjusted to suit rider weight and riding conditions. Variables, such as fork oil capacity, fork spring rate and compression and rebound adjustments, can be modified to overcome various handling complaints. When setting a suspension variable, make one adjustment at a time and then test ride the motorcycle. Keep a record of the changes and how they affect the handling. Work in a systematic manner to avoid confusion and return to the original base settings if handling deteriorates.

### Air Release Screw

The fork is designed to operate without air pressure. Before riding the motorcycle, bleed the air out of the fork tubes as follows:

1. Support the motorcycle with the front wheel off the ground (fork fully extended).

2. Loosen the air bleed screw (A, **Figure 118**) in the fork cap to release built-up air pressure. Then tighten the screw. Repeat for the other fork tube.

### Compression Damping Adjustment

The compression damping adjuster is mounted in the center of the fork cap (B, **Figure 119**). The compression damping adjustment affects the rate of front fork compression. Turning the compression adjuster clockwise stiffens the compression damping; turning the compression adjuster counterclockwise softens the compression damping. **Table 2** lists the standard and the approximate number of compression damping positions.

To adjust the compression damping adjuster to its standard position, perform the following:

**13**

1. Turn the compression damping adjuster *clockwise* until it stops (B, **Figure 118**). This is the maximum hard position.

2. Turn the compression damping adjuster *counterclockwise* the standard number of clicks listed in **Table 2**. This is the standard position.

3. Set both fork tubes to the same damping position.

> *CAUTION*
> *Turning the adjuster past the adjustment range listed in **Table 2** can damage the adjuster.*

> *NOTE*
> *Make sure the compression adjuster screw is located in one of the detent positions and not in between any two settings.*

## Rebound Damping Adjustment

The front fork rebound damping adjuster is mounted in the center bolt in the bottom of the fork slider (**Figure 119**). The rebound damping adjustment affects the front fork extension rate after compression. Turning the rebound adjuster clockwise speeds the rebound damping; turning the rebound adjuster counterclockwise decreases the rebound damping. **Table 2** lists the standard and the approximate number of rebound damping positions.

To adjust the rebound damping adjuster to its standard position, perform the following:

1. Turn the rebound damping adjuster *clockwise* until it stops (**Figure 119**). This is the maximum hard position.

2. Turn the rebound damping adjuster *counterclockwise* the standard number of clicks listed in **Table 2**. This is the standard position.

3. Set both fork tubes to the same damping setting.

> *CAUTION*
> *Turning the adjuster past the adjustment range listed in **Table 2** can damage the adjuster.*

> *NOTE*
> *Make sure the rebound adjuster screw is located in one of the detent positions and not in between any two settings.*

## Table 1 STEERING AND FRONT SUSPENSION SPECIFICATIONS

| | |
|---|---|
| Fork air pressure | 0 kPa (0 psi) |
| Fork spring free length | |
| **CRF250R and CRF250X** | |
| New | 495 mm (19.5 in.) |
| Service limit | 488 mm (19.2 in.) |
| **CRF2450R** | |
| 2002-2004 | |
| New | 495 mm (19.5 in.) |
| Service limit | 488 mm (19.2 in.) |
| 2005 | |
| New | 494 mm (19.4 in.) |
| Service limit | 487 mm (19.2 in.) |
| **CRF450X** | |
| New | 500 mm (19.7 in.) |
| Service limit | 493 mm (19.4 in.) |
| Slider runout service limit | 0.20 mm (0.008 in.) |
| **(continued)** | |

**Table 1 STEERING AND FRONT SUSPENSION SPECIFICATIONS (continued)**

| | |
|---|---|
| Front suspension stroke | |
| 2002 | 305 mm (12.0 in.) |
| 2003-on | 315 mm (12.4 in.) |
| Front wheel axle travel | |
| CRF250R | |
| 2004 | 280 mm (11.02 in.) |
| 2005 | 279 mm (10.98 in.) |
| CRF250X | 280 mm (11.02 in.) |
| CRF450R | |
| 2002 | 270 mm (10.63 in.) |
| 2003-2004 | 281 mm (11.06 in.) |
| 2005 | 280 mm (11.02 in.) |
| CRF450X | 279 mm (10.98 in.) |
| Recommended fork oil | Pro Honda HP 5W fork oil or equivalent |
| Steering | |
| Caster angle | |
| CRF250R | |
| 2004 | 27° 44 minutes |
| 2005 | 27° 50 minutes |
| CRF250X | |
| 2004 | 27° 56 minutes |
| 2005 | |
| CRF450R | |
| 2002 | 27° 50 minutes |
| 2003 | 27° 1 minute |
| 2004 | 26° 91 minutes |
| 2005 | 27° 47 minutes |
| CRF450X | 27° 10 minutes |
| Trail length | |
| CRF250R | |
| 2004 | 112 mm (4.41 in.) |
| 2005 | 123 mm (4.84 in.) |
| CRF250X | |
| 2004 | 116 mm (4.57 in.) |
| 2005 | |
| CRF450R | |
| 2002 | 114 mm (4.49 in.) |
| 2003 | 109 mm (4.29 in.) |
| 2004 | 108 mm (4.25 in.) |
| 2005 | 109.4 mm (4.31 in.) |
| CRF450X | 110 mm (4.33 in.) |

**Table 2 FRONT FORK COMPRESSION AND REBOUND ADJUSTMENT**

| | Total adjustment positions | Standard adjuster position |
|---|---|---|
| Compression damping adjustment | | |
| CRF250R | | |
| 2004 | 16 | 12 |
| 2005 | 16 | 10 |
| CRF250X | 16 | 10 |
| CRF450R | | |
| 2002 | 16 | 11 |
| 2003 | 16 | 8 |
| 2004-on | 16 | 11 |
| CRF450X | 16 | 14 |

(continued)

13

**Table 2 FRONT FORK COMPRESSION AND REBOUND ADJUSTMENT (continued)**

|  | Total adjustment positions | Standard adjuster position |
|---|---|---|
| Rebound damping adjustment |  |  |
| CRF250R | 16 | 8 |
| CRF250X | 16 | 7 |
| CRF450R |  |  |
| 2002 | 16 | 14 |
| 2003 | 16 | 10 |
| 2004-on | 16 | 7 |
| CRF450X | 16 | 7 |

**Table 3 FORK DAMPER OIL CAPACITY**

|  | ml | U.S. oz. |
|---|---|---|
| CRF250R | 195 | 6.6 |
| CRF250X | 192 | 6.5 |
| CRF450R |  |  |
| 2002 | 189 | 6.4 |
| 2003-on | 195 | 6.6 |
| CRF450X | 190 | 6.4 |

**Table 4 FORK DAMPER OIL LEVEL**

|  | mm | in. |
|---|---|---|
| 2002 CRF450R | 5-10 | 0.2-0.4 |
| All other models | 42-47 | 1.65-1.85 |

**Table 5 FRONT FORK OIL CAPACITY AND SPRING RATES***

|  | ml | U.S. oz. |
|---|---|---|
| CRF250R |  |  |
| 2004 |  |  |
| Standard 0.45 kg/mm (25.15 lb./in.) fork spring |  |  |
| Minimum | 320 | 10.8 |
| Standard | 379 | 12.8 |
| Maximum | 416 | 14.1 |
| Softer 0.43 kg/mm (24.13 lb./in.) fork spring |  |  |
| Minimum | 317 | 10.7 |
| Standard | 376 | 12.7 |
| Maximum | 413 | 14.0 |
| Stiffer 0.47 kg/mm (26.42 lb./in.) fork spring |  |  |
| Minimum | 323 | 10.9 |
| Standard | 419 | 14.2 |
| Maximum | 382 | 12.9 |

(continued)

**Table 5 FRONT FORK OIL CAPACITY AND SPRING RATES (continued)**

|  | ml | U.S. oz. |
|---|---|---|
| CRF250R (continued) | | |
| 2005 | | |
| Standard 0.45 kg/mm (25.15 lb./in.) fork spring | | |
| Minimum | 321 | 10.9 |
| Standard | 371 | 12.5 |
| Maximum | 417 | 14.1 |
| Softer 0.43 kg/mm (24.13 lb./in.) fork spring | | |
| Minimum | 318 | 10.8 |
| Standard | 368 | 12.4 |
| Maximum | 414 | 14.0 |
| Stiffer 0.47 kg/mm (26.42 lb./in.) fork spring | | |
| Minimum | 324 | 11.0 |
| Standard | 374 | 12.6 |
| Maximum | 420 | 14.2 |
| CRF250X | | |
| 2004-on | | |
| Standard 0.42 kg/mm (23.52 lb./in.) fork spring | | |
| Minimum | 303 | 10.3 |
| Standard | 345 | 11.7 |
| Maximum | 398 | 13.5 |
| Softer 0.40 kg/m (22.40 lb./in.) fork spring | | |
| Minimum | 308 | 10.4 |
| Standard | 350 | 11.8 |
| Maximum | 403 | 13.6 |
| Stiffer 0.44 kg/mm (24.64 lb./in.) fork spring | | |
| Minimum | 306 | 10.3 |
| Standard | 401 | 13.6 |
| Maximum | 348 | 11.8 |
| CRF450R | | |
| 2002 | | |
| Standard 0.47 kg/mm (26.32 lb./in.) fork spring | | |
| Minimum | 356 | 12.0 |
| Standard | 425 | 14.4 |
| Maximum | 449 | 15.2 |
| Softer 0.45 kg/mm (25.20 lb./in.) fork spring | | |
| Minimum | 361 | 12.2 |
| Standard | 430 | 14.5 |
| Maximum | 454 | 15.4 |
| Stiffer 0.49 kg/mm (27.44 lb./in.) fork spring | | |
| Minimum | 351 | 11.9 |
| Standard | 419 | 14.2 |
| Maximum | 443 | 15.0 |
| 2003 | | |
| Standard 0.47 kg/mm (26.32 lb./in.) fork spring | | |
| Minimum | 323 | 10.9 |
| Standard | 412 | 13.9 |
| Maximum | 419 | 14.2 |
| Softer 0.45 kg/mm (25.20 lb./in.) fork spring | | |
| Minimum | 320 | 10.8 |
| Standard | 409 | 13.8 |
| Maximum | 416 | 14.1 |
| Stiffer 0.49 kg/mm (27.44 lb./in.) fork spring | | |
| Minimum | 318 | 10.8 |
| Standard | 406 | 13.7 |
| Maximum | 413 | 14.0 |

13

(continued)

**Table 5 FRONT FORK OIL CAPACITY AND SPRING RATES (continued)**

|  | ml | U.S. oz. |
|---|---|---|
| **2004** | | |
| Standard 0.47 kg/mm (26.32 lb./in.) fork spring | | |
| Minimum | 322 | 10.9 |
| Standard | 416 | 14.1 |
| Maximum | 420 | 14.2 |
| Softer 0.45 kg/mm (25.20 lb./in.) fork spring | | |
| Minimum | 319 | 10.8 |
| Standard | 413 | 14.0 |
| Maximum | 417 | 14.1 |
| Stiffer 0.49 kg/mm (27.44 lb./in.) fork spring | | |
| Minimum | 316 | 10.7 |
| Standard | 410 | 13.9 |
| Maximum | 415 | 14.0 |
| **2005** | | |
| Standard 0.46 kg/mm (25.76 lb./in.) fork spring | | |
| Minimum | 322 | 10.9 |
| Standard | 382 | 12.9 |
| Maximum | 420 | 14.2 |
| Softer 0.44 kg/mm (24.64 lb./in.) fork spring | | |
| Minimum | 327 | 11.1 |
| Standard | 387 | 13.1 |
| Maximum | 426 | 14.4 |
| Stiffer 0.48 kg/mm (26.88 lb./in.) fork spring | | |
| Minimum | 316 | 10.7 |
| Standard | 376 | 12.7 |
| Maximum | 415 | 14.0 |
| **CRF450X** | | |
| Standard 0.47 kg/mm (26.32 lb./in.) fork spring | | |
| Minimum | 306 | 10.3 |
| Standard | 332 | 11.2 |
| Maximum | 402 | 13.6 |
| Softer 0.45 kg/mm (25.50 lb./in.) fork spring | | |
| Minimum | 311 | 10.5 |
| Standard | 338 | 11.4 |
| Maximum | 407 | 13.8 |
| Stiffer 0.49 kg/mm (27.44 lb./in.) fork spirng | | |
| Minimum | 309 | 10.5 |
| Standard | 335 | 11.3 |
| Maximum | 405 | 13.7 |

*See text and Table 6 for spring identification.

**Table 6 FRONT FORK SPRING IDENTIFICATION MARKS**

| Spring description and rate | Spring identification scribe marks |
|---|---|
| **CRF250R** | |
| Standard 0.45 kg/mm (25.15 lb./in.) | No factory mark; aftermarket 1 mark |
| Softer 0.43 kg/mm (24.13 lb./in.) | 3 marks side-by-side |
| Stiffer 0.47 kg/mm (26.42 lb./in.) | 1 mark and 3 marks 75° apart |
| **CRF250X** | |
| Standard 0.42 kg/mm (23.52 lb./in.) | No factory mark; aftermarket 2 marks side-by-side |
| Softer 0.40 kg/mm (22.40 lb./in.) | 3 marks side-by-side |
| Stiffer 0.44 kg/mm (24.64 lb./in.) | 1 mark |

(continued)

### Table 6 FRONT FORK SPRING IDENTIFICATION MARKS (continued)

| Spring description and rate | Spring identification scribe marks |
|---|---|
| **CRF450R** | |
| 2002-2004 | |
| Standard 0.47 kg/mm (26.32 lb./in.) | No factory mark; aftermarket 1 mark and 3 marks 75° apart |
| Softer 0.45 kg/mm (25.20 lb./in.) | 2 marks 75° apart |
| Stiffer 0.49 kg/mm (27.44 lb./in.) | 1 mark and 2 marks 75° apart |
| 2005 | |
| Standard 0.46 kg/mm (25.76 lb./in.) | No factory mark, aftermarket two marks side-by-side |
| Softer 0.44 kg/mm (24.64 lb./in.) | 3 marks side-by-side |
| Stiffer 0.48 kg/mm (26.88 lb./in.) | 4 marks side-by-side |
| **CRF450X** | |
| Sandard 0.47 kg/mm (26.32 lb./in.) | No factory mark; aftermarket one mark |
| Softer 0.45 kg/mm (25.20 lb./in.) | Two marks side-by-side |
| Stiffer 0.49 kg/mm (27.44 lb./in.) | 3 marks side-by-side |

### Table 7 AMOUNT OF OIL REMAINING IN FORK WITHOUT FORK DAMPER*

| Temperature | Drain Time in Minutes | | | | | | |
|---|---|---|---|---|---|---|---|
| C (F) | 5 | 10 | 20 | 35 | 55 | 85 | 145 |
| 30° (86°) | 7.1 | 5.9 | 4.7 | 4.2 | 3.5 | 3.5 | 3.5 |
| 20° (68°) | 10.6 | 8.2 | 7.1 | 5.9 | 5.6 | 4.7 | 4.7 |
| 10° (50° ) | 11.8 | 8.3 | 7.2 | 6.2 | 5.8 | 4.9 | 4.8 |
| 0° (32°) | 12.9 | 10.6 | 9.4 | 8.2 | 7.9 | 7.1 | 5.9 |

*All units specified in milliliters (ml).

### Table 8 AMOUNT OF OIL REMAINING IN FORK WITH FORK DAMPER INSTALLED*

| Temperature | Drain Time in Minutes | | | | | | |
|---|---|---|---|---|---|---|---|
| C (F) | 5 | 10 | 20 | 35 | 55 | 85 | 145 |
| 30° (86°) | 27 | 15.3 | 10.6 | 9.4 | 8.3 | 7.9 | 7.9 |
| 20° (68°) | 29.4 | 16.5 | 11.8 | 10.6 | 9.4 | 8.2 | 8.2 |
| 10° (50°) | 28.2 | 21.4 | 16.5 | 15.3 | 12.9 | 11.8 | 11.8 |
| 0° (32°) | 30.6 | 22.4 | 18.8 | 16.5 | 16.5 | 15.3 | 14.1 |

*All units specified in milliliters (ml).

**13**

### Table 9 FRONT SUSPENSION AND STEERING TORQUE SPECIFICATIONS

| | N•m | in.-lb. | ft.-lb. |
|---|---|---|---|
| Brake caliper mounting bolts | 30 | – | 22 |
| Brake lever pivot bolt/nut | 5.9 | 52 | – |
| Clutch lever holder mounting bolts | 8.8 | 78 | – |
| Clutch lever pivot bolt | 2.0 | 18 | – |
| Clutch lever pivot nut | 9.8 | 87 | – |

(continued)

**Table 9 FRONT SUSPENSION AND STEERING TORQUE SPECIFICATIONS (continued)**

|  | N•m | in.-lb. | ft.-lb. |
|---|---|---|---|
| Fork cap | 29 | – | 21 |
| Center bolt | 69 | – | 51 |
| Center bolt locknut | 22 | – | 16 |
| Fork damper | 34 | – | 25 |
| Fork protector mounting bolt* | 6.9 | 61 | – |
| Fork tube pinch bolts |  |  |  |
|   Upper |  |  |  |
|     CRF450X | 22 | – | 16 |
|     All other models | 23 | – | 17 |
|   Lower |  |  |  |
|     CRF450X | 20 | – | 14.7 |
|     All other models | 21 | – | 15 |
| Front brake caliper mounting bolt* | 30 | – | 22 |
| Front brake hose guide bolts | 6.9 | 61 | – |
| Front master cylinder mounting bolt | 9.8 | 87 | – |
| Handlebar upper holder mounting bolt | 22 | – | 16 |
| Handlebar lower holder nut | 44 | – | 32 |
| Plug bolt | 1.3 | 11.5 | – |
| Steering stem adjust nut | See text |  |  |
| Steering stem nut | 108 | – | 80 |
| Throttle housing bolt | 8.8 | 78 | – |

*Apply threadlocking compound to threads.

# CHAPTER FOURTEEN

# REAR SUSPENSION

This chapter describes service and adjustment procedures for the rear shock absorber, shock linkage assembly and swing arm. Specifications are listed in **Tables 1-5** at the end of the chapter.

## REAR SUSPENSION

The rear suspension is a progressive rising rate design. Compared to conventional suspension systems, this system allows for increased swing arm travel and provides ideal spring and damping rates over a larger operating range of the swing arm. For example, when the swing arm is slightly compressed, the spring and damping rates are soft, for handling small bumps. As riding conditions become more severe, the swing arm travel increases. This causes the linkage system to pivot into a position to increase the travel of the spring and damper. This provides a progressively firmer shock absorbing action, greater control and better transfer of power to the ground.

The system consists of a single shock absorber and linkage (shock arm, shock link and needle bearings) attached to the swing arm.

## SHOCK ABSORBER

The single shock absorber is a spring-loaded hydraulically damped unit with an integral oil/nitrogen reservoir. To adjust the rear shock absorber, refer to *Rear Suspension Adjustment* in this chapter.

### Shock Absorber Removal/Installation

1. Support the motorcycle with the rear wheel off the ground.
2A. On CRF250R and CRF450R models, remove the subframe (Chapter Sixteen).
2B. On CRF250X and CRF450X models, raise and lock the subframe (Chapter Sixteen).
3. If the spring will be removed, clean the threads on the shock body. Then loosen the spring locknut

14

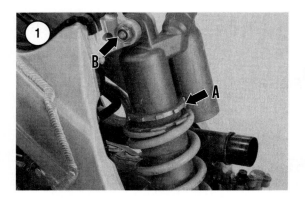

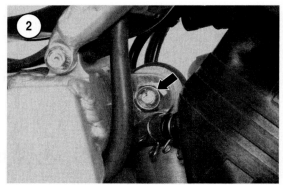

(A, **Figure 1**) with a spanner wrench. If the adjuster turns with the locknut, the locknut will have to be shocked with a punch and hammer so it can turn separately.

4. Remove the upper shock absorber nut and mounting bolt and allow the rear wheel to drop to the ground. See B, **Figure 1** (CRF250R and CRF450R) or **Figure 2** (CRF250X and CRF450X).

5. Remove the lower shock absorber nut and bolt (**Figure 3**), and remove the shock absorber. On CRF250X and CRF450X models, remove the shock absorber from the right side (**Figure 4**).

6. Clean and service the seals, collar and spherical bearing as described in this section.

7. Service the shock spring as described in this chapter.

8. Installation is the reverse of removal. Note the following:

    a. Clean and dry the shock fasteners. Inspect and replace damaged fasteners.

    b. Lubricate the upper and lower mounting bolt shoulders with grease. Do not lubricate the bolt or nut threads. Clean the fastener threads with brake or contact cleaner.

*CAUTION*
*The bolt and nut threads must be clean and dry when tightened; otherwise, the threads may strip if the nuts are tightened with a torque wrench.*

    c. Install the shock absorber with its reservoir on the right side.

    d. Install the upper and lower shock mounting bolts from the right side. Align the flat edges on the upper bolts with the groove in the frame. Align the flat edge on the lower bolt with the stopper on the shock absorber.

    e. Tighten the shock absorber mounting nuts to 44 N•m (33 ft.-lb.).

    f. Install or reposition the subframe (Chapter Sixteen).

**Shock Absorber Inspection**

1. Inspect the shock absorber (**Figure 5**) for gas or oil leaks.

2. Check the damper rod for bending, rust or other damage. If parts of the damper rod have turned blue,

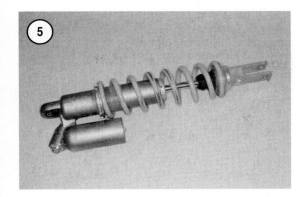

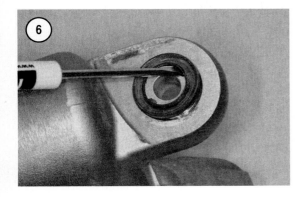

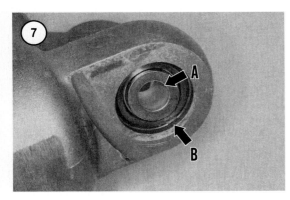

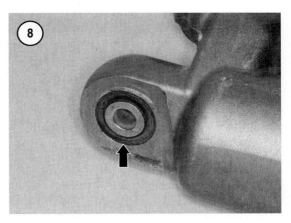

the rod is overheating, probably due to a lack of oil in the shock.

3. Check the reservoir for dents or other damage.

4. Inspect the seals and spherical bearing installed in the lower shock mount as described in this section.

5. Remove and inspect the spring as described in this section.

6. If the shock is leaking, or if it is time to change the shock oil, refer service to a Honda dealership or suspension specialist.

## Seal and Bearing Inspection/Lubrication

Use a waterproof bearing grease when lubricating the seals and bearing in this section.

1. Insert a thin screwdriver or similar tool between the seal and bearing and carefully pry the dust seal from the bearing bore (**Figure 6**). Repeat for the other seal.

2. Clean and dry both seals, then check them for damage. If the seals are not damaged, they can be reused.

3. Pivot the spherical bearing (A, **Figure 7**) by hand. If any roughness, damage or excessive looseness is evident, replace the bearing as described in this section.

4. If the bearing is in good condition, lubricate it with grease.

*NOTE*
*The right side seal (on the reservoir side) has a smaller outside diameter than the left side seal.*

5. Lubricate the dust seal lips with grease and then install them into the shock mount with their *open* side facing out (**Figure 8**). Make sure the outer edge of the seals are positioned flush with the shock body.

## Spherical Bearing Replacement

**Figure 9** shows the seal and bearing assembly used on all models. The stop ring is installed in a groove in the left side of the bearing bore and must be removed before the bearing can be pressed out.

14

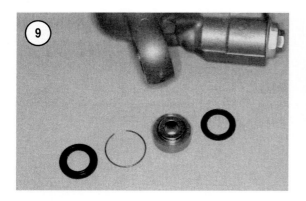

This section describes bearing replacement using a bolt, washers, and pieces of pipe or metal tubing.

> *NOTE*
> *Shock bearing rebuild kits are available from **www.pivotworks.com** (**Figure 10**) or through motorcycle dealerships. Each kit contains all of the parts required to replace the bearing in the rear shock absorber and the shock pivot bearing in the shock arm.*

1. Remove the stop ring as follows:

> *NOTE*
> *During the bearing's initial installation, it was pressed against the stop ring to prevent the stop ring from coming out of its groove. Before the stop ring can be removed, the bearing must be pressed away from it.*

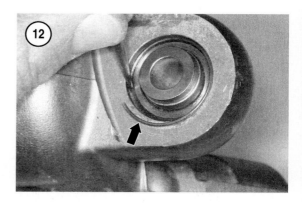

   a. Use a bolt and nut to assemble a piece of tubing (A, **Figure 11**) against the bearing and a thick washer (B) against the shock absorber.

   b. Hold the nut and turn the bolt to press the bearing away from the top ring. Then remove the assembled pieces.

   c. Pry the stop ring out of its groove with a scribe or similar tool (**Figure 12**).

2. Remove the bearing as follows:

   a. Assemble the bolt and pipe assembly against the shock absorber and bearing as shown in **Figure 13**.

   b. Hold the nut and turn the bolt to press the bearing out of the shock mount (**Figure 14**).

3. Clean the bearing bore. Check the bore and stop ring groove (**Figure 15**) for cracks and other damage.

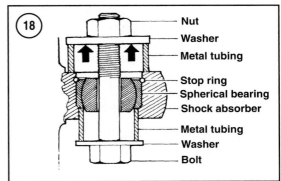

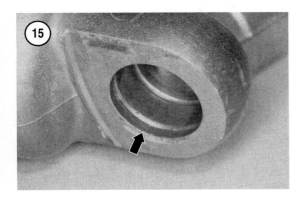

4. Lubricate the new bearing with waterproof grease.

5. Install the new bearing as follows:

   a. Assemble the bolt, spacer, bearing and washer assembly (**Figure 16**) onto the shock mount as shown in **Figure 17**. Make sure the bearing seats squarely in the bore.

   b. Hold the nut and tighten the bolt to press the bearing into the shock mount. Install a new stop ring into the groove (**Figure 12**).

   c. Remove the assembled parts, and then reassemble them onto the shock mount to move the bearing until it seats against the stop ring (**Figure 18**).

   d. Remove the assembled parts from the shock mount. Make sure the stop ring and bearing are properly installed (**Figure 7**).

6. Install new seals as described in this section.

**Spring**
**Removal/Installation**

   Refer to **Table 3** for shock absorber spring rates and identification marks.

1. Support the motorcycle with the rear wheel off the ground.

2A. On CRF250R and CRF450R models, remove the subframe (Chapter Sixteen).

2B. On CRF250X and CRF450X models, raise and lock the subframe (Chapter Sixteen).

3. Clean the threads on the shock body. Then loosen the spring locknut (A, **Figure 1**).

4. Measure and record the spring's preload length (**Figure 19**) for installation. Measure the spring from end to end. Do not include the thickness of the adjuster or the spring seat.

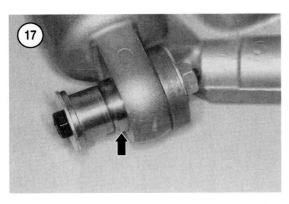

**14**

5. With the shock mounted on the motorcycle, turn the spring counterclockwise by hand (**Figure 20**) to turn and loosen the adjuster. Continue until all of the preload has been removed from the spring.

6. Remove the shock absorber as described in this section.

7. With all of the preload removed from the spring, slide the spring away from the spring seat. Then tap the spring seat (**Figure 21**) toward the spring to uncover the stop ring.

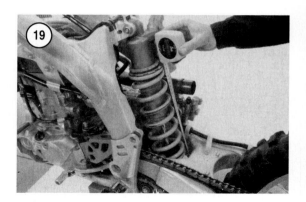

*NOTE*
*The spring seat will be difficult to move if it has been damaged, or if the area between the spring seat and stop ring is corroded or filled with dirt. If the spring seat is tight, tap it evenly across its face to move it without binding it against the stop ring.*

8. Remove the stop ring (A, **Figure 22**) from the groove in the stopper seat.

9. Slide the spring seat (B, **Figure 22**) off the stopper seat.

10. Identity one end of the spring end so it can be installed facing in its original position, then remove the spring.

*NOTE*
*It may be necessary to file burrs or smooth any raised or rough areas on the stopper seat before the spring seat can be removed.*

11. Clean and dry the shock assembly (**Figure 23**).

12. Check the spring for cracks and other damage.

13. Slide the rubber stopper (A, **Figure 24**) to expose different areas on the damper rod and inspect the rod surface for nicks, bluing or other damage. This surface must be smooth.

14. Install the spring facing in its original position.

15. Install the spring seat with its flat edge facing toward the spring (B, **Figure 22**).

16. Lubricate the spring adjuster threads on the shock body with engine oil.

17. Install the stop ring into the groove in the stopper seat (A, **Figure 22**).

18. Turn the spring adjuster to apply preload to the spring. When doing so, make sure the spring seat moves squarely across the stopper seat and seats flush against the stop ring (**Figure 25**). Then adjust the spring preload to the dimension recorded in Step

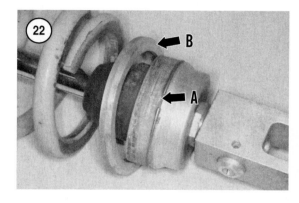

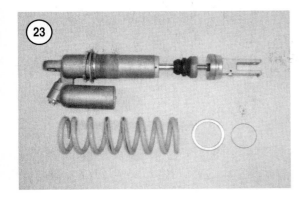

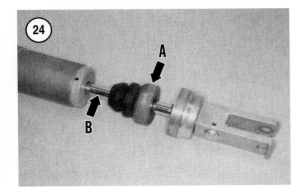

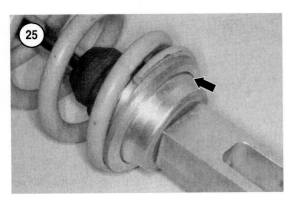

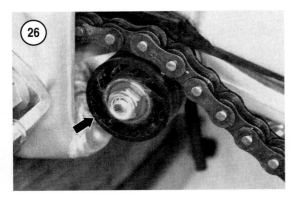

4, or set it within the adjustable length dimensions in **Table 4**. Hold the adjuster and tighten the locknut (**Figure 16**) to 44 N•m (33 ft.-lb.). If it is easier to do so, set the spring preload and tighten the locknut with the shock absorber mounted on the motorcycle.

> *CAUTION*
> *The spring preload must be set within the minimum specifications listed in* ***Table 4****. If the minimum specification is exceeded, the spring may coil bind when the shock nears full compression. This will overload and weaken the spring.*

19. Install the shock absorber as described in this chapter.

## SHOCK LINKAGE

The shock linkage consists of the shock arm, shock link, pivot bolts, seals and bearings. Service the assembly at the intervals specified in Chapter Three. Also, service the shock linkage after riding in extremely muddy or sandy conditions.

### Shock Linkage Removal

1. Clean the shock linkage assembly to prevent dirt from contaminating the bearings when removing the linkage components.

2. Support the motorcycle with the rear wheel off the ground.

3. On CRF250X and CRF450X models, remove the sidestand from the frame (Chapter Sixteen).

4. Remove the bolt and chain roller (**Figure 26**).

5. Remove the following:

    a. Shock absorber lower mounting nut (A, **Figure 27**) and bolt.

    b. Shock arm nut, washer and bolt (A, **Figure 28**) and shock arm (B).

    c. Shock link nuts (C and D, **Figure 28**), washer, bolts and shock link (E).

6. Inspect the shock linkage components as described in this section.

14

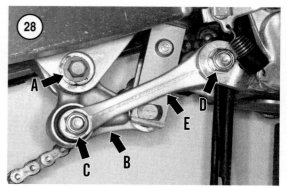

### Shock Linkage Installation

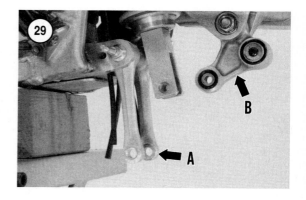

1. Lubricate and assemble the shock linkage components as described in this section.

2. Clean and dry the pivot bolts, washers and nuts. Lubricate the pivot bolt shafts with a waterproof grease and seat aside for installation. Service the bolt threads and seating surfaces as follows:

   a. On 2002 models, do not lubricate the washer or the pivot bolt and mounting nut threads. These threads and washer must be clean and dry when tightened.

   b. On 2003-on models, lubricate the washer and the pivot bolt and mounting nut threads with engine oil. Do not lubricate the lower shock absorber mounting bolt or nut threads.

3. Refer to **Figure 27** and **Figure 28** and install the shock linkage assembly:

   a. Shock link. See A, **Figure 29**.

   b. Shock link bolt from the left side.

   c. Shock arm. See B, **Figure 29**.

   d. Shock arm bolt from the right side.

   e. Shock absorber lower mounting bolt from the right side. Align the flat on the bolt with the stopper on shock absorber.

   f. Raise the shock link and install the shock arm bolt from the left side.

   g. On 2002 models, use brake or contact cleaner to remove any grease that may have been picked up by the pivot bolt threads when installing the bolts through the linkage components.

*CAUTION*
*On 2002 models, the pivot bolt and nut threads must be clean and dry when tightened; otherwise, the*

*threads may strip if tightened with a torque wrench.*

   h. Install the washers and tighten the nuts finger-tight.

4. Tighten the shock arm nuts and the frame side shock link nut to the torque specification in **Table 2**:

   a. Shock link nut at frame (D, **Figure 28**).

   b. Shock arm nut at swing arm (B, **Figure 27**).

   c. Shock arm nut at shock link (C, **Figure 28**).

   d. Shock absorber lower mounting nut (A, **Figure 27**).

5. Install and tighten the lower chain roller as follows:

   a. On 2002-2004 models, install the roller with the arrow mark (**Figure 26**) facing out. Tighten the nut to 12 N•m (106 in.-lb.).

   b. On 2005 models, install the drive chain roller with its recessed side facing out. Tighten the nut to 12 N•m (106 in.-lb.).

6. On CRF250X and CRF450X models, install and tighten the sidestand assembly (Chapter Sixteen).

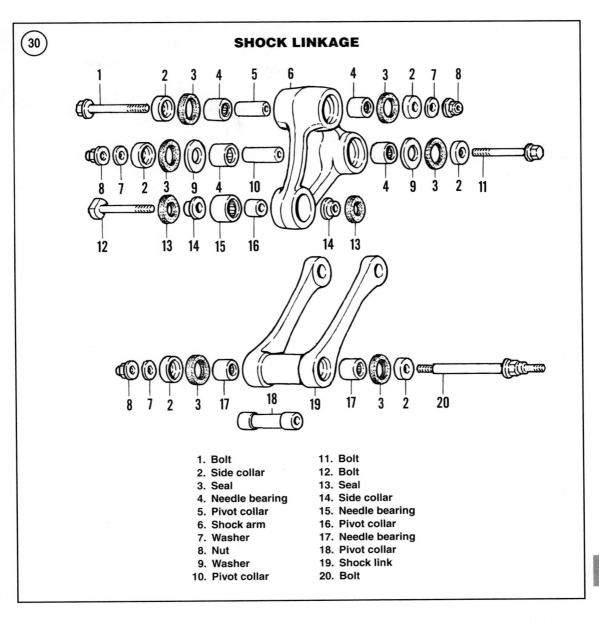

**SHOCK LINKAGE**

1. Bolt
2. Side collar
3. Seal
4. Needle bearing
5. Pivot collar
6. Shock arm
7. Washer
8. Nut
9. Washer
10. Pivot collar
11. Bolt
12. Bolt
13. Seal
14. Side collar
15. Needle bearing
16. Pivot collar
17. Needle bearing
18. Pivot collar
19. Shock link
20. Bolt

14

**Shock Arm**
**Cleaning and Inspection**

Refer to **Figure 30**.

*NOTE*
*Figure 31 shows an original needle bearing and its loose bearing rollers. After removing the pivot collar(s) from these parts, some of the rollers may fall out of their bearing cage. When servicing the shock arm, keep the different bearing rollers separate*

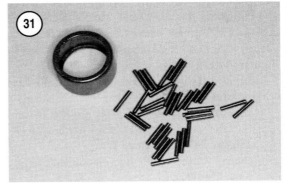

*so the bearings can be assembled correctly. On some aftermarket needle bearings the bearing rollers are permanently mounted in the bearing cage and are not removable.*

1. Remove the side collars, pivot collar and seals from the shock arm (**Figure 32**).
2. If the bearing rollers are not permanently fixed in place, use a magnet to remove them from the bearing cages installed in the shock arm (**Figure 33**).
3. Clean and dry all parts. Remove rust and corrosion from pivot bolt surfaces.
4. Inspect the seals for cracks, excessive wear or other damage.
5. Inspect the pivot collars for cracks, scoring, rust or other damage.
6. Inspect the bearing rollers for cracks, flat spots, rust or color change. Bluing indicates overheating. Inspect the bearing cages for cracks, rust or other damage. Replace damaged bearings as described in this section.
7. Inspect the pivot bolts for cracks, scoring or other damage.

*NOTE*
*Use a waterproof bearing grease during assembly.*

8. Lubricate the bearing cages and bearing rollers with grease. Then install the bearing rollers into their correct cage. Note the number of rollers used in each shock arm bearing:
   a. Shock absorber side bearing (A, **Figure 33**): 27 rollers.
   b. Shock link side bearings (B, **Figure 33**): 32 rollers in each bearing.
   c. Swing arm side bearings (C, **Figure 33**): 32 rollers in each bearing.
9. Lubricate the pivot collars, side collars, washers and seals with grease and set aside for reassembly.
10. Install the shock absorber bearing assembly (A, **Figure 32**) as follows:
   a. Lubricate and install the pivot collar (A, **Figure 34**).
   b. Lubricate the side collars (B, **Figure 34**) and install them through the *inside* of the seals (C, **Figure 34**). See **Figure 35**.
   c. Install the seals with their marked side facing out (**Figure 36**).

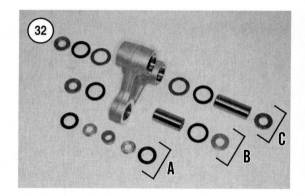
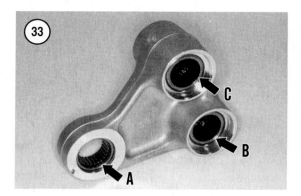
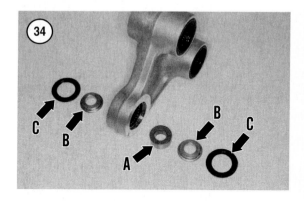

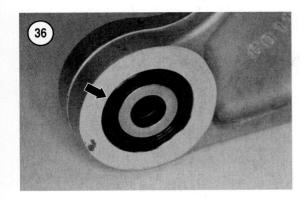

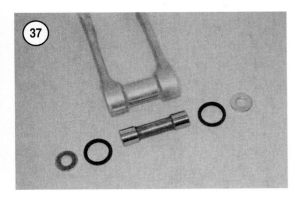

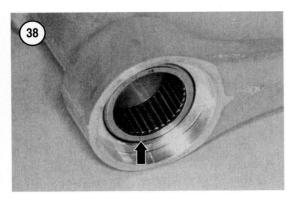

11. Install the shock link bearing assembly (B, **Figure 32**) as follows:

    a. Install the pivot collar (5, **Figure 30**) and center it between both bearings.

    b. Install the seals with their marked side facing out.

    c. Install the side collars through the seals.

12. Install the swing arm side bearing assembly (C, **Figure 32**) as follows:

    a. Install the pivot collar (10, **Figure 30**) and center it between both bearings.

    b. Install the washers (9, **Figure 30**) and seat them against the bearings.

    c. Install the seals with their marked side facing out.

    d. Install the side collars through the seals.

**Shock Link**
**Cleaning and Inspection**

Refer to **Figure 30**.

> *NOTE*
> *Figure 31 shows an original needle bearing and its loose bearing rollers After removing the pivot collar, some of the rollers may fall out of their bearing cage. When servicing the shock link, keep the different bearing rollers separate so the bearings can be assembled correctly. On some aftermarket needle bearings, the bearing rollers are permanently mounted in the bearing cage and are not removable.*

1. Remove the side collars, pivot collar and seals from the shock link (**Figure 37**).

2. Remove the bearing rollers from the cages (**Figure 38**).

3. Clean and dry all parts. Remove rust and corrosion from pivot bolt surfaces.

4. Inspect the seals for cracks, excessive wear or other damage.

5. Inspect the pivot collar for cracks, scoring, rust or other damage.

6. Inspect the rollers for cracks, flat spots, rust or color change. Bluing indicates overheating. Inspect the bearing cages for cracks, rust or other damage. If a bearing is damaged, replace both bearings as described in this chapter.

7. Inspect the pivot bolt for cracks, scoring or other damage.

> *NOTE*
> *Use a waterproof bearing grease during assembly.*

8. Lubricate the bearing cages and bearing rollers with grease. Then install the bearing rollers into their correct cage. Install 32 rollers into each shock link bearing cage (**Figure 38**).

14

9. Lubricate and install the pivot collar (A, **Figure 39**). Center it between both bearings.

10. Lubricate the seals with grease and install them with their numbered side facing out (B, **Figure 39**).

11. Lubricate and install the side collars (**Figure 40**) through the seals.

## Needle Bearing Replacement

This section describes replacement of the needle bearings installed inside the shock arm and shock link (**Figure 30**). Where two bearings are used in the same bore, replace both bearings at the same time.

The needle bearings installed in the shock arm and shock link are installed with a slight press fit and are not generally difficult to remove when using the tools and following the steps described in this section. However, due to their operating environment, corrosion can seize the bearings into the bore. Work carefully to avoid damaging the linkage units when replacing the bearings. Discard the bearings after removing them.

Bearing kits are available from *www.pivot works.com* (**Figure 41**). These kits contain all the seals, bearings and collars required to rebuild the shock arm and shock link.

### *Tools*

The following tools are used in this section to replace the shock arm and shock link needle bearings:

1. Motion Pro Swing Arm Bearing Tool (part No. 08-0213 [A, **Figure 42**]) and a hollow pipe (B). The Motion Pro tool is designed to install the needle bearings using a threaded rod, bearing drivers and thrust bearing. By using the hollow pipe as shown in the text, the tool can also be used to remove the bearings.

2. Motion Pro Blind Bearing and Bushing Remover (part No. 08-0292) or equivalent. This tool is required to remove the bearings installed inside the shock link.

3. Heat gun or propane torch. Applying heat to the shock link or shock arm can ease bearing replacement and may be required for corroded or especially tight bearings.

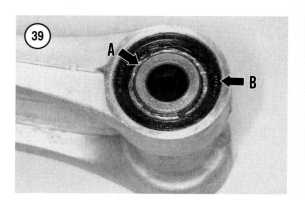

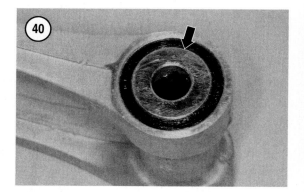

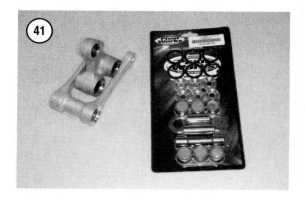

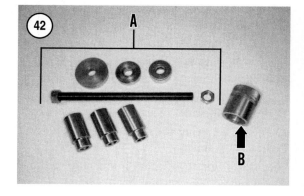

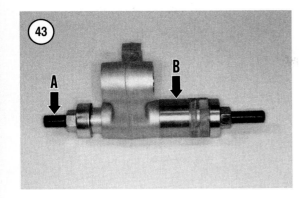

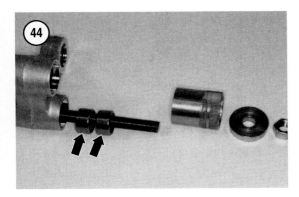

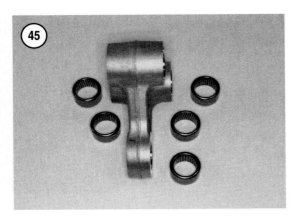

### Shock arm

This section describes how to remove two bearings that are installed in the same side of the bore. However, if the bearings are tight and difficult to move, you may not be able to remove them with the threaded rod tool. If so, consider removing the bearings with a hydraulic press or instead of removing both bearings from the same side, remove each bearing through its adjacent bore opening with a blind bearing remover. See *Shock Link* in this sec-

tion on how to use this tool while following the same service procedures.

1. Refer to **Figure 33** to identify the needle bearings:
   a. Shock absorber side bearing (A, **Figure 33**).
   b. Shock link side bearings (B, **Figure 33**).
   c. Swing arm side bearings (C, **Figure 33**).
2. If previously removed, reinstall the bearing rollers to support the bearing cage when removing it.
3. Measure the bearings installed depth from the top of the bore to the outer bearing surface.
4. Refer to *Basic Service Methods* in Chapter One for bearing removal and installation techniques. Also, refer to *Interference Fit* in Chapter One for using heat for the removal and installation of the bearings. Observe all safety and handling procedures when heating the shock arm.
5. Heat the shock arm with a heat gun or propane torch.
6. Assemble the threaded rod (A, **Figure 43**) and pipe (B) onto the shock arm.
7. Hold the nut next to the pipe and turn the opposite nut to remove the bearing(s). See **Figure 44**. Where two bearings are used in one bore, remove them both from the same side.
8. Repeat for each bearing set.
9. Clean and dry the shock arm. Inspect the mounting bores for cracks, galling and other damage.
10. Lubricate the new bearings with grease.
11. Before installing the new needle bearings, note the following:
   a. Where two bearings are used in one bore, install them from opposite sides (**Figure 45**) with their manufacturer's marks facing out.
   b. On all 2002-2004 models and 2005 CRF250X and CRF450X models, install the shock absorber side needle bearing (A, **Figure 33**) 2.0-2.2 mm (0.08-009 in.) below the shock arm surface.
   c. On 2005 CRF250R and CRF450R models, install the shock absorber side needle bearing (A, **Figure 33**) 3.0-3.2 mm (0.12-0.13 in.) below the shock arm surface (**Figure 46**).
   d. Install the shock link side needle bearings (B, **Figure 33**) 6.0-6.5 mm (0.23-0.26 in.) below the shock arm surface (**Figure 47**).
   e. Install the swing arm side needle bearings (C, **Figure 33**) 4.4-4.7 mm (0.17-0.19 in.) below the shock arm surface (**Figure 47**).

14

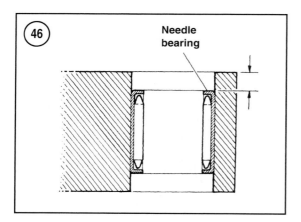

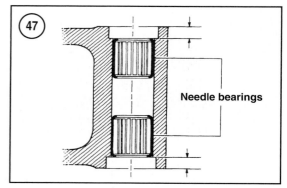

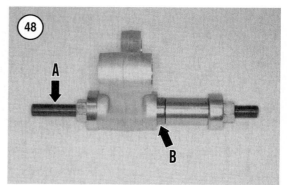

12. Assemble the threaded rod (A, **Figure 48**) and new bearing (B) onto the shock arm. Make sure the bearing seats squarely against its bore. Hold the nut opposite the bearing and turn the other nut to draw the bearing into the shock arm to the depth specified in Step 11. Repeat for each bearing.

### *Shock link*

Because of the shoulders machined inside the shock link bearing bores (**Figure 38**), the bearings can only be removed with a blind bearing removal tool.

1. If previously removed, reinstall the individual bearing rollers to support the bearing cage when removing it.

2. Measure the bearings installed depth from the top of the bore to the outer bearing surface.

3. Refer to *Basic Service Methods* in Chapter One for bearing removal and installation techniques. Also, refer to *Interference Fit* in Chapter One for using heat for the removal and installation of the bearings. Observe all safety and handling procedures when heating the shock link.

4. Wrap a piece of thick rubber or foam around one of the shock link arms and mount the shock link in a vise (**Figure 49**). Secure as much of the shock link arm in the vise as possible.

5. Assemble the blind bearing remover so it locks against the inner edge of one bearing.

6. Heat the area around the bearing bore with a heat gun or propane torch. Do not directly heat the tool or bearing.

7. Operate the bearing remover and remove the bearing (**Figure 50**).

8. Repeat to remove the opposite bearing.

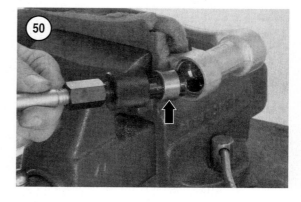

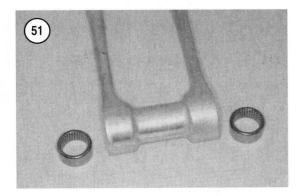

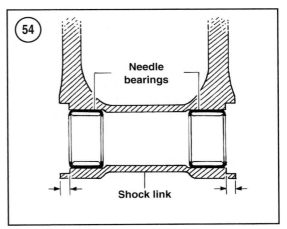

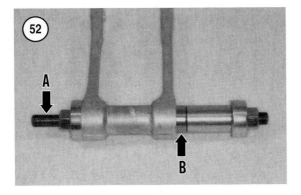

9. Allow the shock link to cool, then clean the shock link in solvent and dry. Inspect the bearing bores for cracks, scoring and other damage.

10. Lubricate the new bearings with grease.

11. Install the bearings as follows:

a. Install the bearings from opposite sides (**Figure 51**) with their manufacturer's marks facing out.

b. Assemble the threaded rod tool (A, **Figure 52**) and new bearing (B) onto the shock link.

Make sure the bearing seats squarely against its bore.

c. Secure the nut opposite the bearing in a vise and turn the other nut (**Figure 53**) to draw the bearing into the shock link until it is 4.4-4.7 mm (0.17-0.19 in.) below the shock link surface (**Figure 54**).

d. Repeat for the opposite bearing.

## REAR SWING ARM

### Preliminary Inspection

Periodically inspect the swing arm bearings with the swing arm mounted on the motorcycle. Inspect the swing arm needle bearings for excessive play, roughness or damage.

1. Remove the rear wheel (Chapter Twelve).

2. Loosen the swing arm pivot shaft nut, then retighten it to 88 N•m (65 ft.-lb.).

3. Remove the shock arm nut, washer and bolt (**Figure 55**) at the swing arm and separate the linkage from the swing arm.

4. Check the bearings as follows:

a. Have an assistant steady the motorcycle.

b. Grasp the rear end of the swing arm and try to move it from side to side in a horizontal arc (A, **Figure 56**). There should be no detectable play in the bearings.

c. Pivot the rear of the swing arm up and down through its full travel (B, **Figure 56**). The bearings must pivot smoothly.

d. If there is play or roughness in the bearings, remove the swing arm and inspect the needle

**14**

bearings and pivot shaft for wear. Inspect the swing arm bearing bores for damage.

5. Install and tighten the shock arm-to-swing arm bolt, washer and nut (**Figure 55**) as follows:

a. Clean and dry the pivot bolt, washer and nut. Lubricate the pivot bolt shaft with a water-proof grease. On 2002 models, do not lubricate the washer or the pivot bolt and mounting nut threads. These threads and washer must be clean and dry when tightened. On 2003-on models, lubricate the washer and the pivot bolt and mounting nut threads with engine oil.

*CAUTION*
*On 2002 models, the washer and the pivot bolt and nut threads must be clean and dry when tightened; otherwise, the threads may strip if the nut is tightened with a torque wrench.*

b. Install the shock arm-to-swing arm bolt, washer and nut (**Figure 55**) and tighten to the torque specification in **Table 5**.

**Removal**

The swing arm can be removed without having to remove the shock linkage assembly.

1. Remove the rear wheel (Chapter Twelve).

2A. On CRF250X and CRF450X models, unbolt and remove the chain guide (**Figure 57**) from the swing arm. This will allow removal of the swing arm without having to separate the drive chain.

2B. On all other models, remove the master link and remove the drive chain from the rear chain guard.

3. Remove the brake pedal (Chapter Fifteen).

4. Remove the shock arm nut, washer and bolt (**Figure 55**) at the swing arm.

*NOTE*
*If the washer is cracked or broken, it may be too thin and is probably not the stock washer. Purchase a new washer and compare the thickness.*

5. Remove the brake hose guides from the right side of the swing arm.

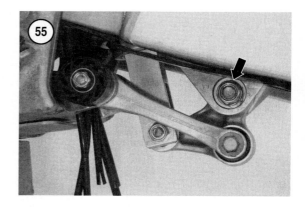

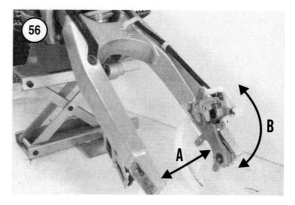

6. Slide the rear brake caliper (**Figure 58**) off the swing arm rail and secure it with a piece of stiff wire.

*CAUTION*
*If the pivot shaft is hard to remove, it may be necessary to drive it out with a hammer and a brass or aluminum rod. Do not damage the pivot shaft threads. If the pivot shaft is stuck, spray a penetrating liquid at both*

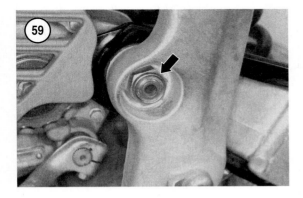

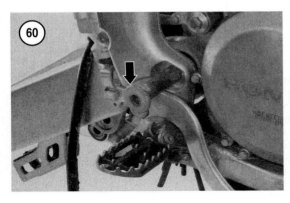

*ends of the pivot shaft and at the swing arm and engine mating areas. Allow sufficient time for it to penetrate before trying to remove the pivot shaft.*

7. Remove the swing arm pivot shaft nut (**Figure 59**), washer, pivot shaft (**Figure 60**) and swing arm.

8. Clean, inspect and lubricate the swing arm bearings as described in this chapter.

9. If necessary, use a wire wheel mounted in a drill to clean the pivot shaft of rust and corrosion.

## Installation

Use a waterproof wheel bearing grease when grease is called for in this procedure.

1. Clean the engine bushings and frame where the pivot shaft passes through.

2. Lubricate the pivot collars and seals as described in this section.

3. Lubricate the pivot shaft with grease and set aside until installation. Do not lubricate the pivot shaft or pivot shaft nut threads.

4. Make sure the notch in the chain slider engages with the tab on the front of the swing arm.

5. Install the swing arm, making sure the side collars did not fall out. If the drive chain is mounted on the drive sprocket, position the swing arm under the upper chain run.

6. Install the pivot shaft from the right side (**Figure 60**). Check that the pivot shaft head enters the cutout in the frame. Wipe off all grease from the pivot shaft threads before installing and tightening the nut in Step 7.

> *CAUTION*
> *The pivot bolt and nut threads must be clean and dry when tightened; otherwise, the threads may strip if the nut is tightened with a torque wrench.*

7. Install the washer and pivot shaft nut (**Figure 59**) and tighten to 88 N•m (65 ft.-lb.).

8. Before connecting the shock linkage, recheck the swing arm bearing operation as described under *Inspection*. If the swing arm movement does not feel correct, remove the swing arm and check the needle bearings and pivot collars for damage.

9. Install and tighten the shock arm-to-swing arm bolt, washer and nut (**Figure 55**) as described under *Preliminary Inspection* Step 5 in this section.

10. Reinstall the brake caliper bracket (**Figure 58**) onto the swing arm rail. Do not twist the brake hose.

11. Align the brake hose with the swing arm and install the hose guides. Tighten the hose guide screws to 1.2 N•m (10 in.-lb.).

12. Install the rear brake pedal (Chapter Fifteen).

**14**

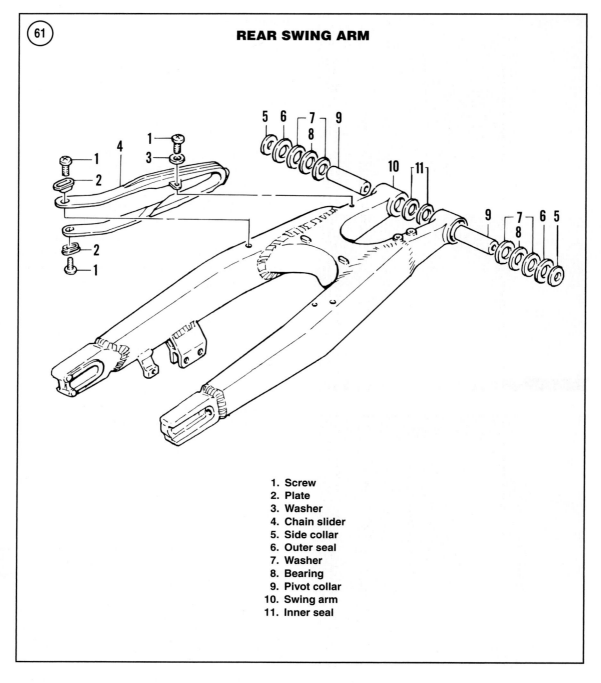

**REAR SWING ARM**

61

1. Screw
2. Plate
3. Washer
4. Chain slider
5. Side collar
6. Outer seal
7. Washer
8. Bearing
9. Pivot collar
10. Swing arm
11. Inner seal

13. On CRF250X and CRF450X models, install the chain guide and tighten the bolt and two nuts to 12 N•m (106 in.-lb.).

14. Install the rear wheel (Chapter Twelve).

15. Make sure the rear brake pedal and rear brake work properly.

**Disassembly**

Do not intermix the left and right bearing assemblies (**Figure 61**). Install the parts in their original positions.

1. Remove the chain slider (**Figure 62**).

2. Remove the chain guard (**Figure 63**).

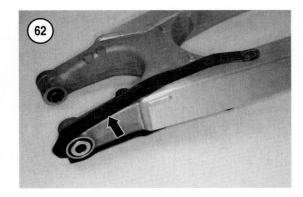

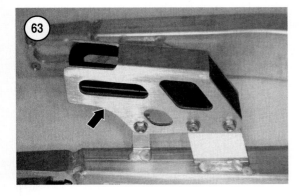

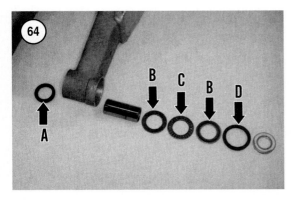

3. Remove the pivot collar, side collar, seal and thrust bearing assembly (**Figure 64**) from each side of the swing arm.

4. Remove the inner seals (**Figure 65**).

**Inspection**

Replace parts that show excessive wear or damage as described in this section.

1. Clean and dry the swing arm and its components. Clean the needle bearings thoroughly with solvent to remove old grease, sand, dirt and other abrasive material. Then clean with soapy water and flush with clean water. Repeat until the bearings look clean.

*NOTE*
*After thoroughly cleaning the needle bearings, the rollers will appear loose. This is normal and is not an indication of wear.*

2. Inspect the pivot collars for scoring, excessive wear, rust or other damage.

*NOTE*
*If a pivot collar is excessively worn or damaged, the mating needle bearing is probably worn also.*

3. Inspect the side collars (5, **Figure 61**) for wear or damage on their outer circumference that could cut the outer seals and allow water and dirt to enter the bearing bore.

*NOTE*
*Refer to **Assembly** for information on lubricating the pivot collars and needle bearings with grease.*

4. Inspect each needle bearing (**Figure 66**) for cracks, flat spots, rust, seizure or other damage. If there is no visible damage, lubricate the pivot collar and needle bearing with grease and install it into the bearing. Turn the pivot collar and check the bearings for any roughness, excessive play or other damage. If play or roughness exists, replace the bearings and pivot collars as a set as described under *Needle Bearing Replacement* in this section.

5. Inspect the thrust bearing assembly (**Figure 67**). The rollers should be smooth and polished with no flat spots, burrs or other damage. Inspect the two-piece bearing case for separation, cracks or

14

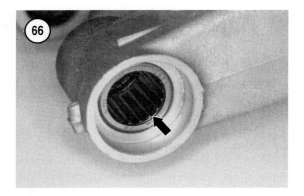

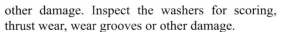

other damage. Inspect the washers for scoring, thrust wear, wear grooves or other damage.

6. Check the swing arm for cracks and other damage.

7. Check the outer seal and thrust bearing bore surfaces for nicks, gouges and other damage. Repair minor damage with a file and then smooth it with fine emery paper. Make sure not to enlarge the bore or to file a flat spot as this may allow water and dirt to enter past the seal and contaminate the bearing. Damage like that shown in **Figure 68** requires professional repair.

*NOTE*
*Refer swing arm repair to a competent welder/machinist. Figure 69 shows the same swing arm shown in Step 7 with the crack repaired.*

8. Inspect the chain slider for excessive wear or missing fasteners. The slider prevents the drive chain from contacting the swing arm. Refer to Chapter Three for information on inspecting the chain slider and drive chain rollers.

9. Inspect the swing arm pivot shaft for scoring, rust, bending and other damage. Install the pivot collars onto the pivot shaft and slide them back and forth by hand. There must be no binding or roughness.

10. Inspect the axle plates for wear, loose fasteners and other damage.

**Assembly**

*NOTE*
*Lubricate the swing arm components with a waterproof bearing grease.*

1. Lubricate the needle bearings with grease. Place grease on your finger and force the grease on and between the rollers. Spin the rollers to ensure penetration behind the rollers. Work around the bearing until all of the rollers are thoroughly lubricated.

2. Lubricate the thrust bearing assembly and pivot collars with a waterproof bearing grease.

3. Lubricate the seal lips with a waterproof bearing grease.

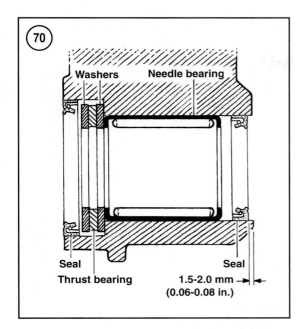

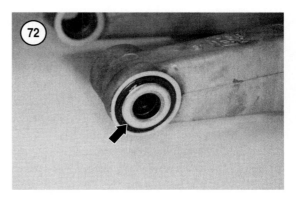

6. Install the outer seals (D, **Figure 64**) with the manufacturer's marks facing out. Press the seals into place until they are flush with the swing arm bore outer surface (**Figure 71**).

7. Install the pivot collars (9, **Figure 61**) into the needle bearings. Then turn the pivot collars to distribute the grease previously applied to both parts.

8. Install the side collars and seat them against the thrust bearing (**Figure 72**).

9. On CRF250R and CRF450R models, install the chain guide (**Figure 63**). Tighten the bolt and two nuts to 12 N•m (106 in.-lb.).

10. Install the chain slider as shown in **Figure 62**. Insert the hole in the chain slider over the tab on the swing arm. Apply a threadlock onto the screw threads and tighten to 3.9 N•m (34.5 in.-lb.).

11. Install the swing arm as described in this chapter.

### Needle Bearing Replacement

This section describes replacement of the needle bearings installed inside the swing arm. Do not remove these needle bearings (**Figure 66**) unless they are going to be replaced. Always replace both needle bearings at the same time.

The needle bearings are installed inside the swing arm with a slight press fit. Due to their operating environment, corrosion can seize the bearings into their bores, making removal very difficult. Work carefully to avoid damaging the swing arm when replacing the bearings. Discard the bearings after removing them.

The following procedures describe bearing replacement using a press or hand tools. Read both

4. Install the inner seals (A, **Figure 64**) with the manufacturer's marks facing out, while noting the following:

    a. On all 2002-2004 models and 2005 CRF250X models, install the seals until they are flush with the swing arm bore outer surface (**Figure 65**).

    b. On all 2005 CRF250R, CRF450R and CRF450X models, install the seals until their outer edge is positioned 1.5-2.0 mm (0.06-0.08 in.) below the swing arm bore outer surface (**Figure 70**).

5. Assemble the thrust bearing assembly. The bearing (C, **Figure 64**) goes between the washers (B, **Figure 64**). Seat the thrust bearing assembly against the needle bearing and collar.

14

procedures to determine which method is most practical.

Bearing kits (**Figure 73**), which contain all the seals, bearings and collars required to rebuild the swing arm, are available from *www.pivotworks.com*.

### Press method

This is the most effective method of removing the swing arm bearings, especially when the bearings are corroded. When using a press, be careful when supporting the swing arm. Applying pressure to the bearing with the swing arm improperly mounted can damage the swing arm.

1. Remove the pivot collar, side collar, seals and thrust bearing components from both sides of the swing arm.

2. Clean the swing arm bore thoroughly to remove all dirt and other abrasive material from the bearing and bore surface.

3. Support the swing arm in a press with a piece of pipe (A, **Figure 74**). The pipe must fit solidly against the swing arm bearing bore and have an inside diameter large enough to allow the bearing to pass through.

4. Place a bearing driver against the inside edge of the bearing (B, **Figure 74**), then pass a driver (C) through the upper bearing and rest it against the bearing driver.

5. Apply pressure against the bearing, while continuing to hold the swing arm, and press the bearing out of its bore. Once the bearing is free of its bore, the swing arm will fall to the floor unless it is being held or supported.

6. Turn the swing arm over and repeat to remove the opposite bearing.

7. Clean and inspect the mounting bores as described under *Inspection* in this section.

8. Lubricate the new bearings with a waterproof bearing grease as described under *Assembly* in this section.

9. Support the swing arm bearing bore as shown in **Figure 75**. The bearing must be installed from the outside of the swing arm.

10. Center the bearing (A, **Figure 75**) in its bore with the manufacturer's marks facing out. Place a socket or driver (B, **Figure 75**) over the bearing and press the bearing into the bore until its outer edge is flush with the bearing bore surface (**Figure 66**).

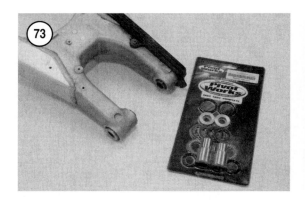

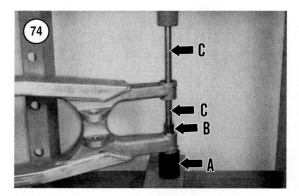

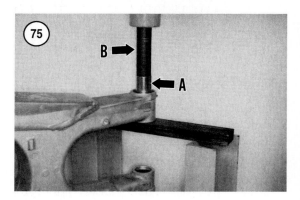

11. Turn the swing arm over and repeat for the other bearing.

### Hand tool method

In the following procedure, the bearings will be removed with a bearing driver and hammer. The bearings are installed with the Motion Pro Swing Arm Bearing Tool (part No. 08-0213 [**Figure 76**]). A similar tool can be made with a length of threaded

76

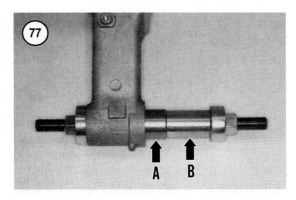

77

A B

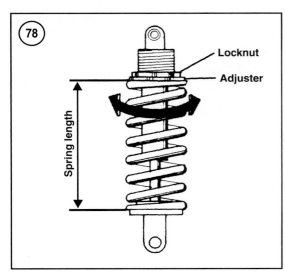

78

Locknut

Adjuster

Spring length

rod, two nuts, large thick washers and a suitable driver.

*NOTE*
*Refer to **Interference Fit** in Chapter One for using heat for the removal and installation of the bearings. Ob-*

*serve all safety and handling procedures heating when the swing arm.*

1. Heat the swing arm around the bearing bore with a heat gun or propane torch. Keep the heat moving and do not overheat the swing arm. Heat the swing arm just enough to expand the bearing bore. Do not apply heat directly to the bearing.
2. Support the swing arm so force can be applied to the inside of the bearing. Then pass a long driver through one swing arm bore and to the back side of the bearing to be replaced. Place a socket or driver squarely against the bearing and drive the bearing out with a hammer.
3. Turn the swing arm over and repeat to remove the opposite bearing.
4. Clean and inspect the mounting bores as described under *Inspection* in this section.
5. Lubricate the new bearings with a waterproof bearing grease as described under *Assembly* in this section.
6. Center the needle bearing (A, **Figure 77**) in its bore with its manufacturer's marks facing out. The bearing must be installed from the outside of the swing arm.
7. Assemble the threaded rod tool as shown in **Figure 77**. Place a socket or bearing driver (B, **Figure 77**) against the needle bearing.
8. Make sure the bearing is positioned squarely over the bore. Hold the inner nut and turn the outer nut to press the bearing into the swing arm. Continue until the bearing is flush with the outer bearing bore surface (**Figure 66**).
9. Turn the swing arm over and repeat to install the opposite bearing.

**REAR SUSPENSION ADJUSTMENT**

**Shock Spring Preload Adjustment**

The spring preload adjustment can be performed with the shock mounted on the motorcycle. Spring preload is adjusted by changing the position of the adjuster on the shock body (**Figure 78**).
1. Support the motorcycle with the rear wheel off the ground.
2A. On CRF250R and CRF450R models, remove the subframe (Chapter Sixteen).
2B. On CRF250X and CRF450X models, raise and lock the subframe (Chapter Sixteen).

14

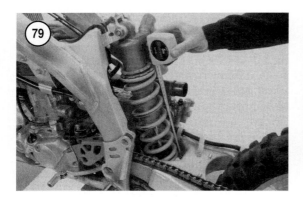

3. Clean the threads on the shock body.

4. Measure the existing spring preload length (**Figure 79**). Measure the spring from end to end. Do not include the thickness of the adjuster or the spring seat. Record the measurement for reference.

5. Loosen the spring locknut (**Figure 80**) with a spanner wrench. If the adjuster turns with the locknut, strike the locknut with a punch and hammer to break it from the locknut.

6. Turn the adjuster to change the spring preload dimension within the limits specified in **Table 4**. Usually, turning the spring by hand (**Figure 81**) also turns the adjuster. Measure and record the dimension for reference.

> *NOTE*
> *One complete turn of the adjuster moves the spring 1.5 mm (0.06 in.). Tightening the adjuster increases spring preload and loosening it decreases preload.*

> *CAUTION*
> *The spring preload must be maintained within the specifications listed in **Table 4**. If the minimum specification is exceeded, the spring may coil bind when the shock comes near full compression. This will overload and weaken the spring.*

7. Lightly lubricate the threads on the shock body with engine oil. Then hold the adjuster and tighten the spring locknut (**Figure 80**) to 44 N•m (32 ft.-lb.).

8. Install or reposition the subframe (Chapter Sixteen).

**Rebound Damping**

The rebound damping adjustment affects the rate of shock absorber extension after it has been compressed. This adjustment has no affect on shock compression. If rebound damping is set too low, the rear wheel may bottom on subsequent bumps.

The rebound damping adjuster is mounted at the bottom of the shock (**Figure 82**). A clicker type adjuster is used; each click of the adjuster screw represents one adjustment or position change. Turning the adjuster one full turn changes the adjuster by four positions. See **Table 2** for standard and total adjustment positions.

For the standard setting, turn the adjuster screw clockwise until it stops (this is the full hard posi-

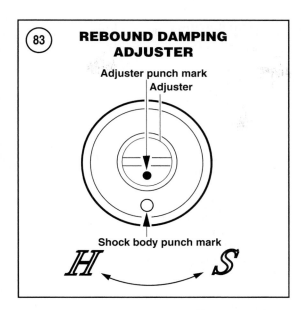

**83** REBOUND DAMPING ADJUSTER

Adjuster punch mark
Adjuster

Shock body punch mark

*H* ← → *S*

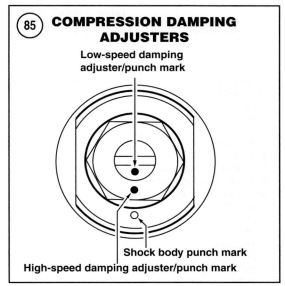

**85** COMPRESSION DAMPING ADJUSTERS

Low-speed damping adjuster/punch mark

Shock body punch mark
High-speed damping adjuster/punch mark

**84**

tion). Then turn it counterclockwise the number of clicks (standard) in **Table 2**. When the standard setting is set, the two index marks on the adjuster align (**Figure 83**).

To increase the rebound damping, turn the adjuster screw toward the H mark (clockwise) on the adjuster. To decrease the rebound damping, turn the adjuster screw toward the S mark (counterclockwise) on the adjuster.

Make sure the adjuster wheel is located in one of the detent positions and not in between any two settings.

## Compression Damping

Compression damping controls the shock absorber rate after hitting a bump. This setting has no affect on the rebound rate of the shock.

The shock is equipped with low- and high-speed adjusters. Both compression damping adjusters are located at the top of the shock absorber (**Figure 84**).

1. To set the high-speed adjuster to its standard setting, turn the hex-head adjuster (**Figure 85**) clockwise until it stops (this is the full hard position). Then turn it counterclockwise the number of turns (standard) in **Table 2**. When the standard setting is set, the high-speed damping adjuster punch mark will align with the shock body punch mark (**Figure 85**).

*NOTE*
*Adjust the high-speed adjuster in one twelfth turn increments.*

2. To set the low-speed adjuster to its standard setting, turn the center adjuster (**Figure 85**) clockwise until it stops (this is the full hard position). Then turn it counterclockwise the number of clicks (standard) in **Table 2**. When the standard setting is set, the low-speed adjuster punch mark will align with the shock body punch mark (**Figure 85**).

3. To increase the compression damping for both adjusters, turn the adjusters clockwise. To decrease the compression damping for both adjusters, turn the adjusters counterclockwise.

## Nitrogen Pressure

Refer all nitrogen pressure adjustment to a Honda dealership or suspension specialist.

**14**

**Table 1 REAR SUSPENSION SPECIFICATIONS**

| | |
|---|---|
| Rear axle travel | |
| CRF250R | |
| 2004 | 312 mm (12.28 in.) |
| 2005 | 313 mm (12.32 in.) |
| CRF250X | 312 mm (12.28 in.) |
| CRF450R | |
| 2002-2003 | 314 mm (12.36 in.) |
| 2004 | 319 mm (12.56 in.) |
| 2005 | 320 mm (12.60 in.) |
| CRF450X | 313 mm (12.32 in.) |
| Rear damper | Remote nitrogen reservoir |
| Rear damper nitrogen pressure | 980 kPa (142 psi) |
| Rear suspension type | Pro-link |
| Shock spring installed length | |
| CRF250R | |
| 2004 | 260.1 mm (10.24 in.) |
| 2005 | 261.3 mm (10.29 in.) |
| CRF250X | 254.4 mm (10.02 in.) |
| CRF450R | |
| 2002 | 256.0 mm (10.08 in.) |
| 2003 | 258.2 mm (10.16 in.) |
| 2004 | 259.4 mm (10.21 in.) |
| 2005 | 256.3 mm (10.09 in.) |
| CRF450X | 258.5 mm (10.18 in.) |

**Table 2 REAR SHOCK ABSORBER COMPRESSION AND REBOUND ADJUSTMENT**

| | Total adjustment positions | Standard adjuster position |
|---|---|---|
| Low speed compression damping adjustment* | | |
| CRF250R | 13 | 7 clicks out from full in |
| CRF250X | 13 | 12 clicks out from full in |
| CRF450R | | |
| 2002 | 13 | 8 clicks out from full in |
| 2003 | 13 | 7 clicks out from full in |
| 2004-on | 13 | 6 clicks out from full in |
| CRF450X | 13 | 10 clicks out from full in |
| High-speed compression damping adjustment* | | |
| CRF250R | | |
| 2004 | – | 1 1/12-2 1/2 turns out from full in |
| 2005 | – | 1 3/4-2 1/4 turns out from full in |
| CRF250X | – | 1 7/12-2 1/2 turns out from full in |
| CRF450R | | |
| 2002 | – | 1-1 1/2 turns out from full in |
| 2003 | – | 1 1/2-2 turns out from full in |
| 2004 | – | 1 7/12-2 1/2 turns out from full in |
| 2005 | – | 1 1/2-2 turns out from full in |
| CRF450X | – | 3/4-1 1/4 turns out from full in |

(continued)

**Table 2 REAR SHOCK ABSORBER COMPRESSION AND REBOUND ADJUSTMENT (continued)**

| | Total adjustment positions | Standard adjuster position |
|---|---|---|
| **Rebound damping adjustment\*** | | |
| **CRF250R** | | |
| 2004 | 17 | 8-11 clicks out from full in |
| 2005 | 17 | 7-10 clicks out from full in |
| **CRF250X** | 17 | 13-16 clicks out from full in |
| **CRF450R** | | |
| 2002 | 17 | 11-14 clicks out from full in |
| 2003 | 17 | 9-12 clicks out from full in |
| 2004 | 17 | 7-10 clicks out from full in |
| 2005 | 17 | 6-9 clicks out from full in |
| **CRF450X** | 17 | 11-14 clicks out from full in |

\*Low-speed compression and rebound damping adjustments are determined by number of clicks. High-speed compression adjustments are determined by number of turns.

**Table 3 SHOCK ABSORBER SPRING RATES AND IDENTIFICATION PAINT MARKS**

| Spring description and rate | Spring identification paint mark |
|---|---|
| **CRF250R** | |
| Standard 5.30 kg/mm (296.7 lb./in.) | Blue |
| Softer 5.10 kg/mm (285.5 lb./in.) | White |
| Stiffer | |
| 5.50 kg/mm (308.1 lb./in.) | Red |
| 5.70 kg/mm (319.3 lb./in.) | Pink |
| **CRF250X** | |
| Standard 4.80 kg/mm (268.8 lb./in.) | Orange |
| Softer 4.55 kg/mm (254.8 lb./in.) | Red and black |
| Stiffer | |
| 5.00 kg/mm (280.0 lb./in.) | White |
| 5.20 kg/mm (291.2 lb./in.) | Blue |
| **CRF450R** | |
| 2002 | |
| Standard 5.40 kg/mm (302.4 lb./in.) | No factory paint mark; aftermarket green |
| Softer 5.20 kg/mm (291.2 lb./in.) | Blue |
| Stiffer | |
| 5.60 kg/mm (313.6 lb./in.) | Pink |
| 5.80 kg/mm (324.8 lb./in.) | Silver |
| 2003-on | |
| Standard 5.50 kg/mm (308.0 lb./in.) | No factory paint mark; aftermarket red |
| Softer 5.30 kg/mm (296.8 lb./in.) | Blue |
| Stiffer | |
| 5.70 kg/mm (319.3 lb./in.) | Pink |
| 5.90 kg/mm (330.4 lb./in.) | Silver |
| **CRF450X** | |
| Standard 5.50 kg/mm (308.0 lb./in.) | No factory paint mark; aftermarket red |
| Softer 5.30 kg/mm (296.8 lb./in.) | Blue |
| Stiffer | |
| 5.70 kg/mm (319.3 lb./in.) | Pink |
| 5.90 kg/mm (330.4 lb./in.) | Silver |

14

**Table 4 REAR SHOCK ABSORBER SPRING INSTALLED LENGTH***

| Model and spring type | Standard mm (in.) | Minimum mm (in.) |
|---|---|---|
| CRF250R | | |
| 2004 | | |
| Standard | 260.1 (10.24) | 251 (9.88) |
| Optional softer spring (5.1 kg/mm) | 260.1 (10.24) | 252 (9.92) |
| Optional stiffer spring (5.5 kg/mm) | 260.1 (10.24) | 249 (9.80) |
| Optional stiffer spring (5.7 kg/mm) | 260.1 (10.24) | 251 (9.88) |
| 2005 | | |
| Standard | 261.3 (10.29) | 251 (9.88) |
| Optional softer spring (5.1 kg/mm) | 261.3 (10.29) | 252 (9.92) |
| Optional stiffer spring (5.5 kg/mm) | 261.3 (10.29) | 249 (9.80) |
| Optional stiffer spring (5.7 kg/mm) | 261.3 (10.29) | 251 (9.88) |
| CRF250X | | |
| 2004-on | | |
| Standard | 254.4 (10.02) | 245 (9.65) |
| Optional softer spring (4.55 kg/mm) | 254.4 (10.02) | 248 (9.76) |
| Optional stiffer spring (5.00 kg/mm) | 254.4 (10.02) | 247 (9.72) |
| Optional stiffer spring (5.20 kg/mm) | 254.4 (10.02) | 250 (9.84) |
| CRF450R | | |
| 2002 | | |
| Standard | 256 (10.08) | 247 (9.72) |
| Optional softer spring (5.2 kg/mm) | 256 (10.08) | 248 (9.76) |
| Optional stiffer spring (5.6 kg/mm) | 256 (10.08) | 249 (9.80) |
| Optional stiffer spring (5.8 kg/mm) | 256 (10.08) | 247 (9.72) |
| 2003 | | |
| Standard | 258.2 (10.17) | 249 (9.80) |
| Optional softer spring (5.3 kg/mm) | 258.2 (10.17) | 251 (9.88) |
| Optional stiffer spring (5.7 kg/mm) | 258.2 (10.17) | 251 (9.88) |
| Optional stiffer spring (5.9 kg/mm) | 258.2 (10.17) | 250 (9.84) |
| 2004 | | |
| Standard | 259.4 (10.21) | 249 (9.80) |
| Optional softer spring (5.3 kg/mm) | 259.4 (10.21) | 251 (9.88) |
| Optional stiffer spring (5.7 kg/mm) | 259.4 (10.21) | 251 (9.88) |
| Optional stiffer spring (5.9 kg/mm) | 259.4 (10.21) | 250 (9.84) |
| 2005 | | |
| Standard spring | 256.3 (10.09) | 249 (9.80) |
| Optional softer spring (5.3 kg/mm) | 256.3 (10.09) | 251 (9.88) |
| Optional stiffer spring (5.7 kg/mm) | 256.3 (10.09) | 251 (9.88) |
| Optional stiffer spring (5.9 kg/mm) | 256.3 (10.09) | 250 (9.84) |
| CRF450X | | |
| Standard spring | 258.5 (10.18) | 249 (9.80) |
| Optional softer spring (5.3 kg/mm) | 258.5 (10.18) | 251 (9.88) |
| Optional stiffer spring (5.7 kg/mm) | 258.5 (10.18) | 251 (9.88) |
| Optional stiffer spring (5.9 kg/mm) | 258.5 (10.18) | 250 (9.84) |

*One turn of the adjuster changes the spring length by 1.5 mm (0.062 in.).

**Table 5 REAR SUSPENSION TORQUE SPECIFICATIONS**

| | N•m | in.-lb. | ft.-lb. |
|---|---|---|---|
| Brake hose guide screws at swing arm | 1.2 | 10 | – |
| Drive chain guide nut/bolt | 12 | 106 | – |

(continued)

**Table 5 REAR SUSPENSION TORQUE SPECIFICATIONS (continued)**

|  | N•m | in.-lb. | ft.-lb. |
|---|---|---|---|
| Drive chain roller nut/bolt | 12 | 106 | – |
| Drive chain slider screw[1] | 3.9 | 34.5 | – |
| Shock absorber nuts |  |  |  |
|   Upper and lower | 44 | – | 32 |
| Shock absorber overhaul |  |  |  |
|   Damper rod end nut[2] | 37 | – | 27 |
|   Damping adjuster[2] | 29 | – | 21 |
| Shock absorber spring locknut[3] | 44 | – | 32 |
| Shock arm pivot bolt nuts |  |  |  |
|   2002 |  |  |  |
|     Shock link side | 79 | – | 58 |
|     Swing arm side | 79 | – | 58 |
|   2003-on |  |  |  |
|     Shock link side[3] | 52 | – | 38 |
|     Swing arm side[3] | 52 | – | 38 |
| Shock link pivot bolt nut at frame |  |  |  |
|   2002 | 79 | – | 58 |
|   2003-on[3] | 52 | – | 38 |
| Swing arm pivot shaft nut | 88 | – | 65 |

1. Apply threadlocking compound to threads.
2. Stake.
3. Lubricate threads and seating surfaces with engine oil.

14

# CHAPTER FIFTEEN

# BRAKES

This chapter describes service procedures for the front and rear disc brakes.

**Tables 1-3** at the end of this chapter list brake specifications.

## BRAKE SERVICE

The disc brake system transmits hydraulic pressure from the master cylinders to the brake calipers. This pressure is transmitted from the caliper(s) to the brake pads, which grip both sides of the brake disc(s) and slow the motorcycle. As the pads wear, the pistons move out of the caliper bores to automatically compensate for wear. As this occurs the fluid level in the reservoir goes down. This must be compensated for by occasionally adding fluid.

Proper system operation depends on a supply of clean brake fluid (DOT 4) and a clean work environment when any service is being performed. Debris that enters the system can damage the components and cause poor brake performance.

Brake fluid is hygroscopic (easily absorbs moisture) and moisture in the system reduces brake performance. Purchase brake fluid in small containers and discard any small quantities that remain. Small quantities of fluid will quickly absorb the moisture in the container. Use only fluid clearly marked DOT 4.

If possible, use the same brand of fluid. Do not replace the fluid with DOT 5 (silicone) fluid. It is not possible to remove all the old fluid and DOT 5 is not compatible with other types. Silicone type fluids used in systems for which they were not designed cause internal seals to swell and deteriorate. Do not reuse drained fluid and discard old fluid properly.

Proper service also includes carefully performed procedures. Do not use any sharp tools inside the master cylinders or calipers or on the pistons. Any damage to these components could cause a loss in the system's ability to maintain hydraulic pressure. If there is any doubt about having the ability to correctly and safely service the brake system, have a professional technician perform the task.

Consider the following when servicing the brake system:

1. When properly maintained, hydraulic components rarely require disassembly. Make sure it is necessary.

2. Keep the reservoir covers in place to prevent the entry of moisture and debris.

3. Clean parts with DOT 4 brake fluid, an aerosol brake parts cleaner or denatured alcohol. Never use petroleum-based solvents on internal brake system components. They cause seals to swell and distort.

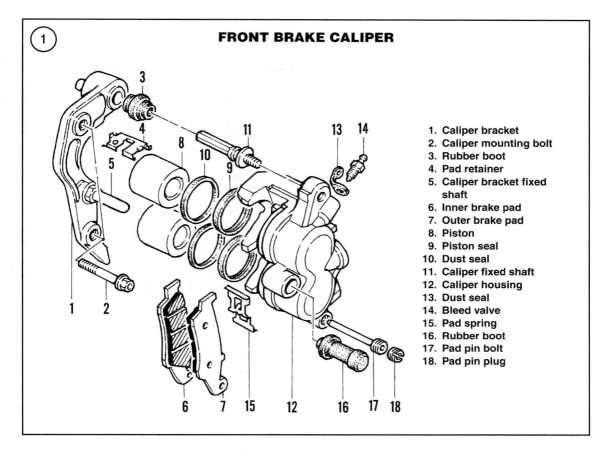

**FRONT BRAKE CALIPER**

1. Caliper bracket
2. Caliper mounting bolt
3. Rubber boot
4. Pad retainer
5. Caliper bracket fixed shaft
6. Inner brake pad
7. Outer brake pad
8. Piston
9. Piston seal
10. Dust seal
11. Caliper fixed shaft
12. Caliper housing
13. Dust seal
14. Bleed valve
15. Pad spring
16. Rubber boot
17. Pad pin bolt
18. Pad pin plug

4. Do not allow brake fluid to contact plastic, painted or plated parts. It will damage the surface.

5. Dispose of brake fluid properly.

6. If the hydraulic system has been opened (not including the reservoir cover), the system must be bled to remove air from the system. Refer to *Brake Bleeding* in this chapter.

> *WARNING*
> *Do not add to or replace the brake fluid with Silicone (DOT 5) brake fluid. It is not compatible with the system and may cause brake failure.*

> *WARNING*
> *Whenever working on the brake system, do **not** inhale brake dust. It may contain asbestos, which can cause lung injury and cancer. Wear a facemask that meets OSHA requirements for trapping asbestos particles, and wash hands and forearms thoroughly after completing the work.*

> *WARNING*
> *NEVER use compressed air to clean any part of the brake system. This releases the harmful brake pad dust. Use an aerosol brake cleaner to clean parts when servicing any component still installed on the bike.*

## FRONT BRAKE PADS

Pad wear depends greatly on riding habits and conditions. There is no recommended time interval for changing the pads in the front brake caliper. The brake pads have wear grooves that allow inspection without removal. Refer to *Brakes* in Chapter Three. Always replace brake pads as a set.

### Replacement

Refer to **Figure 1**.

1. Read the information listed under *Brake Service* in this chapter.

15

2.  Remove the brake disc cover.

> *CAUTION*
> *Do not allow the master cylinder res-*
> *ervoir to overflow when performing*
> *Step 3. If the fluid level is high, re-*
> *move the cover and draw some of the*
> *fluid from the reservoir with a*
> *syringe.*

> *CAUTION*
> *Before pushing the pistons back into*
> *the caliper to make room for the new*
> *pads, check for corrosion and dirt*
> *buildup on the exposed end of the pis-*
> *tons. When the pistons are pushed*
> *back into the caliper, this material can*
> *damage the caliper seals. If there is*
> *residue built up on the ends of the pis-*
> *tons, try to clean the end of the pistons*
> *with a soft brush and denatured alco-*
> *hol while the caliper is assembled or*
> *remove and disassemble the caliper to*
> *clean the pistons.*

3.  Push the caliper body in by hand to push the pistons into the caliper to make room for the new pads.
4.  Remove the pad pin plug (**Figure 2**).
5.  Loosen and remove the pad pin bolt (**Figure 3**).

> *CAUTION*
> *If the pads are to be reinstalled, han-*
> *dle them carefully to prevent damage*
> *and contamination.*

6.  Remove the brake pads (**Figure 4**).
7.  Remove the pad spring (**Figure 5**).
8.  Inspect the brake pads (**Figure 6**) for uneven wear, damage or contamination. Note the following:
    a.  Remove surface contamination by lightly sanding the lining surface with a piece of sandpaper placed on a flat surface. If lining material is contaminated, replace both brake pads.
    b.  Both brake pads should show approximately the same amount of wear. If the inner pad (6, **Figure 1**) is worn more than the outer pad (7), the caliper may be binding on the caliper bracket. This wear can also be caused by worn or damaged dust seals (10, **Figure 1**) that have lost their resilience to self-adjust (returning the pistons and disengaging the brakes after the brake lever is released).

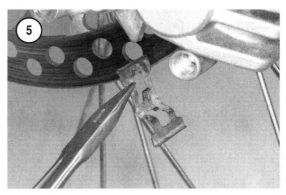

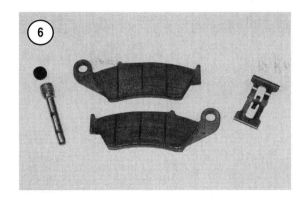

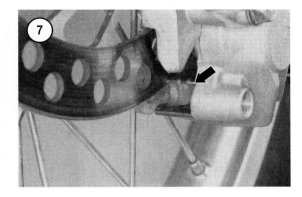

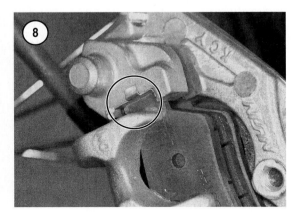

*NOTE*
*A leaking left side fork oil seal will contaminate the front brake pads, caliper and brake disc with fork oil.*

9. Replace the pads as a set if the thickness of any one pad has worn down to its wear groove.

10. Check the caliper for signs of leakage around the pistons. If brake fluid is leaking from the caliper bores, overhaul the brake caliper as described in this chapter.

11. Clean the pad pin and plug. Remove rust and corrosion from the pad pin and inspect for excessive wear, grooves or other damage. Replace if damaged.

12. Inspect the pad spring (**Figure 6**) and replace if damaged.

13. Inspect the brake disc for oil contamination (especially if the fork seal was leaking). Spray both sides of the brake disc with a brake or contact cleaner. Inspect the brake disc for wear as described in this chapter.

14. Install the pad spring (**Figure 5**) so it grips the brake caliper tightly (**Figure 7**). Replace the pad spring if it does not stay in position.

15. Install the inner and outer brake pads as shown in **Figure 4**. Push them in place so the upper end of each pad seats against the pad retainer (**Figure 8**) in the caliper bracket.

16. Push both pads against the pad spring and install the pad pin bolt (**Figure 3**) into the caliper and through the hole in the bottom of each brake pad.

17. Tighten the pad pin bolt (**Figure 3**) to 18 N•m (159 in.-lb.).

18. Install and tighten the pad pin plug (**Figure 2**) to 2 N•m (17 in.-lb.).

19. Operate the brake lever to seat the pads against the disc. The brake lever should feel firm when applied.

20. Check the brake fluid level in the reservoir. If necessary, add new DOT 4 brake fluid.

21. Raise the front wheel and check that the wheel spins freely and the brake operates properly.

*WARNING*
*Do not ride the motorcycle until the front brake is operating correctly. Make sure the brake lever travel is not excessive and the lever does not feel spongy. Either condition indicates the front brake must be bled as described in this chapter.*

22. Install the brake disc cover.

23. Break in the pads by braking slowly at first and then increase braking pressure. Do not overheat new brake pads.

15

## FRONT BRAKE CALIPER

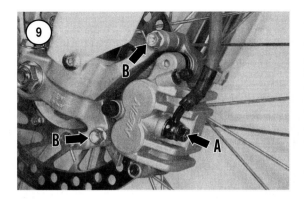

The pistons in the front brake caliper are self-adjusting to compensate for brake pad wear. When the front brake is applied, hydraulic pressure against the pistons causes the piston seals (9, **Figure 1**) to stretch and deflect slightly. This allows the pistons to move out where they contact the brake pads and push them against the brake disc. When the brake lever is released, pressure against the piston seals is reduced and allows them to retract and return to their original shape. This action draws the pistons away from the brake pads and disengages the brake. As the brake pads wear, the pistons will travel farther through the seals in order to contact the brake pads.

### Removal/Installation

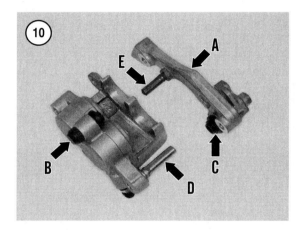

1. Remove the brake disc cover.
2. If the caliper will be disconnected from the brake hose, drain the system as described in this chapter. After draining, remove the brake hose banjo bolt and both washers (A, **Figure 9**) while the caliper is mounted on the fork. Tie a plastic bag over the end of the hose.
3A. If the caliper will be removed from the motorcycle, remove the caliper mounting bolts (B, **Figure 9**).
3B. If the caliper will be left attached to the brake hose:
    a. Remove the caliper mounting bolts (B, **Figure 9**) and secure the caliper with a length of wire. Do not allow the caliper to hang by the brake hose.
    b. Insert a spacer block between the brake pads.

> *NOTE*
> *The spacer block will prevent the pistons from being forced out of the caliper if the front brake lever is applied with the brake caliper removed.*

4. Service the caliper as described in this chapter.
5. Installation is the reverse of removal. Note the following:
    a. If the pads are installed in the caliper, press the caliper pistons back into the caliper so the pads will clear the disc.
    b. Apply a medium strength threadlock onto the front brake caliper mounting bolts and tighten to the torque specification in **Table 3**.

    c. Check the brake fluid level in the reservoir and fill or remove fluid as necessary.

    d. After installing the brake caliper, operate the brake lever several times to seat the pads against the brake disc.

    e. If the brake hose was disconnected from the caliper, install a new washer on each side of the brake hose and tighten the banjo bolt to 34 N•m (25 ft.-lb.). Then fill and bleed the brake system as described in this chapter.

    f. With the front wheel raised, check that the wheel spins freely and the brake operates properly.

> *WARNING*
> *Do not ride the motorcycle until the front brake is operating correctly. Make sure the brake lever travel is not excessive and the lever does not feel spongy. Either condition indicates the front brake must be bled as described in this chapter.*

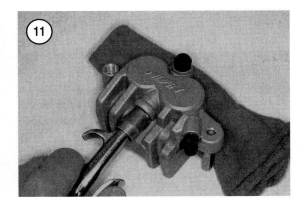

### Disassembly

Refer to **Figure 1**.

#### *Removing the pistons hydraulically*

If the piston and dust seals are in good condition and there are no signs of brake fluid leaking from the bores, it may be possible to remove the pistons hydraulically. However, note that brake fluid will spill from the caliper once the pistons are free.

Read this procedure through to understand the steps and tools required.

1. Remove the front brake caliper as described in this chapter. Do not loosen or remove the brake hose.
2. Remove the caliper bracket from the caliper. Have a supply of paper towels and a pan available to catch and wipe up spilled brake fluid.
3. Hold the caliper with the pistons facing down and slowly operate the brake lever to push the pistons out of their bores. If both pistons move evenly, continue until they extend far enough to be removed by hand.
4. If the pistons do not move evenly, stop and push the extended piston back into its bore by hand, so

that both pistons are even, then repeat. If the results are the same, reposition the extended piston again, then operate the brake lever while preventing the moving piston from extending. Install a strip of wood across the caliper to block the piston. If the other piston now starts to move, continue with this technique until both pistons move evenly and can be gripped and removed by hand. After removing the pistons, hold the caliper over the drain pan to catch the brake fluid draining through the caliper.

5. Remove the banjo bolt with an impact gun (air or electric), if available. Otherwise, hold the caliper in a secure manner and remove the banjo bolt with hand tools. If the caliper cannot be held securely to remove the bolt, stuff paper towels into the caliper bores to absorb brake fluid leaking from the hose and reservoir. Temporarily reinstall the caliper bracket and mount the caliper onto the slider with its mounting bolts to hold it in place, then remove the banjo bolt and both washers.

6. Perform the relevant steps in the following section to complete caliper disassembly.

#### *Removing the pistons with compressed air*

1. Remove the brake caliper as described in this chapter.
2. Slide the caliper bracket (A, **Figure 10**) out of the caliper.
3. Remove the caliper's rubber boot (B, **Figure 10**) by grasping its thick outer edge and pulling it out of its mounting hole. Then remove the rubber boot (C, **Figure 10**) from the caliper bracket.
4. Remove the pad retainer from the caliper bracket.
5. Close the bleed valve so air cannot escape.

> *WARNING*
> *Wear eye protection when using compressed air to remove the pistons and keep your fingers away from the pistons.*

6. Cushion the caliper pistons with a shop rag and position the caliper with the piston bores facing down. Apply compressed air through the brake hose port (**Figure 11**) to *pop* the pistons out. If only one piston came out, block its bore opening with a piece of thick rubber (old inner tube), wooden block and clamp as shown in **Figure 12**. Apply com-

15

pressed air again and remove the remaining piston. See **Figure 13**.

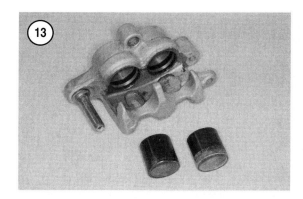

*CAUTION*
*Do not try to pry the piston out. This will damage the piston and caliper bore.*

7. Use a small wooden or plastic tool and remove the dust (A, **Figure 14**) and piston seals (B) from the caliper bore grooves and discard them.
8. Remove the bleed valve and its cover from the caliper.
9. Clean and inspect the brake caliper assembly as described in this section.

**Assembly**

*NOTE*
*Use new DOT 4 brake fluid when lubricating the piston seals, pistons and caliper bores in the following steps.*

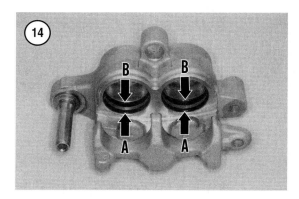

1. Install the bleed valve and its cover into the caliper.
2. Soak the new piston and dust seals in brake fluid.
3. Lubricate the cylinder bores with brake fluid.

*NOTE*
*The piston seals (A, **Figure 15**) are thicker than the dust seals (B).*

4. Install a new piston seal into each rear bore groove (B, **Figure 14**).
5. Install a new dust seal into each front bore groove (A, **Figure 14**).

*NOTE*
*Make sure each seal fits squarely inside its bore groove.*

6. Lubricate the pistons with brake fluid.

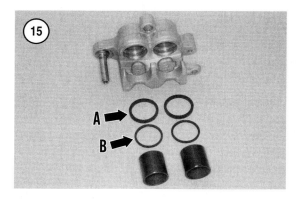

*CAUTION*
*The tight piston-to-seal fit can make piston installation difficult. Do not install the pistons by pushing them straight in as they may bind in their bores and tear the seals.*

7. Align a piston against its bore with its *open* side facing out. Rock the piston slightly to center it in its bore while at the same time pushing its lower end past the seals. When the lower end of the piston

clears both seals, push and bottom the piston in its bore (**Figure 16**). After installing the other piston, clean spilled brake fluid from the area in front of the pistons to prevent brake pad contamination.

*CAUTION*
*In the following steps, use only silicone grease specified for brake use. Do not confuse silicone sealant (RTV) with silicone brake grease. Do not use brake fluid to lubricate the rubber boots or fixed shafts.*

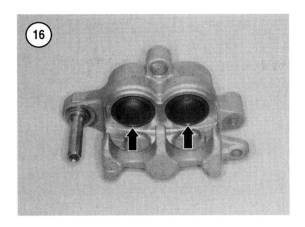

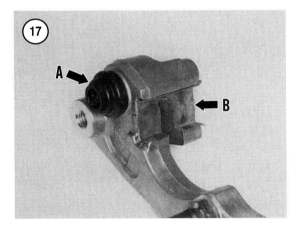

8. Pinch the open end of the large rubber boot and push this end through the mounting hole in the caliper until its outer shoulder bottoms (B, **Figure 10**). Make sure the boot opening faces toward the inside of the caliper. Partially fill the boot with silicone brake grease.

9. Install the small boot into the groove in the caliper bracket (A, **Figure 17**). Partially fill the boot with silicone brake grease.

10. Hook the pad retainer (B, **Figure 17**) onto the caliper bracket.

11. Lubricate the fixed shafts on the caliper (D, **Figure 10**) and caliper bracket (E) with silicone brake grease.

12. Align and slide the mounting bracket onto the caliper body (**Figure 10**). Hold the caliper and slide the caliper bracket in and out by hand. Make sure there is no roughness or binding.

13. Install the brake caliper assembly and brake pads as described in this chapter.

## Inspection

All models use a floating caliper design, in which the caliper slides or floats on shafts mounted parallel with each other on the caliper and caliper bracket. Rubber boots around each shaft prevent dirt from damaging the shafts. If the shafts are worn or damaged the caliper can move out of alignment on the caliper bracket. This will cause brake drag, uneven pad wear and overheating. Inspect the rubber boots and shafts during caliper inspection as they play a vital role in brake performance.

Refer to **Figure 1** when servicing the front brake caliper assembly. Replace parts that are out of specification (**Table 1**) or show damage as described in this section.

> *WARNING*
> *Do not get any oil or grease on any of the brake components. Do not clean the parts with kerosene or other petroleum products. These chemicals cause the rubber brake system components to swell, which may cause brake failure.*

1. Clean and dry the caliper and the other metal parts. Clean the seal grooves carefully. If the contamination is difficult to remove, soak the caliper in a suitable solvent and then reclean. If any of the rubber parts are to be reused, clean them with denatured alcohol or new DOT 4 brake fluid. Do not use a petroleum-based solvent.

> *CAUTION*
> *The caliper bore and seal grooves can be difficult to clean, especially if brake fluid was leaking past the seals. Clean the grooves carefully to avoid damaging the grooves and bore surfaces.*

2. Inspect the caliper bracket, fixed shafts and rubber boots (**Figure 10**) as follows:
   a. Inspect the rubber boots for cracks, tearing, weakness or other damage.
   b. Inspect the fixed shafts on the caliper housing (11, **Figure 1**) and caliper bracket (5) for excessive or uneven wear. If the caliper's fixed shaft is damaged, remove and discard the shaft. Install a new fixed shaft with threadlock and tighten to the specification in **Table 3**. If the caliper bracket fixed shaft is damaged, re-

**15**

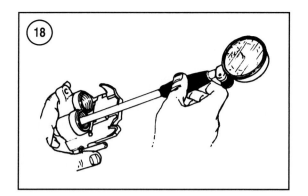

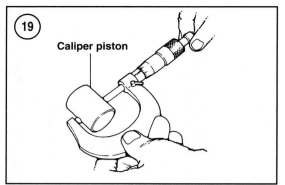

Caliper piston

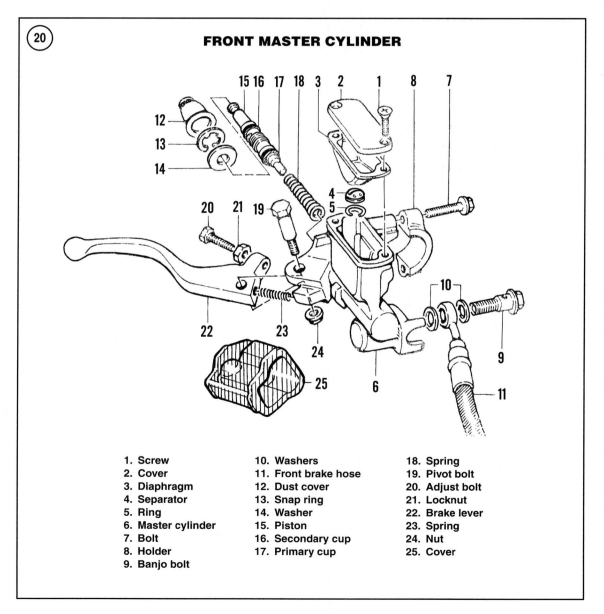

20

**FRONT MASTER CYLINDER**

1. Screw
2. Cover
3. Diaphragm
4. Separator
5. Ring
6. Master cylinder
7. Bolt
8. Holder
9. Banjo bolt
10. Washers
11. Front brake hose
12. Dust cover
13. Snap ring
14. Washer
15. Piston
16. Secondary cup
17. Primary cup
18. Spring
19. Pivot bolt
20. Adjust bolt
21. Locknut
22. Brake lever
23. Spring
24. Nut
25. Cover

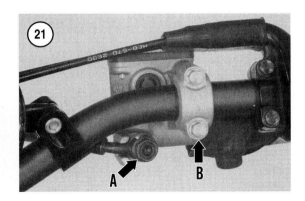

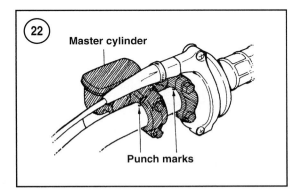

Master cylinder

Punch marks

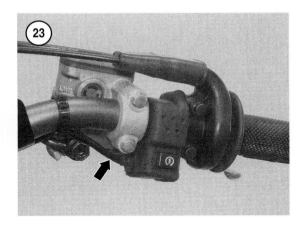

5. Check the pistons for wear marks, scoring, cracks or other damage.

6. Measure the outside diameter of the pistons (**Figure 19**).

7. Check the bleed valve and cap for wear or damage. Make sure air can pass through the bleed valve.

8. Check the banjo bolt for wear or damage. Discard the washers.

9. Inspect the brake pads, pad spring, pad pin plug and pad pin bolt as described under *Front Brake Pads* in this chapter.

### FRONT MASTER CYLINDER

Read the information under *Brake Service* in this chapter before servicing the front master cylinder.
Refer to **Figure 20**.

#### Removal/Installation

1. Support the motorcycle on a workstand.

2. Cover the area under the master cylinder to prevent brake fluid from damaging any component it might contact.

*CAUTION*
*Wipe up any spilled brake fluid immediately as it will damage the finish of most plastic and metal surfaces. Use soapy water and rinse thoroughly.*

3. Remove the master cylinder cover and diaphragm. Use a syringe to draw brake fluid from the master cylinder reservoir. Discard the brake fluid. Reinstall the diaphragm and master cylinder cover.

4. Remove the banjo bolt (A, **Figure 21**) and washers. Cover the end of the brake hose to prevent leakage.

5. Remove the bolts, holder (B, **Figure 21**) and master cylinder.

6. Clean the handlebar, master cylinder and holder mating surfaces with contact cleaner.

7. Install the master cylinder holder with the UP mark on the holder facing up (B, **Figure 21**). Align the edge of the master cylinder clamp surface with the punch mark on the handlebar (**Figure 22**).

8. On CRF250X and CRF450X models, check the starter switch wiring harness (**Figure 23**) to make sure it is not pinched between the master cylinder or the brake hose banjo bolt.

place the caliper bracket assembly. However, if the fixed shaft on the caliper body is loose, remove the shaft and clean its threads and the caliper bracket threads of all threadlock residue. Apply a threadlock to the shaft threads and tighten as described in **Table 3**.

3. Check each cylinder bore for corrosion, pitting, deep scratches or other wear.

4. Measure the inside diameter of the caliper bores (**Figure 18**).

15

9. Install and tighten the master cylinder holder bolts (B, **Figure 21**). Tighten the upper bolt first, then the lower bolt to 9.8 N•m (87 in.-lb.).

10. Secure the brake hose to the master cylinder with the banjo bolt (A, **Figure 21**) and two *new* washers. Install a washer on each side of the brake hose (10, **Figure 20**). Center the brake hose between the arms on the master cylinder (A, **Figure 21**) and tighten the banjo bolt to 34 N•m (25 ft.-lb.).

11. Bleed the front brake as described under *Brake Bleeding* in this chapter.

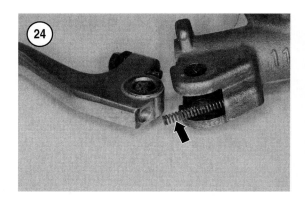

> *WARNING*
> *Do not ride the motorcycle until the front brake is operating correctly. Make sure the brake lever travel is not excessive and the lever does not feel spongy. Either condition indicates that it is necessary to repeat the bleeding procedure.*

**Disassembly**

The long arm snap ring pliers shown in this procedure make the removing of the piston snap ring easy, since they can reach deep into the cylinder. These pliers are available from Motion Pro and Kowa Seiki.

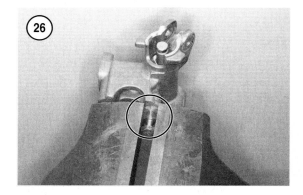

1. Remove the master cylinder as described in this chapter.

2. Remove the brake lever cover.

3. Remove the nut, pivot bolt, brake lever and spring (**Figure 24**).

4. Remove the dust cover (**Figure 25**) from the master cylinder and piston.

> *CAUTION*
> *Do not pry the snap ring out of its groove, as doing so can damage the piston, snap ring groove or bore.*

> *NOTE*
> *Use a bolt and nut as shown in* ***Figure 26*** *to hold the master cylinder in a vise when removing and installing the piston snap ring.*

5. Compress the piston and remove the snap ring with snap ring pliers (**Figure 27**).

6. Remove the washer, piston and spring (**Figure 28**) from the master cylinder bore.

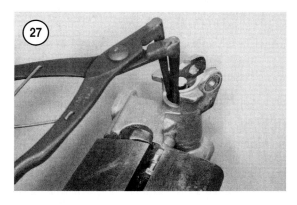

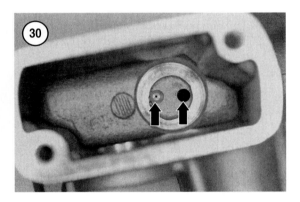

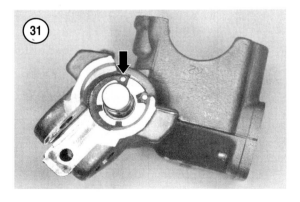

7. Remove the separator and its ring (**Figure 29**) from the reservoir.

8. Before cleaning the master cylinder, examine the filler port (large hole) and the compensating port (small hole) in the reservoir (**Figure 30**). A plugged compensating port causes pressure to build in the brake system and causes brake drag.

9. Perform the *Inspection* procedure to clean and inspect the parts.

**Assembly**

> *WARNING*
> *Do not get any oil or grease on any of the master cylinder components. These chemicals cause the rubber brake system components to swell, which may cause brake failure.*

1. Make sure all the components are clean before reassembly.

2. If installing a new piston assembly, assemble it as described under *Inspection* in this section.

3. Install the spring, small end first, onto the piston as shown in **Figure 28**. It should fit tightly on the piston shoulder.

4. Lubricate the piston assembly and cylinder bore with new DOT 4 brake fluid.

> *CAUTION*
> *Use care when installing the piston. Do not tear the piston cups or allow them to turn inside out.*

5. Install the piston assembly, spring end first (**Figure 28**), by turning and pushing it into the master cylinder bore.

> *NOTE*
> *Before installing the snap ring, mount the master cylinder in a vise (**Figure 26**) as described under **Disassembly**.*

6. Install the washer (**Figure 28**) over the piston with its flat side facing up.

7. Compress the piston assembly and install the snap ring into the master cylinder groove. Make sure the snap ring seats in the groove completely (**Figure 31**). Push and release the piston a few times to make sure it moves smoothly and the snap ring does not pop out.

15

8. Slide the dust cover over the piston in the direction shown in **Figure 25**. Seat the dust cover's large end against the snap ring and install its small end into the piston's groove (**Figure 32**). Push and release the piston a few times to make sure the small end stays in the piston's groove and is not folded incorrectly.

> *CAUTION*
> *The dust cover prevents dirt and moisture from contaminating the end of the master cylinder bore. Make sure it is installed correctly.*

9. Lubricate the separator ring with brake fluid. Install the separator (**Figure 29**) by pushing it into the master cylinder until it bottoms (**Figure 33**).

10. Install the diaphragm, master cylinder cover and screws.

11. Install the brake lever as follows:
   a. Lubricate the pivot bolt with silicone brake grease.
   b. Install the spring into the brake lever (**Figure 24**).
   c. Insert the spring into the master cylinder hole and install the brake lever into position.
   d. Install the pivot bolt.
   e. Install the pivot nut (24, **Figure 20**) and tighten to 5.9 N•m (52 in.-lb.).

12. Install the master cylinder as described in this chapter.

**Inspection**

Replace parts that are out of specification (**Table 1**) or show damage as described in this section.

> *WARNING*
> *Do not get any oil or grease on any of the brake components. Do not clean the parts with kerosene or other petroleum products. These chemicals cause the rubber brake system components to swell, which may brake failure.*

1. Before cleaning the master cylinder, examine the filler port (large hole) and the compensating port (small hole) in the reservoir (**Figure 30**). A plugged compensating port causes pressure to build in the brake system and causes brake drag.

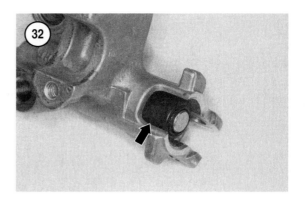

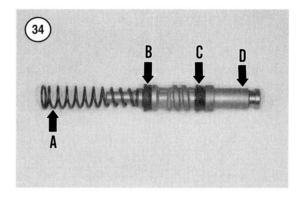

Both ports must be clear for proper master cylinder operation.

2. Clean the master cylinder parts with new DOT 4 brake fluid or with denatured alcohol. If using denatured alcohol, dry with compressed air.

3. Refer to **Figure 34** for piston assembly identification:
   a. Spring.
   b. Primary cup.
   c. Secondary cup.
   d. Piston.

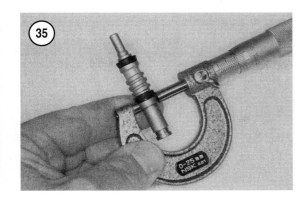

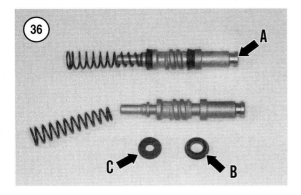

*CAUTION*
*Do not remove the primary and sec-*
*ondary cups from the piston assembly*
*to clean or inspect them. If the cups*
*are damaged, replace the piston*
*assembly.*

4. Visually check the piston assembly (**Figure 34**)
for the following defects:

    a. Broken, distorted or collapsed piston return
       spring.

    b. Worn, cracked, damaged or swollen primary
       and secondary cups.

    c. Scratched, scored or damaged piston.

5. Inspect for a corroded or damaged washer or
snap ring.

6. Inspect the dust cover for tearing and other damage.

7. Measure the piston outside diameter with a micrometer at the point shown in **Figure 35**.

8. To assemble a new piston assembly (**Figure 36**),
perform the following:

*NOTE*
*A new piston assembly consists of the*
*piston, primary cup, secondary cup*
*and spring. Because these parts come*
*unassembled, the new primary and*
*secondary cups must be installed onto*
*the piston. Use the original piston and*
*pistons cups (A, Figure 36) as a refer-*
*ence when assembling the new piston*
*assembly.*

    a. Soak the new cups in new DOT 4 brake fluid
       for 15 minutes to soften them and ease instal-
       lation. Clean the new piston in brake fluid.

    b. Secure the front end of the piston in a tap
       wrench and then mount the tap wrench in a
       vise (**Figure 37**) so both hands are free to in-
       stall the secondary cup.

*CAUTION*
*The piston cups can be difficult to in-*
*stall. Do not pry the cups over the pis-*
*ton with any metal tool as this may*
*damage the cup. Carefully stretch the*
*cups by hand to guide them over the*
*piston's shoulder. The cups have a*
*tendency to turn inside out when in-*
*stalling them, so pay attention to how*
*the cup moves and drops into its*
*groove on the piston. The secondary*
*cup (B, Figure 36) is more difficult to*
*install because of the large shoulder it*
*must pass over.*

    c. Install the secondary cup (B, **Figure 36**) onto
       the piston. Then remove the piston from the
       tap wrench and install the primary cup (C,
       **Figure 36**) onto the piston. Check that both
       cups are positioned correctly and did not turn
       inside out.

**15**

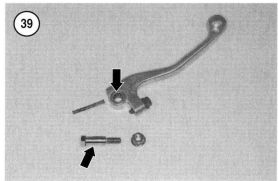

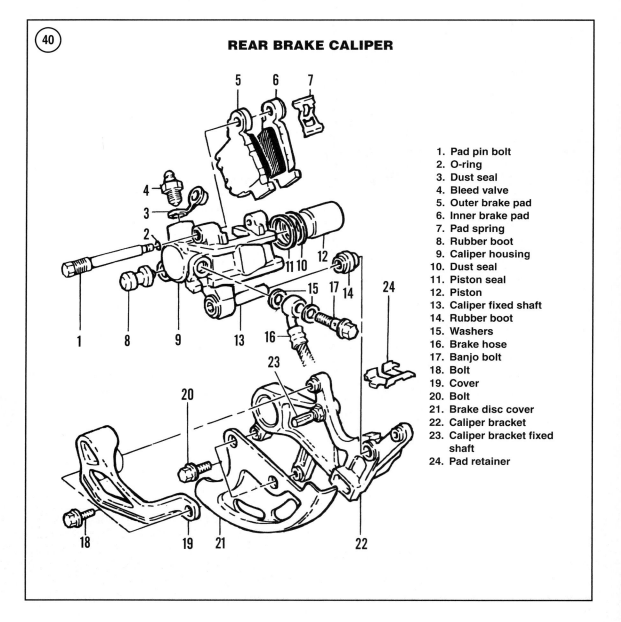

**REAR BRAKE CALIPER**

1. Pad pin bolt
2. O-ring
3. Dust seal
4. Bleed valve
5. Outer brake pad
6. Inner brake pad
7. Pad spring
8. Rubber boot
9. Caliper housing
10. Dust seal
11. Piston seal
12. Piston
13. Caliper fixed shaft
14. Rubber boot
15. Washers
16. Brake hose
17. Banjo bolt
18. Bolt
19. Cover
20. Bolt
21. Brake disc cover
22. Caliper bracket
23. Caliper bracket fixed
    shaft
24. Pad retainer

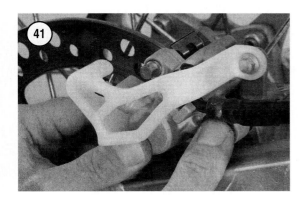

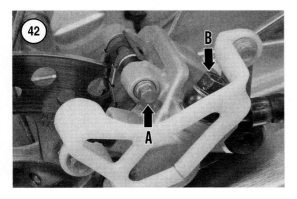

9. Inspect the master cylinder bore for corrosion, pitting or excessive wear. Do not hone the master cylinder bore to remove scratches or other damage.

10. Measure the master cylinder bore (**Figure 38**) with a small hole gauge or bore gauge.

11. Inspect the separator (**Figure 29**) for plugged passages. Replace the ring if damaged.

12. Inspect the master cylinder reservoir diaphragm for tearing, cracks or other damage.

> *NOTE*
> *A damaged diaphragm allows mois-*
> *ture to enter the reservoir and con-*
> *taminate the brake fluid.*

13. Inspect the brake lever assembly (**Figure 39**) for:

    a. Cracks or other damage.

    b. Excessively worn or elongated brake lever hole.

    c. Excessively worn brake lever pivot bolt.

    d. Weak, stretched or damaged brake lever spring.

## REAR BRAKE PADS

Pad wear depends greatly on riding habits and conditions. There is no recommended time interval for changing the pads in the rear brake caliper. The brake pads have wear grooves that allow inspection without removal. Refer to *Brakes* in Chapter Three. Always replace brake pads as a set.

### Replacement

Refer to **Figure 40**.

1. Read the information listed under *Brake Service* in this chapter.

> *CAUTION*
> *Do not allow the master cylinder res-*
> *ervoir to overflow when performing*
> *Step 3. If the fluid level is high, re-*
> *move the cover and draw some of the*
> *fluid from the reservoir with a*
> *syringe.*

> *CAUTION*
> *Before pushing the piston back into*
> *the caliper to make room for the new*
> *pads, check for corrosion and dirt*
> *buildup on the exposed end of the pis-*
> *ton. When the piston is pushed back*
> *into the caliper, this material can*
> *damage the caliper seals. If there is*
> *residue built up on the end of the pis-*
> *ton, try to clean the end of the piston*
> *with a soft brush and denatured alco-*
> *hol while the caliper is assembled or*
> *remove and disassemble the caliper to*
> *clean the piston.*

2. Push the caliper body in by hand (**Figure 41**) to push the piston into the caliper to make room for the new pads.

> *CAUTION*
> *If the pads are to be reinstalled, han-*
> *dle them carefully to prevent damage*
> *and contamination.*

3. Loosen and remove the pad pin bolt (A, **Figure 42**) and both brake pads (**Figure 43**).

4. Check the pad spring (**Figure 44**) to make sure it is firmly attached to the caliper.

5. Inspect the brake pads (**Figure 45**) for uneven wear, damage or contamination. Note the following:

**15**

a. Remove surface contamination by lightly sanding the lining surface with a piece of sandpaper placed on a flat surface. If the lining material is contaminated, replace both brake pads.

b. Both brake pads should show approximately the same amount of wear. If the outer pad (5, **Figure 40**) is worn more than the inner pad (6), the caliper may be binding on the caliper bracket. This wear can also be caused by a worn or damaged piston seal (10, **Figure 40**) that has lost its resilience to self-adjust (returning the piston and disengaging the brakes after the brake pedal is released).

6. Replace the pads as a set if the thickness of any one pad has worn down to its wear groove.

7. Make sure the heat insulators (**Figure 46**) are clamped tightly on the back of each pad. Remove any rust or corrosion from the insulators with a brush.

8. Check the caliper for signs of leakage around the piston. If brake fluid is leaking from the caliper bore, overhaul the brake caliper as described in this chapter.

9. Clean the pad pin bolt. Remove rust and corrosion from the pad pin and inspect for excessive wear, grooves or other damage. Replace if damaged.

10. Replace the O-ring installed on the end of the pad pin bolt (**Figure 45**) if damaged.

11. Inspect the pad spring (**Figure 44**) and replace if damaged.

12. Inspect the brake disc for oil contamination. Spray both sides of the brake disc with a brake or contact cleaner. Inspect the brake disc for wear as described in this chapter.

13. If removed, install the pad spring so it grips the brake caliper tightly (**Figure 44**). Replace the pad spring if it does not stay in position.

14. Install the inner and outer brake pads as shown in **Figure 43**. Push them in place so the upper end of each pad seats against the pad retainer (**Figure 47**) in the caliper bracket.

15. Push both pads against the pad spring and install the pad pin bolt into the caliper and through the hole in each brake pad (A, **Figure 42**).

16. Tighten the pad pin bolt (A, **Figure 42**) to 18 N•m (159 in.-lb.).

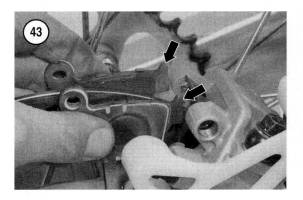

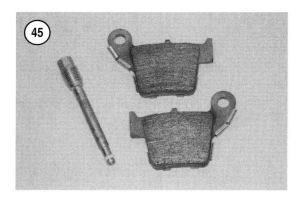

17. Operate the brake pedal to seat the pads against the disc. The brake pedal should feel firm when applied.

18. Check the brake fluid level in the reservoir. If necessary, add new DOT 4 brake fluid.

19. Raise the rear wheel and check that the wheel spins freely and the brake operates properly.

*WARNING*
*Do not ride the motorcycle until the rear brake is operating correctly. Make sure the brake pedal travel is*

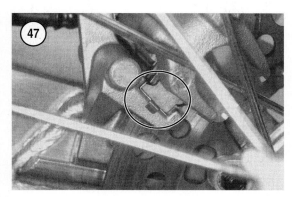

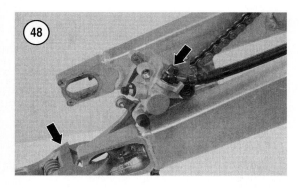

rear brake is applied, hydraulic pressure against the piston causes the piston seal (10, **Figure 40**) to stretch and deflect slightly. This allows the piston to move out where it contacts the brake pads and pushes them against the brake disc. When the brake pedal is released, pressure against the piston seal is reduced and this allows it to retract and return to its original shape. This action draws the piston away from the brake pads and disengages the brake. As the brake pads wear, the piston will travel farther through the seals in order to contact the brake pads.

Refer to **Figure 40**.

**Removal/Installation**

1. Remove the rear wheel (Chapter Twelve).

2. If necessary, remove the brake pads as described in this chapter.

3. If necessary, remove the caliper and brake disc covers.

4A. If the caliper will not be disconnected from its brake hose during this procedure, insert a small wooden block between the brake pads. This prevents the caliper piston from extending out of the caliper, if the brake pedal is actuated.

4B. If the caliper will be serviced, note the following:

    a. The caliper piston can be pumped from the bore while the brake hose is connected and the system is filled with fluid. Do not remove the brake hose or drain the system at this time. Refer to *Disassembly* in this section.

    b. The caliper piston can be removed by using compressed air. Hold the caliper bracket against the swing arm with an adjustable wrench, then loosen and remove the brake hose and both washers (**Figure 48**). Seal the hose to prevent leakage. Remove the caliper bracket and caliper from the swing arm.

5. Remove the caliper bracket from the caliper, if necessary.

6. Install the brake caliper by reversing these steps, and perform the following:

    a. If the brake hose was not disconnected, remove the spacer block from between the brake pads and slide the caliper bracket onto the swing arm (**Figure 49**). Make sure the brake pads were not contaminated with brake fluid.

*not excessive and the pedal does not feel spongy. Either condition indicates the rear brake must be bled as described in this chapter.*

20. Break in the pads by braking slowly at first and then increasing braking pressure. Do not overheat new brake pads.

## REAR BRAKE CALIPER

The piston in the rear brake caliper is self-adjusting to compensate for brake pad wear. When the

15

b. If the brake hose was disconnected, place a *new* washer on each side of the brake hose and position the brake hose against the stop on the caliper (**Figure 48**). Install the caliper bracket onto the swing arm and hold it with an adjustable wrench (**Figure 48**). Tighten the banjo bolt to 34 N•m (25 ft.-lb.).

c. Install the rear wheel (Chapter Twelve).

d. If the brake hose was disconnected, refill the master cylinder and bleed the rear brake as described in this chapter.

e. Operate the rear brake pedal to seat the pads against the brake disc.

> *WARNING*
> *Do not ride the motorcycle until the rear brake is operating correctly. Make sure the brake pedal travel is not excessive and the pedal does not feel spongy. Either condition indicates the rear brake must be bled as described in this chapter.*

**Disassembly**

Refer to **Figure 40**.

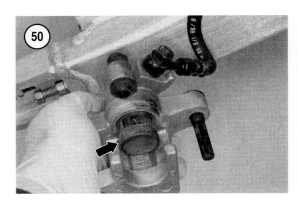

### *Removing the piston hydraulically*

If the piston and dust seals are in good condition and there are no signs of brake fluid leaking from the bore, it may be possible to remove the piston hydraulically. However, note that brake fluid will spill from the caliper once the piston becomes free.

1. Remove the rear brake caliper as described in this chapter. Do not loosen or remove the brake hose.

2. Remove the caliper bracket from the caliper. Have a supply of paper towels and a pan available to catch and wipe up spilled brake fluid.

3. Hold the caliper with the piston facing out and operate the brake pedal to push the piston out of its bore (**Figure 50**).

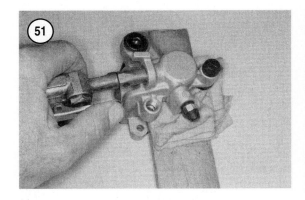

4. Remove the banjo bolt (**Figure 48**) with an impact gun (air or electric), if available. Otherwise, hold the caliper and caliper bracket against the swing arm with an adjustable wrench and remove the banjo bolt with hand tools.

5. Perform the relevant steps in the following section to complete caliper disassembly.

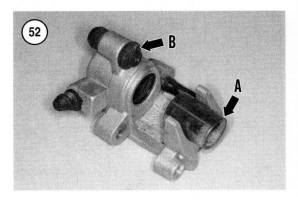

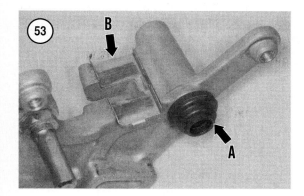

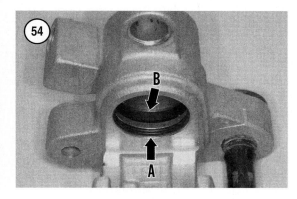

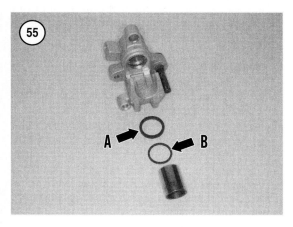

*Removing the piston with compressed air*

1. Remove the brake caliper as described in this chapter.

2. Slide the caliper bracket out of the caliper.

3. Close the bleed valve so air cannot escape.

> *WARNING*
> *Wear eye protection when using compressed air to remove the piston.*

*Keep your fingers away from the pistons.*

4. Cushion the piston with a shop rag and position the caliper with the piston bore facing down. Apply compressed air through the brake hose port (**Figure 51**) to *pop* the piston out. See A, **Figure 52**.

> *CAUTION*
> *Do not try to pry the piston out. This will damage the piston and caliper bore.*

5. Remove the caliper's rubber boot (B, **Figure 52**) by grasping its thick outer edge and pulling it out of its mounting hole.

6. Remove the rubber boot (A, **Figure 53**) from the caliper bracket.

7. Remove the pad retainer (B, **Figure 53**) from the caliper bracket.

8. Use a small wooden or plastic tool and remove the dust (A, **Figure 54**) and piston (B) seals from the caliper bore grooves and discard them.

9. Remove the bleed valve and its cover from the caliper.

10. Clean and inspect the brake caliper assembly as described in this section.

**Assembly**

> *NOTE*
> *Use new DOT 4 brake fluid when lubricating the piston seals, piston and caliper bore in the following steps.*

1. Install the bleed valve and its cover into the caliper.

2. Soak the new piston and dust seals in brake fluid.

3. Lubricate the cylinder bore with brake fluid.

> *NOTE*
> *The piston seal (A, **Figure 55**) is thicker than the dust seal (B).*

4. Install a new piston seal into the rear bore groove (B, **Figure 54**).

5. Install a new dust seal into the front bore groove (A, **Figure 54**).

> *NOTE*
> *Make sure each seal fits squarely inside its bore groove.*

15

6. Lubricate the piston with brake fluid.

*CAUTION*
*The tight piston-to-seal fit can make piston installation difficult. Do not install the piston by pushing it straight in as it may bind in the bore and tear the seals.*

7. Align the piston against its bore with its *open* side facing out. Rock the piston slightly to center it in its bore while at the same time pushing its lower end past the seals. When the lower end of the piston clears both seals, push and bottom the piston in its bore (A, **Figure 56**). Clean spilled brake fluid from the area in front of the piston to prevent brake pad contamination.

*CAUTION*
*In the following steps, use only silicone grease specified for brake use. Do not confuse silicone sealant (RTV) with silicone brake grease. Do not use brake fluid to lubricate the rubber boots or fixed shafts.*

8. Pinch the open end of the large rubber boot and push this end through the mounting hole in the caliper until its outer shoulder bottoms (B, **Figure 56**). Make sure the boot opening faces toward the inside of the caliper. Partially fill the boot with silicone brake grease.

9. Install the bleed valve (C, **Figure 56**) and its seal and tighten finger-tight.

10. Install the pad spring onto the caliper (D, **Figure 56**).

11. Install the small boot into the groove in the caliper bracket (A, **Figure 53**). Partially fill the boot with silicone brake grease.

12. Hook the pad retainer (B, **Figure 53**) onto the caliper bracket.

13. Lubricate the fixed shafts on the caliper (A, **Figure 57**) and caliper bracket (B) with silicone brake grease.

14. Align and slide the caliper bracket onto the caliper body. Hold the caliper and slide the caliper bracket in and out by hand. Make sure there is no roughness or binding.

15. Install the brake caliper assembly and brake pads as described in this chapter.

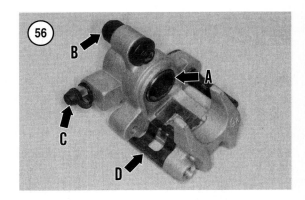

**Inspection**

All models use a floating caliper design, in which the caliper slides or floats on shafts mounted parallel with each other on the caliper and caliper bracket. Rubber boots around each shaft prevent dirt from damaging the shafts. If the shafts are worn or damaged the caliper can move out of alignment on the caliper bracket. This causes brake drag, uneven pad wear and overheating. Inspect the rubber boots and shafts during caliper inspection as they play a vital role in brake performance.

Replace parts that are out of specification (**Table 2**) or show damage as described in this section.

*WARNING*
*Do not get any oil or grease on any of the brake components. Do not clean the parts with kerosene or other petroleum products. These chemicals cause the rubber brake system components to swell, which may cause brake failure.*

1. Clean and dry the caliper and the other metal parts. Clean the seal grooves carefully. If the contamination is difficult to remove, soak the caliper in a suitable solvent and then reclean. If any of the rubber parts are to be reused, clean them with denatured alcohol or new DOT 4 brake fluid. Do not use a petroleum-based solvent.

*NOTE*
*The caliper bore and seal grooves can be difficult to clean, especially if brake fluid was leaking past the seals. Clean the grooves carefully to avoid damaging the grooves and bore surfaces.*

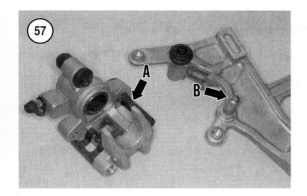

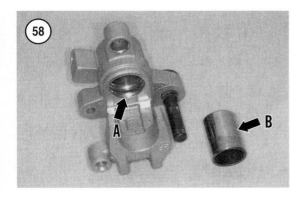

6. Measure the outside diameter of the piston (B, **Figure 58**).

7. Check the bleed valve and cap for wear or damage. Make sure air can pass through the bleed valve.

8. Check the banjo bolt for wear or damage. Discard the washers.

9. Inspect the brake pads, pad spring and pad pin bolt as described under *Rear Brake Pads* in this chapter.

## REAR MASTER CYLINDER

Read the information listed under *Brake Service* in this chapter before servicing the rear master cylinder.

Refer to **Figure 59**.

### Removal/Installation

1. Support the motorcycle on a workstand.

2. Drain the rear brake as described in this chapter.

*CAUTION*
*Wipe up any spilled brake fluid immediately as it will damage the finish of most plastic and metal surfaces. Use soapy water and rinse thoroughly.*

3. Remove the rear brake pedal and disconnect the pushrod as follows:

 a. On CRF250X and CRF450X models, remove the snap clip from the end of the brake pedal pivot bolt.

 b. Remove the rear brake pedal bolt (A, **Figure 60**) and flat washer. Then pivot the rear brake pedal away from the footpeg and disconnect the return spring (B, **Figure 60**). Note the position of the brake pedal seals as they may fall out when the pivot bolt is removed.

 c. Remove the cotter pin and clevis pin connecting the master cylinder pushrod to the rear brake pedal (**Figure 61**). Discard the cotter pin.

4. Remove the banjo bolt (A, **Figure 62**) and both washers. Cover the end of the brake hose to prevent leakage.

5. Remove the mounting bolts (B, **Figure 62**) and rear master cylinder.

6. Service the master cylinder as described in this section.

2. Inspect the caliper bracket, fixed shafts and rubber boots as follows:

 a. Inspect the rubber boots for cracks, tearing, weakness or other damage.

 b. Inspect the fixed shafts on the caliper housing (13, **Figure 40**) and caliper bracket (23) for excessive or uneven wear. If the caliper's fixed shaft is damaged, remove and discard the shaft. Install a new fixed shaft with threadlock and tighten to the torque specification in **Table 3**. If the caliper bracket's fixed shaft is damaged, replace the caliper bracket assembly. However, if this shaft is loose, remove the shaft and clean its threads and the caliper bracket threads of all threadlock residue. Apply a threadlock to the shaft threads and tighten as described in **Table 3**.

3. Check the cylinder bore for corrosion, pitting, deep scratches or other wear.

4. Measure the inside diameter of the caliper bore (A, **Figure 58**).

5. Check the piston for wear marks, scoring, cracks or other damage.

15

## REAL MASTER CYLINDER

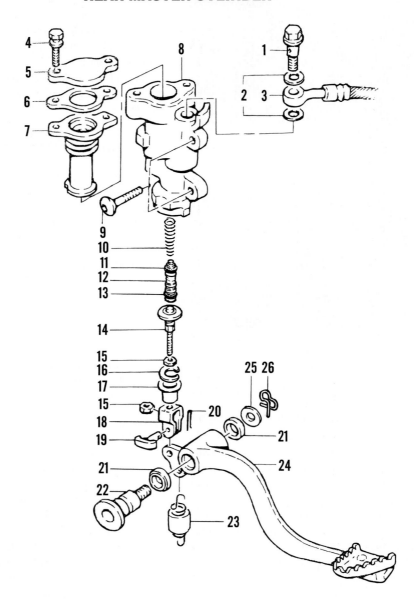

59

**REAR MASTER CYLINDER**

1. Banjo bolt
2. Washers
3. Brake hose
4. Bolt
5. Cover
6. Plate
7. Diaphragm
8. Master cylinder
9. Mounting bolt
10. Spring
11. Primary cup
12. Piston
13. Secondary cup
14. Pushrod assembly
15. Locknut
16. Snap ring
17. Dust cover
18. Clevis
19. Clevis pin
20. Cotter pin
21. Dust seal
22. Brake pedal pivot bolt
23. Return spring
24. Brake pedal
25. Washer
26. Snap clip (CRF250X
and CRF450X)

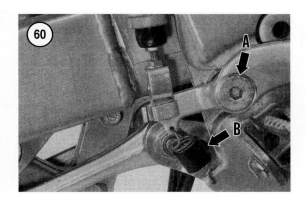

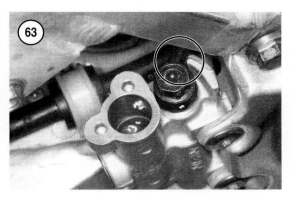

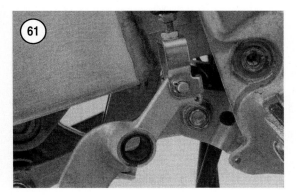

a. Connect the brake pedal to the master cylinder pushrod with the clevis pin and a *new* cotter pin (**Figure 61**). Bend over the ends of the cotter pin to lock it.

b. Reconnect the return spring between the rear brake pedal and frame.

c. Lubricate the brake pedal pivot bolt and brake pedal bore with grease. Do not lubricate the frame or pivot bolt threads. These threads must be clean and dry.

d. Apply a medium strength threadlock onto the pivot bolt threads, if specified in **Table 3**.

e. Install the pivot bolt (A, **Figure 60**) and washer and tighten to the torque specification listed in **Table 3**.

f. On CRF250X and CRF450X models, install the snap clip through the hole in the end of the brake pedal pivot bolt, then hook its arm to lock it.

10. Bleed the rear brake as described under *Brake Bleeding* in this chapter.

> *WARNING*
> *Do not ride the motorcycle until the rear brake is operating correctly. Make sure the brake pedal travel is not excessive and the pedal does not feel spongy. Either condition indicates that repeating the bleeding procedure is necessary.*

**Disassembly**

The long arm snap ring pliers shown in this procedure makes the removing of the piston snap ring easy, since they can reach deep into the cylinder. These pliers are available from Motion Pro and Kowa Seiki.

7. Install the rear master cylinder and tighten its mounting bolts to 13 N•m (115 in.-lb.).

8. Secure the brake hose to the master cylinder with the banjo bolt (A, **Figure 62**) and two *new* washers. Install a washer on each side of the brake hose (2, **Figure 59**) and position the brake hose against the stop on the master cylinder (**Figure 63**). Tighten the banjo bolt to 34 N•m (25 ft.-lb.).

9. Reconnect the pushrod and install the brake pedal as follows:

**15**

1. Remove the master cylinder as described in this chapter.

2. Remove the bolts, cover, plate and diaphragm (**Figure 64**) from the reservoir.

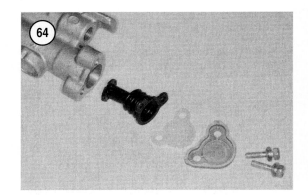

3. Before disassembling the pushrod, measure the pushrod length indicated in **Figure 65**. Record the measurement for reassembly.

4. Hold the clevis (A, **Figure 66**) in a vise and loosen the locknut (B). Then remove the clevis, locknut and dust cover (C, **Figure 66**). See **Figure 67**.

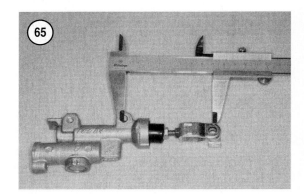

*CAUTION*
*Do not pry the snap ring out of its groove, as doing so can damage the piston, snap ring groove or bore.*

*NOTE*
*Use a bolt and nut as shown in **Figure 68** to hold the master cylinder in a vise when removing and installing the piston snap ring.*

5. Compress the piston and remove the snap ring with snap ring pliers (**Figure 69**).

6. Remove the pushrod and piston assembly (**Figure 70**) from the master cylinder bore.

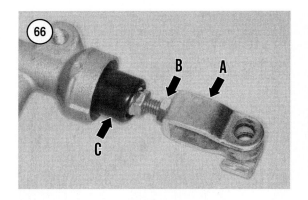

7. Before cleaning the master cylinder, examine the filler port (large hole) and the compensating port (small hole) inside the master cylinder bore. A plugged compensating port causes pressure to build in the brake system and causes brake drag.

8. Perform the *Inspection* procedure to clean and inspect the parts.

**Assembly**

*WARNING*
*Do not get any oil or grease on any of the master cylinder components. These chemicals cause the rubber brake system components to swell, which may cause brake failure.*

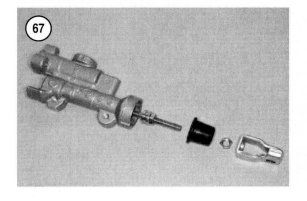

1. Make sure all the components are clean before reassembly.

2. If installing a new piston assembly, assemble it as described under *Inspection* in this section.

3. Install the spring, small end first, onto the piston as shown in **Figure 70**. It should fit tightly on the piston shoulder.

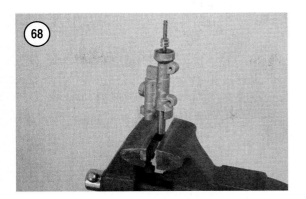

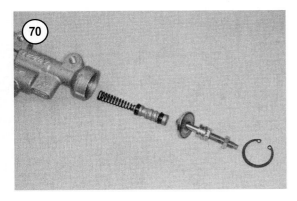

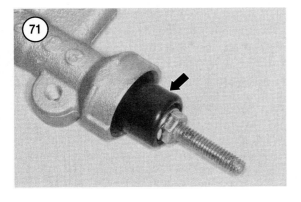

4. Lubricate the piston assembly and cylinder bore with new DOT 4 brake fluid.

*CAUTION*
*Use care when installing the piston. Do not tear the piston cups or allow them to turn inside out.*

5. Install the piston assembly, spring end first (**Figure 70**), by turning and pushing it into the master cylinder bore.

*NOTE*
*Before installing the snap ring, mount the master cylinder in a vise (**Figure 68**) as described under **Disassembly**.*

6. Apply silicone brake grease onto the end of the pushrod that will contact the piston. Then install the pushrod assembly. Compress the piston with the pushrod so the washer on the pushrod is below the snap ring groove in the master cylinder. Continue to compress the piston and install the snap ring (**Figure 69**) into the master cylinder groove. Make sure the snap ring seats in the groove completely. Push and release the pushrod a few times to make sure the piston moves smoothly and the snap ring does not pop out.

7. Slide the dust cover over the piston in the direction shown in **Figure 67**. Seat the dust cover's large end against the snap ring and install its small end into the pushrod groove (**Figure 71**). Push and release the pushrod a few times to make sure the dust cover's small end stays in the pushrod groove and is not twisted or folded incorrectly.

*NOTE*
*The dust cover prevents dirt and moisture from contaminating the end of the master cylinder bore. Make sure it is installed correctly.*

8. Adjust the brake pedal height position as follows:
   a. Thread the locknut (B, **Figure 66**) and clevis (A) onto the pushrod but do not tighten them.
   b. Adjust the clevis position to 79.6 mm (3.13 in.) or to the dimension recorded before disassembly as shown in **Figure 65**. Then hold the clevis and tighten the pushrod locknut (B, **Figure 66**) to 5.9 N•m (52 in.-lb.).

9. Install the diaphragm, plate, master cylinder cover and bolts (**Figure 64**).

15

10. Install the master cylinder as described in this chapter.

## Inspection

Replace parts that are out of specification (**Table 2**) or show damage as described in this section.

*WARNING*
*Do not get any oil or grease on any of the brake components. Do not clean the parts with kerosene or other petroleum products. These chemicals cause the rubber brake system components to swell, which may caues brake failure.*

1. Before cleaning the master cylinder, examine the filler port (large hole) and the compensating port (small hole) in the reservoir. A plugged compensating port causes pressure to build in the brake system and causes brake drag. Both ports must be clear for proper master cylinder operation.
2. Clean the master cylinder parts with new DOT 4 brake fluid or with denatured alcohol. If using denatured alcohol, dry with compressed air.
3. Refer to **Figure 72** for piston assembly identification:
   a. Spring.
   b. Primary cup.
   c. Secondary cup.
   d. Piston.

*CAUTION*
*Do not remove the primary and secondary cups from the piston assembly to clean or inspect them. If the cups are damaged, replace the piston assembly.*

4. Visually check the piston assembly (**Figure 72**) for the following defects:
   a. Broken, distorted or collapsed piston return spring.
   b. Worn, cracked, damaged or swollen primary and secondary cups.
   c. Scratched, scored or damaged piston.
5. Inspect the pushrod assembly (**Figure 73**) for the following defects:
   a. Inspect for a corroded or damaged washer or snap ring. The washer is an integral part of the pushrod and cannot be replaced separately.

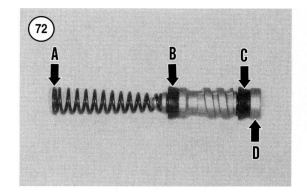

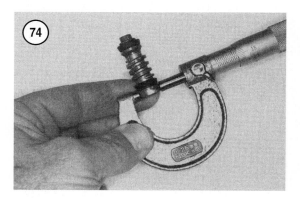

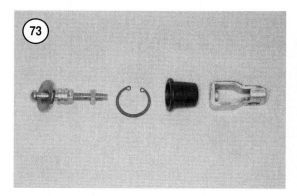

   b. Tearing and other damage on the dust cover.
   c. Bending and other damage on the clevis.
6. Measure the piston outside diameter with a micrometer at the point shown in **Figure 74**.
7. To assemble a new piston assembly (**Figure 75**), perform the following:

*NOTE*
*A new piston assembly consists of the piston, primary cup, secondary cup and spring. Because these parts come unassembled, the new primary and*

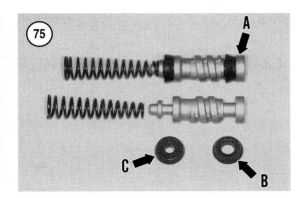

vise (**Figure 76**) so both hands are free to install the secondary cup.

*CAUTION*
*The piston cups can be difficult to install. Do not pry the cups over the piston with any metal tool as this may damage the cup. Carefully stretch the cups by hand to guide them over the piston's shoulder. The cups have a tendency to turn inside out when installing them, so pay attention to how the cup moves and drops into its groove on the piston. The secondary cup (B, Figure 75) is more difficult to install because of the large shoulder it must pass over.*

  c. Install the secondary cup (B, **Figure 75**). Then remove the piston from the tap wrench and install the primary cup (C, **Figure 75**) onto the piston. Check that both cups are positioned correctly and did not turn inside out.
8. Inspect the master cylinder bore for corrosion, pitting or excessive wear. Do not hone the master cylinder bore to remove scratches or other damage.
9. Measure the master cylinder bore (**Figure 77**) with a small hole gauge or bore gauge.
10. Inspect the master cylinder reservoir diaphragm for tearing, cracks or other damage.

*NOTE*
*A damaged diaphragm allows moisture to enter the reservoir and contaminate the brake fluid.*

## BRAKE HOSE REPLACEMENT

1. Drain the brake system for the hose to be replaced. Refer to *Brake System* in this chapter.
2. Before disconnecting the brake hoses, note how they are routed and mounted onto the master cylinder and brake caliper. Install the new hoses so they face in the same direction. Note also how the ends of the brake hoses are routed through guides or positioned next to a stop at the master cylinders and brake calipers. These hold the brake hoses in position when the banjo bolts are tightened. See **Figure 63** and **Figure 78**, typical.

*CAUTION*
*If the end of a brake hose is not positioned correctly, but instead turns as*

secondary cups must be installed onto the piston. Use the original piston and pistons cups (A, *Figure 75*) as a reference when assembling the new piston assembly.

  a. Soak the new cups in new DOT 4 brake fluid for 15 minutes to soften them and ease installation. Clean the new piston in brake fluid.
  b. Secure the front end of the piston in a tap wrench and then mount the tap wrench in a

15

*the banjo bolt is tightened, the bolt may strip the threads in the master cylinder or brake caliper. However, if the bolt does tighten without stripping the threads, the end of the brake hose will be positioned incorrectly. This may shorten the hose in its installed position, which will put excessive stress on the hose and eventually cause it to crack.*

3. Remove the banjo bolts and washers for the brake hose to be replaced.

4. Install the new brake hose in the reverse order of removal and perform the following.

    a. Install *new* sealing washers when installing the banjo bolts.

    b. Tighten the banjo bolts (**Figure 78**, typical) to 34 N•m (25 ft.-lb.).

    c. Fill the master cylinder(s) and bleed the brake(s) as described in this chapter.

    d. Operate the brake lever or brake pedal while observing the brake hose connections. Check for a loose connection or other damage.

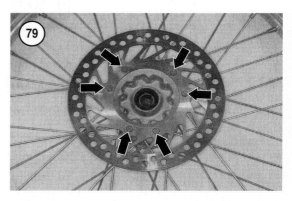

> *WARNING*
> *Do not ride the motorcycle until both brakes are operating correctly. Make sure the brake lever and pedal travel is not excessive and they do not feel spongy. Either condition indicates that repeating the bleeding procedure is necessary.*

## BRAKE DISC

The brake discs are separate from the wheel hubs and can be removed after removing the wheel from the motorcycle. See **Figure 79**, typical.

### Inspection

The brake disc can be inspected while mounted on the motorcycle. Small marks on the disc are not important, but radial scratches that run all the way around the disc surface and are deep enough to snag a fingernail can reduce braking effectiveness and increase brake pad wear. If these grooves are evident, and the brake pads are wearing rapidly, replace the brake disc.

Do not machine a deeply scored or warped disc. Removing disc material causes the disc to overheat rapidly and warp. Maintain the discs by keeping them clean and corrosion-free. Clean the discs with a non-petroleum solvent.

See **Table 1** and **Table 2** for standard and service limit specifications for the brake discs. The minimum thickness dimension is also stamped on the outside of each disc.

1. Support the motorcycle on a workstand.

2. Measure the thickness around the disc at several locations with a micrometer (**Figure 80**). Replace the disc if its thickness at any point is less than the service limit in **Table 1** or **Table 2** or less than the dimension stamped on the disc.

> *NOTE*
> *If the disc thickness is within specifications as described in Step 2, then also check the disc parallelism to locate differences in disc thickness. Excessive parallelism will cause brake grab and a pulsating brake lever or pedal when the brakes are applied.*

3. Check disc parallelism as follows:

    a. Divide the disc into six different points equally spaced 60° apart.

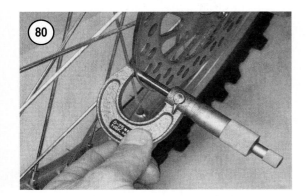

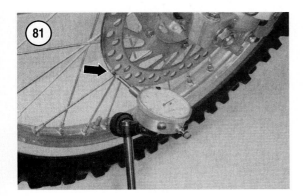

b. Measure the disc thickness with a micrometer at each of these six points. If there is a noticeable variation in disc thickness, replace the disc.

*NOTE*
*Before checking disc runout in Step 4, make sure the wheel bearings are in good condition and the wheel is running true as described in Chapter Twelve.*

4. Measure disc runout with a dial indicator (**Figure 81**). Replace the disc if the runout exceeds the service limit in **Table 1** or **Table 2**.

*NOTE*
*Excessive brake disc runout causes the disc to knock against the pistons, which pushes the brake pads back into the caliper. This condition causes brake chatter and increased brake lever or pedal travel when applying the brakes.*

### Removal/Installation

1. Remove the wheel as described in Chapter Twelve.
2. Remove the nuts and bolts securing the brake disc to the wheel hub. Remove the brake disc.
3. Inspect the brake disc flanges on the hub for cracks or other damage. Replace the hub if damage is evident.
4. Clean the nuts and bolts of all threadlock residue. Replace the bolts if the hex end has started to round out.
5. Install the brake disc onto the hub with the side of the disc marked DRIVE facing out.
6. Apply a threadlock onto the brake disc mounting nuts and tighten to 16 N•m (142 in.-lb.). When tightening these fasteners, hold the bolt and tighten the nut. Reversing this may round out the hex shoulders in the bolt.
7. Install the wheel as described in Chapter Twelve.

## REAR BRAKE PEDAL

### Removal/Installation

1. On CRF250X and CRF450X models, remove the snap clip from the end of the brake pedal pivot bolt.
2. Remove the rear brake pedal pivot bolt (A, **Figure 82**) and move the rear brake pedal away from the footpeg.
3. Disconnect the return spring at the pedal (B, **Figure 82**).
4. Remove the cotter pin and clevis pin that connect the master cylinder pushrod to the rear brake pedal (**Figure 83**). Discard the cotter pin.
5. Remove the seals from the brake pedal.

**15**

6. Clean the pivot bolt, brake pedal and seals of all old grease.

7. Replace the seals if worn or damaged.

8. Lubricate the lips of the seals with grease and install them into the brake pedal with their open side facing out.

9. Reconnect the return spring (B, **Figure 82**).

10. Connect the brake pedal to the master cylinder pushrod with the clevis pin (**Figure 83**) and a *new* cotter pin. Install the clevis pin from the outside. Bend over the ends of the cotter pin to lock it.

11. Lubricate the brake pedal pivot bolt and brake pedal bore with grease. Do not lubricate the frame or pivot bolt threads. These threads must be clean and dry.

12. Apply a medium strength threadlock onto the pivot bolt threads, if specified in **Table 3**.

13. Install the pivot bolt (A, **Figure 82**) and washer and tighten to the torque specification listed in **Table 3**.

14. On CRF250X and CRF450X models, install the snap clip through the hole in the end of the brake pedal pivot bolt, then hook its arm to lock it.

15. Operate the rear brake pedal, making sure it pivots and returns correctly.

### BRAKE SYSTEM DRAINING

Before disconnecting a brake hose when servicing the brake system, pump as much brake fluid from the system as possible. This prevents brake fluid from leaking from the open lines.

The brake system can be drained either manually or with a vacuum pump. When draining the system manually, the master cylinder is used as a pump to expel brake fluid from the system. An empty bottle, a length of clear hose that fits tightly onto the caliper bleed valve and a wrench (**Figure 84**) are required. When using vacuum to drain the system, a hand-operated vacuum pump like the Mityvac (**Figure 85**) is required.

1. Remove the diaphragm from the reservoir.

2A. When draining the system manually, perform the following:

    a. Connect the hose to the caliper bleed valve (**Figure 86**). Then insert the other end of the hose into a clean bottle.

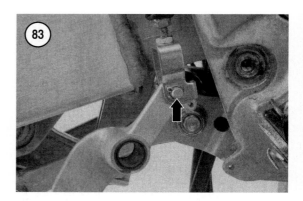

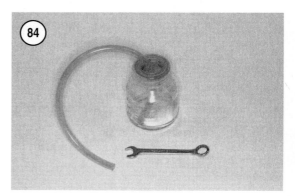

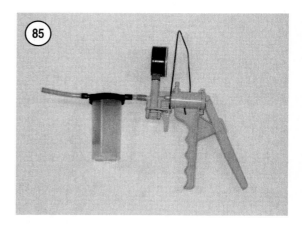

    b. Apply (do not pump) the brake lever or brake pedal until it stops and then hold in this position.

    c. Open the bleed valve with a wrench, then apply the brake lever or brake pedal until it reaches the end of its travel. This expels some of the brake fluid from the system.

    d. Hold the lever or pedal in this position and close the bleed valve, then slowly release the lever or pedal.

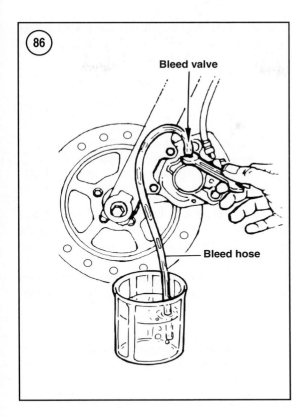

**86**

Bleed valve

Bleed hose

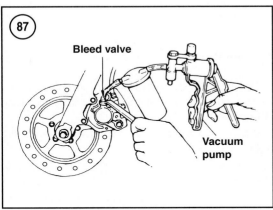

**87**

Bleed valve

Vacuum pump

e. Repeat this sequence to remove as much brake fluid as possible.

2B. When using a vacuum pump, perform the following:

a. Assemble the vacuum and connect it onto the caliper bleed valve (**Figure 87**) following the manufacturer's instructions.

b. Operate the pump lever five to ten times to create a vacuum in the line, then open the bleed valve with a wrench. Brake fluid will

begin to flow into the bottle connected to the vacuum pump.

c. When the fluid draining from the system begins to slow down and before the gauge on the pump (if so equipped) reads 0 HG of vacuum, close the bleed valve.

d. Repeat this sequence to remove as much brake fluid as possible.

3. Close the bleed valve and disconnect the hose or vacuum pump.

4. If necessary, use a syringe to remove brake fluid remaining in the bottom of the master cylinder reservoir.

5. Reinstall the diaphragm cover.

6. Discard the brake fluid removed from the system.

### BRAKE BLEEDING

Whenever air enters the brake system, bleed the system to remove the air. Air can enter the system when the brake fluid level drops too low, after flushing the system or when a banjo bolt or brake hose is loosened or removed. Air in the brake system will increase lever or pedal travel while causing it to feel spongy and less responsive. Under excessive conditions, it can cause complete loss of the brake pressure.

Bleed the brakes manually or with a vacuum pump. Both methods are described in this section.

When adding brake fluid during the bleeding process, use new DOT 4 brake fluid. Do not reuse brake fluid drained from the system or use a silicone based DOT 5 brake fluid. Because brake fluid is very harmful to most surfaces, wipe up any spills immediately with soapy water.

*NOTE*
*When bleeding the brakes, check the fluid level in the master cylinder frequently. If the reservoir runs dry, air will enter the system.*

**Manual Bleeding**

This procedure describes how to bleed the brake system manually by using the master cylinder as a pump. An empty bottle, length of clear hose and a wrench (**Figure 84**) are required.

**15**

1. Make sure both brake system banjo bolts are tight.

2. Remove the dust cap from the brake bleed valve and clean the valve and its opening of all dirt and debris. If a dust cap was not used, use a thin screwdriver or similar tool and compressed air to remove all dirt from inside the bleed valve opening.

*CAUTION*
*Dirt that is left inside the bleed valve opening can enter the brake system. This could plug the brake hose and contaminate the brake fluid.*

3. Connect the clear hose to the bleed valve on the caliper (**Figure 86**). Place the other end of the hose into a container filled with enough new brake fluid to keep the end submerged. Loop the hose higher than the bleed valve to prevent air from being drawn into the caliper during bleeding (**Figure 86**).

*CAUTION*
*Cover all parts that could become damaged by brake fluid. Wash any spilled brake fluid from any surface immediately, as it will damage the finish. Use soapy water and rinse completely.*

4. Remove the diaphragm and fill the reservoir to about 10 mm (3/8 in.) from the top. Do not install the diaphragm until the system is bled.

5. Apply the brake lever or brake pedal, and open the bleed valve. This will force air and brake fluid from the brake system. Close the bleed valve before the brake lever or pedal reaches its maximum limit or before brake fluid stops flowing from the bleed valve. Do not release the brake lever or pedal while the bleed valve is open. If the system was previously drained or new parts installed, brake fluid will not start draining from the system until after several repeated attempts are made. This is normal.

*NOTE*
*As the brake fluid enters the system, the level will drop in the master cylinder reservoir. Maintain the level at 10 mm (3/8 in.) from the top of the reservoir to prevent air from being drawn into the system.*

6. Repeat Step 5 until the brake fluid exiting the system is clear, with no air bubbles. If the system is difficult to bleed, tap the master cylinder and caliper housing with a soft faced mallet to regroup the air bubbles so they can be released.

*NOTE*
*If the brake lever or pedal feel firm, indicating that air has been bled from the system, but air bubbles are still visible in the hose connected to the bleed valve, air may be entering the hose from its connection around the bleed valve.*

7. The system is bled when the brake lever or pedal feels firm, and there are no air bubbles exiting the system. Close the bleed valve and remove the bleed hose.

8. If necessary, add brake fluid to correct the level in the master cylinder reservoir. It must be above the level line.

*WARNING*
*Do not ride the motorcycle until both brakes are operating correctly. Make sure the brake lever and pedal travel is not excessive and they do not feel spongy. Either condition indicates that it is necessary to repeat the bleeding procedure.*

**Vacuum Bleeding**

This procedure describes how to bleed the brake system with a vacuum pump like the Mityvac pump (**Figure 85**).

1. Make sure both brake system banjo bolts are tight.

2. Remove the dust cap from the bleed valve and clean the valve and its opening of all dirt and other debris. If a dust cap was not used, use a thin screwdriver or similar tool and compressed air to remove all dirt from inside the bleed valve opening.

*CAUTION*
*Dirt left inside the bleed valve opening can enter the brake system. This could plug the brake hose and contaminate the brake fluid.*

*CAUTION*
*Cover all parts that could be damaged by brake fluid. Wash any spilled brake fluid from any surface immedi-*

*ately, as it will damage the finish. Use soapy water and rinse completely.*

3. Remove the diaphragm and fill the reservoir to about 10 mm (3/8 in.) from the top. Do not install the diaphragm until the system is bled.

4. Assemble the vacuum tool according to the manufacturer's instructions.

5. Attach the pump hose to the bleed valve (**Figure 87**).

> *NOTE*
> *When bleeding the system with a vacuum pump, the brake fluid level in the master cylinder will drop rapidly. This is especially true for the rear reservoir because it does not hold very much brake fluid. Stop often and check the brake fluid level. Maintain the level at 10 mm (3.8 in.) from the top of the reservoir to prevent air from being drawn into the system.*

6. Operate the pump handle five to ten times to create a vacuum in the line between the pump and caliper, then open the bleed valve with a wrench. Doing so forces air and brake fluid from the system. Close the bleed valve before the brake fluid stops flowing from the valve or before the master cylinder reservoir runs empty. If the vacuum pump is equipped with a vacuum gauge, close the bleed valve before the vacuum reading on the gauge reaches 0 HG of vacuum.

7. Repeat Step 6 until the brake fluid exiting the system is clear, with no air bubbles. If the system is difficult to bleed, tap the master cylinder and caliper housing with a soft faced mallet to regroup the air bubbles so they can be released.

8. The system is bled when the brake lever or pedal feels firm, and there are no air bubbles exiting the system. Tighten the bleed valve and disconnect the pump hose.

9. If necessary, add fluid to correct the level in the master cylinder reservoir. It must be above the level line.

> *WARNING*
> *Do not ride the motorcycle until both brakes are operating correctly. Make sure the brake lever and pedal travel is not excessive and they do not feel spongy. Either condition indicates that repeating the bleeding procedure is necessary.*

### Table 1 FRONT BRAKE SERVICE SPECIFICATIONS

| | New mm (in.) | Service limit mm (in.) |
|---|---|---|
| **Brake disc runout** | | |
| CRF250X | – | 0.25 (0.010) |
| All other models | – | 0.15 (0.006) |
| **Brake disc thickness** | 3.0 (0.12) | 2.5 (0.10) |
| **Brake pad thickness limit** | – | 1.0 (0.04) |
| **Caliper bore inside diameter** | 27.000-27.050 (1.0630-1.0650) | 27.06 (1.065) |
| **Caliper piston outside diameter** | 26.861-26.894 (1.0575-1.0588) | 26.853 (1.0572) |
| **Master cylinder bore inside diameter** | 11.000-11.043 (0.4331-0.4348) | 11.05 (0.435) |
| **Master cylinder piston outside diameter** | 10.957-10.984 (0.4314-0.4324) | 10.84 (0.427) |

**15**

### Table 2 REAR BRAKE SERVICE SPECIFICATIONS

| | New mm (in.) | Service limit mm (in.) |
|---|---|---|
| **Brake disc runout** | | |
| CRF250X | – | 0.25 (0.010) |
| All other models | – | 0.15 (0.006) |
| (continued) | | |

### Table 2 REAR BRAKE SERVICE SPECIFICATIONS (continued)

|  | New mm (in.) | Service limit mm (in.) |
|---|---|---|
| Brake disc thickness | 4.0 (0.16) | 3.5 (0.14) |
| Brake pad thickness limit | – | 1.0 (0.04) |
| Caliper bore inside diameter | 22.650-22.700 (0.8917-0.8937) | 22.712 (0.8942) |
| Caliper piston outside diameter | 22.585-22.618 (0.8892-0.8905) | 22.573 (0.8887) |
| Master cylinder bore inside diameter | 9.520-9.563 (0.3748-0.3765) | 9.575 (0.3770) |
| Master cylinder piston outside diameter | 9.477-9.504 (0.3731-0.3742) | 9.465 (0.3726) |

### Table 3 BRAKE TORQUE SPECIFICATIONS

|  | N•m | in.-lb. | ft.-lb. |
|---|---|---|---|
| Banjo bolt | 34 | – | 25 |
| Brake disc nuts | 16 | 142 | – |
| Caliper bleed valve | 5.4 | 48 | – |
| Front brake caliper bracket fixed shaft* |  |  |  |
|   CRF250R and CRF250X | 23 | – | 17 |
|   CRF450R and CRF450X | 22 | – | 16 |
| Front brake caliper mounting bolt* | 30 | – | 22 |
| Front brake caliper fixed shaft* |  |  |  |
|   CRF250R and CRF250X | 23 | – | 17 |
|   CRF450R and CRF450X | 22 | – | 16 |
| Front brake hose guide bolt | 5.2 | 46 | – |
| Front brake hose guide screw | 1.2 | 11 | – |
| Front brake lever adjuster locknut | 5.9 | 52 | – |
| Front brake lever pivot bolt and nut | 5.9 | 52 | – |
| Front master cylinder holder bolt | 9.8 | 87 | – |
| Pad pin bolt | 18 | 159 | – |
| Pad pin plug | 2 | 18 | – |
| Rear brake caliper bracket fixed shaft* |  |  |  |
|   CRF250R and CRF250X | 13 | 115 | – |
|   CRF450R and CRF450X | 12 | 106 | – |
| Rear brake caliper fixed shaft* | 27 | – | 20 |
| Rear brake disc cover bolt* |  |  |  |
|   CRF250R and CRF250X | 13 | 115 | – |
|   CRF450R | 12 | 106 | – |
|   CRF450X | – | – | – |
| Rear brake pedal pivot bolt |  |  |  |
|   CRF250R |  |  |  |
|     2004* | 25 | – | 18 |
|     2005 | 37 | – | 27 |
|   CRF250X* | 25 | – | 18 |
|   CRF450R |  |  |  |
|     2002-2004* | 26 | – | 19 |
|     2005 | 31 | – | 23 |
|   CRF450X | 37 | – | 27 |
| Rear master cylinder mounting bolt | 13 | 115 | – |
| Rear master cylinder pushrod locknut | 5.9 | 52 | – |
| *Apply medium strength threadlock onto fastener threads. | | | |

# CHAPTER SIXTEEN

# BODY AND SUBFRAME

This chapter describes service procedures for the seat, side panels, footpegs, sidestand (CRF250X and CRF450X) and subframe.

**Table 1** is at the end of the chapter.

## SEAT

### Removal/Installation

1. Remove the two mounting bolts (A, **Figure 1**), washers (2002 CRF450R) and collars. Then lift and pull the seat (B, **Figure 1**) back to remove it.

2. Install the seat by aligning the rear seat hook with the frame (A, **Figure 2**) and the front seat hook with the mounting boss on the fuel tank (B).

3. Install the collars, washers (2002 CRF450R) and bolts and tighten to 26 N•m (19 ft.-lb.).

4. Pull on the front of the seat to make sure it is locked in place.

## SIDE COVERS

### Removal/Installation

1A. To remover the left side cover on CRF250X and CRF450X models, lift the ring (A, **Figure 3**) and turn it counterclockwise to unlock and open the air box cover (B). Remove the bolts (C, **Figure 3**), collars and left side cover (D).

1B. To remove the right side cover on CRF250R, and CRF450R models, remove the bolts (A, **Figure 4**), washers (2002 CRF450R only), collars and side cover (B).

2. Installation is the reverse of these steps. Tighten the seat mounting bolt to 26 N•m (19 ft.-lb.).

## RADIATOR SHROUDS

### Removal/Installation

*NOTE*
*The upper and lower collars used on some models are a different thickness. Identify the fasteners so they can be*

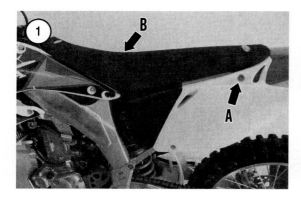

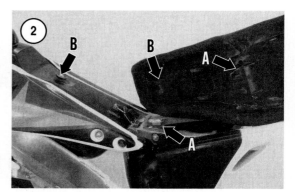

*reinstalled in their original mounting position.*

1. Remove the bolts, collars and radiator shroud (**Figure 5**).

2. Install by reversing these steps. Insert the tab on the rear part of the shroud onto the subframe (**Figure 6**). Tighten the radiator shroud bolts securely.

## ENGINE GUARD

### Removal/Installation

1. Remove the bolt and engine guard (A, **Figure 7**).

2. Install the engine guard and tighten the bolt securely.

## CENTER ENGINE GUARD
## (CRF450X)

### Removal/Installation

1. Support the motorcycle on its sidestand.

2. Remove the bolts and collars. Then remove the center engine guard (B, **Figure 7**) from the coolant reserve tank.

3. Install the center engine guard by aligning its rear tabs with the holes in the coolant reserve tank. Install the collars and bolts and tighten securely.

## NUMBER PLATE
## (CRF250R AND CRF450R)

### Removal/Installation

1. Remove the number plate strap (**Figure 8**) from around the handlebar.

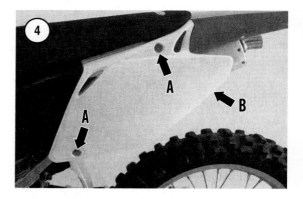

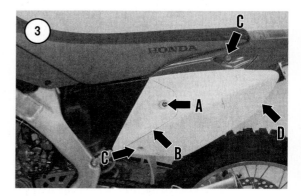

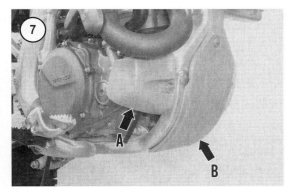

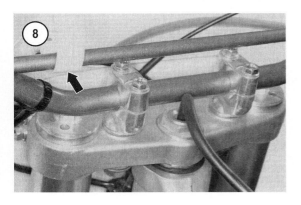

2. Remove the bolt at the top of the number plate and remove the number plate.

3. Install the number plate by inserting its mounting hole over the pin on the steering stem. Make sure the front brake hose is routed on the outside of the number plate.

4. Install the collar and bolt and tighten securely.

5. Secure the number plate strap (**Figure 8**) around the handlebar.

### FRONT VISOR (CRF250X AND CRF450X)

**Removal/Installation**

1. Remove the bolts (A, **Figure 9**) and set the front visor (B) on the front fender.

2. Remove the headlight bulb wiring harness from the clamp (**Figure 10**).

3. Insert a small wooden stick between the connector halves (**Figure 11**) and lift/pry the connector tab to unlock the connectors, then disconnect them.

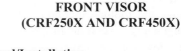

16

4. Installation is the reverse of these steps. Install the front visor by inserting its mounting holes over the two pins on the steering stem.

5. Start the engine and check the headlight operation.

## TRIPMETER AND CABLE (CRF250X AND CRF450X)

### Cable Replacement

1. Remove the front visor as described in this chapter.

2. Disconnect the cable (A, **Figure 12**) at the tripmeter.

3. Disconnect the cable (**Figure 13**) at the front wheel and remove the cable (**Figure 14**).

4. Installation is the reverse of these steps.

### Tripmeter
### Removal/Installation

1. Remove the front visor as described in this chapter.

2. Disconnect the cable (A, **Figure 12**) at the tripmeter.

3. Remove the nuts, washers (B, **Figure 12**) and tripmeter (C).

4. Installation is the reverse of these steps.

## FOOTPEG AND MOUNTING BRACKET

### Removal/Installation

1. Remove the cotter pin, washer, pivot pin, footpeg (**Figure 15**) and spring.

2. To remove the footpeg mounting bracket, remove the upper and lower mounting bolts.

3. Check the pivot pin and replace if worn or damaged.

4. Replace the return spring if weak or damaged.

5. Reverse these steps to install the footpeg bracket and footpeg. Note the following:

   a. Lubricate the footpeg mounting bracket's upper and lower mounting bolt threads with engine oil.

   b. Tighten the footpeg mounting bracket's upper mounting bolt to 54 N•m (40 ft.-lb.).

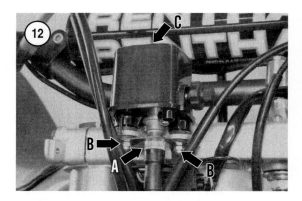

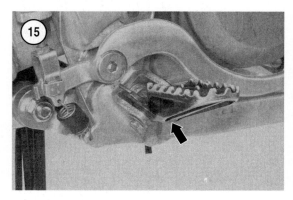

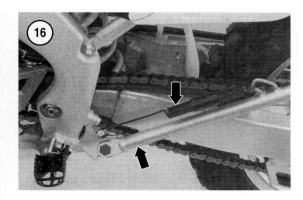

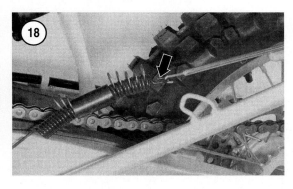

c. Tighten the footpeg mounting bracket's lower mounting bolt to the specification listed in **Table 1**.

d. Secure the pivot pin with a new cotter pin.

e. Lift and release the footpeg. Make sure it returns under spring tension.

## SIDESTAND
## (CRF250X AND CRF450X)

Maintain the sidestand and its spring (**Figure 16**, typical) in good working order to prevent the sidestand from falling down and causing an accident.

### Spring Replacement

1. Support the motorcycle on a work stand.

2. With the sidestand in its down position, insert a number of pennies between the spring coils as shown in **Figure 17**.

3. Raise the sidestand to its up position, then disconnect the spring from the post on the sidestand (**Figure 18**). If the spring coils spread far enough, the spring can be removed without having to apply pressure against the spring.

4. To install the new spring, fit pennies between the spring coils to spread the spring, then install the spring between the two posts. Remove the pennies from the spring to tighten the spring, then operate the sidestand (**Figure 16**) by hand to check its operation.

### Removal/Installation

The sidestand can be removed as an assembly (at the frame or footpeg) or separately by removing its pivot bolt and spring.

1. To remove the sidestand (**Figure 16**) as an assembly, perform the following:

  a. Remove the left footpeg assembly if necessary.

  b. Remove the sidestand mounting bolts and the sidestand assembly.

  c. Tighten the upper mounting bolt to 54 N•m (40 ft.-lb.).

  d. Tighten the lower mounting bolt to 39 N•m (29 ft.-lb.).

2. To remove and install the sidestand at its pivot bolt, perform the following:

  a. Remove the spring as described in this section.

  b. Hold the pivot bolt (A, **Figure 19**) and remove the nut (B). Then remove the pivot bolt and sidestand.

  c. Clean the pivot bolt, nut and sidestand bore.

  d. Lubricate the pivot bolt with grease and reinstall the sidestand, pivot bolt and nut and tighten finger-tight. Do not lubricate the pivot bolt or nut threads. These must remain dry.

  e. Tighten the pivot bolt and nut as described in Step 3.

  f. Reinstall the spring as described in this section.

16

3. Perform the following to tighten the pivot bolt and nut:

   a. Tighten the pivot bolt (A, **Figure 19**) to 10 N•m (88 in.-lb.).

   b. Loosen the pivot bolt (A, **Figure 19**) 45° to 90°, then hold the pivot bolt and tighten the pivot nut (B) to 39 N•m (29 ft.-lb.).

4. Make sure the sidestand locks firmly in place when raised up.

> *WARNING*
> *Do not ride the motorcycle if the sidestand will not lock firmly in its raised position.*

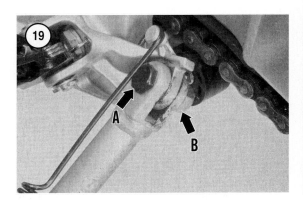

### SUBFRAME (CRF250R AND CRF450R)

**Removal/Installation**

1. Remove the seat and both side covers as described in this chapter.

2. Remove the muffler (Chapter Four or Chapter Five).

3. Disconnect the breather hose from the air filter housing (**Figure 20**).

4. Loosen the rear carburetor hose clamp (**Figure 21**).

5. If the fuel tank is mounted on the frame, disconnect the air filter case cover from the fuel tank.

> *CAUTION*
> *Do not damage the mud guard (A, **Figure 22**) when removing and installing the subframe.*

6. Remove the subframe mounting bolts (B and C, **Figure 22**) and subframe. The 2005 CRF450R uses two upper subframe mounting bolts.

7. Cover the air filter housing boot and the rear of the carburetor with a plastic bags.

8. Installation is the reverse of these steps. Note the following:

   a. Remove the plastic bags from the air boot and carburetor.

   b. Install the two lower subframe mounting bolts (C, **Figure 22**). Then pivot the subframe up and connect the air box to the carburetor. On 2005 CRF450R models, align the carburetor and air box boot alignment points.

   c. Install the upper subframe mounting bolt(s) (B, **Figure 22**).

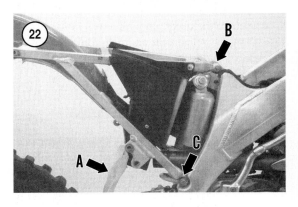

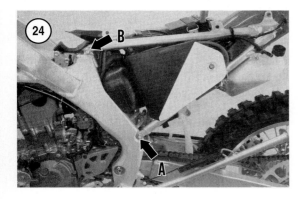

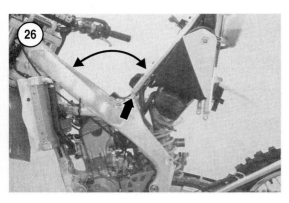

d. Recheck the carburetor-to-air boot connection.

e. Tighten the lower subframe mounting bolts (C, **Figure 22**) to 49 N•m (36 ft.-lb.).

f. Tighten the upper subframe mounting bolt(s) (B, **Figure 22**) to 30 N•m (22 ft.-lb.).

g. On 2005 CRF450R models, tighten the rear carburetor hose clamp so the distance between the clamp ends is 11-13 mm (7/16-1/2 in.). On all other models, tighten the rear carburetor hose clamp securely.

## SUBFRAME
## (CRF250X AND CRF450X)

**Raise and Lock Subframe**

1. Support the motorcycle on a work stand.
2. Remove the muffler (Chapter Four or Chapter Five).
3. Remove the fuel tank (Chapter Nine).
4. Loosen the rear carburetor hose clamp (**Figure 23**).
5. Remove the two lower subframe mounting bolts (A, **Figure 24**). Then loosen the upper subframe mounting bolt(s).
6. On California models, disconnect the air suction hose (**Figure 25**) from the air box.

*CAUTION*
*To prevent damaging the wire harness when raising the subframe, do not exceed the 90° angle specified in Step 7.*

*NOTE*
*Before raising the subframe, pull the air box boot off the rear of the carburetor. This will prevent the boot from disconnecting from the air box if its connection at the carburetor is tight.*

7. Raise the subframe so the subframe and frame form a 90° angle (**Figure 26**). Then tighten the upper subframe mounting bolt(s) (**Figure 26**) to 30 N•m (22 ft.-lb.) to lock the subframe in position.
8. Cover the air boot opening and the carburetor with plastic bags.

*NOTE*
*When lowering the subframe, make sure the mud guard does not bend and contact the rear tire.*

16

9. Reverse these steps to lower the subframe. Note the following:
  a. Tighten the upper subframe mounting bolts (B, **Figure 24**) to 30 N•m (22 ft.-lb.).
  b. Tighten the lower subframe mounting bolts (A, **Figure 24**) to 49 N•m (36 ft.-lb.).

**Removal/Installation**

1. Support the motorcycle on a work stand.
2. Remove the muffler (Chapter Four or Chapter Five).
3. Remove the fuel tank (Chapter Nine).
4. Remove both side covers as described in this chapter.
5. Remove the battery (Chapter Ten).
6. On CRF250X models, remove the radiator reserve tank (Chapter Eleven).
7. Loosen the rear carburetor hose clamp (**Figure 23**).
8. Remove the two lower subframe mounting bolts (A, **Figure 24**).
9. On California models, disconnect the air suction hose (**Figure 25**) from the air box.

*CAUTION*
*To prevent damaging the wire harness when raising the subframe, do not exceed the 90° angle specified in Step 10.*

*NOTE*
*Before raising the subframe, pull the air box boot off the rear of the carbu-*

*retor. This will prevent the boot from disconnecting from the air box if its connection at the carburetor is tight.*

10. Raise the subframe so the subframe and frame form a 90° angle (**Figure 26**). Then tighten the upper subframe mounting bolt (**Figure 26**) to 30 N•m (22 ft.-lb.) to lock the subframe in position.
11. On CRF250X models, remove the air box (Chapter Nine).
12. Loosen the upper subframe mounting bolt (**Figure 26**) and lower the subframe.
13. Remove the plastic bands securing the main relay to the subframe.
14. Remove the ICM and starter relay switch from the rear fender.
15. Remove the upper subframe mounting bolt(s) and remove the subframe.
16. Installation is the reverse of removal. Note the following:
  a. Make sure not to damage the coolant hose (CRF250X) and wiring harness. Check their routing when raising and lowering the subframe.

*CAUTION*
*When lowering the subframe, make sure the mud guard does not bend and contact the rear tire.*

  b. Tighten the upper subframe mounting bolt (B, **Figure 24**) to 30 N•m (22 ft.-lb.).
  c. Tighten the lower subframe mounting bolts (A, **Figure 24**) to 49 N•m (36 ft.-lb.).

**Table 1 BODY AND SUBFRAME TORQUE SPECIFICATIONS**

|  | N•m | ft.-lb. |
| --- | --- | --- |
| Footpeg mounting bracket | | |
| Upper mounting bolt* | 54 | 40 |
| Lower mounting bolt* | | |
| CRF450X | 39 | 29 |
| All other models | 30 | 22 |
| Seat mounting bolts | 26 | 19 |
| (continued) | | |

**Table 1 BODY AND SUBFRAME TORQUE SPECIFICATIONS (continued)**

|  | N•m | ft.-lb. |
|---|---|---|
| Sidestand | | |
| CRF250X and CRF450X | | |
| Sidestand bracket mounting bolts | | |
| at frame | | |
| 10 mm (upper) | 54 | 40 |
| 8 mm (lower) | 39 | 29 |
| Pivot bolt | See text | |
| Pivot nut | 39 | 29 |
| Subframe mounting bolts | | |
| Upper | 30 | 22 |
| Lower | 49 | 36 |

*Lubricate bolt threads with engine oil.

16

# INDEX

17

17

17

17

## 2004-2005 CRF250R

## 2002-2003 CRF450R

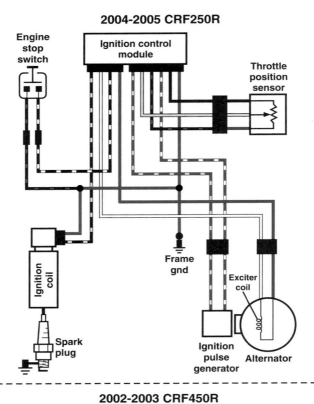

## 2004 CRF450R

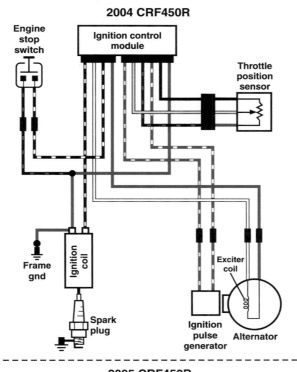

Engine stop switch · Ignition control module · Throttle position sensor · Frame gnd · Ignition coil · Spark plug · Ignition pulse generator · Exciter coil · Alternator

## 2005 CRF450R

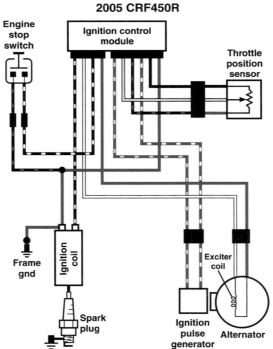

Engine stop switch · Ignition control module · Throttle position sensor · Frame gnd · Ignition coil · Spark plug · Ignition pulse generator · Exciter coil · Alternator

18

**CRF250X (2004-2005)**

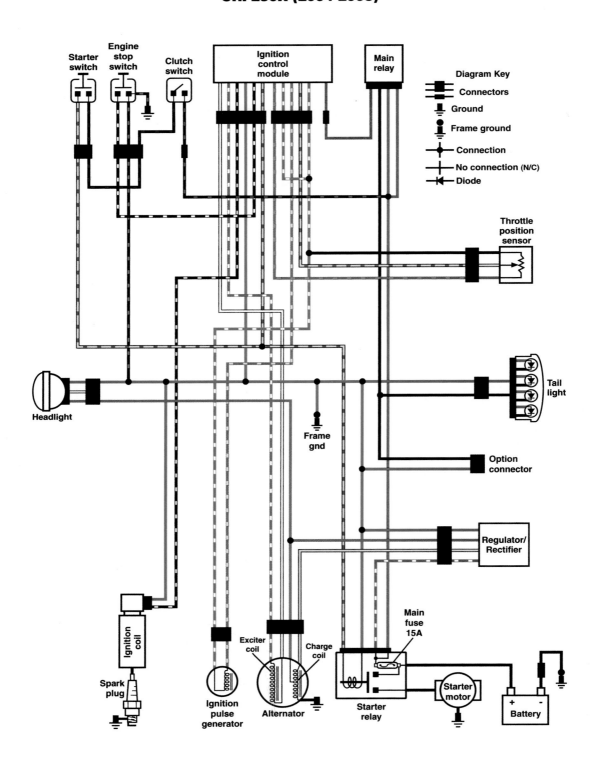